Yugoslavia as History is the first book to examine the bloody demise of the former Yugoslavia in the full light of its history and that of its ethnic mosaic. A Yugoslav idea had already emerged before the First World War, and it led to two states called Yugoslavia, between 1918 and 1941, and from 1945 until 1991. This book examines the origins of that idea among the related but separate peoples who have populated the region over the last 1,000 years, drawing out connections to both states and to the violent end of Tito's Yugoslavia in 1991. The author follows these peoples, their institutions and ideas from their earliest interaction, into the two world wars and the states which resulted from them, detailing the tortuous search for political and economic viability which characterized Yugoslavia as a state. Accessible and authoritative, this book provides a unique insight into the origins of the tragedy that has overtaken the region.

Yugoslavia as History

Yugoslavia as History

Twice there was a country

John R. Lampe

University of Maryland and Woodrow Wilson
International Center for Scholars

CAMBRIDGE
UNIVERSITY PRESS

Published by the Press Syndicate of the University of Cambridge
The Pitt Building, Trumpington Street, Cambridge CB2 1RP
40 West 20th Street, New York, NY 10011-4211, USA
10 Stamford Road, Oakleigh, Melbourne 3166, Australia

First published 1996
Reprinted 1997

Printed in Great Britain at the University Press, Cambridge

A catalogue record for this book is available from the British Library

Library of Congress cataloguing in publication data

Lampe, John R.
Yugoslavia as History: Twice there was a country / John R. Lampe.
p.   cm.
ISBN 0 521 46122 7 (hc). – ISBN 0 521 46705 5 (pbk.)
1. Yugoslavia – History. I. Title.
DR1246.L36 1996
949.7 – dc20 96–10390 CIP

ISBN 0 521 46122 7 hardback
ISBN 0 521 46705 5 paperback

WD

In memory of Michael Boro Petrovich

Contents

List of plates   *page* xi
List of maps   xii
List of tables   xiii
Acknowledgments   xv
Note on pronunciation   xix

Introduction: The search for viability   1

1   Empires and fragmented borderlands, 800–1800   9
     Mountains first, water last   10
     Brief native empires, long remembered   14
     Varieties of Ottoman rule   20
     Varieties of Habsburg rule   27
     Exceptions to imperial fragmentation   33

2   Unifying aspirations and rural resistance, 1804–1903   39
     From Illyrian provinces to Yugoslav idea, 1806–1860   41
     Serbia as a nineteenth-century nation-state   46
     Montenegro as mini-state   56
     Croatian and South Slav ideas in the Habsburg lands, 1860–1900   58
     Bosnia's transition from Ottoman to Austro-Hungarian rule   64
     Dalmatia and Slovenia as Yugoslav outposts   68

3   New divisions, Yugoslav ties, and Balkan Wars, 1903–1914   70
     Fragmented growth and party politics in the Habsburg lands   74
     Serbia's rising reputation and the Bosnian crisis of 1908   81
     Balkan Wars and new Yugoslav prospects, 1912–1914   89

4   The First World War and the first Yugoslavia, 1914–1921   99
     Serbia and the Yugoslav Committee, 1914–1917   100
     Wartime regimes from Slovenia to Serbia   104
     National council in Zagreb and unification in Belgrade   108
     Western policy and border disputes   111
     Economic obstacles to political unification   115
     Divisive elections for a unitary constitution   119

5   Parliamentary kingdom, 1921–1928   126

Prewar politicians, new parties, and the Vidovdan framework, 1921–1926   127
Cultural connections and economic disjunctures   141
Hostile neighbors and distant allies   150
Fatal intersections, 1927–1928   155

6   Authoritarian kingdom, 1929–1941   160

Royal dictatorship, 1929–1934   161
Stojadinović and the royal regency, 1935–1938   173
Balance sheet for the first Yugoslavia, 1921–1939   183
From Serb-Croat *Sporazum* to Tripartite Pact, 1939–1941   190

7   World war and civil war, 1941–1945   197

The destruction of the first Yugoslavia   197
The Independent State of Croatia (NDH), occupation regimes, and
    active opposition, 1941–1942   206
Communist advantages, 1943–1944   213
Consolidating Communist power, 1945   222

8   Founding the second Yugoslavia, 1946–1953   229

Consolidating power under the 1946 Constitution   230
Setbacks and the Tito–Stalin split, 1947–1949   237
First steps down the Yugoslav road   250

9   Tito's Yugoslavia ascending, 1954–1967   260

Balancing between East and West   262
Western markets and self-managed enterprises, 1954–1962   271
Market reform and the fall of Ranković   279

10   Tito's Yugoslavia descending, 1968–1988   293

Opposition comes into the open, 1968–1969   294
From the Croatian crisis to the 1974 Constitution   298
From half-market to contractual economy   308
Foreign policy and the debt crisis, 1979–1985   315
The failure of federal leadership and economic retreat, 1986–1988   320

11   Ethnic politics and the end of Yugoslavia   325

Social strains and regional relations   326
New leaders and new politics   338
Fatal intersections, 1989–1991   344

Notes   357
Selected further reading (in English and German)   393
Index   402

Plates

1.1 The medieval center of Dubrovnik (photograph
    courtesy of Joco Žnidaršić)   *page* 35
5.1 Belgrade in the 1930s (photograph courtesy of the
    Museum of the City of Belgrade)   143
6.1 King Aleksandar in 1934 (photograph courtesy of
    Corbis-Bettman)   163
7.1 Tito and inner circle, 1944 (photograph courtesy of
    Corbis-Bettman)   212
8.1 Communist demonstration, Belgrade 1947 (photograph
    courtesy of the Museum of the City of Belgrade)   244
9.1 Sarajevo Winter Olympics, 1984 (photograph
    courtesy of Joco Žnidaršić, *Delo*)   290
11.1 Mostar, July 1992 (photograph courtesy of Kevin Weaver
    and *Balkan War Report*)   350

Maps

1.1 Former Yugoslavia's physical geography and
    land use   *page* 13
1.2 Medieval states of Croatia, Serbia, and Bosnia   17
1.3 Croatian Military Border and Habsburg borderlands
    in 1780   31
2.1 Illyrian provinces, 1809–1813   43
2.2 Serbia and the Habsburg South Slav lands, 1830–1878   47
3.1 Serbia and Montenegro, 1911 and 1913   95
4.1 Territorial claims and final borders, 1918–1921   113
6.1 Territorial division of the Kingdom of Yugoslavia,
    1929–1939   165
7.1 Division of the former Yugoslavia, 1941–1944   201
8.1 Yugoslavia's internal borders, 1945–1991   231
9.1 Grain land and rural overpopulation, 1970   291
11.1 Ethnic majorities in Bosnia-Hercegovina, Croatia,
    and Kosovo, 1991   331

Tables

3.1	Land distribution (pre-1914 census)	*page* 72
3.2	Population, 1870 and 1910	73
4.1	Regional party shares and seats in the 1920 elections	121
5.1	Population by ethnicity and geographic area, 1921	129
5.2	Parliamentary elections, 1920–1927	135
5.3	Occupational structure, 1921 and 1931	149
5.4	Ethnic voting by party, 1923 and 1927	157
6.1	Electoral support for regime list, 1931, 1935, and 1938	177
6.2	Yugoslavia's foreign trade, 1929–1939	178
6.3	Foreign investment in Yugoslavia, 1928 and 1936	181
6.4	Distribution of income in 1938	187
8.1	Foreign trade, 1947–1953	251
9.1	US aid to Yugoslavia, 1949–1967	271
9.2	Balance and distribution of foreign trade, 1954–1980	273
9.3	Macroeconomic growth, 1952–1970	275
9.4	Socio-economic indicators, 1950–1970	289
10.1	Bank credit and rates of inflation, 1965–1985	311
10.2	Decline of the social sector, 1960–1985	317
10.3	Foreign trade and debt, 1965–1985	319
11.1	Growth of population, 1921–1981	327
11.2	Population and income by republic, 1953–1988	328
11.3	Ethnic populations in Bosnia-Hercegovina, Croatia, and Kosovo, 1961–1991	330
11.4	Socio-economic indicators by republic, 1953–1988	332

Acknowledgments

Following his retirement from the University of Wisconsin in 1987, Michael Petrovich intended to undertake a history of Yugoslavia as a state and an idea. My co-mentor's death the following year prevented him from even starting what has since become an inquest about a vanished state and a vanquished idea. Nor did Fred Singleton live to include Yugoslavia's collapse in an updated edition of *A Short History of the Yugoslav Peoples*, published by Cambridge University Press in 1985 as a successor to its 1968 volume, *A Short History of Yugoslavia*, edited by Stephen Clissold.

I began to prepare the present volume in 1993 in part from a sense of obligation to the work that Michael Petrovich's foreshortened retirement had left undone. But there are other obligations. The works by Fred Singleton and Petrovich came out of the well-established Anglo-American tradition of studying these lands and peoples and deserves my wider acknowledgment. The British tradition is, of course, the longer, dating back to the arrival of anthropologist Arthur Evans in Bosnia in 1875 and extending through the work of Phyllis Auty, Stevan Pavlowitch and others to the Research Unit in Yugoslav Studies at the University of Bradford founded by Fred Singleton. The pioneer generation of American specialists came forward after the Second World War. Among my own debts to them, beyond Michael Petrovich and the grounding in Balkan history I owe to Theofanis Stavrou of the University of Minnesota and in economic history to Rondo Cameron, my primary mentor at the University of Wisconsin, are long associations with Charles and Barbara Jelavich, Peter Sugar, Wayne Vucinich, and George Hoffman. Younger American scholars from whose work I have benefitted are too numerous to list here, well beyond the substantial number referenced in the notes.

Mention should also be made of the younger generation of German historians who have emerged within the past twenty years. They have restored their country's scholarship on Southeastern Europe to the prominence it enjoyed earlier in the century. The work of Holm Sundhaussen and Wolfgang Höpken of the Universities of Berlin and

Leipzig, respectively, have proved especially useful to me, as well as the publications and activity of the Südosteuropa-Gesellschaft in Munich under the direction of Roland Schönfeld.

My own connection to the former Yugoslavia dates from 1965. I served at the American Embassy in Belgrade as a young Foreign Service Officer until 1966 and returned in 1969–70 for doctoral research as a graduate student. Since then, further research as a Professor of History at the University of Maryland and also, since 1987, as Director of East European Studies at the Woodrow Wilson International Center for Scholars in Washington has brought me back numerous times to Sarajevo, Ljubljana, and Zagreb, as well as Belgrade. Within the former Yugoslavia's own pioneer generation of postwar historians, let me cite wider benefits drawn from the works of Janko Pleterski in Ljubljana, Mirjana Gross and Ljubo Boban in Zagreb, Danica Milić and Branko Petranović in Belgrade. At the same time, neither they nor any of the Western scholars mentioned should be held accountable for the volume that follows.

Because of my long association with the former Yugoslavia, a further obligation hovers over these chapters: how to connect the unfinished tragedy of its violent end with its history, more specifically, with its origins in related but separate peoples and places before the First World War and the search for viability that both state and idea pursued twice, from 1918 to 1941 and again from 1945 to 1991? I took the pursuit of these connections, rather than a more comprehensive history of the two Yugoslavias, as my primary task. Urging me on was the pernicious role played in the former Yugoslavia and the successor states by what the Belgrade historian, Andrej Mitrović, has aptly called "parahistory," the distortion of selected sources to indict one side or another for all of Yugoslavia's misfortunes. In the Western world, this mixture of contradictory indictments has encouraged the notion of "age-old antagonisms." Although historically false, the notion has still served to deny to the constituent peoples credentials as Europeans and to portray their current conflicts as primordial problems.

This brief book is intended to bring together enough threads from the mass of available evidence, scholarship, and diplomatic reporting to connect the two Yugoslavias with their origins, their strengths with their weaknesses, and their bloody demise with that full historical context. The text hopefully provides fresh analysis or interpretation that scholars will find instructive. It should also speak to the interested public and responsible public officials as well as university students. The times call for a book that is accessible as well as authoritative and original. The suggestions for further reading, primarily in English but also in German, point to a body of work that in its entirety is larger than for any country in the former Soviet bloc. The notes acknowledge the sizeable scholarship left behind from all parts of the former Yugoslavia and the record left by instructive reports from the British and American embassies in Belgrade and from Radio Free Europe/Radio Liberty in Munich. The notes also seek to identify the conflicting judgments that leave a number of important historical issues, particularly where reliable primary sources are lacking, as with the two world wars, still embroiled in legitimate controversy. The narrative finds its own way through these controversies, reaching conclusions or omitting details that some serious scholars as well as many of those with native experience from the former Yugoslavia will doubtless find controversial in themselves. I have tried to combine my own experience as an outsider there with the broadest scholarly perspective and set of sources I could muster. And I have tried to be fair.

Finally, I wish to express some specific gratitude. The successive chairs of my Department of History at the University of Maryland, Richard Price, Clifford Foust, and James Harris, have offered consistent encouragement, as has Samuel F. Wells, Jr., Deputy Director of the Woodrow Wilson International Center for Scholars. I thank Kristof Nyiri as issue editor for the chance to air my initial approach to the broader subject in "The Failure of the Yugoslav National Idea," *Studies in East European Thought* 46 (1994): 69–89, and co-authors Russell O. Prickett and Ljubiša Adamović for insights in our joint monograph, *Yugoslav-American Economic Relations since World War II* (Durham, NC: Duke University Press, 1990). Roundtable discussions of the proposed table of contents with historians and social scientists in Zagreb and Ljubljana in 1993, and informal meetings with Belgrade and Budapest historians that same year should also be acknowledged.

Secondary or primary sources came from a long list of locations, all with unfailingly helpful staff: the National Archives of the United States in Washington, the Public Record Office in London, the archives of Radio Free Europe/Radio Liberty in Munich, and the several libraries of the Institute of Contemporary History in Belgrade, the Südosteuropa-Gesellschaft in Munich, and the universities of Illinois, Maryland, Minnesota, and Wisconsin. Support for a month of research in Munich from Radio Free Europe in 1993 and a month of writing in Vienna from the Institute for Human Sciences in 1994 was much appreciated.

In the later stages of the enterprise, I received valuable assistance from a variety of critical readers: Gale Stokes, Dennison Rusinow, Sabrina Petra Ramet, Drago Roksandić, Nicholas Miller, Kristin Hunter, Anita Baker Lampe, and the several anonymous readers solicited by

Cambridge University Press. They share none of my responsibility for the final text. The published volume also benefits from copy-editing by Kristin Hunter and the Cambridge University Press, statistical tables prepared by Jonathan Kimball and Philip Birkelbach, and maps by Larry A. Bowring of Bowring Cartographic of Arlington, Virginia. Lys Ann Shore of South Bend, Indiana, ably prepared the index. And I myself could not have completed the volume without the constant support of Anita Baker Lampe, particularly during a year and a half of weekend and evening writing.

Note on pronunciation

The joint language known as Serbo-Croatian in the former Yugoslavia (and since 1991 divided into the historically separable Serbian and Croatian languages) is spelled phonetically, that is, each letter of the alphabet always represents the same sound. The following guide to pronunciation is based on the Latin alphabet, used in the Croatian variant of Serbo-Croatian. Diacritic marks are used with certain consonants to indicate sounds which have a separate sign in the Cyrillic alphabet, used in Serbia, Macedonia, and Montenegro.

A	as in English	a in *father*
B		b in *bed*
C		ts in *cats*
Č		ch in *reach*
Ć	a sound between	ch in *reach* and t in *tune*
D	as in English	d in *dog*
Dž		j in *John*
Dj	a sound between	d in *duke* and dg in *bridge*
E	as in English	e in *let*
F		f in *full*
G		g in *good*
H	as in Scottish	ch in *loch*
I	as in English	i in *machine*
J		y in *yet*
K		k in *kite*
L		l in *look*
Lj		ll in *million*
M		m in *man*
N		n in *net*
Nj		n in *new*
O		o in *not*
P		p in *pet*
R		r in *run* (slightly rolled)

S	ss in *glass*
Š	sh in *she*
T	t in *tap*
U	u in *rule*
V	v in *veil*
Z	z in *zebra*
Ž	s in *pleasure*

Introduction: The search for viability

The avowedly Yugoslav director, Emir Kusturica, originally intended to call his controversial film commemorating the collapse of the Socialist Federal Republic of Yugoslavia "Once There Was a Country," or *Bila jednom jedna zemlja*. His producers, perhaps with an eye to the Cannes Film Festival where it won a Golden Palm in 1995, later abandoned the title of the novel on which the film is based and chose the more marketable and more literal, "Underground." Indeed, the bitterly powerful plot takes us through the half century from 1941 to 1991 in the company of Communist Partisans whose corrupt leader keeps them underground for decades after the Second World War. They stay in a cave underneath the old Belgrade fortress, believing that the Fascists have not been defeated and the war rages on above them. When the leader's scheme finally collapses in the 1960s, he blows up the cave but fails to kill them all. Only with the disintegration of Yugoslavia and the warfare of the early 1990s can the last survivors take their revenge on him.

The title of Dušan Kovačević's novel avoids the allegorical inference that Tito kept Yugoslavia's population "underground," or uninformed about the outside world until his death in 1980. In addition, the plaintive, almost Arthurian original may alternatively be translated as "Once There Was One Country," reminding us immediately that separate if similar parts were put together. The origins and trials of Yugoslav political unification preoccupy this volume. The First World War gave birth to one Yugoslavia that the Second World War destroyed. That same war then created quite a different sort of Yugoslavia.

The subtitle for this book, "Twice there was a country," sounds less plaintive and also reminds us that a first Yugoslavia, 1918–41, preceded the second, 1945–91. Neither deserves idealization as some latter-day Camelot, beyond even the "Yugo-nostalgia" of some former citizens. But damnation as a dictatorship, first royal and then Communist, is also undeserved. The following chapters suggest that these two multi-ethnic states had strengths as well as weaknesses. Both struggled to achieve a viability that eluded them in the end.

1

The bloody end of the second Yugoslavia tempts Western observers to trace the struggles of these South Slav, that is, Yugoslav, peoples and states backward from the present impasse. But going forward into the past makes for bad history. The recent wars of Yugoslav succession, surgically separating Slovenia but dividing Croatia and Bosnia-Herzegovina at terrible human and material cost, have surely made it more difficult for the participants themselves to detach their own history from the past decade. Beginning in the late 1980s, politically manipulated media encouraged Serbs and Croats, the two largest ethnic groups, to think of the other's present intentions as biologically driven by exclusivist, nineteenth-century nationalism and a disposition to repeat the crimes of the two world wars. Too many Serbs saw Bosnian Muslims, the former republic's largest ethnic group, as Turks or Slavic turncoats ready to resume the Ottoman Empire's exploitation of the Serb peasantry with conversion to Islam the only escape. Thus did the respective leaders and media make the others' present populations into "imagined adversaries."[1] They also encouraged foreign observers to assume the revival of old alliances – Serbs with Russians, Bosnian Muslims with Turks, and Croats with Germans – whose historical dimensions all sides have since wildly inflated. The shock of the recent wars and the disruption of everyday life still make the present hard for the survivors to comprehend without falling back on selective historical memory and false analogies. The most heroic character in Kusturica's film is a prisoner of memory and analogy. All the more reason for this volume to track with as much detachment as possible the converging, separate, and ambiguous currents that challenged both Yugoslavias.

Unlike the Nazi destruction of the first Yugoslavia in 1941, the collapse of the second fifty years later came as a shock to the Western world. Most observers had given Yugoslavia's viability the benefit of the doubt since Tito's regime had survived the split with Stalin and the Soviet bloc in 1948. Its widely advertised devolution of economic power to self-managed enterprises and their workers' councils won further respect. Tito's diplomacy balanced artfully between East and West and made Yugoslavia a founder and the only European member of the Non-Aligned Movement. By the 1970s, Tito was an aging Communist leader who, like counterparts in the Soviet bloc, kept too much of the central government's reputation bound up in his own personal authority. Still, open borders and perceptibly higher standards of consumption set Yugoslavia apart from the best of the Soviet bloc. European and American tourists flocked to the Adriatic coast, and over 1 million Yugoslavs, from guest workers to professionals, were employed or studying in the West. Academic exchanges opened many doors. Easy

access, a dramatic past, and an innovative present attracted more
Western scholars and study than any Communist country save the Soviet
Union. In 1961, Ivo Andrić won the Nobel Prize for Literature, and
Miroslav Krleža was also a candidate. Western readers rightly saw
Andrić's work as Yugoslav rather than ideologically socialist or ethnically
nationalist while Krleža's credentials made him a forerunner of the East,
really Central European dissidents of the 1980s.[2]

Contrary to the expectations of *émigré* opponents, no tremors por-
tending disintegration followed Tito's death in 1980. The successful
staging of the 1984 Winter Olympics in Sarajevo and the ongoing
achievements of Yugoslavia's athletes, authors, and film directors told
the outside world that all was still well. Had not the population
continued to rise, to 23 million, and the proportion calling themselves
Yugoslavs climbed past 5 percent in the 1981 census? In any case,
especially for Americans, a federation seemed the appropriate framework
for a multi-ethnic state to address its problems.

The last two chapters of this book detail the deadly problems that did
accumulate by the end of the 1980s. Unemployment rose past 15 percent
and inflation accelerated toward 3,000 percent in 1989. Open ethnic
disputes exploded in Kosovo and at least surfaced in Bosnia, just as the
sort of dissent already challenging Soviet bloc regimes spread from
Slovenia. Meanwhile, Slobodan Milošević tried to step into the vacuum
left in the country's Communist leadership by Tito's death, but
succeeded outside of his Serbian base only in alienating the non-Serb
public and their political élites. When Slovenia's own Communist
leadership joined local dissidents in rejecting a crudely recentralized
Yugoslavia just as Communist power collapsed across the Soviet bloc,
dissolution followed.

In the words of one Belgrade historian, "Yugoslavia began and ended
with Slovenia." The leading Slovenian politician of the first Yugoslavia,
Monsignor Anton Korošec, argued that "even a bad Yugoslavia is better
than no Yugoslavia." Tito's Slovenian ideologue, Edvard Kardelj, had
crafted the second Yugoslavia's federal structure in part to preclude the
large Croatian and Serbian territories that the realignment of internal
borders in 1939 had promised. Without Slovenia to create a broader
balance beyond that between Serbs and Croats, the second Yugoslavia's
framework of six federal republics and two autonomous provinces could
not easily survive. Serbs constituted significant minorities in Croatia as
well as in Bosnia-Hercegovina and Kosovo province. The ethnic politics
that Milošević had launched in Serbia to save Communist power now
came back to threaten, or seem to threaten, those minorities. Imprisoned
by history, although no more than was Croatia's new anti-Communist

leadership, Serb elements were persuaded to force their way out of the hastily recognized new states of Croatia and Bosnia-Herzegovina in 1991–92. (The latter's Bosnian Muslim leadership reverted to the German spelling of Hercegovina so as to emphasize the break with a Serbo-Croatian identity.) Macedonia also declared its independence. Montenegro stayed with a Serbia that now included the previously autonomous provinces of Kosovo and Vojvodina in a rump federation. The second Yugoslavia ceased to exist.

The idea of an inevitable Yugoslavia

Inside and outside what is now the "former Yugoslavia," its costly demise has not surprisingly given new life to the notion that its creation was a mistake from the start. Many insiders now call the country that survived for seventy years in two incarnations an artificial creature whose deformities made collapse inevitable. A Serbian version sees the first Yugoslavia as a burden imposed by the powers at the Paris Peace Conference of 1919 on their wartime ally Serbia and the second as one imposed by the Croatian Communist Tito and an anti-Serbian Soviet Union. A Croatian version cites the disintegration of Yugoslavia as final proof that the Paris peace treaties erred in helping create the first Yugoslavia after the First World War. If the principle of ethnic self-determination introduced by US President Woodrow Wilson justified the dissolution of the multi-ethnic Habsburg monarchy, how could it accommodate another one in the Kingdom of Serbs, Croats, and Slovenes, as the first Yugoslavia was christened? Among the outsiders, some Habsburg historians are attracted to this view. Many Western journalists and politicians unfamiliar with Balkan history have jumped at a more questionable notion, the region's "age-old antagonisms." If primordial hatreds had set Serbs, Croats, and Muslims at each other's throats from the Ottoman conquest forward, they offered both a simple explanation for the recent Yugoslav tragedy and a ready rationale for avoiding any significant involvement.

How different these views sound than the general consensus about Yugoslavia that had prevailed since the 1950s. Most scholars who enlisted in the Western army of Yugoslav specialists, the present author included, simply assumed that the country would and should continue to exist. Officially approved historians of Tito's Yugoslavia went a step further. They called the very creation of their kind of Yugoslavia inevitable. Drawn like many Marxist scholars to the idea of inevitable historical processes at work, they sought like their Soviet counterparts to explain how longer-term forces, and not just the fortunes of war, brought them to power. Instead of reading the origins of industrial capitalism in their lands back to the earliest possible moment, however, they gave pride of place to the inevitable convergence of the South Slavic ethnic groups that Yugoslavia brought together. Each of the six federal republics – Serbia, Croatia, Slovenia, Bosnia-Hercegovina, Macedonia, and Montenegro – had its own history, separate from the others, but to seek any political or economic preeminence from the distinctions was to succumb to "bourgeois nationalism." This tendency was the fatal flaw, rather than "capitalist exploitation," that supposedly undid the first Yugoslavia. Its authoritarian evolution and Great Serb impositions on other ethnic groups were blamed primarily on the Belgrade bourgeoisie, with their counterparts in Zagreb sometimes named as accomplices. In return official Serbian historians could divide the responsibility for the war crimes of the Second World War between the Germans (rarely referred to as Nazis) and the fascist regime of the Independent State of Croatia (NDH). For all Yugoslav historiography, the Serb Chetnik formations could then be held accountable only for their opposition to the Communist Partisans and their collaboration with the Nazi invaders exaggerated. As in the Soviet Union, younger, more able historians avoided the interwar and postwar periods.

A project to write the history of Yugoslavia in a single volume soon put this consensus under pressure. Begun in 1966 at the height of liberal reform, Vladimir Dedijer, et al., *A Short History of Yugoslavia* (New York: McGraw Hill, 1974) was not completed in Serbo-Croatian until 1972. By then Tito had brought the liberal era and its emphasis on political tolerance to an end. The volume's Serb and Montenegrin authorship might not have created such controversy if the two authors of the nineteenth and twentieth-century chapters had not suggested that forces other than foreign domination and bourgeois exploitation stood in the way of unification. The respected Sarajevo historian, Milorad Ekmečić argued that religion, specifically the policies of the Croatian Catholic church, had constituted a serious obstacle to the unification and secular modernization that should otherwise have followed more successfully from a common Serbo-Croatian language. Dedijer was a restless journalist turned historian, after earning renown as Tito's wartime colleague and biographer. His chapters highlighted Croatian crimes against Serbs in both world wars. His case against the Serbian and Croatian bourgeoisies as the bane of interwar Yugoslavia was too sketchy to be convincing. By 1979 Serbian historian Momčilo Zečević was able to open a country-wide conference on the initial unification after the First World War by criticizing the ideological consensus around the Yugoslav idea.[3]

The postwar evolution of Yugoslav scholarship about Yugoslavia should not detain us further. Stevan Pavlowitch and Ivo Banac have provided prudent guides, from somewhat different points of view, through the 1970s and 1980s.[4] The collapsing consensus on an inevitable Yugoslavia did permit more forthcoming and accurate accounts of the world wars and interwar period, first from Croatian and then from Serbian and other Yugoslav historians. Without these historians, as footnotes will attest, this volume could not have been written.

None of them would have the political impact of three works written primarily for polemical purposes during the 1980s. Numerous Western accounts of the country's collapse cite the publication, if not the exact content, of the 1986 Memorandum of the Serbian Academy of Sciences. It protested the abuses that postwar Serbia had supposedly suffered in Yugoslavia in general and Serbs in Kosovo province in particular, thus providing ammunition for Milošević's nationalist campaign. Less publicized in the West were the forbidden but still circulated writings of Franjo Tudjman, the future president of Croatia, cataloguing the injustices that he saw inflicted on Croatia since the First World War, while from Belgrade, Vojislav Koštunica and Kosta Čavoški wrote a volume decrying the way that a Communist political monopoly was imposed on postwar Serbia.[5] In different ways, all three questioned the legitimacy of Tito's Yugoslavia and played a part in its disintegration. But they also posed the question of whether any single Yugoslavia was a legitimate state and by implication raised the prospect of inevitable dissolution.

The search for a viable Yugoslavia

The chapters that follow suspect all inevitabilities. They acknowledge the separate cultural legacies and literatures of these largely related peoples, but neglect their distinctive substance. These brief pages concentrate instead on how these peoples mixed and migrated across proximate lands, and where they intersected with one another – politically, economically, or socially – before and during their unification twice in this century. More specifically, who were they historically and who were their leaders? Tito's individual identity counted; others' did too. What structures and ideas drew them together or divided them? By structures, we mean first the stuff of statebuilding, that is, political culture and legal framework more than ethnic distinctions. We also focus on socio-economic or religious institutions more than class relations and on warfare or other dealings with near neighbors more than with distant powers. The former were generally more important than the latter, supporting the thesis of a leading western scholar of nationalism that the three forces crucial to coalescing ethnic identity into enduring national consciousness have been state-building experience, religious organization and military mobilization.[6] All three forces played their parts, perhaps more than socio-economic structures, in bringing both Yugoslavias together and in breaking them both apart.

By ideas, we mean the various rationales for a new South Slav state that emerged during the nineteenth and twentieth centuries. They confronted a slowly declining Ottoman Empire and a slowly modernizing Habsburg monarchy before 1914. Prior to the nineteenth century, these two empires had divided almost the entire sparsely populated territory between them for nearly 300 years. By the end of the nineteenth century native populations were growing as the imperial hold on them weakened or shifted its ground. Then the First World War swept both empires away. The army of already independent Serbia was essential to the formation of the first Yugoslavia, as were Tito's Partisans to the creation of the second. Still, ideas mattered both times.

Forming the second Yugoslavia seemed initially to pose fewer complications than the first. The Partisan cause brought together people from all the constituent ethnic groups, although precious few Albanians and Hungarians, to fight on the winning side. Its Communist leadership could thereby proclaim a Soviet-style federation under the party's central control. But when the republics received or wrested significant authority from the center, the balance of power across the federation became a crucial issue. Back came the claims and counterclaims that had competed across the interwar period in the first Yugoslavia.

Two modernizing motives favored a single Yugoslavia. They were the same pair that succeeded for Western Europe after the Second World War in building the institutional structures needed to sustain them. One was the promise of a representative government. Surely it could draw some acceptable balance, federal or otherwise, between the provincial parts and the capital city. Between 1921 and 1974, no less than six constitutions and one confederal agreement (in 1939) sought to draw that balance between Belgrade and the rest of Yugoslavia. The second was the attraction of economic integration. It promised a larger internal market and greater comparative advantage in the international trade that revived briefly in the 1920s, but boomed from 1950 to 1980. In addition, as NATO did for Western Europe *vis-à-vis* the Soviet bloc, a single state also afforded Yugoslavia's parts more secure relations with the seven potentially hostile neighbors that ringed its borders after the two world wars.

All three of these state-building rationales – political, economic, and military – played their part in promoting the viability of both "really existing" Yugoslavias. Struggling with them for predominance throughout were three romantic nineteenth-century ideas for the creation of a unitary nation-state – Great Serbia, Great Croatia, and a Yugoslavia founded on the assumption that at least Serbs and Croats, and possibly all South Slavs, were one ethnic group. Any nation-state, it was assumed before 1914, had the potential to assimilate smaller ethnic groups, not by force but by the attraction of the successful European-style modernization that was supposed to follow from political unification. The nation-state's new high culture, secular and open to an increasingly educated population, would assimilate all in its path. Such was in fact the case, Eugen Weber has argued, for nineteenth-century France.[7] Pre-1914 Serbia appeared to start down the same track. Yet it would scarcely be easy for a single state to accommodate three national ideas. A larger, multiethnic Yugoslav state would need and never sufficiently find the sense of common citizenship overriding even the majority's ethnic origin that Rogers Brubaker has called the real distinction of pre-1914 France.[8]

The everyday interaction of peoples nonetheless cut into their ethnic segregation for much of the history of the two Yugoslavias. To the extent that it did, the several state-building rationales held the upper hand over any of the three romantic conceptions of a nation-state. Where it did not, the viability of Yugoslavia was threatened. Two external shocks were still needed to make that threat lethal – the Second World War and the contagious failure in 1989 of the postwar Communist regimes.

1 Empires and fragmented borderlands, 800–1800

What did the 1,000 years prior to the modern era have to do with the development of the two Yugoslav states created during the twentieth century? Or with nineteenth-century ideas and momentum for a state of South Slav, that is, Yugoslav peoples? By 1800 the territories that later became Yugoslavia had suffered even more warfare and forced migration, foreign intervention, and internal division than had their Mediterranean or Central European neighbors. These lands had no chance of sharing in the economic upswing that spread through most of Northwestern Europe during the eighteenth century. Political disarray had deepened economic backwardness during the millennium between the dawn of the medieval centuries and the end of the early modern period.

To understand that disarray, we look first at a small population scattered across a difficult landscape, poorly suited for premodern commerce but accessible to foreign armies. Native ethnic groups, although culturally close, found themselves generally isolated from one another. Yet where they were intermingled, they coexisted constructively. There is scant evidence of the long-standing ethnic hostility that some journalists and politicians, but few scholars, have used to explain the recent warfare on the ruins of the second Yugoslav state. Serbs, Croats, and finally Bosnians established briefly viable, native states during the medieval period. Although their territories overlapped, they did not fight each other and disappeared instead due to internal weakness and external adversaries.

The powerful forces of the Ottoman and Habsburg Empires, advancing from the east and north, respectively, made sure that none of these native states would survive into the early modern period. The Ottoman defeat of Serbian forces at Kosovo in 1389 proved to be the one decisive and long-remembered battle. Otherwise, the two empires left their marks primarily through the institutional frameworks they imposed. Both possessed their own set of coherent institutions, but both failed to apply them uniformly across their Balkan borderlands. Political

9

fragmentation only increased under the long, imperial regimes. After imposing impressive institutional uniformity at the start, the Ottoman Empire allowed different sets of rules and ruling groups to prevail in Serbia, Macedonia, Montenegro, and Bosnia-Hercegovina. For the Habsburg lands, the territories of the present states of Croatia and Slovenia were each divided among four or more distinct jurisdictions. The institutions under civil or military rule differed fatefully.

There were exceptions to the pattern of imperial fragmentation, as we shall see at this chapter's end. Limited commercial connections between the regions developed under the aegis of the multi-ethnic empires and even passed between the two of them. An independent Dubrovnik, Ottoman Sarajevo, and the Habsburg Vojvodina became focal points. Cultural connections that had barely existed within or between the lost native polities of the medieval period now laid groundwork both for their national revival and for a South Slav (or Yugoslav) idea and economy, if not yet a state. The two twentieth-century Yugoslavias would still have to contend with a multiplicity of historical legacies and with the geographic fragmentation nurtured by the wooded mountains that are, in fact, the English translation of the Turkish word, Balkan.

Mountains first, water last

The diversity of geographic features is spectacular, as the late Fred Singleton noted, in a territory whose size, one-quarter million square kilometers, is barely larger than the United Kingdom. The prevalence of uplands poorly suited to cultivation and the absence of an extensive river network for bulk trade kept the density of population strikingly low. An attendant lack of urban centers and intensive agriculture persisted into the nineteenth century. By 1800, despite an eighteenth-century increase, the population of the future Yugoslavia numbered not much more than 5 million, a density of roughly 20 per square kilometer. E. L. Jones has tellingly contrasted this low population count and lack of cities to the higher densities of early modern Western Europe.[1] Both deficiencies reinforced the geographic barriers that were too low to prevent outside penetration but too high to permit widespread integration of any one ethnic group with another.

Stark, striking vistas of the Dinaric mountains lie deceptively close to the soft contours of the Dalmatian coast and long-civilized towns like Dubrovnik. From the earliest centuries, these rugged bands of mountains and uplands, running northwest to southeast and in some places coming within a few miles of the Adriatic Sea, have separated rather than connected. This "vertical north," as Fernand Braudel dubbed the

Dinaric range, confined Mediterranean political influence to the coast and left the dispersed inland settlements isolated from each other and from an adequate food supply.[2] Like the rest of the Mediterranean, the Adriatic coast lacked the fish and arable land needed to make up this deficit. Unlike the rest, it was not short of timber. Ship-building flourished until the modern era and helped link the Dalmatian ports with the wider European world from the medieval period forward.

There were no ties, however, between the coast and the largest, most fertile stretch of lowlands, the region of the former Yugoslavia most capable of producing the grain surplus needed to feed the uplands. A fertile northern plain extends from western Croatia to eastern Serbia. This plain had the preindustrial potential to connect east and west and to feed the south. But the rivers and the valleys through the mountains to the south were too small and too few to permit the bulk trade crucial to population growth in Western Europe.

The Dinaric dividing line, as it turned south, also reinforced the border between Eastern and Western Christianity that proceeded from Bosnia to the coast just south of Dubrovnik. What trade, livestock herding, and other traffic there was between the coast and the hinterland tended to move north and south through mountain valleys, thereby making the economic connections between east and west minimal. Yet the predominant uplands were hardly impassable to foreign armies and domestic populations. Their movements blurred ethnic as well as religious borders, pulling or pushing Orthodox Serbs and Catholic Croats into or out of the same territory. Even when they settled in the same area, the rugged uplands helped keep them isolated in separate villages.

Mountains

Some 45 percent of the territory of the former Yugoslavia rises at least 500 meters above sea-level. While the Julian Alps reach into Slovenia and the Balkan range into Macedonia, it is the Dinaric chain and its periphery that predominates. Its southeasterly course from Croatia to Hercegovina and Montenegro has long been renowned for the high karst (anhydrite) surface that covers fully 10 percent of the area in Map 1.1. Its limestone rock pulls precipitation into underground channels, leaving the arid soil above barren for cultivation of any kind. Access in summer to the water underground does at least support upland grazing for livestock. The northeastern Dinaric terrain of Bosnia and western Serbia, however, consists of crystalline rock that retains surface water. The forest cover that once lay over this more favorable soil also offered better chances for later cultivation and settlement, particularly in the highland plateaus and valleys near the Sava and Morava rivers, in Slavonia and Serbia, respectively.

Lowlands

If defined as land less than 200 meters above sea level, lowlands comprise only 29 percent of the territory of the former Yugoslavia. They are concentrated in the north from the Ljubljana basin in the west, across Slavonia to the Vojvodina in the east. This eastern plain contains the richest, loess-covered soil and accounts for 20 percent of the former Yugoslavia's arable land on less than 9 percent of its territory. But here periodic floods alternate with droughts caused by barely 20 inches of annual rainfall versus nearly 30 inches to the west. Such a climate posed problems for the first Slav settlers comparable in the American experience to the homesteaders in Nebraska. In Macedonia the former lake basins surrounding the Vardar river are too isolated and choked by soil from the erosion of the long-deforested hills to provide a similar center for grain cultivation in the south. The northern Macedonian lands that became a Yugoslav republic lie far enough south, however, to grow cotton and tobacco.

The limited areas higher than 1,500 meters are divided by what geographer George Hoffman called "corridor valleys reaching into the heart of the region," opening it up to "people and ideas from nearby power centers," while the rugged and diverse relief preserved upland isolation and protectionism.[3] The region's accessibility has doubtless contributed to the myriad of east-west lines that geographers have drawn to mark the cultural division between Mediterranean and Central European influences. The lines run from the Adriatic coast and Greek Macedonia, the furthest south, to the Sava and Danube rivers, the furthest north. Over most of this territory, however, these two influences were mixed rather than separate or hostile by the late nineteenth century.

Rivers

The Danube provided the Balkans with its major premodern connection to Central Europe. Navigable from Ulm in German Baden southward through Vienna and Budapest, the great waterway enters the former Yugoslavia in the east as the border between Slavonia and the Vojvodina. The Danube draws on the Drava and Sava rivers, if not their tributaries, to constitute the one commercially useful network for the region. No navigable river flows north from either the Adriatic or the Aegean Sea.

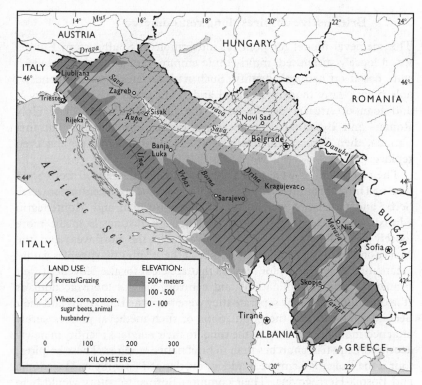

Map 1.1 Former Yugoslavia's physical geography and land use

The longest entirely Yugoslav river, the Sava, is not navigable from its
Slovenian source until halfway to Belgrade, nor are any useful stretches
of its four southern tributaries, from the Una in Croatia to the Drina that
divides Bosnia from Serbia. The Morava river, connecting the Serbian
interior to the Danube, was also unable to carry the bulk trade essential
to modern economic integration and to the growth of large cities. A
Central European regime came down the Danube, with the Habsburg
advance almost to Belgrade by 1700, but its political and cultural
influence south into Serbia and Macedonia would not be significant
before the nineteenth century.

In sum, the geographic contrast between the lands of the former
Yugoslavia and Northwestern Europe could not be more striking. The
latter's fertile lowlands, abundant rainfall, and easy access to the sea or
a river network are all missing. Economic development or integration
without them would be difficult.

Brief native empires, long remembered

The medieval model for political integration in Southeastern Europe was a loosely structured, multi-ethnic empire, rather than a centralized state based on national identity. Such nation-states were not conceivable before early modern England and France finished what Henry V and Joan of Arc set out to do in the fifteenth century. The Holy Roman and Byzantine Empires were instead the regimes that first Croatia, then Serbia, and finally Bosnia sought to replicate and even replace.

Their populations were primarily South Slavs, descended from Slavs who had moved southwest into the region from the sixth century onward. Serbs and Croats, as well as the disputed Bosnian and Montenegrin admixtures, spoke roughly the same language, distinct from the more loosely related languages of the Slovenes in the northwest and the Macedonians to the southeast. Neither of these latter two peoples would create medieval empires for reasons that are clear for the Slovenes (their Frankish German domination) and controversial for the Macedonians (the question being how separate they were from the Bulgarians and their Second Empire). But the populations of such medieval polities surely attached more importance, at the time, to their religious identity in newly accepted Christian churches than to brief native empires. These empires, four if the Bulgarian empire is added, overlapped fatefully in Macedonia and Bosnia-Hercegovina. Their common Bosnian territory would help bring the modern claims for Greater Serbia and Greater Croatia (the native usage is "Great") into conflict.

Croatia

The tribes whose southwestern track toward the Adriatic and conversion by Latin priests marked their initial distinctions as Croats reached the Dalmatian coastal towns by 600. They came as South Slavs, possibly stirred by an Iranian admixture shared with rather than separating them from the Serbs. And they came as pagans, attacking the small Christian population of Romanized Illyrians whom they soon absorbed. The Croats' own conversion to what became Roman Catholicism occurred over the next 300 years, inland under the loose Frankish regime and on the coast from a neglected interplay between Latin and Byzantine influences. Byzantine authorities, anxious to deny Venice the political authority they sought to reestablish for themselves, recognized the regime of the first recorded Croatian ruler, Tomislav, at Biograd in 910. They even swallowed his confirmation as king by the Pope in Rome, already informally independent of the Christian church's eastern center in Constantinople.

Further pressure from an expanding Venetian coastal empire pushed subsequent Croat kings into close cooperation with the growing Hungarian kingdom to the north. Indeed, Venetian rule over most of the Istrian peninsula and the Dalmatian coast continued intermittently from this early date through the eighteenth century. Expanding inland, the Croatian state found its ruling feudal nobility unable to produce an heir to the throne at the end of the eleventh century. In 1102, the Hungarian king assumed the throne under a joint agreement, the *Pacta conventa*. Thus began the separate but unequal existence of Croatia within the Hungarian kingdom that finally ended in 1918. For most of that period, the Croatian nobility kept their titles, their assembly (or *Sabor*), and rural authority in Croatia proper. But in recently acquired Slavonia, that authority was lost to the Hungarians, and in Bosnia, to a series of other regimes beginning with the Byzantine Empire in 1167.

The restoration of a Great Croatian state within its broadest eleventh-century borders, including Dalmatia, Istria, Slavonia, and even Bosnia-Hercegovina, as well as Croatia proper, has attracted advocates from the nineteenth century forward. Croatia proper continued to exist as a separate political entity, even after the 1102 agreement with Hungary, but neither it nor the other four territories were successful in state-building on their own terms. Hungarian, Venetian, Ottoman, and finally Habsburg sovereignty stood in the way.

Religious division also stood in the way of a more unified Croatia. The inland peasantry converted to Christianity under liturgy and a Slavic alphabet (*glagolica*) ministered by native priests who married, wore their hair long like the Byzantine clergy, and knew no Latin. Early in its struggle with Constantinople for control of the Dalmatian coast, Rome felt obliged to accept such priests as a political concession. By the tenth century, papal authorities tried to confine the liturgy to Croatia and suppress the recruitment of any more *glagoljaš* priests. Their principal Croatian allies were the nobility, particularly from the coastal cities that were already well within the Latin orbit.

The struggle over use of the Latin versus Slavic-based glagolitic alphabets continued among Croatian churchmen beyond Rome's formal break with Constantinople in 1054 and even Croatia's inclusion in loyal Hungary in 1102. This marked the low point, according to A. P. Vlasto's authoritative study, for the Slavic language and church in Croatia.[4] Both revived, however, to persist in a number of coastal dioceses for several centuries. Glagolitic served as a secular alphabet for Croatian literature from the fourteenth to the sixteenth centuries. But for the nobility and higher clergy, Croatia became a Latin Catholic domain under the discipline of the papal hierarchy from the twelfth century forward. Only the always locally grounded Franciscan order would survive, as we shall see, to challenge that hierarchy in the modern era.

Serbia

The medieval state of Serbia maintained its full independence longer and faced far less religious division than did the Croatian kingdom. Its greater experience in state-building, supported by its own autocephalous, or independent, Orthodox church, did not produce as centralized a regime as its rulers desired nor as ethnically Serb a population as the nineteenth-century model for a Great Serbia would presume. In fact, with no thought to ethnic consolidation or cleansing, Serbia's medieval rulers pursued a policy of imperial expansion that first won and then lost a territory too extended to permit central control.

After their arrival in the seventh century, the main South Slav (eventually Serb) settlements between the Drina and Ibar rivers at first seemed too far from the Adriatic or the Aegean to generate imperial ambitions or to gain access to Christianity. The patriarchal Serb clans were eventually drawn toward the Adriatic with its winter pastures for livestock and the promise of trade. A combination of Byzantine and Bulgarian influences emanating from Ohrid in Macedonia had deflected their conversion from Adriatic and Latin religious influences to Orthodoxy by the tenth century. Thereafter, several local Serb clan chiefs, or *župani*, used the coastal connections via their base in Zeta (roughly modern Montenegro) to challenge weakening Byzantine authority there. A *župan* named Nemanja from the adjoining area called Raška (Kosovo today) later succeeded, despite a series of Byzantine humiliations, in founding an independent state in 1180. He quickly incorporated Zeta and secured a coastal foothold beyond the Bay of Kotor and Dubrovnik. One son, Stefan, became the "first crowned" Serbian king, in 1196, under papal authority accepted to emphasize independence from Constantinople.

Another son, later canonized as St. Sava, took further advantage of Byzantine weakness in 1219 to establish an independent Serbian church, observing the Orthodox ritual through the Cyrillic alphabet and a Slavic liturgy that would endure. This separate church, recognized by Constantinople, adopted the Byzantine principle that church and state should work together to shape public policy. Yet in the nearly two centuries that this Serbian state survived after the two brothers had apparently merged church and state, the church leaders spent their

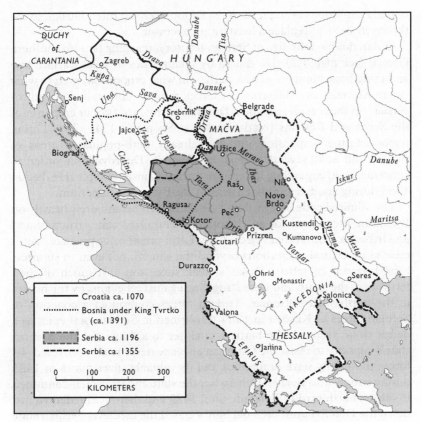

Map 1.2 Medieval states of Croatia, Serbia, and Bosnia

energies on winning the king's support for isolated monasteries like Nemanja's original Studenica, patterned after the still more isolated Mount Athos, the famed peninsular monastery of northern Greece. Church leaders did not oblige the Serbian state to break contact with the Catholic world or force the conversion of Latin Christians. They even allowed Latin priests to proselytize until the mid-fourteenth century.[5]

The subsequent rulers of the Serbian state sought to emulate and challenge the Byzantine Empire, but they let their clan chieftains, who became feudal lords, retain too much authority. Despite their scattered holdings and initially weak control over a largely free peasantry, these nobles were able to deny their rulers the central military authority characteristic of a Byzantine emperor. The nobles nonetheless pressed for further advance into Byzantine territory beyond Macedonia. Their imperial ambitions brought the most famous Serbian ruler, Dušan, to the throne in 1331 to replace a hesitant predecessor.

Dušan doubled the size of Serbian territory, reaching far into southern Greece (see map 1.2). He did so by taking sides in local warfare and accepting large numbers of non-Serbs – in what proportion, even to what extent Macedonian, Bulgarian, or Greek remains uncertain and controversial – in the conquered lands. Dušan was crowned tsar, or emperor, of the Serbs and Romans (read Greeks) at Skopje in 1346. Tsar Dušan forsook further expansion into the already Serb-populated areas of Bosnia and sold several coastal holdings to Dubrovnik in order to concentrate on expanding his empire toward Constantinople. He died in 1355 during another campaign against the Byzantine imperium.

The admired code of laws that Tsar Dušan left behind drew heavily on Byzantine precedents for an elaborately centralized state structure and an Orthodox church that rejected any Latin presence or practice. Yet it created no central institutions beyond the church, not even to suppress local brigands or rebels. Dušan's weak successors lost much of their territory in the south and were struggling against rebellions by the nobles in the north when Ottoman Turkish forces confronted a coalition of Serbian forces as Kosovo in 1389. Enshrined in Serbian oral epics as a defeat to be avenged, the battle was closer to a draw. Yet the Serbian state's capacity to resist the Ottoman advance never really recovered. Its forces did briefly seize Srebrenica and its valuable silver mines in 1425 during a foray into Bosnia. Otherwise, the state and its capital continued to retreat northward to Belgrade until 1429 and then to Smederevo just down the Danube until the final blows ended the medieval Serbian state in 1459.[6]

Bosnia

First set between and then briefly outlasting these medieval Croatian and Serbian empires was a Bosnian state much less celebrated in the historical memories that underpin ethnic self-assertion. Its religious identity remains too ill-defined to bolster the claim that most of the population was consciously either Croat or Serb. To muddy the waters for ethnic identification still further, a significant fraction of its unquestionably South Slav population converted to Islam after the Ottoman conquest that destroyed the Bosnian state.

This Bosnian state did exist long enough to help break the ties that bound the area to the Croatian or Serbian states, ties not vigorously pursued by either polity. In the course of the twelfth century, Bosnia won political independence and added Hercegovina later. Loosely constituted under a single *Ban*, or governor, named Kulin, the Bosnian state rejected both Byzantine and Hungarian overlordships. A set of court officials and a state treasury emerged and a *stanak*, or assembly, of nobles regularly convened. Their social origins fit the pattern of local clan leaders among the Balkan Slavs, Serbs and Croats alike. Traian Stoianovich describes them as župani who controlled the lowland commons or the choice upland pastures for an otherwise free peasant population.[7] Their murky ethnic origins may well have been more Croat than Serb, but this new ruling élite regarded itself as a separate Bosnian entity.

The independent state of Bosnia that survived intermittently until the mid-fifteenth century added much of Hercegovina in 1326 and continued to struggle against Hungarian advances until the Ottoman conquest. Its powers reached their high point under Ban (Governor) Tvrtko. He reestablished independence from Hungary in 1369, crowned himself king of Serbia and Bosnia in 1377, and began construction of a port for Adriatic shipping in the Bay of Kotor in 1382. This link to the Adriatic created the economic base that supported the rise of the Bosnian state. Local merchants and towns soon joined Dubrovnik and other Dalmatian ports to trade with the Bosnian mines for silver, gold, copper, and iron, a concentration of precious metals found nowhere else in southern Europe. Bosnian wax, wool, and slaves were also exchanged for salt and Mediterranean manufactures. Customs revenues from this trade and dues paid by Dubrovnik partially bankrolled the Bosnian court.

The Bosnian rulers still headed a disjointed, isolated regime and as such did not oppose the Manichean heresy that here was called Bogomilism. Spreading from Bulgaria to Bosnia, Hercegovina, and Dalmatia by the thirteenth century, the movement and its dualist belief in the devil as well as the deity were initially tolerated. Papal authorities soon tried to expunge it, perhaps using the excuse of heresy to establish local control over the nominally Latin Bosnian church. Dominicans were dispatched in 1240 and the Franciscans in 1340. Finally in the mid-fifteenth century, a determined Hungarian campaign to eradicate the heresy and to bring the Bosnian church under Rome's hierarchical control forced the weakening Bosnian state to capitulate. Bosnian church leaders had to recant or emigrate to Hercegovina. The powerful Hungarian kingdom reasserted its suzerainty and canceled the payment of tribute to the Ottoman Empire. In 1463 an Ottoman army quickly conquered Bosnia and, by 1483, Hercegovina.

More important than heresy in this dénouement, according to recent research, was the fragmented isolation of the Bosnian church and state. John V. A. Fine, Jr., has identified the Bogomil clergy as only a small group of priests, probably fewer than 100, who isolated themselves in a small number of monasteries and who in general did *not* speak the South Slavic language needed for a mass movement.[8] The larger number of Slavic-speaking village priests using a glagolitic liturgy formed the backbone of the separate Bosnian church. If its priests were not often Bogomils, neither were they typically tied to the hierarchy or authority of the Latin Catholic church. Its monasteries reportedly allowed priests to marry, and its services incorporated a number of Orthodox practices. Village members were too loosely bound for it to endure as a separate Christian church after the Ottoman conquest.

The low density of population (probably fewer than ten persons per square kilometer) contributed to limiting the Ban's authority and, hence, the Bosnian state's capacity to survive. Bosnia's small and scattered population was a weakness shared with the medieval Croatian and Serbian states, as well as an invitation to later disputes about historic claims to ethnic borders. But the inability of the ruler to designate his successor or dispossess those nobles who defied him became a particular, and surely fatal, weakness of the Bosnian state in the face of a coordinated Ottoman advance.

Varieties of Ottoman rule

The Ottoman occupation of Bosnia began just ten years after the conquest of Constantinople in 1453. Larger than any European city at the time and heir to the long Byzantine tradition of a centralized bureaucracy, the now Ottoman capital and the Turkish sultan's staff, or *Porte*, located there became the centers for connecting front line forces with an increasingly bureaucratic system of military occupation for newly conquered territories in the Middle East as well as Southeastern Europe.[9]

The Ottomans successfully imposed a centrally controlled regime of land tenure, tax collection, and native religious rights that in practice approached the responsible local government that the medieval South Slav states had failed to establish. The sultan's cavalry officers, or *sipahi*, were assigned varying amounts of agricultural land, called *timar* after the most common size, to administer for the sultan. Timar holdings were carved from newly conquered land that was considered the sultan's personal property. Officers were to maintain themselves modestly on these holdings and collect a tithe, initially one-eighth of the harvest plus a livestock tax, from local peasants to help provision Constantinople, other towns, or the rest of the sultan's army. These timar holdings and ranks were not heritable. The *devşirme* system of forced recruitment and conversion to Islam of young boys (not the babies of later legends) brought South Slavs into the officer corps. The *millet* structure for the several non-Islamic religious communities (Catholics were excluded as papal adversaries) empowered the native Orthodox (and Jewish) clergy to administer their populations' local religious and internal legal affairs, and even justice if no Muslims were involved. Ethno-religious identity could thus grow at the local level as long as overriding Ottoman authority was not challenged. More specifically the Serbian Orthodox church received rights to local authority that their native empire had never granted. The church's political power would have no native state with which to contend until the nineteenth century.

In the years after its high point under Suleiman the Magnificent (1520–66), central authority weakened and the Ottoman regime lost some of its uniformities. Landholdings eventually became hereditary and taxation more exploitative, while local élites vied with renegade officers and the sultan's loyal representatives for control.

Weakening Ottoman authority contributed to a set of significant distinctions among the four future Yugoslav lands that remained under Ottoman control until the nineteenth century – Macedonia, Bosnia-Hercegovina, Serbia, and Montenegro. Their disparate places in the Ottoman framework, commercial as well as administrative, worked against the creation of common Yugoslav political traditions.

Macedonia

By the late medieval period, within the borders of the post-1945 Yugoslav republic or beyond into Pirin or Aegean Macedonia, there was no Macedonian state to delay the Ottoman conquest. Neither increasingly Greek Byzantium, nor the Bulgarian and Serbian states, in whose territories all of Macedonia alternately found itself, were able to prevent its early absorption as an Ottoman province after the Battle of Maritsa in 1371. Its medieval ethnic composition is the most controversial among any of the future Yugoslavia's territories. No reliable sources exist to determine whether the probable South Slav majority on the future republic's territory was ethnically Macedonian or Bulgarian, or what the size and influence of a Greek minority was in the inland heart of the ancient Greek province of Macedonia. Two features seem more certain. This territory, together with the areas of northern Greece and western Bulgaria that comprised Byzantine and Ottoman Macedonia, was sparsely populated and it attracted the one significant immigration of Turkish peasants into the future Yugoslav lands after the Ottoman conquest.

The Ottoman regime had already established its timar system of state land administered by the sultan's cavalry officers. They were firmly in place in Macedonia's lowland villages by the sixteenth century. But many peasants deserted those lowland villages during the campaigns further north and west that kept Ottoman forces moving back and forth across Macedonia. Its lowland soil was nitrogen-poor because of erosion from surrounding hills. To repopulate such villages, Ottoman authorities encouraged the migration of originally Anatolian peasants and also more of the Vlach herders and traders of livestock. The Tsintsar Vlachs, speaking a language related to Romanian, founded the trade center of Moskopol in northern Greece that endured until the late eighteenth century.

Further commercial connections to the Aegean port of Salonika (Thessaloniki in modern Greece) hardly modernized the Macedonian countryside. Private holdings of heritable lowland villages, called *chiftlik*, were concentrated under more exploitative arrangements (up to one-half of all crops demanded) than elsewhere in the Ottoman Balkans. Rather than local merchants from Salonika responding to capitalist demand, the chiftlik owners appear from recent research to have been Turkish or Albanian officers of the Ottoman cavalry or infantry who took advantage of the weakening political authority of the Porte to seize former timar lands and treat them as their own property.[10] These generally small seizures of less than 50 acres yielded small amounts of grain or cotton for smuggled export from villages. Their peasants often deserted to nearby hills or more distant towns. The struggle of these local warlords with each other and with the central Ottoman authority formed the early political history of Vardar Macedonia, eventually incorporated into Yugoslavia, making it the most chaotic and at the same time the least accessible to native participation or non-Ottoman influence of any South Slav land.

Bosnia-Hercegovina

The Ottoman empire made Bosnia-Hercegovina its furthest western outpost in the South Slav lands, fortifying the province from the start against its principal European adversary, the Habsburg Empire. Unlike the Orthodox, largely Serb populations of Serbia and Montenegro (discussed below), the Bosnian Serbs, and the upland Vlachs who sooner or later assimilated with them initially benefitted from the Ottoman concessions granted to make the border more secure. So too did some Croats, especially those who were granted timar concessions along the western or northern border. In addition the Franciscan order was allowed to continue its ministry to Bosnia's Croat population, thus receiving the equivalent of millet status, a privilege denied to the Roman church elsewhere in the empire.

The bulwark of the Ottoman order became the large number of Bosnian Slavs who converted to Islam. The controversy over those conversions and those converted has contributed enough to the twentieth-century bloodshed in Bosnia to merit further attention. The old presumption that only the adherents of the Bogomil heresy converted to Islam must be questioned. They were far too few, as we have seen. Even membership in the nominally Catholic Bosnian church amounted to maybe one-fifth of the roughly one-half million people in the former Bosnian state of the fifteenth century. Following the Ottoman conquest, a largely unforced process of conversion had made two-fifths of the total population Muslim by the middle of the sixteenth century. Some previous members of the Bosnian church, if only a few Orthodox, were surely included. More significantly, to the considerable degree that religious identity determined ethnic identity in the fifteenth and sixteenth centuries, the extent of the conversion calls into question the consciously Croat or Serb identity of much of the Bosnian population. Those distinct identities were not, however, long in emerging *after* the Ottoman conquest.

What attracted South Slav converts to Islam and what sort of Islam was it? We must not confuse the Sunni mainstream of the Ottoman Empire with the militant and fundamentalist Shiites far to the East. Nor was religious observance and rigor stressed in the Ottoman Sunni framework until the seventeenth century. Although the direct evidence of the Ottoman registers remains to be studied, recruitment through the devşirme system or the conversion of slaves (who could thereby obtain freedom) appears to have been most important in the longer run. In the short run, the legal rights that Muslims received in an urban milieu growing in size and sophistication during the sixteenth century made conversion advantageous.[11] For the overwhelmingly rural population, such rights and tax privileges attracted few of the small surviving nobility, but more of the Serb and Vlach leaders of upland villages that had adopted the "Vlach mode" of livestock pasturing and seasonal soldiering, whether before or after the Ottoman conquest. The Porte had a special role for these converted villages. All of them were designated as "Vlach," thus providing the basis for some later Croatian scholars to claim that "Serbs" outside of Serbia were all descendants of Vlachs. Because only limited imperial forces were available to man their frontiers against the organized military borders of Venice and the Habsburg monarchy, the Ottoman administration adopted their adversaries' system of fortresses garrisoned with local forces. They even called them by the same name – *kapitanates*. The system quickly spread across Bosnia, attracting converts who became eligible to be a captain, especially if they converted their village into the force.

Such captains were most often the Ottoman designees to administer agricultural land and tax collection. By the seventeenth century, they began to impose the higher chiftlik obligations for their own use primarily on the Serb newcomers whose numbers had greatly increased after the Ottoman conquest of Serbia. These impositions on the crops of the unconverted Serb peasantry, called *kmet* or serf, only increased as the permanent Habsburg advances of the late seventeenth century forced the Bosnian and other Muslim élites, who had followed the imperial banner into Hungary under Suleiman the Magnificent, back into Bosnia.

The borders of Ottoman Bosnia would not change again from 1699 to the Habsburg occupation of 1878 and beyond. But within the upland and generally inhospitable countryside, the seeds of the antagonism between rural Serbs (or Croats) and Muslims had been planted. At the same time, a process of three-sided accommodation – four, counting a growing number of Sephardic Jews – was under way in Sarajevo and other towns. The enduring exclusion of Slavs from urban life that became a major burden of the Ottoman regime elsewhere in the Balkans did not persist in Bosnia. Bosnian Muslims had accounted for almost all of Sarajevo's population during its sixteenth-century expansion. Thereafter, the city accommodated Serb merchants and a smaller number of Croats and Sephardic Jews. The business of state and commerce was conducted in the local South Slavic language, the *štokavski* dialect that was the forerunner of Serbo-Croatian. The practices of the native *bektashi* order of Islamic mystics, whose nine cardinal points thoroughly mixed Christian and Islamic tenets, may have also contributed to the overlapping and even borrowing of religious traditions.[12] While twentieth-century anthropologists were overconfidently celebrating them, Serb or Croat nationalists could use such overlapping to argue that Bosnian Muslims were originally Serbs or Croats.

Serbia

Ottoman rule did not subject neighboring Serbia to the complex Bosnian mixture of integration and oppression. The prolonged Ottoman conquest that stretched from the Battle of Kosovo in 1389 to the fall of Smederevo on the Danube in 1459 prompted Serb emigration to Montenegro, Bosnia, and Hercegovina. They left behind scattered lowland clearings in Kosovo that attracted Albanian migration. Yet the forested interior of Serbia proper discouraged the settlement of many

Turks or even an extensive network of timar holdings outside of Belgrade, the fortified towns, and their environs. Serbian presence in those towns was by the same token minimal, but in the countryside their local leaders, drawn from the village's extended family communities, or *zadruge*, maintained their authority from the start.

This small Serbian population, no bigger than the one-half million totals for late medieval Bosnia and Macedonia, nonetheless carried with them the strongest immediate memory of lost statehood among any of the Ottoman's subject peoples. The last Serbian regimes exploited their peasant population too much for the reality of their rule to explain this folk memory. The Ottoman regime itself provided the social framework. Village autonomy and zadruga rights grew with the restoration of the independent authority of the Serbian Orthodox church. The millet system gave it legal as well as religious powers. And to celebrate the church's saints, from St. Sava on, was to celebrate medieval Serbia, thus making the Orthodox millet a major source for the early modern elaboration of Serbian ethnic identity.

A Bosnian Serb, Mehmed Sokoli, rising from devşirme selection through the officer corps to become the sultan's grand vizier, had in fact restored the Patriarchate at Peć in Kosovo in 1557 and appointed his brother as the first Patriarch. Yet the concession also fitted with the general Ottoman tendency to accept special arrangements to secure its borderlands. Peć's forty-one dioceses remained under Serbian control until 1766, when the Patriarchate's flirtation with Russia prompted the Porte to hand them over to trusted Greek clergy. In the meantime, however, the dioceses for Serbs in eastern Bosnia had promoted the spread of a distinctly Serbian Orthodox, ethno-religious identity that had not been prominent in pre-Ottoman Bosnia.[13]

Filling in this Ottoman framework for a separate Serbian identity were two particular sources of historical memory. The Serbian folk tradition of epic poetry passed from village to village and from generation to generation by oral verses as famous to literary historians as their Finnish counterparts. They were sung after the Ottoman conquest precisely to lament the lost Battle of Kosovo (1389) and to praise past native rulers. The seven original cycles of verse center on one or the other of these two, treating the events as tragic and the historical figures as mythic.[14]

Serbian historical memory would also fasten on the Great Migration of 1690, from Kosovo to the Habsburg's newly won Vojvodina north of the Sava and Danube rivers. Led by the Patriarch himself, this mass migration of at least 30,000 villagers followed from the fear of Ottoman reprisals after the Serbian population had supported a Habsburg incursion. When the advance failed to secure Serbia proper, much of its native population simply retreated across the river to the Habsburg border regime in the Vojvodina. The new borderland and its Serb settlements provided a sanctuary for others wishing to leave Ottoman territory and another base for the Serbian Orthodox hierarchy, the only one left after Peć was taken from them in 1766. Perhaps more importantly, the hardships and heroism of the migration itself added Kosovo to Serbian historical memory as a region to which they should return.

Montenegro

Until the nineteenth century, Montenegro was the one future Yugoslav territory whose history was not greatly affected by migration. Its mountainous isolation barred permanent or easy access to its narrow coastline, while its land was too barren even to support much livestock. Local resources typically provided a food supply for two-thirds of the year at best, making banditry almost necessary for survival. Resistance from the small but fiercely warlike population kept the belated Ottoman conquest of 1499 from ever being completed. Much like the Scots highlanders, these upland clans resisted external authority and enforced their own rules. Numbering well under 100,000, they were certainly Orthodox and probably of Serb origin. Part of the original Nemanja province of Zeta, this province became known as Montenegro when it was cut off from a Serbian state forced to shift northward after the 1389 Battle of Kosovo. Ottoman authorities never attempted to apply the timar system of landholding to Montenegro. They relied instead on local clan leaders to collect a poll tax, the only revenue demanded.

The bishops of the Orthodox church, now cut off from the Serbian hierarchy, emerged as the rulers of Montenegro from 1516. Their temporal powers exceeded those of their Serbian counterparts in theory, but how much in practice they controlled the extended, well-armed families is doubtful.

Bishops from the Njegoš clan established a line of continuous succession as religious rulers from Danilo in 1696 forward. Perhaps following the line of least resistance, they pursued foreign alliances rather than internal consolidation. A religious connection to the Russian Orthodox church dated from the sixteenth century. Bishop Danilo's visit to Moscow in 1716 extracted a Russian subsidy that continued until the comic-opera confusion of 1767, when a local imposter claimed to be Stefan the Small, the tsar of Russia, and was soon exposed. The bishops then turned to the Habsburg monarchy for external support, but relied on their own forces to repel a last Ottoman assault on Montenegro. It began in 1785, led significantly (for future ethnic relations) by an

Albanian *pasha* and his force of neighboring Albanians. By the time this assault was finally defeated in 1796, Montenegro had turned back to Russia for external support.

The disproportionately large role that Montenegro played in European diplomacy of the nineteenth century had its roots in this freedom to establish even limited foreign relations.[15] The Ottoman Empire had ceded no such rights to its other territories. Montenegro's long-standing international identity would count for far less in the formation of the first Yugoslavia than the rulers of the independent principality expected, while its upland outlaw tradition helped give Montenegro's Communist Partisans a major role in the formation of the second Yugoslavia.

Varieties of Habsburg rule

Central Europe for these Balkan borderlands consisted primarily of the Habsburg empire. Heir to the Holy Roman Empire and its German lands until the nineteenth century, it is properly called an empire until then. The Habsburg court and administration in Vienna started down the road leading to the enlightened absolutism (read authoritarian bureaucracy) of the eighteenth century more to secure its southern border than to accommodate or compete with any German pattern. The initial Ottoman advance and defeat at the gates of Vienna in 1529 linked the Austrian center of the empire to the retreating Hungarian nobility and their determination to retake their lost kingdom. Only the repulse of the second Ottoman advance on Vienna after 1683 allowed the recapture of these lost lands, which included Slavonia and the Vojvodina. Long before then, the empire had established a broad Military Border (*Vojna Krajina*) on the Croatian side of Ottoman Bosnia-Hercegovina. During the eighteenth century, it extended that border area to northwest and southern Slavonia as well as to the southern Vojvodina. All three border regimes were bound to Vienna, but each was distinct from the other and from the Habsburg administration of Civil Croatia (now cut off from Slavonia) and a similarly subdivided Slovenia (see map 1.3). Thus the press for progress through bureaucratic uniformity – the essence of enlightened absolutism – did not tie the Habsburg borderlands together any more than the Ottoman regimes linked together their Balkan provinces. Only the nineteenth century would bring such centralizing pressures to bear on both sides of the border.

The various Habsburg authorities did not impose a Roman Catholic monopoly on the practice of Christianity. This may seem surprising, given Vienna's commitment to the Counter-Reformation against Protestant denominations and the prominence given to the crusading

Jesuit order.[16] Yet to the south, where the threat of Ottoman attack persisted, the emperor had granted concessions across the Military Border and all of the Vojvodina to Serbs, other Orthodox Christians, and even non-native Protestants. The only native Protestant movement on the southern Habsburg border, in Slovenia, had been rigorously suppressed.

Slovenia under Austria

The Slovenes' ancestors first came to their compact Alpine redoubt in the late sixth century. Already speaking a separate South Slav language that distinguished them from Serbs or Croats, their location close to the Frankish German realms of Central Europe created another distinction. Less than 100 years after their conversion to Christianity in the eighth century, Slovenes lost their political independence to Frankish feudal lords. An immediate influx of German settlers to the plains and valleys pushed Slovenes into the abundant uplands. Before any native political structure could reemerge, the Habsburg rulers who succeeded the Franks as Holy Roman emperors incorporated the several parts of modern Slovenia more closely into their administrative framework than any other future Yugoslav land.

The absence of any serious Ottoman threat to Habsburg Slovenia, an advantage in itself, gave the regime in Vienna a freer hand to deal with the sizeable Protestant movement that sprang up in the early sixteenth century. Luther's tenets attracted Slovene and German adherents, first in the towns and then in the countryside. They openly opposed the authority of the established Catholic hierarchy. Jesuit zeal and military force soon suppressed them. A number of the German townspeople and nobles simply left during the 1590s. Not until the eighteenth century, however, did one Slovene scholar, Tomas Linhart, reject the lingering view that the Slovenes were ethnically German themselves and had no separate Slovene identity.[17]

Several Italian influences helped confirm the separate Slovenian identity that Linhart postulated. Increasing Habsburg control had culminated in 1747 with a provincial government administered directly by civil servants in Vienna. Yet within Carniola, the most heavily Slovenian province, the Counter-Reformation closed the German schools precisely because they were Protestant and replaced them with ones sponsored by Italian universities. The school at Laibach (Ljubljana in Slovenian) that later evolved into a Slovenian university was founded in 1693 on the model of a Roman academy. German waned as the language of instruction sufficiently to open the door to some official acceptance of Slovenian by the later eighteenth century, if only as a device for technical manuals and school primers to teach German.

Commercial access to the Adriatic Sea created another Italian counterweight to German influence. With German Protestants gone, non-Venetian Italian traders were needed to generate taxable income in the coastal towns. They soon set up a network to collect cloth woven by upland peasant households. By 1719 the Habsburg military advantage over Venice was strong enough to proclaim Trieste and Rijeka, on the opposite sides of the Istrian Peninsula, as free ports. Trieste developed more rapidly, but Vienna's state-sponsored Oriental Company and its plans for long-distance trade did not survive the 1730s. When it went under, some Slovenian traders joined a larger number of Italians in taking over a share of the export trade.[18] Favorably located at an economic crossroads between Central Europe and the Mediterranean, the politically subdivided Slovenian population increased to some 700,000 by the mid-eighteenth century, roughly half as much again as Ottoman Serbia or Macedonia.

The Croatian Military Border

What is now Croatia was divided throughout the early modern period into five parts, only three of which lay within the Habsburg monarchy. Istria and Dalmatia remained under Venetian control until the beginning and end of the eighteenth century respectively. The special regime of the Croatian Military Border served among other things to divide the other two Habsburg territories, Civil Croatia and Slavonia.

At its fullest extent by the late eighteenth century, the Military Border extended from the Lika area north of Dalmatia, around the Bosnian border eastward along the Sava and Danube rivers bordering Serbia, and into the Transylvanian border with the Romanian principalities. Its origins were in the western salient, where predominantly Serb refugees from the Ottoman advance into Bosnia were already forming their own frontier bands. From 1553 these bands came under the integrated command of Habsburg officers in units that multiplied with the Ottoman kapitanates appearing on the other side. The terms of Habsburg military service attracted still more border guards, or *Grenzer*: a small grant of free land, no manorial obligations, and freedom for the Serbs to build Orthodox churches and to practice their religion. The grants typically went to the extended families who had migrated together and now received land more suited to raising livestock. As elsewhere in the Balkans where this combination prevailed, these families developed a patriarchal complex of property and working relations called a *zadruga*.[19]

A formal Habsburg statute in 1630 made each zadruga a legal entity, responsible for drafting all males over age sixteen for military service, to fight against Ottoman forces or any other adversaries of the emperor. The surviving Croatian nobility resented the Grenzer because they were exempt from feudal dues. The Grenzer contained a significant proportion of Croats, although probably not the 40 percent recorded in the initial ethnic census of 1819. The percentage of Serbs – over one-half in 1819 – presumably reached its peak after the further migration from Serbia northward that occurred in 1690.[20]

This large Serb presence in historic Croatia might have evolved more fortunately had the initial military purpose drawing them there fostered economic prosperity. It did not. From Lika to the Slavonian border, crop yields were barely half those in Civil Croatia. While the karst-covered foothills blanketing this region may largely explain these low yields, the Habsburg border regime was also an economic burden. Its restrictions limited the maximum holding to 26 acres, barred their sale or transfer, and took the male labor force away on maneuvers for a minimum of several weeks every growing season. The Habsburg Sanitäts Kordon, established along the length of the Ottoman border in 1770 to protect against the bubonic plague and livestock diseases, hindered trade as did Hungarian customs tariffs collected at the Krajina's border with Civil Croatia.

Despite Habsburg legislation to make the Military Border imperial property in 1754 and the brief promise of agrarian reform under Joseph II in the 1780s, the region remained impoverished and isolated. Of its population of 900,000 in 1799, less than 3,000 lived in the largest town of Karlovac. One survey found a quarter of the Grenzer dwellings to be totally isolated and another third clustered in hamlets of twelve or fewer families. Besides emigration, only the forcible seizure of a neighbor's land offered relief from such deep poverty. Yet few such seizures were recorded as late as the eighteenth century, and not just because of the Habsburg military framework. Serbs and Croats lived peaceably without religious antagonism in neighboring hamlets, if not the same ones, and served together without incident in the same regiments.[21] Even along the Military Border, therefore, the brutalities of the past 100 years cannot be explained as "age-old antagonisms."

Civil Croatia and Slavonia

The number of Serbs was far smaller, except for the easternmost Srem in Civil Croatia and Slavonia, than in the Military Border. Yet the principal

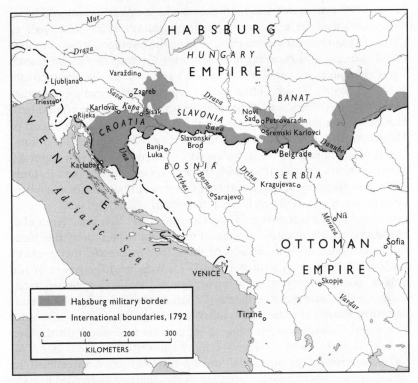

Map 1.3 Croatian Military Border and Habsburg borderlands in 1780

distinctions between these two territories by the eighteenth century were not ethnic but economic.[22] Although working better land, almost 90 percent of the Croats north of the Military Border were estimated to be serfs in a 1784 census. Peasant families owed an onerous number of days of labor to the noble estates (or more precisely, to their private [allodial] property), in return for the modest plots that the peasants were allowed to farm on the estates' wider urbarial holdings. Usually ethnic Croats, noble landowners numbered 9,500 in 1785, nearly four times the population of Agram (Zagreb in Croatian). The town's medieval promise of independence from rural or official rule, like that of other royal free cities south of Vienna and Budapest, had long since withered. Civil Croatia's total population was barely 650,000 people in the wake of Ottoman–Habsburg warfare from the fifteenth through the seventeenth centuries and the urban proportion perhaps 5 percent.

Slavonia's still smaller population and the presence of only 314 nobles in the 1785 census helps explain the smaller number of required labor days that could be extracted from its peasantry – less than half of Croatia's requirements. Even then, sensing the leverage that scarce labor could exercise, and knowing of neighboring Grenzer rights, the mainly Croat peasantry revolted as early as 1573, under the then cruelly executed Matija Gubec. They rose up against their largely Hungarian lords twice in the first half of the eighteenth century. In the second half, Hungarian law and control replaced the civil–military administration of Habsburg Vienna. Feudal obligations cut heavily into peasant incentives, and noble landowners had little reason to introduce intensive methods, given the restrictions on trade with the grain-poor Military Border. Only trade with Hungary, which hardly needed grain imports from the south, became easier late in the early modern period.

The political framework of Civil Croatia, if not Slavonia, resembled Hungary's in significant respects. First warfare and then the mid-seventeenth-century suppression of the Croatian *Fronde*, the revolt of the Zrinski-Frankopan nobles in 1663–71, weakened the power of the nobles' *Sabor* (assembly) in comparison to the Ban appointed from Vienna. The local powers of the Croatian nobility were still intact, patterned exactly after the Hungarian county system. They survived the new Royal Council that Habsburg Empress Maria Theresa proclaimed in 1767 at the expense of taking still more authority from the Sabor. The reforms proposed by Joseph II during his brief reign threatened to eliminate these local powers. Croatian nobles thereupon decided to cede central authority to the Hungarian Diet rather than risk Joseph's regulations surviving him.

A second division of the territory further constrained Croatian state-building within what had been its medieval borders. The Dalmatian coast and much of Istria remained under Venetian control throughout the early modern period. One-quarter million Italians would eventually inhabit these valuable lands until their expulsion after the Second World War. As early as the seventeenth century, however, a Croatian claim to reunite what was now called the Triune Kingdom of Croatia, Slavonia, and Dalmatia found its first voice in the often-cited writings of the Dalmatian nobleman, Pavao Ritter Vitezović. Although he introduced the notion that Bosnian Serbs on the territory that medieval Croatia had once held were in fact Orthodox Croats, Vitezović concentrated on persuading legalistic Habsburg authorities to lay a historical claim to the Venetian-held coast. Ivo Banac calls Vitezović and other Croatian spokesmen of the early modern period advocates of historic state's rights, based on past regimes and their borders rather than on ethnic rights grounded in language and culture.[23]

Exceptions to imperial fragmentation

True, imperial expansion and then division disrupted any South Slav state-building and economic integration of the sort appearing in early modern Western Europe. Native as well as Ottoman and Habsburg Empires fragmented territory and isolated populations more than they brought them together. And the disadvantages of Balkan geography – lack of access to the sea or navigable rivers and the small amount of well-watered lowlands – contributed to divisions between territories taken to buffer imperial centers with a distant land border.

At least by the early modern period, several focal points of integration also appeared and provided a more fruitful legacy for the future Yugoslavia. Although scarcely political centers, an independent Dubrovnik, Ottoman Sarajevo, and the Habsburg Vojvodina created networks for regional trade. They also mixed ethnic groups and opened themselves to intellectual traditions too broad for any one ethnic identity.

Trade centers and networks

The Dalmatian city-state of Dubrovnik was the one territory to escape imperial domination for most of the period before 1800. Known as Ragusa and recognized as a republic throughout this time, the port's Italian commercial connections helped establish it as the principal point of entry for Mediterranean trade with the Ottoman Empire by the sixteenth century. An unsuccessful Venetian effort to monopolize the Adriatic coastal trade at the same time that it confronted the Ottoman advance militarily gave the small republic, extending from the Bay of Kotor to the island of Korčula, the chance to step in as neutral entrepôt. When Venice blocked Ragusa's access to the Italian grain needed to cover the coastal food shortage, its merchants opened a network of trade centers across Ottoman Bosnia, Serbia, Macedonia, and even Bulgaria. Ottoman regulations made direct imports of grain difficult, but the profitable manufacture of raw wool imported across this overland network soon opened the way. The Ragusan legacy of European commercial practice and credit instruments survived the seventeenth-century demise of the network itself when Ottoman–Habsburg warfare cut its lines of communication.[24]

Ottoman Sarajevo was able to draw on this legacy and even assume some of the Ragusan role as a trade center by the eighteenth century. Just as the city was recovering from a Habsburg sacking and subsequent fire in 1697, Venetian weakness opened its way to the Dalmatian port of Split. (Bosnia-Hercegovina would have no port of its own to the present day.) At 50,000 or more, Sarajevo was, with Belgrade and Skopje, one of the few large towns in the early modern territory of the future Yugoslavia. (Ragusa's population in the seventeenth century, for instance, was about 7,000.) At least some of Sarajevo's trade moved east and west, not just north and south to and from the port of Split.

The same could not be said for several Habsburg trade centers that also became important by the eighteenth century.[25] These were the ports of Trieste, Fiume (now Rijeka), on either side of the Istrian Peninsula, and Novi Sad on the Danube and the overland route across the Vojvodina. From the Adriatic ports, commercial traffic moved north to Vienna and Budapest, making literally no connection among the future Yugoslav lands and scarcely any within them. Trieste was by far the more important port, offering the shortest route from Vienna to the Adriatic and accounting for one-third of all Habsburg exports by 1783. Textiles from Austrian and Czech manufacturers thus found their way to Mediterranean but not Balkan markets.

A free port from 1719, Trieste's population was largely Italian. The Slovenian hinterland nonetheless benefitted from the chance to supply the port with labor, cloth collected from cottage industry, and even some merchants after the Habsburgs' mercantilist effort to control trade through a state company had collapsed in the 1730s. Rijeka on the other hand had no connection to the Croatian economy until the nineteenth century.

The Ottoman–Habsburg border in the Vojvodina, stabilized at the Danube and Sava rivers by the Treaty of Karlovac in 1699, promoted the growth of considerable trade. Here the Habsburg authorities set aside their commitment to mercantilist protectionism. Despite the barriers of the Military Border and the Sanitäts Kordon, the value of livestock, cotton, wool, and tobacco imports swamped Habsburg exports five-to-one. Serbia and Macedonia furnished a large share of the goods and also some of the traders, although Greeks and Vlach Tsintsars were probably more prominent. They all moved back and forth across the border, sometimes settling themselves or encouraging others to settle in Habsburg Novi Sad on the Danube or in Belgrade on the Ottoman side, at the confluence of the Danube and the Sava.[26] Such traffic reduced the economic and intellectual isolation that had confined Serbs since the fall of their medieval empire, although little political change was experienced until the nineteenth century.

Mixing populations and ideas

While the Habsburg Vojvodina was the largest arena for mixing ethnic populations and exposing their educated élites to the mainstream of

1.1 The medieval center of Dubrovnik

European ideas, it was hardly the first in the future Yugoslav lands. Three hundred years earlier during the fifteenth century, the Dalmatian coastal towns had begun sending Latin-speaking scholars (not all of them Catholic priests) to the universities of Padua and Budapest. They returned committed to the tenets of pre-Reformation humanism that the Western rediscovery of classical antiquity and the Italian Renaissance had called forth. By the sixteenth century, according to Michael Petrovich, some 200 Croat humanist scholars had emerged from these Dalmatian towns.[27] Latin was a defense against Italianization, as was the simultaneous preservation of the Croat vernacular. But such a defense was hardly needed. Their citizens' cultural identities were from the town itself and from the community of European humanists, who sought to reconnect themselves with the wider cultural heritage of the ancient Romans and Greeks. Italian humanists came frequently and stayed comfortably in these towns, home as well to an uncertain number of Catholic and Orthodox Serbs. Among the Catholic Serbs was the physical scientist whose name later honored the first scientific institute in interwar Yugoslavia, Rudjer Bošković.

More ethnic mixing and religious coexistence emerged in early modern Sarajevo. Although entirely Muslim in the early sixteenth century, native converts vastly outnumbered the Turks and came from a range of ethnic backgrounds. By the end of the sixteenth century, the town's increased population included more Serbs, Croats, or Sephardic Jews than Turks. Neither the Turks nor the ruling Bosnian Muslim majority had access to higher education in their own language. Muslim foundations offered Islamic education in Arabic to primary school students, a few of whom went on to Islamic high schools, *medresa*, that opened in Sarajevo in 1537. There is some evidence of primary schooling for Serb children, although not to the extent that the Franciscan fathers offered to Catholic Croat children throughout Bosnia, using Croatian language textbooks. In sum, Sarajevo's population came from four ethno-religious groups, all South Slav save for the Jews, and did not include a large Turkish garrison. These features made it unique among the major towns of the Ottoman Balkans.

A still larger number of ethnic groups had undoubtedly collected across the Habsburg Vojvodina by the end of the eighteenth century. Initially consisting (after 1699) of the Srem between the Sava and Danube rivers, and the Bačka between the Danube and Tisza, the Vojvodina's addition of the larger Banat region to the east in 1718 marked the start of a considerable Habsburg effort to populate these rich but largely deserted lands. Vienna's policy of what might be called "populationism" sought to place settlers north of the newly extended

Military Border as a further line of defense against the Ottoman Empire. When Ottoman forces counterattacked in 1739 and ended the brief Habsburg occupation of Serbia begun in 1718, "populationism" became an imperative. As it had after 1699, the Vojvodina again attracted Serb immigrants fleeing a resentful Ottoman regime to the south. Religious freedom to practice their Orthodox faith was a further incentive. Germans and others from the north needed more encouragement to settle. Doubling the previous three-year tax exemption on free land and housing soon enticed over 40,000 Germans, who were joined by Slovaks, Hungarians, Croats, and Romanians. Joseph II recruited another 40,000 German Protestants, promising them the same religious freedom as the Orthodox Serbs and Romanians. Those with farming skills were favored, and the Germans in particular introduced iron plows and cultivation techniques that spread widely if not completely throughout the Banat. By 1787 the population of the Banat had swelled to nearly 300,000, with the Bačka and Srem each adding another 20,000.[28]

Not many within this diverse population were even acquainted with the tolerant secular ideals of the European Enlightenment by the end of the eighteenth century. The peasant majority of all these ethnic groups lived peaceably as neighbors, but mostly in separate villages and almost never in marriages that required one partner to change religion. Separate church schools offered limited primary education. In the towns, the Catholic clergy was most interested in using the growing political influence of Hungarian authorities to press for conversion of the Orthodox Serbs. The Serbs' Patriarchate at Karlovac meanwhile concentrated its intellectual energies on defending the religious authority granted it by Austrian authorities.

And yet there were exceptions, enough on the Serbian side to give Novi Sad the reputation, in retrospect, as the "Athens of Serbia." The Orthodox monk, Dositej Obradović, an almost-Protestant traveller, teacher, and encyclopedist, was the most influential figure to join the government of Serbia proper during the First Uprising (1804–13). His rationalist view of the world made him anti-clerical, along the lines of Emperor Joseph II, if hardly an opponent of a separate Serbian identity. His less renowned compatriots included not only the sons of merchants and Grenzer officers but also some of the Orthodox high clergy. Their access to the Enlightenment, interestingly enough, came from French rather than German tracts, despite a Habsburg ban on the import of such publications.[29]

This small band of Serbs attracted to the eighteenth-century Enlightenment should remind us of Croatia's fifteenth-century Humanists. Although their immediate impact was obviously small, both introduced

European traditions of broad, universal values upon which future generations of Serbs and Croats might draw to escape the confines of ethnic exclusivism. Ahead lay the nineteenth century's lure of a single state for each ethnic nation to discourage such an escape. Yet the imperial legacies just reviewed had introduced virtually no political ideas or institutions by which to integrate their territories. They had, however, so fragmented these lands and mixed their populations that such humanist values and some sort of multi-ethnic institutional framework stood the best chance of weaving them together constructively.

2 Unifying aspirations and rural resistance, 1804–1903

Although we can find no real prospect for a Yugoslav state or practice of common politics before the twentieth century, a South Slav, or Yugoslav, idea still emerged during the nineteenth century. According to this idea, the peoples of the future Yugoslavia, and possibly Bulgaria, shared a common ethnic fraternity that should lead them to political unification and independence. Yet there were other unifying ideas, Croatian and Serbian, and an existing Serbian state with which any Yugoslav idea had to contend. Even in independent Serbia, much of the overwhelmingly rural population resisted the institutional framework of the modern state.

Driving all of these unifying aspirations, despite rural resistance to them, was the desire to overcome the various divisions described in chapter 1. The geographic fragmentation imposed by the Habsburg and Ottoman Empires only reinforced the isolation of the rural peasantry, particularly in the upland villages. During the nineteenth century, increasingly modern political administrations in both empires and in autonomous or independent Serbia tried to reduce this isolation, trading taxation and military service for education and public order. Peasant revolts in Bosnia-Hercegovina, Croatia, and Serbia later in the century suggest that many peasants did not welcome this bargain.

At the same time, the administrative capitals for this limited unification – Sarajevo, Zagreb, and Belgrade – were also becoming centers for culture and commerce, if not for industry, modelled on contemporary Europe. They constituted a new, native source of division. These small cities contrasted more and more with the rural sea of backward agriculture and illiterate peasantry surrounding them. Robert Tucker has called the result "differential modernization."[1] The peasant majority might embarrass the increasingly educated urban élite, as in Budapest or Warsaw, but they also inspired them, as in Belgrade or Zagreb. Once educated and armed, the peasants could confront the other principal source of élite embarrassment, the real or presumed hegemony of the European powers. For the future Yugoslav lands, Ottoman and Habsburg hegemony was real, and even at the end of the nineteenth century, still nearly complete. But, by then, the majority of peasants had their own smallholdings and most had small arms. They represented potential opposition to, as well as support for, any new state structure.

By the start of the twentieth century, political élites in Belgrade and Zagreb, if not Sarajevo, were spoiling to push back imperial hegemony, but they hardly agreed on how to do so. Potential plans for Yugoslav coordination had to contend with Serbian and Croatian state ideas that had grown up during the nineteenth century. When stated in that century's rhetoric of romantic nationalism, these two ideas for a unitary nation-state were incompatible with each other and with any wider Yugoslav idea. The Serbian and Croatian ideas sought to build on existing communities, not the "imagined communities" of European colonial construction described by Benedict Anderson. These ideas were still romantic. They staked out huge territories on the basis of medieval claims to ethnic homelands or historic borders. To support their claims, advocates elaborated on actual traditions, such as commemorating the Serbs' Kosovo battle of 1389. The celebration of these events still fits modern nationalism's use of the past for verification, what Eric Hobsbawm has called "invented tradition."[2] Serbian nationalists did so to demonstrate unique suffering during the Ottoman conquest and Croats to show cultural superiority, both wishing to connect their group alone to European civilization. In the process, each claimant began to see or, to paraphrase Benedict Anderson, "imagine" the other as an historical adversary.

One must not jump to the conclusion, urged on by the disastrous end of the two Yugoslavias, that the rhetorical barriers erected by the most narrowly focused nationalists reflect an incompatibility cast in stone. Such a view presumes adverse ethnic relations before ethnic distinctions were much perceived and ignores evidence of socio-economic similarity between Serbs and Croats. It also neglects the later potential of related ethnic groups, particularly the Slovenes, to moderate between them. True, the growth of separate political cultures and trade patterns across the fragmented face of the future Yugoslavia during the nineteenth century did not build on this compatibility. Yet the very political fragmentation of the Yugoslav lands helped promote the search for some unifying framework. How else could their similar and mixed populations be accommodated?

Ethnic accommodation within a larger South Slav framework found its earliest expression in the proto-Yugoslav concept called Illyrianism by its Croatian creators. But were these South Slavs one people or several related ones? The romantic inclination to view them as one would plague the Yugoslav idea from the start.

From Illyrian provinces to Yugoslav idea, 1806–1860

The idea of a single South Slav nationality first surfaced in what became known as the Illyrian movement. Early in the nineteenth century, Napoleonic France tried to introduce the idea as a corollary to its centralized administration of the Adriatic coast and inland parts. It resurfaced in Zagreb during the 1830s as a Croatian cultural strategy detached from practical politics. When the leaders of this Illyrian movement turned toward politics during the next two decades, they discovered that opposition from the Hungarian and Austrian cores of the Habsburg monarchy frustrated them from within, while the existence of an independent Serbia did so from without.

French centralism and the Illyrian provinces, 1806–1813

Napoleon's France revived the ancient term, Illyria, to designate Croatian and Slovenian lands that it wished to mold into a single administrative and cultural unit. The advance of French arms, first at Venetian and then at Habsburg expense, led to the creation of the Illyrian provinces of 1809–13 (see map 2.1). Already by 1806, a French-controlled regime had been imposed on largely Venetian Istria and northern Dalmatia. In 1809 French forces extended this regime down the Dalmatian coast to Dubrovnik and the Montenegrin littoral and north into the Military Border and Civil Croatia just short of Zagreb. The new administrative structure also absorbed Carinthia and much of Slovenian Carniola as well as Istria, all with ethnically mixed populations.

The French administrators had in mind the actual Illyrian province that had been a part of imperial Rome, rather than the fifteenth century revival of the idea by Croatian humanists who sought a reunion with European culture. Napoleon's motive was primarily military, but political integration proved to be a formidable challenge. Habsburg Slovenia had been divided among several provinces, while Civil Croatia and the Military Border lived under radically different regimes.

The long Venetian rule had also divided the Istrian peninsula and Dalmatian coasts. Coastal towns such as Split and Zadar were small, but developed separate communal traditions of self-government patterned after Italian city-states and used the Italian language, if not inhabited by many Italians. The largely Croat élite in these two towns, plus some Orthodox and even Catholic Serbs, held the hinterland's nearly landless peasantry in thrall under a colonate system of contractual sharecropping that dated back to Roman times. But in the territory further inland that they had wrested from Ottoman control by the early eighteenth century, the Venetians introduced a system of free peasant soldiers on state land, similar to the Habsburg Military Border and for the same military purpose.[3] (The most noteworthy example of these once-Venetian districts is Knin, the capital of the Serb Krajina that broke with newly independent Croatia from 1991 until 1995.)

Not until 1810 did French Marshal Auguste Marmont arrive to initiate a full-scale but short-lived effort to turn these disparate territories and populations into a *Département* of Napoleon's central government. He introduced the Napoleonic Code with its provisions for equality under the law and independent courts. Marmont tried to abolish the colonate system and introduce free trade. But he also levied high taxes on landowners and imposed roadbuilding and military obligations on coastal peasants. Both landowners and peasants resisted these new obligations, despite the considerable number of Croatian, Italian, and French administrators dispatched to implement them. The failure of Napoleon's Russian campaign in 1812 soon ended the French regime, but this set of regulations and administrators nonetheless introduced the Yugoslav lands to the centralizing framework of nineteenth-century European state-building.

The French regime left a stronger legacy to the Yugoslav idea that took shape later in the century. Again under Marmont, the fledgling school system made a belated effort to teach one version of the *štokavski* dialect that became Serbo-Croatian and to encourage its use in fledgling local newspapers.[4] Marmont wanted to build more schools than his Italian predecessor had and convert them from teaching in Italian to teaching in štokavski. But local communities would have to cover the cost, and many could not pay. Their schools closed before the French left. The brief experiment introduced the notion that Serbs and Croats did or should speak the same language.

The French administrators simply assumed that Croat and Serb peasants were, or should be, one people. France had rejected the regionalism in its own pre-revolutionary past, and its administrators presumed any distinctions dividing South Slavs on the basis of their imperial or medieval past were equally irrelevant. Thus did the "new nationalism," that Benedict Anderson has identified in the American as well as the French Revolutions with their assumptions of starting from a blank historical slate, bring the idea of a single Yugoslav people forward for the first time.[5] European nationalism of the nineteenth century would not welcome the notion of a blank slate.

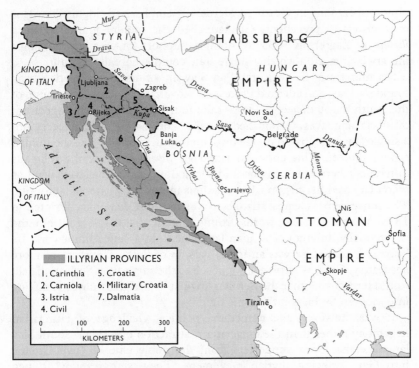

Map 2.1 Illyrian provinces, 1809–1813

Cultural Illyrianism, 1835–1841

A small group of Croatian publicists and nobles fleshed out an early
native definition of the Yugoslav idea in the 1830s. Centered in Zagreb
and other royal free towns of Civil Croatia, most prominently Karlovac
on the Military Border, they sought to unite South Slav "sub-groups"
from the Slovenes to the Bulgarians. Their leader, Ljudevit Gaj, called
this union "Greater Illyria," recalling both the French provinces and the
assumption by early modern Croatian humanists that the South Slavs
were somehow descendants of the ancient Illyrians. The son of a Slovak
pharmacist and a German mother who had settled in the northern
Croatian Zagorje, Gaj grew up in a German-speaking family. He
fastened on the importance of language after a search for his own ethnic
identity that began at the Franciscan monastery library in his native
Krapina. During his university studies in Vienna, Graz, and Budapest,
from 1826 to 1831, he discovered the growing Central European mainstream of ethnic anthropology, following the lead of the Baltic German

philosopher, Johann Gottfried Herder. It emphasized linguistic origins over historical precedent. Gaj launched the literary journal, *Danica ilirska*, in Zagreb in 1835 to mobilize support for creating the single literary language on which a single state could eventually be built.

Starting from the cultural Pan-Slavism of its Czech and Slovak founders, Gaj soon adopted Protestant Slovak Jan Kollar's designation of the South Slavic dialects as one of the four major units in the spectrum of Slavic languages. Gaj pushed ahead to consolidate these dialects into a single language, based on the most common, štokavski, like the French school project. This common language would override the religious differences between Catholic and Orthodox that he believed were as secondary as other historical distinctions imposed by external authority. The movement's clearest manifesto was its short dictionary. Printed in 1835, it amalgamated words from different dialects, even from the substantially different Slovenian language, into a single framework. Its "Illyrian" admixture was an initial version of Serbo-Croatian, or more accurately, Croato-Serbian, as opposed to the single west Serbian dialect from Hercegovina that the Serbian linguist Vuk Karadžić was codifying into modern Serbian at the same time.

It was, however, the immediate political challenge of Hungarian hegemony rather than the longer-term attraction of a single South Slav language that drew supporters from the noble élite of Civil Croatia into Gaj's growing Illyrian movement. They were reacting to two threats, according to Elinor Murray Despalatović.[6] First, the Hungarian language law of 1827 promised to conduct affairs of government, including the parliament to which Croatia sent representatives, in Hungarian rather than Latin. Second, the Hungarian Diet of 1832–36 passed a liberal program of rural reform that reduced the rights of all nobles, Croats included, to control their peasantry. The Croatian nobles reacted by introducing a bill before that body to make "Illyrian" rather than Latin (or Hungarian) the language of government in Slavonia and Dalmatia as well as Civil Croatia, the three components of the Triune Kingdom (meaning the medieval Croatian state) that they sought to reunite. In his *Dissertation*, the Croatian leader, Count Janko Drašković, also laid claim to Slovenian territory. He demanded the return of the Military Border under terms that would revoke the Grenzers' exemption from feudal obligations.

The nobles' alliance with Gaj's young circle of scholars and professionals did not succeed in these broader aims or even in establishing a Croatian cultural society, similar to those of the Czechs and Serbs. They did set up a nework of local reading clubs similar to those in Ottoman Bulgaria and won royal permission to make Illyrian the language of instruction in the elementary schools of all three territories by 1840. Vienna's growing concern with Magyar nationalism elicited sufficient Habsburg support to overcome Hungarian objections.

This widening support did little to attract followers from Slovenia or Bosnia to the movement. Even with the adoption of Gaj's orthography, the Slovenian language was, as their leading Slavicist, Jernej Kopitar, emphasized, too different from the štokavski core. In Ottoman Bosnia, only a few Franciscan (usually Croat) priests were attracted, despite an insignia that combined star and crescent in order to appeal to Muslims as well. Nor did the Serbs in the Vojvodina or in Civil Croatia show much interest, while the large number from the movement's stronghold in the Military Border seemed determined to hang on to a separate Serb identity. Despite some contact between Gaj and Karadžić, Serbians, or those from Serbia proper, bridled at the term "Illyrian," instead of "Serbian" or "Yugoslav." Gaj himself counseled that "a Serb will never be a Croat or a Slovene," but never defined the difference. In addition, he constructed his first notion of these ethnic "sub-groups" uniting under a common language before a Serbian state existed. That such a state was now emerging helps us understand the disposition of Croat nobles, such as Count Drašković, to confine their aims to the presumably medieval Triune Kingdom of Croatia, Slavonia, and Dalmatia. They wished to avoid any connection with the small Serbian principality or the larger threat of Russian influence.[7]

Political Illyrianism and 1848

Before any real connection to Serbia could appear, Gaj and his allies had transformed the Illyrian movement into a political party. The formation in Civil Croatia of a Magyarone Party that rejected the "Illyrian language" and any attendant national identity forced their hand. The urban and noble élite of the Illyrian Party won seats in the local elections of 1841–42. Their victory in Zagreb particularly antagonized the Hungarian authorities. By 1843 Gaj had to give up the leadership of what was now the National Party, lacking the noble pedigree needed to sit in the Sabor. Its noble leaders concentrated on a more specifically Croatian agenda, persuading the Sabor to petition for Croatian control of the Catholic church and to make Illyrian the language of government as well as instruction in the Triune territories.

Gaj returned to the political stage briefly in 1848 when the Hungarian revolt against Habsburg rule led to the suppression of both Croat and Serb activities, from Civil Croatia to the Vojvodina. The Hungarian parliament voted to separate Civil Croatia completely from Slavonia, reaffirmed Latin as the official language, and refused to recognize the hasty Habsburg appointment of Josip Jelačić, a Croat military colonel from the Military Border, as Ban of Civil Croatia and Slavonia. The Croatian Sabor countered by eliminating all feudal obligations for the peasantry. Hungarian troops put down an initially successful revolt by Vojvodina Serbs, led by their Orthodox Metropolitan and supported by volunteers from Serbia and regulars from Jelačić's forces. The Vojvodina Serbs demanded their own linguistic and religious autonomy, including an annual assembly that would have given lay representatives a political forum. Yet they sought no special connection with Serbia. Jelačić too wanted an informal alliance, not a South Slav state including Serbia. Gaj had already made a clumsy effort to discuss such a state with Serbia's recently deposed ruler, Miloš Obrenović. Gaj's entanglement in Obrenović's visit to Zagreb and a subsequent financial scandal ended his own political career.[8]

The wider debacle of 1848 also ended the first efforts to form a Serb-Croat alliance that had any prospect of throwing off Austro-Hungarian control. Military assistance to the monarchy against the Hungarians won the Habsburg Serbs and Croats no political rights in the authoritarian Austrian regime that prevailed from 1849 to 1860. The Croatian Sabor was not allowed to meet again during this period. Vienna ruled both the Vojvodina and Dalmatia even more directly. This sorry end to the Illyrian movement has in part been attributed to Gaj's lack of political experience, but two broader limitations must be emphasized.[9] First, the movement lacked any base in the overwhelmingly illiterate peasantry that made up 90 percent of the Croat population. Their emancipation was the noble-led National Party's last thought, not its first. Second, the movement left the question of any new nation-state's identity unresolved. Gaj, nobles like Drašković, and Ban Jelačić were quick to disagree about what form a new South Slav entity should take and what its relation should be to an already autonomous Serbia (see map 2.2). Arguments over these same issues would plague Croatian politics from this time forward.

Serbia as a nineteenth-century nation-state

Serbia and the future Yugoslav capital of Belgrade spent much of the nineteenth century building the framework for a modern nation-state. This achievement was unique among the future Yugoslav territories. Although it took almost the entire century, Serbia created a modern army and a civilian bureaucracy. If its increasingly democratic constitutions were observed mainly in their breach, the state also acquired a political

Map 2.2 Serbia and the Habsburg South Slav lands, 1830–1878

culture based on more independent experience than any of the other South Slav peoples. While doubling in size and increasing its population from one-half million to 2.3 million between 1830 and 1900, Serbia also became more Serb. After a limited number of Turks, Albanians, and Bosnian Muslims had been forced out and Greek traders had voluntarily departed, its ethnic composition was nearly 90 percent Serb by the end of the century.

The First Serbian Uprising

The still-honored First Uprising against Ottoman rule (1804–13) was too brief and insecure to acquaint its village leaders with European political institutions or military organization. The First Uprising began as a frontier revolt against the latest in a century of rapid reversals of Serbian fortune at the hands of Ottoman forces. In 1690, 1739, and 1791, military alliances with the advancing Habsburg army had prompted successful Ottoman counterattacks. After the third counterattack, a weakened Porte formally conceded one right that Serbian village leaders had sporadically been given throughout the eighteenth century, the collection of local taxes. Moreover, the Ottomans now allowed some of this revenue to finance a popular militia. Displaced Ottoman Janissaries, moving into Serbia after their exclusion from the reorganized Ottoman army, tried to revoke these rights. In 1803 they attempted to kill the village leaders, now called *knezovi* (or princes, according to Habsburg usage), and set off the revolt. Its initial purpose was to restore local Serbian rights within the Ottoman framework. The brutal Ottoman effort to suppress the rebellion, led by the irregular units of Bosnian Muslims that were the closest at hand, helped change what was, by accepted Ottoman practice, a "ritually correct rebellion" against the Sultan's enemies into a Serbian attempt to break free from imperial rule. Also at work, beyond the rallying cries of the knezovi, was the receptivity of Serbian peasantry at the turn of the century to the millennial expectation that St. Sava would return to lead them and drive the Turks "across the blue sea."[10]

A peasant border trader named Karadjordje, or Black George, led the uprising. He used his experience with a regiment of Serb volunteers, organized and trained by Habsburg officers in the 1788–91 campaign, to win initial victories and then to survive a series of Ottoman assaults. After accepting a governing council of twelve locally chosen leaders in 1805, Karadjordje resisted their authority. He replaced them with a larger body of his appointees in 1811, confirming himself as hereditary ruler for life at the same time. His attitude toward representative government may be gauged from his answer to the arguments for constitutional account-ability posed by an educated Serb from the Vojvodina: "Well now, it's easy for this sovereign law of yours to rule in a warm room, behind this table, but let us see tomorrow, when the Turks strike, who will meet them and beat them." If Karadjordje failed to introduce representative government, neither did he conduct a religious war against an enemy seen primarily as Muslim. Serbian Orthodox priests joined in the struggle, but Michael Petrovich discounts the idea that they led a crusade for the "Venerable Cross against the Islamic Crescent."[11]

This First Uprising left other legacies to Serbian political culture beyond the primacy of the military commander in the face of outside attack. The assemblies of village elders, the heads of extended zadruga families or groups of families, lost their right to elect military as well as civilian leaders in 1811, but they had launched the uprising and thus preserved the legitimacy of local government in popular memory as *srpska demokratija*. In addition, educated Serbs from the Vojvodina, *prečani* (literally, those from across the river), came in sufficient numbers to establish their credentials for participating in future Serbian central governments, where their Enlightenment ideas of representative consent would eventually bear fruit.

Foreign intervention was, on the other hand, discredited. Habsburg economic exploitation and pressure for Uniate or Catholic conversion during the occupations of 1718–39 and 1788–91 had already called Vienna's motives into question. The Napoleonic advance into Central Europe precluded any significant military assistance from that source after 1805, and none was offered in any case. The Russian assistance promised in 1806 never materialized, despite the dispatch of a small mission. When Napoleon's attack on Russia ended the Russo-Turkish War of 1806–12, Ottoman forces were free to crush Karadjordje's forces the following year.

Total defeat after a long struggle and the ruthless reprisals that followed linked the First Uprising in Serbian historical memory to the medieval empire's defeat at Kosovo in 1389, a defeat memorialized by an oral tradition of epic poetry. The bloody legend of heroic defiance and cruel defeat now received a transfusion, as did the idea that restoring a Serbian state would be the best defense against future suffering. But no one mentioned restoring the extended borders of the medieval empire or reviving the title of emperor.

Monarchic versus constitutional centralism, 1815–1874

A Second Uprising began further south of the Habsburg border in 1814, and it succeeded in forcing an Ottoman concession of limited autonomy by 1815. Its leader, Miloš Obrenović, left his descendants to vie with Karadjordje's heirs for the Serbian throne. Chances for reconciliation suffered grievously when Miloš had Karadjordje assassinated as the latter tried to return from the Vojvodina in 1818. To his credit, Miloš bargained masterfully with Ottoman leaders in Serbia and in Constantinople during the 1820s to slice Turkish and Bosnian Muslim rights and reduce their presence, particularly in the countryside. He offered incentives to Serbs from neighboring Bosnia-Hercegovina in particular to immigrate, helping swell the largely rural population from 450,000 in 1815 to 700,000 by 1830. When another Russo-Ottoman War broke out in 1828, Miloš was well positioned to parlay for formal autonomy. The sultan's decrees of 1830 first reduced Serbian obligations to permitting a few border garrisons and paying an annual tribute. The decrees of 1833 then agreed to the departure of all Turkish civilians plus the restoration of six southern and western border districts lost in 1813.

Miloš's extraction of such concessions from Ottoman authorities came from an autocratic regime in which he and his associates monopolized the hard won rights of tax collection in Serbia and trade across the Danube. In 1826 his military forces put down another rebellion by local knezovi of the sort that Karadjordje had suppressed in 1811. This marked the demise of oligarchic regionalism. In the phrase of Michael Petrovich, only "constitutional centralism" was left to challenge the native ruler's monarchic powers until the emergence of modern political parties later in the century.[12]

By 1839, however, Miloš had lost his exclusive authority and new, more broadly based opponents forced him to abdicate his position as prince, the first peaceful transfer of power in modern Serbia's history. Miloš had apparently placed the Serbian Orthodox church under his control when he extracted its autonomy from the Greek Patriarch in Constantinople in 1831. He forced out the several Greek bishops and named his own secretary as the new Metropolitan. But by 1835 the educated prečani prelate extracted a statute that allowed the church internal autonomy. Commercial and political opponents, based in Belgrade, forged the first independent opposition. Belgrade was still a small, Ottoman-style town of some 20,000 people in 1830. But the mushrooming livestock export to the Habsburg lands, whose value tripled again in the 1820s and again in the 1830s, had created a new trading class jealous of Miloš's tax and trade monopolies.[13] Prečani members of his regime were also uncomfortable with their subordinate position. In 1838 a combination of domestic opponents and European consuls, the British representative in particular, finally pushed Miloš into agreeing to a kind of constitution.

The document bears comparison with the Organic Statutes instituted under Russian sponsorship for the Romanian principalities a few years earlier. It did not provide for a legislative assembly, but did create separate courts and a governing council to which European-style ministries would be responsible. A coalition of council members, dubbing themselves the Defenders of the Constitution, were soon able to force Miloš across the Danube into exile. The coalition recognized a son of his rival Karadjordje as his legitimate successor in 1842, after clashes with council members ended the brief reign of one of Miloš's sons.

The new prince, Aleksandar Karadjordjević, was too weak to set his own stamp on a long reign that lasted from 1842 to 1858. That period is remembered less for him than for its ministers, the most powerful of whom was Ilija Garašanin. Born near Kragujevac in 1812, he had been educated in Greek and German schools "across the river." Three of the six other Constitutionalist leaders were prečani, born in the Vojvodina. With Garašanin in the central position as interior minister, they sought to modernize the small principality by bureaucratic authority. They expanded police powers accordingly, and wrested state control of the small number of primary schools from the Orthodox church. Their most positive achievement, in the judgment of scholars from Slobodan Jovanović on, was the liberation of village commerce so that peasants from the interior could share in the further expansion of Habsburg trade.[14] The Constitutionalists' unwillingness to share power and their resistance to a genuinely independent judiciary eventually allowed a mix of local and commercial opponents to force them and the Karadjordjević dynasty from power in 1858.

The monarchy soon reasserted its central position. The aged Miloš's brief return in 1859 had little impact, but his son Michael's succession the following year saw power returned to the modest palace. The first Serbian prince with a formal education, Michael worked initially with Ilija Garašanin to eliminate opposition from an increasingly educated and dissatisfied Belgrade élite. A censorship law in 1861 attacked the right to publish views opposing the regime's in the city's nascent newspapers. The prince dismissed a number of tenured civil servants and virtually dissolved the highest court in 1864. Calling themselves Liberals in the contemporary European tradition, opponents led by Vladimir Jovanović refused to abandon their demands for a new constitution and an elected legislature.[15]

Their chance did not come until other opponents of Michael assassinated him in 1868. The minister of war promptly used his troops to make the Regency accept Michael's fourteen-year-old nephew Milan as heir to the throne. The ascendant Liberals were then able to oust conservative ministers and push through a new constitution by 1869. It eliminated the governing council and revived the *Narodna Skupština*, or National Assembly, whose sessions every three years under Michael had been largely ignored. Now all tax-paying males would elect representatives to meet annually. Although freedom of the press was not yet guaranteed, debates in the new Assembly became public occasions. Its major factions, although not yet political parties, felt sufficiently independent by 1874 to force a sitting government to resign.

The right of the Skupština to initiate legislation and to control the state's budget, as well as its election by secret ballot, came only with the 1888 constitution. Those rights would not become real until the accession of a genuinely constitutional monarch, Petar Karadjordjević, in 1903.

National aspirations versus party politics, 1844–1903

As in modern Greece, Serbia's leaders aspired to expand its borders to include fellow Serbs before mass political parties had taken shape. The most complete statement of such Serbian aims was also the first. In 1844 then Interior Minister Ilija Garašanin revised a ten-page draft memorandum prepared for him by a Polish-sponsored Czech advisor. This *Načertanije*, or outline, described in Pan-Slavic terms the unification of all South Slavs in a single, new state. Garašanin substituted Serbs for South Slavs and made the existing Serbian state the center around which surrounding Ottoman territory with Serb populations should be drawn. He added some vague references to the restoration of Tsar Dušan's medieval Serbian empire. This much is well known, as celebrated by later Serbian nationalists as it is damned by their Croatian counterparts. Yet this famed Načertanije remained an internal, uncirculated memorandum read only by a handful of politicians until a Belgrade journal published it in 1906.

More important for the origins of the first Yugoslavia and the end of the second was its ambiguous call for both a Great Serbia and a still larger South Slav state. The document invoked both the romantic nationalism of Serbs standing alone and the *Realpolitik* needed to navigate among the Great Powers. Ilija Garašanin, the future foreign minister, embodied both sensibilities. Even if his designation by David MacKenzie as the Balkan Bismarck goes too far, Garašanin saw the inherent danger of overdependence on Habsburg trade to much smaller Serbia's survival, particularly if Vienna managed to use that leverage politically.[16] Anticipating the breakup of the Ottoman Empire, he sought to deny the Balkans to both Russian and Austrian domination. The Načertanije itself uses the language of romantic nationalism to propose a Serbian state that would include Bosnia-Hercegovina, Montenegro, Macedonia, Kosovo, and northern Albania, with borders assuring access to the Adriatic. Garašanin did not suggest retaking the far borders of Tsar Dušan's Serbia, much less moving the capital to Macedonia. Belgrade and an enlarged Serbia would instead be the center of a still larger entity that would include Bulgarian and Croatian lands but not the large Greek territory that Dušan conquered. Separate ethnic identities were to be respected, and the Croats were promised full religious freedom. Garašanin specifically proposed a network of Serbian agents and educators, but called on them to pay special attention to cooperation with Catholic priests, the Franciscan order in particular. This was well and good, but the implicit designation of an undefined *subsidiary* role for the Croats in some union with an enlarged Serbia including Bosnia made Garašanin's double vision a fatal flaw whenever twentieth-century politicians, Serb or Croat, applied it to either of the two Yugoslavias.

Garašanin himself had two chances to apply his ideas. The first came in 1848, when the Serbs of the Vojvodina revolted against the Hungarian forces they had first joined in a common uprising against Habsburg rule. The Serbian interior minister avoided any formal support for the insurgents, fearing Great Power objections, but sent agents to Dalmatia and aforementioned volunteers to the Vojvodina. He also worked behind the scenes to forge an alliance with General Jelačić, the Croatian Ban and commander of the forces from the Military Border that were crucial to the Habsburg suppression of Hungarian independence by 1849. In return Vienna allowed the Vojvodina Serbs only to reaffirm their religious autonomy, tightening its own political control, as already noted, until handing it over to Hungarian authorities in 1860.

Thus disillusioned with the rewards of maneuvering within the Habsburg lands, Garašanin turned in the 1860s to the Ottoman Empire's European territories.[17] Now foreign minister, he and Prince Michael concluded alliances with Greece and Montenegro in case the revolt his Bosnian Serb network anticipated became a general uprising to expel the Ottomans from the Balkans. The prince had already authorized a large national militia with a potential force of 90,000 men. But the prince's attempted "militarization of Serbia" did not persuade him or visiting Russian officers that the effort to train or equip to European standards what was still a set of local militias had succeeded. He rejected his foreign minister's advice simply to send the new army across the Drina river into Bosnia at the first sign of revolt, against Austrian wishes and with little prospect of victory.[18]

Michael's judgment was vindicated, but only after his assassination the next year. Almost a decade later in 1876, still loosely organized Serbian troops, supported by even more loosely organized Russian volunteers, rushed into Bosnia-Hercegovina to aid Serb peasants who had revolted against their Bosnian Muslim landlords. Ottoman forces quickly repulsed two small thrusts. Their defeat forced post-1878 Serbia to come to terms with Austria-Hungary and to concentrate on domestic issues. It was this domestic focus, rather than aspirations for national expansion, that brought modern parties and mass politics to Serbia.

The Liberal leaders who had ruled Serbia through the 1870s paid little respect to the increasingly active young monarch, Milan Obrenović. Now they were answerable to him and other opponents for a war effort on the Bosnian border and in eastern Serbia that attracted no Russian support and yielded only the modest addition of the southern Niš triangle in the final peace settlement reached at Berlin in 1878. When the Liberals introduced new income taxes to pay for some of the war's expenses and signed the one-sided trade agreement proposed by Austria-Hungary, Milan seized the occasion to dismiss them. The so-called young conservatives, successors to Garašanin's generation, now formed the cabinets of 1880–87. They established themselves as a formal party called the Progressives and created a club for their Skupština members.

The new Radical Party had in the meantime overtaken the Progressives with modern initiatives to attract a mass membership and organize a network across Serbia. Its village organizers and its widely distributed newspaper, *Samouprava* (yes, Self-Management, here meaning local self-government rather than the economic concept of Tito's Yugoslavia) led the way. This party would dominate Serbian politics during the decade before 1914. Moving away from its roots in the utopian rural socialism of Svetozar Marković, which he barely articulated before his early death in 1872, the party's platform for the 1881 elections sought only political change on the pattern of the French Radical program of that same year.[19] The first comprehensive program for domestic reform put before Serbian voters emphasized the primacy of the National Assembly and local government over the monarch and its ministries. Although their increased vote did not win them a majority, they were able to push through a law for free, compulsory village schooling by 1883. The Orthodox hierarchy that might otherwise have blocked secular schools was still embroiled in Milan's dismissal of their Metropolitan for refusing to pay taxes. The Radicals' other demands for democratic constitutional amendments and specific rights for local government might not have prevailed had it not been for a local peasant rebellion that same year.

The Radical victory of 1888 and the fine, Belgian-style constitution that followed from it, drew heavily on wider reaction to the Timok rebellion in 1883. Peasants from this eastern border region rose up against government agents rather than accept a law confiscating peasant rifles and distributing a smaller number of new Mausers to local army commanders. The law was a part of a logical effort to organize a thoroughly integrated European-style army, so as not to repeat the failures of the 1876–78 war in Ottoman Bosnia. Both the Progressive government and Milan, newly crowned as king rather than prince, refused to back down despite Radical support for the rebels and their opposition to the idea of a national army. The Radical Party leader was already the 36-year-old Nikola Pašić, a native of the Timok region and educated as an engineer in Switzerland. The king's peasant regiments held together and put down the revolt, forcing Pašić into brief exile in

Bulgaria.[20] Such local resistance to the power of a modernizing central government was popular enough to help Pašić lead his party to a sweeping victory in the elections of 1888. They won every seat in the Skupština and quickly ratified a more democratic constitution. It gave majority rule from the Assembly the right to dominate the political process and to defy the monarchy. The Radicals were able to force Milan Obrenović from the throne in 1889. Yet his weak successor, Aleksandar, was strong enough by his majority in 1894 to discard the 1888 constitution completely.

In the meantime, party politics had turned away from issues of domestic development and back to the emphasis on expanded borders begun by Ilija Garašanin. The Radicals' 1881 program had endorsed the liberation and unification of all parts of Serbdom. By 1889 Pašić joined Progressive Party Minister Čedomil Mijatović in sponsoring an elaborate commemoration of the 500-year anniversary of the battle of Kosovo, complete with the public promises to reclaim the territory. Here was one issue on which they agreed – a revived if not "invented" tradition – and one which omitted issues of internal modernization entirely. Like Greece's *megali idea* to reclaim the territory of the Byzantine Empire, Serbia's quest for Kosovo would reinforce what Gale Stokes has called "politics without development," a growing state apparatus barely connected to a backward, rural economy.[21]

Peasant agriculture and the Austro-Hungarian connection

Serbia's population and economy had grown significantly since the first years of autonomy. But the structural changes needed to turn growth into sustained development through rising productivity and modern technology had hardly begun. No Serbian government had addressed the issue beyond providing limited support for technical education and a series of European loans to construct Serbia's section of the Orient Express rail line to Constantinople. After the first of these loans collapsed in 1881 with the death of French financier Eugène Bontoux, other borrowing built the line and whetted the government's appetite for more. Debt service already consumed one-third of a ballooning state budget by 1887. More loans helped double that budget again by 1898, but not one more mile of track was built nor any other economic project undertaken with the largely French loans.[22]

Considerable economic growth was nonetheless underway, making state support seem less important. The population of Serbia doubled to reach 1 million from 1834 to 1859 and then jumped to 2.5 million by 1899, including the 330,000 people added by the Niš triangle after the

Treaty of Berlin. Primarily responsible were the high rural birth rate (over 40 per 1,000) and the continuing immigration of Serbs from Ottoman Bosnia-Hercegovina and Macedonia. Extensive grain cultivation on newly cleared land doubled the wheat acreage per capita between 1862–66 and 1896–1900. Output per capita also rose until the absence of modern methods or technology on these peasant smallholdings forced it to decline after 1900.[23]

The major export and major stimulus to urban growth beyond the state bureaucracy growing up in Belgrade was not grain but livestock. Hogs and cattle were herded on foot to Belgrade or other towns on the Danube or Sava rivers for transport across to the Habsburg Vojvodina and on to the Austro-Hungarian market. None of this made any contribution to the tiny industrial sector and little to urban growth. People in towns over 2,000 remained only 14 percent of Serbia's population by the end of the century, less than in any other independent Balkan state and higher only than Dalmatia among the future Yugoslav lands.

The livestock trade's greater significance lay in the export boom and the excessive dependence on the Austro-Hungarian market that it maintained from the 1830s through the 1890s. Led by livestock, Serbian export value tripled from 1835–38 to 1856–60 and then nearly quadrupled by 1896–1900. No one noticed that, by the later date, the population had increased enough to lower the exports' total real per capita value. But Serbian politicians did perceive the consistent direction of 85–90 percent of their total export to Austria-Hungary as a political problem. Such overdependence had already given the Dual Monarchy enough commercial leverage to extract a secret agreement to monitor Serbia's foreign policy in 1881. Then the Hungarian half of the monarchy and its agricultural interests launched the decennial campaign of 1896 for Austrian concessions in order to renew its own customs union for another ten years. Habsburg representatives fastened for the first time on barring rival Serbian livestock exports as a painless concession to Budapest. Serbian traders now began to search for other markets. They paid scant attention to the other lands of the future Yugoslavia because they had the same primary products to export. In fact, Serbian sales to these territories never accounted for more than 2 percent of its own pre-1914 export value.[24]

Montenegro as mini-state

By the modest economic standards just applied and by European political standards as well, the nineteenth-century Principality of

Montenegro was significantly smaller, less developed, and more isolated from the future Yugoslav lands. Yet the Black Mountain (*Crna Gora*) was important for other reasons, as it would be again, during and after the Second World War. On these several occasions, the local inhabitants' military valor on mountainous terrain defied foreign occupation. Here was one reason. Montenegro also emerged as a state separate from Serbia, despite an arguably Serb population, and it conducted foreign relations with the European powers like any of the far larger independent states of the pre-1914 Balkans.

The initially landlocked principality was remarkably small and poor. Its population even by the mid nineteenth century was barely 60,000 and concentrated almost entirely in mountain villages unconnected by any roads. Low crop yields and limited cultivation produced enough grain to feed only a fraction of its people. Livestock trade provided the only export. Either work abroad or banditry at home was more profitable, and both were better respected.[25]

A series of Orthodox bishops based in Cetinje and supported by Russian subsidies had struggled with the leaders of a dozen local clans to establish some sort of central authority since the eighteenth century. They came together only to hold Ottoman suzerainty at bay. Even the last and most famous of these bishops, Petar Petrović Njegoš, better remembered for his powerful, almost epic poetry, could not collect taxes or administer a legal system. He tried to do so, inspired by a sense of wider Serbian identity, based on the Kosovo defeat and the mission of expelling local Turks, rather than by any of the Enlightenment ideas with which he was also familiar. His most moving poem, "The Mountain Wreath" (*Gorski vijenac*), makes such priorities clear. His secular successor in 1851, Danilo, managed to promulgate a legal code and organize a unified army. He increased the new principality's size slightly in 1859, but was assassinated the next year.

Danilo's successor, Prince Nikola, presided over Montenegro as it doubled in size and won access to the Adriatic. On Russia's urging, the European powers recognized Montenegro as an independent state after its forces stayed in the field longer than Serbia's in the Russo-Ottoman War of 1877–78. The subsequent Treaty of Berlin gave the principality less territory than the initial Treaty of San Stefano and put its new coastline under Habsburg oversight. Russian subsidies to its state budget continued. Limited separation of the prince's arbitrary powers after 1879 between executive, legislative, and judicial bodies did nothing to advance the backward economy.

At the same time, Montenegro's population of 117,000 within its new borders grew to 185,000 by 1900. The urban share passed 8 percent.

Pressure to work abroad and the chance to study there grew accordingly. The state allocated a larger share of its budget for education than any Balkan state budget, funding enough primary schools to decrease the urban illiteracy rate of males to less than 50 percent by 1900. Students going on to Zagreb and especially to Belgrade for higher education established intellectual connections with the future Yugoslav lands. But the separate Montenegrin military and political structure continued on its own way, supported by Prince Nikola's ability to navigate his small state between the European powers until the First World War.

Croatian and South Slav ideas in the Habsburg lands, 1860–1900

Among the South Slavs of the Habsburg monarchy, the politics of national aspiration were concentrated in Civil and Military Croatia, at least until 1900. Yet they also made an appearance in Bosnia-Hercegovina, Dalmatia, and Slovenia. Of the three Croatian ideas for national integration, the Yugoslav idea had the shorter life span than either nationalism or liberalism.

Strossmayer's Yugoslav Federation

The first mention of a federal Yugoslavia, and even the first use of those words, came from the 1860s program of Josip Juraj Strossmayer. The Bishop of Djakovo (in eastern Slavonia) since 1849, the liberal Croat cleric with the deceptively German name spent the next decade searching for a way to build a new movement for the cultural integration of the South Slavs on the Illyrian pattern. He found it in what Mirjana Gross has called the "ideological system" of Franjo Rački, another Catholic priest.[26] Rački believed that Herder's political promise of "freedom through culture" could be fulfilled for the educated Croatian élite if only a single South Slav identity could be created to include Serbs as well as Slovenes. Strossmayer and Rački together founded the Yugoslav Academy of Arts and Sciences in Zagreb in 1866 to pursue that goal through secular scholarship and linguistic unification.

How could the Orthodox Serbs be brought into their Yugoslav state? Strossmayer and Rački suggested two unpromising solutions. They crafted Uniate propaganda that asked Serbs to accept loyalty to Rome in return, combining their liturgy with a revived *glagolica*, the medieval Slavonic language of the Croatian church. They also espoused the liberal hope that the two Christian faiths could reconcile their differences if the papacy relaxed its exclusive claims, particularly the late medieval suppression of the glagolitic liturgy.

Strossmayer used his position as a leader of the National Party to pursue political rather than religious goals during the 1860s. He sought Croatian autonomy from Vienna rather than independence as a South Slav state. The February Patent of 1861 allowed the Croatian Sabor to meet again and offered Civil Croatia the chance to send its own delegates to the new imperial *Reichsrat* in Vienna. Strossmayer led the majority of his party in opposing participation. He counted instead on the Hungarians granting Civil Croatia and Slavonia the autonomy for it to become the center of a federation including the Military Border, Dalmatia, and Slovenia. The presumption that Croatia would continue to lead this autonomous part of the Habsburg monarchy emerged only in such details as the Slovenian obligation to give up their language in favor of the štokavski dialect.

Strossmayer did not propose a specific connection with Serbia until 1866. The humiliating Habsburg defeat that year at the hands of Bismarck's North German Confederation allowed the Hungarian leadership to win its case for autonomy. It now made clear its discouraging intentions toward Croatia. Ferenc Deák, leader of the dominant Liberals, called the Croatians a "non-political people" with a separate but lower culture. His attitude accurately foreshadowed the limited autonomy for Civil Croatia and Slavonia alone that Hungary granted in the *Nagodba* of 1868.[27]

Strossmayer's interest coincided with Garašanin's efforts, already noted, to forge a system of alliances that would support a Serbian military confrontation with the Ottoman Empire. As we have seen, Serbia's foreign minister had already concluded agreements with Greece and Montenegro. Now he explored one with Croatian representatives as well. An assistant drafted a proposal for a Bosnian uprising that promised "local administrative autonomy" and equal central authority for the "two poles" of Belgrade and Zagreb in a future federal state. But, as he had with the original draft of the Načertanije, Garašanin revised the text. He eliminated the references to local autonomy and the two poles, stipulating instead that Belgrade was the "natural center . . . for unification of all Yugoslav peoples into a single federated state." What Strossmayer had in mind, on the other hand, was a dualistic arrangement like Austria-Hungary between his Croatian-led federation and Serbia. Nothing came of the bishop's last project as an active politician, but this first conflict between Croatian and Serbian terms for a Yugoslav federation make it significant.[28]

Croatian national and liberal ideas

The Nagodba of 1868, its modest amendment in 1873, and the incorporation of the Military Border into Hungary in 1881 fixed the framework within which Croatian political culture developed for the rest of the century. By the 1870s, two independent currents had already established themselves in Croatian politics. They were the nationalism and liberalism that have survived to the present day in Croatia, as the peasant and socialist currents of the early twentieth century have not.

Both nationalism and liberalism had appeared in Croatia before 1868, but unlike nineteenth-century Yugoslavism, they survived the shock of the Austro-Hungarian Nagodba and Serbia's terms for a joint state. The leading proponents of a separate Croatia were Ante Starčević and Eugen Kvaternik. They founded the Party of Right (read State's Rights) in 1861 to fight the centralized Austrian regime in Vienna that had suffocated the entire monarchy during the 1850s. Kvaternik died young during an abortive 1871 uprising in the Military Border against that authority, while Starčević lived on as a reclusive sage until 1896.

Starčević used his erudition and single-mindedness to put an indelible anti-Serb stamp on the Croatian national idea for the first time. Born on the Military Border of a Croat father and Serb mother, he was an ardent disciple of the Illyrian idea as a student during the 1840s. Even then, the centralized political regime that French rule had brought to the Illyrian provinces attracted him. By the 1860s, he made Napoleon III his political hero because the French emperor supported northern Italian independence from Habsburg rule. His Party of Right would rely even more on Budapest as Vienna's adversary than had Strossmayer. Starčević's subsequent disappointment with the Nagodba did not lead him to withdraw from politics like Strossmayer, but to extend his opposition to Austrian rule of the Dual Monarchy. This disappointment also encouraged his assertion of a purely Croatian ethnic character over the widest possible territory, Serb settlements included.

Still, the mainsprings of his anti-Serb sentiments are as open to question as their powerful impact on later generations of Croatian and Serbian nationalists is not. Did they derive from disillusion with his first ideological allegiance, the failed Illyrian movement? Or from his judgment (and Kvaternik's) that France was a more powerful and modernizing ally for Croatia against the Habsburg monarchy than Serbia's presumed ally Russia? Should a personal search for a single identity to overcome his own mixed, Serb–Croat parentage be included? Positive answers to any of these questions suggest that Starčević was not simply reacting to the 1849 publication of an essay written by the leading Serbian linguist, Vuk Karadžić, in 1836. Vuk's "Serbs All and Everywhere" (*Srbi svi i svuda*) claimed that all štokavian speakers, and thus the majority of Croats, were Serbs regardless of religion. Whatever the origins of Starčević's ideas, he expressed them eloquently and at length. He downplayed religious differences, but argued that the Serbs of Bosnia and the Military Border were really Orthodox Croats who, like the Bosnian Muslims, would voluntarily acknowledge their tie to the historical Croatian nation once it was shown to them. Forced conversion to Croat or Catholic identity was admittedly as far from his mind as were any of the other arbitrary features of Croatia's fascist government during the Second World War. Yet it was he who coined the pejorative term, "Slavoserb," revived by Croatian fascists and again later by some of the Zagreb media during the 1991–92 war to describe an inferior people who were not a nation but "a race of slaves, the most loathsome beasts." Even his colleague Kvaternik objected, as he did to Starčević's assertion that Slovenes were "mountain Croats."[29] In sum the same person whose writings on the organic unity of the Croatian people were the most persuasive to be penned during the nineteenth century also brought the dangerous idea of Serbian inferiority, spiritual if not yet genetic, into Croatian politics.

Both Starčević and his Party of Right played a small role, let it be emphasized, in these two initial decades of Croatian party politics. The two branches of the National Party had split apart in 1863, one favoring cooperation with Hungarian and the other with the Austrian authorities as the better way to gain greater autonomy. Both won more seats in Sabor elections than the Party of Right, as did the Unionist (formerly the Magyarone) Party that welcomed full integration with modernizing Hungary. Support for the modernizing initiatives that swept the new Dual Monarchy after the *Ausgleich* won the Independent National Party a majority in the Sabor by 1871. Its leader was Ivan Mažuranić (Starčević's former schoolteacher who had helped convert him to Illyrianism). He became a leading literary figure after the publication of his masterfully tragic tale of a doomed Ottoman official in Hercegovina, *Smrt Smail-aga Čengića* (The death of Smail Aga) in 1846. Mažuranić favored cooperation with Habsburg Vienna from the 1860s forward. In 1873 that loyalty was rewarded by his appointment to the position that Budapest believed it could always control, the economically powerful Ban.

Mažuranić's slogan for modernization, "from the inside and outside" bore visible fruit in a number of towns, particularly Zagreb. The capital now began to look like a city, growing from 19,000 to 28,000 people during the decade and acquiring the first European-style university in the

Yugoslav lands. Educational reform made primary and secondary schooling more accessible, and its urban infrastructure began to look Central European as well. Mirjana Gross credits him and literary giant August Šenoa with raising Croatia's high culture to a European level.[30] Mažuranić's movement for liberal reform lasted until 1880, longer than counterparts in Austria and Hungary on which it was modeled. In addition, Habsburg Serbs occupied the top three positions in his regime with no significant complaint from the Croatian mainstream.

In 1883 Budapest appointed a young, vigorous Hungarian Ban with instructions to advance the administrative integration of Croatia-Slavonia with the Hungarian Kingdom and spread the use of a single Magyar language. His mandate may well be viewed from the Hungarian perspective as taking central control of modernization. At the time, Croats also blamed the long tenure of Count Károly Khuen-Héderváry (to 1903) for diverting their politics from the liberal path of the period 1860–80. To the extent that the Sabor lost control of tax revenues and the urban élite were confronted with the prospect of creeping cultural Magyarization, this seems a fair charge. The Croat élite now interpreted the count's appointment of Serbs to high official positions, unlike Mažuranić's, as a policy of divide and rule.

The Mažuranić regime nonetheless shared responsibility with its successor for neglecting peasant interests. Peasants predominated in the 98 percent of the population who could not vote and were still over 80 percent illiterate in 1880. The absorption of the Military Border into Croatia-Slavonia in 1881 and the monarchy's occupation of neighboring Bosnia-Hercegovina two years before helped set the stage for a peasant revolt in 1883 that spread more widely than Serbia's Timok rebellion of the same year. Its origins and course had little to do with the Croatian nationalism of Starčević's small party, contrary to the suspicions of Habsburg officials, and nothing to do with anti-Croatian initiatives from the Military Border's sizeable Serb population.

The 1883 peasant revolt and the Military Border

The unrest that spread from northern Croatia into the former Military Border in the autumn of 1883 began in Zagreb as a Croatian nationalist protest. The Hungarian financial director had decided to hang the Hungarian state seal with inscriptions in both languages on his buildings. This was not a trivial gesture. The director's pressure on his staff to use the Hungarian language over the past three years had already aroused Croatian apprehension. An Independent National Party newspaper sounded the alarm, and the streets of Zagreb and several other towns quickly filled with angry demonstrators. But the Party of Right failed miserably in its efforts to turn this urban furor into a rural insurrection against Habsburg rule, even when they invited Serb participation.

Instead, the insurrection became a peasant revolt against *all* tax-collecting authority. It quickly spread from the Zagorje region north of Zagreb to the Banija district of the former Military Border. As Manuela Dobos has demonstrated, peasants rebelled for economic reasons unrelated to the ethnic anxieties of the urban élites.[31] Serious rural problems had emerged across all of Croatia, although not as much in the less populated, more prosperous Slavonia. Both the Hungarian abolition of serfdom in Civil Croatia after 1848 and the 1850 Austrian law to make Grenzer holdings on the Military Border inheritable property had prompted parcellization of peasant land into uneconomically small homesteads by the 1870s. Legal obstacles prevented the dissolution and subsequent sale or mortgage of the larger zadruga communal holdings and also discouraged efficient cultivation. Then, during the decade preceding the peasants' revolt, grain prices fell by half following the world market slump, and land taxes doubled. Peasant resentment of Croatian as well as Hungarian officials, still the largest occupational group in Zagreb, rose accordingly.

The Grenzer counted additional grievances against the rapidly swelling state apparatus. The gradual dissolution of the Border's special status had begun in 1873. The process combined infantry regiments with other Habsburg units, and closed the special stores that furnished necessities like tobacco, salt, and (shades of Serbia's Timok rebellion in 1883) rifles at cost. New indirect taxes followed, and the final absorption of the Border in 1881 gave the Hungarian Financial Directorate the power to impose more. This threat prompted the Serb and Croat Grenzer to join together to expel all officials and even their own priests from a number of Banija villages. Their common adversaries were the *kaputaši*, or frock-coat-wearing urban officials, who only asked for taxes and offered no assistance for agricultural modernisation.

Serb officers in the Croatian Krajina and townspeople in the Slavonian Krajina already saw the Habsburg administration of Croatia-Slavonia as working to their ethnic disadvantage. When the Grenzer delegates admitted to the Croatian Sabor for the first time in 1861 were expelled for rejecting participation in the new Austrian parliament, a number of Serb junior officers defected to Serbia. Some of them helped organize support along the Military Border for Garašanin's Serbian schemes to foment an uprising in Bosnia-Hercegovina against the Ottoman regime.[32]

Such initiatives from Serbia only deepened Hungarian determination to dissolve the Military Border, to which the emperor finally agreed in 1871. Two years later, the liberal Mažuranić introduced a single system of secular schools that threatened the survival of the Serbs' Orthodox church schools in the previously protected Border. Serb townspeople in the Srem, the eastern area between the Danube and Sava rivers bordering Serbia, protested, but there was little response from the countryside. The Serb peasants who joined Croat peasants in 1883 to oppose the threat of higher Hungarian taxes came from the other, western end of the Military Border. They evoked no echo in the Srem, even though pressures on the townspeople there for cultural Magyarization had since mounted. In the meantime, the Serbian government's secret agreement of 1881 had granted Vienna a veto on its foreign initiatives, underscoring Belgrade's inability to prevent the Austro-Hungarian occupation of Bosnia-Hercegovina and keeping Serbia off the international stage.

Bosnia's transition from Ottoman to Austro-Hungarian rule

The three-cornered warfare that bloodied Bosnian Serbs, Croats, and Muslims after the breakup of Yugoslavia in 1991 struck its earliest roots during the period surrounding the end of Ottoman domination. Serb–Muslim antagonism had spread in the several decades prior to 1877 and sharpened thereafter. The hybrid features of Austro-Hungary's post-1878 Bosnian regime also made Serbs and Croats potential adversaries for the first time anywhere on the territory of the future Yugoslavia. Habsburg rule shared one feature with the late Ottoman regime that provoked antagonism. Both empires sought to modernize tax collection, military service, and education by bringing them under central control. The same motive was at work in the policies that led to the peasant uprisings of 1883 in both Serbia and Croatia, but had no consequence there for ethnic conflict.

Ottoman reforms earlier in the nineteenth century had tried to put a modern army in place of the autonomous Janissary corps locally entrenched around the empire. Military reform directly challenged the power of the Bosnian Muslim élite. Their local lords (*begs* and *agas*) commanded the Janissary Corps and held land which was sharecropped by largely Serb peasants. The proportion of Serbs in Bosnia had risen with migration from 10 to 40 percent of the population during the seventeenth and eighteenth centuries. From 1815 Bosnian Muslim forces also held the six western and southern districts of Serbia that Prince Miloš was finally able to bargain back from the Porte in 1833.

By then the Bosnian Muslim élite had already organized a military expedition against the regular Ottoman army. Their force briefly won victories as far away from Bosnia as Kosovo and demanded autonomy, before being defeated. Bosnian Muslims also resisted the efforts of further Ottoman reforms after 1839 to end the system of local commanders entirely. Finally, the arbitrary efforts of a new Ottoman governor to raise taxes and to make the state rather than local landlords the tax collectors triggered a last, failed Bosnian Muslim revolt in 1851.[33]

Serb peasants comprised over one-third of the 1.3 million people in Bosnia-Hercegovina by the 1860s. They had already staged local revolts in 1834 and 1842 against their landlords' impositions, made more severe by the economic decline after the increased transit trade of the Napoleonic era had ended. New 1848 regulations demanded one-third of the grain harvest or forced labor in its place and spawned four more uprisings by 1862. For these rural Serb sharecroppers, all 400,000 Bosnian Muslims seemed to be inextricably implicated in their grievances, not just the 10,000 members of the typically landowning élite. Some of the 250,000 Croats, largely from Hercegovina, also drank from this poisoned well, although they did not have the small commercial élite that was starting to speak up for the Serbs and look to Serbia for relief. But both Croat and Serb peasants, illiterate as they were, had local priests to add a confessional justification to their grievances.

The widespread violence which would surround the transition to Austro-Hungarian rule began with the 1875 uprising in Hercegovina. Both Serb and Croat peasants were ready to take up arms when their demands to reduce a monetary tax burden, tripled since 1850, were rejected after a bad harvest. The killing of a Franciscan priest who had traveled to Dalmatia for the visit of the Habsburg emperor, Franz Josef, ironically set off the Serbs with the support of Montenegro. Ottoman and Bosnian Muslim forces soon put down the revolt and repulsed a brief invasion from Serbia. In the bloody process, some 150,000 people, mainly Serbs, had been killed or forced to flee. This prolonged turmoil persuaded the European powers to add Austro-Hungarian occupation of Bosnia-Hercegovina to the terms of the Treaty of Berlin, concluded in 1878 to rescind Russian gains from its recent war with the Ottoman Empire. Austrian generals had coveted the province since 1854 as a land route to safeguard the Dalmatian coast. They also feared Serbia's interest as a potential Russian client. It took nearly three months of sometimes heavy fighting for Habsburg units to subdue the paramilitary forces assembled from the Bosnian Muslim population. The ensuing departure of more than 200,000 Muslims and Turks for Constantinople and the Ottoman core gave the Serbs a plurality in Bosnia-Hercegovina that would endure until after the Second World War. To add to the legacy of 1878, the victorious Habsburg units were primarily Serbs and Croats drawn from the dissolving Military Border into regular regiments and still led by Grenzer commanders.[34]

A Grenzer general, a Croat, became the province's first governor. Still, the terms of the Austro-Hungarian compromise now placed its administration under a new Bosnian Bureau set up in the joint Finance Ministry. From the start, the province was charged with paying its own way. The resulting pressure to collect taxes encouraged the Finance Ministry to abandon the Croatian governor and his harsh treatment of the Muslim élite in favor of accommodating them and the existing land regime. A hasty cadastral survey also increased the area on which the share-cropping kmet majority of the population owed a recently reduced crop tax. In the meantime, Habsburg authorities encouraged Serb refugees to return to Hercegovina after the 1875–78 uprising by allowing them to form their own paramilitary units. When the returnees realized what taxes they faced and learned in late 1881 of the further Habsburg requirement for compulsory service in the regular army, they rose up in revolt. Several regular army regiments, now more Croat than Serb, put down the rebellion of 1882 but not the banditry that continued for another decade.

Greatly facilitating the restoration of order was the appointment of an able Hungarian, who had become a South Slav scholar during his previous posting to Belgrade, as joint finance minister to head the Bosnian Bureau in 1882. Benjámin Kállay's tenure continued until 1903, and his second-in-command's even longer. Together they oversaw significant additions to urban infrastructure and the rural transport network; they also founded a number of state industrial enterprises. Whatever their long-run economic benefits, these modernizing initiatives demanded higher tax revenues, even though they were introduced for the primary purpose of generating enough revenue to show an annual budget surplus.[35] The resulting tax burden continued to fall most heavily on the Serb and Croat peasants still tied to sharecropping for Muslim landlords.

Kállay's insistence on confessional equality, combined with his inability to advance interconfessional education, contributed to growing tensions between Serbs and Croats. An influx of Croats, including many Habsburg officials, and a newly aggressive Catholic hierarchy made Serb apprehension inevitable. The Franciscan order lost its long-standing monopoly on speaking for the Catholic church in Bosnia-Hercegovina to the Austrian hierarchy. It encouraged other orders, Jesuits included, to send priests and brought an archbishop to Sarajevo. From the 1890s, Archbishop Josip Stadler used those priests to expand the network of Catholic primary and secondary schools. Kállay opposed the identification of religion with ethnicity as "oriental backwardness" unsuited to state-building, but his choice of words revealed a readiness to restrict the Serb Orthodox schools in particular. He abolished the special tax donation to the Serbs' Orthodox schools in 1884 and a number of them subsequently closed. Certificates of political reliability were required from 1892 for Serbs to teach in state schools which had in the meantime been staffed largely with Croat immigrants. In addition Kállay opened a few state interconfessional schools in Serb areas and vetoed a plan for 150 new schools throughout the province in 1894. As a result, while the share of primary pupils in state schools climbed from 31 percent to 74 percent between 1882 and 1900, the Serbian share of all pupils dropped from 55 to 42 percent. The total number of primary schools rose from 40 to 200, but the number per capita was still only half of Serbia's low level. Less than one-sixth of all primary-age children attended school, and adult illiteracy, overwhelmingly rural, remained high at 90 percent.[36]

Kállay must be credited with trying to articulate a common Bosnian consciousness for all three ethnic groups, an effort whose general failure then should not be used to deny such consciousness in Sarajevo and other large towns after the Second World War. His project to prepare a new series of school texts struggled to spell out Bosnia's multi-ethnic identity. The wider Ottoman past and Muslim classics were neglected. His censors' resistance to any specific references to Serbia or Croatia delayed the volume on medieval history until 1901. None of the three groups' contributors to the texts nor the urban élites from which they came could be won over to his idea of *Bošnjaštvo*, a Bosnian identity, more because it admitted no additional identity and demanded allegiance to the Habsburg administration than because of deep religious animosities.[37]

Kállay's refusal to tolerate any form of political organization or expression pushed all three groups toward the separate political parties that emerged during the decade after his death. By that time, the Serbs' connection with Serbia and the Croats' connection with the Catholic hierarchy had hardened (see chapter 3). Nor had Kállay's initial concessions to the Muslim community convinced them that a political party was unnecessary. Neither the office of *Reis-ul-ulema* that he created for their religious leader in 1882 nor the regulation of 1891 that required family consent for conversion (usually from Muslim to Catholic) in mixed marriages persuaded the Muslim leadership in Sarajevo and the other towns that they could trust the Austro-Hungarian bureaucracy to represent their best interests.

The idea that these interests and those of the Bosnian Serbs and Croats might best be served in a single South Slav state crossed relatively few minds by the end of the nineteenth century in this most ethnically mixed part of the future Yugoslavia. Chapter 3 will explore how accelerating urban modernization and new political possibilities after 1900 brought that idea to Bosnia, where distinct Serbian and Croatian ideas already had a foothold.

Dalmatia and Slovenia as Yugoslav outposts

The incorporation of the Military Border into Civil Croatia-Slavonia and Bosnia-Hercegovina into the Dual Monarchy concentrated large numbers of Serbs under administrations that accorded them none of the privileges given them on the Border and relieved none of the burdens they bore in Bosnia-Hercegovina. The territorial changes also shifted the focus of Serbs in Belgrade and Croats in Zagreb toward the lands between them. Austro-Hungarian efforts to point Serbia southward to Kosovo and Macedonia had no lasting success. Croatia was diverted as well and more quickly from multi-ethnic connections with Dalmatia and Slovenia. The Croatian diversions would prove most costly to the Yugoslav idea.

A kind of Yugoslav nationalism appeared in Dalmatia during the 1860s. Some urban Serbs and more Croats united to form the National-ist Party and challenge the Italianizing Autonomists, who had used a tiny franchise to win the first election to a Dalmatian Diet in 1861. They were soon joined by Franciscan priests representing the illiterate peasantry of the hinterland. The Nationalists avoided the name "Croat" in their demands, even though one of their goals was to reunite the Triune Kingdom of Croatia, Slavonia, and Dalmatia. This they did to avoid a name offensive to Italian sympathizers because Grenzer regiments had participated in the recent Habsburg campaign in northern Italy. The name "Yugoslav" also reassured the Serb minority that they would be treated equally with Croats in any Triune state. It promised the coastal towns that their long tradition of municipal autonomy would be restored if not rescued from Austrian centralism.

The Nationalists persevered until they won a majority in the Diet in 1876 and even in the Italian Autonomist stronghold of Split in 1882. By then the entirely separate Serb and Croat tendencies from across the border in Hercegovina led to the creation of a separate Serbian National Party. The remainder in Hercegovina renamed themselves the Croatian National Party a few years later.[38]

The Slovenes' connection with Croatia and the Yugoslav idea was even more brief but portentous. Their population was scattered among six Austrian provinces or territories, most with German or Italian ethnic majorities – hence the appeal of some South Slav support, once the Illyrian insistence on abandoning the Slovenian language had been set aside. Bishop Strossmayer's more accommodating "Yugoslavism" encouraged a small group of Slovenes to draft the Maribor Program for a single Slovene entity within the Habsburg monarchy. The proposal had no practical prospects, but the idea of a larger, South Slav province began to attract large crowds to a series of *tabor*, or town meetings. As a result, some 100 representatives of Serbs and Croats as well as Slovenes were invited to a meeting in Ljubljana in 1870 to decide what to do next. The Slovenian organizers had to expend considerable effort to persuade the Croatian National Party delegates to include a smaller number of Serbs.[39] Nothing came of the meeting, understandably, given their weak political position. The next year, this leading Croatian party accepted the Nagodba with Hungary and after 1878 transferred its attention to winning political rights for the Croat population of Hercegovina.

Slovenian politics turned inward after the 1873 elections and did not turn eastward again until after the turn of the century. By that time the uneven pace of accelerating economic modernization made the lack of Slovenian political leverage within the Austrian half of the Dual Monarchy more painful. Only then did their interest revive in a wider unit from which to bargain. Yet with little economic incentive in 1870, the Ljubljana meeting set a modest precedent for Slovenian mediation as a way to bring Serbs and Croats together.

3 New divisions, Yugoslav ties, and Balkan Wars, 1903–1914

Only the course of the First World War, as we shall see in chapter 4, made it possible to form the first Yugoslav state in December of 1918. Yet calls for some sort of Yugoslavia were increasingly heard after the turn of the century. Change was in the air during this last prewar decade. New political parties appeared, impatient over the promise of mass politics. The status quo looked less promising and less likely to last than it had previously.

The year 1903 appeared to usher in a new era even at the time. In Serbia, what began as a royal assassination and a military coup to install the rival dynasty soon promised to make the independent state truly a constitutional monarchy and a parliamentary democracy. Here was a Serbia to envy or even to join. In 1903, the Illinden Uprising also challenged Ottoman rule in Macedonia, and the twenty-year regimes of autocratic if able Habsburg administrators for Croatia-Slavonia and Bosnia-Hercegovina both came to an end. Across the South Slav lands of Austria-Hungary, ethnically based political parties questioned the existing political or territorial order. Their leaders began to debate alternatives that proposed the unification of all or some of the future Yugoslavia. The very word "Yugoslav" now passed into common usage.

The European economic and political milieu was now pregnant with new possibilities. Accelerating economic growth and political unrest were the rule across the continent. The popular press and other means of rapid communication spread anxiety over international relations to a mass audience. The advance of universal male suffrage made mass politics a reality and gave nationalism a constituency that the new anxiety could mobilize. Partly in response, states large and small were rapidly expanding the civilian and military apparatus of government. Politicians and people were, in Winston Churchill's words, "everywhere eager to dare." By 1914 too many were ready to risk full-scale war. Officials, students, and townspeople from Slovenia to Macedonia shared an impatience for ethnic rights, class interests aside, and for self-determination at any cost. The very sense that precipitous change was under way everywhere made the prospect of a larger, South Slav state more realistic, and gave it far wider appeal than before.

Then Serbia won the two Balkan Wars of 1912–13, absorbing northern Macedonia and Kosovo in the process. Its victories inspired some Croats and Slovenes as well as most Serbs in the Habsburg lands to think about a large, new state as an immediate alternative. These events also reinforced the conviction of the Austrian General Staff that the Dual Monarchy needed a preventive war against Serbia in order to retain its hold on these southern lands, most prominently Bosnia-Hercegovina.

Across the spectrum of South Slav peoples there was continuing disagreement or ambiguity about just what shape any new state should take. Political divisions split the increasingly educated, urban élites of the various ethnic groups. In major towns, new political parties fed on a mass press and mass education. Sharp commercial and industrial upswings after 1900 swelled the numbers of these divided élites at the same time that the advantages of a larger Yugoslav market first became obvious. Modernization, in other words, now mattered as it had not during the nineteenth century, at least outside the expanding structures for state administration and tax collection.

Rural peasants still made up four-fifths of the population of the future Yugoslav lands. They were less divided along political or ethnic lines than the new party leaders, but were more divided economically. Some peasants gained from the economic upswings of the last prewar decade; the majority did not. The natural rate of rural population growth was simply too high, more than 1 percent per year, with no means to buy more land or employ better agricultural methods to increase production. As population growth outpaced what industrial stirrings from Slovenia to Serbia could absorb, a significant number of the disadvantaged peasants consequently emigrated. Permanent or prolonged emigration removed fully 5 percent of the mean populations of Slovenia and Bosnia for 1901–10, and 7 percent in Croatia proper. Seasonal migration prevailed in Serbia and Macedonia, but over 10 percent of Macedonia's population also made prolonged stays from 1890 to 1910.[1]

Croatia-Slavonia's urban population increased its proportion slightly, rising from 16 to 21 percent between 1880 and 1910. Much of that increase came from German and Hungarian immigrants, whose share of total population rose from 7 to 9 percent. Over 90 percent of the rural landowners worked smallholdings of less than 5 hectares (one hectare equals 2.47 acres), as they did in the other territories of the future Yugoslavia. The equal division of property among all sons (done secretly

Table 3.1. *Land distribution (pre-1914 census)*

Land distribution (size in hectares)	Serbia	Croatia-Slavonia	Bosnia and Hercegovina	Dalmatia	Slovenia
Up to 2	18.5	44.3	40.7	61.5	31.6
2 to 5	34.3	27.2	26.4	25.8	19.4
5 to 20	43.1	27.6	18.7[a]	11.4	39.1
20 to 50	3.8	0.7	14.2[b]	0.9	8.5
Above 50	0.3	0.2	–	0.4	1.4

[a]5 to 10 hectares
[b]Above 10 hectares
Sources: Ranko M. Brashich, *Land Reform and Ownership in Yugoslavia: 1919–1953* (New York: Mid-European Studies Center, 1954), 10–15; and Jozo F. Tomasevich, *Peasants, Politics, and Economic Change in Yugoslavia* (Stanford, Calif.: Stanford University Press, 1955), 389.

in Croatia to avoid the tax burden of breaking up the old communal zadruga) split inheritances into ever smaller holdings. Although often on better land in Civil Croatia or Slavonia, the subdivision of the Croat peasants' holdings had gone farther (or started with smaller holdings) than for their Croatian Serb counterparts. The Croat proportion of peasants on holdings under 3 hectares approached 80 percent by 1910, versus 16 percent for Serbs who made up 25 percent of total population (Croats were 63 percent). For larger holdings of 5 to 50 hectares, the Serb share was 37 percent.

Seen in historical perspective, these long-underpopulated lands were now filling up to levels that extensive small-scale agriculture could no longer sustain. Serbian and Croatian population densities that had barely exceeded twenty people per square kilometer in the early nineteenth century approached sixty or more in 1910. Little wonder that the same decrease in hectares cultivated for grain per capita seen in Serbia after 1900 occurred in Croatia-Slavonia as well.[2]

The apparently rapid growth in both export value and industrial production in Serbia and the various Habsburg borderlands after 1900, by as much as 10 percent a year, did little to relieve the pressure in rural areas. Serbia's exports declined in real per capita terms during this decade before the First World War. The Austro-Hungarian periphery probably did not do much better, but this is unclear and controversial from available data. More certain is the combined failure of the several industrial mini-spurts to provide employment in modern manufacturing for even 2 percent of the labor force across all of the future Yugoslav lands by 1912.[3]

Table 3.2. *Population, 1870 and 1910 (in thousands)*

	Serbia		Croatia-Slavonia		Bosnia and Hercegovina		Dalmatia	
	Population	per sq. km.	Population	per sq km.	Population	per sq. km.	Population	per sq. km.
1870	1,302		1,838		1,042		457 (1871)	
1910	2,912	58.3	2,732	62.3	1,898	37.1	625	49.1

	Slovenia		Macedonia		Montenegro		Vojvodina	
	Population	per sq. km.	Population	per sq. km.	Population	per sq. km.	Population	per sq. km.
1870	1,134				67.5			
1910	1,064	65.7	1,665	36.4	238	24.6	1,353	68.7

Source: Werner Markert, *Jugoslawien* (Cologne: Bohlau-Verlag, 1954), 40; Toussaint Hočevar, *Structure of the Slovenian Economy, 1848–1963* (New York: Studia Slovenica, 1965), 81; and Michael R. Palairet, "The Culture of Economic Stagnation in Montenegro," *The Maryland Historian,* 17 (1986): 19–21.

In addition, neither the commercial upswings nor the peasant migrations fostered connections among the future Yugoslav lands beyond the few exceptions to be described below. Trade between them remained minuscule; emigrants went elsewhere, to the Hungarian harvests or to Czech or American factories. (The young Josip Broz, later Tito, ended up in a Prague factory after deciding not to emigrate to the United States from Trieste.) But this still amounted to more economic change than any of these lands had experienced in the last decades of the nineteenth century, enough to call into question their connections to the Austro-Hungarian or Ottoman Empires. None of it, moreover, created economic conflict between native ethnic groups; it even encouraged their cooperation.

Tables 3.1 and 3.2 offer some bench marks by which to compare demographic change and distribution of land in these territories. Behind them lie the common features just recited: backward agricultural sectors overcrowded with peasant smallholdings and substantial urban and industrial growth that fell far short of the promise held out by rapidly rising foreign trade and state expenditure. There were also significant differences, sometimes exaggerated and sometimes reduced by the modern political parties that stepped forward everywhere except in Montenegro and Macedonia.

Fragmented growth and party politics in the Habsburg lands

The prewar economic advance within the largest and most modern market, Austria-Hungary, became sufficiently disjointed to encourage the search for a new political framework that would bring the south Slavs closer together. Austrian or Hungarian restrictions kept franchises for regional assemblies small and made public meetings difficult. Still, the monarchy granted enough press and organizational freedom to allow the practice of modern, if not mass, politics by competing parties. The Austrian extension of universal suffrage in 1907 opened up Slovenian and Dalmatian politics even further. Independent Serbia offered a near universal male franchise from the start and developed new political if not economic connections with its western neighbors in the future Yugoslavia. The connections with Bosnia-Hercegovina and its new ethnic politics deserve particular attention.

Slovenia and Dalmatia

The political division of the Slovenian population among six provincial administrations in the Austrian half of the monarchy may be recalled from chapter 2. It was, however, the increasing economic integration of the future Yugoslavia's largest urban population with Trieste and its rail link to Vienna that first stimulated Slovenian politics after 1900. The port's booming economy became the centerpiece that transformed 28 percent of the Slovenian provinces' population into townspeople and produced four times more industrial output per capita than Serbia by 1912. With the end of Trieste's status as a separate free port in 1891, tariffs were no longer levied on goods entering by land from elsewhere in Austria-Hungary. New port facilities and a second rail line to Vienna opened in 1901 to attract further bank investment, mainly from Vienna, as well as new firms. Trieste's large Italian majority, long commercially preeminent, founded most of the new industrial enterprises in and around the city. The city's population rose to 229,000 by 1910. It included 57,000 Slovenes, nearly equal to the 64,000 in Ljubljana, which was the biggest town by far in the one predominantly Slovenian province of Carniola.[4]

The Slovene minority concentrated in Trieste made louder declarations of Slovenian ethnic identity there than the majority in Carniola. At the same time, the ties to Trieste worked against the emergence of any political program for an economically separate Slovenia. How much more attractive it was for Slovenian managers or enterprises to seek a fair share in the expanding nexus from Trieste north to Vienna. Such motives led to the founding of the Ljubljanska Banka in 1901 and the Jadranska Banka in 1905. Behind the founders stood the powerful Czech Živnostenská Banka of Prague and a group of Croatian investors. The latter, not surprisingly, financed several import-export companies and shipping lines. Both began profitable trade up and down a Dalmatian coast cut off from the Austro-Hungarian railway[5] network south of Rijeka.

For inland Dalmatia and Istria, a cooperative network soon furnished a broader Slovenian connection. The co-founder of the Slovenian Christian Social movement, Janez Krek, launched the network in 1895 with a series of parish-based credit unions on the Raiffeisen model. They offered easy access to loans regardless of the size of the member's account. A new cooperative law in 1903 allowed him to increase the number of credit unions fourfold to 405 by 1912, a total of 115,000 members, and to double the agricultural cooperatives to 170. The rise to preeminence in Carniola of the Catholic National Party – soon renamed the Slovenian People's Party (SLS) – also helped, but Krek steered the party away from political control of the network. No doubt this facilitated its spread beyond ethnic Slovenes to the Croats of Istria and Dalmatia, who accounted for one-quarter of the credit unions by 1912.[5] The network's main bank in Ljubljana also invested in primary and agricultural education for an inland Dalmatian peasantry that was over 80 percent illiterate, in contrast to a rate of less than 20 percent among Slovenian peasants.

Along the coast and inland, Croats and Slovenes also shared a common political adversary, the Italian nationalists in the principal Adriatic towns. Italians were most prominent in Istria, with 38 percent of the province's population in 1910 versus less than 3 percent in Dalmatia. Yet the leading parties of the Croatian and Slovenian political spectrums failed, even along the coast, to create what Serbian nationalists like Nikola Pašić had feared in the 1890s: a united Catholic front led by a Croatian-dominated clerical party. It was instead the clerical leaders of the largest *Slovenian* party, the Peoples' Party, who pursued the policy of "Christian nationalism." They proposed giving up the Slovenian language in favour of Croatian if the Dual Monarchy accepted a third, South Slav, part of the monarchy in return. The urban-centered minority parties, the Liberals and the Social Democrats, refused to consider bargaining away the Slovenian language.[6]

New leaders of the Croatian National Party (founded in Dalmatia in the 1880s – see chapter 2) began to seek out reconciliation with its minority Serb counterpart after the turn of the century. They did not demand or dream that the Serbs would adopt what the Slovene clerical leaders called a "clearly superior" Western religion and culture. Instead, the two secular apostles of Dalmatian Yugoslavism, Frano Supilo and Ante Trumbić, organized the first meetings for Serb-Croat unity in Rijeka in 1905. The resulting Rijeka Resolution, although primarily a statement of political strategy, spoke of one Serb-Croat people who should learn the same history lessons from new textbooks printed in both alphabets, a task that could hardly be left to either of their two clergies.[7]

Croatia-Slavonia

Two features of the economic upswing in the Croatian economy before the war became potential handicaps for the first Yugoslavia, into which Croatia was drawn after 1918. The upswing exaggerated the already sharp regional differences described between Civil Croatia-Slavonia and the former Military Border that had been incorporated into both of them after 1881. Nor did it repair the singular absence of economic contact with the other lands of the future Yugoslavia. At the time, both of these disjunctures helped confine the new coalition of Croats and Serbs (described below) to seeking only the unification of Dalmatia with Croatia-Slavonia or, in other words, the restoration of the medieval Triune Kingdom.

Industrial production rose past 10 percent of the crude estimates of Gross Domestic Product (GDP) on the strength of a growing Slavonian advantage over Croatia proper. Timber production from large estates spawned new sawmills and other wood-working enterprises in the one large town of Osijek (population 28,000 by 1910) and a number of smaller ones like Vukovar. Germans and Hungarians made up half of the new labor force, Croats and Serbs the other half. (Hungarian capital supported the large Beočin cement plant and a few others, but generally held back. Budapest's business interests opposed the rail line to Rijeka on the Adriatic that would have opened alternative Mediterranean markets for Croatian manufactures.) Led by timber, Slavonian industry accounted for over half of the capital and labor in large-scale Croatian industry by 1910 and for most of its advantage in industrial production over independent Serbia. In Croatia proper, Zagreb remained primarily an administrative center. Officials and students made up the largest occupational groups. Within the two groups, Croats held percentages proportional to their five-eighths population share, with Serb numbers trailing their one-quarter share in both. For officials, Germans and Hungarians filled the gap. The Croatian capital was an industrial center only for small firms of fewer than twenty employees, again involving few Serbs.[8]

Estate agriculture in both Croatia and Slavonia led the way in modernizing the raising of livestock, such that their export north to the rest of the Dual Monarchy was triple Serbia's highest value before the war. The rural population in Croatia-Slavonia increased almost three times faster than the real value of grain output for 1900–10, however, reflecting the downward drag of the limited and low yield cultivation along the former Military Border. The old Border's low literacy rates – barely 20 percent – exerted an even greater drag on the joint province's overall literacy rate, holding it to 54 percent in 1910. Industry remained virtually non-existent along the Border, further prompting the emigration of some 300,000 Serbs and Croats to the United States during the last prewar decade.[9]

The prominence of livestock and timber in the exports of Croatia-Slavonia discouraged trade with or migration to the other lands of the future Yugoslavia. Urban Austro-Hungarian markets to the north imported such goods, but the largely rural lands to the east and west had no need of them. From the total export value of manufactures from Croatia-Slavonia in 1912, only 5 percent was sent to Bosnia-Hercegovina, and less than 1 percent to Dalmatia or Serbia.[10] The Croatian-Serbian Coalition that dominated the Croatian Sabor of 1906 contained a number of successful businessmen, but few who were seeking to improve their commercial connections with Serbia or to create some still wider Yugoslav entity.

The Coalition's majority (46 out of 88 seats) in the first freely elected Sabor since the 1870s won out because of the narrower, essentially political agenda of two Dalmatians, journalist Frano Supilo and lawyer Ante Trumbić. Most of the Croat deputies had signed Supilo's Rijeka Resolution of 1905, while the Serbs had supported, with some of them signing, a similar resolution the same year at Zadar. The Serb signatories came from the Serbian Independent Party, long passive but actively expanding since 1903 under the militant, charismatic leadership of Svetozar Pribićević, the youthful editor of the party newspaper. Pribićević embodied the Independents' equally new disposition to present a unified front with the Croats as part of the "same nation." For their part, the Croats sought political support from Hungary, against Vienna, for the union of Austrian Dalmatia with Croatia-Slavonia. Croat signatories reportedly agreed to recognize Bosnia as a Serb "sphere of influence" if Serbia supported the Dalmatian union. Both Croats and Serbs also welcomed the Coalition's "new course" toward ethnic cooperation and its promise of breaking the former Military Border's large Serb minority free from the role of Croatian adversary, in which their appointment to administrative positions by the previous Ban, Count Khuen-Hédeváry, and their support for the Hungarian regime's National Party had cast them. Pribićević decried the past reliance on special privileges rather than constitutional rights that would nonetheless continue to attract the Vojvodina Serbs until the eve of the First World War.

In 1907 the new Hungarian government challenged the victorious coalition by introducing a law requiring use of a single language (Hungarian) on the state railway and by adopting an equally Magyarizing education bill that violated the Nagodba. The Austrian emperor, Franz Josef, also refused to change the status of Dalmatia. The coalition turned toward a policy of confrontation with the Dual Monarchy. The Independents soon became equal partners and increased their contacts with the Independent Radical Party of Serbia. Both parties spoke of the Yugoslav idea, but meant *narodno jedinstvo*, or national unity between ethnic brothers, rather than any federal relationship.[11]

Of the other four parties whose representatives were elected to the Sabor in 1910, the only two that survived to participate in the first Yugoslavia also opposed the state's existence, at least with any place for Serbia. The Pure Right and Peasant Parties won just 14 and 9 of the 88 seats, although from a franchise that had increased from 1.8 to 6.6 percent of the population. The larger number went to the radical nationalist Party of Pure Right. Its Slavonian Jewish leader, Josip Frank, merged it with the clerical faction, "Croatia," to form a Christian-Social Party of Right. Frank had for some time been turning toward Vienna and the Catholic hierarchy. He opposed any separate status for Serbs and advocated a Great Croatia within the monarchy that would include Bosnia as well as Dalmatia. Frank stood the anti-clerical and anti-Austrian direction of Ante Starčević and his original Party of Right on its head in order to serve a stronger, more racist sort of anti-Serbian program.

Had the franchise been universal, the larger vote-getter by far would have been the new Croatian People's Peasant Party (HPSS). The Radić brothers, Stjepan and Ante, founded what became Croatia's largest interwar party in 1904. Ante was an ethnographer who espoused a program of peasant populism. He proposed a cooperative network and other agricultural reforms that would eliminate middlemen and foreign landlords. But the bulk of the program concentrated on folk culture, and saw it rather than religion or historical borders as the element binding peasant Croats together. By this standard, Bosnian Muslims and even Serb peasants were welcome to join. Ante Radić believed peasants should govern because they were by far the largest social class, just as Aleksandar Stamboliiski of the newly organized Bulgarian Agrarian National Union was arguing in Sofia at the same time. Radić's mercurial brother Stjepan, who became the party's leader, neglected economic issues for political even more than Ante. He revelled in the newspaper polemics of the new mass politics. Stjepan pushed the party to support a South Slav unit within the monarchy, but under Croatian leadership and with the same confederal autonomy as the Hungarian lands. Indeed, his own political career had begun in 1895 when, fresh from Prague and his first taste of Tomáš Masaryk's ideas for Slavic self-determination, the young Radić and several other students burned the Hungarian flag at the Zagreb railway station. Radić insisted that they use alcohol rather than oil, a distinction he felt would temper their disrespect for the Habsburg emperor, Franz Joseph, who was then visiting the Croatian capital. Subsequent years of exile and study in Paris, Prague, and Moscow strengthened his rejection of political control from Budapest, as he would later reject control from Belgrade.

At the same time, Stjepan Radić recognized the Serbs as Slavs, ethnically separate from Croats. He suspected that many in Bosnia had Croat origins because of their common peasant culture. His disposition to ethnic tolerance and strongly anti-clerical views barred any alliance with the Party of Pure Right, the Catholic hierarchy in Croatia, or the Slovenian People's Party and its clerical leadership.[12]

Bosnia-Hercegovina

Austro-Hungarian economic policies sought to promote both the province's industrial and agricultural development of Bosnia-Hercegovina. They began with the term of Benjámin Kállay (1882–1903) as joint finance minister for the new province. As they have been described, respectively, in the classic studies by Peter Sugar and Ferdinand Schmid, the first was an initial success and the second a failure throughout.[13] In the first decade of the twentieth century, both Kállay's industrial success and his agricultural failure carried significant consequences for any future South Slav state that included Bosnia-Hercegovina. The state-sponsored industrial growth that he oversaw failed to pursue the foreign trade opportunities or to attract the private capital needed to sustain its fast start. Kállay accepted a land regime dominated by the traditional Bosnian Muslim landlords, opposed agricultural cooperatives, and neglected rural education. All this encouraged the ethnic antagonisms that opened the door to vengeful violence in the two world wars and in the 1990s.

The new administration of Istvan Burian (1903–12) continued to collect impressive revenues. They were spent entirely in the province, unlike Croatia-Slavonia where 55 percent of revenues were transferred to Budapest. Average Bosnian state expenditure after 1900 was three times the Croatian figure per capita and nearly equal to that of independent Serbia. The Habsburg regime for the province conducted the most active state policy to promote economic development in any of the Yugoslav lands. Railway construction continued to lay down twice as much track as in Serbia, although the lines were narrow gauge, had prohibitively high freight rates, and ran only to Budapest. Hungarian representatives in the joint administration also vetoed an Austrian plan to build a line linking Sarajevo with Split on the Dalmatian coast.

In addition, the striking pace of growth in the value of industrial production under Kállay, which had reached 15 percent per year in the 1890s, dropped off to barely 3 percent for 1906–13. Large-scale enterprises, primarily sawmills and iron ore mines, employed three times as many people per 1,000 as in Serbia. But they could not attract the Austrian or Hungarian capital required to keep up the growth launched by start-up subventions and other concessions.[14] This state-subsidized spurt and later slow-down left as one legacy the notion that private enterprise needed political support in order to succeed. Another legacy may lie hidden in the ethnic composition of the 30,000 workers in large-scale enterprises in 1910 if, as scattered evidence suggests, the more numerous Serbs occupied only a small fraction of these high-wage jobs and the newly arrived Croats took a disproportionate share.

More clearly, Austro-Hungarian policy aggravated rural ethnic antagonisms despite several specific efforts to reduce them by promoting agricultural modernization. Conversion of the land worked by largely Serb sharecroppers, or *kmetovi*, to their own smallholdings was made legal, but required the peasant to indemnify the Muslim landlord. The process went slowly, cutting the total of landless sharecroppers only from 90,000 to 80,000 for 1895–1910, until the size of payment was reduced in 1911. Serbs were 42 percent of the rural population, but made up 74 percent of the sharecropping landless, while Bosnian Muslims were 37 percent of the rural total and 91 percent of the landlords. Agricultural production, crop yields, and exports had indeed doubled during the first two decades of Austro-Hungarian occupation, but their rate of growth slackened after 1900 and stagnated after 1906.[15]

Rural population continued to grow rapidly, however. Lack of credit and an Austro-Hungarian ban until 1908 on cooperative organizations discouraged the purchase of new equipment and reduced the number of livestock. The 1908 authorization of cooperatives imposed a new tax in order to set up an official cooperative organization. The tax only goaded the Serbs to set up their own network, as Habsburg officials had feared in the first place. Official restrictions on the use of state forests and pasture lands hurt the Serb peasants who needed it most and did nothing to encourage peasants to switch to widespread cultivation of fodder crops that official programs promoted instead.[16]

Already in 1907, the demands of urban Serbs pushed the Burian administration to grant them the right to set up the sort of ethnic, political organization that Kállay had always forbidden. The Serbian National Organization united three factions that had long pursued educational autonomy as their primary practical goal. Now the number of Serb Orthodox schools, separate from the secular or Catholic schools favored by the Austro-Hungarian administration, nearly doubled by 1914. Both the Bosnian Muslims and Croats received similar rights to organize, in 1906 and 1908 respectively, and placed a similar emphasis on separate school networks rather than economic reform. When the confrontational Catholic archbishop, Josip Stadler of Sarajevo, failed to gain control of the Croat National Organization, he promptly set up his own society. He was, in his own words, "a full-blooded Croat with a German name," who saw Bosnia as a Croatian land. Only the small Social Democratic Party stood for interconfessional organizations and schools, but it failed to win any seats in the first parliamentary elections held in 1910.

The three ethnic parties swept all of the seats. They showed themselves capable of "tactical cooperation," in the words of Robert Donia, during the negotiations with the Joint Finance Ministry that led up to the Constitution of 1910 and even afterward. Leaders of both the Croat and Serb parties were careful to avoid calling for the compulsory liberation of all kmet sharecroppers from their Bosnian Muslim landlords until the Serbs finally broke ranks in 1911. Croats and Muslims quickly reached agreement on opposing compulsory agrarian reform, and the Serb side accepted the subsequent parliamentary vote against their demand for reform. Donia calls this capacity for peaceful coexistence and some cooperation much more significant than the relatively small number of Bosnian Muslims who declared themselves to be Croats, or, more frequently after 1900, Serbs.[17]

Serbia's rising reputation and the Bosnian crisis of 1908

Modern party politics and open debate in the press made the last prewar decade dramatic in independent Serbia. Its economy and political self-confidence were growing, but so were the expectations of an increasingly educated, if still small, urban population. Rapid social or economic change created new uncertainties for those leaving the peasant villages that old leaders like prečani lawyers or Serbian priests could not address. Who would lead the *Došljaci*, or "newcomers," of Milutin Uskoković's biting prewar novel about the struggles of such people to find their way in a rapidly growing Belgrade? Journalists, bank or enterprise directors, army officers, and other professionals were now candidates, not just the handful of lawyers, clerics, and intellectuals who had stepped forward in the nineteenth century.

The aging founder of the Radical Party, Nikola Pašić, already sixty years old in 1904, dominated the political scene during the pre-1914 decade. His inarticulate and elusive public statements make him an unexpected leader in an increasingly vocal political culture and press. Had Serbia not faced a variety of foreign pressures and temptations throughout the period, Pašić might not have survived. Many younger party members had already defected in 1901 when he accepted a royal revision of that sacred Radical text, the constitution of 1888. Instead, his public ambiguity and preference to work secretly behind the scenes (even burning messages in his desk ashtray) enhanced the diplomatic balancing act on which he concentrated his energies. These successes plus an image of inscrutable wisdom, accentuated by his long white beard, kept him almost continuously in power as foreign or prime minister (or both) from 1904 to 1918.[18]

Serbia and Bosnia

For Serbia, the defining external event in the decade before the First World War became the Austrian decision in 1908 to annex formally the province of Bosnia-Hercegovina that it had occupied since 1878. How would the new, native political parties there and in the surrounding territories of the future Yugoslavia react? The annexation proved to be a litmus test for the new political spectrum, to align itself for or against some Yugoslav entity.

The loudest and longest reaction came from Belgrade. Serbs were the largest of the three constituent ethnic groups in the Habsburg province, 43 percent versus 32 percent for the Bosnian Muslims in a total population of 1.9 million, virtually the reverse of the proportions in the 1980s. Insult was added to injury when the Austro-Hungarian foreign minister, Alois von Aehrenthal, arranged the initial Russian approval that made annexation possible. The illusory promise of naval passage through the Straits to the Mediterranean stilled the one diplomatic voice, St. Petersburg, that might have spoken up for Serbia's interests.

The consequences for Serbia and its role in the future Yugoslavia were twofold. The Austro-Serbian antagonism that would lead straight to the First World War and the disintegration of Austria-Hungary deepened irretrievably for Austrian generals and for Serbian officers and students. Second, the annexation crisis sidetracked the promising two- or three-party system that had promoted the democratic politics of domestic reform in Serbia since 1903 in favor of a two-tier system: official consensus around a restrained foreign policy and unofficial support for radical, nationalist agitation outside of Serbia.

Confrontation with the Dual Monarchy had been coming since Petar Karadjordjević succeeded the assassinated Aleksandar Obrenović as Serbia's king in 1903. Karadjordje's grandson, Petar, had spent his adult life in exile before the unanimous vote of the Skupština brought him back to take the throne at the age of fifty-nine. A translator of John Stuart Mill, he deserves credit for his role as a constitutional monarch who allowed the parliamentary majority to govern and otherwise helped restore Serbia's international reputation after the regicide. Both he and the Radical leader, Nikola Pašić, also shared attachments to Russia and to Serbs outside of Serbia. Neither man was disposed to honor the secret agreement of 1881 with Austria-Hungary, binding Belgrade's diplomacy to the foreign ministry on Vienna's Ballhausplatz. Austrian diplomacy bridled at a proposed Serbian–Bulgarian customs union in 1905. The next year, as in 1896, Austrian officials faced a Hungarian campaign to use the decennial renewal of the customs union between the two halves of the monarchy as an occasion to win further political or military autonomy. Once again, Vienna decided to offer Hungarian agricultural interests protection against competing imports of Serbian hogs and cattle in return for renewal. The Dual Monarchy countered Belgrade's refusal to concede an increase in the nominal tariff quickly with a veterinary ban against Serbian livestock. This time the impasse escalated into the long tariff war of 1906–11.[19]

Hostile Serbian reaction to the tariff war encouraged the Austrian decision to annex Bosnia-Hercegovina in 1908. The resolution of the dispute in Serbia's favor by 1911 only emboldened the small state. Each of the three great continental powers added fuel to the fire. The Paris capital market made two large loans to the Serbian government, both officially arranged. The first of them (90 million francs) covered further reequipping of the Serbian army with artillery from Schneider-Creuzot in France instead of the monarchy's Škoda works, and the second (150 million francs) ensured financial survival to the end of the tariff war. For its part, Germany allowed its commercial market to accept the bulk of Serbian grain and processed meat exports, frustrating its ally's trade sanctions. Perhaps most fatefully, the Russian government dispatched a zealous Pan-Slav minister to Belgrade in 1909. Nikolai Hartwig encouraged Serbian governments to forgive the absence of Russian support in the annexation crisis of 1908 and to assume that it was now wholehearted, even if war with Austria-Hungary was threatened.[20]

A German-backed, Austrian ultimatum in 1909 stoked the Serbian disposition to defy the Dual Monarchy. The ultimatum obliged the Radical government of Nikola Pašić to accept annexation of Bosnia-Hercegovina and at the same time agree to confine the activities in Bosnia of the newly formed Narodna Odbrana, or National Defense organization of volunteers from Serbia proper, to support for Serb culture and education. Narodna Odbrana was the first of two organizations operating outside the open system of political parties that had governed Serbia since 1903. The other was a secret society of army officers, whose leaders were conspirators in the assassination in 1903 of the last Obrenović king. They refused to accept the Austrian ban on paramilitary activity in Bosnia. The formal name made their program plain, *Ujedinjenje ili smrt*, Union or Death, and their popular designation as the Black Hand confirmed its underground, potentially terrorist nature. Most members ironically came from the 500 new officers that the king's father, the long-deposed Milan, had brought in from the rural interior to an upgraded military academy under the army reforms of 1897–1900. They included the society's head, an artisan's son named Dragutin Dimitrijević, nicknamed Apis for his bull-like physique. From its founding by Apis in 1911 until its dissolution by Serbia's civilian government in 1917, the society pursued a Great Serbian state stretching from western Bosnia to southern Macedonia. Austrian authorities, the army's general staff in particular, were quickly if falsely convinced that the Serbian government controlled not only these two organizations but also the Croatian-Serbian Coalition in the Zagreb Sabor.[21]

Inside Serbia the patriotic furor surrounding the 1908 annexation of Bosnia had the effect of helping exclude from power the one major party in regular contact with the Coalition and in sympathy with the idea of a new Yugoslav entity, within or beyond the Dual Monarchy. The members of this Independent Radical Party were younger and closer both to urban life and to the more prosperous northern border than Pašić's ruling Radicals. Established in 1901 to protest Pašić's acceptance of King Aleksandar Obrenović's restrictive new constitution, they quickly pushed aside the aging Progressives to become the second largest party. The Independents shared or alternated power with the Radicals in a series of short-lived governments until the onset in 1906 of the tariff war with Austria-Hungary. Afterwards, Pašić was able to play on his greater experience and use Radical ties to Budapest as well as St. Petersburg to keep his party almost continuously in power through the First World War.

Meanwhile, in Serbian towns, the history and geography taught in a rapidly expanding system of secular schools reinforced the Radical view of the ethnic landscape. The number of primary and secondary schools had nearly tripled between 1890 and 1910. Urban literacy jumped past 70 percent, although failure to include much of the huge rural majority, still 87 percent of total population, kept overall literacy under 40 percent. Textbooks were sometimes written by party leaders and always spoke of the lands of a future Yugoslavia as inhabited by Serbs to the virtual exclusion of Croats, Bosnian Muslims, or Macedonians. They may not have turned "peasants into Great Serbs," to paraphrase Eugen Weber, but they surely did not turn them into Yugoslavs.[22] Neither did they turn many promising young townsmen into Orthodox priests. Although Orthodoxy remained the state religion and village priests received state salaries, the Orthodox church and its isolated monasteries now attracted few urban youths. They were drawn instead to secular European ways and ideas, through a Serbian language and school system that prompted the ethnic assimilation of the small minority of Jews, Vlach Tsintsars, and Czechs which had accumulated in Belgrade.

Serbia's capital was a bustling city of nearly 90,000 by 1910 with no less than a dozen daily newspapers. Half of the country's 12,000 secondary or vocational school students studied there, plus another 1,600 in the autonomous university formed from the Velika Škola in 1903. As in Zagreb, the student total was nearly equal to the number of workers in industrial enterprises. Student demonstrations had played a significant part in the successful demand for press freedom in 1903. They helped turn the next year's centenary observation of the First Serbian Uprising into an occasion for welcoming Croat, Slovene, and even Bulgarian delegations to multi-ethnic celebrations of South Slav solidarity. Politically, the city's voters gave more support in the 1906 elections to Independent Radicals in the National Assembly and to the new (since 1903) Social Democratic Party for municipal government than to the Radicals. In other words, a small Central European capital city had sprung up. Its political variety, cultural activities, and even urban amenities like street cars created an appealingly modern milieu. Belgrade's profile made Serbia much more attractive to its South Slav neighbors still under Habsburg or Ottoman rule. Within Serbia itself, the heightened contrast between the capital and the countryside to the south fed the impatience of the urban élite to overcome that contrast somehow. In other words, the process identified at the beginning of chapter 2 as "differential modernization" now promoted politics impatient for change, foreign or domestic. In Belgrade, moreover, the momentum for modernization could easily be confused with Serbianization.

What had become known by the turn of the century as the "Belgrade style" of literary expression seemed to confront Habsburg cultural hegemony as well as help assimilate the small, non-Serb minorities of Serbia. Its emphasis on simple, direct expression, drawing on the popular idiom, took its inspiration from contemporary France, where the founders of the influential new *Srpski književni glasnik* (Serbian literary journal) had been educated. Their criticism of the cumbersome formal language of Austro-German high culture extended to the Croatian literary language of Zagreb. They argued for the more modern Serbian of Belgrade as the language of any new Yugoslav state and won some Croat converts. But could a language from one side overcome the "narcissism of minor differences," in Freud's phrase, that seemed the major distinction between Serbs and Croats?

The two central figures for the newly educated youth of Belgrade and Zagreb suggested that it could not. They were their respective literary mentors, Jovan Skerlić and Antun Gustav Matoš. Similarities between the two went beyond their premature deaths in 1914. Both were attracted to French literature and to the cosmopolitan perspectives of European literary criticism. Both introduced their student disciples to the modernist movement's iconoclastic disdain for tradition. But like many others in the *Moderna* mainstream of early twentieth-century Europe, both became also belligerently enthusiastic, ethnic nationalists. True, Skerlić had promoted the 1904 South Slav congress to bring Serbs and Croats together, and his political hero was the eminently tolerant French socialist, Jean Jaurès. But after 1908, he turned to criticizing the "hymns of indifference" to Serbia's national consciousness written by other modernists like Isadora Sekulić. His celebrations at least did not extend to the denigrations of Serbian proselytizing and separatism that Matoš lumped together with Hungarian and clerical controls as un-Croatian activity. Skerlić may have feared the "terrible tempest" of war that he foresaw, but he urged the youth of Serbia to confront every adversary, including Austria-Hungary, in the name of a new socialist and democratic Serbia rather than any union of South Slavs.[23]

Even the socialists could reach no general agreement on what that Yugoslav partnership should be. Most delegates to the 1909 congress of South Slav socialists that convened in Ljubljana spoke of *jugoslavenstvo*, or South Slavdom, as their goal, but to the Croats and Slovenes this meant some federal reorganization of Austria-Hungary that Serbia and

Bulgaria would have to join if they wished to be included. To the delegates from Serbia, by contrast, jugoslovenstvo meant a Balkan federation organized around Serbia. Their leader, Dimitrije Tucović, of the Social Democrat Party, proposed such a federation as the proper framework for dismissing the national issue in favor of the class struggle.[24]

Croatia and Bosnia

Serbia's reaction to the annexation of Bosnia incensed Croatian Peasant Party leader Stjepan Radić. Serbian hecklers interrupted his speech in St. Petersburg when he emphasized the long Croatian presence in Bosnia and a recent increase in Muslims declaring themselves Croats. He criticized Serbia's politicians for "megalomania" and its government for trying to incite a war between Austria-Hungary and the Ottoman Empire. His party program was promptly rewritten to identify the Serbs of Croatia-Slavonia as "not Serb by origin," thus paralleling the formulation of Frank's Party of Pure Right. From this time forward, Radić regarded Belgrade only as an obstacle to a third, autonomous unit within the Habsburg monarchy, or better, a Danubian federation that would exclude Serbia. His relations with the Serbs of Croatia-Slavonia were also strained by a series of confrontations with the leader of their Independent Party. Svetozar Pribićević had used the principal Serb newspaper, Srbobran (Defender of the Serbs), of which he was editor, to attack Radić ever since Radić refused to join the Croatian-Serbian Coalition. In 1913 Pribićević infuriated him when he would not publish his article condemning assassination and terrorism despite its recent release from official censorship.[25] As effusive and intemperate as Nikola Pašić was secretive and taciturn, Pribićević later became the most prominent Serb politician after Pašić during the first decade after the First World War. His challenge to the more voluble Radić before the war did not bode well for Serb-Croat relations afterwards, as we shall see in chapter 5.

Austrian and Hungarian pressures meanwhile combined to keep the Croatian-Serbian Coalition together and in control of the Sabor in post-annexation politics. Sympathy for Serbia's indignation had generated a few initial demonstrations, but left no lasting marks on public opinion. Then two ill-conceived treason trials in 1909 charged Coalition leaders with maintaining secret links with Serbia. Austrian courts were convened in Zagreb for the first and in Vienna for the second. The first trial dragged on for months with the European press as witness to unconvincing evidence and embarrassingly light sentences. A Viennese historian named Friedjung tried to provide more damning evidence in a second trial, but his documents turned out to be easily demonstrable forgeries. Croats who had looked to Vienna for support against Budapest were disillusioned, and the Coalition got a new lease on life. Hungarian authorities tried vainly to outflank the Coalition. They abruptly adjourned the Sabor elected in 1908 and ruled by decree until 1910. The Budapest government of Croatia's former Ban, Khuen-Héderváry, now Hungarian minister president, next appointed a conciliatory Croatian Ban in 1910 and, as noted above, enlarged the franchise. Yet the officially endorsed new Party of Progress still failed to secure even half the seats won by the Croatian-Serbian Coalition. Again the Sabor was dismissed, and the fully constitutional regime of 1906 was not restored until 1913. Meanwhile, Pribićević and the other leaders of the Coalition were forced to accept too many violations of the original Nagodba of 1868 to persuade Radić, Frank, or the student forces that their future lay with the monarchy.[26]

The growing and restless student populations of Zagreb and Sarajevo turned from frustration to terrorism. Inspired by the Russian revolutionary underground and the suicide of a Croat youth after he failed to assassinate the civil administrator of Bosnia, the Croato-Serbian Radical Progressive Youth Movement struck out on its own after 1910. They staged student strikes at Zagreb University and tried unsuccessfully on a half-dozen occasions to assassinate the Ban or other ranking Habsburg officials in the city. Beyond a commitment to individual terrorism, their romantic, revolutionary notion of Yugoslavism set them apart. The notion was warmly received in Belgrade by unofficial eminences, from literary critic Jovan Skerlić to the editor of *Pijemont*, the mouthpiece for the Union or Death organization in the Serbian officer corps. The organization itself did not endorse either individual terrorism or Yugoslavism until after the Balkan Wars. Until then, its main concern was to win Ottoman Macedonia for Serbia, against competition from similar organizations from Greece, Bulgaria, or the local Internal Macedonian Revolutionary Organization (VMRO).

The strongest advocates of both revolutionary terrorism and romantic, ill-defined Yugoslavism came instead from Bosnia-Hercegovina. The group loosely and only later defined as *Mlada Bosna*, or Young Bosnia, had its origins in the literary or patriotic organizations that the Narodna Odbrana from Belgrade and the Croatian Catholic church from Zagreb had encouraged as exclusivist Serb or Croat organizations. Starting with Bosnian Serb students in 1909, again because of the annexation, the turn to Yugoslavism proceeded apace. Serbs took the lead in forming the Serbo-Croat Progressive Organization in 1911, and its largely student membership included some Muslims. Another member was Gavrilo Princip, the teenage Bosnian Serb who would soon assassinate Habsburg heir Franz Ferdinand. Anti-Hungarian demonstrations early in 1912 led to arrests, trials, and the overtly terrorist network of Young Bosnia in Sarajevo and other towns organized by several young Serbs. Now assassination plans and attempts followed in quick succession, the last of which succeeded in 1914 and started the First World War.

Two questions still haunt the historiography of the Young Bosnian movement. What were its ties to Serbia's government in general and to the Union or Death organization in particular? What legacy did its Yugoslavism, romantic and ill-defined as it was, leave behind? Wayne Vucinich has offered two persuasive answers. Contrary to the enduring presumption of Habsburg historians, the Bosnian students sought out their own connections in Belgrade and among the Union or Death agents dispatched to Bosnia as Narodna Odbrana representatives, rather than the reverse. Vucinich also credits the Young Bosnians with converting some Union or Death members from the idea of Great Serbia to Yugoslavism.[27] That idea surely attracted the young Ivo Andrić to Young Bosnia. He was then a student of Bosnian Croat origin whose eventual identity as a Serbian writer came only with his interwar move to Belgrade. Yet one would search in vain to find some consensus about the shape of a "federal South Slav state" (probably socialist), between youths like Princip and either the wider Bosnian political organizations of the time or his comrades who survived the war into the first Yugoslavia. All they could agree on was a Bosnian Yugoslavism, vaguely defined as the only possible solution to the nationality problem in that province, a solution that both of the two Yugoslavias failed to find.

Balkan wars and the new Yugoslav prospects, 1912–1914

A combustible mixture of Serbian students and army officers was spoiling for war with Austria-Hungary after the 1908 crisis; Serbia's government and ruling Radical Party were not. Neither were Nikola Pašić and his colleagues yet thinking in "Yugoslav" terms. It took the First Balkan War of 1912 to merge their long-standing ideal of a Great Serbia with the aim of a still larger Yugoslav state. The Serbian victory in both Balkan Wars then fanned Croatian and Slovenian enthusiasm anew for some Yugoslav state. At the same time, Serbian policy in just-absorbed Kosovo and Macedonia raised doubts about how a truly multi-ethnic state could be the result. Bosnia-Hercegovina was left to choose between enthusiasm and doubt.

Serbia and Macedonia

Ottoman vulnerability and a flurry of diplomatic activity opened Serbia's way to a Balkan alliance in 1912, outside of Austro-Hungarian control. The alliance made Macedonia the prototype for a powder keg. Why was Ottoman Macedonia particularly vulnerable? A proper answer must return to 1870, when Ottoman authorities permitted the new Bulgarian Exarchate to open Orthodox churches and schools across all of northern Macedonia. Soon afterwards, officially supported groups in Serbia and Greece set up their own schools and sought to persuade the Slav Macedonians that they were Serbs or Greeks rather than Bulgarians. None of this cultural activity would have shaken Ottoman rule had not a small group, first organized in 1893 as the Internal Macedonian Revolutionary Organization (VMRO), staged an abortive revolt on the Illinden holiday in August 1903. Fighting centered in the Monastir *vilayet*. It straddled the later-drawn border with Greece, although there were uprisings in the other two Macedonian vilayets of Salonika and Skopje, as well as a small one in Thrace. Teachers or former students of the Bulgarian school network led the revolt, but controversy continues about whether they sought Macedonia's autonomy as an end in itself or as a stepping stone to union with Bulgaria.[28] In any case, Ottoman forces quickly and brutally suppressed the uprising at the cost of several thousand lives and 50,000 homeless refugees.

The subsequent Mürzsteg Agreement did the local population little good. Under terms that in part anticipated the abortive 1992 Vance–Owen plan for Bosnian cantons, Austria–Hungary and Russia dispatched monitors to set up a new police force and restore order in return for continuing to recognize Ottoman sovereignty. Order was not restored, and locals took European intervention to mean that the days of Ottoman presence were numbered. The defeat of the uprising had weakened both the VMRO and the rival Sofia-sponsored Supremists, encouraging the Serbian side to move into the breach. Further encouragement came from the chaos of the Young Turk Revolution. In 1908, army officers including Kemal Attatürk, later the founder of the Turkish republic, seized power in Constantinople, then renamed Istanbul. Although still pursuing a general rapprochement with Bulgaria as an ally against Austria-Hungary, the Pašić government sanctioned the dispatch of more political and military agents to Macedonia, now devoid of Great Power monitors. The Young Turk regime obliged them to leave, hastening the Austro-Hungarian decision to annex Bosnia-Hercegovina before any Ottoman claim to that province could be revived.[29]

A brief Ottoman–Italian War and new, local unrest or external agitation in Macedonia itself made the three vilayets seem vulnerable again in 1911. The overzealous Russian minister to Belgrade, the aforementioned Hartwig, encouraged an alliance of the independent Balkan states once Italian forces had shown the Ottoman Empire to be too weak to hold on to Libya. He and his equally ardent Pan-Slavic colleague in Sofia brought the two governments crucial to the alliance together after five months of difficult negotiations. The Serbo-Bulgarian treaty of March 1912 proposed a three-way division of the northern Macedonian territory still under Ottoman rule, long a principal zone of contention between them. Both accepted Greek claims to southern Macedonia, to roughly the present border. To its north, Serbia would receive the northwest triangle, and Bulgaria the southeast as far as Ohrid. Russian mediators would decide the fate of the section in between, including Skopje.

Historians from Ernst Helmreich forward have explored the consequences of this agreement and the stunningly successful campaign of the Serbian army that undid it.[30] Some 350,000 men were mobilized into four field armies that swept the Ottoman forces out of northern Macedonia. Crushing victories from Kumanovo in October and south to Bitola in November reinvigorated the heroic legends of Serbian military valor that dated from the lost Kosovo battle of 1389. The 1912 campaign avenged the distant defeat by recapturing Kosovo. The hubris of that achievement, plus some hasty Austrian diplomacy to deny Ottoman Albania to the advancing Serbian army, prompted the Pašić government to refuse any retreat from its Macedonian gains. The Bulgarian tsar, Ferdinand of Coburg, tried to reverse them nonetheless. Bulgarian forces had suffered heavy losses while advancing almost to Istanbul, but Ferdinand and his generals threw them into the Second Balkan War against Serbia in May 1913. With all their former allies plus the Ottoman adversary arrayed against them, the Bulgarians were quickly defeated.

Although won at the cost of at least 60,000 dead and wounded, the two wars were the two greatest military triumphs in Serbian history. They may have convinced Serbian public opinion that it was destined to lead some future Yugoslav state, but its leaders were not ready to risk military confrontation with Austria-Hungary to achieve it. They did, however, turn toward closer economic cooperation with the Slovenes, establishing a joint bank in Trieste and exploring political collaboration with the Croatian-Serbian Coalition that would create the basis for such a state. Although the Radical Party's program was not amended to include a possible future union, Nikola Pašić and other leaders began to talk that way. They did so partly because the permanent break with Bulgaria over Macedonia had isolated Serbia against Austria-Hungary. Active Russian support had not been needed during the Balkan Wars. Why not solicit it now in the name of solidarity with other Slavs in the Habsburg lands? (The Radical leadership assumed that the newly absorbed Slav Macedonian population could be readily assimilated as Serbs, thus supplying no reason for any multi-Slav formulation.) By July 1913, Finance Minister Lazar Paču included Slovenes and Croats in what he now called a Yugoslav state. In April of the following year, Belgrade officially commemorated the 250th anniversary of the last great Croatian revolt against Habsburg rule, the Zrinski–Frankopan uprising of 1667.

The Austrian General Staff and its militantly anti-Serbian chief, General Franz Conrad von Hötzendorf, took full account of this turn. They became even more convinced than in 1909 that a preventive war should be launched against Serbia as soon as possible. The only obstacle to a speedy Serbian defeat, according to Conrad, would be a Russian alliance that could deliver significant military assistance. He therefore argued that Serbia must be defeated before such aid could be mobilized. Conrad refused, moreover, to consider evidence from the Balkan Wars that the Serbian army could, by itself, put up considerable resistance.[31]

Croatia, Dalmatia, and Slovenia

Political reactions in Croatia and Slovenia to the news of Serbia's victories were mixed. In Dalmatia it was more uniformly enthusiastic. Both reactions strengthened Conrad's case for a military assault on Serbia.

The Croatian-Serbian Coalition collected a crowd of 10,000 in Zagreb to celebrate Serbia's triumph and to call for the creation of a South Slav state. Such hopes had already led some Croats to try enlisting in the Serbian army for the Balkan wars, a young Miroslav Krleža twice without success. Nikola Pašić had to restrain Coalition leaders when they called for a "second round" to reverse the annexation of Bosnia-Hercegovina and add it to the new state. Pašić declined their demand to confront Austria-Hungary with the threat of internal revolt and a Serbian attack. Pribićević's Independent Party still strengthened its position by renegotiating the autonomy of the Orthodox church and its popularly elected Congress (see chapter 2) with Hungarian authorities who had engineered its restriction early in 1912.[32] On the other hand, the small Frankist Party (without Frank, who had died), expanded its support for a third, Croatian-led part of the Habsburg monarchy into a program that envisaged the absorption of a defeated Serbia. Some of the Catholic clergy shared this new view. Stjepan Radić, leader of the potentially much larger Croatian National Peasant Party (HPSS) stopped short of such expansionary schemes. He did, however, deepen his opposition to any connection with Serbia, now that the Bulgarians, the other South Slavs he had always spoken of including in any wider association, were out of the picture.

Demonstrations across Dalmatia flaunted Serbia's victories in the face of the Austrian authorities still administering the province from Vienna. Serbian flags flew in Split, Šibenik, Zadar, and Dubrovnik, as well as in many smaller towns. Volunteers from the Dalmatian Serb population enlisted in the Serbian army, and a number of towns collected donations for war relief. The powerless Dalmatian diet even adopted a resolution praising the Balkan alliance against the Ottoman Empire and condemning Austro-Hungarian policies toward its own subjects.[33]

In Slovenia, the clerical leaders of the largest party, the Slovenian People's Party (SLS), remained committed to cautious bargaining with Austrian authorities for educational autonomy at a minimum. They also weighed the Trialist formulation that would add a South Slav entity to the Dual Monarchy, but were worried by probable Croatian domination of such a unit. The younger generation outside of the clerical and peasant network that was the bulwark of the SLS did, however, approach the Dalmatian level of enthusiasm for a new South Slav state linked to victorious Serbia. Some volunteered for service in the Serbian army at the start of the Balkan Wars. Slovenian university students in Zagreb were particularly active. High school students in Ljubljana had already formed their own radical organization, Preporod, and beat the drums for war to break free of the monarchy. Ivan Cankar, the great Slovenian novelist who was also a member of the growing Yugoslav Social Democratic Party until his death in 1918, spoke of cementing the bonds with "our cousins in language and our brothers in blood." But, as Carole Rogel's analysis of pre-1914 Slovene Yugoslavism has argued, Cankar and the student radicals were inspired by opposition to Austro-German urban hegemony rather than by any Illyrian disposition to give up the Slovenian language or culture.[34] Their Yugoslavia, in other words, would have to be some kind of federal state that provided a political basis for cultural autonomy.

Macedonia, Kosovo, and Montenegro

The same conclusion follows for different reasons from the experiences of these three southeastern territories in the wake of the Balkan Wars. The substantial change in their borders may be seen in map 3.1. The first two were transported from the disorder and ethnic rivalry of the last

Ottoman years into an arbitrary regime administered by the Serbian army. Independent Montenegro took over new territory that strained its limited capacities as a separate nation-state.

The Serbian army paid a considerable price for northern Macedonia. Its units suffered more dead and wounded in the Second Balkan War than in the First (38,000 versus 23,000) in order to secure the territory as far south as Bitola. Its officers remembered the atrocities perpetrated against local Serbs by Ottoman and Bulgarian forces. They dismissed their own brutalities as understandable reactions, although the prompt, unbiased Carnegie inquiry found all parties guilty of war crimes against defenseless civilians.[35] The army's high command helped stifle the efforts of the Pašić government to give the largely Slav Macedonian population at least the right to local government. (Pašić himself proposed denying them representation in the Skupština in Belgrade.) Opponents of the Radical regime wondered why the impressive rights of Serbia's 1903 constitution were not extended to these new lands that had increased the population by more than half, from 2.9 million to 4.4 million. Meanwhile, military authorities sanctioned the dismissal of school teachers, priests, and local officials who were not willing to declare themselves Serbs. Officers more loyal to the Union or Death organization than to Serbia's legal government played a prominent role in these initiatives.

Only a couple of Belgrade banks ventured into this legal vacuum to help rebuild the weak, war-torn infrastructure, and no foreign investors appeared. South toward the major port of Salonika, massive emigration and disrupted connections to the European-backed Ottoman railway and Banque Ottomane blocked regional recovery even to the trade levels of 1911. Serbia received little economic compensation for its estimates of military expenditure during the Balkan Wars, 575 million francs, a figure four times the state revenues for 1911 or the most recent French loan of 1909.[36] These economic burdens plus the wartime losses and postwar disarray of the Serbian army regime in Macedonia encouraged General Conrad and his Austrian staff to discount the likelihood of effective Serbian resistance to their "preventive war."

The new Serbian regime made no attempt to demand that the ethnic Albanians, who were a majority of uncertain number in Kosovo, declare themselves Serbs. They were instead placed under a regime of military occupation that was resumed after both world wars and has reappeared in the death throes of Tito's Yugoslavia. The Albanians were accused of having forced some 150,000 Serbs out of Kosovo since the mid-1870s and of conducting a campaign of local terror against the Serbs who remained.[37] Some Albanians emigrated to the new Albanian state or to elsewhere in the shrinking Ottoman Empire. Those who stayed in

Map 3.1 Serbia and Montenegro, 1911 and 1913

Kosovo resisted recognition of Serbian authority whenever they could, starting a tradition that has also persisted.

Like Serbia, the much smaller Montenegrin state had doubled its territory as a result of the Balkan Wars. Its army of 36,000 had fought bravely but without effective central command. Over one-quarter of its soldiers were killed, most dying during the unsuccessful attempt to seize Shköder. Montenegro expanded inland rather than toward the Adriatic, ending at the division of the former Sandžak of Novi Pazar with Serbia. This common border posed two enduring dilemmas. What place would the large Muslim, often Turkish population of the Sandžak have in a Montenegrin state? The answer was not promising. Some 13,000 people converted to Orthodoxy under duress and a comparable number were forced to emigrate across the border to Bosnia-Hercegovina. In the process, Muslim villages were burned and scores settled for past sins against Montenegrin villages, particularly from the warfare of 1876–78.[38]

Even after this forced emigration, Montenegro found itself with a population of 500,000, twice the previous figure. The newcomers included many Serbs who felt a closer bond to Belgrade than Cetinje. They joined the growing number of Belgrade-educated Montenegrins who were dissatisfied with the autocratic, indeed, anachronistic rule of King Nikola. His promise to accept a constitutional monarchy, on the pattern of post-1903 Serbia, had long been given the lie. After two so-called bomb plots failed to assassinate then-Prince Nikola in 1907 and 1910, he used them against the nascent People's Party. Nikola had already forced party leaders out of their parliamentary seats despite mandates from Montenegro's first elections in 1905. Now they and the Serbian government were blamed for the subsequent bomb plots. Nikola alienated Belgrade further when he proclaimed himself king in 1910.[39] Little wonder that the last alliance to be negotiated between the Balkan allies confronting the Ottoman Empire in 1912 was between Serbia and Montenegro.

Nikola had maintained his regime in Montenegro with a combination of tsarist Russian support (even subsidies) and bargaining with the other Great Powers. The new borders moved Montenegro inland toward Serbia, but not toward abdication of a separate identity. The loss of identity implicit in uniting with Serbia versus the difficulty of maintaining a small, isolated nation-state made the third alternative of a larger Yugoslav state attractive to some Montenegrins after both world wars. Yet all three options, brought to the fore by the Balkan Wars and the new common border with Serbia, would retain their supporters.

Bosnia-Hercegovina

The impact of Serbia's victory and expansion was more immediate in Bosnia than in any other territory of the future Yugoslavia. Serb enthusiasm, Bosnian Muslim anxiety, and divided Croat opinion quickly disrupted the peaceful if competitive relations between the three major ethnic groups. Austro-Hungarian authorities did their part by suspending the 1910 constitution and making the military commander, General Potiorek, head of government. Serb–Muslim relations suffered serious wounds from these events.

Their relations were already strained. The long-awaited law for voluntary redemption of properties from Muslim landlords resulted in few transfers of titles to the largely Serb sharecroppers. A scattered uprising of Serb peasants against their landlords in 1910 had helped force through the Austro-Hungarian decree of the following year, but fewer than 6,000 redemptions were recorded in 1912 and an even smaller number in 1913. Nearly 90,000 holdings were left with landlords who declined voluntary redemption. The thirty-one representatives of the Serbian National Organization in the 1910 parliament (versus twenty-four Muslim and sixteen Croat representatives) had pressed for obligatory redemption, but a Muslim alliance with twelve Croat representatives thwarted the Serb plurality. Other politically sensitive decisions, such as the location of new railway lines and the use of German rather than Serbo-Croatian as the language of railway operation, lay entirely outside the limited powers of parliament.[40] All but twelve of the Serbian National Organization representatives to the parliament abandoned their efforts to work within the Austro-Hungarian framework. They stood by as radical students convinced Serbian agents, most likely tied to Union or Death rather than the Belgrade government, that terrorism was now justified as tyrannicide.

Incendiary Serb celebrations that erupted in Sarajevo and other major Bosnian towns in response to the Balkan Wars moved Bosnian Muslim leaders to support the Habsburg regime and to oppose Serbian rule over a significant Albanian population in Kosovo. Ottoman defeats created general anxiety among the Muslim élite. Muslims, whether Bosnian, Albanian, or Turkish, fled from territory newly divided between Serbia and Montenegro into Bosnia-Hercegovina. They posed a new problem. Some of the refugees came from families who had originally left Bosnia-Hercegovina in the wake of the Austrian occupation of 1878. The total number was probably less than 10,000, but rumors quickly spread among the Serb community that many more Muslims had or would come, and all of them would be settled in areas of Serb majority. Further rumors of new lands opening up for Serb settlement in Kosovo or Macedonia offered no consolation.

Some Bosnian Croats joined those Serbs calling for a new Yugoslav state to displace Habsburg rule. Student advocates of such an alliance had already succeeded in attracting Muslims as well to an anti-Hungarian demonstration in 1912. A number of Franciscan priests also lent their support. Archbishop Stadler of Sarajevo and other advocates of the Party of Pure Right program, like their counterparts in Croatia and especially Slavonia, took the demonstrations of the Bosnian Serbs as further proof of Serb disloyalty. The Pure Right sought a third, Croatian-led territory with the same standing as the Austrian and Hungarian parts of the Habsburg monarchy. Stadler's Croatian Catholic Association won only four of sixteen Croatian seats in the 1910 elections. The rival Croatian National Community elected the other twelve, and they stood by the Muslim alliance that Stadler rejected.

Such was the balance, or better, the imbalance of forces in Bosnia-

Hercegovina when Princip and his student colleagues read in a Belgrade newspaper of the Habsburg heir's forthcoming visit to Sarajevo on June 28. The date had been carelessly chosen and coincided with the anniversary of the Serbian defeat at Kosovo in 1389. General Potiorek's arrangements for the archduke's security were equally careless; that much is clear. Austrian scholars still seem convinced that Black Hand officers, admittedly well placed in Serbian army intelligence, acted under orders from the Belgrade government to use the young students for official purposes. The limited amount of direct evidence suggests the reverse, that Princip and his small group took the initiative and used Black Hand officers to help themselves carry out the greatest act of individual terror, tyrannicide to them, that any of the radical students had yet achieved. Their confused motives appear to have been more pro-Yugoslav than pro-Serb, and as much anti-urban and anti-modern as anti-Habsburg. Princip himself complained about women appearing in public in Sarajevo and spoke of "lighting a match" to the city itself.[41]

On June 28, 1914, he found himself the last assassin left in place and fired two shots blindly when Franz Ferdinand's open car inadvertently stopped in front of him. The archduke's driver had misunderstood the new route for leaving Sarajevo, hastily planned after other conspirators had attacked the royal procession that morning. Princip had no idea where the assassination of the archduke and his wife (he had aimed at him and General Potiorek) would lead. But General Conrad and the war party in Vienna knew perfectly well what a gift they had been given. Conrad pressed for an ultimatum that no Serbian government could accept. When Emperor Franz Josef signed it in July 1914, the war parties in the other European capitals made their separate cases for rapid mobilization. Only then were the two rival alliance systems and their military time-tables free to drag them all into the First World War.

4   The First World War and the first Yugoslavia, 1914–1921

The Serbian army's sacrifice and the population's sufferings during the First World War seemed for many survivors to justify Belgrade's upper hand in the Yugoslav state that was created between 1918 and 1921. That sacrifice and suffering deserve respect, but it was the army's survival of the war that made it physically possible to establish such a large, new state. Without its army, Serbia's government could not have convened Croat and Slovene representatives in Belgrade in December 1918 and proclaimed the Kingdom of Serbs, Croats, and Slovenes. Without the disintegration of Austria-Hungary and Italy's ardent territorial claims, Croat and Slovene leaders would not have come to Belgrade on essentially Serbian terms. At the same time, a majority of popular opinion everywhere except Kosovo arguably favored the creation of some sort of Yugoslavia by 1918.[1]

For the next three years, politicians from all of the component parts except Macedonia struggled with neighboring states to resolve a series of border disputes and with each other to agree on a constitutional framework. The first struggle helped draw them together, and the second divided them. The wartime burdens borne by all of the constituent populations, not just the Serbs, barred a return to the pre-1912 order. In any case, the two aging empires surrounding the two small, ethnically compact states of Serbia and Montenegro had broken apart by the end of the First World War. But now what? Border claims had to be settled not just with neighbors but within a framework of broader peace treaties fixed by the Western allies. A single Yugoslav state would facilitate a better settlement for its component parts with its neighbors and peacemakers. Internally the long-term logic of a common market and considerable cultural affinity also argued for a single state. Yet in the short term, economic obstacles to political unification and divisive elections to the constituent assembly made it difficult for even a Serb-dominated majority to reach agreement in 1921 on what sort of Yugoslavia it wanted.

Serbia and the Yugoslav Committee, 1914–1917

By the middle of 1915, both the Serbian government and a newly formed Yugoslav Committee of Croatian and Slovenian exiles had proclaimed war aims that would overturn the pre-1914 order and create some sort of South Slav state. These aims cannot fairly be said to predate the first desperate months of the war. They would not be combined into a single document until a 1917 conference at Corfu, and then without real agreement on what sort of state Serbia and the Yugoslav Committee were proposing.

The Niš Declaration

Serbia declared its war aims on December 7, 1914, from the temporary capital of Niš. A second Austro-Hungarian offensive had driven the Serbian army there well south of Belgrade by that autumn. Its August success in repulsing the original invasion at the battle of Cer was a distant memory. True, Serbia's army had launched its own counter-offensive on December 3, and within two weeks it once again drove the invaders out, at least until December of the following year. But the success of the Serbian attack on an Austro-Hungarian army of 250,000 men that included perhaps 100,000 South Slavs could not be foretold; indeed it was barely and dearly won by desperate heroics from the last line of reserves. The much debated Niš Declaration is therefore best seen as a defensive document intended to attract wartime support from Habsburg South Slavs, at a time when none of the other European battlefronts promised peace, rather than a precise proposal for an imminent postwar settlement.

The coalition government of Nikola Pašić had no prospect of reinforcements from the Russian or Western allies whose Entente had gone to war on Serbia's behalf. Desperate pleas had extracted some shipments of French ammunition by late November. Pašić was even trying to revive good relations with Bulgaria despite the 1913 war over Macedonia. His newly appointed set of scholarly advisors foresaw potential support from Bosnia to Slovenia, and from Croats and Slovenes as well as Serbs. They began their inquiry in August 1914 under the general European assumption that the war would not last long and postwar demands needed to be quickly put in place. Pašić, too, had shared this illusion, speaking openly in September of postwar borders for a Serb-led, South Slav state reaching halfway across Istria. In December, with a long war looming, the Belgrade professors and their leader, the geographer, Jovan Cvijić, argued instead that the three ethnic groups were "tribes of one people," each deserving equal standing in a future but undefined state of South Slavs. The phase "Great Serbia" did not appear in the Niš Declaration. Neither did any recognition of a separate Macedonian "tribe"; they were still regarded as an "unformed" ethnic group that could be easily assimilated as Serbs. Their territory was in any case to be denied Bulgaria and was deemed strategically essential to the survival of a future Yugoslav state.[2]

The Yugoslav Committee

The Pašić government simultaneously sent representatives to meet in Italy with exiled Dalmatian Croat advocates of a South Slav state. The indefatigable Yugoslav spokesmen, Frano Supilo and Ante Trumbić, had agreed by 1913 that if war came they would organize abroad for the destruction of Austro-Hungarian rule. Soon after war broke out, the more ardent Supilo sought French support. On November 22, in Florence, Supilo and Trumbić agreed to accept Serbian financial backing for a Yugoslav Committee. The exile organization was to represent all Serbs, Croats, and Slovenes in their demand for some future Yugoslav state. In the meantime, from Paris, it would solicit Entente support for Serbia's survival. Supilo visited Niš early in 1915 to seek some agreement on the place of non-Serbs in the future state, but came away empty handed.

The Yugoslav Committee moved to new headquarters in London shortly thereafter. Its separate official existence began here, but not because of any disagreement with Serbia's government. Supilo had simply discovered during a March 1915 visit to St. Petersburg that the Entente powers were about to conclude a treaty with Italy, promising its government Istria and central Dalmatia in return for entering the war, essentially against Austria-Hungary. The Treaty of London, the least secret of the secret treaties trading postwar promises for wartime support, was duly signed there on April 26. Trumbić and Supilo probably lacked leverage in Entente circles, and surely the disposition, to concede even limited Italian claims to their Adriatic home ground and thus head off the treaty. Their May memorandum instead claimed for a future Yugoslav state all of Istria plus territory beyond Slovenia's present border with Italy, the same territory that Austrian diplomats were then offering to Italy in last minute efforts to forestall the Treaty of London. Supilo and Trumbić made their claim despite the fact that Slovenes were hardly represented and were not regarded by Supilo as equals within the committee. Gale Stokes has called the Yugoslav Committee's claim to a western border that included largely Italian districts the equivalent of

Serbia's insistence on absorbing Macedonia as its own province.[3] Both claims would bedevil the postwar formation of both Yugoslavias.

Serbia and the Salonika Front

The full weight of a German-led offensive backed by Austro-Hungarian and Bulgarian troops fell on Serbian forces in October 1915. Their epic retreat during a cold December across the uplands of Kosovo and Albania to the Adriatic coast and Corfu reduced an army of 300,000 by nearly one-half. Undeniable privations bravely borne found a permanent place in popular historical memory along with accounts of harassment by local Albanians.

The Pašić government could take no immediate advantage from the army's heroic survival. First, they faced criticism in the rump parliament of prewar deputies that convened on Corfu in October 1916. Pašić soon recessed the Skupština for the rest of the war, but a more serious, prolonged challenge came from the reconstituted and reequipped army of 115,000 that was transferred to Salonika under French command. The pro-Yugoslav regent, Aleksandar, with an army entourage called the White Hand, represented royal authority. Its rival was the same group of Union or Death (Black Hand) army officers around Colonel Dragutin Dimitrijević (Apis), whose assassination of the last Obrenović king in 1903 had brought them together. In 1914 they had wanted war only for Great Serbia (see chapter 3). An alliance between the Pašić government and the increasingly assertive regent finally succeeded in bringing down the dreaded Apis. He and two colleagues were executed in June 1917 after a prolonged court-martial in Salonika on ill-supported charges of plotting mutiny and Aleksandar's assassination.[4] Only a few months before, Pašić had lost his closest international ally when the tsarist regime collapsed in Russia. Now, despite a spring buildup, no breakthrough seemed likely against the Bulgarian troops on the Salonika Front. The Serbian government moved forthwith to meet on Corfu with the Yugoslav Committee and repair its connections. Pašić had strained them badly with his readiness to receive Entente proposals for an Italian Adriatic in 1916 and his arrangements to incorporate Montenegro directly into Serbia in 1917. Frano Supilo urged a break with Serbia and then resigned from the committee before his death that same year.

The Corfu Declaration

Both sides came to Corfu burdened with significant weaknesses. They seemed more concerned with compensating for them than working out an agreed blueprint for a future Yugoslav state. The Pašić government had just succeeded in bringing some 30,000 volunteers, defectors from Habsburg forces or returnees from the United States or elsewhere, directly into the Serbian army. The Yugoslav Committee, whose propaganda had attracted many of these men, wanted to assemble them instead into a separate Adriatic Legion. Of the further 30,000 volunteers recruited in Russia, over one-third refused to serve in any army but a Yugoslav one. Pašić negotiated an agreement with the Yugoslav Committee to allow the Serbian army to qualify as that army, thus denying the Committee the sort of Czech Legion that helped bring Tomaš Masaryk's exile government to power in postwar Czechoslovakia. Serbian officers took charge, ready to weed out any volunteers seeking to spread the Russian revolutionary contagion.

The Committee itself had not yet won Western support for the postwar breakup of Austria-Hungary by 1917. Trumbić was shaken by the May 30 declaration of South Slav representatives in the Austrian parliament that affirmed their loyalty to the monarchy and the new young emperor, Karl I. They supported only a trialist South Slav entity on the dualist pattern of Austria-Hungary. On the other hand, a number of the Croatian and Slovenian delegates accompanying Trumbić to Corfu advocated a unitary state under presumably Serbian leadership. Italian insistence on carrying out the terms of the Treaty of London meanwhile showed no signs of weakening.

Despite more than a month of sessions on Corfu, the two sides could sign only an ambiguous document on July 20. Like some agreements late in Tito's Yugoslavia, the document allowed both sides to claim that it strengthened their own position. Its fourteen points proposed a single state for the "three-named people" of Serbs, Croats, and Slovenes under the Karadjordević dynasty and promised the democratic rights already provided by the Serbian constitution. The equal listing of the three names in Article 5 implied autonomy for all three partners, but did not spell it out. At the same time, Trumbić accepted a simple three-fifths majority, opening the door to a Serb majority in the constituent assembly that *would* define the rights of the "autonomous units" promised in Article 14. He specifically declined to support a federal framework because he believed that it would be too difficult to agree on internal borders.

What legacy did the Corfu Declaration leave to the Kingdom of Serbs, Croats, and Slovenes? Its longer-term importance should not be exaggerated. Belgrade seemed far away that summer of 1917, and signing an agreement to secure a larger Allied force on the Salonika Front may have been Pašić's major motive. He reportedly did not regard the precise terms as binding, terms that in any case left the central government in Belgrade to decide what "local autonomy" would mean.[5] The name itself also represented a victory for the Pašić government in that it preserved Serbia's separate identity. The failure to list constituent peoples other than Serbs, Croats, or Slovenes was not promising. Still, the agreement at least allowed the Yugoslav Committee to tie Serbia's government to a published document whose terms the Western allies might well wish to interpret the Committee's way. Lacking an army, the Committee's only alternative would have been to accept the Treaty of London and forfeit the central Adriatic coast to Italy. This was surely too much to ask of Ante Trumbić.

Wartime regimes from Slovenia to Serbia

The negotiations that passed between the Yugoslav Committee and Serbia's government from mid-1917 until the autumn of 1918 were less important to the legitimacy of the new state than two cumulative reactions. Countering the continuing Italian claim to Gorizia, Istria, and the central Adriatic coast provided one justification for creating some sort of Yugoslavia. The oppressive military regimes of Austria-Hungary and Bulgaria that occupied all of the future Yugoslavia from 1916 forward constituted another.

Italy's claims had the clearest effect on Slovenian political leaders. They led the largest party, the Slovene People's Party (SLS) under Monsignor Anton Korošec, to vote for the May 1917 declaration of support for a new South Slav entity in the Habsburg Monarchy and then, in early 1918, to send representatives to the Yugoslav Committee. By August 1918, Korošec headed a multi-party National Council to prepare for the unification of all the South Slavs, including those outside the monarchy, in a new state. Within weeks, 130 local councils were also in place from Trieste across Gorizia to Carinthia.

The Bulgarian military regime in northern Macedonia ironically had done more to damage the development of a Bulgarian identity than any of Serbia's heavy-handed efforts to destroy it between 1912 and 1915. Mines had been handed over to German authorities for production that was sent straight to the German war effort. Bulgarian military officers from Sofia took control of local administration and requisitioned the needs of their troops from the local population as would an occupying army. A considerable number of VMRO or Bulgarian Supremist supporters, perhaps 100,000, joined the Bulgarian forces, but even their own families suffered from a growing food shortage made worse by German troops sending food parcels home. Then with the collapse of the

Salonika Front in September 1918, both Bulgarian and German forces withdrew, leaving behind few locals in authority to challenge the returning Serbian army.[6]

Austria-Hungary's later wartime regimes in Croatia and Bosnia-Hercegovina also imposed worsening economic hardships on their populations, regardless of ethnic identity. Despite these hardships, the various South Slav contingents accounted for a larger share of the monarchy's military forces late in 1917 than in 1914, 17 versus 11.5 percent. The Croat contingent, slightly larger than the Serb, lost the most men, close to 300,000 dead by 1918. Proportionally, Slovenes and Bosnian Muslims took the highest casualties. Only the Bosnian Serbs served under special restrictions, and only they defected in significant numbers on the Serbian and Russian fronts of 1914–17.[7] At the beginning of the war, both the monarchy's Croatian and Bosnian regimes persecuted some Serbs and made life difficult for many more of them in ways that would be remembered as mistreatment at Croat or Bosnian Muslim hands.

Croatia

The Austro-Hungarian army commanders set aside civil authority and began to arrest or harass Serbs suspected of any ties to Serbia during the autumn of 1914. Although they could not persuade Hungarian Prime Minister Tisza to dissolve the Sabor, they did extract the emperor's permission to proclaim martial law. The new military regime curtailed already limited rights of assembly and free speech and arrested some of the Croatian-Serbian Coalition members in the Sabor. In the meantime, Croatian extremists in the small Frankist Party (see chapter 3) had burned a number of Serb schools. The Ban proposed closing them all after the war. Croatia's Catholic hierarchy split over the issue of preserving Austria-Hungary without change. The bishop of Rijeka and some young followers published demands that all South Slavs be represented in a new third entity in the monarchy. This was to be a more multi-ethnic entity than the Croatian-dominated one proposed by the Party of Right or by Stjepan Radić after he abandoned his support for an Austro-Hungarian victory in 1917.[8]

By then, the Habsburg war effort was imposing a serious economic burden. Peasants hoarded their produce rather than deliver it to the Austro-Hungarian *centrale* set up in provincial towns. The Zagreb Military Command kept promising improvement in the city's provisions, but less and less food was available. In the food-poor areas of Istria and Dalmatia, widespread hunger was reported from 1916 forward. Then came the prisoners of war, primarily Croats, returning from Russia in the course of 1917. They formed the core of the "Green Cadres" who began to seize estates and power in the countryside in October 1918. Croat and Serb soldiers from the disintegrating army of Austria-Hungary greatly reinforced their ranks.[9]

Is it possible to speak of sizeable support throughout the various Croatian lands for a Yugoslav state outside of Austria-Hungary before the monarchy and its forces literally fell apart? No public opinion polls were taken, but the fiercely anti-Yugoslav Habsburg commander of Bosnia-Hercegovina, Stefan Sarkotić, reckoned that while a majority of Croatia-Slavonia was still loyal to the monarchy in May 1918, by August some 60 percent had been "infected with the Yugoslav idea." The proportion in Dalmatia and Slovenia was much higher by all accounts.[10]

Bosnia-Hercegovina

This same General Sarkotić estimated that fully half of the Bosnian population was similarly "infected" by May 1918. Ironically his own draconian regime was responsible for a sizeable share of that half. Because it was also Sarkotić's regime that first mobilized Bosnian Croats and Muslims to persecute Serb civilians after centuries of Ottoman and Habsburg rule, he deserves special attention.[11]

A Croat from Lika whose family had served for generations in a Military Border regiment, he first saw action as a young officer fighting Serb peasant rebels in the 1882 uprising in Hercegovina. By the outbreak of war in 1914, he had risen to command the only Croat–Serb division (two-thirds Croat) in the Austrian army and led it in the war against Serbia. He immediately issued an order for the summary execution of civilians in Bosnia as well as Serbia who aided or supported the Serb guerrilla bands that sprang up. By November 1914, Sarkotić had been promoted to military governor, or *Landeschef*, of Bosnia-Hercegovina. He began to arrest and deport prominent Serbs, including Orthodox clergy. Before he had finished, approximately 5,000 Serbs were interned in camps, joining the small number of Young Bosnia members, like Ivo Andrić, who had been arrested immediately. Perhaps 50,000 were forced from their homes in the Drina valley. Show trials held at Banja Luka in 1916–17 passed death sentences as well as numerous deportation orders. Although amnesties from Vienna prevented more than three executions from being carried out, the number of Serbs forced from their homes and deported or confined in concentration camps approached 100,000 by mid-1917. Muslim dissent was also discouraged, but the regime recruited Muslims as well as Croats into a defense force, or *Schutzkorps*, that grew to 20,000 men. In their "anti-bandit operations" along the Drina border with Serbia, in Foča for instance, they massacred Serb villagers as well as deported them. This first incidence of active "ethnic cleansing" in Bosnia-Hercegovina left grievances that played into the hands of Sarkotić's successors on all sides. Its immediate effect in 1917–18 was to swell the ranks of the Serb guerrillas with deserters from the Austro-Hungarian army, not all of them Serbs. By early 1918, Sarkotić himself estimated their numbers at 50,000. Hungarian opposition prevented him from putting into effect his plan for the administrative unification of Bosnia-Hercegovina with Croatia-Slavonia and Dalmatia even after the new emperor, Karl, had approved it in May 1917. Had Sarkotić succeeded, the resulting repression might have made popular support for a Yugoslav alternative to the Habsburg monarchy broader still.

Serbia

Meanwhile, in occupied Serbia, a less personal Austrian military regime still subjected the local population to treatment that hardened opposition to any restoration of the Habsburg monarchy. General Conrad, long Serbia's arch enemy, had in fact proposed that all officials, professionals or clergy who were politically active, must be "destroyed or banished firmly and for a long time, preventing their return." Belgrade shrank from 90,000 to 15,000 between 1914 and early 1916. Over one-third of the population had already left Belgrade by October 1915, when the Serbian army's retreat left some 30,000 Austro-Hungarian troops to occupy the country. A typhus epidemic spread from the Serbian army to civilians that fall and took a staggering 150,000 lives. Another 40,000 people were deported to Austria-Hungary and 10,000 confined in concentration camps in Serbia. Still more died of hunger and disease during the rest of the occupation, bringing the civilian death total for 1914–18 to at least one-half million. Troop losses of nearly 300,000 matched the South Slav toll for Austria-Hungary, from a pre-1912 population of 8 million versus 3 million for Serbia. One way or another, half of Serbia's male population between the ages of 18 and 55 had perished.

The war also crippled Serbia's capacity to feed itself. Disease and the absence of peasant labor may have been the greater reasons for devastating food shortages, but popular memory would blame the Austrian centrale for requisitioning foodstuffs from the countryside and rationing a shrinking amount back to the towns. Other requisitions took what cloth and metal could be seized from the towns. Habsburg civil authorities had no plans either for developing Serbia's economy or for connecting it to their western territories. Zagreb's Chamber of Commerce was persuaded to make one trip to Belgrade to explore a rail link, but the project went no further. The military command and the German army exploited the mines and a few industrial enterprises for the war effort. Other factories stood vacant or were destroyed, and Austrian or German troops flooded the mines as they withdrew in the face of the Allied advance from Salonika in October 1918. Rail lines and bridges were blown up, and Belgrade's electrical utility put out of commission. As a final gesture, one Austrian army unit broke every window and lock they could find in the city before leaving. Serbia had surely suffered greater losses, human and material, during the First World War than did the other component parts of the future Yugoslavia.[12]

National Council in Zagreb and unification in Belgrade

The Serbian army and government returned in November 1918 to a war-ravaged population and economy, hardly a basis of political strength beyond the popular sense of shared sacrifice. Nor did the Pašić government and the regent, Aleksandar, form a united front, ready to deal with the resumption of party politics in Serbia. The Serbian side was nonetheless in a stronger position to bargain with the Yugoslav Committee about the shape of any new state than it had been on Corfu in 1917. In addition to a victorious army, Serbia now had French support and a potential ally in Zagreb against the Committee itself.

A Yugoslav state would secure the breakup of Austria-Hungary without handing over the Adriatic coast to Italy. This became a French interest as early as April 1918. British and American policy was much slower to promote the breakup of the monarchy; indeed, despite the promise of self-determination in President Woodrow Wilson's famous Fourteen Points of January 1918, Anglo-American diplomacy accepted rather than promoted the monarchy's disintegration. France had sent the most Allied troops to the Salonika Front, and a French general, Franchet d'Esperey, commanded the largely Serbian force that retook Macedonia and Kosovo and liberated Serbia. By October French representatives were telling the Pašić government that they favored a unitary Yugoslav state on the pattern of Italy or Poland. Any federal arrangement would be divisive and, worse, they argued, too weak to stand up to its neighbors. Such support bolstered the Pašić government against the rising criticism of R. W. Seton-Watson and Henry Wickham Steed, long the leading

British advocates of a Yugoslav state on the presumably federal terms of the Yugoslav Committee.[13]

At the same time, Austria-Hungary's declining fortunes had prompted an *ad hoc* body of deputies to the Croatian Sabor in Zagreb to proclaim themselves a National Council (Narodno vijeće). Quickly joined by representatives from Dalmatia, Istria, and a similar Slovenian council (Narodni svet) that had convened in August, they commanded an immediate claim to legitimacy. The Yugoslav Committee, still based in London, could only ask to be their foreign representative. Last to join but constituting a majority when they did were members of the prewar Croatian-Serbian Coalition. By this time, they had come around to the idea of a new state that included Serbia, as fervently championed by their leader, Svetozar Pribićević. They were especially attracted to Serbia's army as a force that could restore order in the countryside and secure their ambitious Western borders, in other words, suppress the "Green Cadres" and turn back the Italian army. Stjepan Radić and his Croatian Peasant Party opposed any such bargain, rejecting the National Council's vote for the Serbian monarchy and army as well as for a single state. His only ally was the Frankist Party of Pure Right. But on November 4, the Council barely halted an Italian advance on Ljubljana with a force of former war prisoners. It immediately dispatched an appeal through Allied representatives for Serbian troops.[14]

At Geneva on November 9, Ante Trumbić staged a last stand for the Yugoslav Committee. He pressed Pašić as Serbia's foreign representative to accept a confederation, comparable to the Dual Monarchy, as the framework for the new government. Both the Serbian opposition to Pašić and the Slovenian People's Party leader, Monsignor Korošec, joined forces with Trumbić to secure the tentative Geneva Agreement. But the Belgrade government, headed by fellow Radical and the regent's favorite, Stojan Protić, repudiated that agreement two days later simply by resigning with a promise to include the opposition in a new cabinet. The continuing advance of Italian forces prompted a majority of the Zagreb National Council to accept the regent's invitation to meet with him in Belgrade. Trumbić stood by in shock as their representatives first repudiated the Geneva Agreement and then, on November 28, asked Aleksandar to proclaim the Kingdom of Serbs, Croats, and Slovenes as agreed on Corfu. This he did on December 1 before delegations from Bosnia-Hercegovina, Montenegro, the Vojvodina, and the National Council as well.[15]

Several groups outside the Council openly criticized the December proclamation. Montenegrin supporters of King Nikola naturally objected, favoring an Italian-backed effort to reclaim his throne. The newly radical Social Democratic Party opposed any agreement with a monarchy like Serbia's that was antagonistic to Bolshevik Russia. The first and loudest denunciations came from Croatia's small Party of Pure Right. Croats from Slavonia and Hercegovina, both bordering Serb concentrations, were particularly attracted to such nationalist opposition, as was the Catholic archbishop of Sarajevo, Josip Stadler. Already an active advocate of a Croatian Bosnia-Hercegovina before the war (see chapter 3), Stadler failed to win over leading clerics from the Bosnian Franciscans and several Croatian orders, especially in Dalmatia, who accepted the unification. The Catholic hierarchy, in other words, was hardly united in opposing the formation of Yugoslavia.[16]

The steadfastly anti-clerical Stjepan Radić and his Croatian Peasant Party did present a unified opposition. Wilfully excluded from any role in the Zagreb National Council by Pribićević, Radić saw the proclamation as the fulfillment of his worst fears. In February 1919, he dispatched a letter to President Wilson appealing for the recognition of a Croatian republic, adding the word "republican" to his party's name the next day. Lacking a better route, Radić sent the letter through the Italian military mission in Ljubljana, a hasty misstep that his opponents in Belgrade turned to their political advantage.

By then, Trumbić and other moderate opponents of the proclamation had agreed to the single interim government that was to prepare a new constitution for ratification by a promised Constituent Assembly. Behind any such government stood the need to rely on the Serbian army. The National Council tried to use its own meager forces to confront a surviving Hungarian unit in Zagreb on December 5 while Serbian army troops watched. The Council's failure marked the end of any military alternative to the Serbian army across the entire territory of the new state. Despite the lack of new arms from the wartime Allies, its forces swelled to 400,000 by mid-1919.[17] Its sheer presence established the authority of the united government as agreed in Belgrade on December 20, 1918. With Protić rather than Pašić as prime minister, again at Aleksandar's behest, the cabinet consisted of ten members from Serbia, nine from former Habsburg territory, and one from Montenegro. Trumbić agreed to join Pašić and Korošec as its representatives at the Paris peace conference.

Internally, Belgrade's representatives rejected a proposal from the Croato-Serbian Coalition for joint or autonomous ministries on the Habsburg pattern. Instead, the Serbian constitution of 1903 became the interim law of the land until January 30, 1919, when agreement was reached on a similar temporary constitution. By March 1919, the Interim National Parliament (PNP) was in place to prepare for the elections to the Constituent Assembly. They were delayed until November 1920, and ratification took another six months. During that long interim period, the struggle to negotiate secure external borders helped bind the new political spectrum together while problems of domestic recovery and public order pushed it apart.

Western policy and border disputes

Allied support during the First World War, first for Serbia and then also for the Yugoslav Committee, did not translate into immediate recognition of the new Kingdom of Serbs, Croats, and Slovenes, let alone international agreement on precisely what its borders should be. None of the victorious powers had recognized the new state when the Paris peace conference convened January 1919. Recognition by the United States followed in February. Britain and France delayed, deferring to Italian opposition because of the Treaty of London's claims to the Adriatic coast. By May both of the victorious powers felt obliged to accept the kingdom's credentials because the newly arrived delegation of defeated Germany had done so.[18]

Before recognition the triumvirate of Pašić, Trumbić, and Korošec that represented the new kingdom could occupy only the three seats at the conference initially granted to Serbia. This weakened their claim to negotiate the new western frontier. To the north, there were further border disputes to be settled with Austria and Hungary, and to the south, with Bulgaria and Albania. Only the Macedonian border with Greece and, after bargaining into the summer of 1919, the Banat border with Romania were not contested. Divisions between Trumbić and Pašić also limited the delegation's ability to present a single bargaining position. Pašić was not yet ready to trade Rijeka to Italy in return for Shköder from Albania, as he would by 1920, but the difference between his emphasis on eastern claims and Trumbić's preoccupation with the western border was already there to exploit.

Istria and Dalmatia

Two initial advantages promised to make up for these weaknesses in the new kingdom's position. First, the moralistic American President Woodrow Wilson had compromised his commitment to ethnic rather than strategic borders in January 1919 by accepting Italy's claim to the Tyrol (and the Brenner Pass). Supported by his geographic advisors, he now determined to refuse any more concessions to Italy, particularly if they honored the sort of secret wartime treaty he had never respected.

Those powerful British persuaders, Wickham Steed and Seton-Watson sought to coordinate support for the Yugoslav claim between Trumbić and Italian liberals opposed to their nationalist foreign minister, Sidney Sonnino. Second, Italian army units moved beyond the border granted them by the 1915 Treaty of London into Rijeka (Fiume) in particular, and further weakened the legitimacy of Italy's case. Allied support grew for the so-called Wilson line proposed by his experts to bisect the Istrian peninsula from north to south and leave the eastern portion plus all of Dalmatia (except for Zadar) to the Yugoslav state (see map 4.1). Some 370,000 inland Slovenes and Croats would remain in Italy, but this was half the number that the London line would have included.[19]

Orlando's insecure government and his intransigent foreign minister refused to accept the Wilson line, leaving the border unsettled. Only in November 1920 did a new, still non-Fascist Italian government use the defeat of Wilson's Democratic ticket (Wilson was not a candidate) in the US elections to extract the signature of the interim Yugoslav government to the Treaty of Rapallo. Its terms drew a border between the London line and the eastern advance of Italian troops that left over one-half million Slovenes and Croats in Italy. Rijeka was to become a free state once the private militia of the Italian poet and irredentist, Gabriele d'Annunzio, that had occupied the port since August 1919 was expelled. Although this was accomplished by January 1921, Mussolini's Fascist regime would move to reclaim Rijeka in September 1923. By that later date, the Italian administrators of Istria and Gorizia had already closed down Slovenian and Croatian language schools, publications, and political organizations. They also disbanded Krek's extensive network of cooperatives (described in chapter 3). Their restrictions drove the Social Democrats and some other Slovenes on Italian territory into the Communist camp.[20] Within the new Yugoslav state, these cross-border grievances and Mussolini's continuing hostility encouraged Slovenia's political leaders to seek out an alliance with Serbian interests. As the Yugoslav capital and army headquarters, Belgrade was the strongest source of diplomatic and military leverage against Italy.

Carinthia and the Vojvodina

Serbian military leverage had also allowed Korošec and other Slovenian leaders to press their claim to the mixed area of Carinthia. Serbian army units ignored Trumbić's ongoing negotiations in Paris to reduce that claim and occupied most of the Carinthian basin, including the largely Austrian German city of Klagenfurt, in May 1919. Italian arms and officers supported a weak Austrian counterattack (the defeated,

Map 4.1 Territorial claims and final borders, 1918–1921

shrunken Austrian state had virtually no army) that regained some ground. British, French, and American representatives at Paris now agreed that the dispute should be settled by two plebiscites, the first one in Carinthia south of the Drava river (Zone A) and then, if it went against Austria, a second one to the north (Zone B). The south voted three-to-two for Austria in July 1920. Some 40,000 to 60,000 Slovenes remained on the Austrian side of the final border and strengthened the Serbian case for refusing to sign the St. Germain peace treaty with Austria, for other reasons related to Macedonia.[21] The Yugoslav kingdom also retained small triangles on either side of the Mur river, Prekomurje and Medjumurje (see map 4.1).

As with Austria, the new state's adversarial relationship with interwar Hungary began over a dispute about their common border. When the Bolshevik regime of Bela Kun seized power in Hungary for four months in 1919, French representatives pressed for a Serbian army division to move northward. No troops were moved, but the invitation strengthened the kingdom's hand in bargaining successfully for most of its claim to the Bačka area between the Danube and Tisza rivers, including the largely Hungarian towns of Sombor and Subotica and the southern triangle of the Baranja between the Drava and Danube (see map 4.1). Since General d'Esperey had authorized it in November 1918, the Serbian army occupied that area and more, reaching into Hungary as far as Pécs and into Romania as far as Timişoara. The *Bunjevci* or *Šokci* of the Subotica area, originally Catholic Serb or Croat immigrants from Hercegovina, had thereupon joined with Serbs in Novi Sad and elsewhere to demand separation from Hungary "in the sacred name of self-determination."[22] France's support at the Paris peace conference secured the claim although it was the strategic argument of the Serbian General Staff that persuaded the French representatives.

Like the interwar Romanian border with Hungary in Transylvania, a relatively small adjustment would have reduced the Hungarian minority of 400,000 in the first Yugoslavia by about one-half. The Vojvodina's ethnic German minority of 500,000 remained in any case. The South Slavs had sought minority rights with mixed success from Austria-Hungary before the war. The new Yugoslav kingdom now faced the dilemma of respecting such rights or encouraging the breakup of the state.

Macedonia and Kosovo

While minority rights would be at least addressed in the north, they were entirely ignored in the south. Serbia's representatives at the Paris peace conference consistently refused to acknowledge the existence of a huge, non-Serb majority in Macedonia or the legitimacy of one in Kosovo. It is easy to condemn this refusal to recognize the Macedonian Slavs as a separate ethnic group in light of the genuine national consciousness that has developed there in the meantime. But at that time, its small educated élite was still divided between Macedonian, Bulgarian, and even local identities, sometimes within the same person. When we consider the irredentist claims of defeated Bulgaria to that territory along with those of an emerging Albania to Kosovo, Belgrade's reluctance to call northern Macedonia anything other than "South Serbia" and Kosovo, "Old Serbia," becomes more understandable, at least in strategic terms. Military arguments were also the grounds for demanding a strip of western Bulgaria from Vidin down to the Strumica river and along the rim of northern Albania to the Drin river (see map 4.1) at the Paris peace conference. The Allies granted only three minor adjustments eastward in the Bulgarian frontier.

A subsequent program (described in chapter 5) to bring Serb colonists to Macedonia and especially to Kosovo and the Sandžak of Novi Pazar sought to secure these border areas in a fashion reminiscent of Habsburg "populationism" in the eighteenth-century Vojvodina. Homesteads for Serb families from Bosnia-Hercegovina, Montenegro, and the Lika region of the old Croatian Military Border were to be carved from Albanian or Turkish lands, allegedly vacated by former Ottoman land-lords or postwar outlaws. The interim land reform passed by the PNP in Belgrade in February 1919 abolished the Ottoman feudal rights by which Muslim landlords had claimed sharecropping levies from Bosnia down to Macedonia.[23]

The ongoing warfare between the Serbian army and assorted Albanian bands around the northern circle of a disputed border with Albania gave the Belgrade government new justification for launching its resettlement policy. So did VMRO raids across the Bulgarian border into Macedonia that continued until 1923.[24] The 1921 conference in Paris of signatories to the peace treaties assigned Albania to Italy's protection under League of Nations provisions, thus making Kosovo seem the more vulnerable of the two territories in the eyes of subsequent Belgrade governments.

Economic obstacles to political unification

Threatening border disputes, particularly with Italy, helped hold together the first Yugoslavia during the long interval before a constitution could be ratified. Meanwhile, the separate postwar problems of the Serbian and Croatian economies impeded political accommodation. From 1918 until the demise of the second Yugoslavia in 1991, Serbs and Croats were the one pair of ethnic groups capable of tearing the state apart if they clashed. When each failed to understand the other's economic misfortunes during and after the First World War, their political relations got off on the wrong foot.

The new kingdom faced formidable problems of economic integration even without the ravages of war being taken into account. Serbia, Croatia-Slavonia, and the other component territories had traded far more with other commercial networks than with each other (see chapter 2). Austro-Hungarian rivalry within the Dual Monarchy had encouraged these alternate connections with two separate rail networks. Across all of the future state, there were four different rail networks, five currencies, and six customs areas and legal systems, all dating from before 1914. Perhaps the one economic feature that Serbia and Croatia-Slavonia had in common was a comparative advantage in the export of live-stock.

The war and its aftermath damaged the largely agricultural economies in every corner of the new kingdom. Transport was disrupted and little manpower reached the fields. Food-poor areas such as Hercegovina faced desperate shortages. The interim land reform of 1919 and its abrogation of Muslim share-cropping regimes may have increased grain production in Bosnia, Macedonia, and Kosovo. But the reform's effects on Croatian agriculture and exports caused political trouble, as did the special burdens borne by Serbia's industry and transport.[25] The mutual resentments that they engendered came to a head in the controversy over a single currency and a central bank.

Agriculture and foreign trade

A series of peasant uprisings shook Croatia during the immediate post-war period and disrupted agricultural recovery in several regions. Bands of returning peasant soldiers sacked the large, foreign-owned estates of Slavonia in particular. Such violence had already prompted the mainly Croatian National Council in Zagreb to call for Serbian troops to restore order by the end of 1918. An interim land reform of April 1919 promised to break up all estate or other holdings over 150 acres. Actual redistribution, however, was slow in coming. Rural order had barely been restored in September 1920 when a still essentially Serbian army started to inventory all draft animals and brand those fit for military use in case of war. Its clumsy campaign sparked a rumor that the livestock was about to be confiscated. Many Serbian politicians assumed that Croatian peasants had profited during the recent war, but in fact Austro-Hungarian authorities had requisitioned animals and grain at centrale in Croatia-Slavonia as well. The new inventories looked like more requisitions. Rural revolts now erupted south and east of Zagreb in Croatia proper and quickly elicited support from Radić's Peasant Party, even though Radić was imprisoned by the Belgrade government. Serbian units soon put down the rebellions, but they contributed to an overall decline, estimated at 20 percent, in Croatian agricultural production for 1918–21 from an already reduced level.[26]

This reduction combined with the desperate demand for foodstuffs in postwar Vienna and Budapest to drive up food prices in Zagreb to several times beyond the Belgrade level. The food-poor areas of Dalmatia, Slovenia, and Hercegovina were left with virtually nothing from Croatia-Slavonia. But the rail links to the struggling new states of Austria and Hungary were still intact. Croatian traders played the interim government's civil and military authorities off against each other in order to obtain exemptions from an Allied ban on exports to those countries. Selling to the highest bidder, they also found buyers in relatively prosperous Czechoslovakia. In the process, Zagreb became the commercial center of the new kingdom, accounting for most of the food exports that were in turn half of the kingdom's total for 1920.

Serbia's own agricultural woes only encouraged the Belgrade politicians to focus on Zagreb's rising role in foreign trade and to neglect any problems of the Croatian peasantry. The Serbian burden from wartime requisitions by the Austro-Hungarian centrale had, of course, been higher. Livestock was reduced to one-third of the prewar total for peasant households. The grain-rich Vojvodina still sent the majority of its produce north, even after the prewar customs barriers had been removed in March 1919. But there were no "Green Cadres" to disrupt the cultivation of the fertile fields of northern Serbia, albeit mainly with wooden ploughs. Their overwhelmingly small properties were also exempt from the land reform and, in fact, produced a better food supply for Belgrade than for Zagreb in the autumn of 1919.

Industry and transport

Serbia's industry suffered more than agriculture, particularly when compared to Croatia and Slovenia. Broken rail connections heightened Serbia's postwar problems. Its rail track per capita was already less than even the Bosnian average (31 versus 74 kilometers) before the war. Retreating Bulgarian troops had destroyed the Niš repair yards and most of the rolling stock that the Austrian forces had not taken with them in the autumn of 1918. To the north, the retreating Austrians had blown up the bridges across the Sava and Danube rivers. Because of these limitations, the postwar coal shortage that interrupted rail service across all of the new kingdom except Slovenia and Bosnia hit Belgrade all the harder.

Prewar Serbia's modest industrial capacity had been concentrated in Belgrade, where it now faced the lack of full rail service until 1922. The occupiers' last-minute flooding of lignite mines delayed the resumption of power, heat, and light for factories through 1919. Denied a place on the Allied commission to divide up the assets of Austria-Hungary, the kingdom's Serbian-dominated government could not bargain for Czech coal supplies that would have offered relief. Indeed, the reparations from both Austria-Hungary and Germany that the government had counted on for Serbia's economic recovery were slow to arrive beyond a number of German locomotives. Meanwhile, Belgrade's association of private industrialists, the Industrijska Komora, consistently failed to win state support for priority over agricultural recovery or military requirements.

Even demands for the nationalization of Austrian and Hungarian firms in Croatia or Slovenia fell on deaf ears.

Two portentous consequences followed from the travails of Serbia's industry. First, the hardships of unpaid wages or unemployment throughout 1919 convinced a significant part of Belgrade's industrial labor force, swollen by returning soldiers, to support the new Communist Party of Yugoslavia in the 1920 elections for the Constituent Assembly. Second, the rapid recovery of Croatian industry now concentrated in Zagreb created a significant economic gap between the two cities. Although roughly equal before the war, the number of industrial enterprises in Zagreb grew to four times the Belgrade figure by 1926 with twice the capital.

Serbian currency and Croatian banks

Much of that capital came from Zagreb commercial banks that refused to participate in the new kingdom's central bank in Belgrade. They left Serbian shareholders to take up almost three-quarters of the joint stock issued for the Narodna Banka Kr. Srba, Hrvata i Slovenaca in 1920 and rarely called on the bank to rediscount their loans in subsequent years. Instead, they turned to investment banking within Croatia, owning or issuing 57 percent of the joint-stock in the entire kingdom by 1921, one year before the central government passed a law authorizing incorporation.

Encouraging this separate and more profitable course was the 1919 dispute over the rate at which crowns from the defunct Dual Monarchy would be converted to dinars, Serbia's long-standing denomination. Dinars had survived the war at virtual par with the French franc: dinar notes had not circulated and Serbia's gold reserves were held in safe-keeping by France. By the summer of 1919, the Austro-Hungarian crown depreciated to one-fifth of its prewar par with the German mark, four to the dollar rather than the dinar's prewar five, on the Vienna and Budapest exchange markets. The Serbian-dominated government's decision to "mark over" crowns or trade them for dinars at a five-to-one ratio may appear to economic historians as a market-based measure, but neither the Croatian nor the Serbian side would remember it that way. The initial Serbian offer of ten-to-one faced a Croatian demand for a one-to-one exchange. Even the two-to-one rate offered by Romanian authorities in Transylvania in order to allow the powerful Bucharest banks to attract deposits had proved wildly inflationary. The five-to-one ratio of crowns for dinars persuaded the Zagreb banks to ignore the new central bank that would manage a money supply of dinars.[27] Irritation over the initial conversion would not fade from the list of Croatian grievances against "Serbian centralism" in the first Yugoslavia.

Divisive elections for a unitary constitution

The constitution of 1921 surely deserved its reputation as a framework for centralization. This was to be a state dominated by the monarch, the Belgrade ministries, and Serbian political leaders. Yet Serbs did not constitute even a simple majority, let alone the overwhelming majority that made such a prescription more workable, even without a king, in France. But if the regent, Aleksandar, and the Serbian army still held the strong hand described above, why was the political process leading to that constitution so long and difficult? Nearly two years passed before a Constituent Assembly was elected on November 28, 1920, and another seven months before that body ratified a constitution. The uncertainty over the peace treaties and Serbia's particular economic weakness were only two reasons. Divisions within the Serbian and other Serbs' camps combined with the abstention of irreconcilable Croatian and Communist parties to fracture the final outcome.

That struggle began in the Interim National Parliament (PNP). It convened on December 10, 1918, and continued to sit until the regent disbanded it exactly one month before the 1920 election for the Constituent Assembly. The PNP remained an unelected body through-out its existence, with the undemocratic exception of twenty-four deputies from Macedonia and Kosovo elected via open ballot by voters approved by Serbian authorities. The rest of the PNP's 296 delegates were selected by the prewar parties in rough proportion to their seats in the last prewar assemblies. Hence, only two token seats were offered to Radić's Croatian Peasant Party (and promptly refused) and none to the new Communist Party. Prewar Serbia, Macedonia, and Kosovo together had 84 seats, Croatia 62, Slovenia 32, Bosnia-Hercegovina 42, the Vojvodina 24, Dalmatia and Montenegro 12 each, and Istria 4. Although a majority of the National Council in Zagreb would have preferred its own separate parliament and Slovenian representatives had asked for 6 more seats, the body was not an unrepresentative one by the available census figures.

Two principal features distinguished the PNP's legislative life.[28] First, although Nikola Pašić's Radical Party organized three of its four cabinets, Pašić headed none of them, and his party commanded only sixty-nine mandates. It sought to counter this disadvantage by alliances with the Slovenian People's Party (SLS) and Bosnia's Yugoslav Muslim Organization (JMO), alliances that would reappear several times during the interwar period. The formation of political clubs for each major party or coalition on the prewar Serbian pattern facilitated the contacts that made such alliances possible. The new Democratic Party held the largest number of seats with 115 and was itself a coalition. Its members, led by Ljuba Davidović, came from Serbia's Independent Radical Party, Pašić's prewar adversary, and the Serbian Independent Party that Svetozar Pribićević had taken into the Croato-Serbian Coalition. Pribićević traded on his close relations with the regent to take centralizing initiatives, but soon squandered support in confrontations within his own party as well as with the Radicals over his arbitrary ways.

Pribićević's divisive role helps to explain the PNP's second major distinction, its failure to pass thirty-five of the forty-seven legislative measures that came before it, including a budget. The only important items on which it could agree were the several peace treaties, a customs union, and the procedures for the Constituent Assembly election. The regent refused the Democrats' demand for elections to the PNP itself in September 1919.

The 1920 elections

The long-awaited balloting for the Constituent Assembly finally took place on November 28, 1920. The Radicals increased their representation largely at the expense of the Democrats. With 419 seats now open instead of the PNP's 296, Pašić's Radicals increased their mandates from 69 to 91, while their Serb Democratic rivals fell from 115 to 92. The total representation for the two parties, 194 versus 183, hardly changed. While the Democrats won more votes, 319,000 to 285,000, and could claim twice as many from Croatia, the Radicals held the same advantage in the Vojvodina and tripled the Democrats' numbers in Bosnia-Hercegovina. Only a similar three-to-one advantage in Macedonia and Kosovo allowed the Democrats to pull ahead in the popular vote, if not the number of seats.

Table 4.1 records the distribution of votes and seats among the various parties within the eight major regions. The balloting brought out a respectable 65 percent of eligible voters, all males twenty-one years or older, barring those with dual (foreign) citizenship. This device conveniently excluded nearly 1 million Hungarians and Germans, residing primarily in the Vojvodina. Serbia recorded the lowest voting percentage, only 56 percent according to one survey, probably reflecting greater economic disaffection with the postwar regime than elsewhere. The low turnout did not hurt the Radicals much. A Radical-influenced distribution of electoral districts compensated for the lower density of

Table 4.1. *Regional party shares and seats in the 1920 elections*

	Percentage	Seats		Percentage	Seats
Bosnia and Hercegovina			*Serbia*		
Yugoslav Muslim			Radicals	20	41
Organization (JMO)	23	24	Democrats	18	32
Radicals	13	11	Communists (KPJ)	9	14
Labor Union	12	12	Agrarian Union	8	14
Croatian Labor Party	8	7	*Kosovo and Sandžak*		
Croatian People's Party	4	3	Democrats	36	13
Democrats	4	2	Radicals	15	6
Communists	4	4	Communists	8	3
Croatia			*Macedonia*		
Croatian Republic			Communists	20	15
Peasant Party (HRSS)	37	50	Democrats	16	11
Democrats	12	19	Radicals	14	6
Radicals	6	9	*Montenegro*		
Communists	5	7	Communists	25	4
Croatian Union	2	3	Democrats	13	2
Croatian People's Party	2	3	Republicans	11	2
Croatian Party of Right	2	2	Radicals	9	1
Dalmatia			Independent list	6	1
Croatian People's Party	16	3	*Vojvodina*		
Labor Party	12	3	Radicals	30	21
Communists	9	1	Democrats	12	10
Radicals	7	1	Communists	10	5
Democrats	6	1	Social Democrats	5	3
Non-party list	4	1	Croatian People's Party	4	4
Croatian Union	3	1	Agrarian Union	2	1

Source: Branislav Gligorijević, *Parlament i političke stranke Jugoslavije, 1919–1929* (Belgrade: Narodna knjiga, 1979), 82–89.

population in both rural and southeastern regions and allowed a smaller number of voters to elect their candidates and some Communists as well.[29]

Leading the parties with lesser percentages were three apparently religious but in reality ethnic parties, Slovenia's clerical-led SLS, the Bosnian Muslims' JMO, and their Albanian counterpart in Kosovo, the Sandžak, and Macedonia, the Džemijet. The SLS and JMO each received one-third of the ballots cast in their regions, making them the largest parties and winning them twenty-seven and twenty-four seats, respectively. These small but significant representations made them ideal partners, despite their religious affiliation, for the Serbian Radical Party in its search for support against Croatian and other Serb parties. The

Džemiyet also won the largest party share in Kosovo, but received no initial representation. They had put forward no specific candidates after forming a pre-election alliance with the Radicals and especially the Democrats. Such an alliance was the best that they could do, given electoral districts gerrymandered to include enough Serbs to outnumber the Albanian majority. This restrictive framework gave the Džemijet eleven votes, all of them cast to ratify the constitution on June 28, 1921.

By that time, the two parties that had won the largest number of seats after the Serb front runners decided to absent themselves. The Croatian Republican Peasant Party (HRSS) had abandoned its efforts of early 1919 to seek separate recognition for a Croatian Peasant Republic and run a list of candidates that swept away the prewar Croatian parties. The Frankist Party of Pure Right, for example, won just 2.5 percent of Croatia's votes. The Radić party took advantage of the newly widened franchise to capture 52.5 percent, or 230,000 votes, exactly twice the total of the two major Serb parties combined in Croatia. Released from prison in time for the campaign, Radić himself continued to oppose any framework other than a limited constitutional monarchy with confederal autonomy for Croatia. He wanted a position comparable to that of Hungary in the Dual Monarchy. There was little chance from the beginning that any of his party's forty-nine votes would be cast for a French-style state with a Serbian king.

The largest opposition party was not Radić's but rather the new Communist Party of Yugoslavia (KPJ). It won fifty-nine seats with fewer votes than the HRSS, less than 200,000. Formed only in April 1919 in Belgrade, it attracted voters from several constituencies to eclipse the Social Democrats, who fell short of 50,000. A number of the 100,000 prisoners of war returning from Russia and Austria-Hungary were ready recruits, later including a certain Josip Broz, who would become the Communist leader, Tito. Difficult conditions for factory and transport employees in Belgrade and Zagreb, plus the example of Bela Kun's brief Bolshevik regime in Budapest, helped the KJP attract 34 and 39 percent, respectively, of the votes cast in the two cities' municipal elections of 1920. The Communists also made their best showings in the Assembly elections in the cities and in less populous Macedonia and Montenegro, both favored as noted above with more districts for fewer people. In Montenegro and Macedonia alike, the KJP won 38 percent of the total votes cast. Much of this vote, as with the 16 percent the Communists received in Dalmatia, was cast as a protest against rule from Belgrade, past or prospective. But the KPJ's 15 percent from Serbia came from the disaffected, often unemployed workers of Belgrade and interior towns. Almost immediately after the election, a coalition government of

Radicals and Democrats passed the famous *Obznana*, or ban, on any sort of organized Communist activity. Although several leading Radicals and Democrats argued against the ban on Western legal principle, it stayed in place. In response the KPJ representatives walked out of the Constituent Assembly barely two weeks before the vote of ratification.[30]

The 1921 constitution

The vote on ratification is remembered as much for who did not vote as for who did. The Communists and the Croatian Peasant Party accounted for 110 of the 158 abstentions, and the Slovenian People's Party (SLS) for another 27. Only 35 delegates were left to vote against the proposed constitution, 21 from the Serbian Agrarian Party and all 7 of the Social Democrats. One independent opponent of the document was noteworthy, Ante Trumbić, the wartime champion of a Yugoslav state. That left the 176 votes of the two largest parties, the 89 Serb-led Democrats and the 87 Serbian Radicals, to dominate the total 223 ballots cast for the constitution. The Democrats' unanimous vote, let it be noted, included their 11 ethnic Croatian and 3 Slovene delegates, as well as several Macedonians and Montenegrins. The Radicals promised Muslim landlords compensation for holdings taken by the interim land reform, helping bring in the 23 votes of the Bosnian JMO and the 11 of the Kosovar Albanian Džemiyet. They accounted for 34 of the remaining 48 aye votes that enabled the constitution to pass by a simple majority, if not by the 60 percent agreed to in the Corfu Declaration.

The strong Serbian position could be seen from the start of the constitutional process. The assembly quickly elected Nikola Pašić, now prime minister for the first time since the war's end, as its temporary president on December 12, 1920. Following an initial meeting, the assembly's constitutional committee stood adjourned for most of the next two months while Pašić and Pribićević negotiated behind the scenes. Only on May 12, when the Radicals had already won the support of the two Muslim parties, did they submit their proposal to an initial ballot. The provisional adoption by 227 to 93 with 96 abstaining forecast the final result. But as brief as the open debate and as unitary as the constitution proved to be, the details of the process deserve greater attention than they usually receive. They mark the first, albeit unsuccessful, effort to work out the compromise between unitary and confederal frameworks that would have been needed to preserve a Yugoslav state.

The debate revolved around four specific issues: (1) the name of the state; (2) the recognition of religious freedom; (3) the need for a second legislative chamber; and (4) the nature of local administration. Serbia- and Bosnia-centered Radicals were able to rebuff the Democrats' preference for "Yugoslavia" and find allies in the other two ethnic groups for the "Kingdom of Serbs, Croats, and Slovenes" with its specific mention of all three. Perhaps strengthening the Radicals' support on this issue was their readiness to grant the Orthodox church no special position, as it had been accorded in the Serbian constitution of 1903, and to stipulate equality and toleration for all recognized religions. The variety of proposals addressing the last two issues, however, revealed more fault lines than the one dividing Serbia and Croatia.

The eminent American historian, Charles A. Beard, reviewed these proposals and concluded that despite occasional references to the United States, Switzerland, and Germany, none displayed a "firm grasp of the practical nature and operation of these three governments [or] . . . a thorough knowledge of any existing federal systems." According to Beard and the eminent Serbian legal scholar and historian, Slobodan Jovanović, the proposal of Pašić's rival, Stojan Protić, came closest to a federal compromise between unitary and confederal extremes.[31] Under his plan, nine historical provinces would receive substantial autonomy under a governor-general with only supervisory powers over adminis- tration and legislation. A French-style state council and an English-style parliament, including an upper chamber, would have constituted the central government. Jovanović emphasized the need for a strong parliament to bind these provinces together, but he worried prophetically that the creation of more than two or three federal units, which he judged too few to avoid irreconcilable conflict, would be difficult for a Yugoslav state. The main Croatian proposal advocated a framework likened by Beard to the American Confederation of 1781–87. Six provinces, including the Vojvodina but leaving Macedonia and Kosovo to Serbia, would each have the right to veto any change in a constitution based on independent administrations and legislatures for the six. The monarch could appoint a principal governor who would replace the central government's interior minister, then the much-resented Pribićević, as countersigner of legislation. Both a strong provincial judiciary and a second central legislative chamber based on territory and local organiz- ations, rather than population like the first, would complement these confederal rights. The principal Slovenian proposal for six provinces and a Dalmatian scheme for twelve granted the central government more residual powers, but also included second provincial chambers intended to strengthen local rights. These Slovenian chambers would have selected representatives from socio-economic organizations, including enterprise councils for certain industries, thus foreshadowing the second

Yugoslavia and the provisions for workers' self-management prominent in its last three constitutions.

In the end, Pašić and Pribićević had the party votes and the Muslim allies to carry through a centralized constitution on the Serbian model of 1903. Their document in turn was based on French principles and the Belgian constitution of 1830. The interior ministry was to appoint police prefects for each of the thirty-three *oblast*, or districts. Regional combinations of districts were forbidden. As a concession to the abstaining opposition, Pašić shifted Pribićević from the ministry of interior to the ministry of education. No second chamber was authorized, and judges were to be centrally appointed. Freedom of the press and religion were, however, generally affirmed, and the legislature could debate measures without government initiative.[32] Radić proposed a separate constitution for a fully autonomous Croatian Republic on June 26 as a last gesture of defiance before the final vote. Pašić set the vote symbolically for June 28, 1921, the celebrated anniversary of the Serbian defeat at Kosovo Polje in 1389.

On that day, the first Yugoslavia came into being as the constitutional, parliamentary, and hereditary Kingdom of Serbs, Croats and Slovenes. The king's powers in foreign affairs, appointments to the proposed high court, and final approval of legislation were considerable. Aleksandar was still regent at the time of the constitution's ratification, but the aged King Petar died in August. Aleksandar was formally crowned in Belgrade on November 6, 1921. The political leaders who had created or opposed the 1921 constitution and its electoral framework would set much of the new kingdom's course over the rest of the decade, until the king abrogated the constitution and dissolved a sitting parliament in 1929.

5　Parliamentary kingdom, 1921–1928

Like the other states that emerged from the prewar empires after the First World War to become Eastern Europe, the new Kingdom of Serbs, Croats, and Slovenes did not enjoy the luxury of long decades to establish a central government and national identity. Barely twenty years lay at its disposal before the Second World War shattered this "first Yugoslavia." The precarious interwar period did not produce political consensus or encourage economic cooperation anywhere in Europe, save possibly in the Scandinavian countries. The Yugoslav kingdom's parliamentary framework at least promised representative government, but survived for less than a decade. Its definition and demise frame this chapter. New cultural connections, a disjointed economic recovery, and a daunting set of international relations also deserve emphasis.

Three years of peacemaking and internal debate created a new state whose administration would have sorely tried any set of elected officials. Border disputes and issues of minority rights remained to be settled with all neighboring countries except Romania. Internally, the long-debated constitution had passed by a bare majority (see chapter 4), if abstentions are counted with negative votes. The separate economies and legal systems of the former Habsburg lands had to be reconciled with the new center in Serbia, not always to Serbia's advantage as it turned out. In the former Ottoman territories, Serbian authorities took full political advantage of the need to reestablish public order. The unification of the Orthodox, Catholic, and Muslim religious communities from previously separate jurisdictions would also pose problems.

There were, lest they be forgotten in the face of formidable problems, some initial strengths. In Belgrade the young King Aleksandar and a number of intellectuals drawn to the new capital from across the country celebrated the South Slavs' cultural affinities. These intellectuals, if not always the king as well, recognized the danger if the constitution's postulate – that Serbs, Croats, and Slovenes were ethnically three tribes of one people – was seen as a formula for assimilation with Serbia. Their goal was the creation of a single state, not a single tribe. Towns in the former Habsburg lands, particularly in Slovenia and Dalmatia, tended to support the idea of one Yugoslavia because it promised a large, integrated economy. The new state's territorial integrity also rebuffed existing claims on its component parts from Italy, Bulgaria, and Albania.

The surviving European powers of Britain and France were not initially concerned with Balkan security. The war had weakened them both, and their only common interest in the region appeared to be keeping Austria and Hungary too weak to reunite. They showed little inclination to support the Yugoslav kingdom as the obvious centerpiece of a new Southeast European order. Also absent throughout the 1920s was the revival of European trade and foreign lending, particularly to governments, to anything approaching prewar levels. As a result, the postwar recovery failed to reassure the various regions of a single Yugoslav economy that they would be better off together than they had been apart before the First World War.

This "first transition," if we may compare it to the East European transition of the 1990s, labored under a major internal handicap as well. Rather than the multi-party system or the bourgeois-led parties typically blamed by Communist historians of the "second Yugoslavia," the predominance of prewar politicians posed the greater problem as elsewhere in interwar Europe. Here, they returned to lead regional Serb or Croat parties in the absence of younger men who might have favored country-wide, multi-ethnic parties had they survived the war. The leaders of the largest Serbian, Croatian, and Croatian Serb parties were also poorly suited to work together. Before the war, they had only confronted or dominated opponents, and their individual personalities were incredibly mismatched (see chapter 3). Nikola Pašić, Stjepan Radić, and Svetozar Pribićević failed to build the kind of coalition governments that three parliamentary elections with no majority party demanded. Of the coalitions that were formed, several tried to unite at least two of this trio, but each of them soon collapsed. Even Pašić's death in 1926 did not relieve the parliamentary stalemate, and the assassination of Stjepan Radić in the Skupština itself two years later only made it worse. The king and his autocratic military advisors had already begun to step forward before taking full power in 1929. By then, some of the younger intellectuals who had gathered there after the war were deserting Belgrade.

Prewar politicians, new parties, and the Vidovdan framework, 1921–1926

A centralized administration with powerful ministries as the prizes fought over by badly divided parties within one legislative body and without recourse to a second chamber or a constitutional court – this was the French prescription for parliamentary government that served the inter-war Third Republic badly and the first Yugoslavia worse. Executive centralization, even from all-powerful Paris, had discouraged legislative consensus. Belgrade was not Paris. France had no Zagreb. In the case of the new kingdom, moreover, the shape and substance of its executive branch made the parliament a court of last resort for Serbs and Croats, but not for the other ethnic groups that made up one-third of the population of 12 million (see table 5.1). That administrative framework is essential to understanding the parliamentary elections and coalitions that followed.

Central government

For some, Serbian dominance explains all the initial failings of the first Yugoslavia. This view assumes that the king and the army leadership worked closely and effectively with Nikola Pašić and a united Radical Party to impose central control from Belgrade across the country. The royal and Radical forces, however, were often divided and sometimes ineffective.

King Aleksandar began his reign with good, if ill-formed intentions toward the creation of a state to which non-Serbs could feel as loyal as Serbs and with an established antipathy toward Nikola Pašić (see chapter 4). Less obvious were the real limits on the king's powers to influence the shape of the central government. He was still young, only thirty-three-years old in 1921, and unschooled in civilian government. His education had consisted of ten years of essentially military training in prewar Russia, and his long regency from 1914 to 1921 was primarily concerned with military matters. A good political marriage to a daughter of the English-born Queen Marie of Romania and the birth of a son and heir in 1923 strengthened his solid position in public opinion. But his constitutional powers were effectively confined to foreign relations. He could not dissolve parliament on his own initiative and chose not to exercise the right to veto legislation, perhaps because too little of importance was ever passed into law. The High Court prescribed by the constitution would have allowed the king to nominate half of its members with parliamentary approval and pass judgment on the nomination of the other half. The Skupština could not agree on its creation.[1]

Leading officers from the former Serbian army also played a limited role in the early shaping of the new central government. To be sure, the king's closest confidants were General Petar Živković and other members

Table 5.1. *Population by ethnicity and geographic area, 1921 (in thousands)*

	Population	Percent of total
Serb and Montenegrin	4,705	39
Serbia proper	2,657	
Montenegro	199	
Croatian	2,889	23.9
Croatia-Slavonia	3,360	
Slovene	1,024	8.5
Slovenia	1,055	
Bosnian Muslim	760	6.3
Bosnia-Hercegovina	1,890	
Macedonian	630	5.3
German	512	4.3
Albanian	484	4
Hungarian	472	3.9
Turkish, Romanian, and Italian	580	4.8
Kingdom of Serbs, Croats, and Slovenes	11,985[a]	

[a]1951 data, later revised to 12,545 per table 11.1
Sources: *Enciklopedia Jugoslavije*, v, III (Zagreb: Jugoslavenski leksikografski zavod, 1983), 263; and Werner Markert, *Jugoslawien* (Cologne: Bohaul-Vorlag, 1954), 40

of the so-called White Hand who had sided with the regent against the Black Hand officers purged in the Salonika trial of 1917. The constitutional provision that barred them from open political activity was not the only constraint on their powers. They also faced the considerable task of reducing military forces from 400,000 in 1919 to 200,000 by 1921, and then the obligation of absorbing some 2,500 officers from the former Austro-Hungarian army and 500 from the Montenegrin army into an officer corps of only 6,000. (One way to maintain control of this enlarged corps was to increase the number of generals, so that by 1927 the total number of flag-rank officers, over 80 percent of whom were Serbian, surpassed that of the French and Italian armies combined.) New equipment was badly needed, as French supplies from wartime stocks were no longer available.[2]

To make matters worse, the new army had tarnished its reputation in November 1921. General Zečević, the war minister, ordered 6,000 recruits into maneuvers with no protection from a winter storm; 300 died, and the minister's refusal to accept responsibility cost him his influence, although not his job. In subsequent years, moreover, the army squandered the initial credit it had received from Muslims as well as local

Serbs from Bosnia to Macedonia for suppressing postwar banditry. Its heavy-handed role in support of local administrations staffed largely by Serbs and run entirely from the interior ministry in Belgrade, made their gendarmerie unpopular in these former Ottoman territories.

The interior ministry's power to appoint provincial prefects and county sub-prefects generated even more resentment against "Belgrade centralism" throughout the new state, particularly in the non-Serb areas. The four Pašić-led Radical governments that ruled from 1921 until the 1923 elections used the French framework that they had written into the constitution to take control of local government. His ministerial commission drew up the thirty-three provincial boundaries in haste, after endless parliamentary debate exhausted the nine months allowed by the constitution. These *oblasti* (provinces) ranged in population from 100,000 to 800,000 and each was subdivided into 4 to 24 counties, or *srezovi*. (The largely Serb Krajina had 24 counties despite its low population.) Pašić enjoyed the king's support for promoting ethnic or economic links that combined provincial populations on both sides of major rivers or divided towns between several counties, rather than observing the historical borders. In Kosovo this laudable purpose served only to attach Serb-populated areas to each of the four provinces so that none had an Albanian majority. Bosnia-Hercegovina's four provinces and Croatia's six provinces were drawn within the historical boundaries of their territory, but not one Bosnian Muslim or Croat was named by the ministry as prefect for any Bosnian province. All four prefects were Serbs, as were all three in the Vojvodina, where the Hungarians and Germans combined outnumbered the Serbs. Only Slovenia escaped a disproportionate share of Serbian officials.

The prefects were required to have fifteen years of previous government service and sub-prefects ten years, a qualification that favored candidates from Serbia's prewar bureaucracy. They soon commanded an army-appointed police force of some 20,000, calculated to be 60 percent Serb. The prefects and other employees pushed the proportion of state employees working for the interior ministry past 50 percent by 1927.

Total state employment rose in turn to 172,000 by 1928, minus army enlistees. Charles Beard reckoned, as did British embassy reports, that this aggregate could have been efficiently reduced by one-third, to bring the per capita total closer to its pre-1914 level.[3] The state's notorious delay in paying for private services helped spread the practice of kickbacks and other corrupt arrangements to assure payment. Temptations within the ministries were also corrupting. At the top, the ministers needed only a single year of service to acquire a lifetime pension and two years for a family pension. At the bottom lay the poorly paid employees of the provinces and counties who, according to the constitution, were to be accountable to elected local assemblies as well as to the interior ministry. But these assemblies were slow in coming. Only the still lower level for municipal government were elected from the start. Unsurprisingly, the Congress of Public Employees, when convened in Zagreb in 1922 by the Pašić regime's main adversaries, made Belgrade's withdrawal from local government their principal demand.

Pašić and Pribićević

Nothing that could be called a comprehensive program of legislation came from the ten cabinets headed by Nikola Pašić between January 1921 and April 1926. Prime minister for all but four months in 1924, he appointed fellow Radical Party members to the key posts of the interior, finance, and foreign affairs ministries. Yet the large number of cabinets reminds us that the Radicals were a minority party unable to form lasting coalitions.

Both the party and its leader bore some responsibility. The Radicals made no appeal to non-Serbs and little to Serbs from outside Serbia or Bosnia. Their aged leadership and lack of a specific legislative program cost them support in Belgrade and other Serbian towns. Pašić had always been an introverted personality and a close-mouthed politician since helping to found the party in 1881 (see chapter 3). First the Bosnian crisis of 1908 and then the Balkan and two world wars had allowed him to escape the experience of coalition politics. He could only see a series of opposition parties challenging his right to rule in what he considered a time of national emergency. Pašić was seventy-five years old in 1921, and for whatever reason, he reportedly took any opposition to a party he no longer tightly controlled as a personal attack.[4]

The Radicals indeed faced sizeable opposition from other parties, most consistently from their principal *Serbian* rival, the Democrats. Its founders had created the Democratic Party in Sarajevo in February 1919 with high hopes of becoming a Yugoslav-wide party uniting Slovenian (if not Croatian) liberals with Serbs and Serbians opposed to the Pašić regime. This new party won as many seats as the Radicals (92 and 91) in the Constituent Assembly of 1920 (see chapter 4). Until the first elections under the resulting Vidovdan constitution were held in 1923, the Democrats repeatedly challenged their Radical partners in an uneasy coalition. Their leader, Ljuba Davidović, was the competent but uncharismatic head of the Independent Radicals, the largest of the three parties from prewar Serbia to become Democrats. While the Independents had been strongest in urban Belgrade and more prosperous north of Serbia (see chapter 3), postwar Democrats won the majority of the votes that the Radicals lost in Montenegro, Macedonia, and the Vojvodina, as well as Serbia. The other votes lost there went to the Communists, who were not allowed to take their seats, and to the Agrarian Union. With leaders best described as agrarian socialists in the tradition of Svetozar Marković, the Union represented peasants dissatisfied with Radicals' plans for land reform which had no provision for a new cooperative network.

Both the Agrarian Union and the Democrats failed to hold their ground among Serbian voters in the initial election of 1923, despite their continued insistence on redistributing the property of Muslim landlords quickly and without compensation. Both paid a high price for their attempts to become parties representing the country as a whole. The Democrats dropped to 51 seats (from 92), losing all but one from Serbia in a parliament trimmed by a Radical initiative from 419 to 315 members, while the Agrarians fell from 39 to 11 (see table 5.2). Unlike the Democrats, the Agrarians would never recover. They kept a sizeable constituency of Bosnian Serbs, but struggled vainly to reach an accommodation with Radić's Croatian Peasant Party in Dalmatia and were plagued by internal dissension in Serbia. Overall, their disdain of any nationalist orientation and preference for peasant candidates worked against them.

Crucial to the Democrats' decline was the split with Svetozar Pribićević, the main Serb leader in the Croatian-Serbian Coalition. After the war, he led his constituency into the Democrats' camp, but only to champion a centralized regime that would secure the position of the Croatian and Bosnian Serbs. Without acknowledging the contradiction, Pribićević also applied his militant energies to enforcing the constitution's questionable postulate that Serbs, Croats, and even Slovenes were one people that external forces had separated into tribes. Confrontational (see chapter 3) and less able to tolerate opposition than any of the major political personalities, Pribićević was ready to break with the Serbian Democrats as early as September 1922. He censured Davidović for daring to attend the Zagreb conference of the Congress of Public Employees, even though Davidović had pointedly refused to join its discussion of a decentralizing revision of the Vidovdan constitution.

Nikola Pašić seized on the Democrats' divided opinion about constitutional revision to exclude them from his last pre-election cabinet. In their place, however, he could only find two Bosnian Muslims from the conservative, clerical faction which by then had been decisively defeated for the leadership of the new Yugoslav Muslim Organization (JMO). The Radicals' failure to sustain an initial agreement with the winning faction reflected the difficulties that Pašić experienced in creating lasting coalitions.

The JMO was plainly a successor to the prewar Muslim National Organization. Yet it quickly became the representative of urban, commercial interests over those of Islamic clerics or rural landlords. The new leader of the JMO, Mehmed Spaho, was a Vienna-trained lawyer who had previously headed Sarajevo's Chamber of Commerce. He and his younger, Yugoslav-oriented colleagues had tried to work with the Radicals to implement two agreements in 1921. Both promised a series of Muslim and Bosnian rights beyond the redemption payments to landlords. The Radicals had quickly agreed to those payments in return for votes in the constituent assembly. Spaho was appointed to two Pašić cabinets, as minister of forestry and then minister of trade and industry, but resigned in February 1922 because the key points of the agreements were not being honored. In addition *Samouprava* and other Radical and nationalist newspapers in Belgrade berated the JMO as an organization based on the Koran and medieval feudalism.[5]

The Radicals searched for other non-Serb allies in Slovenia too, but without success during the Pašić era. The small Slovenian Liberal Party, strong only in Ljubljana and a few other towns, had already committed itself as a founding member of the Democrats. The prewar Slovenian People's Party (SLS) remained the largest by far, now led by a younger faction favoring the Christian Social ideals of Krek's great cooperative network (see chapter 3). It was still a conservative clerical party, but Monsignor Anton Korošec, the party head, had proposed a confederal, socially progressive alternative to the Vidovdan constitution in the 1920 debate and persisted with these "autonomist" demands after it came into force.[6] He and his fellow clerics were particularly alarmed by the heavy-handed proposals of Pašić's education minister, none other than Svetozar Pribićević, to establish a single system of secular schools in place of existing religious networks, of which the Catholics had the largest. The SLS slipped only slightly in the 1923 elections, dropping only one seat with 56 percent of the vote, down from the 61 percent won in the 1920 vote in Slovenia.

The absence of political allies undermined the Radicals' victory in the 1924 elections (see table 5.2). So did the intimidation employed by the interior ministry's local organizations to skew the vote, not only in Kosovo and Macedonia where balloting was rarely secret but also in the Vojvodina, Croatia, and Bosnia-Hercegovina. Vojvodina Hungarians could now vote, unlike in 1920, but abstained in the face of concerted harassment. In Croatia, Pribićević fanned fears of Croatian domination among the rural Serb minority. The Belgrade-appointed police engaged in what a Serbian historian has called the worst violence in any of the three elections in the 1920s.[7] Threats led to beatings; Croat houses were burned, blown up, or confiscated without punishment to the perpetrators. Word of a Croatian response in kind spread to Bosnia, prompting the Serb plurality to mobilize against Muslim villages closer at hand than Croat ones – an eerie precedent for the sequence of events in 1941–42 (see chapter 7) and 1991–92. In March of 1923, the Radicals took 108 seats of 313, but found only isolated support beyond Serbia. Pašić was forced to seek a governing majority by uneasy alliances with his other major political rivals – first Svetozar Pribićević and then Stjepan Radić.

Radić and Pašić

The mercurial Radić set the stage for both alliances. His Croatian Republican Peasant Party won seventy seats in the 1923 election with 37 percent of Croatia's vote. This largely rural vote was achieved despite the violence and the Pašić government's use of the 1910 census, rather than that of 1921, thus allowing Serbia's greater number of war dead to count for proportional distribution. Radić negotiated with the Slovenian SLS and the Bosnian Muslim JMO to form a Federal Bloc of 163 votes, if combined with the Davidović Democrats, but failed to produce a working agreement. Meanwhile, Radić continued to challenge the legitimacy of the state's framework in a series of powerful, provocative speeches.

From July 1923 until August of the next year, Radić delivered his pronouncements outside the country. When he gave a Bastille Day speech comparing the kingdom to that infamous French prison, he had to flee Zagreb for Hungary in the face of an arrest warrant. Radić now embarked on his well-publicized travels from Vienna to London and Moscow. His conversations in London with the increasingly disillusioned British champion of Yugoslavia, R. W. Seton-Watson, may have been more important to him, but his attendance at the Comintern's Peasant International Congress in Moscow made the greater impact in Belgrade.[8] Radić's mere presence there gave Pašić the heaven-sent chance to charge Radić with links to a Bolshevik regime that was anathema to London and Paris and, more importantly, to King Aleksandar. The first pamphlets now appeared, probably with official approval, but based on a proposal from political rival Stojan Protić, to suggest the "amputation" of Croatia from the kingdom because Serbs "could not go on with the Croats."

These tensions brought Pašić and Pribićević together for the first of

Table 5.2. *Parliamentary elections, 1920–1927 (number of seats won)*

Political party	1920	1923	1925	1927
Democrats	92	51	37	61
Independent Democrats (SDS)			21	22
Radicals	91	108	143	112
Communists (KPJ)	59			
Croatian Republican Peasant (HRSS)	50	70	67	61
Agrarian Union	39	11	3	9
Slovenian People's Party (SLS)	27	24	21	21
Yugoslav Muslim Organization (JMO)	24	18	15	17
Social Democrats	10			1
Germans		8	5	6
Montenegrin Federalists		2	3	1
Other	27	21		4
Total mandates	419	313	315	315

Source: Enciklopedia Jugoslavije, v, III (Zagreb: Jugoslavenski leksikografski zavod, 1983), 269.

their two "P-P" regimes. From March to July 1924, a minority combination of some 120 Radical and Independent Democrat deputies, dubbed the National Bloc, managed to survive in the Skupština, but only because Pašić prevented recognition of the mandates of 60 HRSS deputies, who had come to Belgrade for the first time.

Radić returned from abroad shortly before Aleksandar asked the Democrats' Ljuba Davidović to put together a broad coalition government in August 1924. The new cabinet included four Slovenes (SLS) and three Bosnian Muslims (JMO), with four more places reserved for the HRSS. But Radić offered the king little proof that he now favored a British-style monarchy for Yugoslavia rather than a Croatian peasant republic in a Balkan federation. (Radić had proclaimed both views in different speeches.) Several new, anti-monarchical speeches by Radić apparently prompted Aleksandar to dismiss the Davidović government. A second P-P regime was quick to pursue the attack on Radić personally, arresting him in a comic-opera scene in January 1925 as he hid behind a wall in a relative's apartment that doubled as his party's bookstore.[9]

The Pašić–Pribićević National Bloc proved incapable of using Radić's arrest and a series of other advantages, fair and unfair, to win a convincing victory in the second parliamentary elections that they quickly called for in February 1925. Their common platform was "fighting for the state," with the Vidovdan constitution championed as the only alternative to disintegration. They tarred the Davidović

Democrats with their association with the "Bolshevik secessionist," Radić. The election was less violent than in 1923, but reportedly was more corrupt.[10] Still, heavy voting by 77 percent of those eligible gave the National Bloc just one-third of the ballots and a bare 160-seat majority of 315. The Albanians' Džemijet Party was pushed aside in Kosovo, but only after the leader's arrest and more police pressure had split the party. In Montenegro, however, the federalist "Greens" won more votes than the Radicals, signalling the reappearance of autonomous sentiment that the pro-Serbian "Whites" had been able to suppress after the First World War in favor of simply supporting the Radicals. Elsewhere the Radicals saw rival lists submitted by the dissident faction of Ljuba Jovanović competing with their own for twenty-six seats. The British Embassy speculated that Pašić, now eighty years old, was losing control of the party. Worst of all for the National Bloc, Radić's Peasant Party still won sixty-seven seats, only three less than in 1923.[11]

Pašić tried again to arrange the rejection of the HRSS mandates and to form another P-P cabinet, but was forced to make the least comfortable alliance of his long career. The Radić-Radical, or "R-R" government of July 1925 seemed the only way out of the continuing impasse. Royal feelers put out earlier in the year to Radić, who was once again in prison, had revealed that the Croatian leader was ready, as he put it, "to turn his automobile around." The unrelated impeachment of the interior minister, a Pribićević man who had imprisoned Radić for his "Bolshevik connections," created the occasion for his release. He now avowed his acceptance of the monarchy, the constitution, the army, and even military service. He removed the word "Republican" from the party's name as a gesture of good will. The now-HSS mandates were approved, and four of its members received posts in the last Pašić cabinet.

So Stjepan Radić came to Belgrade as minister of education, the post so long held by Pribićević. Zagreb University professors dismissed under Pribićević were reinstated, but others were removed for teaching Yugoslav rather than Croatian history. Radić placed greater emphasis, however, on the importance of primary and vocational education. He believed that the largely rural population would be better off if they did not know too much of city ways. Whether idealist or ideologue, he overflowed with often contradictory proposals whose practical implementation he had not worked out. His scattered approach helped keep his educational reforms from making any sort of start. In February 1926, another of his undiplomatic speeches implied that Pašić himself and other close associates were involved in the financial scandal fast gathering around the prime minister's son Rade. Radić also took the occasion to raise anew the demand for revising the constitution.

By this time, however, Pašić lacked the power to close off the corruption inquiry as adroitly as he could have done in earlier years. Age and infirmity left too much authority in the hands of his ill-regarded entourage. Aleksandar refused to reappoint him after he prolonged the Skupština's Easter recess to play for time. There followed four short-lived Radical cabinets under the long-time minister of public works, Nikola Uzunović. They kept Radić and his HSS colleagues in place until year's end. But the Uzunović coalition could agree on little, bringing Pašić to the palace on December 9 to ask the king's authorization to return to power. The royal refusal left the aged leader speechless with fury, no doubt contributing to the stroke from which he died the next day.

The two post-Pašić years began with a new opposition that united Radić and Pribićević and ended with Radić's assassination. Before proceeding to 1927–28, we need to stand back from the center rings of the Skupština and Belgrade ministries to look at the other concentric circles within and around the new state during the 1920s. Regional law survived, but local government struggled to emerge, and a single, integrated economy was slow to develop. The only circles that encompassed the whole country came from a small Communist Party, a surprising set of cultural connections, and the threat of foreign intervention. None of the three separate sets of prewar religious jurisdictions that were now combined – six each for the Orthodox and Catholic churches and three for the Muslims – covered the country, nor was their final form decided until the 1930s. This complex of religious unifications and how they worked to widen political division, is left to chapter 6.

Regional law and local government

The power of the king and the Belgrade ministries to control the local administration of justice was real but limited everywhere except in Macedonia and Kosovo. The king's authority to appoint and retire all judges remained in force through Aleksandar's lifetime. By 1925 the ministry of justice could dismiss judges or overrule specific decisions, as when a Zagreb court vacated political arrest warrants on its own authority. Serbs continued to be overrepresented in law enforcement, making up more than 60 percent of the officers, officials, and employees.

The regional counterweights were still considerable. Six sets of prewar legal codes including Serbia's remained in force throughout the parliamentary period, despite a series of efforts to create a single criminal or civil code. The special ministry for the unification of laws ceased to function after it completed its work on how to administer the constitution. The Radicals put forward Serbia's penal code as a model, but the Skupština refused to approve its wider application. Croatia, Slovenia, Dalmatia, the Vojvodina, and Bosnia-Hercegovina continued to apply their versions of Habsburg law, and Montenegro its own legal code from King Nikola's era. The number of Croat and Slovene judges was proportional to their ethnic populations, and Serbs only slightly more, supporting Lenard Cohen's conclusion that at least until 1929 "a de facto legal federalism remained intact."[12]

While federal features already existed in the judicial system, they would have to be created in the legislative branch of government. The Skupština approved provincial assembly elections in Slovenia as early as 1922 and, by extension, for the other former Habsburg lands as well. None took place until 1926 in Dalmatia, followed by Slovenia, Croatia, and the Vojvodina in 1927, and Bosnia-Hercegovina in 1928. Radical candidates supported by local Serbs prevailed only in the Vojvodina. The Croatian Peasant Party won control in Croatia and shared it with Ante Trumbić's Federalists in Dalmatia. Mehmed Spaho's Yugoslav Muslim Organization (JMO) took all the major Bosnian towns, aided by an alliance with the HSS. Monsignor Korošec's Slovenian People's Party (SLS) won 82 of 115 seats in the two new Slovenian assemblies in the Ljubljana and Maribor provinces.

For the Ljubljana assembly, the lack of state funds made it difficult to take any initiatives in 1927. The assembly needed commercial loans even to convene. But, by the following year, enough revenue had been collected, amid loud local complaint because of a levy on alcohol, to give the assembly a significant budget outside the control of the Belgrade-appointed prefect. Ljubljana was in the process of taking over health and other social services plus exploring other ways to become a "state within a state," when the royal decree of January 1929 suspended the provincial assemblies, along with the constitution and the Skupština.[13]

Municipal elections to the smaller communal assemblies (*opštine* or, in Croatia, *općine*) were also agencies for empowerment outside the control of the central government, sometimes even in Macedonia, if not Kosovo. The Democratic Party continued to win majorities in Bitola and several other Macedonian towns under the Serbian municipal law in force there. A tradition of independent municipal elections had developed in Serbia before the war. Some 2,200 such elections were now held across Serbia and Montenegro in 1923 and 1926. The ruling Radicals had been able to use their police powers and financial leverage to secure the 1923 elections to the Belgrade opština for themselves, but the Democrats defeated them in 1926.[14] The interior minister could still suspend specific acts of a local assembly, a prerogative much resented by Zagreb and other Croatian municipalities whose Habsburg tradition as royal free towns did not permit such interference. There was, on the other hand, no way of stopping the Independent Workers' Party, a surrogate for the illegal Communists, from running candidates in these local elections.

The Communist Party and the Macedonian question

Historians in Tito's Yugoslavia tended to exaggerate the role of the Yugoslav Communist Party (KPJ) during the 1920s, arguing that the KPJ missed opportunities for decisive influence only because of their "mistakes" and government repression. A new set of exaggerations now tempt post-Yugoslav historians. In Zagreb the KPJ leadership of the Serbian Sima Marković is equated with pursuing Great Serbian goals; in Belgrade the Soviet Comintern's encouragement of the KPJ to promote the breakup of the first Yugoslavia has been backdated and has become primarily a connection to Croatian leaders, from Stjepan Radić to Josip Broz Tito.

Three features seem more decisive in the failure of the only party other than the Democrats to try to win support throughout the country. First, there was the obvious lack of appeal to a peacetime populace, almost half of whom were peasant landowners and another 30 percent peasants aspiring to own their own land. For Serbs, the Agrarian Union provided a better base for peasant radicalism. Industrial labor and artisans together made up barely 10 percent of the economically active population (see table 5.3). Second, the ban against open political activity from 1920 on proved to be a serious liability. Third, left and right factions within the party struggled destructively for control. An assassination by the left made the ban permanent, which in turn attracted some of the KPJ leadership to left advocates of a terrorist alliance against the state. The trade union network remained in the hands of the right. The left quickly sank into the quicksand of Comintern meddling in the Macedonian question, while the right failed to pull in many members or voters from the limited number of industrial workers.

Extremists made terrorism a hallmark of the dispute over Macedonia and cost King Aleksandar his life in 1934. For its part, the Communist left felt frustrated after the Russian Revolution failed to spread elsewhere. The same sort of frustration led a young Bosnian Muslim member of the KPJ to assassinate the Democrat interior minister, Milorad Drašković, in July 1921. Drašković had just invalidated the ten seats out of forty-five that the Communists had won in the Belgrade opština that March, compounding his denial of the KPJ victory the year before. In his often-cited "you or us" pronouncement to party leaders, he bluntly told them,

"Communists cannot have the capital city's government in their hands." His assassination ironically closed off the parliamentary debate on whether the December 1920 *obznana*, or ban, on KPJ activity should be sustained and instead secured easy passage for the more permanent and prohibitive Law for the Protection of the State.

The subsequent failure of Sima Marković and the Belgrade party organization to create an effective base for illegal operations cannot be denied. Yet what more could they have done, pending a European Communist revolution, beyond carrying out more self-destructive acts of terrorism? The bombing of the Sofia cathedral in 1925 by the Bulgarian Communists' Left, on the heels of the party's disastrous 1923 uprising, and the ensuing flight of party leaders stood as an object lesson. Marković argued for creating a surrogate Independent Workers' Party of Yugoslavia (NRPJ) that did indeed operate legally from January 1923. He himself was sent to prison as a consequence of the assassination of Drašković, and after his release later that year, he led his right colleagues away from the Serbian notion of Serbs, Croats, and Slovenes as one people. From the start, moreover, Marković had mercilessly criticized the Pašić regimes for their Great Serbian policies toward Croatia and Macedonia. At the KPJ's May 1923 conference, the Left opposition to Marković and his Belgrade organization still carried the day. They advocated an alliance with Croatian and Macedonian nationalists who rejected both electoral politics and any Yugoslav state. By February 1924, this Left mixture of Croats and Serbs moved into important positions in the front of the NRPJ as well as the KPJ. Marković retained control of the secretary's position his Belgrade organization, and the trade union movement. The stalemate persisted until 1928 when Marković and his Right allies were ousted.[15]

Macedonia rather than Croatia became the focus of the Communist Left's ambiguous efforts to forge an alliance that would break away part of the new kingdom and perhaps destroy the royal regime. Radić and his Croatian Peasant Party colleagues were approached, but he did not respond, despite his 1924 Moscow trip, his membership in the Comintern's Peasant International, and his series of pro-Soviet statements. Radić was, after all, an avowed pacifist and a believer in peasant smallholdings.

Macedonia seemed more promising ground to the KPJ. A quarter of the country-wide Communist vote in the constituent assembly elections of 1920 came from Macedonia, attracting nearly one-half of the non-Muslim ballots cast there. But only 55 percent of those eligible had voted, with many Slav Macedonians abstaining because of a boycott organized by the Internal Macedonian Revolutionary Organization

(VMRO). VMRO leaders could agree only on opposition to Serbian rule; they were otherwise divided between Federalists, who advocated Macedonian autonomy as a separate nationality in Yugoslavia or Bulgaria, and Supremists, who saw their mission as uniting Bulgaria's Macedonian "tribe" with the single Bulgarian nation. The latter unsurprisingly drew support from Sofia once they had joined the *coup d'état* that assassinated the Agrarian prime minister, Aleksandar Stamboliiski, and their nationalist allies had seized power in 1923. By then Comintern representatives were assiduously courting the VMRO factions. Contrary to later claims by Tito and other Communist leaders, the KPJ's December 1923 conference failed to acknowledge the existence of a separate Macedonian nationality and subsequently ignored the Comintern's 1924 Vienna Manifesto that *did* recognize a Macedonian nationality. What followed in and out of Macedonia was a bloody feud between Federalists and Supremists. Two Communist attempts to found a United VMRO, one by the KPJ and one by the Comintern attracted few supporters.[16]

Sima Marković and his supporters on the Communist right were doomed not only by the nationalist initiatives of left opposition but also by the failure of industrial workers, especially in their Serbian stronghold, to join the trade union network or the NRPJ. The network never attracted more than 30,000 members after a promising start in 1920, when some 4 million work days were lost to strikes across the country. That figure dropped to less than 200,000 days by 1921 and fell even further after 1923, when legislation for workers' insurance against illness and accident, if not unemployment or disability, went into effect. Communist unions did not organize a majority of the strikes in the 1920s. Most of their members came from small artisan shops, not the large, mostly state enterprises hit by strikes. Also, the concentration of party membership in Croatia, over 40 percent by the mid-1920s, fore-shadowed the shift of the party's center from Belgrade to Zagreb by the end of the decade. Just as Marković was finally dislodged from his position as party secretary in 1928, the young head of the Croatian leather and metal workers' union, Josip Broz, made his presence first felt as a leader of the Left faction.[17]

Cultural connections and economic disjunctures

If the second Yugoslavia suffered cultural disjunctures against a promising background of economic integration, the experience of the first Yugoslavia was roughly the reverse. Integrating the economies of former Habsburg and Ottoman lands with those of war-torn Serbia and tiny Montenegro posed more daunting problems than those faced by Tito's Communists after the Second World War. Separate land, law, and tax regimes had to be reconciled, and transport networks and banking systems connected. Yet the 1920s were also a decade when cultural activities were relatively free of state supervision and could develop their institutions within civil society. Those currents favored a Yugoslav and a European identity as much as or more than separate ethnic identities. This was particularly true, and particularly important, for Belgrade.

Belgrade and the search for a Yugoslav center

The new capital was the largest city in the future Yugoslavia prior to the First World War, but only by a small margin over Zagreb (95,000 versus 74,000). From 1920 to 1929, its population doubled from 112,000 to 226,000, and made up more than 9 percent of the country's urban total. Zagreb stayed close behind with 185,000. Belgrade's public officials and state-employed professionals accounted for over one-third of that total before the war and were still 30 percent in 1920. Their share dropped to 24 percent by 1929, while the commercial class rose to 19 percent. A rich variety of immigrants from across the new state and Europe as well swelled the number of professionals, business class, and intellectuals. Newcomers from Dalmatia and the Vojvodina played prominent parts in modernizing business practices and stimulating the visual arts. Some of the 30,000 Russian emigrants fleeing the revolution contributed significantly to raising university and cultural standards, especially in opera, dance, and theater, to a European level. Such newcomers made professionals more independent of the state, and some of them, like the stars of the blossoming National Theater, became public personalities to rival political leaders.[18] So did the stars of silent films, such as Charlie Chaplin and Rudolph Valentino. Hollywood films dominated the many new movie theaters and provided what a Belgrade newspaper already called by 1919 a kind of new religion.

Newspapers and publishing houses also flourished to an extent that put public opinion outside the control of the ruling Radical Party. The Radical daily, *Vreme*, trailed far behind the largely independent *Politika* in circulation numbers. Although it received some state funding in the early postwar period, *Politika* went on to become one of the most profitable private enterprises in Belgrade. Among some fifty regularly published periodicals, several economic weeklies touted economic integration from the perspective of European business rather than Serbian politics. The *Srpski kniževni glasnik* (Serbian Literary Journal, see chapter 3) published more work by the preeminent Croatian writer

5.1 Belgrade in the 1930s. View up the Terazije with the Hotel Moskva on the right

of the decade, the left-wing Miroslav Krleža, than appeared in Zagreb. Other journals often published articles from Ljubljana in Slovenian without translation. Geca Kon, a Jewish immigrant from Zemun across the Sava river, was already printing cheap editions of translated European works. They made his book store the most famous in the city by the 1930s, a notoriety that would cost him his life during the first days of the Nazi invasion in 1941.[19]

Central to the increasingly cosmopolitan cultural life were the cafes where authors and artists gathered almost nightly. Of some 700 in the city, the Moskva on the newly fashionable Terazija was probably the most noted. Its closing for two weeks of renovation in 1923 was reportedly a major ordeal for the literary elite. The most colorful and probably the most talented of the Moskva regulars was the Croatian poet Augustin (Tin) Ujević, who spent the 1920s in Belgrade's bohemian circle as a conscious Yugoslav and European. The Serbianized Tsintsar playwright, Branislav Nušić, was the other writer to emerge as a prominent public personality. His most performed work, *Gospodja Ministarka* (Mrs. Minister), satirized Belgrade's official class mercilessly. Nušić also organized the volunteer efforts that opened the remarkable Cvijeta Zuzorić Pavilion in 1927. Named for a Dubrovnik patron of the arts, it functioned as a free performance center for art exhibits, concerts, and literary evenings unable to afford a hall.

Women were increasingly accepted into this cultural milieu.[20] Although promised the right to vote in the 1920 constitution, they did not receive it. Otherwise favoring their independence in postwar Belgrade was the new social acceptability of single or divorced women. Marriages, quipped Nušić, were now shorter, "like skirts and haircuts." The proportion of women at Belgrade University and other institutes of higher education doubled for 1922–28 to approach one-quarter. Their participation in the various arts grew as well, leaving aside literature and the still isolated if impressive figure of the poet and essayist, Isadora Sekulić (see chapter 3). Women became an integral part of the café culture. They were noticeably absent only from the soccer matches that brought mass attendances at sporting events, sometimes over 10,000, to Belgrade for the first time.

Belgrade's connections with the other cultural and intellectual centers of the first Yugoslavia, Zagreb and Ljubljana, were considerable. Zagreb had its established university and an unequaled library, expressionist and folk art, and a variety of scholarly publications; Ljubljana its new university, architectural innovation in the city center, and a developing set of social sciences. A burgeoning cultural and intellectual rivalry between Belgrade and Zagreb did not bode well for the viability of the new state. Imagine nineteenth-century France with a major city to rival Paris. For the first Yugoslavia, a more positive sign was the bonding, interpersonal and interregional, to the new state that occurred in Belgrade. Its mixture of immigrants and visitors from across the kingdom was unique. At the same time, similar debates on the desired nature of the new state took place in all three cities.[21] *Nova Evropa*, the journal originally founded during the war by Seton-Watson to promote a post-war Yugoslavia, led the fight in Zagreb for a genuine federation against the "vulgar unitarism" of Pribićević and the confederalism (at best) of Radić. The same battle lines in Ljubljana found fewer supporters on the confederal side. In Belgrade, perhaps the most respected intellectual leaders, theater critic Milan Grol and lawyer/historian Slobodan Jovanović, the son of that first Serbian liberal, Vladimir Jovanović (see chapter 2) were ready by 1922 to sacrifice unitarism in order to preserve a state whose survival they saw threatened more by the Serbian side than the Croatian.

Set against this emerging civil society and Yugoslav dialogue was the less positive role that the central government played in Belgrade's postwar development. Interference by the ministries and bureaucratic delay frustrated the General Plan of 1923 for the badly needed renovation of the city center. Only the new Skupština and a couple of government buildings were ever completed. Constant changes contributed to a cost-overrun that was projected to exceed the opština government's entire revenue for the decade. The lack of a cadastral survey and interference by ministerial property owners (Pašić included) combined with its enormous cost to sink the much debated plan.

Meanwhile the city centers of Zagreb and Ljubljana took on a more contemporary European appearance, thanks to the readiness of their municipal governments to give a free hand to modernist architects. Most prominent were two students of Vienna's Otto Wagner, Viktor Kovačić and Jože Plečnik. Kovačić designed a number of buildings in Zagreb and trained students at the university's new architectural faculty. They promoted enough new construction to be called the Zagreb School by the 1930s. Plečnik was responsible for the graceful baroque bridges, embankments, and arcades that gave Ljubljana the most coherent city center in the interwar kingdom.

Belgrade's university increased its faculties from three to five and its enrollment (primarily law students). German reparations and donations from the American Carnegie Endowment funded construction of an impressive library and other facilities. Yet the university lacked the legislation to guarantee its independence. Enrollment in the primary schools controlled by the ministry of education declined during the

1920s. Textbooks left over from the prewar period posed a greater problem for the future of the new state. Svetozar Pribićević's heavy-handed efforts to introduce new textbooks glorifying the monarchy and the idea of a single nationality with three tribes quickly failed. The resulting furor frustrated any compromise during the parliamentary period, so that schools continued to use prewar texts that slighted any common multi-ethnic heritage in Croatia, unless Habsburg-sponsored, and simply omitted it in Serbia.[22]

Land reform and colonization

Centralized administration from the Belgrade ministries generally failed to provide Serbia with the economic advantages during the 1920s that adversaries assumed it was afforded, agriculture included.[23] One major exception was land reform. It favored Serbia because it was largely inapplicable there. Serbia had few large holdings and none of the foreign-owned estates that its politicians had been promising to break up in Macedonia since the Balkan wars. In 1917 the Pašić government had promised 5 hectares (12.5 acres) to all volunteers who joined the Serbian army. The Narodno vijeće in Zagreb had given similar assurances in 1918 to the "Green Cadres," primarily Croats from the disbanding Habsburg army who were taking over Slavonian estates on their own.

The interim decree of February 1919 had ratified the end of share-cropping obligations (*kmetsvo*) and rents while promising to redistribute land from large holdings (see chapter 4; "large" was undefined in the former Habsburg and Ottoman lands). The state was to indemnify previous owners. But the actual indemnification and distribution took longer and offered less clear title than peasant recipients anticipated. Meanwhile, beginning late in 1920, a Special Commission of the interior ministry made limited awards of choice land in Bosnia, Macedonia, Kosovo, and the Vojvodina to Serb war veterans from impoverished uplands like Hercegovina. These awards of land somehow forfeited by their former owners created resentment among the lowland populations. Thus, the land reform and these colonist migrations both had unintended political consequences.

By the time it had finally run its course in the 1930s, the reform of 1919–21 had redistributed about 10 percent of the country's agricultural land, or 2.5 million hectares, and 20 percent of all arable land to one-quarter of the country's 2 million peasant families and paid at least some indemnity to the 10,000–12,000 owners. Of these 518,000 families who received land, only 43,500 were Serb or Montenegrin colonists or wartime volunteers. Although they generally received a bit more than the average dispensation of 5 hectares, they were not noticeably more prosperous and were often less so.

Jozo Tomasevich, whose critical appraisal of its impact remains the most comprehensive, calls the reform a political and socio-economic necessity in Bosnia, Macedonia, and Kosovo.[24] The semi-feudal, sharecropping regimes of the Bosnian Muslim, Turkish, and Albanian landlords over largely Serb tenants were neither efficient nor politically sustainable, given their wartime opposition to the new state. At least the former Bosnian Muslim officials, or *aga*, who owned large properties, had promptly received half of the 255 million dinar indemnity offered for their political support in ratifying the 1921 constitution. The rest of their payment and all of that paid to the more numerous sharecropping landlords (*beg*) came from state bonds, which were not even issued until 1929. Landlords in Macedonia and the Sandžak of Novi Pazar finally received cash payments in the 1930s. Most of the 10,300 colonist families, half Serb and half Montenegrin, also received an average of 7 to 8 hectares of fertile Macedonian land at that late date. Despite receiving no further state assistance, the Macedonian colonists were generally successful. Their Bosnian counterparts, nearly 7,000 immigrant families, had arrived earlier during the 1920s, but made much less headway. Their more upland, largely forested holdings amounted to only 3.5 percent of the total redistribution in Bosnia-Hercegovina. The bulk of the Bosnian total went to 113,000 former kmet families, who were mainly Serbs. These transfers plus those given under the land reform to a Serb plurality of 42 percent in the province's interwar population lie behind the Bosnian Serbs' recent claim to have owned 64 percent of private Bosnian land (the 1991 census recorded 41 percent, or 19 percent of all land).

Still more portentous politically was the work of the Belgrade government's Special Commission during the 1920s. It brought Montenegrin and Serb families from Croatia and Hercegovina to Kosovo to settle on land supposedly abandoned by Turkish or Albanian owners. The Commission paid a small amount of compensation to a few of the 40,000–80,000 who emigrated. In their place eventually came some 12,000 families of Serb colonists, totalling 60,000 people by the 1930s. They often struggled to survive economically and quickly became active in political campaigns against any revival of Albanian influence.[25]

On the northern grain-growing plains where the estates had been large, consolidated farms operating close to European standards before the war, colonization by landless peasants from food-poor areas to the south should not have been expected to work well. And in the Vojvodina, the one such territory where there was significant colonization, it did not.[26]

Hungarian land was distributed to 12,000 families invited to colonize and to another 5,000 uninvited. Poor yields and the lack of assistance from Radical regimes that they initially supported drove many of these colonists into political opposition by the 1930s. Meanwhile, tens of thousands of landless peasants still struggled to survive in the Vojvodina, three-quarters of them Hungarian.

The economic balance sheet for the reform, all the same, was surprisingly good by the end of the 1920s.[27] The Skupština had belatedly given the peasants clear title to their new land, and hence the right to mortgage it to buy badly needed equipment. Even before then, the small-holdings that replaced large estates in Croatia and Slavonia do not seem inefficient if judged by the record of crop yields for the major grains. By 1931 holdings under 5 hectares (12.5 acres) in Croatia-Slavonia covered precisely 75 percent of agricultural land versus 62 percent for Serbia. And precisely in Croatia-Slavonia, yields dipped slightly below the 1909–13 average during 1921–23 and then significantly increased by 1928–30. There, and even more in Slovenia, a network of agricultural cooperatives helped make up for the lack of mortgage credit or the absence of the national Agricultural Bank that was finally established in 1929. Cooperative savings deposits and imports of modern agricultural machinery rose, supported by a labor supply less depleted by wartime losses than Serbia's and by proximity to the Austrian and Czech markets. Serbia saved its prewar market for prune export, but otherwise found the Vojvodina a difficult competitor even in its domestic market.

Industry, finance, and economic policy

Serbia, and Belgrade in particular, also lost ground in industrialization relative to Croatia. Zagreb got off to a fast start (see chapter 4) because of the demand and capital flowing from Austria and Hungary in the immediate postwar period. It now became the largest single industrial and import center in the new state. By 1923 the city accounted for 6 percent of total industrial employment and 45 percent in Croatia. Zagreb's advantage over Belgrade in industrial horsepower was particularly striking, 22.5 versus 5.4 percent of the country's total. Such industrial growth, primarily in timber and metal processing, helped relieve the loss of employment and income when Zagreb ceased to be the center of provincial government. Sarajevo and Skopje suffered this same loss after the war, but did not get the industrial growth to compensate for it. New competition from Croatian manufactures also trimmed the artisan sectors of both cities.[28]

The capital and entrepreneurship for this Croatian advance was largely

Table 5.3. *Occupational structure, 1921 and 1931*

	1921		1931		Growth
	(in thousands)	(%)	(in thousands)	(%)	in %
Agriculture, livestock, and fishing	4,840	81.1	5,099	76.3	−4.8
Industry and crafts	509	8.5	717	10.7	2.2
Trade, credit, and transport	190	3.2	272	4.1	0.9
Public services, army, and free professions	228	3.8	306	4.6	0.8
Other	202	3.4	289	4.3	0.9
Total	5,969	100	6,683	100	

Sources: *Enciklopedia Jugoslavije*, v, III (Zagreb: Jugoslavenski leksikogravfski zavod, 1983), 349.

homegrown, but several thousand Czech and Austrian businessmen also arrived in place of the Hungarian officials who departed. They provided valuable business experience, particularly in the complexities of postwar foreign trade. The Zagreb općina did not wait for the parliament in Belgrade to pass a law for industrial encouragement (which did not happen until 1934) and granted its own set of exemptions from import duties and taxes for industrial inputs. But the major source of support for Croatian industry were Zagreb's large commercial banks. After the initial postwar boom, they continued to attract foreign capital (some 40 percent of their assets were Austrian and 20 percent Hungarian). They channelled it and their own deposits into long-term credits or investment in industrial enterprises. The Prva Hrvastka Štedionica, for instance, made more long-term loans to industry than the National Bank in Belgrade, which was set up for commercial lending as well as being a central bank. The principal Belgrade banks abandoned their prewar entrepreneurial ways and concentrated on short-term bills of exchange supported by discounting from the National Bank. As a result, the large Zagreb banks now held larger assets than their Belgrade counterparts, reversing their prewar position and by 1928 accounted for fully one-half of bank assets in Yugoslavia.[29]

We should not make too much of Yugoslav industrial growth during the 1920s. Table 5.3 reveals an occupational structure still missing the significant shift of labor from agriculture to industry necessary for growth to become development. The Radical regime's economic policy concentrated on tariff protection for domestic manufactures and currency stabilization to attract foreign loans of the sort so generously accorded to the independent Balkan states before the war. Neither effort was very successful. The 1927 tariff set modest rates by interwar East European standards. As elsewhere, they boosted textile production, but left flour and other agricultural processing operating well short of capacity. The German-trained and British-connected finance minister, Milan Stojadinović, imposed a rigorous one-third reduction in real per capita note issue on the National Bank from 1924 to 1926 in order to stabilize the dinar, probably overvalued at 125 to the dollar. He claimed that this cut plus new land taxes would reduce the state's budget deficit and the burden of prewar debt, thus opening the way to new loans that the overvalued dinar would help to attract. Few new loans came, as we shall see, and the deflationary impact of the stabilization cut commercial credit and tax revenue, particularly from agriculture during the bad harvest and price slump of 1926.[30]

State budget expenditures nonetheless continued to climb for 1926–30 to twice Serbia's real per capita level of 1911. Their distribution did little for the economy, however. The rail network, for instance, badly needed new construction to link east with west and Bosnia with the Adriatic coast. By 1930 fewer than 500 miles had been added to the 6,000 miles of track that existed before the war; half of these new lines were in Serbia and the Vojvodina, and barely 10 percent in Bosnia-Hercegovina.

Hostile neighbors and distant allies

Foreign trade grew enough during the 1920s to become the most positive feature in parliamentary Yugoslavia's relations with the seven neighboring states. The new kingdom recorded the highest rise in real per capita exports of any Balkan economy during the decade. Their value for 1921–25 climbed to 129 and to 161 for 1926–30, if Serbia's 1906–10 figure is taken as 100. Their variety of exported goods was also the greatest, as the value of cereal grains predominant elsewhere fell to just 17 percent. More to the present point, Italy was the new state's largest market, absorbing just over one-quarter of Yugoslav exports for 1921–30. A large export surplus with Italy and a small one with South-eastern Europe and Turkey trimmed down what would otherwise have been a huge trade deficit because of unfavorable balances with the rest of Europe. Austria and Hungary along with Czechoslovakia and Poland accounted for 45 percent of import value, versus 25 percent for Germany and Northwestern Europe.[31]

Parliamentary Yugoslavia did not enjoy correspondingly good political relations with any of its neighbors by the late 1920s, despite initial improvement during the period 1922–26. Italy posed the most persistent

and threatening problems. Border or minority disputes with other neighbors further aggravated relations with Italy, particularly after Mussolini's
Fascist regime brought Albania into a close, dependent relationship.
Neither France nor Britain, although allies in the recent war, were
willing to commit their full weight to the Yugoslav side for fear of
disrupting their own relations with Italy or losing leverage in prolonged
negotiations over Serbia's wartime and prewar debts. Germany played
a benign but distant role. So did the United States, despite the
promise of the 1923 Blair loan that was to have raised $100 million
for rail construction from Zagreb and other inland locations to the
Adriatic.

The regional diplomacy of Britain and France during the 1920s
concentrated on preventing the reemergence of the Habsburg monarchy.
Hanging over American, British, and French relations with the new
state was the same problem that bedeviled the other winners in the First
World War: how to repay wartime loans from larger, Western allies
whose postwar capital markets were ill-disposed or unable to resume
lending prewar amounts on prewar terms? The American Blair loan was
a case in point. Until Serbia's wartime obligation could be negotiated
down to $62 million and officially settled in 1926, the New York capital
market held back a second Blair installment of $45 million (the first
amounted to only $15 million). Agreement on Britain's wartime lending
was finally reached in 1927 and on France's sizeable prewar loans the
following year. In the meantime, the new state had been forced to
stabilize its currency without benefit of a League of Nations loan. A few
small private loans added only 3 percent to the real value of Serbia's
prewar debt by the end of the decade.[32]

The regional diplomacy of Britain and France during the 1920s
concentrated on preventing the reemergence of the Habsburg monarchy.
For this reason, French policy came to support the Little Entente
between Yugoslavia, Czechoslovakia, and Romania. Still counting on a
close connection with Poland, the Quai d'Orsay had initially opposed
this set of bilateral alliances created by Czech initiative in 1920. Some
discussion of a Franco-Yugoslav military alliance with arms credits from
France surfaced in 1922, but came to nothing. By 1924 the Pašić
government concluded that the Entente agreement had only tied
Yugoslavia to French or Czech priorities with no immediate prospect for
the explicit treaty with France expected as a reward. When that treaty
finally materialized late in 1927, it yielded only a vague military protocol,
modest deliveries of obsolete arms, and condemnation from London as
a "retrograde step."[33]

By the mid-1920s, Belgrade's relations with Austria and Hungary
improved despite disputes over reparations and minority rights. The
Slovene-backed claim to two zones in Austrian Carinthia had foundered

by 1921 (see chapter 4). In violation of the League's agreement on minority rights that Yugoslavia finally signed in 1922, Austrian officials and teachers in Slovenia were dismissed, as were their Slovenian counterparts in Carinthia. The SLS leader, Monsignor Korošec, attempted to pursue the issue with the Austrian prime minister, Ignaz Seipel, in 1927, but Pašić's foreign minister, Momčilo Ninčić, had already turned away from the Slovenian case. Ninčić also moved to establish correct, formal relations with Admiral Horthy's Hungary, once Yugoslav army troops were withdrawn from the Pécs region by 1921. By 1926 it appeared that the two states were ready to sign an agreement ending the long dispute over Hungarian reparations with the promise of some coal deliveries.

The friendless Hungarian government accepted this improvement despite the lack of political representation for more than 400,000 Hungarians in the Vojvodina. As already noted, Hungarians had been denied the right to participate in the postwar land reform and the right to vote in the 1920 elections for the constituent assembly. The local Serb plurality of more than one-half million plus the 70,000 Croats or one-time Catholic Serbs, called *bunjevci*, collaborated with the Belgrade ministries to control local government in the three provinces and their counties until the local elections of 1927 offered some Hungarian representation. That year's parliamentary elections also saw the first Hungarian representatives actually seated.[34]

Until 1927 the new state's relations with Bulgaria were not as bad as might have been expected nor relations with Greece as good. The cloud of Bulgaria's irredentist claim to Macedonia, frustrated by Serbia in the First Balkan War of 1912 and again in the postwar settlement, hung low over Yugoslav–Bulgarian relations throughout the interwar period. The 220,000 refugees from Macedonia and Thrace that streamed into Bulgaria in 1918 provided manpower for both the autonomist and supremist factions of the VMRO. As we have already seen, however, internecine warfare would cut into each side's strength. The Agrarian prime minister, Aleksandar Stamboliiski, had agreed to reduce border raids and accept Yugoslav sovereignty over "South Serbia," culminating in the joint Treaty of Niš signed in 1923. The prominent VMRO role in assassinating him shortly thereafter, precisely because of that signature, has typically been seen as ending these improved relations on the spot.[35] In fact they persisted through 1926. The Pašić regimes valued them as a way of preventing any Bulgarian alliance with Italy. There was also a brief effort in December 1924 to win visiting Bulgarian Prime Minister Aleksandar Tsankov over to a new anti-Bolshevik front. The Pašić–Pribićević regime was already touting the Bolshevik threat as a justification to Britain and France for keeping Radić's Peasant Party banned. Of greater importance to the persisting truce in relations with Bulgaria was the prolonged dispute with Greece over access to the port of Salonika.

The new Yugoslav state renewed the Serbian demand of the First World War for control of the old Oriental Railway line from its southern border to Salonika and for a free port there. By 1923 a Belgrade syndicate had purchased the requisite rights to that line from the remains of the original French company. Greek authorities refused to man the railway with anyone but Greek employees and stalled over granting the Yugoslav side a free port. They even resisted a request to stop calling the Slav Macedonian population of Greek Macedonia "Bulgarians." By 1924 the Belgrade government threatened to renounce the 1913 treaty of alliance with Greece. A compromise agreement in 1926 apparently resolved the dispute, but it quickly reemerged when the Greek government of General Pangalos that had negotiated it was overthrown. On the Greek side, final resolution had to await Eleutherios Venizelos' return to power in 1927; French diplomats thereupon pressed King Aleksandar to sign an agreement with Greece in return for resolution of Serbia's considerable prewar debt to France.[36]

The troubled Yugoslav relationship with Albania moved in tandem with Italian involvement in the small state. Albania was surrounded by the new kingdom and Greece, but lay less than 50 nautical miles from the Italian mainland. Secret agreements at the Paris Peace Conference in 1919 had promised all three neighbors some Albanian territory, and all three had troops on that territory. But once local Albanians expelled Italian troops in June 1920, subsequent Italian governments abandoned their readiness to share influence there. The Pašić government also continued its policy of intervention. In 1921 a group of Albanian Catholics in the northwestern Midrits area attempted to set up a border republic with Yugoslav backing, but Muslim Albanians with Italian support quickly put it down.

Internationally recognized by the end of 1921, the Albanian government found the Pašić regime still unwilling to recognize its border roughly as the Great Powers had fixed it in 1913. Tirana also contributed to the ongoing dispute with the Yugoslav state by supporting a Committee for the National Liberation of Kosovo that Albanian refugees from the province founded in 1918. Several of its members became ministers in the Albanian governments of the next few years. Belgrade held them accountable for the continuing violence by *kachak* bands raiding across the border into Kosovo. This set the stage for the decision of the Pašić regime to back the Committee of Kosovo's staunchest foe, the warlord interior minister, Ahmed Zogu, from 1923 forward. When his opponent in the 1923 parliamentary elections, Fan Noli, took power early the next year with support from peasants demanding land reform, Zogu fled across the border. By year's end, however, he returned with Albanian conscripts from the Yugoslav army and White Russian mercenaries to overthrow the Noli government. His agents set about liquidating the leaders of the Committee of Kosovo, and the kachak raids into Kosovo ended shortly thereafter.[37] In 1926 the last Pašić government signed an agreement with Zogu, finally recognizing the 1913 border. All might have been well between the two states if the Italian government had now kept its distance.

The year 1926 nonetheless marked the end of the truce in the Yugoslav–Italian antagonism that surprisingly had begun with Mussolini's rise to power. Not long after a 1922 speech in which he appeared to respond to pleas for *Dalmazia italiana,* he silenced the Fascists of Fiume (Rijeka) and accepted the conventions of the 1920 Treaty of Rapallo with Yugoslavia. In 1923 he initiated direct negotiations with the Pašić regime to trade Italian annexation of Fiume for the incorporation of the rest of the Free State's territory into Yugoslavia. These negotiations proceeded successfully through the summer's crisis with Greece over Italian bombardment and invasion of Corfu. The Rome treaty of January 1924 not only settled the Fiume issue but included a five-year friendship agreement. When Stjepan Radić objected to any agreement without some softening of the Italianization under way against Croats in Istria, Mussolini replied simply, "I stick to the Serbs," meaning the Belgrade government.[38]

By 1926, however, he had changed his mind about both the Serbs and his conciliatory policy toward Yugoslavia. That year, the last Pašić regime failed again to secure parliamentary ratification of the complex commercial agreement with Italy called the Nettuno Conventions. Generally favorable to Italian interests, they had been signed in July 1925, just as Radić and his Croatian representatives joined the government. Radić took the lead in organizing Croatian and Slovenian resistance into a campaign against Italy. Foreign Minister Ninčić failed to overcome their opposition after Mussolini rejected a tripartite alliance with France and Yugoslavia in February 1926. In addition, the Italian dictator proclaimed 1926 his *anno napoleonico.* Ahmed Zogu met the revived taste for Italian expansionism more than half way. As early as 1925, he confounded his Belgrade backers by sounding out chances for the superior diplomatic and financial support that Italy could provide. Here was an offer that Mussolini could no longer refuse. The comprehensive Italian–Albanian Treaty of Tirana in November 1926 prompted

Ninčić to resign in protest. The next year would be the most dangerous one of the decade for Yugoslav–Italian relations.

Fatal intersections, 1927–1928

The rapid deterioration of the first Yugoslavia's relations with Italy and other neighbors in 1927 fed internal tensions and divisions. Together they created the parliamentary confrontation and violence of 1928 that persuaded King Aleksandar to suspend the Skupština and the Vidovdan constitution on January 6, 1929. Neither the much delayed alliance with France nor the economic upturn following the dinar's stabilization came in time to head off these fatal intersections. The largely rural electorate that went to the polls in the last parliamentary election in September 1927 was still suffering from the austere domestic policies and the bad harvests of the previous year. Serbia's Radical Party and the Croatian Peasant Party both lost votes. While the Zagreb élite worried about economic competition from Italy, their Belgrade counterparts were more concerned about the political threat of a hostile Italy gathering all of the new state's neighbors into an alliance against it. Ethnic groups voted for ethnic parties in 1927 parliamentary elections as much as they had in the first one in 1923 (see table 5.4). The Democrats' early promise to become a Yugoslav Party that would represent at least Croats and Slovenes as well as Serbs remained unfulfilled.

Radić and Pribićević

It fell to the country's two most contentious politicians to try to navigate through these rough constitutional waters. The increasingly divided Radical Party gave way to an opposition that brought together the last and most unlikely combination among the three preeminent politicians of the decade, Stjepan Radić and Svetozar Pribićević. After the king's refusal to let Nikola Pašić form new cabinets in April and December 1926, the Radicals' inconspicuous minister of public works, Nikola Uzunović, headed a succession of six weak governments. Already excluded from the second of these cabinets, Radić left three of his colleagues in their positions until December. With their withdrawal, the Croatian Peasant Party ended its brief participation in the Belgrade government. During his stay in the city, however, the voluble, cosmopolitan Radić developed the best personal relations with Aleksandar of any party leader, markedly better than those of the taciturn Pašić.

The September elections did not produce a mandate for any of these increasingly divided parties. Mainly because of a decline in Croatia, overall voter participation fell to 69 percent of eligible voters, down from 77 percent in 1925. The post-Pašić Radicals split into three factions, leading to separate lists of candidates in Serbia and part of Bosnia and cutting their representation from 143 to 112 seats. The Democrats stepped into the breach, boosting their representation from 37 to 61, but were themselves now divided. Radić's HSS Party lost 6 of its previous 67 seats, as support fell off in Zagreb and other towns. Pribićević's SDS barely held its ground with the same 22 seats. In Montenegro its federalist allies lost 2 of the 3 seats they held, one to the strident Serbian nationalist, Puniša Račić. The results were too inconclusive even to provide the basis for rearranging the interim cabinet that had adjourned to await the outcome of the elections. Radić and Pribićević, until then the bitterest of personal adversaries, stepped into the breach and agreed in October to form an opposition coalition of their two parties, calling it a Democratic Bloc.

The new coalition succeeded only in forcing a weak minority government to resign in February 1928, with calls for a "concentration cabinet," representing all major parties, to take its place. Aleksandar exerted his rising influence to defy the fading Radical establishment and to ask Radić himself to form this government. Despite his recent assertion that he now considered Serbs and Croats, at least in Croatia, to be one people, Radić was unable to persuade any of the Radical factions to join. Both he and Pribićević then proposed a non-party government headed by an army general. King Aleksandar declined, reluctantly turning back a cabinet that included Slovenian SLS leader Monsignor Korošec as well as the JMO's Spaho.

Death and dissolution

Radić made his ill-fated return to the Skupština in June 1928. What followed is often portrayed as proof of how the Serb–Croat antagonism made a parliamentary government under majority rule with a loyal opposition impossible. Such a conclusion overlooks not only the personal inability of Stjepan Radić or Svetozar Pribićević to be any majority's loyal opposition, but also the absence of a working majority even for the Radical Party. It also overlooks the issue that triggered the violent and fatal debate in the Skupština on June 19–20.

That issue was the persistent Radical and royal effort to secure ratification of the Nettuno Conventions with Italy. When the Vukićević government raised this issue again in May, the Radić–Pribićević opposition spoke out sharply, denouncing the whole regime as corrupt and unsupportable. Demonstrations erupted in several Dalmatian towns

Table 5.4. *Ethnic voting by party, 1923 and 1927*

	1923 election				
	Serbs	Croats	Slovenes	Others[a]	Total
Radicals	103			5	108
Croatian Republican Peasant Party (HRSS)		68		1	69
Democrats	33				33
Yugoslavs (Slovenian People's Party (SLS) and Bunjevci		1	21	2	24
Yugoslav Muslim Organization (JMO)		17		1	18
Independent Democrats (SDS)	10	4	1		15
Džemijet (Albanians)	2			12	14
Germans				8	8
Undeclared	7	3			10
Total	155	93	22	29	299

	1927 election				
	Serbs	Croats	Slovenes	Others[b]	Total
Radicals	102	2		8	112
Croatian Peasant Party (HSS)	2	59			61
Democrats	56	2		3	61
Independent Democrats (SDS)	13	5	4		22
Slovenian People's Party (SLS)		1	20		21
Agrarian Union	9				9
Yugoslav Muslim Organization (JMO)	1	11		6	18
Germans				6	6
Small groups		2	1		3
Total	183	82	25	23	313

[a]Includes undeclared Germans, Albanians, Turks, and Romanians.
[b]Includes undeclared Germans, Hungarians, Albanians, and Turks.
Source: Branislav Gligorijević, *Parlament i političke stranke Jugoslavije, 1919–1929* (Belgrade: Narodna knjiga, 1979), 293–94.

and then in Belgrade. Without its passage, there was little chance of a much desired British loan. But Radić was adamant; he had already called for recognition of the USSR as a rebuff to the British in particular for "letting Mussolini into the Balkans." Meanwhile in Belgrade, the greater threat appeared to be Italian agreements with increasingly hostile regimes in Bulgaria, whose border incursions had resumed, and Hungary, where extreme Croatian nationalists were organizing. Italian diplomats were also promoting a new tripartite alliance with Greece and Turkey.

Domestic deadlock and foreign danger, as perceived differently by the several sides, thus created the general tension that surrounded the return of Radić and his nephew Pavle to the Skupština in June. The exchange of epithets even in formal sessions now passed all bounds.[39] By June 19, Radić himself said that the rhetoric was creating "a psychological disposition to murder." Puniša Račić, the new Radical deputy from Montenegro, a Chetnik war veteran and militant Serbian nationalist with no political experience, promised that "heads will roll . . . until Stjepan Radić is killed there will be no peace." The next day, this same Račić called for a psychological examination of Radić and then stepped forward to fire a revolver at the assembled Croat leaders. He killed Radić's nephew Pavle and one other instantly and wounded three more people, only Radić himself seriously. The Croatian leader appeared to be recovering from his stomach wound after a hasty return to Zagreb, but he died unexpectedly on August 8. His last statements forsook further Croatian participation in the Belgrade parliament or allegiance to the Vidovdan constitution.

A new government of national consolidation was hastily formed by the Slovenian Korošec. It could not overcome the misplaced Croatian assumption that the Radical Party and army officers close to the king had arranged the attack in the Skupština. Eighty-seven representatives, all but four from the Croatian Peasant Party and the Independent Democrats, walked out of the parliament, and sixty-one Democrats soon threatened to follow. The rump parliament narrowly ratified the Nettuno Conventions, but this gesture failed to secure the anticipated British loan. Both the Croatian and Serbian sides charged the other with reviving Radical dissenter Stojan Protić's 1924 proposal simply to sever Croatia and Slovenia from the Serbian core. Pribićević demagogically claimed that he and the convalescing Radić had prevented such an amputation that July. He called the Vidovdan constitution a dead letter and threatened that Croatia and Bosnia would withhold further payments on the state's international debts. British diplomats asked Korošec whether it would help if Belgrade posted some Slovene and Croat officials to Southern Serbia, that is, Macedonia. It was too late for that, he replied. Even the king raised the prospect of *amputacija* briefly, if only to elicit a public rejection from Radić's successor, Vladko Maček. Maček then could counter with vague demands for a new federal structure that the Radicals refused to discuss. They also rejected Pribićević's proposal for elections to a new constituent assembly.

The first Yugoslavia's parliamentary government survived only until

December 1928. The first day of the month was the tenth anniversary of Aleksandar's proclamation of the new state. The king and Korošec agreed to downplay its celebration in Belgrade in favor of an October commemoration of the breakthrough on the Salonika Front. General Franchet d'Esperey, who commanded the offensive, was invited to emphasize the French connection. But on December 1, student protests in Zagreb turned into riots and a dozen students were killed when police broke them up. Minister Korošec replaced Zagreb's provincial prefect with a Belgrade army general without the Skupština's approval. Leading Democrats in his rump coalition threatened to resign. When Korošec resigned instead on December 30, the king decided to banish the unfortunate parliament from what now became the Kingdom of Yugoslavia.

6   Authoritarian kingdom, 1929–1941

In 1929 King Aleksandar redesignated the Kingdom of Serbs, Croats, and Slovenes as the Kingdom of Yugoslavia. The name's official debut did not augur well for democratic government: the king had just abolished the 1921 constitution and disbanded an elected parliament. Ahead lay the full weight of the Great Depression and the rise of Nazi Germany. As British Ambassador Neville Henderson commented in 1933, "it is easier to say Yugoslavia than to make it." The country would remain a "crossword puzzle" to him until his posting to Berlin a few years later. The political puzzle is better understood if divided into three periods, 1929–34, 1935–38, and 1939–41.

The authoritarian framework by which Aleksandar intended to hold Yugoslavia together and make it into a nation-state has been dubbed a royal dictatorship. It surely started that way. Yet the king, and his army generals, could not retain the hallmarks of dictatorship – direct powers to make all political decisions and to suppress all opposition – even for the five years left of his life. After Aleksandar's assassination in 1934, the most skillful Serbian politician of the decade, Milan Stojadinović, needed a coalition government to retain power from 1935 to 1938. He also failed to come to terms with his most powerful Croatian opponent, Vladko Maček.

By early 1939, the dilemmas of assuring equal rights to a Croatian minority in Yugoslavia and, at the same time, to a Serb minority in Croatia remained unresolved, while the issue was not even raised for Bosnian Muslims. A compromise agreement, the *Sporazum* of August 1939, addressed the first dilemma at the expense of the second. The others were simply ignored, as this confederal arrangement for Croatia still left the rest of the country under central administration from Belgrade. Hitler's war began barely a week later. The resulting uncertainties worked against the broader compromise needed from both sides. Then in 1941, the Second World War spilled over into the Kingdom of Yugoslavia and split it apart.

To see these three periods as a whole, we need to square Aleksandar's authoritarian framework with the political parties that formally or informally supported or contested it during the dozen years between 1929 and 1941. We must also go beyond the domestic politics emphasized in chapter 5, where a real if flawed parliament grappled on center stage with executive power, Radical and royal. By the 1930s, Yugoslavia found itself trapped in the wings of a wider international stage, first economically and then diplomatically. Like several East European neighbors, its government turned to Hitler's Germany to help find a way out of economic dilemmas after 1935. Only after 1939 did that diplomatic gamble become a dead end from which there could be no honorable escape save war.

Domestic economic policies now became more important. One set deepened the impact of the Depression, and the next contributed to a greater recovery than is generally recognized. Both sets of policies relied on state power, extending the reach of the central government in Belgrade to the detriment of Serbian relations with the other ethnic groups. Further regional or social imbalances also encouraged ethnic resentments.

Looking across the entire interwar period, however, we should take note of assets as well as liabilities, among them the intellectual survival of the Yugoslav idea and some progress toward a common culture and modern economy. A balance sheet for 1921–39 therefore precedes the chapter's final section on the reconfigured Yugoslavia of 1939–41.

Royal dictatorship, 1929–1934

Aleksandar announced his decision to dismiss the elected Skupština and ban all ethnically based political parties or organizations on January 6, 1929, the eve of the Orthodox Christmas. The date had symbolic weight for the Serbs and forced all political actors to wait until the three-day holiday had passed to react. The king's proclamation spoke of state duties and the need to pursue "new paths toward Yugoslavism," but it was his condemnation of the parliament and the parties that persuaded a clear majority of public opinion. Western criticism was muted because, as a British Embassy report noted, a united Yugoslavia best served international interests.

Even Vladko Maček, Radić's successor as head of the Croatian Peasant Party (HSS) welcomed the dissolution for throwing off that "badly buttoned vest," the Vidovdan constitution. He and the other leading Croatian politician, the now venerable Ante Trumbić, had sounded out the Czech and French capitals in late 1928 on the prospects for recognition of a separate Croatian state or status. They got no response. The Croatian Serb leader, Svetozar Pribićević, told the king at the same time that he could accept royal intervention, but not royal arbitration between Serbia's parties and his coalition with the Croatian Peasant Party.[1]

The initial decree assigned dictatorial powers to the monarch. In the absence of a parliament, his directives received the force of law. All remotely political organizations were disbanded and their property and records confiscated. Only the Masons and a couple of veterans' organizations escaped. The Masons also would not have been spared, so the joke ran in Belgrade, had the city not hosted their World Congress in 1926. Nearly one-third of the country's newspapers and journals were closed down on grounds of party affiliation, and the others were placed under censorship supported by a new press law. Most ominously, the king appointed his closest military advisor and wartime White Hand leader, General Petar Živković, as prime minister. The only non-Serb of regional standing in his cabinet was the Slovenian People's Party (SLS) leader and head of the last brief parliamentary regime, Monsignor Anton Korošec.

A flurry of constructive and centralizing reforms during the new regime's first year won it initial approval, at least outside of Croatia. Joseph Rothschild's generally critical survey of interwar Yugoslavia lauds the "show of political energy" and cites the "general relief" that followed the overdue reforms.[2] The reforms merged four ministries with larger ones, while reducing corrupt overpricing and delays in government contracting. They combined six different legal codes from the pre-1914 period, criminal and civil, and finally unified the tax structure. Political prisoners from the parliamentary period were granted amnesty, Communists excepted, while some thirty-six generals and fifty diplomats from the top-heavy state bureaucracy were retired. All of this plus a controversial effort to create a single system of public education with common textbooks took effect on October 3, 1929, the same day that the country officially became the Kingdom of Yugoslavia.

Alexsandar's "new path" is most remembered for another feature which aroused instant controversy. His proclamation on October 3 eliminated the thirty-three provinces of the Vidovdan regime, but put in their place nine regional units (*banovine*). The reduced number recalled Stojan Protić's plan for what might be called "unifying decentralization." Indeed, the promotion of Yugoslav unity was the overriding goal of the new arrangement. River valleys furnished the focal points for the new regions, partly to promote economic integration, and the rivers a number of their names. Although the designation of these new divisions as banovine was a bow to Croatia's historical sensibilities, the internal

6.1 King Aleksandar of Yugoslavia on the eve of his assassination in 1934

borders that they created were not historical in the main. Only Drava and Zeta banovine largely corresponded to historical Slovenia and Montenegro (see map 6.1), the latter also enlarged at the expense of Hercegovina and the Sandžak of Novi Pazar. The Sava banovina, centered on Croatia, gave up Dalmatia to the new Primorje, the Srem to Dunav, and some of the Military Border area to Vrbas, where there was a Serb majority in Lika and around the capital of Banja Luka. Vrbas was one of four banovine dividing Bosnia-Hercegovina so that none had a Muslim majority. Serbia was also split into four, but along favorable lines that assured Serb majorities for Macedonia (Vardar), the Vojvodina (Dunav), and eastern Bosnia (Drina), as well as one centered on "narrow Serbia" (Morava). Beyond these nine, a separate prefecture was provided for Belgrade as the capital city, now 289,000 people, including its environs. The nine varied in population from about 900,000 in Primorje and Zeta to three times that number in Sava, which not coincidentally encompassed Zagreb-centered Croatia.

Problems of authoritarian politics

King Aleksandar intended to provide the personal center for the new regime. His ideas and intentions cry out for a scholarly biography.[3] In his own words, he chose "Yugoslavism over federalism," but what those ambiguous terms meant to him is unclear. If he was not autocratically minded, it would also be hard to demonstrate that he was democratically minded. The parliament of the 1920s appeared to him as a privilege whose terms he was entitled to define rather than as a right to be maintained under any circumstances. And until he could trust the country's political leaders to share his commitment to a single Yugoslav state, regardless of how ill-defined the idea, he was not likely to restore an unrestrained parliamentary system. Certainly his Serbian prime minister, General Živković, did not wish to do so. Even British Embassy reporting, which tended to give Aleksandar the benefit of the doubt, noted that the king's lonely upbringing had inhibited his capacity to trust a wider circle of advisors and encouraged him to rely excessively on a few poorly chosen intimates.[4] His political impatience and personal insecurity – a revolver was always within reach when he went out of doors – were qualities often associated with dictators, but his lack of self-confidence and of a clear ideology were not. Nor was Aleksandar's sense of royal obligation to a traditional European order that makes the old Communist epithet of "monarcho-fascist" for his regime a contradiction in terms. All this furnishes some psychological background for a retreat from the royal dictatorship that he began in 1931.

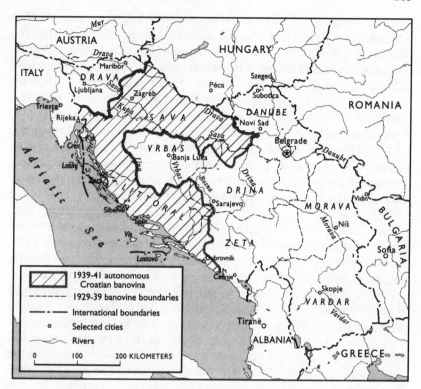

Map 6.1 Territorial division of the Kingdom of Yugoslavia, 1929–1939

During the previous year, a series of long-standing religious problems had fueled regional discontent. Bosnian Muslims protested the 1929 laws that abolished their religious community's hard-won Autonomous Statute of 1909 in favor of a single Islamic community for the country. They were now denied the right to elect their own administrative bodies and found themselves lumped together with the Macedonian Turks and Kosovar Albanians, neither of whom had a historical or ethnic connection with these Bosnian Slavs. Many Slovenes were already smarting from the December 1929 decision to abolish their *Sokol* sport clubs as political organizations. Then General Živković demanded that Monsignor Korošec make local speeches supporting the regime just as a cabinet colleague proposed to close all church schools. Korošec promptly resigned in September 1930. Yet in 1931, the Serbian Orthodox church was allowed to promulgate a fulsome new constitution for itself that finally unified its six regional bodies under a single set of regulations and targeted a number of towns in Croatia for new churches or schools. The Orthodox hierarchies of the six distinct jurisdictions – Serbia, the Karlovac patriarchate for Croatia and the Vojvodina, Bosnia-Hercegovina, Montenegro, Macedonia, and Dalmatia – had accepted a commitment to unify in 1920 as a revived patriarchate of Peć (see chapter 1), with royal approval and the Metropolitan of Belgrade, Dimitrije, as their new patriarch. But each jurisdiction continued to operate according to its own set of customs and regulations through the 1920s. This only added to the insecurity that Orthodox churchmen felt in a new state where their nominal membership was only 48 percent (versus 37 percent for the Croatian and Slovenian Catholic churches) and where lay participation had declined since the war.[5]

The most serious opposition to the royal dictatorship came from Croatia, but not from its Catholic clergy. Both Pribićević and Maček had become fully disillusioned with the new regime before the end of 1929. The outspoken Pribićević was peremptorily jailed under the new Law for the Protection of the State. He sat in prison until permanently exiled in 1931. A State Court created to enforce the expanded law promptly dragged the leader of the disbanded Peasant Party, Maček, into the dock with twenty-four Croats accused of bomb attacks in Zagreb the previous December. Maček's subsequent acquittal made a smaller impression across Croatia than the spectacle of his initial imprisonment or the revelations that other Croats had been tortured to confess at the trial. The regime's appointment of four HSS members to a reshuffled Živković cabinet failed to reassure Croatian public opinion.

Diplomatic pressure from Paris, supported by the promise of a badly needed French loan, helped persuade Aleksandar to concede a new constitution in 1931. So did the cautionary tale of Spain's republican revolution. In any case, his regime seemed to have run out of creative energy. After introducing 163 new laws during its first year, most of them major, only the expanded judicial powers for state security could be called a major initiative in 1930.

Perhaps Aleksandar was also waiting for an "opportune moment for the diminution of his powers," as British Ambassador Henderson hopefully suggested. If so, the terms of the September 1931 constitution suggest no return to an independent parliament. Its famously restrictive electoral provisions stipulated two legislative houses. A restored Skupština of 306 (eventually 373) members was to be elected by open ballot from country-wide lists. Candidates needed 60 signatures from more than 300 of the electoral districts plus 200 signatures from their own districts to run. The list winning a plurality, presumably the government's, would then receive two-thirds of the seats. A senate of some ninety-six members was to be equally divided between royal appointees and nominees from banovina councils under indirect control. The king could in any case arbitrate between the two houses or exercise a preemptive veto. The new constitution promised to free judicial appointments from royal intervention, but only after five years had passed. Elections for municipal self-government were specifically denied to Belgrade, Zagreb, and Ljubljana.

Large numbers in non-Serb areas abstained from the November elections to the regime's restricted National Assembly. The regime claimed that 65 percent of all those eligible had voted, and 35 percent in Croatia, where the HSS was denied the right to run numerous candidates because of the 300-district requirement. British Embassy estimates cut 10 percent off both of the regime's figures. In any case, Serbs won 219 of the 306 seats, compared to 55 for Croats, 25 for Slovenes, 3 for Bosnian Muslims, 2 each for Macedonians and Montenegrins, and 1 each for Germans and Hungarians. This represented a still larger ethnic share for Serbs, 71 percent, than the 49 and 58 percent shares (see table 5.4) for the 1923 and 1927 elections. The assembly's majority passed no noteworthy legislation and made no appeal to an opposing minority that included representatives from the seven major parties from the previous decade, all still formally illegal.

In March 1932, Aleksandar decided to abandon the last Živković government. The king tried to persuade first Aca Stanojević, the aging head of the left-wing Serbian Radicals, and then Vladko Maček himself, to join a more broadly based cabinet. When they refused, he finally chose Milan Srškić. Aleksandar's poorest choice for prime minister stayed in office until January 1934, distinguished only by the series of grievances he aggravated. The Bosnian Muslims remembered Srškić as an adversarial interior minister and an architect of their division among four banates. "Bosnia-Hercegovina, both as a regional individuality and a geographic concept, must disappear forever," he openly declared. It was just those historic borders that the Yugoslav Muslim Organization had insisted on preserving and that even the Serbian Democrats advocated maintaining as a buffer zone between Serbia and Croatia.[6] Minor adjustments in banate borders accompanied the new constitution, but did not mollify the Croatian Peasant Party. The promise of autonomous administrations for the banates also remained unfulfilled. The HSS therefore joined the Independent (Serb) Democrats, Trumbić's Federalists, and even several separatist leaders in drafting the twelve so-called Zagreb points, or *punktacije*, of November 1932. They demanded cultural autonomy and a renegotiated constitution. A similar Slovenian list from Korošec's SLS and others followed in December, partly as a reaction against one local call to abandon the Slovenian language for Serbo-Croatian.[7]

The two punktacije elicited two responses from the royal regime. First, it conceded a looser electoral law, requiring only thirty signatures from half of the electoral districts across just six of the nine banates in order to stand for assembly election. The winning list would then receive only three-fifths of the total seats. But no new elections were held. Secondly, the regime invoked the Law for the Protection of the State and ordered the arrest not only of Maček but of Trumbić, Korošec, and the three Muslim leaders in early 1933.

Failures of liberal economic formulas

The burden that the Great Depression placed on a large agricultural, partly integrated economy added to the grievances that Aleksandar sought to suppress. The precipitous drop in international agricultural prices and the drying up of Western capital markets hit all the small economies of Eastern Europe hard. Yugoslavia's case differed significantly in two respects. First, the impact of collapsing prices was slower to strike Yugoslavia's agricultural exports, which were more varied than the rest of Southeastern Europe's. The primary blow on total export value and prices landed in 1932, the year of the two punktacije and other protests. The collapse followed a long winter, poor fodder crop harvests, and higher taxes on sugar and electricity for revenue to offset a yawning budget deficit. By 1934 the price of an export ton fetched 40 percent less than in 1922–30, and total export value was down by 58 percent.[8] Secondly, the regime implemented liberal Western prescriptions to deal financially with the Depression through Belgrade-based institutions. These prescriptions made the impact of Depression appear to hit some regions harder or more unfairly than others. Emanating from the Belgrade ministries or the central bank, they fed the political opposition's complaints about Serbian centralism.

The liberal antidotes were intended to attract the first French loan of the interwar period. These funds would help the dinar make a stable transition to the gold standard and, as a result, provide further access to international credit that should have come with convertibility. The timing could not have been less fortunate. The largely French loan of 1 million francs (about $45 million) materialized in June 1931, in the midst of the worst financial crisis in Central European history. In May the Creditanstalt of Vienna, the largest single lender to Southeastern Europe, failed. A number of German and Hungarian banks collapsed later that summer. The Creditanstalt's financial troubles prompted the

American initiative, known as the Hoover Moratorium, to end the German obligation to pay war reparations.[9] This decision cost Yugoslavia an expected annual payment of $16 million. Then in September, Britain went off the gold standard, making the prize of convertibility that Yugoslavia had coveted worth much less.

Policies copied from the Western canons of fiscal orthodoxy sought to keep the dinar on the gold standard nonetheless. The regime cut state budget expenses and currency issue more severely than any of its neighbors. Yugoslavia avoided import quotas if not the clearing agreements that accounted for over half of both exports and imports across Southeastern Europe by 1932. The central bank, now the Narodna Banka Kr. Jugoslavije, raised its discount rate in an effort to maintain the dinar at par value. None of this encouraged exports in a shrinking European market. Nor did exports respond when speculation against the dinar in 1932 finally forced the central bank to offer a premium for foreign exchange that essentially devalued the dinar by 22.5 percent. Export value plummeted to 60 percent of the previous year's total and barely 40 percent of the 1922–30 average.[10]

Regional disparity now raised its head. The regime had no way to compensate Croatian banks for their financial losses, but could offer some relief to Serbian peasants. Recall that 43 percent of commercial bank assets were concentrated in twenty-nine Zagreb banks by 1929. Because of the concentration there of Central European (primarily Austrian) assets, they lost more than their share of the 41 percent decline in commercial bank deposits by 1933. The collapse of the Creditanstalt alone cost the Zagreb banks nearly 10 percent of the one-quarter reduction suffered by all the commercial banks between 1930 and 1932. By far the largest number of such banks were small Serbian institutions that had survived the 1920s by lending to peasant farmers rather than investing in industry or other longer-term ventures as had the Croatian banks. Two state initiatives favored both banks and peasants in Serbia and the Vojvodina. Loans from the new State Agricultural Bank, finally launched in 1928, favored these areas partly for political reasons but also because they lacked the more developed cooperative networks of Croatia and especially Slovenia. These cooperative networks had given Yugoslavia the highest amount of cooperative assets and lowest peasant debt per capita in Southeastern Europe by 1930. As their loanable funds now fell with the moratorium on the repayment of peasant debt declared in 1933, the State Bank still had the resources to step into the gap for Serbia.

In addition the regime had established a grain purchasing agency, Prizad, in April 1930, to pay peasants higher prices for exportable grain by eliminating commercial middlemen as the cooperatives had already done. The agency extended its purchases to domestic grain sales the following year and intended them to help all peasants equally, including those in the grain-poor areas of Croatia and Bosnia who had paid exorbitant prices for shipments from the rest of the country. The scheme rapidly ran up losses that no government budget could have sustained in the Depression. Its discontinuation in 1932 seemed to Croat and Bosnian peasants especially to be more evidence of Belgrade's centralism consciously working against them. The rapid rise of the HSS's cooperative network, Gospodarska Sloga, from a few thousand members to one-third of all peasant households in Croatia by 1940 was in part a response to Prizad's failure.

Extremists and assassination

The economic crisis and political deadlock of 1932 not surprisingly spurred on several extremist movements. The royal dictatorship had already hardened its resolve against any compromise. Neither the Yugoslav Communist Party (KPJ) nor the Internal Macedonian Revolutionary Organization (VMRO) were able to take significant advantage of this domestic distress. Only Croatian separatist émigrés acted, seizing the chance to found the eventually infamous Ustaša as a propaganda and terrorist organization. Despite their small numbers, all three organizations deserve attention because of fateful international connections and the assassination of King Aleksandar in 1934.

Before proceeding, some care should be taken to exclude the Croatian Peasant Party and its leader, Vladko Maček, from the list of subversive separatists. In the wake of the Zagreb punktacije, he spent virtually all of 1933 and 1934 in prison. Neither this incarceration nor his previous sentences had the radicalizing effect it might have had on others. He remained more ready than Radić had been to talk with the Serbian political parties; indeed, he had futilely joined with the Democrats' leader, Ljuba Davidović, in trying to persuade the other Serbian parties to accept the punktacije. His narrow views and self-contained style made him a less flexible bargaining partner than Radić, and he was increasingly committed to the same goal of confederal autonomy for Croatia. Yet Maček also paid far more attention to organizing the Peasant Party to operate legally within Yugoslavia.[11]

Perhaps the smallest and least successful of the parties questioning the existence of the Kingdom of Yugoslavia was the Communist Party (KPJ). In 1929 it had immediately called for violent revolt against Aleksandar's dictatorial regime, but could only scatter some leaflets and provoke a couple of shoot-outs with local police. The call for violence came directly from the Comintern's 1928 congress, where the expectation of imminent war by the West against the Soviet Union made it essential to disable all potential adversaries. The congress also issued an instruction, much maligned by Serbian historians in the 1980s, to the various non-Serbs to advocate the breakup of Yugoslavia as a creature of the West's "Versailles system". Party members spent more time, however, struggling against the small Social Democratic Party or disputing the resistance to literary conformity from maverick leftists such as the leading Croatian writer, Miroslav Krleža, than promoting secession. In any case, their membership amounted to less than 500 in 1932.

It did not increase much under the new party secretary appointed that year to hold the KPJ closer to the Comintern line. Comintern youth leader Josip Čižinski, known as Milan Gorkić, fled his native Bosnia in 1923 to avoid arrest as a party member, as had his Czech father two years before. Even as party secretary, he continued to spend the majority of his time outside the country, leaving the small front party of Independent Workers and its trade union network to survive on their own. Čižinski promoted one of the younger leaders released from prison in 1934 to the Comintern network and sent him back into Yugoslavia to organize the clandestine party congress at Ljubljana the same year – a certain Josip Broz.[12] Delegates took immediate secession off the KPJ agenda, but affirmed their intention to establish separate Communist parties for Croatia, Slovenia, and Macedonia and to maintain ties to the secessionist parties as well.

One of these secessionist parties was the Macedonian VMRO. Beset with internal struggles, it was further weakened by new governments in Sofia, previously its source of greatest support. First, a coalition of Agrarians and others won the 1931 Bulgarian elections, replacing Andrei Liapchev's regime and its toleration of the VMRO enclave in the Pirin region, bordering Yugoslav Macedonia, as a law unto itself. Then in 1934, the Zveno, or Link group of military officers overthrew the government in an almost bloodless coup dedicated to restoring order through a non-party regime. Virtually its first act was to arrest the VMRO leaders and intern a number of followers.[13] Only support from Fascist Italy for a few hundred émigré members allowed it to continue.

The other major secessionist organization also had its headquarters in Italy and an equally modest membership. Yet its wider international connections, narrower goals, and less divided leadership had already set the *Ustaša-hrvatska revolucionarna organizacija* (Uprising-Croatian Revolutionary Organization) apart, long before Nazi Germany installed it as the ruler of wartime Croatia in 1941. And before it drafted a formal constitution in 1932, indeed from the day after the royal dictatorship was proclaimed in January 1929, the movement dedicated itself to the overthrow of Aleksandar's Yugoslavia.

The Ustaša's self-proclaimed leader was Ante Pavelić, a lawyer born in 1889 in Hercegovina. After the First World War, he had tried to revive the Frankist Party of Right, minus its now obsolete allegiance to the Habsburg monarchy. Pavelić succeeded in attracting a student following and winning election to both the provincial and national assemblies of 1927. That same year he defended a group of accused VMRO terrorists in Zagreb and met with Fascist officials in Rome to sound them out on support for Croatia's seceding. Zagreb's outrage at Radić's assassination in 1928 allowed him to attract some members to his new paramilitary organization, Hrvatski domobran. At the same time, fellow Ustaša founder and Josip Frank's son-in-law, Slavko Kvaternik, set up student clubs named after his grandfather, Eugen, who had been martyred in an 1871 uprising (see chapter 2).

Fleeing Zagreb for Vienna, Sofia, and then Milan in 1929, Pavelić quickly came to financial terms with Mussolini's Fascist regime. General Sarkotić, the notorious Croat commander of Bosnia in the First World War (see chapter 4), and his aging coterie were camped in Vienna, still hoping to restore the Habsburg Monarchy. They opened doors to the like-minded Hungarian regime under former Admiral Miklós Horthy. Hungary provided a training camp for the Ustaša at Janka Puszta, near the Slavonian border, that soon attracted a few hundred recruits. As in two similar Italian camps, those attracted were Croat emigrant workers, more often from Belgium than the Americas. The uniforms, symbols, and pseudo-military organization and hierarchy, to which they were bound by a blood oath and over which Pavelić held supreme authority as the heroic leader (*poglavnik*), all on the Italian model, make it difficult to resist the conclusion that this was a fascist movement from the start.[14] Its program was vaguely corporatist, but consisted mainly of (un-Italian) racist rhetoric blaming all of Croatia's misfortunes, including the failure to include all of Bosnia-Hercegovina within its borders, on Serbs or their partners.

The initial Ustaša foray into the Lika area of the former Military Border, home to leading lieutenant Mile Budak, did not produce the peasant uprising that was expected. Predominantly Serb gendarmes put down an attack on a village police station, but the expedition brought the local organizer from Gospić, Andrija Artuković, later the wartime interior minister, back to Italy.

Individual terrorism now seemed their only recourse and King Aleksandar their main target. His first visit to Zagreb since the royal dictatorship offered an obvious chance, but the lone assassin failed. The announcement of the king's visit to Marseilles on October 9, 1934, to meet with French Foreign Minister Louis Barthou, invited a second attempt. Barthou's intended French–Italian rapprochement threatened to include Hungary and close the camp at Janka Puszta just as Aleksandar's recent meeting with King Boris of Bulgaria (on the Orient Express during a stop in Yugoslavia) spelled the end of VMRO's Bulgarian base. The VMRO leader's chauffeur was recruited to attack the two statesmen. Lax security at dockside allowed him to fire over a dozen shots into Aleksandar and Barthou before he was seized and lynched.

Whether or not Aleksandar lived long enough to utter the portentous last words "preserve Yugoslavia," his death gave the kingdom a second wind and dealt his killers a serious setback. Although the French trial in Marseilles for his murder trod lightly on the Ustaša's Italian and Hungarian connections, the latter two governments took immediate action to repair their international images. The Hungarian camp was promptly closed and the Italian membership interned on the island of Lipari. Pavelić and the leaders were put under house arrest.

Over 200,000 mourners in Zagreb paid their respects to the king, who lay in state there for a day, prior to being brought back to flag-draped Serbia for his funeral. Monsignor Korošec, the Slovenian leader, was released from prison to attend. "We ought to work and live for Yugoslavia now," he said, "everything else is forgotten." By December Maček too was released.

Stojadinović and the royal regency, 1935–1938

Much of course was not forgotten from the rest of the 1930s down to the commonly held Serbian sentiment of the 1980s: if Aleksandar had lived, he could have avoided both internal division and war. At least until Hitler changed maps and rules in 1938, he might easily have done better than his successors. The new regents and a familiar cabinet fumbled away the first months of public support for a "new path" to honor the king's memory and then settled on the past and present finance minister, Milan Stojadinović. He tried to engineer a limited "small solution" to the Croatian problem and made real economic progress after the crisis hit bottom in 1934. But his gamble on the greater German market paid off only in the short term. After a promising start, he overestimated its political advantages and barely won in the elections of December 1938. He was forced to step down a few months later.

Stojadinović's ascent began in the weeks following Aleksandar's assassination. According to the king's secret will, his unloved cousin Paul was named as senior regent along with two others. He was to fulfill royal obligations until Aleksandar's son Petar reached his eighteenth birthday in September 1941. Paul's English education and connections persuaded him to push Stojadinović, who represented several British companies in Belgrade, into the new cabinet that General Živković, Srškić, and others from the old regime had cobbled together in December 1934. They hoped that the new prime minister, Bogoljub Jevtić, the former foreign minister and relatively young at forty-five, could win the convincing election victory that had eluded them in 1931. They were soon disappointed.

Disputed results marred the May 1935 election. Open balloting gave the Jevtić list a revised 60.6 percent and Maček's Opposition Bloc, 37.4 percent. With support from Croatian Serbs and Bosnian Muslims, the Maček list won eight of every thirteen votes in Croatia and the western districts of Bosnia-Hercegovina. Although winning 303 of 370 seats in the new Skupština, Jevtić still sought to discredit the opposition. When his minions accused Maček of complicity in the king's assassination, that was too clumsy even for General Živković. He and four other ministers, including Finance Minister Stojadinović, resigned in June 1935. Živković expected to be named prime minister, but Prince Paul, encouraged by British Ambassador Henderson, picked Stojadinović instead.[15]

From Yugoslav Radical Union (JRZ) to Concordat

To some, the long-time Radical Stojadinović embodied the prewar political approach of Nikola Pašić. He began his tenure with initiatives to broaden domestic support but came to rely on playing politics (unlike Pašić through economics) with the Great Powers. He relaxed newspaper censorship and restrictions on public assembly and granted amnesty to over one thousand political prisoners plus those arrested during the recent elections. Although General Živković stayed in the cabinet, Stojadinović brought in the Bosnian Muslim and Slovenian leaders, Mehmed Spaho and Anton Korošec, as well. Spaho was rewarded the next year with restoration of the 1909 autonomy statute for the Bosnian Muslims that had been revoked in 1931. To conciliate the Croats, the regime signed a Concordat with the Vatican in 1935 promising authorization for church schools and freedom for the organization, Catholic Action, to operate legally like its Orthodox counterpart, if only the Skupština would ratify it.

Most important, in August, Stojadinović proclaimed the creation of a new government party, not just an election list as earlier in 1935 or in 1931. This *Jugoslovenska Radikalna Zajednica* (JRZ), or Yugoslav Radical Union, had as its slogan "one state, one people, one king." Its slogans promised wide powers of *samouprava*, meant here as local self-administration. Stojadinović brought real advertising skills with him, offering more slogans for his proposals and nicknames for his adversaries than any previous prime minister. Spaho and Korošec agreed to be "vice-presidents" of the JRZ in order to suggest that it was a unified body rather than a coalition. Korošec now made his Slovenian Peoples' Party (SLS) legal again simply by calling it the JRZ. On the Serbian side, younger men were attracted to replace some of the aging or intractable Radical regulars. When General Živković and others objected to these outsiders and to the partnership with the Bosnian Muslims, Stojadinović forced them out between December and March 1936.[16]

Stojadinović also promised a "political reversal" in Croatian relations, but it did not materialize. Maček refused to join the JRZ unless the constitution was open to revision. He continued to boycott the Skupština along with the other deputies of the Opposition Bloc outside Serbia. Yet Maček insisted, with some justification, that he was not one of the Croatian separatists. He dismissed their strength as only a few thousand. In November 1936, Prince Paul asked him point blank, "Do Croats want this state?" Yes, Maček replied, but under either a new constitution or a non-party government. That September's local election for some 4,000 rural and small town opštine had given the new JRZ over two-thirds of the seats, with majorities everywhere (topped by 91 percent of the Bosnian Muslim vote) but Croatia. Maček's agenda may have seemed out of reach, but he kept on negotiating.

In January 1937, Stojadinović promised him an eventual "big solution," but only after an initial "small solution." The HSS was to accept five cabinet posts and field candidates for the new Skupština elections. Both the prince and the prime minister misjudged Maček's party. To them, it was still too shattered after the 1929 dissolution to enter any election without agreeing to join a government coalition. In the meantime, however, Maček had transformed the HSS into the cohesive, broadly based organization that Radić had failed to establish, although at the cost of including right wing or clerical support that Radić would have shunned. In spring 1937, Maček held the party's center firmly enough to accept the offer of Serbia's United Opposition of Democrats, Agrarians, and Republicans. Their coalition began to discuss a single Bloc of National Agreement.

This latest and largest bloc would probably not have become a reality in October 1937 without the political damage that Stojadinović inflicted on himself in Serbia. Ratification of a Concordat with the Vatican to regularize the position of Catholic clergy and schools was still pending two years after its signature in July 1935 (and fifteen years after negotiations had been initiated). Approval now, he judged, would appease Mussolini and strike blows against both the Communists and the presumably anti-clerical Maček. The Slovenian and Croatian Catholic hierarchies were naturally eager for ratification, especially since the new 1931 constitution of the Serbian Orthodox Church had authorized comparable rights. The Orthodox effort in 1934 to make the 700-year anniversary of St. Sava's birth into a country-wide celebration had further angered the Catholic hierarchy. Stojadinović reckoned incorrectly that he could win Skupština approval like "sending a letter in the mail." Instead, a summer storm of opposition blew up in Serbia. Led by the Orthodox patriarch, Varnava, a suddenly united opposition objected to everything from state school subsidies (the Catholic church would receive a 35 million dinar annual subsidy as compensation for property lost in the land reform versus 46 million for the Orthodox church and 13 million for Islam) to a proposed Catholic church in Niš. Then the relatively young Patriarch (57) died on the very night that the Skupština passed the Concordat by a single vote. Rumors that the regime had poisoned him spread throughout Serbia. By the time that Stojadinović withdrew the ill-fated document, in October 1937, Maček and a Serbian opposition led by the old Independent Radicals and erstwhile Democrats, Ljuba Jovanović and Milan Grol, had already reached a formal agreement.[17]

The Bloc of National Agreement did not win the elections of December 1938, but it came close enough to bring down the Stojadinović regime. Its platform affirmed Croatian acceptance of the dynasty and the kingdom's borders, but asked that Croatia be recognized as "an equal state factor that can make decisions affecting the state's future from its own free will." Prince Paul sought another meeting with Maček to resolve the impasse with the Stojadinović government, but was refused. A crowd of nearly 100,000 people welcomed Maček when he came to Belgrade for a conference of Bloc leaders in August 1938. So much for the notion that irreconcilable antagonisms had closed off all options for Serb–Croat reconciliation, at least at the popular level below the political leaderships.

Having played the religious card and lost, Stojadinović could only respond in the fall election campaign with green-uniformed youths shouting *vodja*, or leader, at his speeches. The election results reflected the failure of such proto-fascist trappings to attract support from the Serbian electorate even approaching what they later received in post-

Table 6.1. *Electoral support for regime list, 1931, 1935, and 1938 (in percent)*

	1931	1935	1938
Savska (Croatia)	55	23	14
Primorska (Dalmatia)	34	26	16
Belgrade (Serbia)	58	40	44
Dravska (Slovenia)	52	41	53
Vrbaska (Croatia, W. Bosnia and Hercegovina)	64	44	37
Dunavska (Vojvodina)	71	51	52
Drinska (Bosnia-Hercegovina and Serbia)	79	51	45
Vardarska (Macedonia)	72	60	51
Moravska (Serbia)	80	63	58
Zetska (Montenegro)	79	64	49
Yugoslavia	65	45	40

Source: *Enciklopedia Jugoslavije*, v, III (Zagreb: Jugoslavenski leksikografski zavod, 1983), 274.

Munich Hungary or in Romania. Nor did he win many votes for congratulating himself on abstaining from Czechoslovakia's losing encounter with Nazi Germany, thus "sparing Belgrade's citizens the chore of digging air raid shelters like the Londoners." The JRZ won only 54 percent of the popular vote and the Bloc of National Agreement, 45 percent. In Croatia the Bloc received over two-thirds of the ballots cast. By 1938 the JRZ's fraction of eligible voters had fallen to 14 percent in Croatian Savska and 40 percent in all of Yugoslavia (see table 6.1). In January 1939, Croatian representatives agreed with Maček to assemble in Zagreb instead of coming to the new Skupština in Belgrade. Acknowledging the impasse, Prince Paul asked Stojadinović and his new government, now minus Monsignor Korošec, to resign.

Economic upturn and the German gamble

Stojadinović's political problems leave us to wonder how he stayed in office without interruption, longer than any other interwar prime minister including Nikola Pašić. Economic policy, geared to international trade and aided by the general upturn from the depths of the Depression that characterized all of Eastern Europe after 1935, provides the answer. The other political leaders of the first Yugoslavia in the 1930s – from King Aleksandar and Prince Paul to Maček, Korošec, and the several Serbs – had no general understanding or specific program with which to confront the Depression; Stojadinović had such a program.

Table 6.2. *Yugoslavia's foreign trade, 1929–1939[a] (percent of total value in current prices)*

	Northwestern Europe		Germany and Austria		Eastern Europe		Italy		Southeastern Europe and Turkey	
	Exports	Imports	Exports	Imports	Exports	Imports	Exports	Imports	Exports	Imports
1929	9	13.7	24.1	33	13.4	26.3	24.9	10.8	22.1	3.6
1930	10.5	14	29.4	34.4	16.1	25.2	28.3	11.3	9.7	4.3
1931	10.5	16.8	26.5	34.5	23.2	24.9	25	10.3	8	2.8
1932	10	18.1	33.3	31.3	19.4	20.8	23.1	12.7	5.5	4.3
1933	12.3	19.1	34.6	29.3	15.5	17.9	21.5	15.9	5.2	3.2
1934	14.8	21.5	31.8	26.3	16.2	16.6	20.6	15.5	5.9	5.7
1935	13.3	21.1	32.4	28.1	20	18.9	16.7	10	4.6	4.2
1936	21.1	18.3	38.4	37	17.5	20.3	3.1	2.5	7.3	5.7
1937	26.2	14.8	35.2	42.7	11.9	15	9.4	8.2	4.7	4.5
1938	22.3	16.5	42	39.4	13.7	15.3	6.4	8.9	4.6	3.8
1939	21.6	11.6	31.9	47.7	20	5.7	10.6	11.7	4.4	4.3

[a]In 1929, total exports in billions of dinars were 7.5 and imports 7.9 billion; in 1932, exports dropped to 2.8 billion and imports to 3.0 billion; and exports and imports rose again in 1937 to 5.1 and 6.2 billions of dinars, respectively; and in 1939 exports were 4.7 billion of dinars and imports 5.5 billion.

Source: John R. Lampe and Marvin R. Jackson, *Balkan Economic History, 1550–1950* (Bloomington, Ind.: Indiana University Press, 1982), 460–62.

In a decade of declining agricultural prices and shrinking grain markets, the prime minister made an increase in industrial and processed agricultural exports his highest priority. In order to force their development, he abandoned the then liberal principles of financial austerity and free markets that he had used to stabilize the dinar in the 1920s.[18] Appointed finance minister again in December 1934, Stojadinović pushed through a long delayed law for industrial encouragement, consisting mainly of tariff exemptions, but added specific tax concessions to industrial enterprises. Peasants themselves received some tax relief, harvest insurance, silo construction, and state credit for their cooperatives. Stojadinović artfully announced these measures just before the above-mentioned local elections of September 1936. The following month he ended the moratorium on repayment of peasant debt, a move welcomed by the private banks. One-quarter of large debts and one-half of smaller debts were wiped out. But the state's Agricultural Bank was to pay off the remaining obligations over a twelve-year period with support from the state budget and lottery.

To support his initiatives in both agriculture and industry, Stojadinović promoted Germany as Yugoslavia's principal trading partner. By the early 1930s, he had already become disenchanted with France and the other members of the Little Entente as commercial partners. By 1935, Yugoslav exports to France had shrunk to less than 15 percent of their 1930 level. The shift to Germany began as an effort to observe the League of Nations embargo against Italy after its 1935 conquest of Ethiopia. If Yugoslavia observed the sanctions, it would hurt Mussolini's hostile government and win Western approval at the same time. When the French government failed to reward Stojadinović by relaxing its protectionist tariffs, he readily responded to the offer of favorable export prices tendered by Hitler's finance minister, Hjalmar Schacht, in June 1936.

The shift inadvertently tilted regional development away from Croatia. The drop in Italian trade in 1935 and then its collapse in 1936 (see table 6.2) severely hurt the export of Dalmatian cement and Croatian and Bosnian timber. Stojadinović promised to continue the construction of better rail links between the coast and the interior, but little came of it. A rail line connecting Serbia to Romania was completed, however, and some progress made in the development of three sectors to which he had promised special attention: the Vojvodina's agriculture, the Serbian chemical industry, and Bosnian iron and steel production that would turn the Zenica area into a "Yugoslav Ruhr."[19]

The gamble on the German market seemed at the start to come with no political strings attached. Stojadinović's German education and his admiration for the Nazi economic recovery, which he attributed to his financial colleague, Hjalmar Schacht, opened the way. So did German demand for Yugoslav copper and bauxite that had already boosted exports in 1935. Industrial crops from the Vojvodina, such as the vegetable oil that found few takers in Italy, fitted nicely into the German market even without the Nazi's developing plans for strategic autarky. Primarily because of German purchases, industrial crops rose from 5 to 11 percent of total Yugoslav export value between 1934 and 1935–38. By 1937 trade with Germany had climbed to one-third of Yugoslav export and import value. Now unsanctioned exports to Italy revived, but to less than half of their one-fifth share in 1934. The German share, meanwhile, jumped past 40 percent with Hitler's acquisition of Austria in 1938.

German investment capital and management came too, but its extent has been greatly exaggerated, primarily on the basis of the Krupp concession to develop the Zenica iron works into Yugoslavia's first modern steel mill. Stojadinović consciously chose Krupp in 1936 over bidders from France and Czechoslovakia. But even when a number of Austrian and Czech interests in Yugoslavia were added to the German total in 1938–39, its share of Yugoslav foreign investment capital amounted to only 11 percent.[20] A considerable rise in the Western but non-German share of joint stock in Yugoslav enterprises had already occurred (see table 6.3) by 1936. Dependence on German or Czech military supplies became important only after 1939.

Until then the Stojadinović strategy mainly expanded the state sector of the Yugoslav economy. The German-backed iron and steel complex at Zenica became the state enterprise Jugočelik (Yugoslav Steel) when it opened in 1937. By 1938 all state enterprises and monopolies accounted for 15 percent of industrial capital and provided nearly half of budget revenues. In order to reflate the money supply and provide the initial investments for state enterprises, the dinar had to be protected from the rigors of international convertibility that Stojadinović had worked to achieve in the mid-1920s. Schacht's bilateral clearing agreements offered an artificial exchange rate that paid prices 30 percent above world levels. They were an ideal vehicle for such protection. From 1935 to 1938, the share of Yugoslav trade tied to clearing accounts climbed from 60 to 80 percent. At the same time, note issue through the central bank jumped by one-third. So did deposits in state banks, particularly the mortgage bank, to provide two-thirds of all loanable funds. The resulting rise in real industrial output averaged 10.7 percent a year for 1936–39, but derived more from the newer metallurgical and chemical production of Bosnia and Serbia than from the older Slovenian and Croatian enterprises that had prospered during the 1920s.[21] As war drew nearer in

Table 6.3. *Foreign investment in Yugoslavia, 1928 and 1936*

	Percent share of total joint stock investment	
Sector	1928	1936
Banking	6.4	11.1
Trade	3.3	30.2
Industry	20.2	52.8
Transport and communications	1.9	13.1
Insurance	0.1	51.7
Public finance	67.7	
Other	0.4	

Source: John R. Lampe and Marvin R. Jackson, *Balkan Economic History, 1550–1950* (Bloomington, Ind.: Indiana University Press, 1982), 438 and 509–10.

the late 1930s, a half-dozen enterprises in Serbia and several in Bosnia received the largest share of rising state investment in military production for the army and air force. Such regional concentration of investment, in a Depression decade where any gain was assumed to be someone else's loss, did not go unnoticed in Croatia.

Nazi Germany as a diplomatic dead end

Growing commercial dependence did not mean German control of the Yugoslav economy, contrary to the assumption of many Western observers at the time. But the gamble on the greater German market was also a gamble on Hitler's Germany as better insurance for improving relations with Italy and other neighbors than Britain or France, let alone the Little Entente, could provide.

Stojadinović had taken office promising to improve the often troubled relations with those neighbors. He shared the disillusion with the French connection that had spread after the long-awaited loan of 1931 failed to provide new markets, military supplies, or diplomatic support. Then came Aleksandar's assassination and the French government's failure to demand the death penalty or to pursue the obvious Italian and Hungarian involvement at the conspirators' trial.

If the stage was indeed set for Yugoslav movement toward the German side, there remains the controversial question of how much Stojadinović himself sympathized with the Nazi regime.[22] Certainly he expressed admiration for Hitler as a political leader and propagandist, both qualities on which he prided himself. He also appreciated the Nazis' anti-Communism, especially after Czechoslovakia's 1935 treaty with the Soviet Union. To Stojadinović, that pact discredited the Little Entente for good. The shrewd Italian foreign minister, Count Ciano, did judge him to be a fascist "by virtue of his conception of authority, of the state, and of life." Yet Stojadinović lacked a fascist program or even a fascist disposition to act arbitrarily without consultation or support. Where is the evidence of a corporatist plan to reshape Yugoslavia's state and society, of an expansionist foreign policy, or even of a readiness to silence domestic opponents or perceived ethnic adversaries by force? As for his rhetoric, Stojadinović called the assassination attempt against him in 1936 "fascist methods" and spoke of the need to "return to democratic and civil freedoms."

What does emerge is the picture of a political opportunist who bet on Nazi Germany for immediate economic advantage, in the belief that Germany would have no wider geopolitical purpose in threatening Yugoslavia. When Hitler himself received the prime minister during a January 1938 visit to Berlin, Stojadinović made much of the Führer's comment to him that "in the Balkans, we want nothing more than an open door for our economy." Stojadinović replied that Austria was a purely German matter. Even after the Munich pact that October, Hitler seemed to him to be a man of peace who needed only "a colony or two" before readily turning to the architectural redesign of Berlin and Munich that were presumed to be his real passions. In the meantime, with words reminiscent of British Prime Minister Neville Chamberlain's ill-starred celebration of the Munich pact, Stojadinović claimed that he had ensured "peace on our borders."

Measures of gratitude and dissembling doubtless mixed in with the Yugoslav prime minister's misjudgment of Hitler's intentions. Hitler had personally persuaded Mussolini to reach an understanding with Yugoslavia in 1936 and pushed the Horthy regime in Hungary to concentrate on their minority problems with Czechoslovakia. The large German minority in the Yugoslav Vojvodina was urged to remain quiet. Mussolini immediately made a speech calling for better relations between the two neighbors and a treaty spelling out the details was signed in March 1937. Those details included Mussolini's explicit agreement to continue the Croatian Ustaša members' internment and the ban on Macedonian VMRO activities as well. Then in 1938, German diplomacy discreetly helped to nudge a reluctant Bulgarian government into the so-called Balkan Entente with Greece, Turkey, and Yugoslavia.

At the same time, Stojadinović worked with Prince Paul to keep the

British option open, so as not to tie the German knot too tightly. The prince's trip to London in 1938 seeking subsidized trade to trim the dependence on Germany may have failed, but was still significant for having been tried. During the same October that Stojadinović was celebrating his success in keeping Yugoslavia away from the threat of war at Munich, he also rejected a German economic emissary's offer to consign half of Yugoslav exports to Germany. In return Germany would have processed non-ferrous ores from British or French concessions and provided a variety of German technical assistance and training.

Stojadinović was taking a calculated risk that worked as long as Hitler kept the peace. But Hitler was eager for war by 1938 and was furious when the Munich pact denied him the chance.[23] After his chance finally came in 1939, distant Yugoslavia did not remain outside the reach of Germany's geopolitical priorities nor beyond Hitler's readiness to achieve them by force of arms.

Balance sheet for the first Yugoslavia, 1921–1939

By the start of the Second World War in September 1939, the first Yugoslavia had existed as a sovereign state for less than two decades. Although the idea of a Yugoslav state had by then gained greater acceptance, the idea itself could not, as Joseph Rothschild concludes, create political consensus. He assigns the major responsibility for this failure to Serbian politicians for "squandering the moral capital that Serbia's heroic performance in World War I had earned for Yugoslavia." But the Croatian policy of boycott, he adds, helped account for the often cited Serb predominance in the officer corps, civil service, and cabinet positions – 452 of the 656 ministers serving between 1921 and 1939 versus 26 party-approved Croats and 111 unapproved.

Serbian and Croatian politicians produced a political culture not unlike that of nineteenth-century France. No party was large enough to win a parliamentary majority, and few of their leaders were tolerant enough of the other parties to work together for a coalition for long unless they were in opposition. Such a stalemate tempted King Aleksandar to rule like Louis Napoleon on the basis of restoring order, under an initial dictatorship and then with the aid of arranged elections. The Second World War made sure that Yugoslavia of the 1930s, unlike France of the 1860s, would have no chance to reestablish its political parties in the next decade. Ethnic disputes as well as international pressures crippled the coalition of shadow parties that tried to emerge after 1934. Their failure to come together created an opening for the new sort of non-party coalition that Aleksandar had wanted and the Second World War allowed Tito to construct. This eminently European political culture flawed the first Yugoslavia, together with regional disputes over ethnic representation and the absence of a coherent program for economic integration from any political quarter.

The record of economic growth (still short of self-sustaining development), land reform, public education, intellectual and religious freedom, and even the rule of law was positive for Yugoslavia as a whole. Yet the reality or perception of regional imbalance clouded every area of advance. Although the authoritarian regime of the 1930s relaxed its initial centralization of the Islamic hierarchy and restored relative autonomy to the Bosnian Muslims, religious freedom otherwise failed to reassure the Catholic Croat and Serbian Orthodox clergy about one another. The "legal federalism" cited in chapter 5 endured for Croats and Slovenes as well as for Serbs. They were proportionally represented among the country's regional and district judges in 1937. Bosnian Muslims and Albanians were conspicuously absent.

Against such ethnic imbalance, the Wilsonian optimism that trusted universal suffrage and constitutional safeguards to create a transcending democratic consensus did not prove any more successful than in most of interwar Europe. As elsewhere, pre-1914 tolerance and faith in the future survived through a free-standing, intellectual or cultural flowering, but lost out in political life. The clearest casualty was the suspicion of state power shared by nineteenth-century liberals and twentieth-century conservatives.

Economic development and industry

The new state's economy grew at a respectable rate across the interwar period, despite the lack of prewar trade and transport links made worse during the First World War by the damages done to infrastructure. If the 1909–12 average for Gross Domestic Product is 100, the detailed calculations of Ivo Vinski show recovery from 93 to 104 for 1920–23, a jump to 141 by 1929, and recovery from the 1932 Depression low of 122 to 145 by 1936 and to 168 by 1939. These index numbers put Yugoslavia's economic growth per capita in the upper ranks for interwar Eastern Europe.[24]

A small but growing industrial sector accounted for about two-thirds of this increase. It came from light manufacturing in Croatia and Slovenia during the 1920s and from metallurgy and mining in Bosnia, Kosovo, and Macedonia during the 1930s. Manufacturing grew almost twice as fast – 4.8 versus 2.6 percent a year – for 1918–28 as for 1929–38 overall, but in the latter period metallurgy and mining led all of

Southeastern Europe with annual increases that averaged 10 percent. These sectors were primarily responsible for boosting industrial production by 31 percent between 1936 and 1939. British and French investment provided most of the capital in joint-stock enterprises for processing non-ferrous minerals, and new German investment, as we have just seen, for ferrous metallurgy. This European capital made up for the significant reduction in commercial bank funding, foreign and domestic, available to manufacturing after the 1920s. It increased the share of foreign investment in industrial joint-stock companies from 20 to 52 percent. The one sector of light manufacturing to move ahead during the 1930s also advanced the regional tilt away from Croatia. This was textile production, buoyed by tariff protection to become Yugoslavia's most successful import substitute. Lower wages and taxes in Serbia and especially Macedonia began encouraging firms from Croatia to move there, or new ones to open. The shift compounded the Croatian perception of discrimination created by Stojadinović's aforementioned state investments in Bosnia and Serbia.[25]

While industry had grown to account for perhaps 30 percent of national income by 1938, its workers still earned slightly less than 30 percent of that income. Poor working conditions for men and especially for women drove the number of strike days for 1936 up to twice their total of the decade before, although it was barely one-fifth of the 1920 figure. Industry still lagged far behind agriculture in creating employment. In an economically active population of nearly 7 million, manufacturing enterprises provided just 300,000 jobs and the mining sector less than 50,000 – a total of 5 percent. Table 6.4 records the preeminence of agricultural employment, still growing in absolute numbers. Two-thirds of the peasants worked smallholdings of less than 5 hectares (12.5 acres) according to the last interwar census in 1931. Thus, the rural share of total population – 76 percent in 1921 and 75 percent in 1938 – hardly budged during the interwar period. That total had in the meantime risen from 12 million to 15.5 million, boosting the population density from 48.1 to 62.2 per square kilometer. Competition for good land grew fiercer, particularly in Bosnia-Hercegovina, which recorded the largest jump (36.9 to 52.9).

Agriculture and land reform

Agricultural output made slower but still measurable progress during the interwar period. Per capita growth exceeded 1 percent for most years, with the bad harvest of 1926–27 the most notable exception. Cereals and industrial crops led an overall rise of nearly 20 percent for all crop value from 1926–30 to 1936–38. Animal products held steady after nearly recovering from the severe losses of the First World War. Regional disparities between the grain-surplus areas in the north and the grain-deficit areas to the south (one axis that did not divide Serbia from Croatia) kept the average area of crop cultivation per capita down to one-half the Bulgarian or Romanian average of 1 hectare. Table 6.4 reflects a share of national income for peasants with holdings under 5 hectares that was only one-half their 54 percent share of the economically active population. As in Bulgaria, peasant families reacted to limited incomes by reducing their size, dropping the overall birth rate from 34.2 per 1,000 for 1926–30 to 27.4 by 1936–40.

The perception of regional disparity grew not from these aggregate numbers, unnoticed at the time, but from the land reform of 1919–21. It took a long time to implement, as noted in chapter 5, and was widely believed to have reduced efficiency in Dalmatia and Slavonia. The colonate system of sharecropping persisted in Dalmatia into the 1930s; the rate of compensation to previous owners was not even fixed until 1933 and then at too high a rate for the state budget to afford. The large Slavonian estates had been sold off by the mid-1920s to financial interests who delayed the fixing of maximum holdings and compensation into the early 1930s. The smallholdings carved from such estates were finally given their titles during the depths of the Depression. They were understandably less efficient and profitable than the original properties. In Bosnia and Macedonia, landlord rents due on arable crops ended only after peasants received full title in the late 1920s. The leading Western specialist on interwar agriculture in Eastern Europe, Doreen Warriner, reckoned that farm incomes rose thereafter by 50 percent. The Croatian Peasant Party opposed the implementation of the reform from the start partly because a member of the Serb-dominated Democratic Party was made minister for land reform. In this way, Warriner noted, the otherwise successful transfer of 2 million hectares to 637,000 families also added to the Serb-Croat conflict.[26] And, as some Croatian critics of the Yugoslav state complained at the time, so did the hard evidence of Croatian peasant poverty persuasively assembled by Rudolf Bićanić in his detailed 1937 study of the "passive," or the food-deficit regions, *Kako živi narod* (How the people live).

Public education and employment

The classic liberal prescription for rural poverty was of course providing the higher education needed to move away from it. By Balkan standards, interwar Yugoslav averages of funds spent on education were respectable

Table 6.4. *Distribution of income in 1938*

Occupation	Economically active population		Wages, salaries, and entrepreneurial income[a]	
	(in thousands)	percent	millions of dinars[b]	percent
Agriculture				
Peasants and agricultural workers	2,113	31	8,003	13
Peasants holding 2–5 hectares	1,631	24	9,185	15
Peasants holding 5–20 hectares	1,560	23	13,346	21
Peasants holding over 20 hectares	124	2	2,671	4
Others	263	4	499	1
Non-agriculture				
Non-agricultural wage-earners	453	7	3,488	6
Salaried employees and public servants	357	5	6,858	11
Artisans and minor entrepreneurs	296	4	5,726	9
Senior government officials (including high clergy and Royal Court)	19	0	1,120	2
High managerial staff	12	0	760	1
Professions	20	0	980	2
Major entrepreneurs	79	1	9,645	15
Total	6,927	100	62,281	100

[a]Excludes income originating from the ownership of dwellings.
[b]1938 value in dinars.
Source: Lenard J. Cohen, *The Socialist Pyramid: Elites and Power in Yugoslavia* (Oakville, Ont.: Mosaic Press, 1989), 102.

despite their small share of the state budget – less than 6 percent in 1938. They upped the percentage of primary school enrollments to 51.5 percent of five-to-fourteen-year-olds by 1938–39, overcoming a long-standing Bulgarian lead. Illiteracy fell accordingly from over 48 percent in 1929 to 38 percent by 1937. Secondary school students were 17.2 percent of their age group, the highest proportion in Southeastern Europe, although university enrollment still struggled to reach 1 percent. Among university students, 40 percent were now enrolled in scientific or technical departments rather than the law faculties that had attracted a large majority of students during the 1920s. The rates of school attendance and literacy in Bosnia, Macedonia, and Kosovo lagged far behind these modestly promising averages. In addition, there was little progress in the introduction of new school textbooks that had been promised since 1929 to replace the prewar volumes. For Kosovo and Macedonia, the old Serbian texts whose bias was noted in chapter 3 continued in use. Wrangling between Serb, Croat, and Slovene educators kept any new textbooks from entering classrooms until 1937.[27]

Shrinking opportunities for public employment, still the major job opportunity for secondary or university graduates, posed a further problem for Serbia. Peasant families who managed to send their sons off to the local *gimnazija* or, more rarely, to university in Belgrade, did so with an official's future in mind. After 1933, however, the steady increase in state employment that had begun with the royal dictatorship in 1929 came to an end. Career officers in Southeastern Europe's largest army (800,000 if fully mobilized) were cut by one-fourth to 28,000. The interwar pattern gave Serbs roughly two-thirds of all official positions, civil and military. Only Slovenes joined the Serbs in exceeding their share of the population and then only in civilian positions.

Intellectuals and the Yugoslav idea

Against the combination of intolerant political culture and regional imbalances, Wilsonian liberal assumptions of a democratic future in a multi-ethnic state had little chance of survival by the 1930s. Their advocates nonetheless continued to play a leading intellectual role in Belgrade, Ljubljana, and Sarajevo. Only in Zagreb, despite or perhaps because of its position as the longest-standing university center, did the clerical right and the Communist left, plus the Peasant Party's middle position, leave virtually no room for what Miloslav Janićijević has called the liberal intelligentisa.[28]

In Belgrade, according to his unique survey of Yugoslavia's interwar intellectuals, some three-quarters of university faculty opposed the conservatives of the Serbian Radical Party, and their grounding of all authority in the state and the Orthodox church. Nor was there broad support for the notion of an ethnically pure Serbia, most notoriously advanced in the 1937 proposal of the Agrarian Union's Vasa Čubrilović to expel all Albanians from Kosovo. A majority of the faculty wished instead to be part of the European mainstream, which many had discovered during prewar travels or during time spent at French universities under special wartime dispensations given to Serbian officers. By the 1930s, such people spoke of the need for a modern European society based on "the productive individual" rather than "state power." They were joined by the bulk of the city's considerable literary and artistic élite, including dramatist Branislav Nušić and poet Isadora Sekulić. But these intellectuals took virtually no part in politics, other than the small number who had joined the Republican Party of the 1920s or supported the Agrarian Union. Their interest in the Serbian peasantry was usually minimal. Their students actively sought a new political direction and moved increasingly toward the Yugoslav Communist Party, once it had abandoned separatism for non-Serbs. The Spanish Civil War, in particular, had fired their imaginations.

The same could not be said for Zagreb where the Croatian Peasant Party attracted intellectual interest and political support. Maček had said, "We are the people, not a class." By 1935, urban intellectuals and officials made up 44 percent of the party's representatives, an increase from just one-third in the 1920s. At this later date, the party had strengthened its stranglehold on the Croatian political spectrum, but at the cost of accepting the clerical alliance that Radić had always resisted. Clerics led by the young Jesuit, Alojzije Stepinac, already archbishop by 1937, were less imbued with the Catholic internationalism that some Serbian historians have subsequently emphasized than with opposition to any political framework outside of Croatia, whether Yugoslav or Communist.

The clerics' most formidable opposition came, not from the tiny number of Zagreb-based "Yugoslavs," but instead from a growing Croatian left, led less by such Communist activists as August Cesarec than by the versatile and hugely talented writer Miroslav Krleža. Born in Zagreb and an urban creature to his toes, Krleža doubted that the peasant question was the key to Yugoslav politics. He questioned Radić's assumption that peasant solidarity could solve the Serb–Croat problem and called "unthinkable" the notion that a nineteenth-century Serbian utopian like Svetozar Marković and his ideas of communal democracy could appeal to Croats. And within the small Communist party, Krleža continued to joust against the confines of Soviet-style socialist realism, enough to earn condemnation from Tito himself as a "helper of Trotskyists" by 1939. University students not attracted by the Ustaša or clerical appeals were drawn instead toward his brand of intellectual Marxism, rather than to Belgrade's Communist activism.

After fading into the background during the 1920s, Slovenian liberals stepped forward during the 1930s. They broke with literary critic Josip Vidmar over his idea that Slovenia possessed a language and culture separate from "unnatural, uncultured, and unreal" Yugoslavism. The aging liberals attracted small-town but not peasant support for their counterattack. They argued for free enterprise and said it was best secured in a single Yugoslav market and state, given the growing German threat to peace. Their slogans, however appealing today, attracted less support than the liberal movement inside the clerical party (SLS). True, Monsignor Korošec remained unchallenged as leader of this largest party and head of its cooperative network. But the young Eduard Kocbek used his new literary journal, *Dejanje*, to push the party toward more internal democracy and away from the conservative, anti-Semitic Korošec, charging that "Slovenian clericalism is closer to the Japanese Communist Party than to Slovenian liberalism." Among the large bloc of socialist supporters, the Communist Edvard Kardelj was able to push aside the Masaryk-trained group that drew on Czech principles of social democracy. The Masaryk group argued against central planning under the dictatorship of the proletariat and for decentralized workers' self-management, as the better alternative to private enterprise. Kardelj, its post-1950 champion, resisted the notion at this time.

For Bosnia-Hercegovina, the one commitment to a democratic Yugoslavia came from the Bosnian Muslims. By the 1930s, the Yugoslav Muslim Organization as well as the few Communists among them favored turning away from the emphasis on Islam and traditional ways of the prewar landlords' élite. Both began to speak of a multi-ethnic Bosnia as a model for the rest of Yugoslavia. But Serbs or Croats who might have joined them in this broader view had either died in the war or had gone to Belgrade or Zagreb, the start of a migration that would resume with greater intensity by the 1970s. Those remaining flocked to the right wings of the Serbian Radical or Independent Radical parties on one side and of the Croatian Peasant Party or the Ustaša on the other. They could agree only on their fears of a Muslim predominance in the governing or educated élite of Sarajevo and other towns, an ominous preview of coming attractions.

From Serb–Croat *Sporazum* to Tripartite Pact, 1939–1941

Only once during the history of the first Yugoslavia did Serbian and Croatian representatives agree on the restructuring of the state. And then external forces inadvertently combined to encourage a hasty set of terms whose imposition only insured further dissatisfaction. Without Hitler's war plans, however, that dissatisfaction might not have destroyed the state.

Serb–Croat agreement

By January 1939, Prince Paul had lost confidence in Milan Stojadinović's ability to resolve the impasse with Maček and his Croatian Peasant Party deputies. Maček rejected Paul's overtures to bring his HSS deputies to Belgrade as long as Stojadinović remained as prime minister. In

February the prince asked the less assertive Dragiša Cvetković, previously minister of social welfare and then head of the new state workers' union, JUGORAS, to form a government. In order to reassure a Nazi government that had come to value Stojadinović as an agreeable foreign minister, Paul put the current ambassador to Germany, Aleksandar Cincar-Marković, into that position. Mussolini was not reassured. He rushed to occupy Albania in April 1939 before the new government could renege on Stojadinović's promise to allow him a free hand there in return for restraining the Ustaša.

In the meantime, the new government dutifully pursued the agreement with Maček for which it had been installed. The Croatian leader, in Joseph Rothschild's apt phrase, "was simultaneously heating three mutually incompatible irons in his political fire." One was indeed reconciliation with the prince's government, but the second was the "united front from below" which he had agreed to form with Serbia's opposition leaders (the Opposition Bloc). The third revolved around exploratory talks with Mussolini's foreign minister, Count Ciano, about Italian support for Croatian independence. Much ado has been made about these talks over the years, with each party claiming that the other initiated them and disputing whether Maček sought support for a confederal or an independent Croatia.[29] More importantly for the fate of the first Yugoslavia, Maček soon decided against relying on either the Italian connection or the Serbian opposition.

Over the threatening summer of 1939, both sides hurried to reach some agreement. Maček worried about the internal problems of rising Ustaša support in Croatia and the weak showing by his Serbian allies in the 1938 elections. Prince Paul worried about external pressures. The Nazi military might displayed for him during his June trip to Berlin only convinced him that war was coming. Yugoslavia's gold reserves were dispatched to New York the next month, not to return for nearly a decade. On August 20, less than two weeks before Hitler's attack on Poland, Maček and Cvetković finally came to terms.

Their *Sporazum*, or agreement, divided Yugoslavia on terms reminiscent of the 1867 Ausgleich between Austria and Hungary. It created a separate Croatian banovina that encompassed roughly 30 percent of the kingdom's territory and population. Croatia now included not only Dalmatia from the former Primorje but added Dubrovnik from Zeta, some of the former Military Border from Vrbas, two parts of the Srem including Vukovar from Dunav, and three parts from Drina that cut a border across Bosnia from Brčko south to Travnik and Mostar (see map 6.1). The banovina's population of 4.4 million included 168,000 Muslims mainly in Bosnia-Hercegovina and 866,000

Serbs. Leaders of the Serb minority had not been consulted, and many Serbs feared for their indeterminate position in the new banate. Bosnian Muslims discovered that their presence in the districts assigned to Croatia had simply not been counted; only the ratio of Croats to Serbs was used. The new leader of the Yugoslav Muslim Organization, replacing Mehmed Spaho who had just died, put the best face on the agreement by calling it the prelude to a separate confederal arrangement between Bosnia and Croatia.[30]

The government of this confederal Croatia was to consist of its own elected Sabor and a Ban appointed by the monarchy. The Regent Paul promptly named the trusted Ivan Šubašić, a Croat who had served with the Serbian army at the Salonika Front in the First World War and who would return to play a brief part after the Second World War. Budgetary and internal affairs were to be autonomous, but there were no specific provisions for minority rights (as there would be none in the Croatian constitution of 1991). The Belgrade government retained control of foreign affairs, foreign trade, defense, and going beyond the Ausgleich's terms for Austria-Hungary, transportation and communications. The central government's authority over the remaining banates was unaffected. Debate raged, especially in Belgrade, about their territorial and even administrative reorganization to include a comparable Serbian banovina, but nothing was done before the war. Nor did elections to the new Croatian Sabor or for a new Skupština in Belgrade ever take place. Maček and the four designated HSS members did, however, join the reconstructed Cvetković government.

Opposition to the agreement spread from Serbs and Bosnian Muslims in the new Croatian banate to others, but its importance should not be exaggerated. While delaying the new elections that the Sporazum had promised, domestic disagreement over the deal probably would not have destroyed the first Yugoslavia in the absence of the Nazi invasion. But a more confederal structure with Serbian and possibly Slovenian banates joining the Croatian one might have emerged as the only basis for a long-term agreement. The sources of opposition – in ascending order of their importance to the state's survival – were the Communist Party, the Croatian Ustaša, the Serbian Cultural Club, and Serbia's Democratic Party.[31]

Membership in the illegal KPJ had risen from the start of the Popular Front period of Communist opposition to Nazi Germany and consolidation of its leadership in the hands of Josip Broz Tito by 1937. The policy of preserving Yugoslavia within its existing borders won student support in Belgrade. The appearance of a formally separate Communist Party of Croatia attracted attention in Zagreb. The few thousand members in 1934 increased to more than 6,000 by late 1939 and then 8,000 by early 1941, with several times that many sympathizers. The Serb–Croat agreement and the Hitler–Stalin pact of August 1939 were both setbacks for the KPJ. Its members tried that autumn to sabotage army mobilization in Macedonia, Kosovo, and Montenegro according to the new Comintern line, but failed miserably. The Sporazum took away the chance, however unrealistic, of a "united front from above" with Maček's HSS and the Serbian opposition. The Yugoslav Communist Party's fortunes revived in 1940 with the Comintern's quiet approval of a "united front from below" to oppose the Axis powers despite the Soviet pact with Nazi Germany. It also allowed the KPJ to condemn the Sporazum particularly for its treatment of non-Serbs outside of Croatia. Tito's impressively orchestrated fifth national party conference of the KPJ in a Zagreb suburb in October 1940 included the first Macedonian, albeit pro-Bulgarian, central committee member and delegates from a growing Slovenian contingent. Although a proposal to include Bosnian Muslims in the list of Yugoslav ethnic groups was voted down, other conference resolutions promised self-determination to Montenegro and Macedonia, as well as to a united Bosnia-Hercegovina. But the disposition of none of these other territories could have threatened the survival of Yugoslavia, then or later, had the Serbs and Croats agreed to stay together.

The Ustaša recruited membership on the explicit assumption that the two peoples could not coexist even in the Sporazum's confederation. The choice of "Šubašić, the Salonika Front man" as Ban showed its ultranationalist members that Serbian influence was still pervasive. In addition they objected to the borders of the new banate, particularly their failure to include all of Bosnia-Hercegovina. The Ustaša claimed it not only as historic Croatian land but, more ominously, on the basis that Bosnian Muslims and some Serbs were originally Croats. The Sporazum allowed Ustaša members to return from Italy and to recruit new supporters at Zagreb University and in other centers of support – Mostar, Travnik, Gospić, Vukovar, and Split. Still, actual membership of the Ustaša remained small, perhaps 2,000, with half in Zagreb plus another 250, including the poglavnik, Ante Pavelić, still in Italy. Members were also divided between pro-German and pro-Italian factions. Estimates of their popular support in Croatia barely exceeded 5 percent.

Opposition to the Sporazum in Serbia soon swelled to a larger if undetermined fraction of public opinion. Its smallest source was the openly fascist *Zbor* Party of Dimitrije Ljotić. A lawyer who ended his brief tenure as minister of justice in 1931 when the king rejected his proposed constitution as too authoritarian, Ljotić founded the Zbor, or Rally Party, in 1935. He won no seats and a bare 1 percent of votes cast in the next two elections. By 1940 his violent opposition to the Sporazum attracted perhaps 5,000 members and a student organization of *Beli Orlovi* (White Eagles, the same name adopted by Vojislav Šešlj for the paramilitary units he sent into Bosnia in 1992). In December the regent's regime came down hard on the movement, interning several hundred members and forcing Ljotić into hiding.[32]

The larger Serbian opposition by far came from two sources that had different but significant changes in mind for any confederal Yugoslavia. To some extent their memberships overlapped. These were the Serbian Cultural Club, founded by respected lawyer and historian Slobodan Jovanović and others in 1937, and the Democratic Party. One club member called the Sporazum a "Serbian Munich" because of the Serb minority, particularly in Bosnia, included in the Croatian banate. Democratic leader Milan Grol withdrew his party's earlier support for a separate Bosnia-Hercegovina and now demanded that the sections not in the Croatian banate be included in a single Serbian banate. Grol's vision of Serbia also included the Vojvodina and "the backbone of the national organism," Macedonia. Where Slovenia would fit in such a division of the rest of the country was not discussed. The leading Slovenian politician and Prince Paul's close confidant, Monsignor Korošec, had died in December 1940. Even without war, some new but still confederal structure was likely once Aleksandar's son Petar became king on his eighteenth birthday in September 1941.

Tripartite Pact and war

The Stojadinović strategy had been to prevent war with Italy by relying on Germany's lack of military interest in the Balkans. By 1940 the Cvetković government saw no effective way to escape this strategy, which included a rearmament program based on deliveries of Czech as well as German equipment. Now Czech deliveries had come under Nazi control, as had Italian policy for the time being. Count Ciano tried again to tempt Maček into an agreement over an independent Croatia and an Italian Dalmatia, but got nowhere. When Mussolini lost patience and proposed to attack both Yugoslavia and Greece in March of 1940, Hitler abruptly told him to stay out of the Balkans. This was to be the last dividend paid from Stojadinović's portfolio.

Prince Paul and his prime minister spent the next twelve months trying to escape the sort of formal commitment to Nazi Germany that would be required for any further dividends.[33] The threatened Italian attack prompted the regent to explore closer links with Britain and

France. He was particularly concerned about the security of Salonika. General Weygand offered to dispatch a force of French troops to the northern Greek port, but the Chamberlain government would not have it. Then the Nazi blitzkrieg of May swept away the French army and government. The shock in Belgrade prodded the anti-Communist regime to seek out diplomatic relations with the Soviet Union. Negotiations at Ankara in late June ended the longest-standing refusal of any successor state to establish relations with the USSR. Whether an earlier tie could have offered the Kingdom of Yugoslavia any greater security is of course doubtful.

Mussolini finally drew Hitler into the Balkans with his ill-considered invasion of Greece on October 28, 1940. The Italian advance quickly bogged down and turned into retreat. German troops had just been dispatched to North Africa to reverse the mauling that large numbers of poorly trained and equipped Italian troops were taking at the hands of a small British expeditionary force. Once in North Africa, German commanders wanted supplies sent by the shortest route, which ran through Yugoslavia and Greece. The Churchill government that came to power during the fall of France needed to protect its one force effectively fighting the Nazis. London made the decision in February 1941 to send several divisions to northern Greece, not to the border but southwest of Salonika along the Aliakmon river.

Some Western scholars have argued that the British decision to enter Greece was the final blow to what otherwise might have been a successful effort to keep Yugoslavia out of the war. The most detailed Yugoslav account counters that as early as July 1940, Hitler had turned against Yugoslavia, despite his refusal to give Mussolini a green light to attack later that year.[34] This seems doubtful, but we may speculate that even wholehearted adherence to the Tripartite Pact would not have saved Yugoslavia from an obligation to the German war effort like that of Bulgaria, which declared war on Britain and the United States as well as providing supplies and full transit rights.

The regent and the Cvetković government must be credited with doing all that they could to stay out of the German–Japanese alliance that became the Tripartite Pact when Italy joined in September 1940. Hungary's Horthy government signed up that month as well, but Yugoslavia's adherence would be more useful. It would rebuff any British or Russian presence in the Balkans as well as shortening supply lines to North Africa. General Milan Nedić, the Yugoslav army commander and a German sympathizer from the Stojadinović era, proposed that Yugoslavia join the Axis powers. To cement the bond, the Yugoslav army should then seize Salonika from Greece to prevent the entry of British troops. The regent dismissed Nedić on November 5, just as the Cvetović government began to arrange for the surreptitious supply of munitions and horses to the Greek army. The British and now the American embassies offered belated encouragement. William Donovan visited Belgrade in January as President Roosevelt's representative to deliver just such a message. These efforts helped sustain the government's resolve to resist the pact until March 1941.

But as Prince Paul told the American ambassador, Arthur Bliss Lane, "You big nations are hard. You talk of our honor, but you are far away."[35] The Bulgarian government's adherence to the pact on March 1 and the subsequent arrival there of 350,000 German troops made it impossible for the regent and his regime to hold out any longer. The prince refused to sign on the spot during a secret visit to Berchtesgaden on March 4. Afterwards, Foreign Minister Joachim von Ribbentrop formally amended the German offer to exclude the passage of German troops (but not supplies) through Yugoslavia or any request for military assistance. A secret provision promised Yugoslavia subsequent "free access" to Salonika, a German blandishment that seems not to have persuaded Belgrade as much as anticipated. Even after agreeing, the Cvetković government instructed its ambassador in Berlin, Ivo Andrić, to delay a promise of signing. Its intelligence sources, like a number of others, had heard rumors of an impending German attack on the Soviet Union. The invasion might have sidetracked further pressures, but it did not come soon enough. On March 25, the Cvetković government formally signed the Tripartite Pact despite its repeated warnings to the German ambassador about the Serbian public's reaction to joining a side that they still saw as their enemy from the First World War.

Two days later, Serbia's political spectrum and the Belgrade public gave full support to the military coup that overthrew the Cvetković government and proclaimed the still underage Petar king in place of the regent. The March 27 coup and Hitler's immediate decision to "destroy the Yugoslav state as it currently exists" signalled the end of the first Yugoslavia even though German forces did not invade until April 6.

7 World war and civil war, 1941–1945

The Second World War shaped the second Yugoslavia even more than the First World War did the first. The Nazi-led dismemberment of the first Yugoslavia destroyed virtually all existing institutions. Without the opening it offered the Yugoslav Communists to champion resistance and to replace those institutions, Tito's small party of 8,000 members could not have dreamed of taking power in 1945 and defying the Soviet Union a few years later. This chapter explores the connection between the most rapid seizure of power by any Communist regime in Eastern Europe and the most complex, controversial subject in the history of Yugoslavia, the Second World War.

The war itself has elicited a mountain of secondary accounts, but left less primary evidence for an agreed, definitive history than elsewhere in Europe. This is particularly true of the domestic dynamics that were crucial to the Communist seizure of power and, most prominently, to Serb–Croat relations. The respective roles of Britain, the United States, and the Soviet Union have become clearer, but it now appears that none of them were decisive.

More can be learned by concentrating on the direction of domestic events. First came the physical destruction of the Kingdom of Yugoslavia from April to June 1941. The power and brutality of the successor regimes that divided up the country peaked in 1942, setting the stage for a growing Communist advantage on rural ground by 1943–44. They gained their advantage, however, in a civil war with the non-Communist Serb resistance. That war accompanied and sometimes overshadowed the struggle against foreign occupiers, their collaborators, or the native fascist regime turned loose in Zagreb.

The destruction of the first Yugoslavia

Although the German attack of April 6, 1941, dealt the Kingdom of Yugoslavia mortal blow, the details of its destruction stretched from late March into June. Only then was the geographic crazy quilt of division complete. On June 22, Hitler's attack on the Soviet Union brought the Yugoslav Communist Party (KPJ) actively into the open resistance that had already broken out in Hercegovina and was ready to erupt in Montenegro and Serbia.

If time had permitted, the leaders of the bloodless Belgrade coup of March 27 intended to revise the non-Croatian conditions of the 1939 agreement governing Yugoslavia even at the risk of violent revolt from the Bosnian Muslims. A Serbian banovina would surely have included all of Bosnia-Hercegovina not under Croatia. But there was no time for anything. Hitler determined to destroy the new regime from the day it took power, despite its accommodating statements. The new prime minister, General Dušan Simović, had commanded the large Yugoslav air force and was one of a number of Serbian officers being courted by the British Embassy. But neither Simović nor his deputy, Bora Mirković, who orchestrated the participation of military units in the coup and support from key figures in the Serbian Cultural Club, received enough support or instruction from contacts with British intelligence operatives in the air attaché's office to justify any claim that London had directed the coup.[1] Nor did it matter to Hitler that the Simović regime was able to persuade Croatian leader Vladko Maček to join their cabinet or that it immediately made every diplomatic effort to assure the German Foreign Ministry that the terms agreed to on March 25 would be strictly observed.

How could Yugoslavia have remained a neutral island through 1941, lying as it did on the southern flank of Hitler's Russian front and across the shortest route to Rommel's Afrika Korps and the eastern Mediterranean? German preparations for Operation Maritsa, intended to occupy all of Greece, were already in place; adding the Yugoslav campaign was a small, further step. British inducements to draw the Yugoslav army into an attack on Italian forces in Albania that spring only added to Hitler's readiness to settle accounts with the "Serbian renegades" he blamed for starting the First World War.[2] The massive demonstration of support for the coup and for the Western allies that clogged the central streets of Belgrade on the morning of March 27 confirmed his judgment. So did Winston Churchill's famous reaction to the coup that "now Yugoslavia has found its soul."

After the war, Communists would claim that their supporters took the lead and dominated the Belgrade demonstrations. Propaganda photographs had clocks cut out of them to obscure the fact that the KPJ did not join these otherwise spontaneous crowds until late morning. Only then were their slogans demanding alliance with the Soviet Union seen alongside the early banners calling for "better war than pact" and "better grave than slave." Tito was in Zagreb and needed to approve a decision to participate that would openly flaunt the Hitler–Stalin pact of 1939. Perhaps Tito or other party leaders already knew of the full-scale German preparations for an attack on the Soviet Union, whose onset would obviously shatter the pact. More probably they had learned of the pending non-aggression treaty with the USSR that Prince Paul had authorized. (It would be signed hours before the German attack and dated the day before.) They had received Comintern instructions earlier, in 1940 (see chapter 6), to begin preparing a "united front from below" to oppose Nazi expansion, but this was to be the first act of open opposition.

A Yugoslav military attaché in Berlin had warned the new Simović regime of the German-led attack a couple days after the coup. The regime did nothing, but what could it have done? The Balkans' largest air force of 459 planes included only 87 modern fighters to face the 1,500 aircraft that the Germans would dispatch. Nazi troop concentrations already in Bulgaria and Hungary enabled a German force of 24 largely mechanized German divisions to join 23 Italian and 5 Hungarian divisions to strike from all sides. They swept through a Yugoslav army stretched thin by the long frontier they attempted to hold. Some 700,000 men had been mobilized, but their thirty divisions were understaffed and their armament and mobility grievously deficient. These handicaps would have proved fatal, it should be added, even if the officer corps had been drawn proportionally from the major ethnic groups across the territory to be defended, rather than being over 70 percent Serb. The ten-day blitzkrieg faced less opposition and found more collaborators in Croatia than elsewhere, but it was not noticeably slowed by the greater opposition encountered from scattered units in Serbia and Slovenia. German units lost fewer than 200 men and the Yugoslav forces at least 3,000.[3]

The partition of the first Yugoslavia that followed is too complex to comprehend without looking at a map. Various annexations (see map 7.1) divided Slovenia between Germany and Italy and gave the Dalmatian coast from Zadar to Split, the Montenegrin coast to Italy, areas north of the Drava and Danube rivers (the Slavonian Medjumurje and Prekomurje plus the Vojvodina's Baranja and Bačka, including Novi Sad) to Hungary, and Kosovo and western Macedonia to Italian Albania. Bulgaria occupied the rest of Macedonia, Italy the rest of Montenegro, and Germany all of Serbia, with a separate German administration for the Vojvodina east of the Tisza river (the Banat). Note also the east–west line dividing German from Italian military responsibility in what was called the Independent State of Croatia (NDH). Most fateful for the future of any Yugoslav state in these first months of the war were conditions in the NDH and in German-occupied Serbia.

Serbia

The German attack itself inflicted far more physical damage and psychological shock on the capital of Belgrade than on any other part of the country. Waves of German bombers pounded the city from early Sunday morning to the afternoon on April 6 and returned again the next day, killing some 2,300 people, close to the losses suffered by the entire Yugoslav army. A comparable number of buildings were destroyed or heavily damaged, including the national library and many government facilities. All essential services were cut. The bombing wounded many more than it killed and prompted still more people to flee the city, including the leaders of government. King Petar and the Simović cabinet minus Maček and a few others reached Pale near Sarajevo on April 11 and flew from Nikšić in Montenegro to Athens on April 14 and 15.

In the first days of the occupation, the Germans made sure that there was no interruption in the terror administered to Belgrade and then to all of Serbia.[4] After authorized looting from April 12 to 14, Nazi troops took direct control of all urban centers. A proclamation on April 16, one day before the formal surrender was signed, required all Jews to register with the police. Some, such as the prominent publisher Geca Kon, were simply executed out of hand. A number of municipal authorities were persuaded to collaborate, but the members of the new special police unit hastily recruited in Belgrade were *Volksdeutsche* from the Vojvodina. They joined German army units to enforce curfew and other regulations that amounted to martial law. Several concentration camps around Belgrade were soon set up for offenders. All cultural life quickly came under German control as well, and a single authorized newspaper, *Novo vreme*, began publication in May.

To compound the shock throughout Serbia, the Nazi occupiers deported nearly 200,000 officers and men from the Yugoslav army to prisoner of war camps in Germany. These soldiers, like the great majority of the more than 300,000 initially captured during the German attack, were Serbs from Serbia. The 10,000 or more officers held in Germany included many reservists who together had constituted a large part of Serbia's political and professional élite.

One of the officers who had not been captured was the career army colonel, Draža Mihailović. His earlier experience had scarcely prepared him to lead the non-Communist Serbian resistance to the occupation. Passed over for promotion to general because of a drunken misadventure

Map 7.1 Division of the former Yugoslavia, 1941–1944

in the First World War, he had also received several reprimands in the late 1930s, once for a nationalist proposal to divide the army into separate Serb, Croat, and Slovene units. In the April war, he narrowly escaped an engagement with German tanks in Bosnia and made his way back to the rugged west Serbian uplands with a company of men that numbered only thirty-one by the time they arrived at Ravna Gora on May 12. Thus began the odyssey of one of the most controversial figures of the Second World War in Yugoslavia. Mihailović was a man in whom defeated Serbia and a defiant Churchill government soon placed exaggerated hopes. His subsequent dealings with Italian and German authorities raise still-debated questions of how significantly he collaborated with them and how much control he exercised over his scattered *četnik* forces. These forces would in any case lose the civil war started by the Croatian Ustaša and finished by Tito's Partisans.

Mihailović himself chose the name *četnik* for his forces, formally known first as the Ravna Gora movement and later the Yugoslav Army in the Fatherland. Their exploits would bring "Chetnik" into the English language. Taken from the Serbian and Macedonian terms for upland guerrilla bands opposing Ottoman rule, the name surfaced earlier during the First World War, especially among Bosnian Serb guerrillas. It then became the designation for local militias that King Aleksandar allowed to reemerge informally after his 1929 decree had disbanded the Croatian Serbs' and Serbia's two formal organizations. Together the two had huge, inactive membership lists of close to one-half million men, later used to identify and persecute them. But we should not confuse the largest of the successor militias, headed by the aged Kosta Pećanac, with Mihailović's Chetniks.[5] Pećanac chose to collaborate with the German occupation in August 1941.

Mihailović's Chetnik movement took shape during these initial months of the war. He attracted some 10,000 men to his bands in western Serbia, enough to spread wishful thinking across Serbia that active resistance was under way. He was, in fact, husbanding his forces for Germany's eventual defeat, perhaps passing assurances to the German command that he would not challenge their current authority. Belying Communist charges that collaboration was uppermost in his mind, Mihailović pressed to establish contact with the royal government-in-exile. The Simović government of eight Serbs, two Croats, and one Slovene minister was initially welcomed in London and won recognition by June 21. The war minister and the small military staff remained in Cairo. Two days prior to the recognition, a Chetnik messenger reached Istanbul. He reported that Mihailović's forces had asked for recognition as an army readying itself to fight the German occupiers in Serbia and, more immediately, to render assistance to the Serb villages in Bosnia and Croatia being massacred or cleansed by Ustaša units of the NDH. By this time, a leading Chetnik ideologue, Stevan Moljević, had drafted a memorandum and an accompanying map that proposed a huge, "homogeneous Serbia." Moljević, a lawyer from Banja Luka in northern Bosnia, became one of two civilians, Dragiša Vasić was the other, prominent in Mihailović's Central National Committee. He reckoned that 1 million Croats would have to be expelled in order to create a Serbia covering two-thirds of a reconstituted Yugoslavia. A rump Croatia and a Slovenia enlarged by Istria would make up the rest.

The Nazi invasion of the Soviet Union at just this time, June 22, brought the Communist Party of Yugoslavia instructions through the Comintern, to proceed "without wasting a moment, organize Partisan detachments, and start a Partisan war behind enemy lines." The KPJ began a campaign of coordinated sabotage on July 4, confirming other evidence that its military preparations were already well under way. Belgrade was the logical center. Its size, status, and university had attracted the largest concentration of members to the KPJ. The party and its Communist Youth organization grew by one-half between April and July, reaching 12,000 and 30,000 members, respectively. Tito arrived in Belgrade from Zagreb on May 8 and set about organizing units and collecting arms for active resistance.

Yugoslav patriotism did motivate some members of the party, especially those in its youth organization, to prepare for fighting the Germans with the Hitler–Stalin pact still in force. Two qualifications must be quickly added. By this time, the widely circulating reports of an impending Nazi attack on the USSR had surely reached Tito. Secondly, according to Milovan Djilas, the top leadership saw as its enemy not only the Croatian Ustaša but also "the groups of (Serbian) officers hiding in the mountains of western Serbia," who would be rivals for postwar power.[6] The KPJ leaders expected an early German defeat, reflecting the general Communist confidence in the Red Army to defeat any adversary. Even though they shared the Ustaša as a common foe with the Chetniks and though most of their members who mobilized for resistance were Serbs, the Communists must be still credited with considering themselves a Yugoslav rather than a Serbian movement. Tito summoned representatives from all the major ethnic groups to attend a May meeting of the Central Committee in Belgrade. Leaders of the confederal Slovenian and Croatian parties attended, although not the Macedonian leader, Šarlo. He like most of the Macedonian leadership had transferred his allegiance to the Bulgarian Communist Party after April 19. On that date, Bulgarian troops crossed the border and authorities from Sofia took control of most of Macedonia. They faced no serious opposition and initially were welcomed by significant numbers of Macedonians.

Croatia

The small Ustaša minority led by Ante Pavelić had not been the first choice of German authorities to rule the fully separate Croatia created by the Wehrmacht's destruction of the Yugoslav state. Both the leader of the majority Croatian Peasant Party, Vladko Maček, and Hungary's Horthy regime were hastily solicited on the eve of the attack. Neither accepted the German invitation, and the representative of Nazi Foreign Minister von Ribbentrop turned to a Zagreb lieutenant of Ante Pavelić, the Ustaša leader who had been sustained and sometimes confined in Italy since 1929. Slavko Kvaternik, a former Habsburg officer who was now Pavelić's military commander, agreed to terms on April 5. The Ustaša readily accepted Italy's above-mentioned annexation of central Dalmatia and a titular Italian king for Croatia in return for the chance to take power. The Independent State of Croatia would incorporate all of Pavelić's native Bosnia-Hercegovina and the Srem region of eastern Slavonia, from Vukovar on the Danube to Zemun across that river from Belgrade.

Ante Pavelić and his small retinue rushed to Zagreb by April 15, but Kvaternik had already proclaimed the Independent State of Croatia (*Nezavisna Država Hrvatska*, NDH) on April 10, barely four days after the invasion. Other long-time followers also awaited Pavelić, led by chief propagandist Mile Budak and the new interior minister, Andrija Artuković. The 1939 Sporazum had allowed them to return and had given them a freer hand to attract new members. Party membership, by 1941, still numbered no more than the 12,000 in Communist ranks. Total support was still less than 10 percent of politically active Croats, significantly less than their counterparts, the Hungarian Arrow Cross and the Romanian Iron Guard.[7] Pavelić nonetheless proclaimed himself *poglavnik* (leader), named a cabinet, and appointed a series of *župani* (district leaders) from his party faithful without wider consultation or German–Italian approval.

The German and Italian troops that streamed into Croatia soon established a permanent presence behind the east–west lines in map 7.1; a central zone running from north of Mostar to south of Karlovac on the Italian side was to be left unoccupied. The powerful Axis presence may have put the Pavelić regime in power, but it did not control it or set its agenda. From this regime sprang the most savage intolerance seen anywhere in Europe during the Second World War, outside of the Nazi regime itself. Its overriding purpose was to create an ethnically pure Croatian state from which Serbs, Jews, and gypsies would be permanently cleansed.

The immediacy with which the Ustaša program was announced belies its apologists' claim, that it was a response to Serb rebellion. A decree on April 17, the day of Yugoslavia's formal surrender, established a series of three-man people's courts empowered to impose the death penalty with no appeal for any person who spoke against the regime, supported the Communist Party, or advocated smaller borders. Local Ustaša authorities abused even this wide latitude. Sometimes using lists of interwar Serb organizations, they began executing suspected opponents and encouraging their local militias to evict Serb families for deportation to Serbia. Deportations began on June 4. On April 25, another decree banned the use of the Cyrillic alphabet and designated the Serbian Orthodox church as the "Greek Eastern faith." By May, Muslim representatives from Bosnia-Hercegovina asked Italian commanders for protection in the unoccupied central zone. They suffered discrimination and some persecution despite the fact that Pavelić regarded Bosnian Muslims as the purest Croats, the "flower of the nation." From late April until June, the number of Serbs executed out-of-hand, primarily in Krajina towns like Glina and Knin, reached into the thousands. Jews were ordered to wear identifying patches on April 25 and had to be further identified as "non-Aryans" in an April 30 decree. They were barred from public facilities by June 4, the same date that Serbs began to be deported to Serbia. Locally, Jews were also obliged to perform labor details such as the destruction of the Serbian Orthodox church in Banja Luka.

During May and June, Pavelić's leading lieutenants used a series of propaganda meetings in thirty-five towns across their expanded territory to proclaim that Serbs and Jews had "no place in Croatia" because they "endangered Croatian existence." On June 22, in Gospić, in the center of the Krajina killing fields, Pavelić's education minister, Mile Budak, openly announced that one-third of the new state's 1.9 million Serbs would be deported to Serbia and another third converted to the Catholic church and thereby Croatianized (or reconverted, given the wild Ustaša claim that 200,000 Croats had been forced into Orthodoxy under inter-war Serb pressure). The other third, he added, would simply be killed.[8]

What role did the Croatian Catholic church and its ardently nationalist but politically naive archbishop, Alojzije Stepinac, play in these infamous events? With Mihailović and Tito, he was another of the war's most controversial figures. Stepinac did not encourage, much less initiate, the criminal propaganda and acts spreading outside of Zagreb. But he did, during these early months, welcome the new regime openly and enthusiastically, congratulating Kvaternik on his proclamation of the NDH two days afterwards and meeting formally with Pavelić on April 16. Stella Alexander argues that the coincidence of that procla-mation with the 1,300 year anniversary of Croatia's first link to Rome provided a religious justification that overcame Stepinac's doubts about Ustaša association with pagan Nazis and Fascist Italy's seizure of Dalmatia.[9] His encyclical to the clergy of April 28 spoke of "pride and rejoicing" at letting "the blood with its mysterious links with the country" speak instead of the tongue. It is easy, he concluded, "to see God's hand at work here." He also approved of a variety of new strictures, from prison sentences for swearing to the death penalty for abortion. But by May 22, he was protesting to Interior Minister Artuković against the regulation that compelled Jews to wear identifying badges in public, although conceding that they should be obliged at least to buy them. The archbishop's notorious trial by the postwar

Communist regime relied heavily on this early evidence and ignored his growing if private disenchantment with the Ustaša regime. Still, his narrow dogmatic view of the world, more comparable in Croatian history to Maček's than Radić's, continued throughout.

The Independent State of Croatia (NDH), occupation regimes, and active opposition, 1941–1942

From the summer of 1941 through 1942, the most senselessly brutal and politically disjointed events of the Second World War scarred what was the first "former Yugoslavia." Once the bulk of German troops left as planned for the Russian campaign and half of the much larger Italian force of 200,000 was withdrawn, open revolt broke out against the occupiers in Serbia, Montenegro, and Slovenia. But it was the Bosnian bloodbath launched by the NDH regime in Hercegovina that drove the Communist and Chetnik resistance to civil war with each other, led Italian forces into open conflict with Ustaša militias and alliance with some Chetnik units. New infusions of German troops also returned to pursue Tito's Partisans. Their first setbacks prompted the Bosnian Serb and Montenegrin Partisans to impose their own Red Terror on territories under their control. Yet they killed fewer innocent civilians than did the Chetniks, Germans, or Italians, and far fewer than the Ustaša. Meanwhile, the prospect of diverting German troops or supplies away from North Africa to Yugoslavia attracted the attention of the British government, further persuaded by Yugoslavia's leadership, exiled in London, that Mihailović's Chetniks were a large, coordinated, and active force.

NDH and Bosnia-Hercegovina

Ustaša militias and a hastily appointed gendarmerie, each eventually totalling some 20,000 men, fanned out across Bosnia-Hercegovina as well as the Croatian Krajina in the summer of 1941. A law unto themselves, they first tried to herd as many Serbs as possible into camps for expulsion to Serbia. Any resisters were killed. When expulsion became increasingly difficult, they killed many in their villages or dispatched them to one of several death camps.

The number of Serbs expelled is more certain than the number killed. By July 1941, German authorities in Serbia had recorded nearly 140,000 people pushed across the border, with perhaps another 40,000 unrecorded. The German military command in Belgrade responded by cutting the number of authorized border crossings to two, then to one, and by the autumn to none. The Ustaša regime's only alternatives were conversion or killing. Buttressed by pseudo-historical propaganda that the Serbs of Bosnia-Hercegovina and the old Military Border were largely Croats or Vlachs forced to convert to Orthodoxy in Ottoman times or the interwar period, the regime and many local, often Franciscan, priests launched a campaign of forced conversion. Roughly one-quarter million Serbs accepted this unchristian offer during 1941–42. A much smaller number joined the "Croatian Orthodox church." The regime hastily erected the denomination, headed by an available Russian priest, in 1942 as if to admit that the conversion campaign could go no further. Perhaps another 50,000 Serbs escaped to Serbia by year's end despite the German prohibition.

Controversy still surrounds the number of Serbs killed outright on the territory of the NDH by the end of 1942. That much disputed figure surely surpasses 300,000 men, women, and children.[10] Local massacres accounted for most of the early killing. A series of small camps near Gospić and elsewhere accounted for roughly 50,000 deaths, and finally the two explicit death camps of Jasenovac and Stara Gradiška were responsible for perhaps twice that number, not including the thousands sent to Auschwitz by 1943. Postwar Communist historians claimed that over one-half million people, Jews and gypsies included, died at Jasenovac alone, a figure doubled by recent Serbian pseudo-history and then rightly reduced to slightly less than 100,000 by Croatian scholars. It has since been further reduced and its consciously racist purpose denied by Croatian pseudo-history. Both pseudo-histories have diverted attention from the guilty verdict that hangs over the Ustaša regime as its only epitaph. The executions at villages like Knin, Glina, Pakrac, and Bijeljina, sowed more seeds of family revenge than did Jasenovac itself.

The Ustaša leadership tried to annihilate all of Croatia and Bosnia's small Jewish population of 36,000. Pushed ahead by its own anti-semitism rather than by German instructions or a popular Croatian mandate, the regime began the systematic arrest and execution of this defenseless urban population in June 1941. Barely 4,000 survived the war, while some 26,000 perished in the Croatian death camps or at Auschwitz. Among their "crimes," according to Ustaša leader, Eugen Kvaternik, Slavko's son, were the "several hundred thousand abortions" performed in interwar Croatia "by Jewish doctors so as to reduce the Croatian population." Underlying these persecutions, however, was the racist assumption that Croats were Aryans of Goth or Iranian origin who would be contaminated by contact with non-Aryan Jews or Slavs.

A number of the Catholic hierarchy and the leaders of the Croatian Peasant Party, as well as some leaders of the Bosnian Muslims, soon expressed opposition to the Pavelić regime.[11] They made passive protests calling on the regime to mend its ways rather than exhorting active opposition, but they still deserve recognition. If Archbishop Stepinac did not dismiss criminal clergy or threaten to resign himself, he did protest privately to the Ustaša leadership against forced conversions and mistreatment of Jews on several occasions. His discreet initiatives saved thousands of individual lives. Nor did he plead the regime's case with the Vatican representative who was quickly dispatched from Rome to Zagreb. The NDH never received the diplomatic recognition by the Holy See that Pavelić ardently desired. One-third of the Croatian Peasant Party (HSS) leaders selected by the regime for the Sabor, or National Assembly, of 1942, refused to serve. The party's village rank and file typically withdrew into their families. HSS leader Vladko Maček refused repeated pressures to express public support for the regime and was transferred from house arrest to Jasenovac for his defiance.

The Ustaša courtship of the Bosnian Muslims as the "pearl of the Croatian nation" never persuaded more than a minority to abandon their Bosnian identity. Muslim religious and town leaders were already organizing protest meetings by the autumn of 1941. The Ustaša had elevated pro-Croat Muslims from the interwar period to several high positions in the NDH hierarchy and the restored land seized in the agrarian reform to a number of leading begs. This could not compensate for the regime's denial of non-Croat identity in Bosnia and the crimes committed against some of the Muslims, many Serbs, and almost all Jews. Muslim resolutions in Sarajevo, Tuzla, Banja Luka, and Bjieljina protested the persecution of Serbs in particular. Bosnian Muslims in those towns, moreover, were largely responsible for hiding the 2,000 Jews (out of 14,000 before the war) who survived.

The first active opposition to the Ustaša regime came, not surprisingly, from the rural Serbs of the Krajina, Dalmatia, and Bosnia-Hercegovina. The initial uprising began spontaneously in eastern Hercegovina in June 1941. Confronting the region's two-thirds Serb majority were a murderous new government and their local agents. Most of the latter were drawn from Muslims who made up the other third of the population and whose ancestors had been landlords to Serb sharecroppers until 1919. Uncoordinated groups of rebel Serbs spread from there. They had two features in common. First, their leaders were local men who belonged to the Agrarian Party or to one of the interwar Chetnik organizations or both. They were not officers in the royal army nor initially under the direction of Mihailović's Chetniks. Secondly, while these Hercegovinian Serbs attacked Ustaša authorities and facilities, they also conducted murderous raids against vulnerable peasant villages, more likely to be Bosnian or Sandžak Muslim than Croat. The largest massacre of over one thousand men, women, and children occurred in the east Bosnian town of Foča.

The array of forces in Yugoslavia and their relation to one another during the Second World War, especially in this early going, was a more complicated business. In order to understand the most fateful of these relations, Chetniks versus Partisans, we must first distinguish between the roles played by German and Italian forces in the NDH. True, a coordinated Chetnik force collaborated with the two German offensives of 1943 against a growing Partisan army, but their actions grew out of more defensible precedents from 1941. In the earlier period, uncoordinated Chetnik units had formed alliances with the Italian divisions recalled to push aside the marauding Ustaša militias and restore order. These early arrangements established Italian authority in towns if not in villages. German military presence north of the NDH demarcation line had meanwhile been reduced to two divisions as the Russian campaign wore on. The disdain of the German military attaché in Zagreb, General Edmund Glaise von Horstenau, for the NDH further limited Nazi support. A former Habsburg officer, his animosity toward the Ustaša regime as well as the Italian presence left only von Ribbentrop's ill-prepared diplomatic representative, the one-time Baltic Nazi, Siegfried Kasche, to speak for the regime.

The regime's excesses fueled the readiness of the one large Axis force, the Italian army, to confront it. Their mutual antagonism opened the way for the Chetnik movement in the NDH.[12] The Partisans' failure in early 1942 to hold the allegiance of many initial followers widened the opening. Partisan commanders' brutal treatment of entire villages suspected of Chetnik sympathies or of resisting local Communist authority has been called the "left deviation" by Communist historians and the Red Terror by others. The Partisans' lack of food and arms, a condition less severe for the Chetniks because of their Italian connections, also played a part in the Chetniks' ascendancy in Hercegovina. So did the decision of the London government-in-exile, now headed by Slobodan Jovanović, to appoint Mihailović minister of war in January 1942. Driving that decision, in addition to the Red Terror, were Chetnik–Partisan relations in Montenegro and Serbia.

Montenegro and Serbia

The Partisan model for an armed uprising intolerant of the slightest opposition came from Montenegro. Italian occupation authorities let a small group of *zelenaši*, or autonomist Greens seeking to separate

Montenegro from Serbia, persuade them that the titular independence of Montenegro under an Italian king would meet little opposition. Most Italian troops could therefore proceed to withdraw. But on July 13, 1941, the day after an Orthodox holiday on which the Green group proclaimed independence, armed villagers and a number of surviving Yugoslav army officers and men rose up in opposition. They quickly seized control of the upland majority of Montenegro. Milovan Djilas, the highest ranking Montenegrin in the Communist leadership, and Arso Jovanović, later the highest ranking army officer to side with Stalin against Tito, were dispatched from Serbia to fan the scattered flames into a single bonfire. Only three weeks later, an Italian division returned to put down the uprising and to turn loose their allies, the largely Turkish Sandžak Muslims, to loot and burn. Djilas himself has described how the retreating Partisans now summarily executed any opponents, after merely punishing them in July.[13]

Word of these arbitrary executions encouraged Partisan desertions and swelled the ranks of the Chetnik units that regrouped with Italian approval across Montenegro and also eastern Hercegovina by early 1942. Although the three major groups of Montenegrin Chetniks were all commanded by officers from the former Yugoslav army, they did not constitute a unified force. Only the eastern commander, Pavle Djurišić, was openly pro-Mihailović and was probably in contact with Chetnik headquarters in Serbia. But rather than pursue any coordinated operations, Djurišić concentrated on raids of revenge against the Sandžak Muslims, many of them innocent villagers.

In Serbia, several attempts at coordinated resistance proved abortive, and Chetniks were fighting Partisans by the end of 1941. At the same time, German army units decimated the Partisan forces in Serbia. Tito had to move his headquarters to eastern Bosnia. Survival now depended on attracting new recruits from the NDH and Montenegro. Mihailović meanwhile tried to preserve his Serbian base by winning British support for the longer run and negotiating German tolerance for the time being. He succeeded in neither.

The Partisan–Chetnik conflict further complicated the civil war that the Ustaša had started in the NDH. Only Slovenia, as we shall see in the next section, could confront the occupying forces with something like a united front. Several Chetnik units had joined and even collaborated with the Partisan forces that began their campaign of sabotage and small-scale attacks against German forces on July 4, 1941. Disruption of German lines of communication south to Salonika, the very danger that the invasion was supposed to preclude, brought fast reaction. The German army commander for Serbia replaced the small Commission of

Administrators, a set of Serbian collaborators in Belgrade, with a full-fledged puppet government led by General Milan Nedić. Prince Paul, it may be recalled, had dismissed Nedić early in 1941 for advocating a German alliance. The interwar Chetnik leader, Kosta Pećanac, and the one genuinely fascist Serbian leader, Dimitrije Ljotić, added their respective contingents of 8,000 and 4,000 men to the Serbian State Guard that Nedić assembled primarily from the old gendarmerie. Together their numbers roughly matched the Ustaša militia's total of 30,000, but they never operated independently nor did they initiate the serious war crimes that stained the soil of Serbia in the late fall of 1941. Instead, according to recent scholarship, Wehrmacht instructions and a largely Austrian contingent of local German commanders bore that responsibility.[14]

German army units, recalled explicitly to stop the attacks and destroy the rebel forces launched the new round of war crimes. By September an infantry division and an armored unit had arrived, further armed with a new directive from the Wehrmacht's High Command that 100 civilians were to be executed for every German soldier killed in the future and 50 for each one wounded. Partisan attacks and attendant killings continued into October despite advertised reprisals. General Franz Böhme, the former Habsburg officer who was the German army commander for Serbia, decided to set a still harsher example. At Kraljevo and Kragujevac, German and Vojvodina Volksdeutsche units, supported by Serbian State Guards, cordoned off the towns in order to execute all the adult males. When too few adults could be found in Kragujevac on October 21, schoolboys were taken as well to swell the total past 2,000. They were marched to a field outside of town, lined up in rows, and shot down the next morning. "Go ahead and shoot," said an elderly school teacher, "I am conducting my class."

The massacre was a watershed. It occurred just a few days before the arrival of the first British officer to reach the Mihailović headquarters at Ravna Gora, Captain William Hudson of the Special Operations Expedition (SOE), and one week before Mihailović's second and last meeting with Tito. The slaughter of so many Serbs reinforced Mihailović's resistance to the Communist strategy of consciously provoking German reprisals in order to drive survivors into the hills and into their ranks. Mihailović's instructions from London and his own instincts were to husband his resources and Serbian lives until Germany had been defeated or at least until a new Salonika front was established, as it had been in the First World War. Hudson's arrival confirmed his expectation that British arms would help him prepare for that distant day. Only Tito's promise to share the arms already being produced at the

7.1 Tito as Partisan commander, 1944, flanked by Ranković, Vukmanović-Tempo and Djilas on the right, and Kardelj, Žujović and Bakarić on the left. Andrija Hebrang does not appear.

Partisan headquarters in Užice in the southwest persuaded Mihailović to sign a tentative agreement at least to avoid conflict with one another. But several clashes scuttled the agreement by the end of October.

The German field commanders took no notice of this division and pressed ahead with reinforcements sufficient to destroy all active resistance. In the process, they executed some 25,000 civilians. Mihailović understandably concluded that his force of less than 20,000 men, ill-armed and in scattered units, could not survive against a larger, far better equipped German force. By November 11, 1941, he initiated talks with German representatives to negotiate a *modus vivendi*. But when the Germans demanded total surrender, he abandoned his headquarters and scattered his forces still further. This genuine weakness and the passive strategy it encouraged escaped British notice. Churchill's commanders were still ready to believe what the Yugoslav government-in-exile told them about Mihailović and were eager to trumpet any evidence of resistance inside Hitler's Europe. Mihailović was thus able to maintain the image, in Walter Robert's words, of "Allied Hero" through 1942.[15] He was presumed to control the Chetnik forces in Hercegovina and Montenegro discussed above, and they were assumed to be fighting the Axis occupiers.

The German offensive had meanwhile forced Tito and his main force of barely 10,000 men and women to abandon Užice for Foča in eastern Bosnia at the end of 1941. There they barely survived the second of what would be seven German assaults by 1944. By the end of 1942, however, a reversal of fortune and reputation had begun.

Communist advantages, 1943–1944

That reversal has generated much more controversy than any other aspect of the Second World War in Yugoslavia. The continuing debate derives not only from the greater availability of primary evidence, much of it in English, but also from the temptation of anti-Communist Serbian and Croatian authors to assume that British and later American policy must have been decisive in the rise of this small Communist party. After all, it received no assistance from the Soviet Union until a small military mission arrived in February 1944 and none of significance until the Red Army entered Serbia from Bulgaria that September. Surely, the argument ran, the British government's decision in 1943 to switch its support from Mihailović to Tito and the increasing flow of American supplies to the Partisans in 1944 was crucial. But the weight of Western scholarship suggests that it was not.

Neither was Allied policy irrelevant. Let us sketch its main features and their consequences before turning to the internal developments that proved to be decisive. Churchill's government was responsible for Anglo-American planning in Southeastern Europe and he himself enthused on several occasions about the possibility of an Allied landing on the Dalmatian coast. Each time, however, his general staff and the American command quickly persuaded him to stick to the strategy agreed on in 1943. That strategy, for Greece as well as Yugoslavia, was to promote the deception that there would indeed be such an invasion in order to divert German troops away from first Sicily and then Italy. And it worked. Successive deceptions convinced not only Hitler but also Tito, Mihailović, and the Greek resistance leaders that a landing in great force was pending. In fact, as Churchill told the Commonwealth (then Dominion) leaders whose troops were heavily involved in Mediterranean operations, in May 1944, "there had never been any question of major action in the Balkans."[16]

Allied strategy as perceived at the time encouraged Mihailović and worried Tito. Would there be an Anglo-American military presence in Yugoslavia during (and then presumably after) the war? In the event, the wartime deception that the Western allies were preparing to come inadvertently worked to Communist advantage by drawing more German troops into the region and onto their trail. Simply by escaping them, Tito won more local and Allied support than by pursuing the civil war with the Chetniks into which the disconnected brutalities of 1942 were drawing him. And at war's end, there would be no western forces on the ground to contend with or to prevent the settling of local scores.

The road to Communist power by 1945 could never have been traveled even under these circumstances had the Partisan forces not grown in size, unity, and, to a lesser extent, in popular support from 1943. At the same time, the Chetniks lost followers outside of Serbia, and the Ustaša regime forfeited effective control of most NDH territory outside of Zagreb. In addition, Communist leadership of a Slovenian uprising against the Italianization measures of 1941 was able to sustain the one united opposition front anywhere in the former Yugoslavia, even after disunited rivals appeared in 1943.

Ranking the several sources of Communist strength in Slovenia and elsewhere, the Churchill government's decision to abandon Mihailović in favor of Tito was not high on the list. Some British studies of the Special Operations Executive (SOE) have blamed its Cairo headquarters for Communist sympathies that denied Mihailović a fair hearing. Others have argued that London conservatives prevented earlier support to the more active Partisan units. Both biases existed, but neither one could eliminate the other nor overcome the evidence from both electronic intelligence and SOE missions on the ground – nearly twenty by the end of 1943 – that the Partisans were doing more damage to the German war effort. Brigadier Fitzroy Maclean, a Conservative friend of Churchill's, dispatched the testimony on November 6 that was decisive only because it confirmed what Ultra decoding of top secret German military messages was revealing.[17]

Nor could the quarrelsome and increasingly ineffective Yugoslav government-in-exile command the respect necessary to override that evidence. The exiled government's decision to promote Mihailović to general and minister of war in January 1942 enabled the civilian cabinet to dispense with a military candidate for prime minister, namely the difficult General Simović, leader of the 1941 coup and sponsor of an effort to remove the members of the pre-coup General Staff in Cairo. But no significant military force could be assembled in Cairo or London. The new prime minister was the much respected but 72-year-old and politically inexperienced Slobodan Jovanović. He could not prevent the feckless young king, Petar II, from pushing him out just as he, Jovanović, had persuaded his Serbian colleagues to accept a federal reorganization of Yugoslavia after the war. By August 1943, the king had installed his personal cabinet of civil servants, not because they disapproved of reorganization, but because they would approve of his pending marriage. Churchill also approved, but the king was too isolated by 1944 to claim that he represented a political consensus even among the exiles. To cite the sympathetic appraisal of Stevan Pavlowitch, "Whatever the Yugoslav government represented, it was not unity."[18]

British disillusionment with Mihailović first surfaced in February 1943. He berated British officers for London's failure to supply him with the arms he had requested or to understand his reasons for not attacking German targets more often. SOE mission chief S. W. Bailey, who had only reached the Montenegrin headquarters two months before, radioed out a verbatim transcript that made it all the way to Churchill's desk. The Mihailović tirade triggered a reaction that followed accumulating evidence of some Chetnik units collaborating with Italian or even German forces and, more important, of almost no Chetnik units disrupting them. It is doubtful, however, that these reports, many of them from Partisan sources passed on to the admitted British Communist, James Klugman, and other sympathizers in SOE, would have reversed British policy by the end of 1943 if not for three decisive events on the ground, all detailed for Anglo-American intelligence by Ultra intercepts.

First, the main Partisan force of some 25,000 men survived Operation Weiss, the largest of the seven German-led offensives against them during the war. They endured heavy losses in heroically crossing and recrossing the Neretva river to escape German units from Sarajevo and then scattered a Chetnik force of 12,000 that awaited them. From this point forward, the Partisan forces from Bosnia to Montenegro began to attract new members, some from the Chetnik side. (Had the Chetniks succeeded against the Partisans in that battle, they would have faced disarmament at German hands.)

The next German offensive was Operation Schwartz. In May an amalgam of German, Bulgarian, Italian, and Ustaša units whose numbers exceeded 100,000 tried to pin Tito's main force, barely 20,000 men, against the Zelengora mountain in southeastern Bosnia. Again they escaped, although the massacre of their rear guard and their wounded at Sutjeska brought total losses for the engagement to 6,500. Zelengora became a second turning point because Ultra intercepts allowed a British mission led by a friend of Churchill's, F. W. (Bill) Deakin, to arrive precisely in time to witness it all, including some belated Chetnik aid to the offensive. Reports like Deakin's of German divisions being diverted to pursue the Partisans began to accumulate. Still, this intelligence might not have persuaded the British to switch their support to Tito if they had known of his lieutenant Milovan Djilas' contact with German representatives that March. According to Walter Roberts and now Djilas himself, the Communists were ready to accept a cease fire with the Germans in return for a free hand against the Chetniks; according to a German participant, they even considered an alliance in the event of a large British landing on the Adriatic coast.[19] Hitler would have none of such bargaining, and it went no further.

Then in September 1943, Italy left the war. This third turning point went beyond the Italian equipment that fell into Partisan hands. Italian commanders had already decided that summer to abandon their own alliance with the Chetniks, going so far as to disarm a number of units. This decision caused more Chetniks to defect to the Partisans and guaranteed that there would be no Italian effort to turn over arms and equipment to the Chetniks when their divisions departed in September. By the autumn of 1943, Tito's forces had grown sufficiently to make further bargaining with the Germans unlikely. As the Italian windfall compensated for limited Anglo-American supplies, the Partisans' total strength now swelled past 100,000 to face a German force that had doubled to thirteen divisions.

The Partisans' survival and ascendancy in 1943 combined with the Allied offensives of 1944 to settle the outcome of the Second World War in Yugoslavia. By the end of 1943, Mihailović had retreated to Serbia, where his total force of 50,000 had to strike a variety of arrangements with the German occupiers to remain in place. Tito's force of twice that number stood behind his decision to convene a second meeting of the Anti-Fascist Liberation Movement for Yugoslavia (AVNOJ). It had assembled on a much slimmer base in Bihać the year before. Now on November 29, 1943, his 143 delegates set up a provisional government at Jajce in central Bosnia. He proclaimed a National Committee for the Liberation of Yugoslavia. Bill Deakin looked on without a Soviet observer present or prior approval from Moscow. The Jajce program denounced the royal government and proposed a federal structure that would include separate units for Bosnia-Hercegovina and Macedonia plus minority rights for Albanians and others. The objections of Moša Pijade and other Serbs to a Bosnian republic were overcome, but not to the extent of recognizing the Bosnian Muslims as a constituent group. In order to understand what sort of Yugoslavia they would actually begin to govern and reshape simultaneously less than a year later, let us look briefly at the separate legacies left to Slovenia, Croatia, Bosnia-Hercegovina, and Serbia by the final stages of the war. These legacies would return to haunt Tito's Yugoslavia after his death and help to destroy it.

Slovenia

The most benign of the legacies was Slovenia's. Barely two weeks after half of Slovenia was annexed to Italy and the other half putatively to Germany, the Nazi attack on the Soviet Union in June freed the Slovenian Communist Party to form a Liberation Front (OF) for resistance. Repressive Italianization in the southern zone and a Nazi plan to deport over one-quarter million Slovenes from the north to make room for German immigrants fanned popular resentment. Fewer than 20,000 Slovenes were eventually forced to leave for Serbia or Bosnia, but 35,000 were sent to the Reich for "Germanization." In any case, the German military presence was too formidable to challenge quickly in the north. But, in the south, a Communist leadership experienced in underground activity was able to attract followers from the larger Christian Social Party and Sokol youth organization. Italian forces put down their uprising during the summer of 1941, executing 9,000 Slovenes and imprisoning 35,000 more in concentration camps. These abuses helped draw in more members over the next two years.

Italian and then German reprisals against resisting Slovenian villages opened the way for Mihailović's one effort to win non-Serbs to the Chetnik banner. Both his Blue Guards and Italian-sponsored White

Guards were able to assemble some units during 1943–44. Their numbers plus those of the Slovenian Peoples' Party (SLS) units slightly outnumbered the Communist-led Liberation Front in 1943, even after the acquisition of Italian arms boosted the Partisan ranks from 2,500 to 6,000. But the Partisans' greater unity and clearer purpose gave them the advantage before the general tide of battle turned. The high point of the Front's unity came at the AVNOJ congress at Jajce in 1943. The Christian socialist leader of SLS, dissident Eduard Kocbek, spoke eloquently there of "Communists and Catholics working together." Their uneasy alliance lasted through the war, encouraged in 1944 by the one American mission to take a leading role on the Partisan side. A small OSS unit worked successfully with the Slovene Partisans of Styria to destroy the only double-track rail line connecting central Germany through Vienna with the Italian front via the Ljubljana Gap.[20]

Croatia and Bosnia-Hercegovina

The Independent State of Croatia (NDH) left larger footprints across the last years of the Second World War than its limited territorial authority or its subordinate role in fighting the Partisans might suggest. Nor was this because of widespread popular support. The Ustaša survived in Zagreb until May 1945 because the German army needed to protect its line of retreat. To the last, Archbishop Stepinac and the Catholic hierarchy made no public statement disavowing the Ustaša regime, despite the abovementioned private protests and efforts to protect threatened individuals. The archbishop even celebrated the regime's fourth anniversary with *Te Deums* on April 10. No Kocbek stepped forward to suggest an agreement with the Communists or any need to try Franciscan zealots or others for war crimes. First Communist politicians and then Serbian historians would use the unredeemed record of the NDH to question any postwar initiative, however unrelated, from Croatian politicians or clergy.

While its early war crimes left scars that would be slow to heal, the NDH's later loss of control makes other issues equally important for the creation of the second Yugoslavia. These were (1) the economic catastrophe that the NDH precipitated in Croatia; (2) the rise of the separate Croatian Communist liberation front; and (3) the choices that Bosnian Muslims made between the Partisans and the belated Nazi effort to win the allegiance forfeited by the NDH.

The economic incompetence and corruption of the Ustaša cadre soon derailed Nazi plans to include Croatia in the greater German economy (*Grossraumwirtschaft*). By 1943, according to the authoritative study by

Holm Sundhaussen, both sides received far less than they had bargained for.[21] The problems went beyond the Partisans' disruption of transport, largely confined to Bosnia and Dalmatia before 1944. Ustaša officials could not deliver to Germany the promised quantities of bauxite and other non-ferrous metals. They could not collect the grain needed to feed the smaller towns, despite their effort to seize the recently expanded cooperative network of the Croatian Peasant Party (HSS) and use it for that purpose. Their trade deficit with the Third Reich added to a rate of inflation that by 1943 had reduced the *kuna*, a medieval denomination resurrected to distinguish it from the Yugoslav dinar, to less than 10 percent of its 1941 value. By year's end, industrial production had dropped to 20 percent of its prewar level. Only the one-quarter million Croatians who worked at one time or another in the Reich itself made a significant contribution to the German war effort.

Croatian opposition to a regime that had done nothing good for anyone, except its 50,000 Ustaša officials and officers, grew apace in 1943–44. The passive policies of Maček and other HSS leaders who had not gone over to the Ustaša left the Partisans to benefit. Italian annexation of Dalmatia allowed local Communists to attract Croats and Serbs to a Partisan force of a few thousand. From a largely Dalmatian contingent that was perhaps 10 percent of the 20,000 Partisans in 1942, the Croatian share had grown by early 1944 to some 30 percent of a total exceeding 100,000. Party leader Andrija Hebrang and his lieutenants attracted this wider support by emphasizing the separate structure of the Croatian Liberation Council (ZAVNOH). The Council dated from the same Bihać conference of 1942 that had founded the all-Yugoslav AVNOJ. Tito had authorized ZAVNOH to disguise its connection to a Communist resistance that was 90 percent Serb and Montenegrin at the start. Hebrang pushed the distinction hard through the rest of the war. By May 1944, he had proclaimed ZAVNOH to be the reincarnated Croatian Sabor, promising more autonomy after the war than the 1939 Sporazum had offered from "the Serb clique from Belgrade." Although Hebrang made some effort to reassure the Serb population, he spoke too much of forthcoming Croatian autonomy and "his own telegraph agency," in Tito's words. By the summer of 1944, Tito removed him as ZAVNOH leader.[22]

Bosnian Muslim losses occurred primarily at Chetnik hands but increasingly from Ustaša units. In 1942, several Muslim leaders sent a memorandum to Hitler protesting Ustaša depredations and touting their own Gothic origins. Their offer of a Bosnian Muslim Legion in return for autonomy within the NDH remained a dead letter until SS chief Heinrich Himmler took it up, as another of his belated efforts to raise new, non-German divisions. The Pavelić regime violently objected to such a division, despite the absence of any German promise of Muslim autonomy. The Handžar, or Scimitar Division, did assemble at least 12,000 men. But they were quickly dispatched for a long training period in France and Germany, distinguished mainly by a mutiny. When they finally returned to Bosnia in February 1944, some units carried out enough indiscriminate murder and other atrocities against Serb villagers to surpass what the Schutskorps had done in the First World War. Yet more Bosnian Muslims had joined the Partisans directly or defected from the division by mid-1944 than had committed war crimes on the German side, and a slightly greater percentage of Muslims died during the war than did Bosnian Serbs.[23] None of this would matter by the 1990s to the descendants of the dead villagers or to the Bosnian Serb politicians who played on their memories.

Serbia

The Serbia to which Draža Mihailović returned in mid-1943 had seen less actual warfare, but suffered more at Nazi hands than any other part of the former Yugoslavia. Two German divisions, a large Gestapo complement, and the subordinate State Guards of General Nedić maintained order only by executing several hundred people every month under the OKW reprisal order of 1941. Occupation costs were six times the per capita amount of those levied on the NDH. Little meat reached Belgrade after the middle of 1943, while the inflation rate was 50 percent more than Zagreb's high level. Forced labor extracted only half of prewar production of lead from Trepča and copper from Bor. Over 100,000 laborers were taken to the Reich, constituting Serbia's main contribution to the German war effort. The mid-1943 mission of Hitler's new Balkan emissary, the former I.G. Farben executive, Hermann Neubacher, eased reprisals as part of a new anti-Communist campaign, but made no economic concessions or other improvements.[24]

The Neubacher mission did succeed by the end of 1943 in drawing Mihailović's commanders in Serbia into negotiating with the Germans. They reached agreements for four zones where Chetnik forces could at least survive as long as they stayed isolated in rural areas. As 1944 began, the beleaguered Chetnik movement and a bewildered Mihailović convened a large congress at Ba where he tried to stem the turn to collaboration. Still loyal to the monarchy, Mihailović now advocated a federal and democratic Yugoslavia. He set aside the homogeneous Great Serbia on which Moljević and his other political advisors had insisted in 1941, but offered no further proposal for a federal alternative. Nor did

Mihailović oppose the Chetnik truces with German forces that soon covered all of Serbia.

By September 1944, Anglo-American planes had been bombing Belgrade for six months, and the Red Army entered Bulgaria unopposed. As Tito's main force of 80,000 approached from Bosnia, Mihailović could now muster barely half that number. Most were from Serbia, in contrast to a Partisan force with disproportionate numbers of Montenegrins, Bosnian Muslims, and Bosnian and Croatian Serbs in their ranks. Chetnik defectors were already joining the Partisans before Mihailović's last surreal gamble, to greet the Red Army in Belgrade and join forces, failed in early October. King Petar had acceded to British demands the month before and broadcast a radio appeal for all Yugoslavs to support the Partisans. Also in September, President Roosevelt accepted Churchill's request that the ambiguous OSS mission led by Robert McDowell be withdrawn from Mihailović's headquarters. It had arrived in July to evacuate US airmen who had bailed out over Serbia if their planes could not make it back from bombing the Ploeşti oil refineries in Romania. This they did, but with enough sympathy for the Chetniks to convince Tito that the Americans were providing Mihailović with weapons. While the Americans inadvertently stiffened Chetnik resolve, they did not augment the capacity of Mihailović's units to offer more than scattered resistance to the Partisan forces that entered Belgrade on October 20.[25]

Tito had been busy in the meantime. Following a close escape from a German attack on his Drvar headquarters in May 1944, a British plane bore him to the island of Vis and then in August to Italy. Already resplendent in a uniform worthy of the marshal's rank he had adopted, the former Josip Broz drew on the Habsburg manners to which he was attracted as a young worker in Prague and Vienna to impress his hosts with his "un-Balkan" respectability. Meetings with the British army command and Churchill also established his political acumen. Tito left political plans for postwar Yugoslavia and for the king artfully vague, but denied any intention to install a Communist government. He declared himself ready instead to work with the new head of the London government, Ivan Šubašić. They would arrange a democratic postwar transition on the basis of the Jajce program, just as the two of them had agreed during their June meeting on Vis.

Stalin was less impressed with Tito's bearing and claims of domestic support than were the British leaders. He nonetheless acceded to Tito's request that the main Partisan force liberate Belgrade along with the Red Army. He also promised to provide arms for twelve Partisan divisions by the end of 1944, thus ending the dependence on Anglo-American aid.

The Partisan leader's secret trip from Vis to Moscow in September reminded Western policy makers that they were still dealing with a Communist. By November 1944, that clever Communist and his colleagues were in Belgrade while the Red Army had moved north into Hungary, in hot pursuit of German forces who were not ready to make a serious stand until Budapest. In contrast to the rest of Eastern Europe, neither the Red Army nor Soviet political supervision would be decisive in the consolidation of Communist power that founded the second Yugoslavia.

Consolidating Communist power, 1945

The Partisans' heroic survival, multi-ethnic composition, and promised federal program allowed the KPJ to consolidate postwar power even in the absence of Soviet troops. Tito adopted a ruthlessly Stalinist and centralizing set of tactics to seize that chance. Even then, such tactics might not have succeeded but for the justification that settling wartime accounts and repairing wartime devastation provided. The execution or trial of wartime opponents, all painted in the villainous black that only the Croatian Ustaša and Ljotić's smaller Serbian movement deserved, set a precedent for the intimidation or arrest of all political opponents.

By the end of 1945, a newly elected Constituent Assembly, in which the Communists' National Front held all the seats, swept aside the provisional coalition that included Šubašić. Despite a political monopoly, Tito and his inner circle devoted considerable attention to striking a workable ethnic balance. The new internal borders they fixed and compensating movements of populations they proposed would trouble the second Yugoslavia but mainly after Tito's death.

Settling civil war accounts

The Tito regime made its first priority for 1945 the defeat of the domestic military forces still arrayed against it. The bulk of surviving Chetnik units from Serbia, Montenegro, and Bosnia were concentrated under Mihailović's command in eastern Bosnia, but they split up in March. Montenegrin units under Pavle Djurišić headed for Slovenia to join the last stand that the fascist Dimitrije Ljotić and his small Serbian Volunteer Corps were organizing there with Slovenian Blue Guards and Croatian or Bosnian Serb Chetniks. Most never made it through German or Ustaša lines. Mihailović and some 12,000 men headed south. But in May 1945, before they could reach Serbia, Partisan army and now air forces trapped them against the same Zelengora mountain from which

Tito's troops had barely escaped less than two years before. Mihailov and a few survivors eluded capture until March 1946, but his capacity for military resistance was finished. Meanwhile, the pursuit of individual Chetnik supporters, strongest in eastern Bosnia and Hercegovina and western Serbia, justified the rapid growth and unchecked authority of the Partisans' wartime security service. Tito told Aleksandar Ranković, the head of the Organization for the Peoples' Defense (OZNa), that its wider purpose was "to strike terror into the hearts of those who did not like this sort of Yugoslavia." Mihailović's show trial from June into July of 1946 allowed the regime's prosecutor to add previous members of the London government, even Slobodan Jovanović, to the list of those accused. The "whirlwind of events and strivings" that Mihailović lamented in a last, dignified statement before his execution swept perhaps 100,000 people to their deaths during 1945–46.[26]

An unrecorded number died in the one other significant military campaign waged by the new People's Army after the Red Army and the retreating Germans had taken the Second World War out of Yugoslavia. Italian-controlled Albania had incorporated Kosovo after the destruction of Yugoslavia in 1941. The Kosovar Albanians had already proved to be the most difficult minority for Tito's Communists to coopt, Germans aside. The Kosovars' Skenderbeg SS Division had conducted a reign of terror against any Serbs they found in Kosovo or Montenegro. Even Kosovar Communists, most of them Albanians, had endorsed postwar union with a Communist Albania at the end of 1943 in a controversial meeting in Bujan, just across the prewar Albanian border. Tito disavowed such a union, but Serbian historians in the 1980s would hold the meeting itself against him. In 1944 Tito sent Svetozar Vukmanović-Tempo bearing vague promises of some sort of Balkan federation to win support in Kosovo and Macedonia. Now some of the Kosovars who had used local authority under the Italians to drive out the Serbs in 1941 mobilized other Albanians fearing Serbian subordination. They launched an armed rebellion against Partisan authority near the Albanian border in December 1944. The revolt spread as far northeast as the Trepča lead mines and escalated into fierce battles for a number of towns. Army and OZNa units were not able to extinguish it until the summer of 1945.[27]

For Kosovo there followed a repressive regime based on a small Communist core that remained in place under Serbian or Albanian leadership throughout the second Yugoslavia. Tito barred the return of interwar Serb colonists, some of them Chetniks, but also others who had simply fled for their lives. Partisans or their supporters were to be given homesteads in the Vojvodina or their native region as part of a new colonization program described in the next section. The Kosovo ban did not, however, give local Albanian Communists much authority nor did it open the border to massive migration from Albania.

Croatia and Slovenia suffered the largest death toll accompanying the Communist consolidation of power. The Ustaša and Slovenian White Guard or Chetnik units who had surrendered directly to the Partisans in April–May of 1945 or were handed back by the British army were executed out of hand. Many members of the much less accountable Croatian Home Army (*Domobran*) and Slovenian Village Guard were caught up in this supremely unjudicial process, although the majority survived in detention camps. Upwards of 30,000 people, guilty of collaboration but not war crimes, were shot in the Slovenian forests at Bleiburg and Kočevski Rog, acts never acknowledged officially until the last years of the second Yugoslavia.

Judicial proceedings also played a significant, officially trumpeted role in the Communist consolidation of power in Croatia. By June 1945, trials began with the well deserved conviction of leading figures from the Jasenovac death camp and those Ustaša leaders who had not escaped to Germany or Italy. The trials quickly grew to include a significant number of Catholic priests, some of whom were guilty of forced conversions and war crimes. Archbishop Stepinac and other high churchmen insisted on their own innocence and pointed to their success in saving, among others, several thousand children of Serbs and Partisans. Stepinac had none the less made too many public gestures implying support for the NDH for his authority to survive unless he accepted the Communist regime with open enthusiasm. This was beyond him, let alone taking Tito's hints that he make the Croatian church independent of the Vatican or that he simply leave the country. As new measures for civil marriage, the inclusion of church property in the land reform, and limits on Catholic schools and press cascaded down on the Croatian church, Stepinac responded openly with more and harsher criticism than any he had directed at Ustaša leader Ante Pavelić.[28] His own trial and conviction became inevitable. If the evidence of his responsibility for the crimes of the lower clergy is still in dispute, the results of his conviction are not. His November 1946 sentence to prison, later commuted to house arrest until his death in 1960, barred him and the Catholic hierarchy from any role in shaping the second Yugoslavia. Requirements for teaching licenses cut away the church's presence in Croatia's system of education. Perhaps most important, many Serbs remained certain of his guilt and many Croats presumed his innocence, transforming the issue of Catholic religious rights into an ethnic dispute open to later exploitation.

Internal borders and an early election

Tito's Communist Party and Partisan army were well positioned to consolidate political power during the course of 1945. They were simply not prepared to tolerate legal opposition or a critical press, whatever their anti-fascist credentials. Strong credentials were hard to come by in Croatia, where the one large democratic party from the prewar period, the HSS, had fractured badly during the war. Many leaders and supporters had gone over to the Ustaša or to the Partisans. Party chief Vladko Maček had done neither, but said little before choosing emigration over likely arrest by zealous Croatian Communists. The remaining HSS democrats tried to rally around Marija Radić, the widow of party icon Stjepan Radić, but they faced opposition from Tito's coalition partner, their own colleague Ivan Šubašić, as well as from the Croatian Communist Party and its powerful ZAVNOH apparatus. Šubašić clung to the belief that he could preserve a separate HSS identity within a Communist-led coalition.

In Serbia the leaders of the three surviving parties were ready to join in creating a new Yugoslavia, even one without the monarchy. They never had a chance either, as the seminal post-Tito critique of Vojislav Koštunica and Kosta Čavoški made clear to Serbian readers during the 1980s.[29]

Serbia's Democratic, Republican, and Agrarian Parties faced a Communist Party of Yugoslavia whose membership had risen by 1945 to a formidable 140,000. The previous December, its leadership had adroitly transformed the wartime National Liberation Front into a new National Front that would contest the elections to the constituent assembly in place of the KPJ. By September 1945, Tito's AVNOJ delegates and a separate Croatian *Republican* Peasant Party, set up by Partisan supporters to exclude poor Šubašić and his few representatives, dominated the Provisional Assembly. It confirmed the election date for November 11, barely six months after Partisan forces had secured the western regions. Their struggles had salvaged some honor and hope from a disastrous war, and their Communist leadership benefited from much genuine support.

While the elections themselves were fairly conducted by secret ballot, the campaign that preceded them was a travesty of democratic practice. In Croatia, Communist election officials simply struck huge numbers of eligible voters from the rolls on grounds of wartime Ustaša activity. In Slavonia the fraction approached 40 percent. Marija Radić was able to publish only one edition of an independent HSS newspaper before it was banned. In Serbia, where less than 5 percent of voters were excluded, the fate of the largest opposition party and the one opposition newspaper is instructive. The editor of *Demokratija*, Milan Grol, also headed the Democratic Party and the United Opposition, which together with Agrarians and Radicals entered the 1945 campaign. His prewar views on Bosnia and Macedonia as Serbian patrimonies left him open to justified criticism, as did his postwar failure to reach out to non-Communists in Croatia. Yet the Communist press tarred Grol as a figurehead for "fascist émigrés" and warned his supporters that "the people cannot stand idly by." More explicit physical threats followed. Grol and his United Opposition withdrew from the campaign in protest by the end of September. He tried to continue publishing *Demokratija*, pointing out the irony of Communists doing to opponents before these elections what had been done to them after the 1920 balloting for a Constituent Assembly (see chapter 4). Belgrade Communists organized a student attack on the paper's offices and used a printers' boycott to stop publication several weeks before the election.

The only way to express opposition in the subsequent balloting was to check the "box without a list" that posed no alternative candidates. Republican leader Jaša Prodanović had originally suggested it, but Tito's lieutenant Edvard Kardelj fastened upon the device once the United Opposition withdrew. In the elections for the new Federal Chamber, Slovenia recorded the highest share of "empty box votes," 16.8 percent, followed by the Vojvodina with 14.6, Serbia with 11.4, and Croatia with 8.5. Only in Serbia were there a large number of outright abstentions, 20.8 percent, thus reducing the fraction of eligibles who voted for the National Front to 68.3 percent. Even that figure was enough for the Communists to trumpet the result as a mandate to shape a new Yugoslavia to their desires. The Communists received a somewhat less convincing mandate in balloting for the Chamber of Nationalities, with 10–20 percent opting for the empty box except in Bosnia-Hercegovina, Macedonia, and Montenegro.

A new set of internal borders was needed to replace the controversial and inconsistent set of 1941 – basically an enlarged, confederal Croatia and an indeterminate Serbia still supported by a country-wide monarchy. Now the monarchy stood no chance of regaining its authority. Tito and the AVNOJ delegates had already determined that there would be six republics, with a separate Macedonia, Montenegro, and Bosnia-Hercegovina joining Serbia, Croatia, and Slovenia. The fact if not the form of Kosovo and the Vojvodina's adjunct status to Serbia would presumably bar a return to interwar administration from Belgrade. Bosnia-Hercegovina had the one set of entirely internal borders. Well established before the First World War, they were reaffirmed with the addition of Neum to provide an outlet to the Adriatic. The only borders of the new Macedonia republic, proclaimed in August 1944, to raise controversy were those with Bulgaria and Greece. Tito had initially proposed to incorporate the Pirin region on the Bulgarian side, and many Greeks concluded that their Aegean region was also to be included.[30] Slovenia saw its western border expanded to include ethnic fellows previously under Fascist Italy, if not the largely Italian port of Trieste that Tito also coveted. Although the Pirin question would persist until 1948 and the Italian border would be disputed until 1954 (see chapter 8), the internal borders of two other republics posed longer-term problems.

The borders fixed for Croatia and Montenegro drew the Communist leadership into ethnic adjudication that would openly be held against them by the 1980s.[31] Absorbing the larger part of the Istrian Peninsula from Italy made Croatia a net gainer, but condemned the 250,000 Italians living there to an effective if largely bloodless campaign of ethnic cleansing that began in 1945 and continued into the early 1950s. That gain was seen as compensating Croatia for a loss further down the Adriatic coast. A largely Montenegrin population up to the Bay of Kotor on the southern end of the historically Dalmatian coast justified the bay's award to Montenegro, which also received the largest part of the Sandžak of Novi Pazar and its minority of Turkish Muslims. Historically and ethnically, the Sandžak was closer to Bosnia-Hercegovina, but the disproportionate role of the Montenegrin Partisans in the Second World War made their republic the safer custodian of this volatile region for the Communist regime.

Finally there was the border between Croatia and the Vojvodina. Its large German minority had fled, but an equally large and presumably unreconciled Hungarian minority was still in place. In June 1945, Tito appointed Milovan Djilas to preside over a commission specially charged with drawing that border. Its northern and southern reaches were troublesome. To the north, the population of the Subotica area bordering Hungary was largely Hungarian or *bunjevci* Catholics, who by this time considered themselves Croatian. Yet the area was deemed too sensitive for Serbia and too important to Communist plans for new colonization to be cut off from Belgrade. In the south, the long-Habsburg but largely Serb Srem had been given to the Croatian banate under the 1939 Sporazum, much to the indignation of Serb nationalists. Now it was fatefully divided. Counties from Vukovar and Borovo north went to Croatia and several southern counties to Serbia. In the middle of Croatia's share was what Branko Petranović has called a Serbian oasis. Yet neither it nor the several larger Serb areas in Croatia received any separate standing. Tito had long since rejected Moša Pijade's wartime suggestion that one or more autonomous Serb regions be created in the new Croatian republic. Ethnic reconciliation might be better served, Djilas argued in 1945, by moving the capital from Belgrade to Sarajevo. The other party leaders quickly rejected the suggestion on the grounds that the Bosnian city lacked infrastructure and an accessible location. One may well wonder what difference the move would have made. At the same time, of course, Communist power seemed too solid and monolithic as the new Constituent Assembly convened in January 1946 to make serious debate of such territorial issues necessary.

8   Founding the second Yugoslavia, 1946–1953

What sort of state emerged from the limited popular mandate of the Partisan war effort and the unlimited power left in Communist hands at the end of the war? It was easy to make the second Yugoslavia a republic. Communist representatives of the Popular Front dominated the newly elected Constituent Assembly. It convened in Belgrade on November 29, 1945, a date chosen to mark the second anniversary of AVNOJ's proclamation of a provisional Partisan government in Jajce. The delegates voted unanimously to abolish the monarchy, ending the regency of the exiled King Petar II, in whose name Tito had ruled as prime minister since March. The new Federal People's Republic of Yugoslavia (SNRJ) now took its place.

The second Yugoslavia had precisely twice as much time as the first to establish itself. Its birth was as bloody as the first. Like the First World War, it cost nearly 2 million dead and unborn, if all of the likely losses of 1945–46 are added to those of the Second World War. The international environment after 1945 proved to be more favorable, beginning with the addition of the Istrian peninsula from Italy. The new federation nonetheless failed to survive the collapse of the Soviet bloc, from which it had spent virtually the entire postwar period differentiating itself. This chapter explores one major source of that post-1989 breakup. Yugoslavia as a socialist federation simply did not change as much during the formative period from 1946 to 1953 as its theories of local democracy and workers' self-management promised. The initial intent was simply to follow the Soviet model, where a hierarchical party apparatus controlled a fictional federation and pursued rapid development of heavy industry. The famous Tito–Stalin split of 1948 only strengthened a postwar siege mentality.

The various drawbacks of the Soviet model, plus the desire to repudiate it publicly, still pushed Tito's Politburo toward a new theory of decentralized socialism. Specifically intended to replace the Soviet-style constitution of 1946, the 1953 constitution embodied the new theory. The new practice was not a cynical exercise, but its principal effect was to endow local Communist-led committees, not the famous workers' councils, with the arbitrary, unchallenged authority of the Communist leadership, police, and army. How confident they all were that Lord Acton's classic caution, that absolute power corrupted absolutely, would not apply to them. Only Milovan Djilas had doubts early on. Even he did not suspect that the devolution of arbitrary authority would reconcentrate later at the republic rather than the federal level, there to stoke the fires of ethnic self-interest and exclusivism that Tito and his Partisan élite claimed to have put out.

Consolidating power under the 1946 Constitution

Like the first Yugoslavia and Serbia before it, the second Yugoslavia invested considerable energy in a series of formal constitutions. In January 1946, the Constituent Assembly ratified the first of four constitutions according to which Tito's Yugoslavia was ruled, all drafted under the guiding hand of Edvard Kardelj. Not a single dissenting vote was cast against the curious 1946 covenant. It was closely modeled after the Soviet constitution of 1936, yet none of its 139 articles used the word "socialist" or made any reference to the Yugoslav Communist Party (KPJ). Only six central ministries were created – a postal service plus five others dealing with military or foreign affairs. Other ministries were mixed in with counterparts from the six republics, effectively setting up six separate regional bureaucracies. The republics received the same formal right to secede from the federation as their Soviet counterparts, and somewhat greater fiscal authority. The guarantee of greater religious freedom marked the document's only other significant departure from the Soviet model. That guarantee, as we shall see, was not worth much until the 1960s.

The new bicameral National Assembly became "the supreme organ of state authority." The Federal Council was unitary, based on one deputy for every 50,000 citizens much like the parliament of the 1921 constitution. The Council of Nationalities was a federal body: each republic had thirty representatives, although the Vojvodina received twenty as an autonomous province of Serbia and, without explaining the distinction, Kosovo got fifteen as Serbia's second autonomous region. The slate of Popular Front candidates already elected to the Constituent Assembly in November 1945 served the first four-year term. Initially an eight-party coalition, the Front had put forward candidates who were either KPJ members or had been approved by internal Communist decision. Opponents could only check the "empty box" for abstaining votes (see chapter 7). After the ratification of the 1946 constitution, however, the

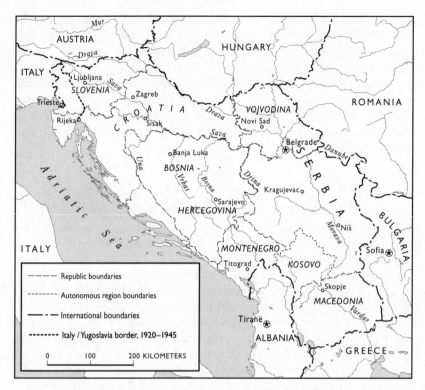

Map 8.1 Yugoslavia's internal borders, 1945–1991

Popular Front became a Communist mass organization, first in the minds of the party leadership and then in fact.

No proposal from Tito's new cabinet faced any opposition beyond the individual objections of those few non-Communists who continued to regard the Popular Front as a coalition of separate parties.[1] Dragoljub Jovanović, the fiery leader of Serbia's left-wing Agrarian Union, protested the loudest, but was shouted down. Jaša Prodanović, the more restrained head of Serbia's small Republican Party, could only complain in the pages of his *Republika*, Belgrade's one non-Communist newspaper to survive 1945. Inside both chambers, Communist delegates railed at such objections and demanded unanimous votes as a rebuke to these "saboteurs of homogeneity" and their alleged "foreign masters." How under these circumstances could anyone make use of the legislative right to annul executive regulations under Article 129 or hold the new peoples' courts or public (in fact, political) prosecutors to the standards of the independent judiciary set down in Articles 115–128? The action was obviously elsewhere, as it was for the Supreme Soviet that brought the pejorative "rubber-stamp parliament" into Western political vocabularies during the 1930s.

"Elsewhere" consisted of the KPJ's efforts to mobilize political support, suppress the slightest opposition, and promote economic recovery. We examine this mixture of party and ministerial initiatives to those three ends before turning to the role played by Western aid and confrontation.

Mobilization and repression

Party propaganda attempted to rally popular support around the ideology of Yugoslavism rather than federalism or socialism, and at first it succeeded. Neither the ideas nor the institutions of the two legs – federal and socialist – on which Tito and his Politburo intended their state to stand over the longer run received much attention. Their Yugoslavism confidently emphasized the common experience in a single Partisan struggle, disregarding the separate parties and liberation councils for Croatia, Slovenia, and Macedonia as wartime expedients. Party propaganda attributed the greater part of their wartime success to solving the national (ethnic) question. Look what Yugoslavism based on *bratsvo i jedinstvo* (brotherhood and unity) had done, they said, to expel the fascist invaders. We should not underestimate the legitimizing power of this charter myth among the first postwar generation.

The 1946 constitution itself enshrined *bratstvo i jedinstvo* in what Aleksa Djilas has called the four equalities.[2] All citizens had equal rights and duties regardless of ethnicity or religion. So did all republics, their minority as well as majority populations. Third, all South Slav "peoples and other groups" deserved equal standing, and, finally, all were presumed to have made an *equal* contribution to the war effort. The list of ethnic peoples included Macedonians and Montenegrins as well as Serbs, Croats, and Slovenes; Bosnian Muslims were at least recognized as a separate group according to Kardelj's prewar formulation (see chapter 6). Hungarians and Albanians were not listed, nor were Germans and Italians. They could be counted only as Yugoslavs, a category that others, particularly Bosnian Muslims, were encouraged to adopt.

The new regime was particularly popular among rural youth. They constituted roughly three-quarters of the 140,000 party members by mid-1945 and the same fraction of the further 330,000 added by 1948. In and outside the party, many people were eager to reject the ethnic exclusivism that had taken more lives in wartime than had the Nazi and

Fascist occupiers. But the Central Committee's Department of Agitation and Propaganda (Agitprop), headed by Milovan Djilas, missed this opportunity and instead stressed the joint struggle against the Germans, thus introducing a theme that would persist in Yugoslav history texts into the 1980s.

The Communists' near monopoly of the press used the Belgrade show trial of Chetnik leader Draža Mihailović in 1946, like the Zagreb trial of Archbishop Stepinac later that same year (see chapter 7), to turn collaboration with foreign powers into the most monstrous of crimes. Such an atmosphere made contacts with the West suspicious at a minimum. The Stepinac trial sent the message to the Catholic clergy that contact with the Vatican should be avoided. The Croatian church's prewar publications, roughly 100, were not allowed to resume. Communist-sponsored associations of priests, established for each republic by 1947, sought to subvert the authority of all the religious hierarchies, Orthodox and Muslim as well as Catholic. Least representative was the association for the Croatian Catholic church.

Aside from religion, however, the Communist approach to cultural policy remained cautious.[3] Even the vague Soviet slogan of "nationalist in form and socialist in content" was modified to replace the word "socialist" with the still vaguer "generally humanist and democratic." While the press continually celebrated the "common Yugoslav spirit" that had emerged from the war, the educational system was allowed to split into the separate republic paths that contributed to the later lack of interregional understanding. The 1946 constitution left standing the republic ministries of education that had been created the previous year, but eliminated the comparable federal ministry.

This decision marked the end of a debate within the KPJ about the centralized preparation of uniform school texts. Representatives from Montenegro, Macedonia, and Bosnia-Hercegovina had argued that uniform texts were good Soviet practice and that their republican resources were too limited to publish their own texts anyway. Croatian, Slovenian, and some Serbian representatives wanted to publish their own textbooks. They prevailed in the crucial cultural disciplines of history and literature on what was supposed to be a temporary basis. A variety of federal councils were created over the years, beginning in 1948, in order to reverse this decision, but none succeeded.

The same fate befell the film industry by July of 1946, although with far less malign consequences in the long run. Film studios in Zagreb and Ljubljana resisted surrendering their equipment and projects to the central film enterprise that the party had established in Belgrade the year before. A Belgrade public weaned on Western cinema since the

1920s flocked to the theaters showing Hollywood musicals and ignored the party's propaganda films.

If this inconsistent cultural policy did not win wider urban support for Yugoslavia, Communist control of the judicial system made political opposition riskier than it had ever been in the first Yugoslavia. Tito designated Aleksandar Ranković, a member of his inner circle and wartime head of his security service, the OZNa or Department for Protection of the People, to head the new interior ministry and the new State Security Administration, or UDBa. Created in March 1946 to replace the OZNa, the UDBa exercised unrestricted powers to arrest, imprison, and even execute political opponents without public charges or trials. One of Serbia's few leading Communists to survive the war, Ranković had risen from provincial origins and an embittering prison sentence as a teenage party member to head the political committee for Serbia by 1937. As with OZNa during the war, he relied heavily on Serbs or Montenegrins to staff the new organization and its paramilitary units. He recruited agents "in every block of flats, in every street, in every village and in every barrack room," according to a British observer.[4] Rough estimates vary, but the numbers of people the UDBa executed in 1946–47 probably ran to five figures and those held in concentration camps at least to six.

Convictions from the new network of people's courts, judges, and public prosecutors (the latter specifically created to root out political opposition) added to the camp population. The system worked without regard to due process or defendants' rights, in the fashion of the military courts that continued to operate after the war. When Agrarian Party leader Dragoljub Jovanović complained that the new Communist prosecutors had become "the all-powerful organs of the judiciary," he only hastened his own arrest and nine-year sentence in April 1947. His judge doubtless met the "fundamental moral qualifications," which the party's chief prosecutor at the Mihailović trial, Miloš Minić, explained as "infinite loyalty" regardless of prior legal training.[5]

Economic recovery and the United Nations Relief and
Rehabilitation Agency (UNRRA)

Familiar features from the Communist consolidation of power across Eastern Europe should not obscure those that set Yugoslavia apart. The large Yugoslav National Army (JNA), as the Partisan forces had been redesignated in 1945, was one. Soon cut by half and still 400,000 strong, the JNA was a source of legitimacy and control for the regime. Tito remained its commander-in-chief. The regime also enjoyed some genuine popular support. Adding to it was an economic recovery that peaked in 1946, largely due to local Communist-led initiative and Western assistance.

Four years of more continuous fighting than anywhere in Europe had killed 1 million people and left another 700,000 unborn. It had also done monstrous material damage to Yugoslavia, particularly to its infrastructure. The transportation network suffered most of all. All rail lines and roads needed repair, rolling stock and repair facilities had been cut to at least one-half, and virtually no motor vehicles remained. Some 15 percent of prewar housing, 40 percent of industrial facilities, and over 50 percent of the livestock and agricultural machinery had been destroyed or heavily damaged. People in large, food-poor areas from the Croatian Krajina to the Serbian south faced starvation if relief supplies did not reach them.

Yet reach them they did, over a rapidly rebuilt rail and road network. Adriatic ports were reopened to receive imports, while domestic agricultural production passed 90 percent of the 1936–39 level by 1947. Flour and saw mills resumed operation, as did most large industrial enterprises and mines, including the Trepča lead and Bor copper mines. Industrial production allegedly exceeded the 1939 level by 1947, well ahead of the recovery recorded elsewhere in Eastern Europe. Although we may question the regime's industrial statistics in particular, the recovery for the largely rural population seems clear. How did it happen?

Sport-like competition between Communist-organized youth brigades provides part of the answer.[6] The centralized party hierarchy tried to coordinate their projects, but their successes stemmed primarily from young Communist leaders, often Partisan veterans, working without much supervision at the local level. JNA conscripts and a significant amount of forced labor played further parts. Many brigade leaders did not hesitate to intimidate or impress local youth into their ranks or to mobilize separate brigades of prisoners from the concentration camps.

Much of this unpaid effort would have been in vain had it not been for the $415 million in aid delivered by the United Nations Relief and Rehabilitation Agency (UNRRA). The largest UNRRA delivery to any European country, the sum was double the 1938 value of Yugoslavia's imports. Shipments of food, clothing, and medical supplies amounted to $237 million. Equipment to rehabilitate agriculture, industry, and the transport network accounted for the rest. Enough railway track and bridge struts, rolling stock and locomotives, river barges and port facilities to restore 90 percent of the inland transport network, minus roads, arrived by 1946. UNRRA replaced almost the entire prewar fleet of 15,000 trucks.

The largest part of UNRRA deliveries – close to $298 million worth, or 72 percent – not surprisingly came from the United States, undamaged by the war and its economy in high gear. Neither the American nor Yugoslav governments appreciated the large US role.[7] American officials and a number of Congressmen suspected that the Yugoslav army was diverting coal and other supplies for its own use. Tractors were indeed being dispatched to the small number of new state farms, but an UNRRA mission sent by its new director, Fiorello Laguardia, the former New York mayor and briefly before then US consul at Rijeka, failed to substantiate the other charges. And despite the fact that UNRRA named a Russian to head the Yugoslav operation, the Tito regime suspected that the 300 Americans attached to the operation were also connected with the US military mission in Belgrade. Their travel to remote areas in US uniforms fed the false suspicion. In addition, Communist leadership still wished to credit the Soviet Union or its allies as the only source of assistance and thus refused to acknowledge publicly that most of UNRRA aid came from the United States.

Confronting the Western allies

Trouble had been brewing between Tito's regime and the Anglo-American alliance since 1943. Compounding Communist consternation about a possible British landing on the Adriatic coast was the mis-interpreted American mission to Mihailović in August 1944 (see chapter 7). Then the United States and Britain insisted that Partisan forces withdraw from Trieste in favor of the Anzac units that had lost the race to the valuable port at the head of the Adriatic in May 1945. The ensuing border dispute with Italy continued to fester until 1954, but at this initial stage, the Yugoslav side saw it as a hostile Anglo-American initiative. As the Soviet confrontation with the Western alliance mounted in Eastern Europe, a relentlessly hostile US ambassador, William Patterson, arrived in Belgrade. The pugnacious postwar confidence of Tito's inner circle heated the whole brew still further.

Several new ingredients brought relations with the United States to boiling point in 1946. A new nationalization law that would take effect by year's end threatened to make permanent the takeover of those foreign firms, already sequestered, which were under German or Italian control during the war. US officials pressed the case for the few American firms hard, using as their principal point of leverage the $46.8 million gold reserves of the Yugoslav National Bank that had been shipped to New York for safe keeping in 1941.

The disputes concerning Trieste and American overflights were more incendiary. They were also related. In the summer of 1946, an American proposal for a common border put Italian territory (Zone A), including Trieste, further east into territory claimed by Yugoslavia (Zone B) than any of the proposed British, French, or Russian lines. Trieste's Slovenian minority and the Italian Communist Party (PCI) joined forces in a series of demonstrations and strikes. As Yugoslav army units moved forward to the French line that had become the border of Zone B, Tito's air force commanders took increasing exception to the unauthorized overflights of American planes. Their spotters undoubtedly exaggerated the numbers and turned transport planes into bombers, but the American crews also used any excuse to take the shortest route from Vienna to Rome. Perhaps to prove to a doubting Tito that the overflights were occurring, his air commanders in Ljubljana ordered a trespassing C-47 transport plane to be forced down in early August.[8] When they shot down another C-47 two weeks later, killing the entire crew, American officials and public opinion were outraged.

Yugoslav propaganda did not retreat. The press endorsed all Soviet indictments of Western policy, despite a noticeable lack of Russian support over Trieste. Yugoslav support for the Communist cause in the Greek civil war went beyond propaganda. The new Macedonian republic became a safe haven for the Greek Communists, where they sometimes received arms and other equipment to carry back to the war that had erupted again in 1946.

Tito's regime seemed to have burned its last bridges to the United States. What did American credits or loans from the fledgling International Bank for Reconstruction and Development matter? The economic *obnova*, or renewal, was well under way, and party membership was mushrooming. Also, Yugoslavia had just signed a series of bilateral trade agreements with the Soviet Union, its East European clients, and prewar partner Czechoslovakia. Their favorable terms were thought to ensure the success of the ambitious Five Year Plan ready for launching in 1947, a year ahead of any other East European regime. Surely the resultant upswing would mold a socialist society of Yugoslav citizens loyal to the new regime and the Soviet Union.

Setbacks and the Tito–Stalin split, 1947–1949

The celebrated break with the Soviet bloc in 1948 made Tito's Yugoslavia unique in Eastern Europe and eventually led to the best set of relations with the West among any of the Communist regimes. But it did not start out that way. The party's economic program was badly troubled in 1947. The regime's initial reaction to the dispute with Stalin and the bloc's economic embargo made matters worse, while the West was slow to offer assistance. At least the overconfidence that had spread from Tito's inner circle to party cadres was now brought up short. Their stalwart defiance of Stalin also revived support among the Yugoslav public. Outside the public's view, however, the purges of party members and extra-legal punishment of all potential opponents deepened the siege mentality that became a damaging legacy of the split. Some of the political brutalities also damaged the idea of Yugoslavism based on a "nation-blind" federation.

Economic setbacks

Yugoslavia's first, and by Soviet standards, last Five Year Plan was by all accounts a spectacular failure.[9] Eager to replicate the Soviet advances in heavy industry and armaments of the 1930s, Tito brushed aside the objections of Andrija Hebrang, his first chairman of the powerful Economic Council and minister of industry, and rushed into a full-scale plan for 1947–51. Hebrang stood little chance in 1946 of making his case, economic realities aside. Tito had removed him two years earlier (see chapter 7) as head of the Croatian Liberation Movement (ZAVNOH) for "nationalist tendencies" and now replaced him with the more trusted Slovenian Politburo member, Boris Kidrič. He had just returned from a crash course in Soviet planning in Moscow. With no other training, Kidrič became the regime's leading economist until his death in 1954. Hebrang hung on briefly as head of the new Federal Planning Commission until Kidrič assumed that position as well in December 1946.

Kidrič and a small army of young party members in the Commission hastily cobbled together a Five Year Plan as immensely detailed as it was wildly ambitious. An aggregate of local plans, its volumes eventually weighed a ton and a half when the weekly instructions and reports that passed between fully 215 Belgrade or republic ministers and all state industrial and agricultural enterprises were added to some 16,000 provisions. National income was supposed to double its 1939 level by 1951, primarily on the strength of a fivefold increase in industrial production. Over 1,000 miles of new railway track were to be laid. Kidrič dismissed the complaints of several fellow Slovenes that the large industrial investment proposed for the less developed republics was a "false solidarity" from which no one would profit. In any case, the fledgling planners overestimated existing industrial capacity and the number of trained personnel by at least one-half. By the end of 1947, Yugoslav planners could see that only the most blatant exaggeration of quantities produced, at whatever low quality, would meet targets that Soviet advisers, suspicious of the local components, had criticized from the start. Even with sizeable exaggeration, only the developed industrial sectors of Slovenia, Croatia, and Serbia came close to hitting their targets for 1947. Yugoslav statisticians subsequently deemed the 1947 data too unreliable to record in future yearbooks.

How had Kidrič and his new planners expected to succeed? Their later accounts emphasized how much they had counted on accelerated deliveries of equipment and raw materials from the Soviet Union, Hungary, and Czechoslovakia. All three economies had their own post-war problems and, for whatever reason, none of them met the increased delivery schedule projected for 1947 on the terms of delayed or barter payment. Perhaps 5 percent of the credits promised by the three countries in 1947 were actually granted before Yugoslavia's mid-1948 split with the Soviet bloc. Yugoslav imports from the three declined slightly to 44.8 percent of a higher total value from 1946 to 1947 (see table 8.1). At the same time, Western imports rose from 15.1 to 23.6 percent. Yugoslav planners still hoped to finance both Western imports and their own investments in heavy industry, if agriculture could make a massive contribution.

The several bodies responsible for agricultural policy all agreed that a huge surplus should be extracted from the peasantry, not only to furnish food for a large army and a growing number of industrial workers as in the Soviet case but also, by 1947, to earn substantial export revenues. With such earnings, Yugoslavia could then pay for necessary Western or (until the 1948 Communist coup in Prague) Czech imports. Yet, only the Agrarian Council headed by the prewar Agrarian Union leader, Vasa Čubrilović, now minister of agriculture, advocated large-scale invest-ment in agriculture and a contractual system that would attract peasants into state farms or producers' cooperatives. Two more influential bodies, the Economic Council and the new Federal Planning Commission of 1946, foresaw an increasingly powerful state sector dominating agri-culture and subordinating the peasantry by force if necessary. This had been the aim of Andrija Hebrang since his wartime efforts to suppress the Croatian Peasant Party. Smallholding Croatian peasants had formed the backbone of that previously predominant party and its extensive cooperative network, Gospodarska Sloga (see chapter 6). In 1945 Hebrang seized on that summer's drought to press for the forced collection of grain quotas at low, fixed prices, or *otkup*, by regional Communist authorities. By September, he called for the arrest of those peasants who withheld grain as enemies of the people. Kidrič merely revived this policy when he replaced Hebrang as head of both the

Economic Council and the Federal Planning Commission and prepared to launch the first plan in April 1947. Kidrič may be held to account only for keeping the agricultural share of state investment projected for 1947–51 to 7 percent.

That meager fraction, subsequently increased to 10 percent, was not the principal reason for the serious shortfall in agricultural production. An ambiguous, shifting set of Communist policies toward peasant smallholdings contributed more to this deficiency and also prompted widespread resistance to the new regime in the countryside. KPJ representatives, Hebrang included, had promised throughout the war that private smallholdings would be preserved. As if to redeem that promise in August 1945, the regime proclaimed an agricultural land reform that redistributed land from eight categories, the largest of which were former German holdings (40.7 percent), estates over 45 hectares (15 percent), and church lands over 10 hectares (10.5 percent). Peasant smallholders and newly created state farms or other agencies each received about half of these lands, amounting to about 10 percent of the arable total (compared to the 20 percent redistributed in the 1919 reform; see chapter 5)). Although maximum holdings of private land were now limited to 25–35 hectares, the considerable backlog of peasant debt was also canceled.[10]

The Communist leadership believed that these gestures would draw peasants voluntarily into the General Agricultural Cooperatives that it created in 1946 to replace the prewar networks. They were quickly disillusioned. The new cooperatives occupied less than 3 percent of the redistributed land. Peasants saw them primarily as an agency for collecting otkup obligations. Their resistance to the cooperatives continued to grow through 1946, despite the decision in April to exempt up to half of the privately cultivated grain harvest from such obligations, allot fixed amounts to households for livestock feed, and allow local authorities leeway in making the otkup purchases. Arrests and land confiscations for evading even the reduced deliveries multiplied over the summer, so much so that the regime was obliged to pardon many offenders and return their land in order to collect the harvest. When less than half of the projected otkup deliveries for 1946 were realized, the regime reverted to harsher terms under recentralized administration. Obligations for deliveries and land sown were now presented in advance and, if not met by the autumn, peasant landowners were prosecuted. *Borba* and the rest of the Communist press trotted out the Soviet pejorative "*kulak*" in order to rail against the resisters as capitalist hoarders. But once again, arrests were so numerous that the regime had to declare another amnesty in order to collect the 1947 harvest. Kidrič and his associates were already tempted to abandon the effort to control private agriculture in favor of Soviet-style collectivization just as Stalin had abandoned comparable NEP policies in 1928. Then the 1948 dispute gave them the further ideological reason of confirming their Communist credentials.

Confrontation with Stalin's Soviet Union

Of all the postwar Communist regimes in Eastern Europe, Yugoslavia's was the only one capable of falling out with the Soviet Union. Tito and his Politburo had not dreamed of doing so, despite his own first-hand knowledge of how foreign Communists were treated during Stalin's prewar purges and the wartime failure of Soviet military support to materialize until the drive on Belgrade in October 1944. Once in power, the Yugoslav Communists were eager to demonstrate their loyalty by supporting Soviet foreign policy and the initiatives of Communist parties across Europe. Yet their inner circle included none of the so-called Muscovites who had spent the war or a longer period in the USSR. Such men and one woman, Ana Pauker in Romania, were crucial figures in the Communist regimes that took power elsewhere in Eastern Europe from 1946 to 1948, with Red Army and Soviet security units backing them up. Tito's regime assumed power in 1945 with a cadre drawn from the Partisan struggle on home ground. Soviet military presence was minimal; it had come and gone by late 1944.

When Stalin's political agents began to treat the Yugoslav "people's democracy" like the transition regimes in Romania or Hungary, they could find no Muscovites to do their bidding and celebrate it at the same time. Soviet economic enterprises and security agents quickly wore out their welcome. Moscow had already failed to endorse Tito's claim to Trieste or his support for the Greek Communist uprising. By 1947 the creation of a new international organization of Communist parties (the Cominform) and the phoney issue of a Balkan federation (the Macedonian question in disguise) were pushing the two sides toward open disagreement. The first meetings of Yugoslav leaders with Stalin himself had reassured them; the last one only made matters worse.

In sum, a raw struggle for political power in Yugoslavia lay at the bottom of the Tito–Stalin split. Ideological differences played no significant role, according to any of the extensive Yugoslav testimony.[11] Economic frictions surfaced in 1946, but Stalin appeared to resolve them with a wave of his hand the following year.

Tito's representatives had welcomed the discussions about joint Yugoslav–Soviet ventures when they began in 1945. Such deals seemed to promise Soviet raw materials and equipment for the rapid development of heavy industry that the Communist regime was eager to launch. By early 1946, the two governments had signed a general agreement for economic cooperation. The Soviets immediately proposed a series of mining ventures as well as a joint airline (JUSTA) and Danubian shipping company (JUSPAD).

The sorry Yugoslav experience with JUSTA and JUSPAD helped abort any of the proposed deals for oil, coal, iron ore, or the non-ferrous minerals in which Yugoslavia was particularly rich. Its Soviet director general used JUSTA to take over traffic control of Yugoslav air space and to confine the fledgling Yugoslav airline (JAT) to a few lesser domestic routes. The shipping company began to operate the Yugoslavs' Danubian fleet in return for a promised Soviet investment, less than 10 percent of which was provided. JUSPAD charged rates for Soviet goods that were half those on Yugoslav products, whose unloading in the USSR was then delayed inordinately. In addition to this mistreatment, Soviet representatives insisted on terms for the various mineral enterprises which were far too exploitative to be accepted. The Yugoslavs were unaware of the grievous economic weakness that Stalin sought to conceal from the West and to repair as soon as possible with whatever resources Eastern Europe could provide. Tito's lieutenants could not know that one reason for the Soviets' objections to the grandiose targets for industrial production in the Yugoslav Five Year Plan was the drain it would impose on Soviet resources.

Stalin himself then defused these economic issues in the summer of 1947. He took the occasion of a meeting with Edvard Kardelj to reject any further discussion of joint enterprises. They were suitable to the transition regimes elsewhere in Eastern Europe, he granted, but not to a people's democracy like Yugoslavia. Stalin proposed investment credits instead, to the generous sum of $135 million. Less than $1 million worth would be delivered before the break. For the time being, however, according to the inside account of Vladimir Dedijer, the Yugoslav leaders were "elated by this attitude. Stalin . . . convinced us that he was fair and the Soviet bureaucracy alone was responsible for our difficulties."[12]

If Stalin therefore stopped short of vetoing the overconfident projections for the Yugoslavs' Five Year Plan, he was not prepared to compromise on international coordination of Communist Party policy. He seems to have singled out the KPJ for particular blame when the conference of European Communist parties that he convened in Poland in September 1947 failed to accept Andrei Zhdanov's proposal to create a permanent Council of Communist Parties. The delegates could only agree to establish an Information Bureau, or Cominform, that might coordinate their activities "when necessary, on the basis of mutual consent," but whose principal task would be to publish a series of periodicals from a headquarters to be located in Belgrade. The Soviet intelligence service of Lavrenti Beria's interior ministry (MVD) used the location in the Yugoslav capital to press ahead with the recruitment of local agents already launched by Red Army intelligence. The widespread UDBa network of Aleksandar Ranković's interior ministry could not fail to notice that the Soviets were setting up a rival network.

Yugoslavia's vocal and material support for the Greek Communists in Aegean Macedonia hardened Stalin's determination to bring the KPJ leadership under control by 1947. The Yugoslav intervention was undermining his 1944 commitment to Churchill to leave Greece to the West, in return for a free hand in Romania and Bulgaria. The Soviet leader saw his chance when the old wartime proposal for a Balkan federation reemerged. Kardelj had originally floated it in late 1944, as a mechanism for bringing Bulgaria as well as Macedonia into Yugoslavia's new federation, but in the subordinate positions of the sixth and seventh republics. The Bulgarian Communist Party (BKP) balked and demanded equal standing for Bulgaria with all of Yugoslavia. After the war, Tito's Macedonian party leaders argued that their own position in the Vardar region was still too weak without some tie to Bulgaria's Pirin region of Macedonia. This sense of weakness contributed to the Bled agreement of August 1947, signed by Tito and BKP leader Georgi Dimitrov as a prelude to a customs union. More significant for the two Communist parties was its immediate provision, soon resented by the Bulgarians, for more than 100 teachers from Skopje to begin teaching a newly distinct Macedonian language and spreading information about a separate Macedonian culture across the Pirin region.[13]

More significant for Stalin was the conclusion of the Bled agreement without prior approval from Moscow. He summoned both the Yugoslav and Bulgarian leaders to Moscow in February 1948. Tito sent Kardelj and Djilas in his place. After upbraiding a hapless Dimitrov for proposing a still wider federation, Stalin then turned on the Yugoslavs. What did they expect to achieve from Greece's civil war? Had they not intended to send a JNA division into Albania without consulting Moscow, another "inadmissible" failure? (Never mind that Stalin had invited Djilas to "swallow Albania" at a drunken dinner the year before.) If they wanted a federation with Bulgaria, Stalin demanded that they agree on the spot to its formation, presumably on Bulgaria's 50–50 terms with some shared responsibility for northern Macedonia. The Yugoslavs did not agree, and there would be no more meetings with Stalin.

8.1 Communist demonstration in Belgrade promising the doubling of wheat production in 1947, dominated by Tito's picture

The Soviets proceeded to orchestrate a series of events that brought the split into the open. Stalin confidently expected that the Yugoslav party would quickly find a new set of more compliant leaders, once "I shake my finger." He withdrew Soviet military advisers on March 19 and their civilian counterparts the next day. Tito sent a pained letter of surprise and protest. Stalin responded by suspending the long-term trade agreement and dispatching a bill of particulars on March 27, a date consciously chosen to remind the Yugoslavs of the coup that had so easily overthrown the regency of Prince Paul in 1941. "We think the political career of Trotsky quite instructive," its text threatened, referring obliquely to Trotsky's murder by Stalin's agents in 1940.

Badly shaken but confident that this was a temporary misunderstanding, the Yugoslav Politburo endorsed Tito's two letters of rebuttal. They denied the charges that the KPJ was "undemocratic" and its program unsocialist. Tito's second letter in April affirmed the KPJ's love for socialism and the Soviet Union, but added the famous phrase that an honorable party member could "in no case love his own land less." In May Aleksandar Ranković ordered the first arrests of KPJ members suspected of siding with the Soviets. Among them were Politburo members Sreten Žujović, a Serb, and the long controversial Andrija Hebrang, a Croat. Soviet diplomats demanded that they be allowed to attend the trial of these two leaders. The faithful Moša Pijade seized the chance to score propaganda points by comparing the demand to the Austrian terms whose rejection had led to the First World War in 1914 (see chapter 3). A much greater windfall for mobilizing public support, especially in Serbia, had already arisen with the Bucharest meeting of the Cominform. Stalin's representatives chose another date, thought to be intimidating, to expel "Tito's clique" formally from the Cominform. But June 28, the anniversary of the Kosovo battle in 1389, the assassination of Franz Ferdinand in Sarajevo, and the proclamation of the first Yugoslavia's constitution in 1921 only posed a dramatic challenge.

Siege and the initial Stalinist response

Flagging support for the regime probably revived with the Soviet challenge, although there are no reliable indicators of public opinion. What seems much clearer is that the loss of Soviet approval meant much less to the Yugoslav Communist Party than Stalin reckoned it would. Few Partisans believed that the Soviets had done much during or since the war to assist their Yugoslavia. Notions that Serbia shared Montenegro's traditional ties to Russia made no more sense in 1948 than they have for the rump Yugoslavia that survived the state's disintegration in 1991. (See chapters 1–3 for the limited and uninspiring historical connection between Russia and Serbia.) KPJ membership nearly doubled during 1948, from 285,000 to 483,000. Tito and his Politburo plainly interpreted this increase to mean greater popular approval.

Whatever the reason, the split prompted the regime to rededicate itself to the Soviet practice of socialism. Party leaders spoke of pursuing the true Leninist path. But if repressive Stalinist methods were needed to collectivize agriculture as well as to suppress any Soviet sympathizers, so be it. As for industry, the resultant Soviet siege slashed imports and boosted defense spending. All of this fed the same autarkic mentality that lay at the heart of the Soviet Five Year Plans of the 1930s.

In 1949 the Communist leadership launched a campaign to collectivize a significant share of Yugoslavia's predominant peasant smallholdings as the new centerpiece of its efforts to restore its standing with the Soviet bloc. Earlier efforts had made no impression. In April 1948, Tito had rushed through a law to nationalize the service sector. His speeches at the KPJ Congress in July had resounded with praise for Stalin and the great Soviet Union. He acknowledged the break, but called it a "temporary misunderstanding." Yugoslav diplomats supported the Soviet position in the international negotiations over riparian and transit rights on the Danube that convened later that month in Belgrade. The Soviets nonetheless accelerated their propaganda offensive against the Tito regime, and the other Cominform members fell in line.

The Central Committee plenum of January 1949 did not reach its decision to end the primary reliance on private agriculture easily. Even Ranković raised objections because of the peasant resistance he feared would follow. As we have seen, however, the decision to launch a collectivization campaign went beyond responding to a major Soviet indictment. Relaxed terms for otkup, or obligatory, grain sales at minimal prices had failed to collect even half of the projected amounts from the generally good harvest of 1947. Economic chief Boris Kidrič had tried reimposing a stricter system early in 1948. He offered otkup exemptions to those peasants voluntarily joining the Peasant–Worker Cooperatives (SRZ) that were the nearest equivalent of the Soviet *kolkhozi*, but few responded. The SRZs still accounted for barely 4 percent of arable land, versus 3 percent for the state farms that were copied from the wage-paying Soviet *sovkhozi*. The 1948 harvest fell short of the previous year's, and compulsory otkup sales failed to collect a higher percentage. In addition some of the Serb colonists from the food-poor areas of Croatia began leaving the new smallholdings that they had been given. In the Vojvodina, the loosely structured General Agricultural Cooperatives had also failed to tie the colonists together.[14] Their return pushed back up the number of purely private farmers. (Where poor Croats had taken over former Serb properties, they now resisted Serb returnees, exacerbating postwar ethnic relations.) The few state farms, largely on former German land in the Vojvodina, had also not prospered. The small amount of agricultural investment budgeted in the Five Year Plan compounded the problems that came with promoting inexperienced young Partisans from agriculturally backward regions to be farm managers.

During the course of 1949, party propagandists and the UDBa apparatus fanned out across the countryside to force 250,000 peasant households into the SRZs, raising the total to 324,000 on 23 percent of arable land. By June 1950, they had added another 100,000 households, although the arable total rose only to 28 percent. Resisters were branded as kulaks however small their holdings. Some peasants now joined the SRZs in hopes of escaping compulsory sales. Initial recruitment was most extensive in the Vojvodina, boosting the collectivized amount of Serbian arable land to 21 percent, slightly more than the Bosnian figure for June 1950. Macedonia and Montenegro were the leaders in SRZ land (with 55 and 80 percent of the arable land), while Croatia and Slovenia lagged significantly behind at 14 and 12 percent. Although the General Agricultural Cooperatives were left in place, Kidrič and the Politburo expected that the larger part of grain production would now come from the SRZs. That failed to happen. Over 90 percent of the reasonably good harvest in 1949 came from private smallholdings, in or out of the General Cooperatives. Wheat yields overall achieved a slight increase from 1933–37 levels, but the lack of mechanization and efficient management cut into the SRZ contribution.[15]

While it seems clear that the great majority of peasant households were coerced into joining the Peasant–Worker Cooperatives, there is no country-wide evidence of peasant resistance beyond the poor production totals noted above. The end of Communist Yugoslavia has not opened the interior ministry files now available elsewhere in Eastern Europe. Recent scholarship has however surveyed significant resistance in central Croatia and detailed a massive uprising around Bihać in northwestern Bosnia.[16] The arrest there in December 1949 of several Bosnian Muslims for resisting the collectivization drive did not intimidate the area's peasants as expected. The Bosnian rebels came from Velika Kladuša, the site of the successful Austrian egg-producing project (see chapter 3), and the Agrokomerc conglomerate of Fikret Abdić in the 1980s. In May 1950, an armed uprising broke out against local Communist authorities. Serbs and some Croats readily joined Bosnian Muslims to resist external control of what had been a relatively prosperous area since the above mentioned Habsburg project of 1908. UDBa and even army units from outside the area were called in to put down the multi-ethnic revolt. They succeeded after killing several hundred peasants.

Such ethnic alliances were not supposed to occur outside the KPJ, but Tito's initial reliance on leaving Bosnian Serb Communists to rule Bosnia-Hercegovina had forfeited the party's opportunity to install a multi-ethnic framework. These same Serbs represented the largest number of Bosnian Partisans, and their leaders had to be persuaded to accept a republic separate from Serbia after the war. They had, since then, obliged the majority of Bosnian Muslim party leaders to declare themselves Serbs, leaving only a few who called themselves Yugoslavs. Strengthening the Bosnian Serbs' position were several trials between 1946 and 1949 that convicted members of the small Young Muslims organization, including a youthful Alija Izetbegović.[17] Insubstantial charges of Islamic extremism obscured their real crime, trying to establish a successor to the Yugoslav Muslim Organization (JMO), the interwar political party (see chapters 5 and 6).

The state's growing security apparatus put KPJ members themselves under closer scrutiny than any other group in Yugoslavia during the split with the Soviet Union, just as Soviet Communists had been during Stalin's purges of the 1930s. Now Stalin counted on the large Yugoslav party, swollen to almost one-half million by the end of 1948, to overthrow Tito's loyalists. For Ranković's UDBa and army intelligence (KOS), the arrest in April of two Politburo members (Hebrang and Žujović) and the August shooting of General Arso Jovanović as he attempted to cross the frontier into Romania were not enough. Other *ibeovci*, or Inform Bureauists as they were called, had found their way to Bucharest and Moscow and were prophesying Tito's imminent overthrow. Nor did the simple expulsion of suspected Soviet sympathizers from the party, a figure that rose from 13,000 to 27,000 between 1948 and 1949, seem sufficient. In the eyes of the KPJ leadership, arrests and "hard time" were needed to send an effective message to the party's large membership.

The 16,000 members whose arrest was later acknowledged (the actual number was probably higher) did indeed do hard time. In general, their ethnic proportions fit their overall share of the general population, as Ivo Banac has demonstrated, with the exception of the hugely overrepresented Montenegrins (21 percent or almost one-third of the republic's party).[18] The Serbs were slightly overrepresented (44 percent), and the Croats and Slovenes underrepresented. Less than one-fifth even received a trial, civilian or military. Most were simply seized under the "administrative procedures" to which all party members could be subjected. From 1949 on, they and other political offenders were dispatched arbitrarily to one of a dozen camps around Yugoslavia, like the protagonist of Emir Kusturica's damning 1987 film, *Otac na službenom putu* (Father away on a business trip). The most notorious of these was the Naked Island, *Goli otok*. Its Stalinist work regimen, abominable conditions, and enforced beatings of new prisoners by the inmates shocked even Milovan Djilas during a 1951 visit. Even though only 400 prisoners died during their time there, the psychological damage was typically lifelong. The party's reputation did not suffer until the details of Goli otok were made public during the 1980s. Yet by 1953, Aleksandar Ranković admitted that nearly half of the 36,000 formal arrests for all major crimes in 1950 had been unjustified. The number of people detained or placed under investigation was certainly much larger, some 22,000 in Croatia alone according to one estimate. When and to what extent did the two-thirds majority of Serbs and Montenegrins in the UDBa and the military's KOS make the Stalinist excesses of 1948–50 seem like ethnic discrimination against non-Serbs? The question remains to be answered.

Finally, the Soviet siege pushed the newly nationalized industrial sector toward autarky and its investment funds into defense production, particularly in Bosnia-Hercegovina. Still at just half of its prewar level in 1947, the value of Yugoslav foreign trade fell by another third from 1948 to 1950. Imports from the Soviet bloc fell from 47 percent of the Yugoslav import total in 1948 to 14 percent in 1949 and then to nothing for 1950 (see table 8.1). Exports followed a similar pattern, and the West was slow to make up the difference, for commercial as well as political reasons. There would be no significant American aid until late 1950.

The siege hit the regime's favored investments in heavy industry hardest. Some 90 percent of their imported equipment and raw materials were slated to come from the Soviet bloc. Barely 5 percent of the deliveries scheduled for 1948–49 were received before they ended altogether. Those offered under Stalin's promised 1947 credits stopped coming in 1948 from the USSR and in May of the next year from Eastern Europe. The beleaguered Yugoslav regime naturally gave the defense industry priority and pushed those projects to proceed as fast as possible. In addition, a number of plants located in Serbia, Slovenia, and Macedonia were moved away from these frontier republics to Bosnia and, to a lesser extent, Croatia. Workers went too or had to be replaced, more than 100,000 for Bosnia alone. The share of national income spent on defense, narrowly defined to obscure some of this investment, nearly doubled, rising from 9.4 percent in 1948 to 16.7 percent in 1950.

The threat of a Soviet-led invasion, intended by Stalin to appear real, also justified a bigger Yugoslav National Army (JNA). Still large in 1947, its troop strength was increased by fully 50 percent, to 600,000 by 1951. Tito had decreed that the army's top leadership should be roughly balanced among the major ethnic groups, but Serbs and Montenegrins already comprised 60 percent of the huge officer and non-commissioned officer corps in 1946. Croats and Slovenes were proportionally represented, but other ethnic groups hardly at all.[19] The greater size of the JNA after the Soviet split fed the perceptions of Serb predominance outside of Serbia. On the other hand, the combined effects of the collectivization drive, the campaign against Cominformists and the relocation of defense production could appear directed more against Serbia than any other republic. We should remind ourselves that at the time, both the regime and its supporters saw these measures as means to preserve Yugoslavia's independence and Communist power and not as devices to gain ethnic advantage.

First steps down the Yugoslav road

The Soviet siege liberated as well as constrained Tito's regime. In order to survive, it had to move closer to the West economically and away from the Soviet Union ideologically. Western scholarly celebrations of Yugoslav socialism usually made 1950 the specific date for this turn away from agricultural collectivization and political factories, and toward workers' councils and self-managed enterprises. The first law postulating workers' self-management did indeed follow that June after the famous exchanges within Tito's Politburo and Central Committee.[20] By some accounts, it began with a three-way conversation in a parked car between Milovan Djilas, Edvard Kardelj, and Boris Kidrič. The first two argued for transferring the control of state enterprises from the unwieldy apparatus of central planning to autonomous but presumably Communist-led workers' councils. Their strictly ideological argument proposed to "start creating Marx's free association of producers." It took longer to convince Kidrič, the chief central planner after all, about the new socialist centerpiece than it did Tito. Once packaged for the marshal with Kidrič's endorsement as "a radical departure from Stalinism," he readily agreed.

The Communist leadership had in fact begun to explore ways of distinguishing Yugoslav from Soviet practice as early as 1949. More importantly, their innovations would proceed at a slower pace and have less to do with the market mechanism than many Western observers assumed. What of the Western, largely American, aid that started to flow in 1950 and peaked in 1953? Its arrival also facilitated the primary fea-

Table 8.1. *Foreign trade, 1947–1953*

	Exports (US $ mil.)	Western share (%)	Imports (US $ mil.)	Western share (%)	Trade balance
1947	173	19.3	279	23.6	−106
1948	323	24.7	378	25.3	−55
1949	193	60.3	333	51.5	−140
1950	162	70.4	287	75.8	−125
1951	186	75.9	434	78.8	−248
1952	249	80.6	393	69.1	−144
1953	183	65.7	418	78	−235

Sources: John R. Lampe, Russell O. Prickett, and Ljubiša S. Adamović, *Yugoslav-American Economic Relations Since World War II* (Durham, NC: Duke University Press, 1990), 41 and 70–71; Jozo Tomasevich, "Immediate Effects," in *At the Brink of War and Peace: The Tito-Stalin Split in a Historic Perspective*, ed. Wayne S. Vucinich, vol. X, *War and Society in East Central Europe* (New York: Brooklyn College Press, 1982), 105–6; and Dragana Gnjatović, *Uloga inostranih sredstava u privrednom razvoju Jugoslavije* (Belgrade: Beogradski ekonomski institut, 1985), 78–79.

ture of the new Yugoslav road to socialism – the decentralization of continued Communist political control over industry. The new 1953 constitution sought to ratify that control while guarding against the dangers of genuine autonomy for the republics themselves. The result left the party, despite its redesignation as the League of Yugoslav Communists (SKJ), with too much central or arbitrary power for one member of the inner circle, Milovan Djilas. His two long prison sentences and the several-sided ascent of Tito's Yugoslavia from 1954 to 1967 (see chapter 9) kept his second thoughts about the second Yugoslavia from having any wider impact.

Workers' self-management or Communist decentralization

The inner circle's second thoughts, in which Djilas was involved from the start, clearly began with a reappraisal of centralized Soviet practice. It had not been serving them well even before the Tito–Stalin split. We may identify several initiatives to decentralize the year before the ideological turn of mid-1950. As early as May 1949, the principal organs of local government, the People's Councils (NO), were allowed to begin maintaining their own budgets and holding their own public meetings to mobilize support. That December's Central Committee plenum approved further measures. In addition to retracting some of the compulsory pressures for collectivization, the plenum also authorized the largest 215 defense-related enterprises to experiment informally with workers' councils. Less happily in the long run, it also gave formal approval to the existing organizations of education at the republic level. By early 1950, a related initiative reduced the number of state and party jobs in the central apparatus. Roughly 100,000 jobs were sliced away in the next six months, reducing the central total by one-half. The Belgrade directorates for the various branches of light industry had been transferred to the republics by early 1950, followed by heavy industry later that year. The transfer of all previously "federal" economic enterprises to republic or local control was also under way, leaving only the railways, postal service, and river and air transport under central control by April 1951.

The ideological centerpiece of socialism with an un-Soviet face was ready almost a year before. On June 27, 1950, the Federal Chamber rubber-stamped the new Law on the Management of State Economic Associations by Work Collectives. Workers' councils were now formally authorized, and "workers self-management" entered the lexicon of official propaganda. Real power or the chance for non-Communist members to assert themselves would not come to the councils for another decade. True, the Law on Planned Management left a power vacuum at the center in December 1951. The large Planning Commission in Belgrade had already been abolished. It would now become a small institute charged with preparing a Five Year Plan pared to twenty pages of broad guidelines. These guidelines could only estimate the proportions that the new General Investment Fund might allocate to the various sectors of the economy through the National Bank. Bargaining for its funds did indeed shift to the local level, but not to the new enterprises or their workers' councils. During the course of 1951, too many councils had used even the limited control they received over enterprise earnings to vote for wage bonuses for skilled workers rather than to fund their own investment. In order to compensate, they let go enough unskilled workers to push unemployment in the social sector past 5 percent. The new councils essentially lost bonus, if not dismissal, rights to a set of fixed percentages by early the next year and did not regain them until 1961 (see chapter 9). A framework of regulated rather than market prices would endure as a substitute for the planning mechanism into the 1980s.

The power to bargain for investment funds passed by 1952 to a reduced number of local committees. Their administration became the main prerogative of the local party apparatus. Trimmed from 7,104 to 3,834 to conform to communal (opština) boundaries, the new committees were grouped only by county (srez) or city limits, not by republic. Once introduced in April 1952, they held all the powers of local government in their hands. In addition to drawing up their own budgets as their predecessors had done since 1949, they now received the right to a guaranteed share of the profits from economic enterprises in their area. These social contributions, or *doprinosi*, would hobble enterprise initiative throughout the history of the second Yugoslavia. Less than 5 percent of net profit accrued to the workers' councils by 1954, although the local share of the rest was still much smaller than the federal share. Equally important in these formative years was the committees' control of all access to higher authority, republic and federal, and their two votes in the selection of enterprise directors to the workers' councils' one. According to American Embassy reports, Tito and his inner circle debated the issue of how to decentralize without losing political control and decided that price controls and the party's hierarchical organization were, for the time being, better guarantees than workers' class-consciousness.[21]

The role of US aid

Extensive diplomatic reporting and attention to Yugoslavia became one of the several longer-term consequences of the US aid that began to flow in 1950. On the Yugoslav side, the aid prompted more accurate economic reporting according to Western standards, a practice that would later benefit not only the more competitive Yugoslav enterprises but also help open the door to $4 billion of World Bank loans after American assistance ended in the early 1960s. Yet as aid ended and attention continued, the Embassy's mandatory location in the capital of Belgrade invited the presumption in Zagreb and Ljubljana that the Americans, like the preeminent British Embassy of the interwar period, saw Yugoslavia through Serbian eyes.

This chapter emphasizes the considerable short-term consequences of the largely American effort to support the first Communist regime to break with the Soviet bloc.[22] That effort started slowly, despite US Embassy reporting as early as June 1947 that Yugoslav officials were surprisingly independent of Soviet control and "must eventually be irked at Russian tutelage." Through 1948 and most of 1949, however, both governments remained wary of each other. American officials wondered whether the split with the Soviets was permanent, if not an outright ruse. Tito and his inner circle suspected the capitalist superpower and worried about the Soviet reaction to American aid. The American government, together with the British and French, had also proposed to place the entire Free Territory of Trieste under Italian sovereignty on March 20,

1948, just one week before Stalin's aforementioned rebuke. Only the release of the $30 million in prewar gold reserves held in a New York bank since 1941 could be negotiated for 1948, and two loans totalling $45 million from the official Export-Import Bank in Washington for 1949.

A significant supply of agricultural aid began in 1950, soon joined by a US military mission and a joint venture with Britain and France to shore up the growing imbalance of payments in Western trade. Its delivery did more than "keep Tito afloat," in the phrase of British Foreign Minister Ernest Bevin, and discourage a Soviet-led invasion. It also helped the regime to abandon collectivization, but also to maintain its large army and, ironically, its commitment to the rapid development of heavy industry on the Soviet pattern.

The severe droughts of 1950 and 1952 obliged the Tito regime to seek emergency food shipments from the United States. The newly collectivized SRZs of the fertile lands from Slavonia to Serbia to the Vojvodina had failed to produce the cumulative surpluses that could have now been used to feed the food-deficit areas to the south. The new American ambassador, George V. Allen, successfully urged fast action in 1950. The example of assistance to Greece and Tito's decision to withdraw support for the Greek Communist insurrection also encouraged the Truman administration. A special act of Congress promptly launched the delivery of US food stocks totalling $32 million by March 1951. Further shipments from the West European accumulation under the Marshall Plan, by then the Economic Cooperation Administration, and other sources increased the 1951 and 1952 totals toward $100 million apiece.

If American representatives pressed the Tito regime to turn away from collectivized agriculture in return for food shipments, poor results and peasant resistance, most dramatically in the Bihać triangle, pushed in the same direction. Kidrič abolished Machine Tractor Stations, a Soviet device to control farm management in September 1950, and the much-resented otkup deliveries the following year. The retreat from the SRZs themselves began in 1952 and reduced their acreage to 14 percent of its 1951 peak by the end of 1953. The regime still resisted offering any encouragement to peasant smallholdings and cut their maximum size from 25–35 hectares to 10.[23]

The United States provided a variety of military assistance to the Yugoslav National Army (JNA), but not much armament. Only $43 million of the $296 million officially delivered during 1952–53 could be called weaponry. The rest nonetheless proved essential to maintaining armed forces of 600,000 in the midst of two droughts and a general shortage of supplies. The military assistance group (MAAG) of

American personnel that arrived in 1951 did double duty. They provided training that helped complete the JNA's transition from guerrilla to regular army that Soviet advisors had begun. Their very presence, small as it was, may also have discouraged a Soviet-led invasion, for fear of US involvement despite the lack of any formal alliance. As the large number of provocative border incidents and Soviet-staged maneuvers declined after 1951, the regime's capacity to survive became an essentially economic question.[24]

How to export enough to Western Europe and the United States, with the Italian market still restricted because of the Trieste dispute, to pay for the imports that the Soviet bloc would have provided for rapid industrialization? The Yugoslav economy could not answer this question by itself unless its leaders abandoned their Marxist commitment to industrialization or came to terms with Stalin. They could do neither, and would struggle to find an answer long after economic relations with the Soviet bloc were fully repaired. They began with, and continued to expect, Western grants or loans to balance their international payments in the face of recurring deficits on current account (trade in goods and services).

The initial infusion of American aid had cut the huge import surpluses of 1950–51 down to manageable deficits on current account, but the payments problem threatened to derail projected imports for 1952–53. The limited economic advance since the split made it essential that those imports arrive. While the real value of industrial production had managed to grow by 5.4 percent a year for 1948–52, agricultural output had declined by 2.9 percent to leave the Yugoslav concept of Gross Social Product (goods and services of the socialist sector) with a modest annual increment of 2 percent.[25] The two major agencies for international lending, the International Monetary Fund and the International Bank for Reconstruction and Development (later the World Bank), were still too small and their criteria too strict for Yugoslavia to receive much relief from them. The United States was left to take the lead in forming a Tripartite Agreement with the British and French governments in 1952. Despite a sharp drop in the British share for 1953, an increased American contribution of 85 percent allowed the agreement to cover most of that year's Yugoslav deficit on current account. These grants and other economic assistance for 1950–53, of which the United States furnished three-quarters or $620 million, did succeed in covering 88 percent of four consecutive current account deficits. The fact that Western or international *credits* could be found to cover only 12 percent of those deficits raised doubts over how such shortfalls could be sustained in future without further grants.

The American answer was to press Tito personally in 1952 for a more competitive and export-oriented economy. He agreed to the first devaluation of the Yugoslav dinar, from 50 to 300 on the dollar, some restructuring of prices to reflect relative scarcity, and most promisingly, to seven market-oriented guidelines for reducing the huge number of industrial projects that had been launched with state investment funds. Only the devaluation came to pass. Aggregate investment in industry for 1953 did not slack off from an annual increase that averaged fully 16 percent for 1952–53. Yugoslav authorities justified four-fifths of the projects as essential to the national defense, a hard argument to refute in 1953. Continued American insistence on a smaller number of projects resulted in reductions primarily in light industry or consumer goods, the very sectors best suited to export markets.[26]

In sum, the initial American assistance to Yugoslavia allowed the Communist regime to continue starving the agricultural sector in favor of heavy industry and defense. Against these liabilities, however, we must balance the preservation of Yugoslavia's independence from the Soviet bloc. Had a change of Communist leadership occurred under Stalin's terms, its likely mandate may be judged from the unfortunate Romanian experience. The transfer of power to Gheorghe Gheorgiu-Dej in 1952 strengthened central planning for industry, made full collectivization of agriculture inevitable, and put an end to regional autonomy for the Hungarian center of Transylvania. Would the primarily Serb and Montenegrin Cominformists have treated Croatia and Slovenia any differently? Instead, Tito's Yugoslavia had the chance, as chapter 9 will demonstrate, to make its Western economic ties and domestic commitment to decentralization work to its unique advantage.

Second constitution and first dissent

The new constitution of 1953 spoke bravely of decentralization and other departures from Soviet practice, but its specific provisions did not point in that direction. Partly obscuring these contradictions was another feature that would persist in the two subsequent constitutions of 1963 and 1974. They were bewilderingly long. While the last one would exceed 400 articles, the 1953 constitution consisted of 115 new articles supplemented by a majority of the 139 articles from the 1946 document. Two of the party's leading ideologues shared the responsibility for the new constitution. Moša Pijade had chaired the legislative committee of 1952 that was charged with drafting a document to replace its predecessor, an embarrassingly close copy of Stalin's 1936 constitution. Edvard Kardelj then took his turn, seeking to elaborate on but clouding instead with his impenetrable prose the old marxist theme of "the withering away of the state." The other major ideologue, Milovan Djilas, stood aside and would soon object to the Communists' continuing monopoly of power, however reduced or restructured in a renamed party.

Three major provisions of the 1953 constitution suggested that it was actually directed toward the withering away of the republics.[27] First, they lost their rights of secession and sovereignty, granted in 1946. Sovereignty now reposed with the people, somewhat imprecisely defined as the unified Yugoslav working class. Their single, socialist consciousness would create a single Yugoslav one to replace the various nationalisms that had discredited themselves during the Second World War. Thus did the Yugoslav idea of the nineteenth-century Illyrian movement and the notion of the "three-named people" before and after the First World War (see chapters 2–4) reappear redefined but under the same name, *jugoslovenstvo* (still *jugoslavenstvo* in Croatian). Its Communist sponsorship would not help it to survive even the Tito era. We must also acknowledge that a number of related provisions limiting the republics' powers in the administration of justice were intended to preclude the abuses for which the public prosecutors in the *republics* had become notorious.

Two other sets of provisions made specific changes in the federal government that hardly advanced the chances for representation of republic interests. One reconfigured the bicameral Federal Assembly. The Federal Chamber of undifferentiated party or party-approved representatives now absorbed the previous Chamber of Nationalities, adding 70 representatives from the republic and provincial (Kosovo and the Vojvodina) assemblies to the 212 chosen for every 60,000 voters. The new Chamber of Producers favored industry over agriculture, by 135 delegates to 67, the better to represent the workers' councils and their presumably socialist Yugoslav consciousness. A second provision named Tito president and created a new Federal Executive Council (SIV) to replace the Council of Ministers. Kardelj intended to separate the SIV from administrative responsibilities in order to advance the withering away of the state. Its members would be free to concentrate on coordinating the new connection between self-managed institutions and a reduced state structure.

What happened instead was the creation of dual authority at the federal level. Both the SIV and the ministries were free to staff their offices in Belgrade without regard to the ethnic balance that was supposed to be a hallmark of Tito's Yugoslavia. A heavy predominance of Serbs and Montenegrins in the SIV leadership emerged only for a brief period in the late 1950s (20 of 34 in 1958). But a disproportionately small Croatian fraction at the top and a heavily Serb and Montenegrin staff had already become permanent patterns by 1953.

The 1953 Law on Legal Status of Religious Communities did not change the pattern of discrimination against the Catholic, Orthodox, and Muslim clergies that had begun in 1945, other than to reduce the number of physical attacks by local Communists. The Catholic hierarchy's objections to the separate associations of priests that the regime had sponsored in Slovenia, Bosnia-Hercegovina, and Croatia had only led to a break in diplomatic relations with the Vatican in 1952. The Orthodox bishop of Tuzla had been assaulted simply for suggesting that the 1953 law guaranteed the church's right to hold services.[28]

These religious and ethnic issues played no part in the official rhetoric or the dissent registered by Milovan Djilas concerning the new constitutional framework. A principal concern was the role of the Communist Party. Tito had told the Sixth Party Congress, convened in Zagreb in November 1952, that Stalin's "complete betrayal of socialist principles . . . (for) state capitalism and an unprecedented bureaucratic system" demanded that the KPJ itself step back from direct control of the central government. Here was the first talk of the party's need to persuade rather than command, a propaganda theme for the rest of Tito's life. The delegates promptly voted to change the party's name to the League of Yugoslav Communists (SKJ) and the Politburo's to the Executive Committee. The Popular Front became the Socialist Alliance of Working People (SSRNJ). Prominent writer Miroslav Krleža made the speech that rejected socialist realism as a cultural standard, appropriately given his 1930s criticism of it (see chapter 6). The Agitprop agency to feed such material to the media was soon abolished. Djilas pressed hard to change the party's name, arguing that Marx himself had called for a looser league rather than a hierarchical party. The regime's chief propagandist seemed to be taking Tito at his word when the marshal prophesied the eventual downsizing of the Communist Party in March 1952. Stalin's death the following March promised the chance to make domestic changes more easily.

Djilas had been agonizing over the need for drastic political reform since 1950 with a rigor that reminded his biographer, Stephen Clissold, of a Bogomil "Perfect."[29] Dismayed at visiting Goli otok and hearing Western criticisms of such methods, he told Tito that regular judicial procedures were needed. Kardelj countered that "we need the camps desperately now," and Tito agreed. Then on his first visit to London in 1951, Djilas met with the stormy petrel of the Labor party, Aneurin Bevan, currently his government's health minister and a soul mate from the start. Djilas came away impressed with the gradual progress toward socialism in Britain under a multi-party system. By the fall of 1953, this impression and a growing sensitivity to the petty abuses of power within the SKJ prompted the series of critical articles in the party newspaper *Borba*. They began with his argument that the upcoming elections should go beyond offering two party-approved candidates from the Socialist Alliance to compete for the same position. "Conscious social forces" deserved the right to separate representation from outside the "official Communist bodies." Subsequent articles called "the continuous struggle for democracy" society's highest goal, one that might be best served by a new socialist political organization separate from the SKJ. This was obviously going too far. In the party meetings hastily called to confront Djilas, Kardelj accused him of reverting to the pre-1914 parliamentary socialism of Eduard Bernstein, the famed German revisionist. Pijade charged him with "political pornography." By January 1954, Djilas had been expelled from the Central Committee and had turned in his party card by March. His further defiance would put him in prison by 1956.

Djilas' initial defiance in 1953 was more significant for the shape of the second Yugoslavia. Only then did he speak from the inner circle with some chance of rallying others to his objections. None did, other than some personal support from Vladimir Dedijer. The huge party had grown by another two-thirds since 1948 to 780,000 members. The new Socialist Alliance could claim 7 million members, and the party hierarchy had a firm hold on any initiatives that might come from their ranks. The SKJ leadership and its unchallenged head, now President Josip Broz Tito, counted on these two organizations to keep the new workers' councils, off to a bad start in improving efficiency, and a decollectivized peasantry, on the path to a socialist Yugoslavia. Tito's Communists had maintained an independent Yugoslavia against all that Stalin could do until he himself had died. Their success revived the postwar confidence that nothing could stop them.

9   Tito's Yugoslavia ascending, 1954–1967

The new constitutional framework of 1953 promised Communist control only from the bottom up. Yet it left too much authority with the top party leadership or its appointed *nomenklatura* to anticipate that Tito's Yugoslavia would distinguish itself from the other East European regimes by the 1960s. Members of the redesignated League of Communists (SKJ) continued to dominate the newly strengthened communal committees as well as the still secondary workers' councils at each enterprise. How could these local members be expected to stand up to a party hierarchy still headed by Tito himself? Against all odds, the "old man" (*stari*) had emerged victorious first from the war and now from the struggle with Stalin. Where his power or prestige was insufficient, several economic mechanisms or Ranković's security apparatus could still exert central control that bears comparison to counterparts in the Soviet bloc. But by 1966, the market mechanism was being welcomed as Ranković was abruptly forced out for abusing his special powers.

In the process, Yugoslavia became a more open and better place to live than anywhere in the nearby bloc. It recorded rates of economic growth throughout the remainder of the 1950s that matched any in Eastern Europe. As in other Communist economies, the emphasis on heavy industry left the standard of living to lag behind. But during the 1960s, standards improved significantly for a majority of the population. Domestic production and Western imports brought in a better supply of food and consumer goods. Visiting Poles, Czechs, and Hungarians rarely failed to notice the difference. Western tourists and scholars also began to testify. People could speak, study, or travel more freely than in any other Communist state. Some of them, whether party members or not, began to feel like Yugoslavs with legal rights as individual citizens. How this happened and why the process went no further than it did are the focal points for this chapter.

Josip Broz Tito played a prominent part both in these advances and in their limits. The latter came from his career-long commitment to the

Communist left. He must also be judged the most skillful political personality in the history of the two Yugoslavias. Already sixty years old in 1952, Tito remained physically vigorous and mentally agile through the 1960s. Never a powerful public speaker, he did not otherwise hesitate to use the unchallengeable authority that his reputation, party position, and personality cult gave him. No joint leadership like that which failed so badly in Eastern Europe after Stalin's death was foisted on him. No internal crisis confronted him in 1956, as it did Poland and Hungary. Long afterwards, Tito continued to visit major construction projects, coming armed with knowledge of the technical details and leaving with even more garnered from talks with foremen and other key personnel. Some of the genuine popular approval he generated rubbed off on the regime.

Tito made his greatest contribution in the first of four areas that set Yugoslavia apart from and to some extent above its East European neighbors. His diplomatic skills were indispensable in the country's successful balancing act between the Western powers and the Soviet bloc. By encouraging competition for his political favor, he extracted valuable economic concessions for Yugoslavia from both sides. Tito's personal role in founding the Non-Aligned Movement fed the competition further.

Other Yugoslavs – professionals in the economy, the media, and education as well as party members – deserve more of the credit for the other three distinguishing features of this promising period. First came the opening to the West European markets, especially Italy's, that pressured some enterprises to improve their efficiency and some party leaders to relax political controls. This allowed some skilled labor to work in the West and, if they returned, to expect still more change. Second was the economic reform of 1965, the most ambitious set of market-oriented changes undertaken anywhere in the Communist world prior to 1989. The momentum that launched them also swept aside their principal opponent, Aleksandar Ranković. Finally, the regime granted some real breathing space to intellectual freedom by the 1960s. Educational standards rose, a more open if still monitored media began to have an impact, and the free expression of opinion and the practice of religion benefited from significant concessions. Urban culture prospered, its audience swollen by rural migration to the main cities. Ethnic mixing, exposure to Western training, and easier access for women buoyed most professions. Such distinctions promised a political transformation that would make Yugoslavia's ascent self-sustaining. Why this larger promise was not kept will concern the end of this chapter and all of the next two.

Balancing between East and West

During the decade following Stalin's death, Tito's Yugoslavia went from being one of the most isolated states in the world to one enjoying good diplomatic relations with a longer list of other countries than any other government. He and his representatives began by reestablishing relations with the Soviet bloc on essentially Yugoslav terms. They made connections with most new states of the decolonizing Third World, carried forward by the Non-Aligned Movement that Tito was instrumental in founding. All of this, various representatives of Yugoslavia managed to do without alienating the West. They soon converted the emergency aid of the early 1950s from the United States into regular economic assistance, which in turn opened the way to considerable credits from the World Bank and other international lenders by the early 1960s.

Coming to terms with the Soviet Union

Yugoslavia did not abandon the original unwavering Communist intention to make heavy industry the leading sector of the economy. If it were to go forward, Tito's regime needed somehow to use Stalin's death to lift the embargo imposed on Yugoslav trade with Eastern Europe and the Soviet Union. But ending the blockade also promised to loosen the siege mentality that favored those in the party who were opposed to market reforms, more open borders, or greater civil rights within them.

Any break in the blockade had to begin in Moscow. Stalin's death in April 1953 provided the opening. The joint leadership which Nikita Khrushchev soon dominated sought some accommodation with Yugoslavia as early as August 1953. Chief of state Georgi Malenkov spoke in public of normalizing relations. The two countries exchanged ambassadors and started talks on a trade agreement. But the Soviet side went no further, avoiding the slightest political concession until the following year. Then the expulsion of their severest critic, Milovan Djilas, from the League of Communists allowed the Soviets to blame both Djilas and their former security chief, Levrenti Beria, for poisoning mutual relations. Now both were gone, Beria executed soon after Stalin's death and Djilas ousted. Yugoslav leaders nonetheless resisted this formulation, even after they signed a trade agreement with the USSR early in 1955.

Soviet party Chairman Khrushchev wanted a political reconciliation as well. He resisted the hardline demand that Tito come to Moscow for political talks and instead led a high-level delegation to Belgrade in May 1955. The meeting did not go his way. Khrushchev's brusque comraderie culminated in a drunken display at a formal dinner. The confident Tito, resplendent in his marshal's uniform, drove a hard diplomatic bargain. He refused to reestablish interparty relations or even a common ideological formulation. The Belgrade Declaration of June 2 dealt only with relations between the two states. The text that Edvard Kardelj and others had prepared with Tito prevailed over a Soviet draft. Kardelj's language recognized Yugoslavia's right to built socialism and conduct its foreign relations without external interference.

A full set of relations between Moscow and Belgrade, and therefore with Eastern Europe, had to await the Moscow Declaration of June 20, 1956. This more specific document restored connections between the two ruling Communist parties on the basis of "complete voluntariness and equality."[1] It also contained a carefully worded ideological consensus. The importance of the Moscow Declaration can be measured by its constant citation in the Yugoslav press, usually in the first sentence of the articles covering the numerous high-level visits that followed.

The 1956 agreement did not mean that relations with the Soviet Union and its East European allies proceeded smoothly for the rest of Tito's life. He was an old Bolshevik whose ideological disposition was fairly represented in the Moscow Declaration. Yet his readiness to resist Soviet domination was also real. It might have led to another complete break had not the Sino-Soviet split of the early 1960s pushed him and Khrushchev back together.

The eruption of the Hungarian Revolution in late October 1956 seemed at first to threaten an early end to the rapprochement ratified in Moscow only a few months before. Tito and his lieutenants still resented Mátyás Rákosi and then Erno Gerö, the last two Hungarian leaders before the revolt, for their bitter opposition during the dispute with Stalin. And they appreciated the new leader, Imre Nagy, for his pro-Yugoslav sentiments, interest in workers' councils, and ties to some of Belgrade's diplomats in Budapest. Khrushchev felt Tito's position important enough to fly with Malenkov to his island retreat at Brioni during these first days and feed his doubts about the sort of "counterrevolutionary forces" that were gathering around Nagy, Communist though he was. Between October 31 and November 1, Belgrade's leading party paper, *Borba*, dropped its earlier support for the Nagy government, as "in any case . . . not a counter-revolution," and now criticized its connection to "right-wing elements." This new tack suggests that Tito was ready to accept the second and brutally successful Soviet military intervention against the revolt. A week later Tito called the attack regrettable but necessary for "saving socialism in Hungary." Nagy ironically sought refuge in the Yugoslav Embassy, but was handed over on November 22 ostensibly to Hungarian authorities. They did not resist his seizure by the Soviets a few blocks away.[2]

Khrushchev was cautiously grateful to Tito for belated support that, had it been withheld, might have encouraged other East European populations to rise up against their Communist regimes. In 1957 the Soviet leader ousted the last old Stalinist, long-time Foreign Minister Vyacheslav Molotov, specifically because of his "erroneous stand on the Yugoslav question." Once a joint project for East Germany and the USSR to finance Yugoslav aluminium manufacture had been recalled to life, Tito forfeited his diplomatic relations with West Germany by recognizing the DDR. The value of imports from the Soviet bloc for 1956–57 now climbed past 30 percent, with the USSR accounting for half (see table 9.2).

The famous wartime commander, General Georgy Zhukov, and Yugoslavia's minister of defense exchanged visits at the end of 1957, marking the resumption of contact between the two officer corps. A flow of Soviet arms began that soon swamped the modest stock of American equipment. Cut back to 500,000 by 1955, the size of the Yugoslav People's Army (JNA) now dropped to 300,000. The Hungarian Revolution had evidently failed to revive the Yugoslav fear of Soviet military intervention. That fear and its capacity to pull the country together never entirely vanished. It surfaced periodically, making its last appearance after the Soviet intervention in Afghanistan in 1979. Souring Soviet–Yugoslav relations in 1959 explain why 126 Partisan brigades were incorporated into the military planning of the JNA as guerrilla war units and formally integrated into the JNA as territorial militias.[3]

What some observers have called the second Yugoslav–Soviet split was well under way by then.[4] The two parties had already clashed in November 1957. The Soviets proffered a Peace Manifesto to be signed in Moscow by all Communist parties on the occasion of the fortieth anniversary of the Bolshevik Revolution. Soviet delegates demanded their party's recognition as *primus inter pares*. Yugoslav party representatives simply refused to accept this formula, calling it a violation of the Moscow Declaration. Their defiance surfaced again at the League of Communists' Seventh Congress, held in Ljubljana in April of 1958. Tito's opening remarks were purposefully conciliatory, but both Kardelj and Ranković followed with hard, uncompromising speeches. All of the Soviet and East European observers, except one from Poland who was asleep, walked out in protest. The draft (and final) program explicitly denied the Soviet party "a monopoly position in the workers' movement."

The Soviet response came quickly. Within a few weeks, *Pravda* reprinted some harsh criticism by the Chinese of Yugoslavia's sort of socialism. Moscow soon cancelled a proposed visit by Marshal Voroshilov and, more importantly, a set of economic credits. Promised deliveries of wheat did not arrive. Trade with the Soviet Union declined to half of the 15 percent share of export and import value it held in 1957. Yugoslav representatives struck back by protesting the execution of Imre Nagy, who had been imprisoned by the Soviets in Romania and then in Hungary since 1956.

Moscow's more serious split with Mao Tse-tung and the Chinese Communist Party came to the rescue of relations with Tito's Yugoslavia. By the early 1960s, the Chinese ideological attack made revision of Stalinist Leninism the major sin of the Soviet party and pointed to the Yugoslav case as damning evidence of how far such revisionism could go. The same shrill criticisms echoed from Albania. Enver Hoxda's Communist regime had by this time shifted its allegiance from Moscow to Beijing. A Chinese alliance seemed to offer Albania a better chance to meet Hoxda's two priorities, excluding Western influence and confronting Yugoslavia, its surrounding neighbor and most threatening adversary. Early in 1961, Albanian security officers arrested a group of high officials on charges of conspiring with Yugoslav and Western agents. When the Albanian admiral who was its ringleader turned out to be a *Soviet* agent, diplomatic relations between Moscow and Tirana disintegrated. The personal connection between Tito and Khrushchev, resumed after their 1960 meeting at a United Nations session in New York, also helped to put an end to the hostile Yugoslav–Soviet exchanges of the late 1950s.[5]

Relatively good relations with the USSR and all bloc members except Albania and Bulgaria survived the fall of Khrushchev in 1964. They continued improving until the Soviet invasion of Czechoslovakia in 1968. Both sides gained a considerable economic advantage. Yugoslavia's natural resources provided less than half of the energy needed to keep pace with the continued growth of urban settlement and heavy industry. Soviet oil and gas and Polish coal became particularly valuable imports. Since the 1950s, moreover, Yugoslav industry had developed the capacity to export a variety of relatively high-quality manufactures, from electrical appliances to cargo ships. Such "hard goods" now commanded favorable terms in the bilateral agreements by which all members of the Soviet bloc conducted their foreign trade. Foreign trade throughout the Bloc took off after 1960, growing more rapidly than any other economic indicator even though the Soviet-sponsored Council for Mutual Economic Assistance (CMEA) hardly promoted free, multilateral trade in the fashion of the European Economic Community or the European Free Trade Association.

Yugoslav exports to CMEA countries peaked in 1965 at 42 percent of total value, thanks to a contract for ship construction following Tito's successful visit to Khrushchev's successors. While it slipped to 36 percent for 1966, the CMEA share of Yugoslav import value rose several points to a postwar high of 31 percent.[6]

Yugoslavia's role in the emerging Non-Aligned Movement also helped its relations with the Soviet Union advance comfortably through most of the 1960s. For Khrushchev and his successors, that role apparently outweighed the undesirable momentum for market reform and more open contact with the West that was plainly building in Yugoslavia. A more comfortable Soviet connection was one of the several dividends that Tito's effort to create an international coalition outside the two alliance systems and outside of Europe seemed at first to offer.

Early dividends from the Non-Aligned Movement

Yugoslavia's search for support against the Soviet Union at the height of the Tito–Stalin split had ironically stimulated its first contacts with what soon became known as the Third World. The search began in the United Nations. A charter member since 1945, Yugoslavia had nowhere else to turn for immediate support when the confrontation with the Soviet Union began in 1948. Yugoslavia's representatives at first continued to support all Soviet positions in the General Assembly. By December, however, Foreign Minister Kardelj used a speech whose major theme was the need to strengthen the United Nations as an independent body to make his initial suggestion that socialism was "no longer a matter only for a single country." Yugoslavia's election to the Security Council for 1950–51 increased the prospect of UN assistance if the Soviet bloc actually tried to invade. With that prospect in mind, the Yugoslav representative voted with the United States and the rest of the council, minus the unwisely absent Soviet delegation, to defend South Korea from the North's invasion in June 1950.

Yugoslavia's election to the UN's Economic and Social Council in 1952 led to its diplomatic pursuit of development aid with key Asian and African states. Their joint efforts failed throughout the 1950s to promote an enlarged special fund for technical aid (SUNFED), but finally convened the first UN Conference on Trade and Development (UNCTAD). Held in Geneva in 1964, it owed much of its success to the consensual Yugoslav role in bringing together all interested parties, including Israel and South Africa. Yugoslavia would maintain its reputation as one of the world body's most active members for the rest of the Tito era.[7]

Another Yugoslav set of Third World connections started with India and Burma, soon spread to Egypt and Indonesia, and then coalesced as the Non-Aligned Movement. During the UN debate over defending South Korea in 1950, both Burma and India displayed independence from Western control that took Yugoslavia's representatives by surprise. They came away genuinely impressed. Yugoslavia's first ambassador to India celebrated a 1951 speech by Prime Minister Jawaharwal Nehru that called for an "unaligned" foreign policy, adding that Burmese and Indonesian diplomats in New Delhi were talking the same way. The range of representatives who attended their Zagreb conference on ways to end the Korean War further impressed the Yugoslavs with the potential for such an international coalition. By 1953, Tito had decided to send delegates to the first Asian Socialist conference in Rangoon. The next year, he invited Emperor Haile Selassie of Ethiopia to visit Belgrade and then traveled himself to India and Burma at the start of 1955. The emergence of coordinated policy between these founding members dated from Tito's 1956 meeting with Nehru and the man who became his closest associate among these leaders, President Gamal Abdel Nasser of Egypt. The three leaders assembled expressly to accomplish more than the previous year's Bandung conference of Asian and African states had been able to do without a Yugoslav presence.

According to Alvin Rubinstein, two dividends accrued during this initial period from 1956 to 1967.[8] The first made relations with the Soviet Union easier than they would otherwise have been. Khrushchev's growing desire for influence in Egypt facilitated rapprochement with Yugoslavia after the Soviet suppression of the Hungarian Revolution. Nasser had by then defied the British and French for control of the Suez Canal, and Israel had clearly failed to become a Soviet ally in the Middle East as some of Stalin's advisors had hoped. The presence since 1953 of an able Yugoslav ambassador to Egypt, Marko Nikezić, and the supply of arms by Yugoslavia to Nasser and the Algerian FLN opened a number of doors for Soviet representatives. The movement's initial meeting, bringing delegates from twenty-five countries to Belgrade in 1961, also smoothed the way toward ending the second Soviet–Yugoslav dispute. In addition to the generally anti-Western and anti-capitalist rhetoric that dominated visitors' speeches, Tito himself opened the meeting with a surprise reference to the recent Soviet resumption of nuclear testing. Departing from a prepared text that US Ambassador George Kennan had already communicated to Washington, he noted the Soviet resumption with regret, but added that it was quite understandable in the face of hostile Western policy. The aforementioned improvement in trade relations with the Soviet bloc soon followed. Later in 1967, Tito's personal decision to support Nasser's disastrous attack on Israel offered comfort to Soviet policy just before Yugoslavia would again confront the Soviets over the invasion of Czechoslovakia the next year.

The third dividend lasted longer than the capacity of the movement to carve out a genuinely independent place for itself in international diplomacy. Nehru died in 1964 and that year's Cairo conference failed to live up to the promise that most delegates had attached to the first. Afterwards, the movement nonetheless remained Yugoslavia's best forum for propagating the theory and practice of workers' self-management. Official missions to a long list of countries, from Peru to Algeria to Indonesia, promoted general support for its positions in the United Nations (see chapter 10) and opened the way for more profitable business activities in the Third World than any member of the Soviet bloc. This experience further combined with Yugoslav promotion of SUNFED and UNCTAD to ease access to some $4 billion in World Bank loans from 1960 to 1990.

Continuing the American connection

Such prolonged support also owed something to the $1.75 million in grants, soft loans, and dinar sales that the United States provided to Yugoslavia between 1953 and 1964. This amounted to three-quarters of the $2.5 billion in US assistance to Tito's Yugoslavia, following the $298 million of UNRRA deliveries in 1946–47 and $497 million of emergency aid during 1949–52 (see chapter 8). The last allotment of this aid required the Yugoslav side to submit development proposals that put their representatives on the road to compete successfully for international credit when American grants and soft loans virtually ended after 1961.

The larger issue in Yugoslav relations with the United States and its West European allies, Britain in particular, was of course not economic development but rather Tito's independence from the Soviet Union. To the extent that Yugoslavia maintained its independence and prospered in the process, the Western alliance could challenge the Soviets' East European allies to loosen their ties to the bloc. The fiercely anti-Communist John Foster Dulles, secretary of state for most of the Eisenhower administration, became the strongest champion of this view. American assistance could thus be expected to contract when Yugoslav–Soviet relations improved and increase again when they deteriorated. Yet the more immediate effect on Yugoslavia would be the encouragement that this aid and consequently close diplomatic relations offered to the market-oriented reforms and economic potential of the mid-1960s. Chapter 10 returns to a longer-term, less fortunate legacy – the exemption of Yugoslavia's political and legal process from the scrutiny that the Western world applied to other Communist governments, particularly after the Helsinki accords of 1976.

Tito and his diplomatic representatives soon recovered from their initial surprise that assistance could continue on any terms after 1953 and bargained hard, primarily for the soft purchase of American agricultural goods in dinars. The imminent threat of a Soviet-led invasion had passed. Neither Yugoslavia's role as an ideological model for Third World socialism nor the economic necessity of repairing ties to the Soviet bloc made these negotiations easy. Yugoslav authorities nonetheless deemed them necessary, partly for political insurance against the Soviet Union but also for a compelling economic reason. The initial break with the Soviet bloc had opened Western markets and sources of supply without which an independent economy could not survive. Such early access to Western markets had stimulated more efficient, consumer-oriented production, but it did not guarantee export sales. Surging imports had already created a significant deficit on current account (goods and services sold and purchased) that was more than twice the value of hard currency exports by 1953. Short-term credits offered no solution. Repayments due to various West European lenders by 1954 threatened a debt service ratio that would consume 20 percent of that year's export earnings and force sharp reductions in imports for the next year. American officials at first responded by calling for a wider creditors' conference on rescheduling payments, of the sort that the US, Britain, and France had convened two years earlier. By 1954 neither the British nor the French governments were ready to continue their contributions to deficit relief. Washington soon reconsidered and cancelled the conference for fear that the Yugoslavs would use the occasion to ask for still more emergency aid from the United States.[9]

By 1955, however, Tito had persuaded Dulles that Yugoslavia would never return to the Soviet camp, and the United States provided $153 million of new economic assistance, more than in the previous peak year of 1953. Over two-thirds came from the grant or dinar sales of American grain and cotton, both in plentiful surplus, under the new PL 480 program. For good measure, Dulles certified the sales under the Mutual Security Act. The provision for military supplies had meanwhile dropped sharply after averaging $173 million a year for 1951–54 to $26 million for 1955–58 before ending entirely. For the rest of the 1950s, agricultural deliveries rose or fell with the US Congress's perception of Yugoslav–Soviet relations. The peak years were 1957, when Tito received undue credit for opposing Soviet intervention in Hungary, and 1959, at the height of the second Yugoslav–Soviet dispute. Despite the repair of these relations by 1962–63, the annual totals again passed $100 million. Yugoslavia's reputation for independence was sufficiently established by that time for the Kennedy administration to defeat the Congressional minority that threatened Yugoslavia's most-favored nation status several times.

Yugoslavia's reputation for investment projects credit-worthy by Western standards received its most significant American assistance from a series of small development loans between 1959 and 1961. Totalling less than $100 million, these nine long-term loans funded the construction of steel, chemical, and electrical plants to Western specifications. They also delivered to the Yugoslav railways a fleet of diesel locomotives known as "Kennedies," even though they arrived before John F. Kennedy became president. The public's sentimental attachment to the slain president aside, the investment projects approved by the Development Loan Fund made a greater impact than the delivery of locomotives. Yugoslav applications had to meet the new, rigorous standards of the American process for economic assistance, through what became the Agency for International Development by 1961. And meet them they did, completing projects on time as specified and making payments on schedule. Yugoslav authorities made the last payment in 1983. Their record and experience reopened a door closed since 1950 to credit from the independent US Export-Import Bank. From a $50 million loan in 1961, the total extended by 1990 would reach almost $1 billion. Access to $4 billion from the World Bank, mentioned above, started the same year.

The United States continued through the 1980s to play the role of Yugoslavia's lender of last resort. Yugoslavia had first called on the United States to repair a desperate imbalance of international payments in 1952. The next call went out in 1960. The Eisenhower administration contributed $100 million and took the lead in putting together an international package of longer-term credit totalling $275 million.

When the last wave of soft PL 480 sales under the Kennedy administration is added to emergency aid after the Skopje earthquake of 1963, the United States had covered 60 percent of Yugoslavia's current account deficits from 1950 to 1964. One rough estimate for the 1950s reckons that American aid contributed as much as two points to an annual average increase of 7.5 percent in Gross Domestic Product.[10] It remains questionable how much this aid, primarily agricultural, added to the efficiency of an economy that still strangled the modernization of its large private agricultural sector and concentrated its own resources on the excessive development of the same heavy industrial base in almost every republic. The continuation of American aid and the revival of

Table 9.1. *US aid to Yugoslavia, 1949–1967 (US $ mil.)*

	Marshall Plan 1949–52	Mutual Security Act 1953–61	Foreign Assistance Act 1962–67
I. Economic assistance: total	186.8	1,038	536.4
Grants	186.8	617	91.9
Loans		422	444.5
A. Aid and predecessor	124.4	454	12.5
Grants	124.4	265	12.1
Loans*a*		189	0.4
Security supplemental assistance	(109.2)	(321.2)	(10.7)
B. Food for peace (PL 480)	24.8	585	523.9
Grants	24.8	352	79.8
Loans		233	444.1
C. Other economic assistance	37.6		
II. Military assistance: total	310	412	1.8
III. Total economic and military assistance	496.8	1,450	538.2
Loans		1,422	445.9
Grants	496.8	1,028	92.3

*a*Includes capitalized interest on prior-year loans.
Source: John R. Lampe, Russell O. Prickett, and Ljubiša S. Adamović, *Yugoslav-American Economic Relations Since World War II* (Durham, NC: Duke University Press, 1990), 70.

Soviet bloc trade nonetheless provided the major economic benefits gained from the artful balancing act that had become Yugoslavia's foreign policy.

Western markets and self-managed enterprises, 1954–1962

Neither of those benefits coaxed the Yugoslav economy toward market-oriented reform as much as trade with Western Europe. First West Germany and then Italy came forward as the most important partners. Together, their equipment and consumer goods provided high quality imports meeting high standards that no member of the Soviet bloc could match. By the late 1950s, access to such imports became the prize that expanding agricultural imports, improving industrial exports, or developing tourist facilities might earn. Although some enterprises began to respond, most did not, and the structure of self-management still left the local party apparatus in a commanding position. A single, centrally controlled General Investment Fund (GIF) allocated most new capital, with no competition from Western investment. An overvalued exchange rate for the dinar also discouraged exports and encouraged imports, as it had done in interwar Yugoslavia and pre-1914 Serbia when access to Western capital was the prize pursued by such a policy.

By the early 1960s, however, both workers' councils and communal banks had enough autonomy to begin responding to the signals of Western markets. The dinar was devalued, although not enough, in 1961. Price controls on the Soviet pattern remained in place. Momentum was building for the great party debate that culminated in the sweeping reforms initiated in 1965. Prior to that debate, the issues of ethnic rivalry and the rights of the republics remained submerged, but they were nonetheless real.

From Trieste to the Italian market

As long as the dispute over Trieste and the nearby border continued, trade relations with neighboring Italy stagnated. Then in October 1954, exactly one year after a clumsy American attempt to force a settlement by threatening the withdrawal of the Anglo-American occupation force from Zone A, including Trieste, a more sophisticated Anglo-American mediation produced a settlement. All four parties signed a memorandum of understanding in London, giving Yugoslavia sovereignty over Zone B plus the right to use a free port area in Trieste in return for Italian sovereignty over Zone A (see map 8.1). The border dispute that had bedeviled Yugoslav–Italian relations off and on throughout the interwar period was apparently over.[11]

Only two months after the London agreement of 1954, Italy and Yugoslavia concluded a trade pact that included credit provisions for Yugoslav imports. The volume of their trade promptly doubled by 1956 and rose again the following year to make Italy Yugoslavia's largest trading partner. Yugoslav exports to both Italy and West Germany recorded surpluses over imports that promised further expansion, in contrast to the huge deficit that would drag down the still large trade with the United States by the 1960s.

Macroeconomic growth and limited reform by 1961

Yugoslavia's economy grew at a faster pace from 1953 until 1961 than most others in the world, including those of the Soviet bloc. The indicators in table 9.3 are impressive indeed. The value of industrial production led the way with an average annual increase of 12.7 percent by official statistics, reduced only to 11.2 by the critical recalculation of John Moore.[12] Employment in the "social sector" (industry and services

Table 9.2. *Balance and distribution of foreign trade, 1954–1980*

	Exports and imports (annual average in US $ mil.)		Western Europe and the US[a] (percent of total)		USSR (percent of total)		Other E. Europe (percent of total)	
	Exports	Imports	Exports	Imports	Exports	Imports	Exports	Imports
1954	246	265	76.8	81.1	0.5	0.3	2.8	0.7
1956	329	495	65	68			23[b]	22[b]
1958–59	475	701.5	58	70.7			29.6	26.2
1960–62	620	817.3	51.9	29.7	8	6.8	20.6	18.7
1963–64	1394.5	1695	65.7	56	11.9	7.2	24.6	18.6
1965	1092	1182	42.2	66.9	17.2	8.4	24.8	21.4
1966–68	1246.3	1550	48.5	57.6	16.6	9.8	18.6	18.1
1969–71	1658	2529.3	50.3	69.3	14.4	7.7	18	14.7
1972–80	1657.3	2712.5	34.7[c]	45.4[c]	20.7	12.3	20.1[d]	14[d]

[a]Between 1954 and 1959 the United States accounted for 28.5% of all imports and 9.7% of all exports.
[b]Includes the USSR.
[c]Only members of the European Economic Community and the US.
[d]Includes China.
Sources: Vinod Dubey, *Yugoslavia: Development With Decentralization* (Baltimore, MD: Johns Hopkins University Press, 1975), 403–4; Dragana Gnjatović, *Uloga inostranih sredstava u privrednom razvoju Jugoslavije* (Belgrade: Beogradski economski institut, 1985), 78–79; *Jugoslavija, 1918–1988 Statistički godišnjak* (Belgrade: Savezni zavod za statistiku, 1989), 300–5; *OECD Economic Surveys: Yugoslavia 1979 and 1988–89* (Paris: Organization for Economic Co-operation and Development, 1980 and 1990), 67 and 101.

plus state farms) grew from 1.8 to 3.2 million workers. Despite a modest increase in labor productivity that averaged only 3.9 percent, industrial wages rose by 6.2 percent a year and controlled prices just 3 percent. Unemployment in the social sector had climbed close to 200,000 by 1961, or 6 percent, but the number of peasants on private farms dropped from 5.1 to 4.3 million. Higher prices and a series of good harvests, culminating in the record crops of 1959, helped to hold up agricultural production.

Industrial growth prompted an average annual increase of 11 percent in exports for 1953–61, led by machinery and transportation equipment that climbed from 5 to 15 percent of total value at the expense of raw materials. Agricultural exports, which had accounted for 37 percent of total value in 1935–39 had already fallen to 20 percent by 1952–56. Finished manufactures jumped from 7 percent in 1952, barely above the 6 percent recorded in 1939, to 43 percent by 1962.

These advances fit the pattern of *extensive* growth familiar to students of Soviet-bloc economies. Heavy doses of capital and labor outpaced gains in productivity. The share of economic investment in Gross Domestic Product stayed high, still 35 percent for 1957–59 or roughly twice the West European level, and four times the interwar level for the first Yugoslavia. Consumption was correspondingly low, at 48 percent. Political authorities fixed the prices of domestic raw materials at artificially low levels to encourage industrial production. But a variety of taxes and contributions claimed over half of gross value added. The largest of these went to the government's General Investment Fund, which after 1956 allocated investment through the new Yugoslav Investment Bank, also located in Belgrade. The fund accounted for 71 percent of all investments in 1957 and favored capital-intensive heavy industry of producers' goods in standard Soviet fashion.[13]

Still, from 1954 forward, Yugoslavia had witnessed more continuous discussion of how to disengage from this top-heavy mechanism for investment than any member of the Soviet bloc. In 1955, Tito's Executive Committee simply sought to cut industrial investment and increase consumption and agricultural investment from the top. The committee member with the most responsibility for such decisions, Svetozar Vukmanović-Tempo, frustrated their efforts with his erratic choices for priority investments. Aptly characterized by Dennison Rusinow as "an eager primitive spirit and self-confident economic illiterate," Tempo had almost single-handedly derailed American agricultural assistance with his precipitous demands during a 1955 visit to Washington. His transfer to head the moribund network of Soviet-style trade unions in 1958 was doubly fortunate, not only removing him from any influence over investments but also placing his redoubtable energies on the same side as the workers' councils.[14] Neither they nor the still weaker unions had enough influence in 1957 to prevent a spontaneous strike at the major Slovenian coal mines that soon spread across much of the republic. At the heart of the "work stoppage," the Yugoslav euphemism for a strike, and a growing list of complaints from other workers' councils, were demands for distribution of more enterprise income as wages. These pressures prompted the Executive Committee to authorize the inclusion of wages in enterprise calculations of retainable net income, an advantage it immediately negated with a new tax on that income. Tempo and his trade unions protested to no avail.

The revived practice of Five Year Plans, now investment guidelines devoid of specific, Soviet-style production targets for the vast matrix of inputs and outputs, provided a focus for open discussion of how to proceed for the period 1957–61. A majority of the leadership, minus both Kardelj and Ranković, argued for redirecting investment to consumer

Table 9.3. *Macroeconomic growth, 1952–1970 (annual change in percent)*

	1952–60	1961–65	1965–70	1952–70
Real GDP	6.7	6.2	4.8	6
Manufacturing and mining	12.3	10.7	6.1	10.1
Construction	4.9	9.5	4.7	6.1
Consumption	4.8	4.7	6.3	5.2
Real personal income	1.3	9	5.9	7
Exports	12.5	12	8.2	11.1
Imports	8.4	8.3	11.7	9.8
Gross fixed investment	9.7	7.5	6.3	8.2
Type of investment (in %)				
Economic	77.6	67.1	60.1	63.6
Non-economic	22.4	32.9	39.9	36.4
Sector (% of total)				
Manufacturing and mining	36.7,[a] 26.7[b]	25.2	23.3	
Agriculture	11.7,[a] 16.4[b]	11.7	9.7	

[a]1952–1956
[b]1957–1960

Source: Vinod Dubey et al., *Yugoslavia: Development with Decentralization* (Baltimore, Md.: The Johns Hopkins University Press, 1975), 54–60, 385–86.

goods, to the tourist facilities that were moving Austria and Greece out of their interwar poverty, and to the processed agricultural goods that promised the greatest profit as exports to Western Europe. The General Investment Fund kept its place, as did the party training schools, which reopened after the Hungarian Revolution. But after Tempo's transfer, some investment was in fact redirected. Led by allocations for state farm purchase of domestically produced equipment, the agricultural share of gross investment in social (non-private) enterprise doubled from 7.6 percent for 1953–56 to 15.9 percent for 1957–58.[15]

In addition, a 1958 reorganization cut the number of communes from nearly 4,000 to 800, making the allocation of the 28 percent of all budget and investment funds they received potentially more efficient. Enterprises still needed independent access to investment funds, however. Both they and the republics received smaller shares – 17 percent apiece – of the aforementioned budget and investment total than either the communes or the federal government.

Dilemmas of regional imbalance and enterprise management

Two interrelated dilemmas confronted Yugoslavia's system of self-managed socialist enterprises by the end of the 1950s. Although the cumbersome constraints of detailed central planning were long gone, the General Investment Fund's favoring of heavy industry in the less developed republics and regions had begun to hold back aggregate growth at the expense of the more developed areas. Economists in Slovenia and Croatia, also closer to the booming Italian market, concluded that federal institutions like the Belgrade-based Fund and the Investment Bank, were working to their disadvantage. After an initial increase in efficiency, the structure and leadership of most enterprises had failed to respond further to the decentralization of authority in 1952–53. Only a minority were developing the market mentality for serving customer needs that carried many West European firms forward by this time. The top party leadership trumpeted the new Five Year Plan for 1961–65 as the occasion for a series of reforms to improve enterprise efficiency even in the less developed republics and to integrate the national economy enough to remove any question of regional discrimination. When both the 1961 plan and reforms quickly failed, the stage was set for regional politics to come into the open.

Investment policy favored the less developed republics, while low price ceilings for energy and the other raw materials that were their major sectors did not. The disparity between them and Slovenia, Croatia, and Serbia only continued to grow. At the opposite ends of the spectrum, Slovenia's per capita income was three times that of Kosovo in 1950 and five times by 1960. If, however, Yugoslavia's overall investment in fixed assets relative to Gross Material Product (goods minus services) equals 100 for the period 1952–60, the ratio for Macedonia, Montenegro, and Kosovo was 126 and for the three developed republics, just 92. Bosnia-Hercegovina recorded 114 on the strength of investment in arms production that had been largely completed by the late 1950s.[16]

Capital poured into military manufacture there provided the rationale for excluding the Bosnian republic from the "guaranteed investment" that the Fund showered on Macedonia, Kosovo, and especially Montenegro. Perhaps the most famous of the "political factories," in Tito's own phrase, was a plant to manufacture refrigerators perched on a mountain top and accessible only by an unpaved road that was impassable for the better part of the year. Yet the plant was located in an area that had supported the Partisans during the war and was in Montenegro, the one hugely overrepresented republic in the KPJ leadership, that included the investment tsar, Vukmanović-Tempo, when it was built. Overall, Montenegro received 230 dinars for every 100 invested in Yugoslavia during the period. Yet its per capita income barely advanced in comparison to the Yugoslav average and the majority of republics. Only Croatia and Slovenia made significant advances (see table 11.2), while Bosnia-Hercegovina lost ground, as did Kosovo. The loyalty of sizeable areas, particularly in Hercegovina, to the Croatian Ustaša or to the anti-Communist Chetniks probably played a part in this decline, although no statistical evidence is available.

More apparent at the time, and certainly more debated, were the obstacles to enterprise efficiency. Three seemed most pressing by the early 1960s. First, Yugoslav industrial enterprises were large, like their counterparts in the Soviet bloc. Those with more than 4,000 workers employed 62 percent of the labor force and those with over 125 workers employed 97 percent. Management mattered, particularly in the largest enterprises where serious underutilization of capacity had dragged the national average of 77 percent down to 70 percent by 1961. Unlike their Soviet counterparts, such enterprises could dismiss workers and they started to do just that. Unemployment in the social sector reached 7.3 percent by 1962. Second, too many directors were not just political appointees, but were men (always men) selected by the communal council because of their wartime credentials. Minimally educated peasants who had joined the Partisans as teenagers most often fit the bill. They were ill-prepared for their positions in general and easily tempted to divide retained earnings as bonuses with their workers' council rather than invest them in improvements. Third, retained earnings remained severely limited in any case. After a variety of taxes, contributions, and the payment of 6 percent interest on total assets to the General Investment Fund, only 43 percent of 1959 earnings stayed with the enterprise.[17]

The upsurge in aggregate growth during the late 1950s seemed to belie these problems. Had not the Five Year Plan for 1957–61 that began retroactively at the end of 1957 reached all of its general targets by 1960? The bumper crop of 1959 had apparently cleared the way for the sharp 1960 reduction in soft purchases of US grain sales for dinars. The US share of total Yugoslav imports fell by one-half from 20 to 10 percent. But the 1960 harvest was predictably smaller, and when short-term trade credits for West European imports continued to mount, Yugoslav authorities faced a huge deficit on current account. The deficit did not favor their recently submitted application for membership in the General Agreement on Trade and Tariffs (GATT). Yugoslavia's plea for renewed assistance yielded an American-led package of $275 million in short-term credits by the end of 1960. In return, the Yugoslavs promised to cut tariffs and devalue the dinar to a single exchange rate, both basic conditions for GATT membership in any case. The dinar was duly devalued from 300 to 750 and a variety of special rates, some of which made raw material imports irresistibly cheap, eliminated.[18] Yugoslavia won associate membership in the GATT. But to take advantage of the reduced price of Yugoslav exports and to sell enough to surpass the loss in unit revenue, enterprises had to operate more efficiently.

The new Five Year Plan for 1961–65 therefore contained a series of reforms intended to bring market pressures to bear on industrial enterprises without changing the socialist structure of their management. First, enterprise directors and workers' councils were again authorized to include wages in the net income whose distribution they controlled, without the new taxes that negated the privilege in 1958. Indeed, a flat rate of taxation on enterprises replaced the progressive scale that had cut into the profit incentive. Second, the distribution of most short-term credit passed from the Yugoslav National Bank in Belgrade to the 380 communal banks that had sprung up since 1955. For 1961, they dispensed nearly twice the enterprise credits that they and the National Bank had provided just two years before. Both reforms exerted inflationary pressures. So did the higher prices for imports after the devaluation. The inflation that characterized the second Yugoslavia for the rest of its days had begun. Wholesale industrial prices rose 10 percent from 1959 to 1962, and the cost of living jumped by 30 percent.[19]

Tito's government responded, as it would for the rest of *his* days, by putting the brakes on the market mechanism. It retreated from liberalizing foreign trade and used the GIF plus the state banks in Belgrade, now three with the addition of the Foreign Trade Bank in 1958, to boost the share for producers' goods in industrial investment back over 50 percent. The regime reigned in other investment and froze wages by 1962 in the face of too many enterprises choosing wage bonuses and new borrowing over reinvesting their own income. Industrial production actually declined for 1961–62. As a result, the new Five Year Plan had to be abandoned a year and a half after it had been proclaimed.

Tito reacted by emphasizing the need for the party to take the lead in integrating the economy into a single unit. In a heralded speech at Split in May 1962, he linked economic integration to the "uniform socialist Yugoslav culture" whose priority the party congress of 1958 had proposed. A socialist division of labor, as Kardelj vaguely explained at the Ljubljana congress, would create this new sort of *jugoslovenstvo*, or Yugoslav consciousness, not the prewar concept of assimilating of the various ethnic groups into a single entity.[20] But what else could it mean? Ethnic unity seemed far away, given the paltry number of people – some 317,000 – who had declared themselves Yugoslavs in the 1961 census. A new constitution in 1963 moved it further away, before the economic reform of 1965 could attempt to advance the country's integration.

Market reform and the fall of Ranković

The period from 1963 to 1966 witnessed the most intensive political debate over economic reform in the history of the second Yugoslavia. The new constitution of 1963 offered reform advocates more political representation, but hardly resolved the issue of how reform might proceed. Instead the debate intensified. Creating other political parties or an enterprise framework other than workers' self-management was not at issue. Privatization was not a prospect. Many Croatian and Slovenian economists simply advocated greater freedom from what they saw as a central rather than federal government in Belgrade. They and a smaller number of Serbian and Macedonian colleagues also shared a wider goal, dubbed "liberal" by their opponents. They wanted to replace the personal authority of the local as well as central party hierarchy with the impersonal rules of the Western markets where they wished Yugoslav enterprises to compete more effectively. Some also supported a more open society and intellectual atmosphere, still supervised indirectly by the League of Communists, still the only political party, but more pluralist and less regionally divided. It proved easier to agree on economic devolution.

The major opponent of market reform, Aleksandar Ranković, used political pressure behind the scenes to deter it and was disgraced in 1966, precisely for such methods. The liberal hour seemed to have struck. As early as 1967, however, there were signs that Communist reluctance and ethnically based resistance were stronger than the lure of a competitive economy integrated internationally as well as internally. Surely rising educational standards and growing religious and intellectual freedom, with media and cultural institutions to match, would overcome this reluctance and resistance. Or so it appeared to many Western observers, this author included. No one realized that reaching a turning point did not assure its being turned. What Yugoslavia entered instead, in the retrospective metaphor of Russell Prickett, was a period comparable to a stretch of the Mississippi river south of Minneapolis, where the river appears to be rounding a bend but never does. It is called Point No Point.

The 1963 constitution and the end of Yugoslavism

Tito's 1963 speech in Split signalled for a renewed centralization to extend from socialist culture to the economy. A regulatory campaign against private enterprise closed down a large number of small repair shops and craftsmen, but customer complaints forced their reopening. The party's Executive Committee authorized a set of commissions to oversee the distribution of net enterprise income set free the year before. None of this represented a turning point in economic policy, and Tito admitted as much by mid-1962. Yet by the end of 1964, he appeared to join the ranks of the market reformers. With his change of mind, the movement for real change in 1965 became irresistible.

The movement began, according to Dennison Rusinow, with two meetings of the Yugoslav Association of Economists in December 1962 and January 1963, and two studies of the Yugoslav economy, called the Yellow and White Books.[21] The first meeting convened specifically to discuss the economic provisions of the draft for the new constitution. The second met in Zagreb with its Institute for Economic Planning as co-sponsor. Some economists favored the middle course of the Yellow Book and others the decontrol advocated by the Croatian liberals who authored the White Book. As the debate came out into the open after 1963, the liberal decontrollers won allies outside of Croatia. Their position prevailed with the help of bad economic news. That year's economic upturn failed to reign in the excessive investment and imports that had led to the 1961–62 slump.

The new constitution of 1963 drew in more supporters. Crafted primarily by Kardelj, as usual, its new legislative framework attempted to isolate separate republic or ethnic interests still further. While the small Chamber of Nationalities remained a part of the large Federal Chamber, another four specialized chambers were created. They would deal with economic questions, education and culture, welfare and health, and organizational policy. Kardelj intended the specialized chambers to constitute a second, more representative legislative body. Enterprises and institutions would nominate delegates, and some 400 communal assemblies would elect them. He introduced the principle of *rotacija* to deny delegates to the assemblies and workers' councils from serving simultaneously and to prevent more than two terms being served. But the delegates were also more representative in a way that worked against the closer socialist integration of Yugoslavia sought by Tito and Kardelj. Almost all were party members, but many were specialists in their respective fields, economists and managers included. They proved more prepared to debate controversial issues within their areas of expertise than the delegates to the Federal Chamber. By January 1964, such people were demanding decentralization. They soon pushed that larger chamber into a full debate on economic reform. Media coverage of the Federal Chamber debate brought such issues into the public eye.

Arguments that spoke of "de-étatization" rather than decentralization won Tito and Kardelj over to the reform side. The withering away of the state had been one of their original points of distinction in the dispute with the Soviet Union. Now the drive for "de-étatization" sounded the death knell for jugoslovenstvo, even though the right of the citizens to declare themselves Yugoslavs survived a challenge in the drafting of the 1963 constitution. For the first time, the considerable powers of the federal government and even the Community Party's central hierarchy itself were reduced, to the specific advantage of the republics and regions. The statement of general principles that prefaced the constitution restored to the republics their rights to secession, if all agreed. Article 226 codified the existing practice of a balanced republican representation on the Federal Executive Council that became the equivalent of a ministerial cabinet. A new constitutional court could also hear republics' appeals against federal laws that infringed on their rights, as well as federal appeals against their legislation.[22]

More important than any article in the constitution, the Eighth Congress of the League of Communists in December 1964 authorized the republics and regions to convene their conferences immediately before the joint party meeting in order to prepare their respective positions. Thus began the confederation of the League of Communists of Yugoslavia (LCY), even though Tito still towered over any set of contending republic leaders and the country's legislative framework continued, at least until 1967, to make the practice of republic or ethnic politics difficult.

The economic reform of 1965

The issue of economic reform occupied too much public space, it must be emphasized, for ethnic politics to intrude during this crucial period. The failure of the 1965 reform to do better and the question of whether or not it should have gone farther invited the same regional infighting that later accompanied the catastrophic inflation of the 1980s. But hopes were higher twenty years earlier, the West European economies were more welcoming partners, and the party's self-confidence as a single unit still intact.

The year began with the disquieting news that the economic upsurge of 1963–64 seemed to be slipping out of control. The rate of inflation for 1964 jumped to 10 percent, the largest yet in a single year, and the import surplus nearly doubled, from $188 to $323 million over 1963. Simply clamping down on investment outside of priority projects as was done in 1962 would only produce another recession and no long-term solution. And it might not work now. Too many enterprises had come to rely on short-term credits from their local communal bank, increasingly rolled-over on demand to become de facto long-term credits. These considerable if uncertain sums must be added to the great majority of formal investment in fixed assets that was now outside the direct control of the federal government. That fraction had risen from 63 percent in 1961 to 93 percent by 1964, as the share under communal or bank control had jumped from 27 to 59 percent. The transfer of the General Investment Fund's assets to the Yugoslav Investment and Foreign Trade Banks in Belgrade accounted for the largest part of this shift, raising the further issue of whether the banks would operate on commercial principles or cater to the political demands of the Serbian republic in which they were located.[23]

The structure of banking and credit therefore commanded initial attention. The legislation of March 1965 proposed a drastic reduction in the number of banks, virtually abolishing the existing network of 380 communal banks in favor of 30 to 40 larger regional banks. Their capital and, to some extent, direction would come from changing their principal enterprise and institutional depositors who now became shareholders. The new banks would operate on a commercial basis, providing long- and short-term credit to the borrowers most likely to repay their loans, but also lending within the guidelines of the government's Social Plan. While they would accept applications for credit from the entire territory of Yugoslavia, their new management was to include representatives of major depositors; these were invariably the largest enterprises from their own area or republic. The three large Belgrade banks with state assets, the Investment, Foreign Trade, and Agricultural Banks, would face worthy competitors to ensure that they operated along the same commercial lines.

The rest of the reform was announced with great fanfare in July. It consisted of five major provisions.[24] (1) Taxes on the turnover of goods were reduced and made more uniform, the tax on an enterprise's net value added was abolished, and the tax on their fixed assets trimmed to 4 percent. As a result, the enterprise share of its net income was to rise from less than 50 percent to 70 percent. (2) The Fund for Accelerated Development of Less Developed Republics and Kosovo (FADURK) that had been created in 1963 now received significant resources from a new tax of 1.85 percent on the gross income of all social enterprises. (3) Aiming for the goal of full GATT membership by 1966, the dinar was again devalued, from 750 to 1,250 to the dollar and divided by 100 to 12.50, to seem sounder like the new French franc. Customs duties were cut from 23 percent to a 12 percent average for imports, and the export subsidies that had mushroomed to 20 percent of export value by 1964 were reduced. (4) Agricultural and raw material prices were still controlled, but increased by an average of 60 percent and industrial prices 30 percent, in order to bring them closer to world levels. (5) Peasants working private land were allowed access to bank credit to purchase the tractors and other agricultural equipment they needed to shore up their lagging productivity.

Had the rest of the economy responded to the 1965 reform as did the 50 percent of private farms located in the fertile lowlands, Yugoslavia might well have turned the corner to intensive growth and market-based development. Even the modest access to bank credit actually allowed during the period 1965–70 boosted the number of privately owned tractors from barely 5,000 to 39,000. Fertilizer consumption increased by one-half. Although the size of the average landholding now slipped below 4 hectares, the amount of cultivated land also dropped by 7 percent as more peasants left the land from 1960 to 1970. Still, while the rural share of the population fell from 60 to 50 percent for this period, wheat and corn yields on private land rose by one-half. Private farms continued to produce nearly two-thirds of total grain, meat, and egg yields, leaving the state farms with higher yields only for sugar beets and sunflowers. Private production climbed 6 percent a year for 1966–70, and took the lead in reducing the share of foodstuffs to 8 percent of import value, roughly the interwar level.[25]

The rest of the reform did not go nearly as well. The restructuring of the banking sector closed some efficient communal banks, replacing them with larger banks, whose small number and cautious loan policies, particularly outside their particular republic, created a credit squeeze by 1966. Fixed net investment in constant prices fell for the rest of 1965 and through 1966 by 15 percent. Wage increases absorbed too much of the newly freed enterprise income for it to pick up the slack in investment. Gross Domestic Product barely rose a percentage point for 1966, but import value jumped 23 percent to reinstate the trade deficit that had temporarily vanished the year before. All of this generated an inflation of 28 percent in manufacturing costs, versus a rise in value added of 16 percent.

Harold Lydall's critical analysis of the reform identifies two troubling portents for the longer term.[26] First, the long postwar rise of largely manufacturing employment in the social sector broke off. Sector totals for industry fell from 1965 to 1968. Official figures for unemployment rose steadily in the social sector over the same period, from 6 to 9 percent. The number of "guest workers" in Western Europe (Croats in West Germany were initially the largest group) surged up from 50,000 to surpass the number of registered unemployed, 280,000 by 1968. With more migration still to come from the countryside, opponents of market reform could point to the specter of "socialist unemployment" as a reason for retreat.[27] Such opponents failed to consider the legacy of Yugoslavia's large, inefficient, capital-intensive enterprises, ironically concentrated in the less developed regions where unemployment was highest. Greater investments of capital in smaller more labor-intensive enterprises might have provided more employment as well as increased the productivity of capital. But they could not serve the defense needs that still contended with production for comparative market advantage. Second, inflation emerged as a chronic problem. Because the economy as a whole could no longer afford to extract investment by forced cuts in consumption, the politically motivated creation of credit from any source, domestic or foreign, would only cause inflation. Serbia's authorities promptly did just that, offering an ominous preview of the Milošević regime's raid on the money supply before the December 1990 elections. The republic's gross fixed investment rose by 21 percent in current prices for 1965–66, versus 5 percent for the rest of the federation. Fueling the inflationary expansion were funds from the three large Belgrade banks and the determination of Aleksandar Ranković to resist the reform at least in his native republic.

Ranković's fall and the liberal hour

With the reform in serious economic trouble by the middle of 1966, its leading political opponent suddenly fell from power. A broad coalition of liberals from every republic except Bosnia-Hercegovina wanted desperately to bring him down. Tito and Kardelj offered them decisive support. Kardelj had favored devolution over the market mechanism from the start, but had never been close to Ranković. According to his wife's account, Kardelj also blamed Ranković for failing to prevent an attempt to assassinate him in 1959. More certainly, Tito's decision to appoint Ranković instead of Kardelj to the potential successor's position of vice president prescribed by the 1963 constitution, must have rankled.

Tito was still president for life and might not have been won over, despite his acceptance of the reform, if not for a bizarre sequence of events in the summer of 1966. Rumors began to circulate that the former UDBa, now the Service for State Security (SDB) since 1954, had used its unchecked powers for electronic surveillance to bug the offices and even residences of the highest officials and party leaders. Only Ranković could have given the authorization. Not trusting the SDB to look into the matter, Tito asked the rival military intelligence service, KOS, to check for evidence. What they found in June allegedly included a device over Tito's bed. Ranković was summoned a few weeks later to appear before a SKJ plenum hastily assembled at Tito's island retreat on Brioni. Army units in Belgrade went on alert that first week in July, but there was no significant reaction in the capital or elsewhere in Serbia to the announcement that Ranković had been removed.[28]

The liberal coalition, it must be emphasized, included party leaders from Serbia and Macedonia as well as Croatia and Slovenia. Whether these leaders were strong enough in the two eastern republics or free enough from regional grievance in the two western republics to have prevailed without Tito on their side remains a doubtful proposition. But after the fall of Ranković, the road ahead of them seemed clear of obstacles. The Serbian strongman's closest supporters were gone, and his earlier efforts to court allies in the less developed republics had yielded only a series of agreements with the smallest one, Montenegro. The Macedonian party and in particular its leader, Krste Crvenkovski, resisted the offer of continued investment subsidies in return for a political alliance. In the Serbian party itself, economic policy had been liberal since Mijalko Todorović had succeeded Vukmanović-Tempo in 1958 as the Executive Committee member responsible for investment policy. The mid-1960s ascent of Foreign Secretary Marko Nikezić from the diplomatic service and Latinka Perović from the university community to high party positions signalled a political change coming in Belgrade as well. The momentum seemed unstoppable if a Serbian alliance with the Croatian and Slovenian economists and with Croatian party leader Vladimir Bakarić held firm.

To what extent was ethnic antagonism waiting in the wings to unseat them? It took two more immediate problems to summon such antagonisms to the stage even in non-violent form. Then they came only under prompting from economic uncertainty and the international turmoil of 1968. Once the liberal alliance had unraveled, however, Yugoslavia's political leadership was left poorly prepared to deal with an aged, still unchallengeable, and increasingly inflexible Tito during the last decade of his life. The federation's political decline, obscured from view by the export of labor and then the import of capital is detailed in chapter 10. We can already discern the outline of the two basic problems that followed the fall of Ranković. One was the dilemma of truly reforming a ruling Communist Party, a feat accomplished nowhere without loss of monopoly on power, and the other, the related pressures of regional economic rivalry. The old Djilas proposal to make the huge Socialist Alliance, which all workers in social enterprises were obliged to join, into a second political party surfaced briefly in 1966. Yet liberals like Nikezić and Bakarić rejected it as quickly as the surviving centralists. Only the further devolution of Communist power to the republic or local level could create a sense of democratic reform on which both sides could agree. Arguments to maintain the party's monopoly of power could still carry the day, particularly for Tito and Kardelj. Such arguments prevented prompt passage of the final piece of the 1965 reform, a law to encourage foreign investment. No investment would be approved until 1967, and then it hardly encouraged Western investors. Its terms remained roughly what they had been before Ranković's fall, authorizing only joint ventures under a Yugoslav director with the foreign partner remaining a minority on the governing board and owning no equity.[29]

Regional rivalry over the increasingly scarce sources of domestic investment rose with the reform's creation of the FADURK fund for less developed republics. It allocated fully 2.63 percent of Gross Material Product (GMP) for investment and social costs to four eastern recipients, Bosnia-Hercegovina, Kosovo, Macedonia, and Montenegro. The two western republics, Croatia and Slovenia, accounting for the largest republic shares of GMP, complained about the diversion of their "tax dinars." Serbia's representatives would later complain about Kosovo receiving the largest relative share of the FADURK funds. Yet Bosnian party leaders were the first to object, pointing out that their republic received only one-third of what Kosovo did on a per capita basis. The liberal coalition ironically had pushed FADURK forward in early 1965 precisely to keep the less developed republics on their side. The fund began, instead, to divide this wider alliance as soon as Ranković's departure had removed the threat of Serbian (or better, centralist) dominance that had held it together.[30]

Positive signs and public opinion

Despite the Communist monopoly of political power, modernizing urban institutions trained enough professionals to make the prospects for an integrated Yugoslavia still seem real. Some credit for that process belonged to the political regime and its relations with the West. The greater credit, as argued at the start of this chapter, belonged to the managers and workers, professionals from schools, social services, or the media, and to a lesser extent, the clergy, who were bringing their institutions into the European mainstream. How far had they come toward an integrated Yugoslavia? Some accounting is needed to understand why so many citizens and most close observers of Tito's Yugoslavia continued to give its prospects the benefit of the doubt. The socioeconomic indicators (table 9.4) suggest that overall progress was considerable.

Enterprises and schools led the way. For all its general failings, the system of workers' self-management produced some directors and workers' councils who chose to use the freer hand they received in 1961 and 1965 to invest their profits in making more competitive products rather than dividing them up as bonuses. By 1965 the US Department of Commerce listed several hundred Yugoslav enterprises as meeting the standards for Western competition. The separate economic institutes headed by Ivo Vinski in Zagreb and Aleksandar Bajt in Ljubljana had already acquired an international reputation that no Soviet bloc institute could match. The same could be said for projects from the department of international economics at Belgrade University.

The economists, managers, and workers that appeared in the various chambers of the National Assembly after its 1963 reconstitution and helped push for the 1965 reform were not the aging Partisans who still dominated the army, the security services, and the party hierarchy. They were younger men, and an increasing number of women, with high school or university education, often with some training or travel outside the country. Access to higher education had grown significantly from 1952 to 1960. Student enrollments as a fraction of their age group had nearly doubled to 23 percent for secondary schools and 5 percent for universities. Three new universities had opened in Sarajevo, Skopje, and Novi Sad, while the established ones at Belgrade, Zagreb, and Ljubljana had added faculties and students. Here and in the professions, as opposed to the enterprises, women occupied a higher percentage of positions than their one-quarter share in all social employment for university graduates.[31] The objectivity of research and the quality of instruction also improved, benefiting noticeably from a variety of faculty and student exchanges with Western Europe and especially the United States by the mid-1960s. The famed Fulbright program began operation in Yugoslavia in 1964, after some political hesitation, and grew quickly to become the largest in Europe after West Germany's. All of this created an improved reservoir of human capital, ready to work harder within the system than their counterparts in any Soviet bloc country.

The Yugoslav media had also become significantly less restricted than its bloc counterparts. Although most journalists were still party members, the principal newspapers in Belgrade, Zagreb, and Ljubljana, *Politika*, *Vjesnik*, and *Delo*, respectively, published often independent analyses. The newscasts on radio and television in those cities as well were increasingly informative and reliable. Weekly journals like *NIN* or *VUS* were even more forthright. Taboo subjects, such as criticism of Tito or the single-party system, could be counted on two hands. Across the country, the number of radio stations jumped from 21 to 77 for 1962-66. The number of radios rose by one-half and television sets five-fold to nearly 800,000.[32]

Among the 23 dailies and 150 weekly publications that appeared by 1966 were a number of religious publications. Their appearance symbolized the long-delayed readiness of the Communist hierarchy to find a working arrangement with both the Catholic and the Orthodox churches. The legal status promised to them and to the Muslims and Protestants in the 1953 constitution had little value throughout that decade. After the death of Archbishop Stepinac in 1960, however, the regime began long negotiations with the Vatican that finally resulted in a joint protocol by 1966. The education of priests and the publication of the weekly *Glas koncila* could now go ahead with a minimum of inter-ference. Similarly, the Orthodox hierarchy of Serbia had been able to bargain with its Communist counterpart for the right to revive its seminaries and publish a variety of publications, culminating with the weekly *Pravoslavije* in 1967. Perhaps more importantly, the Serbian church was able to build 181 new churches and restore another 841 by the end of the decade.[33] Only in areas such as Knin and eastern Hercegovina where the population had overwhelmingly favored the Chetniks over the Partisans during the war was the restoration of Orthodox churches destroyed by the Ustaša regime more difficult.

The neglect of the former Chetnik areas and an inquiry by a Franciscan order that revealed the disproportionately high number of Serbs holding police and other official positions in Croatia were indeed storing up trouble for Yugoslavia after Tito's death. At the time, the primary features of religious life in Yugoslavia hardly seemed threatening. Churches were again becoming a fact of social life, mainly for weddings and funerals, but even the most active, the Croatian Catholic church, failed to strike the deeper political or even religious chords in its population that, for instance, the Polish church was finding. The proportion of the population reporting religious belief in Croatia remained higher than in the Orthodox eastern republics, but it still reflected the country-wide decline that had begun in the 1950s. By 1964, religious belief had slipped to 70 percent, on its way to less than one-quarter twenty years later with a Croatian figure of 33 percent. In public opinion polls, now becoming reliable by Western standards, all republics identified manifestations of ethnic nationalism as a backward phenomenon for which the lack of economic modernization could be blamed. Except for Slovenia, respondents did not blame the religion or the ethnic culture of the economically underdeveloped areas for the nationalist resentments presumed to be their exclusive province.[34]

The massive movement of the Yugoslav population, first into urban areas and then into Western Europe if no satisfactory job was available, also played its part in creating a secular, Europeanized culture that did

Table 9.4. *Socioeconomic indicators, 1950–1970*

	1950	1960	1970
Per capita GDP (1966 prices)	216	333	520
Infant mortality (per 1,000 live births)	118.6	87.7	55.2
Illiteracy rate (% of population ten years and above)	25.4	19.7	15.2
Population per doctor	3,360	1,474	1,010
Radio receivers (per 1,000 persons)	21	78	166
Automobiles (per 1,000 persons)	0.4	2.9	35
Population			
% Urban	21	28	39
% Non-urban	79	72	61
% Rural	64	50	38

Sources: Vinod Dubey, *Yugoslavia: Development with Decentralization* (Baltimore, Md.: The Johns Hopkins University Press, 1975), 54–60 and 385–86; and *Jugoslavija, 1945–1985* (Belgrade: Savezni zavod za statistiku, 1986), 52.

not fully owe its existence to the Communist regime. The urban share of a population approaching 20 million had passed 30 percent by 1966, with only Bosnia-Hercegovina lagging significantly behind at the 20 percent of the first Yugoslavia. But that was because increasing numbers of rural Croats and especially Serbs were leaving Bosnia-Hercegovina permanently to settle in the towns of Croatia and Serbia. Better economic chances rather than any hint of harassment from the Bosnian Muslims led them away. "Guest workers" back on holidays from Western Europe, and a larger number of Western tourists were now bringing significant income into the country. Both groups brought a further infusion of Western popular culture and consumer demand that pressured the Yugoslav Communist regime to respond, a process still unfamiliar in the Soviet bloc. Such market pressures and human capital were accumulating within a socialist framework that seemed to offer Tito's Yugoslavia a way to overcome the immediate problems of the 1965 reform and to distinguish itself safely from the Soviet bloc in the years that lay ahead. Tito still steered a shrewd diplomatic course until his death in 1980. Yet the domestic corners remained unturned, and his longevity proved to be one of the reasons.

Repairing regional imbalance at its rural roots would prove to be the most difficult of these domestic corners. The largely urban advances of the twenty years of Communist rule had indeed moved Yugoslavia's level of aggregate development ahead more rapidly than had the interwar state. Industry obviously led the way, boosted by a far more favorable international economy as well as Communist priorities for domestic

9.1 Sarajevo Winter Olympics, 1984, opening ceremony

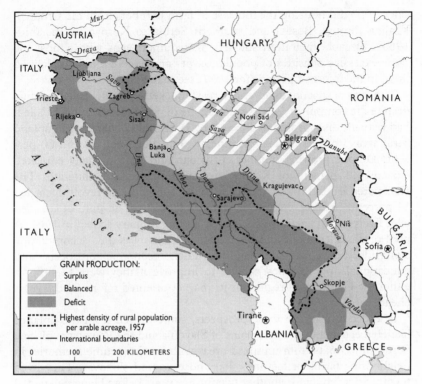

Map 9.1 Grain land and rural overpopulation, 1970

investment. Overall industrial employment had reached 1.25 million by 1964, roughly five times the 238,000 in 1938. The real value of production grew even more rapidly, sixfold rather than fivefold. Serbia's employment, minus Belgrade, now surpassed Bosnia-Hercegovina, while all regions to the south or east of Slovenia and Croatia increased their share of total jobs from 40 to 60 percent.

A majority of the still substantial rural population did not benefit from a comparably balanced distribution of agricultural growth. That growth was not unimpressive.[35] After a slow start in the wake of the abortive collectivization drive (see chapter 8), crop yields for 1957–77 were roughly half again those of 1930–39, with arable acreage for fodder and industrial crops gaining at the expense of food grains. Yet small, typically upland holdings still divided by strip farming and not producing a marketable surplus continued to account for half of all private farms and over one-third of all farmland. The chance to buy, sell, or lease their land since 1953 did not stop the increase in farm numbers from the Croatian Krajina through Bosnia and southern Serbia to Kosovo by the mid-1960s. Sizeable migration still left this southern axis with almost the same excessive densities of population per arable acre that had plagued them in the interwar period (for 1957, see map 9.1).[36]

The axis also contained the largest pockets of illiteracy persisting despite the compulsory, eight-year regime of primary education. While it had virtually disappeared in Slovenia by 1961, rates of illiteracy in upland rural areas from the Krajina southeast ranged between 30 and 60 percent. Despite growing numbers of urban and professionally educated citizens, 41 percent of Kosovo's population was still illiterate. The Cazin area around Bihać, the scene of the 1950 peasant revolt, recorded 51 percent. In all of Yugoslavia (table 9.4), nearly one-third of children over five years of age were still not attending primary school in 1961. A pool of unskilled labor and uneducated citizens was thus accumulating alongside the educated majority. Their economic prospects and educational opportunities needed to improve if they were to support either the Communist regime or its market-oriented reform in the years ahead.

In order to improve these prospects, some moved from the uplands like Hercegovina to the rich plains of Slavonia and the Vojvodina, placing Serbs and Croats from unmixed areas with harsh wartime memories in neighboring farms or factories, like those around Vukovar. They lived together peacefully for another twenty-five years before being persuaded to turn on each other in 1991.

10   Tito's Yugoslavia descending, 1968–1988

Tito's Yugoslavia descended slowly and then not steadily from its most promising period – the late-1960s – to the ominous 1980s. The political crisis that Yugoslavia's émigré detractors had predicted the moment Tito died in 1980 did not come into the open for another eight years. But by the mid-1980s, federal–republic relations in Kardelj's convoluted constitutional framework had deadlocked disastrously. Only some fundamental restructuring could save Yugoslavia. Much was discussed, constitutional amendments proposed, but little was done. By 1988 the League of Communists' federal prime minister and his cabinet were forced to take the previously unthinkable step of resigning.

A demoralizing economic decline had started with the second international oil crisis in 1979, but deepened too relentlessly over the next five years to be blamed on its lingering effects.[1] Registered unemployment in the social sector rose steadily from a 1977–81 plateau of 13.8 percent to reach 16.3 percent by 1985. Real earnings in the predominant social sector fell by a full 25 percent between 1979 and 1985. After turning slightly upward in 1985, they resumed their steady decline the following year, propelled in part by an annual rate of inflation that now passed 100 percent. Aggregate inflation for 1979–85 already exceeded 1,000 percent, compared to a European average of less than 50 percent. The exports needed to maintain imports and service a foreign debt already out of control by the time of Tito's death could hardly flourish given such a disparity. Another American-led package of debt relief and the Sarajevo Winter Olympics of 1984 came and went; neither led to the anticipated domestic reforms.

Most of the population was now worse off than when Tito was alive, and the fear of political crisis that followed his death had worn off. His longevity had allowed Edvard Kardelj to continue elaborating an incomprehensible electoral framework that made sense only as a device to prevent the organization of any rival to Communist power on the local, republic, or federal level. Then Kardelj died in 1979, the year before

Tito, and in little more than a decade, so did the Yugoslav experiment that took a modern European country down with it.

Ethnically based disturbances already challenged the Communist political order as early as 1968–69. Yet they did not lead inexorably to the ethnic battle lines drawn as a substitute for democratic politics some twenty years later. Had they been followed by more market-based economic reform and a chance for country-wide pluralist politics, even within the League of Communists, these ethnic grievances might have stayed where they were for most of the population throughout the 1970s – in the back of their minds. In the forefront were individual efforts to study or work in an expanding, modernizing economy. These growing connections to the wider world nourished a common sense of Yugoslav identity. They also encouraged the same set of multiple or parallel identities – as individuals and Europeans as well as Yugoslavs and Serbs or Croats or other ethnicities – that was transforming Western Europe into a much different place than it had been in the interwar period.

This chapter must weigh the assets bequeathed to post-Tito Yugoslavia against a number of liabilities. Three seem most serious: the consequences of the confederal constitution of 1974, the subdivision of workers' councils into Basic Organizations of Associated Labor in 1976, and the foreign debt crisis of the early 1980s. All three liabilities were rooted in the Communist leadership's response to opposition from outside and inside the party during the period 1968–71. All three contributed to the federal failure to restructure Yugoslavia's political and economic framework in the years after Tito's death. Into that federal vacuum stepped the destructive ethnic politics (see chapter 11) that carried social strains and regional rivalries beyond Communist control.

Opposition comes into the open, 1968–1969

Both international relations and the domestic economy seemed to be working in favor of Tito's Yugoslavia as the 1960s drew to a close. The Soviet invasion of Czechoslovakia in August 1968 pulled both public and party opinion closer together. If Soviet forces could occupy a fellow bloc member with impunity, did not the old danger of attack against heretic Yugoslavia become real again? In addition, Tito's defiant criticism of the invasion and official refusal to send back any of the thousands of Czechs and Slovaks who had been vacationing on the Adriatic raised Yugoslavia's stock in the West. Tito's determination to back Egypt in the Six Day War with Israel in 1967 and break diplomatic relations had damaged Yugoslavia's position. Now its market value rebounded.

Domestic developments also looked promising in several respects.

Gross Domestic Product (GDP) of goods and services turned up in 1968 and the following year practically equalled the high rates of 1963–64 without comparable current account or budget deficits. Exports rose, while the severalfold jump in tourist and remittance revenues allowed imports to rise even more without reopening a serious payments deficit. The reform begun in 1965 was promoting better management in at least some enterprises, despite restrictions on domestic credit and foreign investment (see chapter 9). An internationally-minded set of individuals, openly called liberals, took over the leadership of Serbia's League of Communists by the end of 1968. The number of professionals and managers trained to a European standard continued to grow, and a number of them won places in the multiple-candidate elections to the Federal Assembly held in 1969.

The first open challenge to the party and state regime had nothing to do with ethnic issues, unlike the subsequent opposition in Kosovo, Slovenia, and Croatia. Students went on strike at Belgrade University in June 1968 after riot police charged into a small group of them fighting with youth brigade workers one evening. Police fired pistol shots into the much larger crowds that assembled the next day. A full-scale strike quickly spread to the universities of Zagreb, Ljubljana, and Sarajevo. The protest echoed the student unrest unfolding across Western Europe and the United States. Their demands for some voice in university affairs and better facilities were the same.

The students' more general opposition to growing economic inequality and to anything smacking of capitalism might have sounded the same, but it had a more specific target – the economic reform of 1965. Behind the New Left slogans decrying its capitalist consequences and the affluence of the party élite lay the movement for "Marxist humanism" that had captured the imagination of a number of influential faculty members. Their bible was the Zagreb-based journal, *Praxis*. Since its first issue in 1964, *Praxis* editors had hammered away at the failings of Yugoslav self-management from the left. Socialist idealism rather than market motives, they argued, should dissuade enterprise management, and the party leadership, from profiting by its position. The resonance in Belgrade was particularly strong. Mihailo Marković, eventually a nationalist convert to the Milošević regime of the early 1990s, was among the leading voices of a group exiled from the university in the 1970s and celebrated thereafter as the "Belgrade Eight." In June 1968, they successfully persuaded the university's party organization to support the strike. Their hostility to the market reform of 1965 bears some responsibility for the failure to carry it forward, beyond the economic difficulties of its first years. The same hostility suffused a student press freer to speak out in the more relaxed political atmosphere since the fall of Aleksandar Ranković in 1966.[2] As a result, the universities offered no theoretical support, outside of the various economic departments, to the practical task of reducing the monopoly power of the party and its appointees in favor of economic efficiency.

Demonstrations calling for the withdrawal of the 1965 reform continued for a full week, evoking some recognition of their demands in the officially supervised media. *Borba*'s coverage, in particular, suggests that Tito and the party's Executive Committee now decided to coopt the students. Taking care to keep the demonstrators from reaching factory gates to solicit worker support, officials also silenced those party functionaries who in the spirit of the Ranković era simply wanted to suppress the students. Then, on June 9, Tito spoke on television to affirm that he himself was "with the students." A number of university reforms did indeed follow, but the whole experience helped convince Tito, Kardelj, and many of the Communist leaders that enlightened public opinion would support putting socialism, however ill-defined, ahead of the market mechanism in Yugoslav self-management.

Kosovo

Later that summer a different sort of discontent surfaced in Serbia's autonomous region of Kosovo-Metohija. Two years had passed since the downfall of the Albanian Kosovar majority's principal oppressor, Aleksandar Ranković. His internal security forces (the SDB, formerly the UDBa) in the province, manned mostly by Serbs, no longer possessed powers of arbitrary arrest and secret trial. A group of Kosovar Albanians convicted of espionage for Albania in an open but rigged trial in 1956 were exonerated. Otherwise, little had changed for the 70 percent of the population who were ethnically Albanian. A shortage of schools and Kosovar teachers plus the patriarchal practice of keeping females away from school held the literacy rate below 50 percent. Investment from the new federal fund for less-developed regions (see chapter 9) went to capital-intensive industry and produced very few new jobs for this region whose unemployment rate was by far the highest in Yugoslavia, at over 20 percent. Kosovo's per capita income continued to slip behind other regions and republics, dropping to less than one-quarter of Slovenia's by 1967. More importantly Serbs and Montenegrins still accounted for over half of the professional and official employment in the province, the police and SDB included.

Local Kosovar party members carried these grievances with them into the public meetings organized that summer by the Federal Assembly's constitutional commission. They saw elevation to the status of a separate republic as the most promising solution to all of their problems. With those problems went a sense of isolation from the rest of Yugoslavia and a desire for some connection with neighboring Albania despite its still lower living standard and ruthlessly oppressive Stalinist regime. Yugoslavia's Communist leadership, and not just its Serb members, saw this disposition – it was hardly a coherent plan – as a prelude to secession. Since the preamble to the 1963 constitution had included language almost universally regarded as reinstating the republics' right to secede, the party hierarchy resisted any suggestion of making Kosovo a republic. The region's Albanian language newspaper, *Relindja*, nonetheless floated the idea in August. The autumn produced only marginally greater Albanian representation in the region's party apparatus, and then over the objections of several prominent Serbian party members, including the writer and later nationalist leader, Dobrica Ćosić. Yugoslavia's Liberation Day fell on November 29, the anniversary of Albania's independence. The coincidence brought Kosovar demonstrators into the streets of Priština, the capital, and several other towns. Hundreds of rioters smashed windows and cars, moving *en masse* and battling the police who tried to stop them. Similar violence exploded in Tetovo and other northwest Macedonian towns with large Albanian populations. Forces under the interior ministry quickly and brutally restored order at the cost of many injuries and several lives. Enough separatist and anti-regime slogans appeared for the ringleaders to receive prison sentences of five-to-seven years and for the handful of party members implicated to be expelled.[3]

The concessions granted to Kosovo seemed insignificant at the time. Metohija was dropped from the name of what shortly became a province, equal to the Vojvodina, and permission was granted to fly a black-eagled Albanian flag under the flag of Yugoslavia. More significantly, the Kosovar party leaders could restaff all official positions except the SDB security apparatus with fellow Albanians; they also won approval for a university in Priština. It opened a year later under the exclusive control of a provincial government now dominated by Kosovar Albanians and under the assumption that at least two-thirds of the students would be Kosovar as well. The director of the expanding Relindja publishing house led a delegation to Tirana, the capital of Albania, where they signed a fateful agreement. It flooded the university and the entire school system with Albanian-language textbooks, otherwise in short supply, which seemed to speak against the integration of Kosovo into Yugoslavia.[4] Even before the university had opened its doors, Serb and Montenegrin officials and professionals, whether displaced or simply distressed, had begun to move out of the province. Their departure, plus the high Albanian birth rate, pushed the Kosovar majority in the province to 74 percent in 1971 and 78 percent by 1981. By then, the Kosovar share of employment in social enterprises was even higher.

Slovenia

Of more immediate impact was the dispute over road-building that flared up between the various republic party leaderships during the summer of 1969. Anxious to expand the republic's access to West European markets and tourists, Slovenian officials had carefully prepared an application to the World Bank for part of the $30 million that Yugoslavia was seeking for several projects. They won initial approval in 1968 meetings with representatives from other republics for the division of these funds between Slovenia, Croatia, and Macedonia. Yet when the loan came through the next June, the Federal Executive Council (SIV) in Belgrade voted to exclude the Slovenian segment that extended to the Austrian border. Slovenia was still to receive over one-half of the loan, but Slovenian public opinion as well as the party hierarchy bristled at the charge that they had not adequately secured their portion of the costs and resented the absence of the responsible officials from Ljubljana at the Belgrade meeting. Their fellow Slovene, SIV prime minister Mitija Ribičič, tried to prevent a public outcry, but was rebuffed. Some Slovenians were already smarting from a new federal law that tried to prohibit commercial operation of privately owned trucks weighing over 5 tons. They correctly judged that Slovenia would be more affected by such a restriction than any other republic. The dispute helped to drive a wedge between the liberal coalition of party leaders from the three republics in question and Serbia as well. Steven Burg has convincingly argued that this first republican protest against a federal decision undermined the mutual trust and confidence needed for the fledgling liberal coalition to endure.[5]

From the Croatian crisis to the 1974 Constitution

The crisis over Croatian cultural and economic interests probably did more to shake that mutual confidence than any other problem of the late 1960s. Before the coalition finally dissolved in 1972, Tito had dismissed the liberal leaders of the Croatian, Serbian, and Slovenian parties and demoted their Macedonian counterparts. Edvard Kardelj was also authorized to draft a new constitution from amendments of 1971–72 that made any one republic's right to protection from the others paramount.

Within the maze of provisions that became the 1974 constitution, contractual procedures for conflict resolution formally replaced the budding practice of coalition politics. A confederation of one-party regimes was left to govern a single state and economy, with only an army potentially duplicated by the republics' defense forces to guarantee survival.

Croatian complaints and the liberal coalition

A number of Croatian intellectuals had openly voiced cultural complaints as early as 1967. Some had long entertained second thoughts about the 1954 agreement at Novi Sad to create a common Serbo-Croatian orthography and dictionary that could fairly be called Croato-Serbian as well. Their reservations turned into public protests when the first two volumes of the dictionary were finally published thirteen years later. Serbian variants of these two, overlapping, grammatically identical languages were consistently chosen over the Croatian variants. Croatia's genuinely separate and longer literary tradition, unbroken since the Middle Ages, seemed forfeit in the process. The renowned writer and party intellectual, Miroslav Krleža, hardly a past advocate of ethnic exclusiveness as we have seen, joined with prominent Croatian linguists to lead the protests. The linguists' March 1967 declaration demanded recognition of a separate Croatian language and its public use by all officials, Croatian Serbs included by implication. So began what Sabrina P. Ramet has called "four-and-one-half years of Croatian national renaissance."[6] The language controversy afforded the cultural organization, Matica Hrvatska, both political attention and mass circulation. Its jousting with Novi Sad's Matica Srpska over the next several years finally killed the project for a single dictionary. Their exchanges eluded direct Communist control and drew the Zagreb and Belgrade media into choosing sides rather than seeking consensus.

The easier political climate also allowed the Croats to voice their dissatisfaction with the economic results of the 1965 reform, which in turn encouraged the cultural dispute to spread. Such latitude frightened Kardelj and other old Partisans, who moved to counteract its genuinely democratic features as quickly as possible.

The loosening had begun in April 1967 with the first of forty-one amendments to the 1963 constitution. Under pressure from the liberal coalition of Croatian, Slovenian and Macedonian party leaders, the long subordinate Chamber of Nationalities (actually a chamber of republics and provinces) received broader powers and the right to meet separately. By 1968 a further amendment abolished the long dominant Federal

Chamber. Its 120 communally elected delegates were, in practice, often centrally nominated and outnumbered the 70 delegates allotted to the republics (10 each) and provinces (5 each) as the Council of Nationalities. Beginning with the 1969 elections, the Council's membership doubled to 140, larger than any of the other four specialized chambers of 120 delegates, set up under Kardelj's 1963 constitutional framework. The Council, later the Chamber of Republics and Provinces, also became responsible for introducing legislation. By this time, too, the new liberal leaders of the Serbian party had accepted the right of the Kosovo and Vojvodina assemblies to elect and instruct their own delegates to the enlarged federal Council, like any republic.

None of these changes would have been significant had it not been for the new type of party members who now stepped forward in elections permitting more than one candidate. Multiple-candidate slates, already the rule in communal assembly elections, slipped into the 1967 balloting for fourteen seats in the Federal Assembly. Two years later, multiple candidates declared for a majority of the 120 seats in the direct elections that had just been authorized for the Socio-Political Chamber in the Federal Assembly. That body, which had been reconstructed from the Federal Chamber, had to approve all legislation introduced into the Council of Nationalities before it could become law. All the chambers of the republics and provinces, with 2,769 seats, and the communal assemblies, with 40,279 seats, also held direct elections in April 1969. Approximately 7 million eligible voters chose from among 80,000 candidates.[7]

A significant number of candidates were now enterprise managers or professionals with credentials beyond their party cards. Such people were the ascendant group in party membership, as workers and peasants fell back to one-third of the total by the late 1960s and women stayed at one-fifth. They seemed the natural allies of the liberal coalition. Then all sides backed away from further progress toward direct competitive elections. Kardelj and his old Partisans found unlikely allies in a number of enterprise directors who had fared poorly against non-party candidates representing ethnic interests. Better to let the party complicate the nomination process even further, as Dennison Rusinow has explained the logic, and rely on an informal alliance with party liberals in order to allow enterprises the greater freedom promised by the 1965 reform.[8]

Croatian complaints about the reform now came to the fore. They combined economic and regional grievances as the Slovenes had in the road-building crisis of 1969.[9] Revenue was mushrooming from the tourist traffic along the Croatian Adriatic coast, but profits lagged behind rates of investment and income from tourist facilities. It was tempting if not always accurate to overlook excessive costs and blame corrupt deals favoring large Belgrade trade enterprises like Generalexport. And did not the three big Belgrade banks still control over four-fifths of hard currency credit and half of the overall total? By 1971, the weekly newspaper of the Matica Hrvatska was trumpeting such complaints to a circulation of 100,000. Related rumors revived the old notion that Serbia wished to secure its presumed economic advantage along the coast by promoting a Dalmatian republic or province separate from Croatia.

A second economic issue fed on the old fear of demographic decline shared by many ethnic groups. Primarily as a result of urbanization, the Croatian birth rate had dropped below that of all other republics except Slovenia, according to the 1971 census. Like the censuses of 1961 and 1981 (or of 1931, see chapter 6), the results magnified ethnic anxieties. The share of Croatia's labor force working abroad in West Germany or elsewhere approached 10 percent, while Serbia's was less than 4 percent. Serbs migrated internally from less developed areas, Bosnia-Hercegovina in particular, to Croatia as well as Serbia. Such migration boosted a Serb presence in the Croatian party that was already double its 12 percent share of population. Meanwhile the large Croatian contribution to FADURK for those areas seemed to be having little effect.

Without these economic issues, the continuing cultural complaints of Matica Hrvatska and a newly assertive Catholic hierarchy could not have brought the otherwise liberal leaders of the Croatian League of Communists into conflict with their coalition partners, and Tito as well, by 1971. The battle was already joined in 1970 when a leading Croatian Communist, Miloš Žanko, shifted from attacking Matica Hrvatska for nationalist excess to leveling the same charge at leading liberals. The Croatian party leaders were now Mika Tripalo and Savka Dabčević-Kučar, both Dalmatians in their mid-forties with solid liberal credentials and Bakarić's personally anointed successors in the Croatian party leadership. They promptly forced Žanko from his high position. By 1971 the Croatian Communist leaders found themselves obliged to support or at least not openly reject an escalating list of demands for a revised Croatian constitution.

The final demands went well beyond their own liberal agenda. Further amendments to the 1963 federal constitution had by this time created five interrepublic committees whose powers to negotiate common policies between the republics recall the Habsburg committees that settled domestic issues between the Austrian and Hungarian halves of the monarchy after 1867. Younger Croatian Communists like Marko Veslica or student leader Dragan Budiša joined with the Matica Hrvatska to demand a separate bank for Croatia, and what amounted to a separate army and representation in the United Nations as well.[10] Clearly Tito could not permit even the airing of such demands, or the glorification of old anti-Communists like Stjepan Radić and his "kulak organization," the Croatian Peasant Party. Tito worried that "it was 1941 all over again." The demands of Radić's successor, Vladko Maček, that culminated in the *Sporazum* of 1939 (see chapter 6) would have provided the more accurate parallel.

The Belgrade media led the way in dramatizing the Croatian crisis. Television news and some of the press reported domestic news more openly after Ranković's demise, but they were quick to charge that the protesting voices in Croatia were linked to Croatian émigré opponents of any Yugoslav state. In April 1971, two Croatian terrorists from the Ustaša remnants abroad managed to break into the Stockholm Embassy and assassinate Yugoslavia's ambassador to Sweden, fresh from a mission to Australia to investigate émigré activities.[11] At the same time, the Croatian émigré publication most vehemently claiming legitimacy for the wartime NDH regime began touting the latest Soviet disenchantment with Tito's Yugoslavia. It proclaimed Moscow's interest in a "Soviet Croatia," independent except for a projected Soviet naval base on the Adriatic. Several Belgrade weeklies linked this implausible scenario to unconfirmed evidence that the KGB had helped finance the Stockholm assassination. Perhaps, they implied, further links existed to the *maspok*, or mass movement, that Matica Hrvatska, the Zagreb students, and a reluctant Communist leadership had mobilized in Croatia. Although such foreign links seem fanciful, the maspok's nationalist content still posed the first serious challenge to the Communist leadership's political monopoly in postwar Yugoslavia. The aging Croatian eminence and Tito's wartime colleague, Vladimir Bakarić, warned him of "the appearance on the political stage of people who are not ours." As for the wild notions of a vast Croatian conspiracy, he told the old man that the "Belgrade *čaršija*," or Turkish marketplace, was up to its familiar (read interwar) tricks of spreading malicious gossip.

Exit the Serbian liberals

Indeed, the most fateful consequence of the prolonged Croatian crisis of 1967–72 may have been the chance it gave Tito and Kardelj to bring down the new liberal leadership of Serbia's party. A liberal Serbia linked with the other coalition liberals from Croatia, Slovenia, and Macedonia could refocus the 1965 *Reforma* on the market mechanism and make the direct multi-candidate elections of 1969 the basis for more pluralistic, if still single-party, politics. The years 1970–71 offered Yugoslavia a last chance to turn Point No Point during the Tito era.

The Serbian party had the best chance to lead the turn. Tito was determined to replace Petar Stambolić and the other party leaders who had failed to prevent the Belgrade student demonstrations of June 1968 from erupting. Stambolić and his allies were strong enough, however, to designate their successors. He pried a reluctant Marko Nikezić loose from his favored position as foreign minister to defeat the more conservative candidate for president of Serbia's central committee at the republic's party congress. Born in 1921 to a French mother and a Montenegrin father who had traveled abroad as an interwar trader, Nikezić spent some of the 1930s in Paris on the Left Bank as a budding Communist intellectual. His rapid rise through the foreign ministry to the position of ambassador to the United States and then head of the foreign ministry by 1965 also kept him outside the domestic struggle to depose Ranković. A young liberal with academic credentials, Latinka Perović, won the other major post as party secretary. She was also uninvolved in the Ranković affair, and his former allies consented to her ascension as well.

The Serbian liberals advocated five goals: (1) a market economy; (2) a modern Serbia; (3) liberation from the "ballast" of Serbian Yugoslavism and self-absorption; (4) support for "technocrats"; and (5) cooperation rather than confrontation with the other republics. Nikezić's later reflections suggest that the last four goals were genuine commitments.[12] "We cannot expect unity within the country," he maintained, "if the feeling continues that Serbs are the foundation for Yugoslavia . . . If Yugoslavia is necessary, then it is necessary for all, and not just Serbs." As for self-management, he acknowledged that it had been too much a "cultural revolution . . . not created to weaken political power but to strengthen it." It also contradicted the need for more open, modern enterprise management.

Tito removed Nikezić and his allies from the Serbian leadership in October 1972. Once the Zagreb student strike of the previous November finally persuaded him to dismiss the Croatian liberal leadership, he could use the excuse of ethnic balance to dismiss all of the other republic leaderships as well. During the famous showdown in December 1971 at his Karadjordjevo hunting lodge, Tito had demanded the resignations of the Croatian triumvirate of Tripalo, Dabčević-Kučar, and Pero Pirker. They resisted for a week, but then complied. In addition, over 1,000 members were later purged from Croatia's party apparatus, 90 percent of them Croats. Yet a series of specific grievances also encouraged Tito to remove the Serbian leaders in favor of the conservatives who, ironically, had been close to Ranković.

Tito's past dissatisfaction with Nikezić dated from the latter's opposition as foreign minister to Yugoslavia's break in diplomatic relations with Israel after the Six Day War of 1967. As Serbia's party president, Nikezić had later sided with Mijalko Todorović against Edvard Kardelj to advocate reliance on the market mechanism in further economic reform. Nikezić had also refused Tito's direct request to dismiss a high-ranking colleague in the Serbian party and raised objections to a number of the decentralizing constitutional amendments pushed through in 1971–72. Most important was his resistance to the forced Croatian resignations at Karadjordjevo and the subsequent reestablishment of central party authority.[13]

How much opposition Nikezić also faced within Serbia is debatable. Among the eighty members of the top leadership, only eight rose to criticize him at a meeting in Belgrade convened to condemn him. Tito presided personally and abruptly adjourned the meeting when the great majority defied him. Functionaries lower in the Serbian party hierarchy probably sided with Tito from the start, although comparable evidence is lacking. There was no resisting the old man in any case. By October he had orchestrated the resignations of both Nikezić and Perović, replacing them with weak, unknown figures. By 1973 the same number of party functionaries as in Croatia – just over 1,000 – had resigned, been expelled, or replaced.

The same sort of purge had also reached into Macedonia and Slovenia. Kardelj criticized the Slovenian party leader, Stane Kavčić, for not realizing that readiness to accept the consequences of a market economy would mean "political dependence" on the West. Others went so far as to call him "pro-Bavarian," whatever that might mean, but Kavčić's dismissal more probably reflected a purely domestic anxiety: his pro-market interpretation of self-management would undermine Tito's program to reestablish the party's commanding position. No imposed changes took place in Bosnia-Hercegovina, where the party leadership could hardly be called liberal.[14] Everywhere else the liberal coalition of the 1960s had vanished by the end of 1972.

Confederal amendments and a new constitution

Now free from the coalition, party leaders wishing to maintain or reestablish unchallengeable authority at the local, republic, or federal levels joined Tito and Kardelj in preparing yet another constitution. By 1970 the previous document had been amended nineteen times since its passage in 1963. A further package of twenty-one amendments in March 1971 reduced the power of the federal government by allowing individual republics, for instance, to control their earnings of foreign exchange or to rule on their social plans before the federation could put them together. Such concessions came at a time when Tito still supported the Croatian party triumvirate. The new republic leaderships that emerged after the purges of 1971–72 now confronted a complex framework by which Edvard Kardelj hoped to restrict their power as well as the federal government's.

His last constitutional commission had already started its inquiry in the summer of 1970, just as Tito had agreed at the age of seventy-eight to authorize a collective state presidency. The commission's subsequent proposals revealed the direction in which the 1971–72 amendments were leading the new constitution. Tito remained president of the republic and now became president of the presidency. Its twenty-three members were soon trimmed to fourteen, two for each republic and one for each of the two autonomous provinces of Kosovo and the Vojvodina. Their staffs were also chosen on a republic or provincial basis, leaving only the Federal Executive Council (SIV) exempt from the "key" system of ethnic balance that, from 1971, applied to all high federal positions, civil or military. Until their ouster, the Croatian leadership had pressed for veto rights in the presidency for all republics. Why, once they were gone, did Kardelj still accept the *de facto* right of veto in the requirement for a reconciled, unanimous vote, or *usaglašavanje*? Serbian legal scholar Jovan Djordjević has called such unanimity a "back-door veto." Kardelj was intent on cutting away enough power from the federal and republic governments so that this provision would not matter. When it later spread to party decisions as well, as Tito had been determined it should not, it would of course matter a great deal. In the meantime, the responsibilities of the new presidency overlapped with those of the one coherent body for central government policy, the Federal Executive Council (SIV).[15]

The 1971 amendments had also created five interrepublic committees within the SIV. Their responsibility for working out common policies also threatened to displace the authority of the council itself as well as the Federal Assembly. The interrepublic committees were supposed to deal precisely with economic policy and the areas most crucial to market integration: regionally balanced development, monetary policy, foreign trade and hard currency, market mechanisms, and financial regulation. The committees did nothing to prevent the Croatian crisis of December 1971. Despite that failure, they resolved over 90 percent of the issues brought before them until their downgrading two years later. Their members, let it be emphasized, voted under strict instruction from the republics or provinces that they represented, the same confederal procedure that already applied to delegates to Yugoslav party congresses and to the assembly's Chamber of Republics and Provinces. The committees' very success in arranging working agreements between the republics made the federation's legislation process and representatives, whether elected or delegated, seem irrelevant..

Kardelj and his constitutional committee understood that the document they prepared by 1974 should reduce some of the confederal elements and also the mind-boggling complexity that had become the government of Yugoslavia. They were also determined to reinsert a role for the League of Communists as a whole that would prevent another political crisis like the one in late 1971. Steven Burg has dubbed their work the "search for a regulatory formula" or, more specifically, a formula for conflict resolution.[16] Their compromise between central party control and republic autonomy exempted the Federal Executive Council staff from the requirements of the ethnic key. It gave sole authority over the armed forces, still under Tito's overall command, to a three-man military committee of the presidency that included the JNA chief-of-staff. At the same time, the republics received formal authorization to maintain the Coordinating Committees for Economic Relations abroad that had sprung up after 1970 as extensions of their Chambers of Commerce. A number of them now attempted to usurp functions from the federal foreign ministry. In addition the two autonomous provinces became virtual republics, lacking only the rights of citizenship and secession.

The constitution presented for ratification in February 1974 became the world's longest with 406 articles, now surpassing that of India. Kardelj had indeed simplified the legislative structure, reducing the number of federal chambers from five to two, but he also created the most complicated electoral system seen anywhere during the twentieth century. Few Yugoslavs ever understood it fully or felt that they received any real representation under it. The smaller of the two chambers was also the stronger. Legislation affecting republic interests had to be reconciled there, by unanimous agreement of all eight sets of deputies rather than by majority rule. Most of the important measures proposed by the Federal Executive Council, therefore, came to this new eighty-eight member Chamber of Republics and Autonomous Provinces. The six republic assemblies each sent twelve deputies and the two provinces, eight, to the Chamber. Each set voted under the direction of its home assembly. The minimum of eight votes required to introduce a measure allowed either Kosovo or the Vojvodina to do so on their own.

The same regional formula also applied to the larger Federal Chamber of 220 deputies, with 30 seats for each republic and 20 for each province. The right to make majority decisions reflected the relative unimportance of its deliberations. But the deputies' indirect election by layers of delegates weakened the public presence of both chambers. The requirement for unanimous agreement among the republic and provincial representatives in their Chamber as well as in the collective presidency proved to be the major political failing of the 1974 constitution from the top down.

The new procedure for selecting delegates did the most damage from the bottom up. Three rounds of elections that began in April 1974 selected an astounding total of 840,000 delegates representing 12,000 local communities and 60,000 work units. These delegations of ten or more, divided among 500 communal chambers for labor, local government, and social-political interests, voted with party, union, and Socialist Alliance representatives to select a second level of delegations who would elect three comparable chambers at the republic and provincial level. Those assemblies then voted in a third round of elections that finally named the delegates to the chambers of what was now the Assembly of the Socialist Federal Republic of Yugoslavia. Kardelj claimed that this system of delegations rested on an "imperative mandate" to follow instruction by the larger group from below and thus prevented full-time politicians from dominating the political process. In fact the party's cadre commissions at the next *highest* level selected the delegations without recourse to the open political competition that Kardelj had never trusted. Delegates were usually younger and less experienced than their predecessors. They were also required to continue in their regular jobs while serving. This requirement discouraged the most active enterprise managers and professionals from participating. "The whole undertaking," according to Laszlo Sekelj, "actually meant absolute control over the electoral procedure by informal, non-elected, non-institutionalized, and uncontrollable local oligarchies."[17]

The delegates who emerged from behind these successive layers of curtains were almost entirely party members, but were also anonymous to a voting public who had elected only the original 820,000. Such delegates became even less visible than the increasingly unknown members of the collective presidency. In a decade where television and films in particular were making public personalities more recognizable, the Yugoslav public was left with Marshal Tito and little else. When other members of the collective presidency appeared on movie screens in major cities, for instance, audiences broke into laughter and openly exchanged jokes about who these anonymous figures might be.

Tito saw the dangers to the legitimacy of Communist rule in the new system. Too many of the newly elected delegates, he concluded, lacked strong political presence or commitment. In addition the League of Communists had lost almost 150,000 of its 1 million members by 1969. While recruiting drives filled in new members by 1974, the newcomers had less education or fewer skills. At the Tenth Party Congress in June 1974, one month after the election cycle had been completed, Tito did what he could to reassert control by reshuffling the Central Committee. With managers and professionals suspect and in short supply, he sought to outnumber them with two other groups – younger industrial workers and old Partisan army officers. According to the calculations of Lenard Cohen, Tito's initiative tripled the workers' share in the Central Committee from 1969 to 19 percent and doubled that of military officers to 11 percent.[18] Almost all of them belonged to the same aging, wartime generation as Tito himself. A majority were also Serbs or Montenegrins, making the two ethnic groups 41 percent of the Central Committee. The number of Slovenes and Macedonians dropped in favor of Bosnian Muslims, Albanians, and Hungarians. Croats remained under-represented demographically at 15 percent. Otherwise, the ethnic balance of the League's leadership was roughly proportional to population. The new JNA members were seen primarily as Tito's men.

From half-market to contractual economy

What if the economy continued to expand as it had in most years since the mid-1950s? Might not the way have stayed open to post-Tito political experimentation – to broader representation in a more direct electoral system? Perhaps, especially if Tito and Kardelj had vacated their commanding positions earlier, before 1979–80. There still remained the inefficient system of workers' self-management and the increasingly inflationary economy needed to support it. Both of them evolved during the 1970s to the disadvantage of any political configuration in post-Tito Yugoslavia.

A considerable number of trained enterprise managers tried to pursue market-oriented growth and cost-efficient production, but they operated under a series of new handicaps after 1970. Far freer than most counterparts in the Soviet bloc to choose their product line and to compete for customers, they found themselves constrained in other respects. They were one of the main groups, lumped together with other educated professionals as "technocrats," which Kardelj's 1974 electoral system had been designed to exclude politically. As noted above, they did not belong to the "previously uninvolved strata" that were supposed to dominate the new delegations. Their enterprises struggled under two further constraints that encouraged inflation and subverted market behavior – politicized access to credit and the subdivision of workers' councils.

Banking, basic organizations, and bad business

The failure of the 1965 reform to create a network of commercial or investment banks operating across the entire country soon prompted a number of enterprises to begin crafting credit agreements among themselves. They simply struck informal agreements to accept or receive delayed payments for goods delivered. Reminiscent of the clearing accounts for German trade with Central European states during the 1930s, these deals were now dubbed "grey emissions." And rightly so, because by the early 1970s they constituted a significant if short-term addition to the money supply. The sum of unpaid enterprise trade debts equaled one-quarter of Gross Domestic Product (GDP) for 1970 and exceeded 40 percent of total enterprise liabilities. The common agreement to carry these debts masked enterprise losses that exceeded 4 percent of GDP.

The 102 commercial or investment banks that had replaced the 480 communal banks after 1965 had by this time been reduced to 55 mixed, or universal, banks. Typically limited by republic borders and local political control, they extended long-term, low-interest loans to favored enterprises. When combined with credit from the three large investment banks surviving in Belgrade, they provided 51 percent of domestic fixed investment for 1970–71. Politically encouraged concessions, called selective credits, pulled the actual rates charged to below even the 10 percent legal maximum or 6 percent norm.[19] That widened the "negative interest rate" for borrowed funds, given an annual rate of inflation that averaged 18 percent for 1970–79. Table 10.1 identifies the social sector's dependence on such credit and an accelerating rate of inflation that was already nearly twice the world average for the 1970s. The oil shock of 1972 hit world price levels at least as hard as Yugoslavia's and may thus be factored out of any comparison.

By 1972, the Belgrade journal, *Ekonomska politika*, joined a number of economists from Zagreb and Ljubljana to press for further bank reform. The growth of the money supply had been running ahead of inflation even before adding grey emissions. Their consensus targeted the low ceiling on interest rates and the lack of central bank authority to restrict currency emissions. But Kardelj and the political consensus framing the 1974 constitution had other priorities. They took the occasion to break up the Investment Bank in Belgrade by turning its various republic branches into independent *udružene banke,* or associated banks. Instantly the largest banks in their respective republics, these associated banks contributed further to the decentralization of investment that had already boosted the republics' share in the federal budget to 14 percent in 1972, up from 4 percent the year before. Lest the lending policies of these nine large new investment banks stray too close to strictly commercial principles, a further law on banking and credit in 1976 bound them to work with republic and local authorities in observing the guidelines for allocation laid down in the official Social Plan for 1976–80.[20] The law reinforced Kardelj's intentions. He wanted to replace any recourse to the market mechanism with a set of contractual bargains, or "social compacts," in which the League of Communists could continue to exert its authority through its local or republic hierarchies. This decentralized but political allocation of credit became one major cause of Yugoslavia's excessive inflation throughout the 1970s.

The upward pressure on wages from the workers' councils provided the other. Heavy taxation and other deductions had already reduced wage incomes to as low as one-third of their gross value early in the decade. The 1974 constitution promised to increase that inflationary pressure by subdividing some 4,000 workers' councils into Basic Organizations of Associated Labor, or Osnovne Organizacije Udruženog Rada (OOUR).

By the time that it was ready, in November 1976, the Law on Associated Labor ran to 671 articles and was promptly nicknamed "the little constitution."[21] As early as 1959, large firms had received the right to subdivide their councils according to function or location. Now all social enterprises in industry, agriculture, or the service sector were required to create a set of these smaller councils, totalling 19,000 by 1978. They increased in overall membership to 700,000, but took more time away from the productive process for regular meetings, usually five-to-six hours a week. Workdays began at 7 a.m. and finished at 2 p.m. in order to free women in the afternoons for shopping or preparing meals. Personal activities took large chunks out of the first and last hours of the workday, and now more time was lost in more meetings.

The new OOUR subdivisions within a single enterprise invited two sorts of corruption. An agile director might play the OOURs off against each other and thus subvert any real role for the employees in management. More often, political bargaining among the various subdivisions or between them and the director replaced any coherent process for making business decisions. In either case, the efficiency of the enterprise suffered, while few workers felt that the decision-making process

Table 10.1. *Bank credit and rates of inflation, 1965–1985*

	1965–70	1970–79	1980–83	1984–85	
Consumer prices (annual % increase)	12	17.7	36	63	
	1960	1970	1975	1980	1984–85
Interest rate	6	6	6	6	67
Bank credit % of social sector investment	1	43	43	47	33

Sources: Jugoslavija, 1918–1988, Statistički godišnjak (Belgrade: Savezni zavod za statistiku, 1989), 160–66; and *Jugoslavija, 1945–1985* (Belgrade: Savezni zavod za statistiku, 1986), 72, 239.

had become more democratic.[22] Further wage increases at the expense of the enterprise's own contribution to investment offered the line of least resistance. Most OOURs and enterprise directors accepted the offer.

The law's major initiative to improve efficiency targeted labor discipline. Strikes known as "interruptions of work" had been a fact of industrial life in Yugoslavia since the late 1950s. By the 1970s, the number of strikes had tripled to more than 1,000 a year. Still more prominent was the rise in absenteeism. By 1976, days missed led the way in pulling down the productivity of industrial labor by 1.5 percent. Despite the law's specific provisions to punish absenteeism and reward increased productivity, the OOURs themselves worked against enforcement by diluting the direct authority of enterprise management.

Yugoslav enterprises were already inordinately large and overstaffed (see chapter 9). They now faced a labor market that continued to swell during the 1970s due to the postwar baby boom and reduced opportunities to work in Western Europe. The pressure not to dismiss surplus employees, as had been done following the 1965 reform, rose accordingly. While social sector employment had risen by less than 1 percent a year for 1966–70, the increase for 1971–78 averaged 4.3 percent, nearly twice the addition to labor productivity. The 1 million new jobs created matched the ongoing rural exodus. But 300,000 of the 1 million working abroad had returned to Yugoslavia, half in 1975 alone. The number of registered unemployed doubled for 1971–75 and then jumped another 200,000 by 1978 to constitute 13.6 percent of domestic wage-earners.[23]

Two factors worked against any rapid reduction of this socially dangerous level of unemployment, already exceeding 20 percent in Kosovo and Macedonia. Too many industrial enterprises were too big, and the small, predominantly agricultural, private sector still faced obstacles that discouraged peasants from staying. From 1970 to 1977, the 130 largest Yugoslav manufacturing and mining enterprises had increased their share of social employment from one-third to one-half. The 10 largest employed over 30,000 workers apiece, and the rest typically over 10,000. Separate studies by Saul Estrin and Stephen Sachs have demonstrated that the weight of such enterprises in the Yugoslav economy, twice the American average for employment and assets, gave them the same sort of monopoly powers that we associate with enterprises in the Soviet bloc.[24] New domestic competitors were virtually excluded from entering, and access to domestic capital could be negotiated politically under any sort of market rate. Large, politically monitored enterprises ignored the surplus of job-seekers and continued to grant inflationary wage increases. Capital-intensive strategies continued to be a rational choice for individual enterprises, adding to the inflationary pressure for credit creation. According to Sachs' set of case studies, the subdivision of operations under the Basic Organizations rarely provided the increased responsiveness to market demand or the more precise targeting of investment that was being achieved by a number of Western enterprises at the same time.

Smallholding peasants continued to account for most of the private sector. Their shrinking numbers, down to one-third of the labor force by 1978, helped hold up modest increases in per capita income for an aging rural population. The 1974 constitution failed to remove the maximum limit of 10 hectares on private holdings, although enforcement was sometimes lax, particularly in the Vojvodina. Larger farms, employing seasonal labor from Bosnia or Macedonia, helped the province's per capita income to rise faster than that of any other Yugoslav region during the decade. Elsewhere, the regime's rhetoric generally discouraged private enterprise. Punitive taxation and restrictions on inheritance confined the private sector to tourism, construction, and artisan manufacture. Remittances from work abroad continued to provide almost as much income as legally registered, private enterprise through the 1970s.[25]

Case studies of success and failure

Our concentration on this flawed framework obscures the significant number of Yugoslav enterprises, many more than anywhere in the Soviet bloc, that operated or tried to operate according to market standards.

Readers unfamiliar with economic aggregates may also gain a clearer sense of what a Yugoslav enterprise could actually do if we look at some representative cases of success and failure.

The success stories summarized by Bruce McFarlane share a common reliance on reinvesting profits rather than seeking a state subsidy, a foreign investor, or a commercial creditor.[26] From its founding in 1962, the Tucović sugar refinery near Belgrade ploughed back half of its net profit after taxes, rather than investing the typical 30 percent and turning to bank credit for the rest. Efficiency improved noticeably following an early decision to cut the number of decision-making units in half. After the 1965 reform, the management and workers' council of the huge Bor copper refinery, already modernized as a major Anglo-French investment by the 1930s, turned away from the large subsidies that had sustained its underpriced production since the war. Despite the significantly higher price it now charged, its reliable delivery of higher-quality product soon increased sales. The resulting profits furnished the funds needed for further modernization. Slovenia's huge Iskra enterprise for electrical goods and the Kluž clothing enterprise of Belgrade relied primarily on Western export markets for their success. By the late 1960s, both were exporting some three-quarters of their annual production. Iskra pioneered the marketing agreements with West European partners that assured the Slovenian enterprises of predictable delivery and prices for essential imports. Kluž continued to boost annual profits per worker into the 1980s by gearing wage increases to productivity and financing its own expansion. Similar stories abounded in all regions save, significantly, Kosovo, the Krajina, and Hercegovina. Well into the 1970s, a majority of the extensive Western scholarship on Yugoslav self-management still expected this best practice to spread and eventually change the system itself.

Political resistance helped to prevent it from spreading more widely. Western markets and creditors also shared some of the responsibility in combination with the absence of a major role for direct foreign investment. The oil shocks of 1973 and 1979 cut back the steady growth of Western markets since the mid-1950s at the same time that Western banks found themselves with a flood of petrodollars deposited and demanding profitable deployment. Yugoslavia's own restrictive legislation for foreign investment deflected over 98 percent of Western funding into short-term or medium-term credit rather than long-term investment.

The joint venture law of 1967 (see chapter 9) denied foreign investors both majority ownership and freedom of management, as well as placing profits and their repatriation under a variety of restrictions. Subsequent amendments to the law in 1971 and 1973 relaxed these restrictions and then tightened them in 1976, only to replace the entire law in 1978. These frequent changes created uncertainty. In addition investors now faced requirements for local and federal approval under the new law. Little wonder that the modest total of $325 million in foreign investment attracted during the period 1967–77 did not much increase until the law was finally revised to permit majority ownership in 1984 and unrestricted operation in 1988.

Although the United States accounted for the largest single share, at 35 percent, the early successes of McDonnell Douglas, John Deere, and Armand Hammer in arranging countertrade through large Yugoslav export-import enterprises like Genex and Inex did not lead to major investments in manufacturing. The largest single US venture, Dow Chemical's joint construction of a petrochemical refinery with the large Croatian petroleum firm INA, was launched with great fanfare in 1976, but had to be abandoned at a substantial loss by 1982. The two managements shared responsibility for failing to judge the world market accurately and to coordinate with each other. Another effort by the United States to finance $125 million in imported American processing equipment for the FENI ferro-nickel plant in Macedonia also misjudged the world market, in addition to suffering under poor local management.[27] The attendant import credit was also significant for being one of the few foreign commitments to any of the underdeveloped republics or to Kosovo. Serbia proper, the Vojvodina, Croatia, and Slovenia accounted for 83 percent of the foreign capital invested in joint ventures by 1980.

The country's largest auto manufacturer, Crvena Zastava of Kragujevac, provides perhaps the most revealing case study of the combined failings of the self-managed enterprise, the world market, and Western investment. Established in 1954 as a successor to the Serbian state arsenal there, the enterprise and its able director attracted $30 million and attendant training from Fiat of Italy in 1959. Growing demand by the early 1960s from the domestic market and Eastern Europe as well found a new, much improved plant in place and ready to respond. Domestic and Western borrowing doubled capacity again by the end of the decade. But then, because he resisted political interference and the impending OOUR restructuring, the director was pushed out by 1974. Afterwards, the new management doubled the labor force under local political pressure, and the number of cars produced per worker dropped accordingly. According to Michael Palairet's detailed critique of Zastava operations, increasingly serious deficiencies and delays in the parts supplied under subcontracts with other firms across Yugoslavia combined with shortcomings inside the Kragujevac complex to keep roughly two of every five vehicles produced from being fit for sale.[28]

By the 1980s, Zastava had accumulated too much hard currency debt for the enterprise and its labor force of 50,000 to survive without selling in at least one Western market. A controversial Canadian entrepreneur, Malcolm Bricklin, tried to make that market the United States. He founded his Yugo America, Inc., on the assumption that a slightly improved model licensed from Zastava and priced just under the average cost of a used car would find a niche in the American market. But bad reviews and minimal profit margins on American sales between 1985 and 1988, partly traceable to costly defects and delays in Yugoslav production, forced the Yugo enterprise into bankruptcy by 1989. Zastava took it over completely, but with little chance of success.

Foreign policy and the debt crisis, 1979–1985

Tito's foreign policy left one negotiable legacy to Yugoslavia. His balancing act between the two Cold War sides kept the door open for a final infusion of Western assistance, even after his death. When Western creditors finally refused to continue the reckless lending that had begun in the 1970s, an American-led consortium called the "Friends of Yugoslavia" assembled significant debt relief in 1983–84. The sum of Yugoslavia's foreign indebtedness had already doubled from 1968 to 1972, approaching $4 billion. But that relatively modest total doubled again by 1976 and then rose still faster to touch $20 billion by 1982. To make matters worse, the plethora of economic enterprises, banks, and federal and local institutions contracting for loans made it difficult for any central agency to keep track of the total, let alone control it.

The borrowing binge sustained the rapid growth of the economy through the 1970s. Gross Domestic Product (GDP) per capita grew at 5.1 percent annually in constant 1972 prices for the period 1970–79, but foreign debt by fully 20 percent a year. An overvalued dinar made the import of intermediate goods to support domestic investment less expensive. Such goods accounted for two-thirds of import value and fed an inflationary rise of gross fixed investment as a share of GDP, from 28 to 35 percent during the decade. So did easier access to domestic than foreign credit. Both the money supply and internal loans tripled in nominal value between 1976 and 1980, and then doubled again by 1982. Enterprise credit, now often sanctioned by bank guarantees, still accounted for nearly 40 percent of internal lending.

The rate of inflation rose accordingly, while the balance of trade deteriorated beyond the capacity of tourism and workers' remittances to cover the payments deficit. In 1979 the cost of living rose by 21 percent and the payments deficit reached 6 percent of GDP, both new records. Sharp reductions in imports and investment for the period 1980–82 combined with new Western loans to trim the payments deficit, but inflation continued to accelerate. Retail prices climbed 42 percent for 1981. Exports remained too little specialized and too much subsidized to take advantage of the dinar's belated depreciation. What Harold Lydall has aptly called "the great reversal" of 1979–85 had begun.[29] His calculations (see table 10.2) highlight the negative numbers that now dragged production and consumption down. During those six years, a standard of living whose previous growth had muted most regional grievances and legitimized continued Communist rule declined by fully one-quarter.

Tito's successors were aware of the impending crisis by the early 1980s. The old man's death at the start of the decade sharpened everyone's senses. Their first thought was to look for external assistance, and they soon found it.

Foreign policy before and after Tito's death

Western support to shore up the walls of Yugoslavia's financial house might not have been forthcoming had its mid-1970s tilt toward the Soviet bloc and the Third World persisted. It did not, thanks to Soviet and Cuban foreign policy as much as to Tito's.

Yugoslav relations with both the Soviet Union and the Non-Aligned Movement reached high water marks during 1976. Tito set aside a long-proclaimed reluctance and attended that June's Soviet-sponsored gathering of European Communist parties in East Berlin. On the anniversary of Yugoslavia's expulsion from the Cominform in 1948, Tito met privately with Soviet party secretary, Leonid Brezhnev, and Yugoslav delegates announced that their country belonged to the "Communist world." Despite the summer's trial of a few presumably pro-Soviet Cominformists in Belgrade, Brezhnev visited the Yugoslav capital in November. He reassured Tito and a collection of party leaders, curiously including no Croats, that his party now regarded the SKJ as equal partners.[30]

Relations with the United States had become more contentious than at any point in thirty years. The Yugoslav press, frequently hostile since the Vietnam and Arab–Israeli wars, turned up the heat when the much misrepresented "Sonnenfeldt Doctrine" seemed to endorse a Soviet sphere of influence, and presidential candidate Jimmy Carter hypothetically rejected going to war if the Soviet Union attacked Yugoslavia.

Table 10.2. *Decline of the social sector, 1960–1965*

	Average change per annum (in percent)			Total
	1960–70	1970–79	1979–85	1979–85
Social product, 1972 prices (adjusted)	6	5.6	–0.5	–3.1
Personal consumption per capita, 1972 prices	5.7	4.5	–1.3	–7.7
Gross fixed investment, 1972 prices	6.7	7.1	–7.5	–32.2
Real product per worker in the social sector	4.3	1.8	–3.6	–19.5
Real net personal income per worker in the productive social sector	6.8	2.1	–4.7	–27.9
Registered job-seekers, monthly average (000)	320	76		1040

Source: Harold Lydall, *Yugoslavia in Crisis* (Oxford: Clarendon Press, 1989), 41.

American press publication of a Croatian émigré attack on Yugoslavia as the price for ending an airplane hijacking built the fire higher. The American ambassador, Lawrence Silverman, threw on the last logs with a strident if justified campaign to free a Yugoslav-born US citizen comically accused of industrial espionage. Tito declared Silverman *persona non grata*, and the State Department announced his withdrawal the day that Brezhnev left Belgrade.

Meanwhile, the fifth summit of the Non-Aligned Movement in Colombo, Sri Lanka, in August suggested that Yugoslavia could rely on its standing in the Third World to assure some security against both East and West. Representatives of 112 countries attended, up from 87 at Algiers in 1973. Drawing on the successful Yugoslav aid missions and construction projects in a number of member states, Tito spoke of the need for a new international economic order. He identified only one threat to international peace – Israel, and by implication its principal backer, the United States. But by the next summit in Havana in 1979, a series of events and the quick reaction of Yugoslav diplomacy had moved the government back toward the West.[31]

The Soviet invasion of Afghanistan in December 1979 was the last and most decisive event. If Soviet troops could move across their border without international consultation or sanction, what would protect Yugoslavia if relations soured again some day? The Non-Aligned Movement had no movable military forces and was being pushed toward a pro-Soviet position by aggressive Cuban leadership. During his last international trip to the Havana summit in August, an increasingly frail

Tito could barely rally enough votes to reject the Cubans' several resolutions to endorse Soviet leadership for the movement. The empty economic promise of the movement had by this time come fully clear to the Yugoslav leadership. The latest oil shock had already raised the unwelcome prospect of further dependence on petroleum imports from the Soviet Union and the large surplus of export earnings in non-convertible currency they seemed to require. With Tito's health deteriorating by December, Yugoslav diplomats began to speak favorably of the NATO alliance as the principal guarantor of European security.

And then Tito died. After four months in a Ljubljana hospital and the ominous amputation of his right leg, the old man expired on May 4, 1980, a few days before his eighty-eighth birthday. Although long prepared by medical bulletins, the public reacted with genuine shock and grief across the entire country. In one incident, typical of the domestic reaction, football players for two leading Belgrade and Zagreb teams, Crvena Zastava and Dinamo, spontaneously suspended their crucial game at the announcement of Tito's death and left the field with tears streaming down their faces. This was the same Zagreb stadium where the last match between these two teams would be abandoned a decade later because of Serb–Croat violence in the stands. Huge, reverent crowds packed the stations from Ljubljana to Zagreb to Belgrade as the funeral train crossed the country. Tito's black-bordered picture stayed in many shop windows for the next several years, and nearly half the country's population visited the austere grave site in Belgrade. The birthday pageant at a Belgrade stadium culminating in a youth relay bearing "his torch" across the entire country would continue until 1988 (see chapter 11).

The foreign reaction to Tito's death was more fateful. The funeral brought representatives from 122 states to flag-draped Belgrade. Of the major countries, only the United States failed to send the head of government. Yet its ambassador, the second of the last four to serve in Yugoslavia after a previous tour of duty there, took the lead in persuading Western governments and the International Monetary Fund to rally around Yugoslavia. That subsequent effort and the demonstration of wider international respect at the funeral itself offered Tito's successors the breathing room needed for necessary reform. At the same time, however, such international respect also seemed to sanction the existing political system and its capacity to frustrate the market reforms that most Yugoslav economists now recognized as the only way out of the debt crisis. Simply reducing imports to restore a positive trade balance did not itself pay the interest due on the accumulated foreign debt (see table 10.3).

Tale 10.3. *Foreign trade and debt, 1965–1985*

	Exports-imports (US $ mil.)	Net interest paid[a]	Current account balance[a]	Net foreign debt (US $ mil.)
1965	–90			
1970	–958			
1975	–2,984	–1	–3.5	5.75
1977	–3,788	–0.7	–4	8.5
1979	–6,069	–1.1	–6.5	13.75
1981	–3,165	–2.4	–1	18.75
1983	–1,231	–2.7	0.5	18.75
1985	–588	–3.3	1.7	18.75

[a]Percent of adjusted social product at current prices.
Sources: John R. Lampe, Russell O. Prickett, and Ljubiša S. Adamović, *Yugoslav-American Economic Relations Since World War II* (Durham, NC: Duke University Press, 1990), 98; and Harold Lydall, *Yugoslavia in Crisis* (Oxford: Clarendon Press, 1989), 66.

The Friends of Yugoslavia

Who did Tito's long rule over an otherwise faceless presidency leave in place to deal with that crisis or any other? Surely not his replacement as head of the nine-man presidency, an unknown Macedonian who served for less than two weeks before giving way to an equally obscure successor for the one-year term that the rotation agreement fixed to begin in May. The deputies that Kardelj's tiers of delegates had sifted into the two chambers of the national Assembly were obscure and closely bound to vote under instruction from the republic party leaderships. Only the chair of the Federal Executive Council (SIV), voted by the assembly to a four-year term, was in a position to act as prime minister. The first post-Tito choice came up in May 1982, and it was a fortunate one. True, Milka Planinc could not be called a liberal according to credentials from her days as a young Croat Partisan in the Krajina to her role as the hard-line replacement for Dabčević-Kučar as head of the Croatian Central Committee during the 1970s. And true, the republic leaderships probably did not expect the SIV's only woman to be a strong chair. Yet she would soon force a reluctant set of republic leaderships and assembly delegates to face squarely the alternatives posed by the debt crisis.

The crisis had already descended on the Yugoslav leadership by the time that Planinc took office. In December 1981, the largest American creditor, Manufacturers Hanover Trust of New York, had tried to put together a syndicated loan of $500 million to the Yugoslav National Bank in order to allow some payment of interest due on the $19 billion debt.

By February, as Poland defaulted on its still larger debt, the New York bank had not found enough takers. Another New York bank attempted to collect a smaller sum and also failed. Once Planinc had authorized an official international effort to prevent default, American Ambassador David Anderson and his staff dispatched what became known as the "crossroads cable." According to Russell Prickett's first-hand account, its call for a massive package of debt relief and consolidation also promised to rein in domestic credit and cut away still substantial price controls.[32]

The existing Paris Club of Western lenders, buoyed by the promised participation of the International Monetary Fund, agreed to offer Yugoslavia a package for rescheduling their debt. The Planinc government resisted both the word "rescheduling" and the sponsorship of the private Paris Club. The US Deputy Secretary of State and former Ambassador Lawrence Eagleburger took the lead in officially assembling the separate consortium called "the Friends of Yugoslavia." Private banks led by Manufacturers Hanover offered an initial loan of $600 million and the refinancing of another $1.4 billion. All three international institutions – the IMF, the World Bank, and the Bank for International Settlements – provided another $1.4 billion in loans for 1983 and then "consolidated," rather than rescheduled repayment of $1.1 billion on easier terms in subsequent years. With the IMF Standby Agreement came Yugoslav commitments to dinar devaluation, tighter currency issue and credit, and interest rates at least 1 percent higher than the rate of inflation. The National Assembly was prepared to reject these conditions until Planinc herself confronted them with the "black option" of default and an end to all international credit in the early morning of June 3. Yugoslavia reversed its deficit on current account to record a small surplus for 1983 and earned another $3 billion package of refinanced debt and new credits for 1984.

The failure of federal leadership and economic retreat, 1986–1988

When Branko Mikulić was chosen to succeed Milka Planinc as chair of the Federal Executive Council in May 1986, hopes were high that he might proceed with domestic restructuring as well as meeting international obligations. The fears of a hostile international environment that followed Tito's death had now worn off. Trade and other relations with the Soviet Union survived its ill-fated incursion into Afghanistan. The United States had demonstrated that Yugoslavia still merited special treatment through the debt relief described above.

Representatives from the Yugoslav republics could afford to be more assertive at the Thirteenth Party Congress in June 1986 than they had been four years earlier. Tito's collective state and party presidencies, with their rotating system of one-year presidents, remained in the background. Abstentions in the 1986 elections for the initial layer of delegates that led to the selection of the Federal Assembly were higher than in 1982, reaching 20 percent among Croatia's Basic Organizations (OOUR) in social enterprises. Yet substantial federal power still seemed to reside with the new chair of the Federal Executive Council (SIV). Now that the Planinc regime had used that authority to bargain for breathing space to service the foreign debt, the next SIV could presumably implement the longer-term proposals for a unified market economy and more efficient enterprises that the Kraigher Commission for Economic Stabilization had prepared during 1982–83.

Yugoslavia's difficulty in finally carrying out the market reforms first promised in 1965 began with the seventeen commission reports themselves. One Western economist called them "frustratingly vague and repetitious."[33] They did identify specific problems in each sector of the economy and demand a convertible currency market, real interest rates, relief from indirect taxes, and an end to inefficient inter-enterprise bargaining. The Slovene head of the commission, Sergei Kraigher, had pushed hard for the 1965 reform and then departed from the party's Central Committee, returning only to fill Edvard Kardelj's seat in 1979. But the longer-term recommendations continued to endorse social ownership and even the 1976 subdivision of enterprises into Basic Organizations. They prescribed only price increases and tax exemptions for insolvent firms to restore market equilibrium, thus inviting enterprises to expect further help and pay any price for supplies. More inflation would surely follow. Capital-intensive exports were still favored over the labor-intensive goods that might relieve mounting unemployment. Before these prescriptions could be tried, the Mikulić regime had to enforce the measures sorely needed for macroeconomic stabilization.

Mikulić came from the party presidency. He had been one of them since 1979, after rising to become secretary of the Bosnian League of Communists in 1965. A Bosnian Croat who resisted any flirtation with liberal or nationalist stirrings of the late 1960s, he survived the purge of 1972 that swept away most other republic leaderships. Mikulić maintained a close alliance with Hamdija Pozderac and other Bosnian Muslim party leaders in Sarajevo if less with the previously predominant Serbs. Together they made Bosnia-Hercegovina the republic that restricted dissent most sharply and in the process tainted the multi-ethnic secularism that they invoked as justification. Yet Mikulić's access to army assistance facilitated the forced draft organization of the 1984 Winter Olympics and made it an apparent success. The resulting reputation for economic efficiency helped him to win the SIV position when a majority of republic leaders balked at accepting a Serbian "prime minister" for the first time since Tito's death. Only the Slovenian representatives opposed Mikulić's candidacy until concessions on republic control of the federal budget won them over.

The Mikulić regime assembled a council that seemed ready to pursue stabilization if not restructuring. Thirteen of his twenty-eight nominees were younger people coming from positions in enterprises or educational institutions. Mikulić announced their intentions to reduce a 90 percent rate of inflation and keep the trade deficit from reemerging, despite the decision forced on the Planinc government by the republic leaderships in 1985 to abandon the discipline of IMF guidelines and further Standby credits. Yet her government's agreement with international creditors in May 1986 to accept informal "enhanced monitoring" for multiple-year repayment was overturned in the party congress late the next month, as the new Mikulić cabinet stood by.

The long-awaited report of the party's commission for political reform, headed by the Croatian Josip Vrhovec, gave anti-liberal members the ammunition they wanted to resist further austerity. The report avoided discussion of democratization and concentrated instead on criticizing even the limited market reforms advocated by the 1983 Kraigher Commission, calling them "incompatible with a truly socialist system of self-management."[34] Political pressure focused on the high rates of interest, at least one point over the rate of inflation, to which the IMF had "tied Yugoslavia hand and foot." The relaxation of these rates during the second half of 1986 pushed inflation up to 150 percent by June 1987. A patchwork of price controls proved to be no barrier to the demands from all the republic leaderships for easier credit and new currency emissions that the National Bank in Belgrade was powerless to prevent. Domestic confidence in the SIV resumed its downward plunge according to media-conducted polls, dropping from 36 percent in 1983 and 20 percent in 1985, to a minimal 10 percent in 1987. Unprecedented demands that Mikulić and his cabinet resign now appeared in major newspapers.

The prime minister had in the meantime discovered to his dismay that the republic leaderships would permit a comprehensive change in economic policy only through the cumbersome process of constitutional amendment. His government succeeded in introducing a package of 130 largely economic amendments by February. Some thirty-nine were passed in November, despite Slovenian objections that the amendments had not undergone the full legislative review that would have allowed any republic or province to veto them. By that time, it was clear that the renewed price freeze would not halt the inflationary spiral or boost export earnings.

In addition a combination of front-loaded debt obligations due in 1988 obliged the Mikulić government to reopen negotiations with the IMF and its principal creditors for another Standby agreement and for further support to cover the anticipated shortfall. The Friends of Yugoslavia assembled for one last time and pledged $1.3 billion. Well they might, given Yugoslavia's repayment of considerable debt *principal* to Western creditors from 1985 to 1987 from a current account surplus based on earnings from tourism, worker remittances, and reduced imports. From perspectives respectively favoring and opposing market reforms, Russell Prickett and Susan Woodward have questioned the wisdom of transferring a nearly $1 billion surplus to pay down the debt instead of relieving the shortage of investment capital which was helping drive up the rate of inflation.[35] But this alternative presumes that the $1 billion surplus would have been invested profitably and generated new jobs to relieve social strains. Food processing, electrical appliances, and tourist facilities were obvious but otherwise neglected candidates. The Western support that was part of Tito's last legacy had now become part of the problem: it legitimized the political stalemate and its distribution of economic resources in return for the guarantee of debt repayment.

A Western initiative to address the distribution problem did appear belatedly in the conditions attached to the 1987 agreement. The included the familiar demands that export and import prices be freed from distorting controls, but now asked that the federal government enforce bankruptcy regulations and assert central control over the supply of money and credit. The Belgrade location of the only institution capable of such control, the National Bank of Yugoslavia (NBJ), guaranteed resistance from the western republics. The bank law of 1987 promised the necessary powers to the NBJ and allowed it to apply them by majority vote of republic representatives, not the unanimous decision that otherwise continued to hamstring the federal government. But majority support for reduced currency emissions and a fixed exchange rate on the dinar did not materialize. Such rigor threatened too many enterprises in the less developed republics with collapse if added to the law's "inflation-accounting" requirements that forced the 154 commercial banks to charge a positive rate of interest on any new credits. Opponents of the law claimed that 7,000 enterprises faced bankruptcy, but interenterprise credits and selective exceptions granted by the NBJ to these banks kept the actual number to a handful.[36]

Strengthening the federal case for increased financial authority at the center later in 1987 was a scandal that also weakened the Mikulić government and shook the Bosnian Muslim commitment to the Communist regime. Records retrieved from a warehouse fire revealed that Agrokomerc, one of the largest and apparently most successful Bosnian enterprises, had drawn credit on as much as $865 million worth of unsecured promissory notes due to other enterprises, but guaranteed by over sixty Yugoslav banks, most prominently the reputable Ljubljanska Banka. The sum was simply too large for Bosnian prosecutors to ignore, even if their Serb-dominated ranks had not welcomed the chance to tie the offender to Mikulić's main Bosnian Muslim ally and now a vice president of the federation, Hambdija Pozderac. His intervention had clearly kept bank authorizations flowing to Fikret Abdić, also a Muslim, and his Agrokomerc conglomerate. Based in Velika Kladuša and a successor to the successful Habsburg project to produce eggs (see chapter 3), the postwar enterprise started small in 1963, but grew geometrically to 12,000 employees after the young Abdić, then twenty-eight years old, became its director in 1967. He was hardly alone in overextending his enterprise's activities through unsecured credit still endorsed by the banking system, but Agrokomerc did account for perhaps 10 percent of the resulting debt reckoned to be outstanding in 1987.[37] The trial sentencing Abdić to prison sent a warning to other banks and other enterprises that they should change their ways.

At the same time, the forced resignation of Pozderac from the Presidency and his brother's dismissal from the SIV itself weakened Mikulić's authority even within the federal structure. When the rate of inflation accelerated to 250 percent in 1988, the pressure from all sides on Mikulić to resign became irresistible. He stepped down in December, leaving the position of the federal government even weaker than when he entered office.

11 Ethnic politics and the end of Yugoslavia

What began after Tito's death as rivalry among the republics' Communist parties turned into full blown ethnic politics by the late 1980s. The coincident collapse of Soviet bloc regimes in 1989 also played a part in the turbulence that followed. These dramatic events cost Yugoslavia more than its strategic importance to the West. They also eliminated the legitimacy of one-party rule across Eastern Europe. The League of Communists lost the mandate to maintain its political monopoly or to speak for a single Yugoslavia. Its federal leadership had already failed to face down the accelerating economic crisis before 1989. A more constructive leader, Ante Marković, now came forward, but he could not forge the political consensus needed to sustain support. It was too late simply to restructure the economy. The post-Tito power vacuum at the federal level had already opened the way for new leaders of the republic parties to assert themselves. In 1986 two younger men seized this chance – Milan Kučan of Slovenia and Slobodan Milošević of Serbia. The other republic leaderships remained unchanged and silent, except in Bosnia-Hercegovina where fateful disarray followed decades of tight control under a closed if multi-ethnic hierarchy. By 1989 Milošević had marshalled half of the eight votes in the federal presidency to support his view of how Yugoslavia should restructure itself politically. Kučan opposed his unitary approach, but could not bring the other four votes – Bosnia-Hercegovina, Croatia, and Macedonia, plus Slovenia – to agree on a common alternative.

The two Communist approaches to restructuring interacted with new ones after 1989 to break Yugoslavia apart over the course of the next two years. Multi-party elections at the republic level provided a seemingly democratic centerpiece. A single League of Communists simply ceased to exist, leaving the Yugoslav Peoples' Army (JNA) and its Serb-dominated officer corps as the only guarantor of the federal framework. The cost of ethnic politics in such a setting was prohibitive, derailing first the belated market reforms that showed stunning promise early in 1990. The disintegration of Yugoslavia followed in a fashion that subverted legitimate interests seeking a peaceful parting. Warfare and other disruptions have left the fate of the independent states created by former republics still uncertain. Their leaders can agree only on the impossibility of returning to a single political unit.

Before turning to the new leaders and ethnic battle lines of Yugoslavia's final years, we must understand why both state and society were so vulnerable to the volatile combination of forces that emerged after 1989. An inadequate federal framework and a fractured Communist leadership kept the state from addressing fundamental disjunctures. The party commissions of the early 1980s (see chapter 10) had wrestled with the obvious need for change in economic structure, but could only agree on a stabilization program that was never implemented. Forty years of the second Yugoslavia left society to face a series of disparities in living standards, employment, and education that migration to cities, other republics, or Western Europe could no longer ameliorate. Real incomes shrank with inflation from year to year, creating a new sense of uncertainty among soldiers as well as civilians. Further aggravating this accumulation of social strains was a popular culture that presumed the right to a West European standing of living and information. The modern and therefore sensation-hungry media of Serbia, Croatia, and Slovenia exposed social problems and individual abuses of power, but stopped short of confronting their own republic's Communist leadership. They suggested instead that the disadvantages suffered by their republic came at the others' advantage. Intellectuals growing restive over the spreading corruption tended to question the framework of the federation more than its troubled system of social ownership. These were the ingredients, rather than "age-old antagonisms," for the ethnic endgame that destroyed the Socialist Federal Republic of Yugoslavia.

Social strains and regional relations

The specter of declining real income, down by one-quarter from 1983 to 1988 and one-third from 1979, worked its way through a society grown nervous and skeptical. Public opinion polling in 1987 found 79 percent of the respondents doubting that there was any avenue open to escape the accumulated economic problems. Unemployment in the still predominant social sector had risen steadily for the period 1981–86 from 13.8 to 16.6 percent. Some 60 percent of the unemployed were now under twenty-five years of age and almost that fraction had at least a secondary education. Over one-half were women. The growing number of jobless citizens formed a political barrier to the downsizing of

Table 11.1. *Growth of population, 1921–1981*

	1921	1931	1948	1961	1971	1981
Total population						
(in 1,000s)	12,545	14,534	15,841	18,549	20,523	22,425
Birth rate (per 1,000)	37	34	28	23	18	16
Death rate (per 1,000)	21	20	14	9	9	9
Percent of total population						
Serb	38	41	42	40	36	36
Croat	24	24	23	22	20	20
Agricultural (percent)	79	76	67	50	38	20
Literacy (percent)	50	55	75	79	85	91
Density (per sq. km)	49	57	62	73	80	88

Source: *Jugoslavija, 1918–1988, Statistički godišnjak* (Belgrade: Savezni zavod za statistiku, 1989), 38–44.

inefficiently large enterprises that would be needed to reverse the decline in labor productivity since 1982. So did the escalating number of "work stoppages," or strikes, which more than doubled between 1982 and 1987 to involve 7 percent of those employed in the social sector.[1]

These aggregate figures, troubling as they were, masked the regional or ethnic disparities in population growth, income, and employment that posed the greatest political problems. An increasingly sophisticated set of Yugoslav social scientists delineated these regional imbalances during the 1980s. The ethnic features of their findings preoccupied the popular media and a variety of cultural critics. Such coverage often distorted the data, heightening political tensions in the process. There is no avoiding the fact, however, that the combined Serb and Croat share of Yugoslavia's population decreased from 65 percent in 1948 to 56 percent in 1981. Let us review the actual patterns of social and regional imbalance before returning to the political turmoil that their perception as ethnic issues helped generate. The overall declines in the birth and death rates, in illiteracy, and in the agricultural share of a growing population (see table 11.1) masked these imbalances. Table 11.2 reflects the growth of regional disparities between 1953 and 1988.

Migration, employment and education

The multi-ethnic migration that had moved or mixed the peoples of the Yugoslav lands since the medieval period did not end with the Second World War. Country-wide and urban integration made real progress, but remained incomplete. The massive movement away from peasant

Table 11.2. *Population and income by republic, 1953–1988*

	1953			1971		1988		
	Pop. % of total	GMP/ capita %	Fixed assets/ worker %	Pop. % of total	GMP/ capita %	Pop. % of total	GMP/ capita %	Fixed assets/ worker %
Yugoslavia	100	100	100	100	100	100	100	100
Croatia	23.2	122	101	20.4	127	19.9	128	109.9
Slovenia	8.8	175	122	8.3	187	8.2	203	133.7
Serbia (proper)	26.3	91	112	25.1	96	24.8	101	91
Vojvodina	10	94	95	9.3	118	8.7	119	101.6
Kosovo	4.8	43	89	6.9	32	8	27	91.8
Bosnia-Hercegovina	16.7	83	82	18.6	67	18.8	68	94.9
Macedonia	7.7	68	69	8.3	66	8.9	63	74.2
Montenegro	2.5	77	46	2.7	72	2.7	74	136.6

Source: Dijana Pleština, *Regional Development in Communist Yugoslavia: Success, Failure, and Consequences* (Boulder, Colo.: Westview Press, 1992), 180–81.

villages that began in the 1950s accelerated during the 1970s and increased the non-farm share of the population to 80 percent by 1981. Some 8 million people moved in the process. A majority of migrants stayed in their native republic, and many did not move to urban centers. The urban share of the 1981 total amounted to just 47 percent. A number of large enterprises were located in small towns and drew heavily on rural labor. Yet few such enterprises were to be found in the area of highest rural density per arable acre outlined in map 9.1. In addition many of the unskilled peasant laborers who did move to large cities resisted assimilation in the center or settled in semi-rural areas on the periphery which were then incorporated. The "rurbanization" of Belgrade as it grew from 250,000 in 1944 to 1 million by 1967 and 1.6 million by 1985 is the most striking case, but the rising Kosovar and Serb populations on the peripheries of Skopje and Sarajevo, respectively, should also be mentioned.[2]

Over 1 million people in a labor force of 9 million had also gone abroad by 1972. Within a decade, some 300,000 had returned, mostly to the republic from which they came. There was, however, a portentous Bosnian exception to this rule for returning workers and for migrants in general. The share of the labor force from Bosnia-Hercegovina and Serbia working abroad rose during the 1970s, catching up with an initial Croatian predominance (see chapter 9). Many of the Serbs and Croats among the Bosnian "guest workers" joined their more trained or educated compatriots from the republic and relocated to Serbia or Croatia, primarily Belgrade or Zagreb, during the 1960s and 1970s. The departure of nearly one of every four Serbs by 1981 reversed the demographic plurality of 1948 in favor of the Bosnian Muslims. The Serbs made up 42 percent of the population of Bosnia in 1948 and the Muslims 30 percent, giving way to a Muslim predominance over the Serbs of 40 percent to 32 percent by 1981, and 44 to 31 by 1991 (see table 11.3). The republic's share of Yugoslavia's overall population had meanwhile moved up 16.7 percent in 1953 to 18.8 percent by 1988, on the strength of the Bosnian Muslim rate of natural increase (births minus deaths). Bosnia's Gross Material Product (goods without services) per capita had declined as a proportion of the Yugoslav average over the same period, more than in Montenegro and Macedonia, if less than in Kosovo (see table 11.2).

The dynamics of Bosnian urbanization also increased the Muslim presence. Starting slowly with the lowest urban proportion of any republic after the Second World War, Bosnian municipalities jumped from 19 to 36 percent of the republic's population from 1961 to 1981. Bosnian Muslim migrants accounted for the larger share of this growth,

Table 11.3. *Ethnic populations in Bosnia-Hercegovina, Croatia and Kosovo, 1961–1991 (in percent)*

	1961	1971	1981	1991
Bosnia-Hercegovina	100	100	100	100
Serbs	42.8	37.3	32.3	31.4
Muslims	25.6	39.6	39.5	43.7
Croats	21.7	20.6	18.4	17.3
Yugoslavs	8.4	1.2	7.9	5.5
Others	1.5	1.3	2	2.1
Croatia	100	100	100	100
Croats	80.2	79.4	75.1	78.1
Serbs	15	14.2	11.6	12.2
Yugoslavs	0.4	1.9	8.2	2.2
Others	4.4	4.5	5.1	7.5
Kosovo	100	100	100	100
Albanians	67	73.7	77.5	90
Serbs	23.5	18.4	13.3	10
Montenegrins	3.9	2.5	1.7	
Others	5.6	5.4	7.5	

Sources: Jugoslavija, 1918–1988, Statistički godišnjak (Belgrade: Savezni zavod za statistiku 1989), 160–66; and "The National Composition of Yugoslavia's Population, 1991," *Yugoslav Survey* 1 (1992), 3–24.

helping Muslims overall to record a more than proportional increase in income; the incomes of Bosnian Serbs and especially Croats declined slightly at this time.[3] The more able or educated young Serbs and Croats were simply leaving the republic for Belgrade or Zagreb, but recorded none of the complaints about discrimination or harassment heard from Kosovo. Sarajevo, rather than becoming a more Muslim city, was instead blossoming into the most Yugoslav of all the republic capitals. Nearly one-fifth of the city's population declared itself Yugoslav in the 1981 census, while the country's most fertile secular culture emerged around them.

By then, according to table 11.3, the demographic balance had shifted against the Serbs not only in Kosovo but also in Bosnia-Hercegovina and to some extent in Croatia. In 1991, as seen in map 11.1, areas of compact Serb settlement in Croatia still bordered some of the sizeable but disconnected Serb areas within Bosnia. Their potential alliance with each other or with the Serbs of Serbia would prove more explosive in the break-up of Yugoslavia during 1991–92 than the problem that was generally regarded as most dangerous throughout the 1980s – Serb–Albanian relations in Kosovo. The demographic difficulties in all

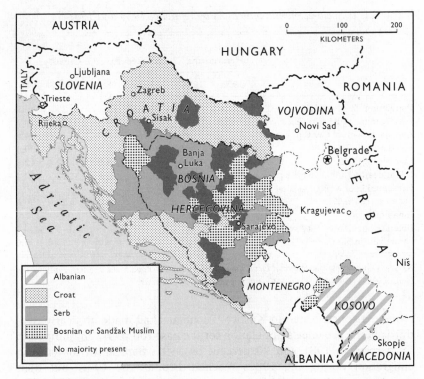

Map 11.1 Ethnic majorities in Bosnia-Hercegovina, Croatia, and Kosovo, 1991

three regions are better understood when we note their close coincidence with Yugoslavia's most densely populated land *per arable acre* as outlined in map 9.1.

For Yugoslavia as a whole, postwar population growth had reduced Serb and Croat shares by 5 percent each, to 36 and 20 percent, respectively, by 1981. Slovenes, Macedonians, and Hungarians had also seen their proportions drop in favor of Yugoslavs, Bosnian Muslims, and Kosovar Albanians. According to the republic data in table 11.2, Slovenia and Croatia could console themselves with rising per capita shares of Yugoslavia's Gross Material Product and fixed assets. Only Serbia's share of fixed assets declined from 1953 to 1988.

The numbers for the Kosovo province carried the greatest political consequences. Its population increased from 4.8 to 8 percent of the Yugoslav total on the strength of an Albanian ethnic share that passed 9 percent. Some had moved to other republics for employment, but they

Table 11.4. *Socio-economic indicators by republic, 1953 and 1988*

	Bosnia-Hercegovina		Montenegro		Croatia	
	1953	1988	1953	1988	1953	1988
Population (% of total	16.7	18.8	2.5	2.7	23.2	19.9
GMP/capita (SFRJ = 100)	83	68	77	74	122	128
Average growth of GMP per capita	4.6	3.3	5	3.9	4.6	4.8
Fixed assets/worker	82	94.9	46	136.6	101	109.1
Live births/1,000	35.1	15.3	28.9	15.8	22.4	12.8
Infant deaths/1,000 live births	125.6	16.1	41	15.6	112	12.4
Participation of women in total labor force (in %)	15.7	32	20	32.6	27.9	39.6
Inhabitants/doctor	3,314	680	4,473	674	1,947	477
Illiterate population 8–10 years and over (in %)	44.9	14.5	26.4	9.4	15.6	5.6

Source: Dijana Pleština, *Regional Development in Communist Yugoslavia: Success, Failure, and Consequences* (Boulder, Colo.: Westview Press, 1992), 180–81.

remained concentrated in Kosovo. Albanians had made up nearly two-thirds of the province's population for the past 100 years, but jumped to 78 percent in 1981 and 90 percent by 1991. Serb and Montenegrin emigration during the 1980s reached 100,000 by 1987, but their departure only accounted for a few percentage points of the shift.[4] The rest belonged to the Kosovars' natural increase of 27 per 1,000 for 1981–90, far exceeding the Serb (and Croatian) average of 2.2 and even the 15.6 average of the Bosnian and Sandžak Muslims. That increase proceeded despite, and partly because of, the province's inordinately high rate of infant mortality and lack of physicians (see table 11.4).

Let us stipulate that Kosovar misdemeanors against persons and property, rather than the high crimes charged by some on the Serbian side, encouraged a significant fraction of the Serb emigration. Over two-thirds of those leaving came from areas of mixed population. Most reported harassment, but the interethnic murder and rape so often stressed in the Serbian media remained minimal, below the country's average in official figures.

Kosovar Albanians suffered from two conflicting trends that troubled all of Yugoslavia, but were most acute in their province: rising levels of higher education and diminishing chances for graduates to find employment. As the fraction of Kosovars with secondary education or higher moved toward 50 percent during the 1970s, unemployment among graduates grew rapidly. The new university in Priština was turning out

Table 11.4 (*cont.*)

Macedonia		Slovenia		Serbia proper		Kosovo		Vojvodina	
1953	1988	1953	1988	1953	1988	1953	1988	1953	1988
7.7	8.9	8.8	8.2	26.3	24.8	4.8	8	10	8.7
68	63	175	203	91	101	43	27	94	119
5.1	4.1	5.2	4.5	5.1	4.3	5.1	2.6	5.3	4.8
69	63	122	133.7	112	91	89	91.8	95	101.6
35	18.5	22.4	14.2	23.1	12.6	38.5	29.1	24.4	11.5
136.1	44.7	81.3	11.4	91.2	21.6	133	51.8	129.7	11
16.7	31	32.3	44.5	21.7	34.3	10.5	20.7	29.2	36
4,324	530	1,704	496	2,104	440	8,527	1,092	2,556	511
40.3	10.9	2.4	0.8	27.4	11.1	62.5	17.6	11.8	5.8

graduates far faster than the province's capital-intensive industrial sector of already over-staffed enterprises could absorb. The Serbs who emigrated from Kosovo tended to have higher levels of education as well, leaving behind fellow Serbs whose education level by 1980 was lower than the Kosovars. When the austerity of the early 1980s pushed the province's overall rate of unemployment past 50 percent in the social sector, rivalry between Kosovars and Serbs for the remaining jobs sharpened, whatever the political context. Across Yugoslavia, educated workers in skilled employment saw their wage differential over unskilled labor shrink to barely two-thirds more.[5]

The rise in literacy and access to higher education had seemed one of the least ambiguous achievements of Tito's Yugoslavia. After a slow start in the 1950s, the rate of illiteracy fell steadily from 21 percent in 1961 to 9.5 percent by 1981. The regional spread remained alarmingly large, from less than 1 percent in Slovenia and 5.6 percent in Croatia to 14.5 percent in Bosnia-Hercegovina and 17.6 percent in Kosovo (see tables 11.1 and 11.4). One-quarter of all women over forty years of age were illiterate in 1981, and it was closer to one-half for these two territories. Yet the rates for women as well as men under thirty years were minimal. Primary school enrollment (ages 7–15) had risen from 65 to 95 percent of those eligible between 1961 and 1974. Full-time students in the various universities and institutes passed 10 percent of the primary school graduates by the early 1980s, doubling since 1961.[6]

While the educational system had not integrated textbooks nor even some curricula among the republics or between Serbia and Kosovo province, it still provided ready access to employment at least in the home region, Kosovo excepted, until the 1980s. Now it could not promise jobs to roughly one-half of the new graduates at salaries near the Western standard of consumption that had prevailed during the 1970s. By 1984 one-quarter of all families in Yugoslavia had fallen below the poverty line. Average income was just 70 percent of the sum reckoned necessary for a family of four.

Media, popular culture, and religion

This looming socio-economic crisis confronted a popular culture partly integrated by Yugoslav-wide and European influences, but divided by separate sets of republic or provincial media and by rising religious influence. Spectator sports were probably the leading intra-Yugoslav activity. Soccer and basketball leagues covered the country with intercity rivalries, drawing large crowds and television coverage that did not identify teams as ethnic representatives. Both sports produced world class athletes whose performance on teams representing Yugoslavia in international competitions drew the populace together. Other sports flourished as well. Yugoslav athletes won Olympic medals without the centralized apparatus or pervasive political control that set the Soviet bloc programs apart. This background explains the genuine enthusiasm for hosting the 1984 Winter Olympics in Sarajevo. Local television coverage sought to meet the standards of Eurovision, the West European network to which Yugoslavia, but not the bloc members, had been linked since the 1960s.

So-called "city music" from the major republic capitals blended with the styles of the Dalmatian coast to produce ballads that won European pop music contests during the 1970s. The folk rock of Bosnian Muslim singer Lepa Brena became wildly popular in Serbia during the 1980s. Pirated copies of the earlier hit albums have now spread across much of the former territory by the mid-1990s, as perhaps the one widespread evidence of "Yugonostalgia."

Popular culture did not always unite. The rise of punk rock by the mid-1980s, particularly the proto-Nazi presentations of the band, Laibach (German for Ljubljana), provided the most striking instance. Especially for Serbian audiences, the combination of Central European youth culture and conscious flaunting of Partisan taboos seemed to carry the same ideological message as though performed in Nazi uniforms in the midst of the Second World War.[7] The media of the separate republics made it easy to spread such separate and divisive impressions, particularly in the looser political atmosphere that followed Tito's death in 1980.

The relative sophistication and reliability of Yugoslavia's press, radio, and television gave them a far greater influence over public opinion than in any of the Soviet bloc countries. The circulation of 27 daily newspapers reached over 2 million people by 1983, and some 200 radio stations reached many more. The 175 television sets per 1,000 persons matched the level for Ireland and approached that for Austria. Their combined impact magnified the failure of the "delegated" Federal Assembly to capture any of the public attention that Western parliamentary debates attract. It should not be surprising therefore that, under new management, first the Belgrade and then, after 1989, the Zagreb medias became effective vehicles for ethnic politics and propaganda. Their counterparts in the Soviet bloc had no such influence to exert.

The often independent Yugoslav film industry, centered in Belgrade and Zagreb and in Sarajevo by the 1980s, did not succumb to nationalist manipulation. Notable examples of its independence were the multi-ethnic films of Emir Kusturica, set in Sarajevo, and the 1988 *Film With No Name* (*Film bez imena*) that used the Romeo and Juliet scenario to portray the ironies of the Serbian–Albanian conflict. But the spread of television and home videos cut deeply into attendance at the small, unrenovated movie theaters for all but the most popular Hollywood films by the mid-1980s.[8] Soon afterwards, the ongoing economic crisis made it impossible for Yugoslav companies to continue producing the roughly thirty films a year that they had averaged since the 1960s.

The three major religions – Catholic, Orthodox, and Muslim – had not received much access to the rising electronic media. The new republic laws on religious rights passed during 1976–78 denied them legal use of radio or television. Their church publications (see chapter 9) could continue, but so did the ban on believers in the League of Communists and on separate religious education for children. The public schools' required instruction in atheism made no inroads into the number of believers, but urban, secular culture did. A 1985 survey found that the Catholic proportion of religious believers had fallen below one-third and the Orthodox and Bosnian Muslim fractions below one-fifth, all down by at least one-half since 1960.[9]

The Catholic hierarchy of Croatia contested the republic's religious law, and its newspaper *Glas koncila* raised repeated objections. Beginning in 1975, the hierarchy undertook annual celebrations of "The Great Novena – Thirteen Centuries of Christianity among the Croats." These huge public meetings continued until 1984, attracting as many as 400,000 people that year. Meetings always included the displays of Croatian national symbols and the singing of national anthems that Communist regulations forbade. Otherwise, the principal initiatives for religious unrest among all three clergies came from their lower ranks. The Franciscans of Bosnia-Hercegovina, by far the largest Catholic order, struggled with Mostar's diocesan authority from the mid-1970s forward. Franciscan promotion of the Madonna's miraculous appearance to children in Medjugorje and the subsequent international pilgrimages there strengthened the order's bargaining power. A 1982 letter from Serb Orthodox clergy in Kosovo complained to a previously quiescent patriarch about harassment and damage to church property by Kosovo Albanians. When complaints continued, the Orthodox newspaper, *Pravoslavije*, published its first real criticism of the Communist regime in 1984. As compensation for the relatively slow reconstruction of Orthodox churches in some other parts of the country, the Patriarchate was allowed to restart the construction of the huge Church of St. Sava in the center of Belgrade that the Second World War had halted.

Only the Bosnian Muslim clergy remained silent by the mid-1980s, constrained by the republic's comprehensive Communist censorship, but consoled by the new right to offer children separate religious instruction and the recent construction or renovation of some 800 mosques. The hierarchy's very restraint helped to push the lay Muslim scholar, Alija Izetbegović, and several others to speak out for Islamic values in the face of the mounting socio-economic crisis. Their prompt trial and imprisonment in 1983 on the unsubstantiated charge of advocating a Muslim government for Bosnia ironically did more to stimulate educated interest in Islam in Sarajevo and other towns than anything the hierarchy had done.[10]

Party and army

Both the League of Communists and the JNA were also feeling the consequences of the prolonged socio-economic crisis by the mid-1980s. The party's membership peaked in 1982 at 2.2 million, up from 1 million in 1972, thanks to successful recruiting drives among managers in the mid-1970s and among students after the Soviet invasion of Afghanistan in 1979. But industrial workers never exceeded 30 percent of total party membership, despite special efforts to attract them. After 1985, workers and students began to leave the party, particularly in the big cities, and the number of members overall started to decline, falling to 1.5 million by 1989. According to a poll taken in the mid-1980s, nearly 30 percent of all members rated the party's reputation as poor and half of all young people, up to 88 percent in Slovenia and 70 percent in Croatia, said that they did not wish to join.[11] Serbs and Montenegrins continued to make up over half of the membership, although they constituted barely 40 percent of the total population. Among the other ethnic groups, Croatian and Slovene party numbers were already declining by 1981, down to one-fifth despite their 30 percent share of the population. Only the Bosnian Muslims showed a significant increase after 1971, with party membership just surpassing their 7.8 percent share of population.

The one institution where party membership stayed high throughout the 1980s regardless of ethnic origin was of course the Yugoslav People's Army, the JNA. Yet its manpower and budgetary resources faced reductions in the face of economic austerity. By 1984 military spending had fallen by one-third from an already reduced target for 1980–84, and its forces from 270,000 to 220,000. The army remained the largest component of the military. It boasted a troop strength of 180,000, some two-thirds of the draftees serving fifteen-month tours that were then reduced to twelve months. Two features distinguished the career officers and non-commissioned officers who made up the other one-third of the army. Almost all were members of the League of Communists. And by ethnic origin, some 60 percent were Serbs and 8 percent Montenegrins, leaving only 14 percent for Croats and 6 percent or less for any of the others. The sharp decline in applications for these positions from urban centers and Slovenia in particular, beginning in the 1970s, explained much more of the disproportion than did any discrimination against non-Serbs.

In any case, this frequently quoted and sometimes exaggerated imbalance proved less important during the 1980s than changes at the top.[12] Serb leverage advanced there significantly. The shift away from strictly applying the "key system" of ethnic balance to the high command began in 1982 when Admiral Branko Mamula, a Croatian Serb who had been army chief-of-staff since 1979, became minister of defense. A Serbian general took his place, and together they put a number of other Serbs, mainly from Croatia or Bosnia, into strategic positions in the high command, while leaving the overall balance largely in place. Mamula had other far-reaching plans to "simplify," in fact, to tighten the army's central control over its troops and resources. He sought to subordinate the republics' Territorial Defense Forces to the JNA and combine the country's defense system into only a few regions. He also promoted new federal investment in arms production, in order to make Yugoslavia self-sufficient by the end of the decade and in the meantime to generate some export earnings for his beleaguered military budget. Each of these initiatives provoked political controversy, particularly in Slovenia.

New leaders and new politics

The crisis in federal institutions and socio-economic strains on Yugoslavia's population finally opened the political stage to a new cast of characters in 1986. The first to step forward, as noted above, were the new leaders of the Serbian and Slovenian League of Communists, Slobodan Milošević and Milan Kučan. The Kosovar Albanians and the JNA became their respective adversaries in the now open practice of ethnic politics. They and the other republic leaderships also faced new actors, unconnected with the Communist apparatus who were eager to play speaking parts in what promised to be the most unrestrained political performance seen in Yugoslavia since the Second World War.

Kosovo and the rise of Milošević

Serbia's League of Communists faced an accumulation of problems by 1986, only one of which was the minority position of Serbs in Kosovo. The republic's leading positions were too heavily staffed with the provincial cadre who had seemed the most reliable replacements for Marko Nikezić and his Belgrade allies after the 1972 purges (see chapter 10). Now, in Belgrade itself, despite a rate of population growth exceeded only by Skopje, the huge city was showing the effects of long being denied the federal funds for investment in urban infrastructure available to the other republic capitals, on the grounds that it was the federal capital. Belgrade's unsuccessful campaign to host the 1992 Summer Olympics in the capital revealed how much would have to be done just to repair accumulated deficiencies. The city's rate of unemployment rose throughout the decade, reaching 25 percent by 1989. Several years earlier, some of the Belgrade party bosses joined in the growing restlessness with the cautious, but market-oriented leadership of Ivan Stambolić.

Belgrade's powerful media and academic community could not resist the conclusion that the other republics were somehow using the federation to discriminate against Serbia in other ways as well. But in what other ways? The economic crisis tempted all of the republics to similar suspicions about their own troubles. Serbia's party leaders sought to address this immediate crisis only through the lengthy process of further constitutional revision and market reform. Earlier revision in

1974 had left Kosovo, and the Vojvodina as well, with the separate votes in federal proceedings that reduced Serbia's voice to one in eight.

Ivan Stambolić had become the League's leader at the age of forty-four, immediately after Tito's death in 1980. The nephew of Petar Stambolić, Tito's choice to neuter the Serbian party in 1972, Ivan could not overcome the inertia that had characterized the republic's party since then. Nor did he himself generally speak about the hard political choices that now had to be made without resorting to the ambiguous, convoluted rhetoric of federal politics – "Yugospeak" as some called it. But there were two exceptions. Stambolić endorsed market reform and also made clear his opposition to "nationalistic poisoning of the young" and ethnic politics. In 1985 he was targeting the notions heard in and out of the party that the Yugoslav Communists had come to power through an anti-Serb coalition and that Mihailović's Chetniks had been misrepresented as war criminals for opposing this coalition. Such views, Stambolić emphasized, "must be beaten everywhere and at all times." But by invoking censorship rather than scholarship and by tying his attacks to the myth of an unimpeachable Communist legacy, he failed to persuade enough of the Belgrade intellectuals who should have been his natural allies.

Waiting in the wings to strike an unlikely bargain with those allies and then a more natural one with the provincial party cadre was Slobodan Milošević. Just 44-years-old by 1985, Milošević became Belgrade party chief under the direct sponsorship of Stambolić. They had met at Belgrade's law faculty in the early 1960s, when Milošević was newly arrived from the Serbian interior and quick to seek a place on the sort of ideological committee that helped young provincials advance. His subsequent advance to the directorships of Technogas (1970–78) and Beobanka (1978–82) neatly followed Stambolić's tenure in those positions. So did his further ascent from the Belgrade party leadership to head the Serbian Central Committee when Stambolić became the republic's president in May 1986. Throughout this entire period and on into early 1987, Milošević followed the unwritten rules of any such client–patron relationship. He supported Stambolić on all matters of policy, opposition to the dangers of Serbian nationalism included.[13]

Of Kosovo, Milošević said almost nothing until the evening of April 24, 1987, when at Stambolić's urging he joined local Kosovar party leaders to address the disgruntled Serbs and Montenegrins of Kosovo Polje at their town's cultural center. Close by the site of the 1389 battle that sealed the fate of medieval Serbia, he watched as a contingent of police beat back a huge, chanting crowd too big for the hall. "No one should dare beat you," he shouted spontaneously and proceeded to spend the next twelve hours listening to a litany of grievances. Much celebrated by his followers in the years ahead, this cathartic event did not change Milošević's political behavior until it presented him with the chance to depose his mentor Stabolić. That time had obviously not yet come in June when Milošević followed up his muted criticism of the 1986 Memorandum of the Serbian Academy of Arts and Sciences with a sharp attack on it as "nothing else but the darkest nationalism."

The Memorandum, or more precisely the seventy-four-page draft leaked to the official media that October, pulled together the grievances that various Serbian writers and historians had been voicing outside of the Communist framework in the looser but less certain political climate since Tito's death. They found that voice by reexamining the past. The historical novels of the young journalist, Vuk Drašković, and the long expelled party leader, Dobrica Ćosić, lamented Serbia's sufferings in the two world wars as unique. More lamentations appeared in the detailed celebration of the Orthodox church's presence in Kosovo in the second volume of the sumptuous new *Istorija srpskog naroda*, in Veselin Djuretić's unscholarly but unprecedented critique of Allied policy for betraying Mihailović and Serbia in the Second World War, and in the rambling documentary collections stitched together by Vladimir Dedijer that questioned Tito's exemplary role during the war.[14] The accumulating economic crisis fed the great popularity of such publications or their sensation-seeking summaries in Belgrade's weekly magazines. Lurid accounts of persecution supplied by Serbs leaving Kosovo helped bring a massive crowd to the 1983 funeral of the disgraced Aleksandar Ranković, now unofficially praised for keeping Kosovo "under control." The several historians who drafted the Memorandum, Ćosić by his account not among them, sought to focus public attention on Kosovo. Its first half mixed abstract principles for revising the 1974 constitution, minus any endorsement of the market mechanism, with coherent complaints about Serbia's economic position in the federation. The document's second half made Kosovo the litmus test to prove that an "anti-Serb coalition" had formed to ensure "a weak Serbia." It charged that the Stambolić leadership was allowing "genocide" there while its Kosovar regime voted independently with rights equal to Serbia in the federation.

Milošević moved adroitly to the nationalist side, but with what conviction is *still* not known, in the autumn of 1987. When his successor as Belgrade party chief lit into the excesses of the "nationalist media" at the Central Committee's September plenum, Milošević seized the moment. He mobilized enough support to force him out and thus condemn Stambolić by implication. Within a few weeks, he orchestrated the dismissal of leading figures in *Politika*'s press complex and in

Belgrade television who had criticized either the media's nationalist excesses or his own ascendancy. These key elements of the Belgrade media thereupon joined Milošević and his provincial party supporters in a campaign to oust Stambolić as president of Serbia. They succeeded by December, and the JNA's chief-of-staff took his place. True, the new leader carried on an initial flirtation with market reform, codified in a report prepared by the liberal Belgrade economists quickly appointed to what was called the Milošević Commission. Yet Milošević and his reconstituted party leadership spoke only of the need for recentralizing authority, first in Serbia and then across Yugoslavia. During 1988 he moved at a dizzying pace not only to consolidate political control in familiar Communist fashion but also to stage a series of huge public meetings in and around Serbia. They encouraged unprecedented assertions of Serbian nationalism, including the display of Chetnik insignia. The November meeting in Belgrade assembled perhaps 1 million people, some mobilized by local party leaders but more by the media or individual grievances. Mass demonstrations of Serbs in the Vojvodina laid the groundwork for replacing party leadership there, already vulnerable for protecting its own privileges while doing nothing to ameliorate the economic crisis. Milošević's own speeches played a central role. He spoke in short, clear sentences to express a variety of popular frustrations and then reduced them all to manifestations of how Serbia and Serbs were suppressed.[15]

By the end of 1988, similar agitation had also toppled the leadership of Montenegro's League of Communists and launched the amendment of the Serbian constitution to reabsorb both Kosovo and the Vojvodina. Demonstrations also encouraged the aforementioned resignation of the federal prime minister, Branko Mikulić. The fading authority of the Federal Executive Council left the federal presidency as the only other civilian authority that might hold Yugoslavia together. The other republics' party leadership and general public had been watching Milošević's speeches and the threatening demonstrations they attracted on television. They bridled at his failure to give up the separate votes held by the two provinces in the presidency. Together with Serbia and Montenegro, they would give the newly formed Milošević camp four of the eight votes needed to approve any decision. Half of the scenario for stalemate or confrontation was in place.

Slovenia versus the Yugoslav army

The other half started in Slovenia and spread from there to Croatia, Bosnia-Hercegovina, and Macedonia. Still the republic with the highest standard of living and with far less unemployment than the others, Slovenia's rate of economic growth had nonetheless fallen sharply by the mid-1980s. Improving connections with neighboring Austria, Italy and Hungary seemed a better way to revive that growth than to respond to Belgrade's call for closer economic integration with the rest of Yugoslavia. Paying for one-quarter of the federal budget with only 8 percent of the population already seemed too much integration for some Slovenes. This purely economic issue helped to make Slovenia the only other republic besides Serbia where the League of Communists turned to new, younger leadership before 1989.

Milan Kučan had completed his law studies in Ljubljana in 1963, one year before Milošević, and had risen more rapidly to head a Slovenian youth organization by 1968. But as a supporter of Slovenian party head Stane Kavčić, he barely survived Tito's 1972 purge of Kavčić and other liberal leaders. From 1973 to 1986, he held a series of top positions in Slovenia's Socialist Alliance, National Assembly, and Communist youth league, but none in the party's inner circle, still controlled by Stane Dolanc and his hard-line allies. Kučan's elevation to head the Slovenian party in 1986 did not initially pose any confrontational issues with the other republics outside of the same economic ones that Milošević had raised to that point. Yet when controversies erupted with Serbia over Kosovo or with the JNA over Slovenian civil rights, he would follow where they led, even into ethnic politics and a campaign for independence that few had imagined possible at the start.

The fateful controversies began around the youth culture which emerged as a social movement. Although Communist-authorized, the new *Nova Revija* and the restructured weekly youth magazine, *Mladina*, had already spun out of control and begun to protest official policy in 1985. They attacked the official media's renewed criticism of the Partisans' best Christian Socialist ally during the Second World War, Edvard Kocbek, just at the end of his life. The two journals also objected to Defense Minister Mamula's proposed reorganization of the JNA for its subordination of republic defense forces to the federal League of Communists. It would be better to plan, they argued with provocative reference to the Marxist phrase that Kardelj had applied to the state, for the JNA "to wither away."

Student leaders at Ljubljana University seized on the public support implicit in the defeat of a tax referendum in November 1986 to put forward four petitions. All of them challenged the existing federal order. The two that received the greatest attention were demands for an alternative to military service and an end to the "antique ritual" of celebrating Tito's May 25 birthday with a youth relay bearing a torch through all the republics to a final stadium ceremony in Belgrade. The federal presidency, aware that the ceremony increasingly focused attention on its own anonymity, abandoned it in 1988. By then Slovenian students and the two now independent journals were locked in conflict with the JNA leadership and the Milošević media in Belgrade. They tagged Defense Minister Mamula a "merchant of death" for the exports of Yugoslav military equipment to the Third World that were to offset some of the budgetary cuts imposed on the JNA. They scorned his plan to reconfigure military regions and tighten political control of the JNA. He had already retired in some disarray when army intelligence (KOS) arrested several Slovenian journalists, including Janez Janša (later a prominent political figure), in May 1988. They published a list in *Mladina* of prominent Slovenians whom the JNA would detain under the new plan in the event of a military emergency. Although the list's authenticity has been questioned, the accused won the sympathy of the Slovenian public because JNA authorities insisted on a closed trial in their own court, conducted in Serbo-Croatian rather than Slovenian. The journalists served their sentences under house arrest arranged by the Slovenian authorities to prevent their incarceration in an army prison. Meanwhile, the spectacle of Milošević's mass demonstrations and his demands that Kosovo be brought under Serbian control turned the Slovenian television audience against any sort of easy reconciliation with Belgrade.[16]

Kučan and the Slovenian member of the federal presidency, Janez Stanovnik, now moved from passive acceptance of these challenges to positive signs of support. The limits on what could be criticized in any of the Slovenian media were formally relaxed, and a number of *émigrés* long critical of Tito's Yugoslavia were allowed to visit. Kučan's leadership curtly rejected the Serbian proposal to hold a November 1988 referendum on the proposed set of constitutional amendments, some of them aimed at restoring rational central controls. The Milošević regime had confirmed the Slovenian public's suspicion of Belgrade as a center for rational administration. Kučan himself then attended a February 1989 rally organized by Slovenia's Socialist Alliance on behalf of protecting human rights for the Kosovar Albanians. He had already approved the dispatch of Slovenian television crews to Priština to cover an unfolding confrontation that Belgrade's media, it was argued, could no longer be trusted to report accurately.

For Slovenian and Croatian public opinion, Kosovo now became a "watershed," as Branka Magaš aptly dubbed it, for their loyalty to the "really existing" Yugoslavia.[17] That November's strike at the Trepča mines protested Milošević's preparations for ending the province's autonomy and his dismissal of the popular Azem Vllasi as party leader. The miners' subsequent march to Priština mushroomed into five days of demonstrations that assembled one half-million Kosovar Albanians. The miners struck again in February and forced Milošević to abandon the former police chief whom he had appointed to succeed Vllasi. But they could not prevent the absorption of Kosovo into Serbia the next month nor Vllasi's long detention on the specious charges, eventually dropped, that he had instigated the February strike. The amended Serbian constitution of March 28 formally ended the autonomous rights of both Kosovo and the Vojvodina, but did not deprive the Milošević regime of their two places in the federal presidency.

Fatal intersections, 1989–1991

The Slovenian and Serbian party leaderships were at loggerheads by the start of 1989. During the course of the year, their confrontation widened to engage all of the Yugoslav republics and provinces. First Croatia and then Bosnia-Hercegovina and Macedonia were drawn into a loose coalition with Ljubljana that saw the latter two trying futilely at times to play a balancing role. Perhaps the one element uniting them with Slovenia was their ability to marshall four federal votes against the four that Milošević's Serbia had assembled by handpicking and installing three new Communist leaders, first in Kosovo and the Vojvodina late in 1988 and then in Montenegro in January 1989.

The political stalemate ironically coincided with the March selection of a new prime minister and the May rotation to the presidency of two committed market reformers. From mid-1989 to mid-1990, the Croatian technocrat, Ante Marković, and the youthful Slovenian economist, Janez Drnovšek, worked well together as prime minister and president of the presidency. They ended the accelerating hyperinflation and instituted a series of sweeping reforms that finally put in place all the building blocks for a market economy. But they did so without a federal League of Communists; it had ceased to exist after January 1990. Then the stalemate spilled over into the various republic elections of 1990 and left the survival of Yugoslavia to new parties and ethnic politics.

The end of the League of Communists

The previous year, in the same month of February that Milan Kučan and other Slovenian party leaders attended the Ljubljana rally for "peace and togetherness" in Kosovo, the more passive Croatian leadership accepted several initiatives to amend their republic's constitution. Among them was the fateful language that permitted the creation of new political parties. The head of the federal League of Communists in 1989, Stipe Šuvar, was himself a Croat and ironically a hard-line advocate of one-party rule under a recentralized regime and, as we have seen, a more ideological system of education. From his location at the League's headquarters in Belgrade, however, he had no way of stopping such an initiative. He was already embroiled in an effort to bring party discipline down on the Milošević forces for overturning the leaderships of the two provinces and now Montenegro. In response, Milošević led an effort, albeit unsuccessful, to force Šuvar to resign from the League's presidency before his brief term expired in May. That same month in Serbia, however, Milošević extended his base of power outside the party by winning the republic's presidency with 86 percent of the votes cast in the referendum he had called.

In June 1989, all of the other republic party leaderships were obliged to attend the Serbian party's mammoth celebration of the 600-year anniversary of the Battle of Kosovo. Surrounded by an unruly crowd of at least one-half million, they heard Slobodan Milošević deliver a threatening speech that recalled how Serbs had fought for their rights in the past. The need to fight for them again in the future "should not be excluded." The other leaders and the television audiences back in their republics saw a Serbia whose leadership of a larger coalition to restructure the federation they could never accept.

Kučan's Slovenian party stood aside that summer while a number of alternative political movements, not yet legally parties, formed alongside the Slovenian Democratic Alliance, the Demos. They had already constituted themselves in January 1989 and were demanding the right to form a separate political party. By September a series of amendments to the republic's constitution gave it to them, along with the promise of multi-party elections by early 1990. The fifty-four amendments concentrated on rights to nullify unwanted federal legislation, but also included, contrary to Article Five of the 1974 constitution, the right to secede from the federation *without* the mutual consent of the other republics.

The Milošević forces countered with the demand that Ljubljana host one of their mass "meetings of truth," to which some 40,000 Serbs and Montenegrins would travel to persuade the Slovenes how wrong they were about Kosovo. Kučan and his colleagues occupied a far stronger position than had the aging, passive nomenklatura of the Vojvodina, who had been unable to stop such a meeting or to keep their positions afterwards. Confident of support from the alternative movements and the public, the Slovene leaders rejected Serbia's demand. In a final exchange, the Serbian party's Socialist Alliance lent official support to the boycott of Slovenian consumer goods, generally regarded as the best produced in Yugoslavia, that had begun a year earlier. Over 300 Serbian firms now cancelled contracts and ended all business relations with Slovenian firms. The Slovenian side cut its contribution to the federal budget by 15 percent and sent its contribution to the federal fund for underdeveloped regions (FADURK) directly to Kosovo rather than through Belgrade.

A stormy stage was thus set for the federal party's 1990 congress, moved forward six months to January because of the growing domestic confrontation and the dramatic collapse of one East European Communist regime after another during the previous November and December. The JNA leadership had been urging an extraordinary meeting since 1986 in order to reestablish the authority of the federal party. Now the meeting was advertised as the "Congress of Salvation" only because it promised the multi-party elections that their former Soviet bloc neighbors were already scrambling to announce. Croatia's League of Communists had finally turned out Šuvar and his associates in December 1989, naming the forty-year-old liberal, Ivica Račan, to head the party. The new leadership promptly approved the right of other political parties to exist and to contest the forthcoming elections. The Croatian Democratic Union (HDZ) had in fact already established itself that previous February, without authorization, under the leadership of Franjo Tudjman. A former Partisan and retired JNA general who had turned nationalist historian by the late 1960s, he was twice sent to prison as such in 1972 and 1982–84. Nonetheless allowed to travel abroad, he had assembled considerable support among the large number of politicized Croat émigrés by the late 1980s. During the summer of 1989, extremist followers of the HDZ in Dalmatia mounted enough physical attacks on local Serbs to make the new party's nationalist rhetoric seem truly threatening. Krajina Serbs staged their own confrontations with local Croats and, encouraged by the Milošević media, began to demand autonomy within Croatia, cultural if part of Yugoslavia and political if not. A direct Serb-Croat confrontation had always threatened the very survival of any Yugoslavia, from the first such fatal intersection in 1927–28 forward (see chapter 5).

By 1990 the federal party had little leverage, outside of the JNA, with which to face these predominantly rural tensions when it assembled in Belgrade that January for the last time. The delegates never had the chance to address the Serb-Croat issues. The Slovenian representatives quickly introduced a proposal that would have made their recent constitutional amendments the framework for a still looser confederation that was little more than an economic union. Neither they nor the Milošević proposals for tightening the federation could win a majority, and the Slovenian delegation promptly walked out of the congress. Because the four Milošević votes now outnumbered the three of the remaining republics, Croatian representatives refused to continue without Slovenia. The Slovenian party left the League of Communists two weeks later and renamed itself the Party of Democratic Renewal. At this point, the federal party effectively ceased to exist.[18] Yet the promise of market reform and multi-party elections allowed the Socialist Federal Republic of Yugoslavia to survive for another year and a half.

Shock therapy and the Marković interregnum

Real momentum for market reforms had surfaced briefly in 1965–66 (see chapter 9). It belatedly reemerged toward the end of 1988. Under pressure from the international financial community, the Mikulić regime had launched three promising initiatives that were already at work by the time Ante Marković became head of the Federal Executive Council in March 1989. Under a new agreement with the International Monetary Fund, Yugoslavia freed imports from the variety of quotas and special tariffs that still restricted access to 90 percent of import value at the start of 1988. By year's end, the figure fell to 45 percent, and to 13 percent by December 1989. The latest law on foreign investment finally removed the inhibiting restrictions on ownership and profits that had left the 1967 law a dead letter. The 1988 law also gave private investors the chance to acquire a stake, albeit ill-defined, in social enterprises. By replacing the 1976 Law on Associated Labor, it mercifully ended the ill-fated subdivision of enterprise workers' councils into Basic Organizations (OOUR). In February 1989, a third law on financial operations required social enterprises to declare bankruptcy if they lacked the actual resources to cover their debt obligations. Supporting labor legislation removed the requirement that enterprises guarantee employment to the existing labor force. Although the procedure did not go as far as the media speculated it would, it still put one of every fifteen social enterprises, employing one-half million workers, on notice that they were insolvent and their employees' jobs were at risk.[19]

The burden of domestic price controls, ineffective in stopping inflation but still capable of distorting the allocation of resources, remained to be lifted. Marković made free pricing one of three priorities for the rest of 1989. By the year's end, he had freed three-quarters of all producers' and retail prices for industrial goods and was pushing to free the rest. The immediate result, of course, turned the 250 percent inflation of 1988 into a hyperinflation of 2,500 percent during 1989. The price explosion actually served his subsequent effort to establish a stable rate of exchange for the dinar and a centrally controlled supply of money. Whereas the rate for one dollar slipped only from 12.5 to 20 during the period 1965–79, the dinar had entered free fall during the 1980s, passing 300 by 1985 and 1,000 by 1988. The currency's collapse ended the longstanding overvaluation of the dinar relative to domestic inflation that had favored imports over exports through the 1970s.[20] Western creditors applauded, as it generated the current account surpluses needed to service and also reduce foreign debt. The hyperinflation of 1989 made it clear to Ante Marković, if not to all Western interests, that the foreign investment needed to balance newly liberated imports would never come unless their profits could be earned in predictably stable and convertible dinars.

By June he had appropriately fastened on to the National Bank of Yugoslavia (NBJ) as the lever by which the supply of money and credit, and hence the rate of inflation and exchange, could be reined in, much as the Balcerowicz regime in Poland would do so successfully in 1991–92. The Marković initiative stripped the NBJ of its right to offer "selective credits" to politically favored enterprises or projects at interest below the rate of inflation. The basic banks and the federation also lost their access to automatic credits from the NBJ. Most importantly, he extracted from the various republic representatives an agreement to allow the bank to enforce these and other decisions by majority rather than unanimous vote.

Once the hyperinflation of 1989 had wrung the last dinar reserves out of enterprises trying to buy their way around the new market mechanisms, Marković used the NBJ and federal reserves of hard currency to support the complete revaluation of January 1, 1990. The new dinar was pegged at eleven to the dollar, its convertibility at that rate fully backed by the aforementioned reserves and its issue closely controlled by the NBJ to prevent inflation from reappearing. The bank's initial success in maintaining this discipline made observers muse over what a difference such steps would have made if instituted long before. The rate of inflation quickly declined to nil, and the huge holdings of hard currency to which many enterprises and individuals had resorted began to be converted to dinars. By May the inflow of foreign exchange significantly exceeded the outflow. By summer a booming tourist season and an improving trade balance made it seem that Yugoslavia had finally turned Point No Point, after failing to do so in 1965–66 (see chapter 9). Some domestic advantage seemed at last to beckon from the current account surpluses and the redirection of exports to the OECD countries (over one-half by 1988) that had been achieved during the 1980s.[21] Public opinion polls showed Ante Marković to be the most popular politician in Yugoslavia half way through 1990.

What went wrong during the second half of 1990 to restart inflation and derail the economic confidence that convinced Yugoslavs to hold dinars instead of marks or dollars? Real economic pressures were of course accumulating. Positive interest rates and a still heavy burden of taxes – federal, republic, and local – made it difficult for an increasing number of enterprises to pay even their frozen wages on time, let alone invest in expansion. These pressures plus the end of state subsidies and the new bankruptcy procedures threatened, or could be seen to threaten, fully half of the labor force in social enterprises with the loss of their jobs. Under such conditions, the National Bank proved unable to prevent the republic governments from forcing additions to the money supply on their territory. Slovenia and Croatia started and the others followed suit. In September and October, Yugoslavia's monthly rate of inflation reached 8 percent, or 120 percent if continued for a full year.

Serbia's authorities finished off any chance for resuming monetary restraint in December. On the eve of the republic's elections, they took half of the drawing rights of the entire federation, $1.5 billion worth of dinars, without NBJ authorization and used the money to pay back wages, pensions, and bonuses to enterprise and government employees. The Milošević leadership of what had become the Socialist Party of Serbia put an ironic end to his own 1988 program for reintegrating the Yugoslav economy under tighter monetary and fiscal discipline. By 1990, however, even Milošević had abandoned reintegration. Marković's restructuring and austerity could not survive the resistance to federal authority that emerged from that year's election campaigns in every republic. Nor could Marković's own popularity continue, once the republics had left the early fruits of those reforms to wither.

Elections and ethnic politics

The breakup of the League of Communists that January prompted the last prime minister to predict that Yugoslavia could survive as a state without the SKJ. He failed to recognize that the state still needed a country-wide election or party. With one or the other, some sort of single if confederal entity might have endured even at this late date. Early in the year, Marković's Federal Executive Council (SIV) put forward plans for a country-wide referendum, scheduled for December 1990, but the still Communist leaderships of the various republics could not agree on the questions to be posed. By that time a series of elections in all the

11.1 Muslim woman returning to East Mostar in July 1992 after Serb forces were defeated by an initial Croat/Muslim alliance in June

republics had swept some of the Communists aside or left others, led by Slobodan Milošević, who were least suited to negotiate a country-wide compromise or to agree on country-wide elections.

Ante Marković belatedly acknowledged the need for a new country-wide party and took the leadership of an Alliance of Reform Forces that he proclaimed before a large Bosnian crowd on July 29. But it was not large enough. By December the SIV's own polling showed that the Alliance was attracting just 14 percent of Bosnian voters and less than 5 percent in all republics.[22] The other new party to speak for Yugoslav unity only frightened away more of the undecided public. This was the reconstituted League of Communists, the Movement for Yugoslavia (SK, Pokret za Jugoslaviju) that Serb and Montenegrin members of the military's top leadership had established in November. Its small following did not extend much beyond the officer corps and failed to record any success even in Serbia's elections.

Serbia's elections were among the last of the multi-party campaigns that set Yugoslavia's political stage for the country's disintegration the following year. Some sixty parties had already declared their intention to participate in the various republic elections by early 1990. By the time that they were held, 235 parties had declared themselves in some fashion. The much-analyzed elections that drew them forth made a significant contribution to disintegration and the bloody business that began in 1991. Of the six republic elections, Communist adversaries won four, although in every republic except Bosnia-Hercegovina a former Communist won the presidency. Milošević's four votes in the still existing Yugoslav presidency had become two, Montenegro and a Serbia that included Kosovo and the Vjovodina in this more decisive arena. Here he could never hope to impose his terms for a unified Yugoslavia, and he would reject all others. With these elections, what Dennison Rusinow has correctly called an "avoidable catastrophe" had become unavoidable.[23]

The Slovenian elections, appropriately, came first in April 1990. Nearly 60 percent of the public still favored some sort of Yugoslavia, but fewer than 20 percent were willing to grant primary powers to any set of federal authorities (compared to the more than 80 percent in Serbia and Montenegro who would). This confederal, rather than secessionist, disposition led many Slovenes to split their votes in parliamentary and presidential elections. The reconstituted Communist Party (ZKS–SPD) won only 14 of 73 seats in the still surviving Socio-Political Chamber, while the Demos' coalition of six opposition parties took 47. But Milan Kučan won the presidency over the Demos' candidate, on the basis of what he had done as a Communist leader since 1986, as well as his party's new "European Union" flag and demands for financial independence from the federation. By the December referendum on whether to remain in the federation on any terms, 95 percent of the equally large turnout of eligible voters opted for independence.

Croatian voters could not split their ballots because the new Sabor, or parliament, that replaced the Social-Political Chamber was empowered to elect the president. During the first round of April–May elections to the Chamber, the two parties representing the reformed Communists (SKH–SDP) and the liberal Centrists did much better than their Slovenian counterparts, winning 57 percent of the vote versus 35 percent. But their division allowed the largest single vote-getter, the Croatian Democratic Alliance (HDZ) to prevail with 42 percent. Favored by the absence of proportional representation as well as a flood of émigré financing for their nationalist campaign, the HDZ took 54 of 80 seats. Their comparable advantage in the Sabor made the May 30 vote, which elected party leader Franjo Tudjman as president of Croatia, a foregone conclusion. Although the new government did not conduct a referendum proposing independence until May 1991, its media campaign exulted in "a Croatia for Croatians only." This campaign encouraged the excesses of local supporters and returning émigrés. They forced Serbs not only out of local police forces as authorized, but from administrative and enterprise positions as well. In the areas where the Serbs were most concentrated, along the old Habsburg Military Border, such wholesale dismissals seemed to confirm the worst local fears. At the same time, local Croats also sacked or seized Serbian-owned vacation houses along the Adriatic coast. Few Croatian Serbs listened to the more judicious statements of Franjo Tudjman once he had been elected president. Nor did they credit offers for conciliation from the coalition government formed under Stipe Mešić, the Communist whom Tudjman soon named to replace the implacably hostile Stipe Šuvar in the Yugoslav presidency. The rioting between Serb and Croat fan clubs that broke up the last soccer match in Zagreb with a Belgrade team, between the same two whose players had jointly wept over Tito's death in 1980, gave public opinion a different preview of coming attractions. Thus did ominous portents for an independent Croatia feed the further fears of an Ustaša return to power about which the Milošević media in Belgrade and local Croatian Serb leaders were already fantasizing. They endlessly cited Tudjman's early campaign speech to a HDZ conference packed with returning émigrés where he denied that the wartime Independent State of Croatia (see chapter 7) was simply "the creation of fascist criminals" and argued that "it also stood for the historic aspirations of the Croatian people for an independent state."[24]

The specter of a reincarnated Independent State of Croatia admirably served Milošević's campaign to preserve the power of both his party and his presidency. Of all the republic party leaders in 1986, he was the only one to survive with his party still on top. The first step was to convert Serbia's League of Communists into a new party. This he did virtually overnight on July 16. A hastily called League congress simply voted to change the party's name to the Socialist Party of Serbia (SPS). His media's coverage obscured the fact that 111 of the 135 members of the new party's ruling committee came from the old nomenklatura. Instead they dutifully trumpeted a slogan attributed to Milošević's wife and new party vice president, Mirjana Marković, that "the time of the Left is ahead of us." Milošević's picture now replaced Tito's in public places. The Serbian media linked Tudjman's campaign rhetoric minimizing Serb losses in the Second World War with the real local abuses that Croatian Serbs were facing. Despite this propaganda offensive, despite the earlier currency raid to provide back salaries, and despite the restricted access to the media given a half dozen opposing parties, the SPS fell short of an absolute majority in the December elections to the new Serbian parliament. But the same lack of proportional representation as in Croatia gave them 194 of 240 seats. Milošević himself won 65 percent of the votes for the presidency. One of his first acts as president was to allow the interior ministry to set up the Serbian Voluntary Guards. This permitted individuals such as Željko Ražnjatović, alias Arkan, a wanted criminal in Western Europe and a known associate of the former Yugoslavia's security service (SDB), to form a paramilitary group calling themselves the Tigers. Helsinki Watch would identify Arkan's Tigers as the perpetrators of war crimes in Bijeljina and other Bosnian towns in the summer of 1992.[25]

The Macedonian and Montenegrin elections produced results suggesting that Yugoslavia might still somehow survive. Over 1,000 candidates from 16 parties and some independents competed in the November elections for the 120 seats in the Macedonian parliament. The six major parties all agreed on the desirability of preserving Yugoslavia and of persevering with the Marković reforms. His Alliance won 19 of the seats and the restructured League, 30, more than the 37 captured by the nationalist coalition using the name of the Internal Macedonian Revolutionary Organization (VMRO) from the interwar period (see chapter 6). The resulting parliament elected the reform Communist, Kiro Gligorov, as president. In the Montenegrin elections of December, the young reform Communist, Momir Bulatović, preserved the power that Milošević had given to him and his equally young colleagues in 1988 by winning the presidency and also two-thirds of the parliamentary seats for his reconstituted Communist Party. Both Gligorov and Bulatović supported the Marković reforms as well as the continued existence of Yugoslavia.

The December elections in Bosnia-Hercegovina should have given the Marković reforms and his Alliance their strongest endorsement. Instead, the Alliance won only 13 of 240 seats in the first round and none in the second. A reconstituted Communist Party, independent of the Milošević forces, captured 18 seats. All of the others went to the three ethnic parties or their ethnic rivals. The Muslim Party of Democratic Action (SDA), under the dissident Alija Izetbegović, released from his 1983 prison sentence in 1988, took 80 seats in the second round, with 13 also going to the more secular but émigré Muslim leader, Adil Zulfilkarpašić and his MBO Party. Hercegovina was largely responsible for giving the Bosnian branch of Tudjman's HDZ 44 of the 49 seats won by Croat candidates. Finally, the strident nationalist, Radovan Karadžić, and his Serbian Democratic Party (SDS) took 72 of the 85 positions won by Serbs. During the campaign, each of the three ethnic leaders had maintained that they could work together as the Communists never could to protect Bosnia-Hercegovina's separate interests inside Yugoslavia. Once the campaign was over, however, they quickly turned to the separate ethnic programs which would help to drag them into the wars of Yugoslav succession by 1992. The three parties each immediately restaffed with their own people the local government of all districts where they had won a majority. They all agreed to begin redividing Sarajevo's school population along strictly ethnic lines before classes began again in the autumn of 1992. In the absence of almost any other agreement between the three parties, the authority asserted by the new "Muslim presidency" of Alija Izetbegotić provided the challenge that Karadžić sought in any case. Izetbegović had some brief success in overcoming SDS objections to his government with a proposal for preserving a "Yugoslav state community of independent former republics" as an asymmetric federation. It promised to keep Bosnia closer to Serbia than to a largely independent Slovenia and Croatia. The proposal endured in some form until early 1992, although its terms were never spelled out.

It was already too late. The previous summer, Slovenia had come through its brief, artfully provoked confrontation with the JNA to win independence. Croatia's war with the JNA and an admixture of Croatian Serb and Serbian militias was under way. The ethnically mixed élites of urban Sarajevo and Tuzla nonetheless remained confident that their cities and their celebrated cultural integration would make it impossible for war to spread to Bosnia-Hercegovina.[26] Their confidence survived the October decision of Karadžić and the SDS to leave the parliament in

Sarajevo and establish a rival one in the Bosnian Serb center of Banja Luka. It even survived the SDS-led boycott of the February 29, 1992, referendum to proclaim Bosnian independence, as evidenced by the huge demonstration in Sarajevo for peaceful reconciliation of all differences the day after the election.

The city's confidence failed to reckon with the momentum of the SDS's paranoid propaganda, reinforced from Belgrade, and the JNA's long-standing concentration of men and especially equipment in the republic. The SDS would make a fatal connection with the shrinking Serb population of the republic, particularly in the upland areas where resentment of cosmopolitan Sarajevo was combined with grievances from the Second World War against the local Muslims, whom these Serbs still called Turks. The SDS leader, the Montenegrin psychiatrist and amateur poet, Radovan Karadžić, stoked their anxieties with his reckless predictions of Serbs subjected to a fundamentalist Islamic regime if Izetbegović were to head an independent state. Karadžić seemed at first to welcome the belated effort of the European Community (EC) in February 1992 to create a cantonal formula for living together in a single state. Izetbegović did not, but reluctantly agreed to the plan put forward in Lisbon by the EC's Portuguese mediator, Jose Cuthiliero. On returning to Sarajevo, the Bosnian president's own misgivings and objections from his own party prompted his change of mind, rather than the brief conversation with American Ambassador Warren Zimmermann that some accounts have called crucial. An EC meeting in Brussels to enhance the role of a Bosnian central government succeeded only in provoking Karadžić's rejection of the plan.[27]

At the same time, neither the Izetbegović government nor the radical Hercegovina wing that took over leadership of the Croats' HDZ could face the prospect of continuing in the rump Yugoslav federation. The departure of Slovenia and Croatia had left a Milošević majority of Serbia, Kosovo, the Vojvodina, and Montenegro. The Bosnian declaration of independence on March 3, 1992, virtually guaranteed that the Bosnian Serbs, supported by Milošević's Serbia and the JNA leadership, would follow Karadžić's inflammatory lead and consolidate a separate, entirely Serbian territory unless the declaration were withdrawn. Neither President Izetbegović's decision to mobilize territorial defense units on April 4 nor the much debated European and American decision to recognize Bosnia-Hercegovina on April 6, then postponed by a day so as to coincide with the anniversary of the Nazi invasion of Yugoslavia and the bombing of Belgrade in 1941, should be considered primary causes of the cruel war that began two days later. Rather they gave former JNA units, reconfigured since January to be nearly

90 percent Bosnian Serbs, and militias from Serbia as well as Bosnia a final reason to initiate the widespread warfare and notorious ethnic cleansing that followed. Such JNA units had already stood by while Arkan's Serbian militia savaged the Muslim residents of Bijeljina on April 1, several days before the mobilization order or international recognition. Bosnian Croat militias supported from Croatia soon began cleansing their own strongholds. When the Bosnian government responded by expanding its tiny, predominantly Muslim forces, and Serbia's government refrained from sending more than logistical support and individual officers from its own JNA units across the border, the conflict inevitably turned into a civil war.[28]

What ended in Bosnia-Hercegovina in 1992 was the long search for a Yugoslav identity, in the very republic whose ethnic diversity made it a microcosm of what any Yugoslavia had to be, however the idea behind it was abused. Now, after seventy years of two Yugoslavias created by two world wars and their survivors, another war has incinerated even the identity. Perhaps the saddest of the present survivors are those for whom the ashes still glow. For they were Yugoslavs, and once, or twice, they had a country.

Notes

INTRODUCTION: THE SEARCH FOR VIABILITY

1 See Mark Thompson, *Forging War: The Media in Serbia, Croatia, and Bosnia-Hercegovina* (Avon: The Bath Press, Article 19, 1994); and for the historical raw material, Djurdja Knežević, "The Enemy Side of National Ideologies, Serbia and Croatia," in *Pride and Prejudice: National Stereotypes in 19th and 20th Century Europe East to West*, ed. Laszlo Knotler (Budapest: Central European University, 1995), 105–17.

2 A Bosnian of Croat birth, Andrić became a Belgrade-based diplomat for the first Yugoslavia and its last ambassador to Germany. By the end of the interwar period, he considered himself a Serbian writer. In his most famous work, the episodic 1945 novel, *The Bridge on the Drina* (Chicago: University of Chicago Press, 1977 ed.), he portrayed the capacity for multi-ethnic accommodation between individuals and, in the face of frequent natural disasters, between groups that sometimes bridged the mistrust that foreign domination along a mountainous fault line between East and West had bred in his native Bosnia. And sometimes not, but because of his resignation to ethnic divisions in a fractured landscape rather than any defense of them. Krleža, born in Zagreb in 1893 the year after Andrić and Tito, defended Croatia's distinctive literary heritage but was otherwise a life-long Marxist scourge of "true-believers" in any narrow ethnic or ideological identity. See the instructive comparison of Krleža and Andrić in Ralph Bogert, *The Writer as Naysayer: Miroslav Krleža and the Aesthetic of Interwar Central Europe* (Columbus, Ohio: Slavica Publishers, 1988), 82–87.

3 Zečević berated the notion of "an ancient and unlinear aspiration, created before the formation of nations, that was coordinated in its motives and interests and constantly on the rise," as cited in Ivo Banac, "Historiography of the Countries of Eastern Europe, Yugoslavia," *American Historical Review* 97, 4 (1992): 1085. For Zečević's more recent views, see his "Slovenci i jugoslovenska država, 1917–1989" (Slovenians and the Yugoslav state), *Istorija 20og veka* 12, 2 (1994): 31–46.

4 Stevan K. Pavlowitch, *The Improbable Survivor: Yugoslavia and its Problems, 1918–1988* (Columbus, Ohio: Ohio State University Press, 1988), 129–42; and Banac, "Historiography of the Countries," 1084–1104.

5 Vojislav Koštunica and Kosta Čavoški, *Party Pluralism or Monism? Social Movements and the Political System in Yugoslavia, 1944–1949* (New York: Columbia University Press, East European Monographs, 1983). Tudjman's

only translated work is *Nationalism in Contemporary Europe* (Boulder, Colo.: East European Monographs, 1981); but far more revealing is the controversial early edition, since revised, of *Bespuća povijesne zbilnosti: Rasprava o povijesti i filosofiji zlosilje* (Impasses of historical reality: A discussion of the history and philosophy of malevolent power), 2nd ed. (Zagreb: Matica Hrvatska, 1989).

6 See Anthony D. Smith, *National Identity* (London: Penguin Books, 1991), 26-28.

7 Eugen Weber, *Peasants into Frenchmen: The Modernization of Rural France, 1870–1914* (Stanford, Calif.: Stanford University Press, 1975).

8 Rogers Brubaker, *Citizenship and Nationhood in France and Germany* (Cambridge, Mass.: Harvard University Press, 1992). On the moderating power of several "interlocking identities," see Yael Tamir, *Liberal Nationalism* (Princeton: Princeton University Press, 1993), 153–63.

1 EMPIRES AND FRAGMENTED BORDERLANDS, 800–1800

1 E. L. Jones, *The European Miracle* (Cambridge: Cambridge University Press, 1981). On the population density in the early modern period, particularly in the Ottoman Balkans, see Bruce McGowan, *Economic Life in Ottoman Europe: Taxation, Trade, and the Struggle for Land, 1600–1800* (Cambridge: Cambridge University Press, 1981), 2–14. On the role of the Danube in the Balkans, the classic source remains David Mitrany, *The Effect of the War in Southeastern Europe* (New Haven, Conn.: Carnegie Endowment for International Peace and Yale University Press, 1936), 6–14.

2 Fernand Braudel, *The Mediterranean and the Mediterranean World in the Age of Philip II* (New York: Harper and Row, 1972), I: 25–44, 137–47.

3 George W. Hoffman, *Regional Development Strategy in Southeastern Europe* (New York: Praeger, 1972), 3–20.

4 A. P. Vlasto, *The Entry of the Slavs into Christendom* (Cambridge: Cambridge University Press, 1970), 187–203. On Croatian origins and their medieval state more generally, see John V. A. Fine, Jr., *The Early Medieval Balkans* (Ann Arbor, Mich.: University of Michigan Press, 1983), 49–59, 248–91; and on the considerable Byzantine connection, see Ivo Goldstein, *Bizant na Jadranu* (Byzantium on the Adriatic) (Zagreb: Latina and Graeca, 1992).

5 Vlasto, *Entry of the Slavs*, 213–23.

6 On medieval Serbia generally, see Fine, *Early Medieval Balkans*, 202–47; and the second volume, Fine, *The Late Medieval Balkans* (Ann Arbor, Mich.: University of Michigan Press, 1987), 219–312. A recent view of the Serbian role in Byzantine history is Donald M. Nicol, *The Last Centuries of Byzantium, 1261–1452*, 2nd ed. (Cambridge: Cambridge University Press, 1993), 118–21, 129–30, 176–79, 229–30.

7 Traian Stoianovich, *Balkan Worlds: The First and Last Europe* (Armonk, NY: M. E. Sharpe, 1994), 151–68. In this survey of social estates across the medieval Balkans, he stresses both their relative complexity and the lack of rigid, European-style, barriers between them.

8 John V. A. Fine, Jr., *The Bosnian Church: A New Interpretation* (New York: Columbia University Press, 1975); and more broadly, Noel Malcolm,

Bosnia: A Short History (New York: New York University Press, 1994), 13–42. An excellent summary of Yugoslav scholarship on medieval Bosnia is the offprint volume in English from the unfinished second edition of the *Enciklopedia Jugoslavije, The Socialist Republic of Bosnia and Hercegovina* (Zagreb: Jugoslovenski leksikografski zavod, 1983), 60–67.

9 The most extensive Western survey of the Balkans' Ottoman period, with careful attention to native scholarship, is Peter F. Sugar, *Southeastern Europe under Ottoman Rule 1453–1803* (Seattle, Wash.: University of Washington Press, 1977). Concise, informed treatments of the Ottoman land regime and *millet* system, respectively, may be found in Fikret Adanir, "Tradition and Rural Change in Southeastern Europe during Ottoman Rule," in *The Origins of Backwardness in Eastern Europe*, ed. Daniel Chirot (Berkeley, Calif.: University of California Press, 1989), 131–76; and Kemal Karpat, "Millets and Nationality: The Roots of the Incongruity of Nation and State in the Post-Ottoman Era," in *Christians and Jews in the Ottoman Empire*, ed. Benjamin Braude and Bernard Lewis (New York: Holmes and Meier, 1982), I: 141–69.

10 On early modern Macedonia, see Fikret Adanir, *Die makedonische Frage: Ihre Entstehung und Entwicklung bis 1900* (The Macedonian question: its origin and development to 1900) (Wiesbaden: Franz Steiner Verlag, 1979); and Nikos Svoronos, *La commerce de la Salonique en XVIIIe siècle* (Trade in Salonika in the eighteenth century) (Paris, 1956).

11 Fine, "The Medieval and Ottoman Roots of Bosnian Society," in *The Muslims of Bosnia-Hercegovina*, ed. Mark Pinson (Cambridge, Mass.: Harvard University Press, 1994), 1–21; Malcolm, *Bosnia*, 51–70; Sugar, *Southeastern Europe*, 55–59. On Ottoman Bosnia, see also the encyclopedia article by Ahmed Aličić "The Period of Turkish (Ottoman) Rule," *Enciklopedia Jugoslavije, The Socialist Republic of Bosnia and Hercegovina*, 67–77.

12 Smail Balić, *Die unbekannte Bosnien* (The unknown Bosnia) (Cologne: Bohlau Verlag, 1992), 101–7. On the Bosnian Muslims, see also Srečko Džaja, *Konfessionalität und Nationalität Bosniens und der Hercegowina: voremancipatorische Phase, 1463–1804* (Religion and Nationality in Bosnia and Hercegovina: The preemancipatory phase) (Munich: R. Oldenbourg Verlag, 1984).

13 Michael B. Petrovich, "Religion and Ethnicity in Eastern Europe," in *Ethnic Diversity and Conflict in Eastern Europe*, ed. Peter F. Sugar (Santa Barbara, Calif.: ABC Clio Press, 1980), 383–90; and also Petrovich, *A History of Modern Serbia* (New York: Harcourt Brace Jovanovich, 1976), I: 7–18, provide the best brief accounts.

14 On the battle's role in that tradition, see Wayne S. Vucinich and Thomas A. Emmert, eds., *Kosovo: Legacy of a Medieval Battle* (Minneapolis, Minn.: Minnesota Mediterranean and East European Monographs, 1991); on Serbian epics, *Serbian Poetry from the Beginning to the Present*, ed. Milne Holton and Vasa D. Mihailovich (Columbus, Ohio: Slavica Publications, 1988).

15 On early modern Montenegro, see Barbara Jelavich, *History of the Balkans* (Cambridge: Cambridge University Press, 1983), I: 84–87.

16 The recent critique of early Habsburg history by R. J. D. Evans describes the Habsburg Counter-Reformation as incomplete everywhere, first retreating in the face of local superstitions and then vulnerable to the rationalist challenge of Emperor Joseph II in the 1780s. See the epilogue to his *The Making of the Habsburg Monarchy, 1550–1570* (Oxford: Clarendon Press, 1979), 346–50. For a more comprehensive survey of earlier Habsburg history, see Charles Ingrao, *The Habsburg Monarchy, 1618–1815* (Cambridge: Cambridge University Press, 1994).

17 Francis Dvornik, *The Slavs in European Civilization* (New Brunswick, NJ: Rutgers University Press, 1962), 132, 419–27; and for details, see *Zgodovina Slovencev* (A history of the Slovenes) (Ljubljana: Cankarjeva založba, 1979). On Linhart, see Michael B. Petrovich, "The Rise of Modern Slovenian Historiography," *Journal of Central European Affairs* 22, 4 (January 1963): 440–67.

18 Toussaint Hočevar, *The Structure of the Slovenian Economy, 1848–1963* (New York: Studia Slovenica, 1965), 6–14.

19 On the distribution of the patriarchal *zadruga* of fifteen or more members, across the Yugoslav lands primarily around the Habsburg Military Border and in Montenegro and central Serbia, see Maria N. Todorova, *Balkan Family Structure and the European Pattern: Demographic Developments in Ottoman Bulgaria* (Washington, DC: American University Press, 1993), 133–58.

20 On the Croatian Military Border, the seminal works in English remain Gunther E. Rothenberg, *The Austrian Military Border in Croatia, 1522–1747* (Chicago: University of Chicago Press, 1960); and Rothenberg, *The Military Border in Croatia, 1740–1881* (Chicago: University of Chicago Press, 1966). On the efforts of some upland Croat and Serb migrants to stay free of either imperial border regime by marauding along the Adriatic coast, see Catherine Wendy Bracewell, *The Uskoks of Senj: Piracy, Banditry, and the Holy War in the 16th Century Adriatic* (Ithaca, NY: Cornell University Press, 1992).

21 See Drago Roksandić, *Srbi u Hrvatskoj* (Serbs in Croatia) (Zagreb: Vjesnik, 1991), 55–70.

22 Jozo Tomasevich, *Peasants, Politics, and Economic Change in Yugoslavia* (Stanford, Calif.: University Press, 1955), 70–72; Slavko Gavrilović, *Agrarni pokreti u Sremu i Slavoniji na početkom XIX veka* (Agrarian movements in Srem and Slavonia at the start of the nineteenth century) (Belgrade: SANU, 1960), 9–14.

23 Ivo Banac, *The National Question in Yugoslavia: Origins, History, Politics* (Ithaca, NY: Cornell University Press, 1983), 73–74. On early modern Croatian history, see Stanko Guldescu, *The Croatian-Slavonian Kingdom, 1526–1792* (The Hague: Mouton, 1970).

24 John R. Lampe and Marvin R. Jackson, *Balkan Economic History, 1550–1950* (Bloomington, Ind.: Indiana University Press, 1982), 51–55. On early modern Dubrovnik, see Francis W. Carter, *Dubrovnik (Ragusa): A Classic City-State* (London: Seminar Press, 1972).

25 Lampe and Jackson, *Balkan Economic History*, 56–61.

26 Ibid., 62–66; and Traian Stoianovich, "The Conquering Orthodox Balkan Merchant," *Journal of Economic History* 20 (1960): 243–313.

27 Michael B. Petrovich, "Croatian Humanists and the Writing of History in the Fifteenth and Sixteenth centuries," *Slavic Review* 38, 4 (December 1978): 624–39.

28 Lampe and Jackson, *Balkan Economic History*, 62–66.

29 Roger V. Paxton, "Identity and Consciousness: Culture and Politics among the Habsburg Serbs in the Eighteenth Century," in *Nation and Ideology: Essays in Honor of Wayne S. Vucinich*, ed. Ivo Banac, John G. Ackerman, and Roman Szporluk (New York: Columbia University Press, 1981), 101–18.

2 UNIFYING ASPIRATIONS AND RURAL RESISTANCE, 1804–1903

1 Robert Tucker, *The Marxian Revolutionary Idea* (New York: W. W. Norton, 1967).

2 These seminal works are Benedict Anderson, *Imagined Communities: Reflections on the Origins and Spread of Nationalism* (London: Verso Books, 1983); Eric Hobsbawm, *Nations and Nationalism since 1780*, 2nd ed. (Cambridge: Cambridge University Press, 1990). See also Ernest Gellner, *Nations and Nationalism* (London: Basil Blackwell, 1983).

3 Jozo Tomasevich, *Peasants, Politics, and Economic Change in Yugoslavia* (Stanford, Calif.: Stanford University Press, 1955), 115–17.

4 See Jaroslav Šidak, *Hrvatski narodni preporod Ilirski pokret* (The Croatian national renaissance, the Illyrian movement) (Zagreb: Školska knjiga, 1990); for a discussion of the best Croatian scholarship on both the Illyrian provinces and the later movement, see especially pages 26–35.

5 See John R. Lampe, "The Failure of the Yugoslav National Idea," *Studies in East European Thought* 46, 1–2 (June 1994): 127–47.

6 Elinor Murray Despalatović, *Ljudevit Gaj and the Illyrian Movement* (New York: Columbia University Press, East European Quarterly, 1975), 71–78.

7 Elinor Murray Despalatović, "The Illyrian Solution to the Problem of a National Identity for the Croats," *Balkanistica* 1 (1974): 82–84. On Hungarian reactions to Illyrian pressures, see János Varga, *A Hungarian Quo Vadis: Political Trends and Theories of the 1840s* (Budapest: Akadémiai Kiadó, 1993), 89–109.

8 Bogdan Krizman, "The Croatians in the Habsburg Monarchy in the Nineteenth Century," *Austrian History Yearbook* 3, pt. 2 (1967): 116–58; and Drago Roksandić, *Srbi u Hrvatskoj* (Serbs in Croatia) (Zagreb: Vjesnik, 1991), 86–87.

9 Philip Adler, "Why Did Illyrianism Fail?," *Balkanistica* 1 (1974): 95–103; and Despalatović, *Ljudevit Gaj*, 197–201.

10 Traian Stoianovich, *Balkan Worlds: The First and Last Europe* (Armonk, NY: M. E. Sharpe, 1994).

11 Michael B. Petrovich, "The Role of the Serbian Orthodox Church in the First Serbian Uprising," *The First Serbian Uprising, 1804–1813*, ed. Wayne S. Vucinich (New York: Columbia University Press, East European Monographs, 1982), 259–302.

12 Michael B. Petrovich, *A History of Modern Serbia, 1804–1918* (New York: Harcourt Brace Jovanovich, 1976), I: 103–28.

13 On the economy of Miloš Obrenović's Serbia, see John R. Lampe and Marvin R. Jackson, *Balkan Economic History, 1550–1950: From Imperial Borderlands to Developing Nations* (Bloomington, Ind.: Indiana University Press, 1982), 109–19; on its social structure, see Stevan K. Pavlowitch, "Society in Serbia, 1791–1830," *Balkan Society in the Age of Greek Independence*, ed. Richard Clogg (Totowa, NJ: Barnes and Noble, 1981), 137–56.

14 The classic work in any language remains Slobodan Jovanović, *Ustavobranitelji, 1838–1858* (The defenders of the constitution) (Belgrade: Geca Kon, 1912).

15 On the place of Jovanović and his colleagues in the framework of contemporary European liberalism, see Gale Stokes, *Legitimacy through Liberalism: Vladimir Jovanović and the Transformation of Serbian Politics* (Seattle, Wash.: University of Washington Press, 1975); on the wider Serbian framework, see Stevan K. Pavlowitch, "The Constitutional Development of Serbia in the Nineteenth Century," *East European Quarterly* 5 (January 1972): 56–67.

16 See David MacKenzie, *Ilija Garašanin, Balkan Bismarck* (New York: Columbia University Press, East European Monographs, 1985).

17 Wayne S. Vucinich, "The Serbs in Austria-Hungary," *Austrian History Yearbook* 3, pt. 2 (1967): 4–8; David MacKenzie, "Serbian Nationalist and Military Organizations and the Piedmont Idea, 1844–67," *East European Quarterly* 16, 3 (1982): 323–33.

18 Stokes, *Legitimacy through Liberalism*, 115–20; Petrovich, *History of Modern Serbia*, I: 313–30.

19 Gale Stokes, *Politics as Development: The Emergence of Political Parties in Nineteenth Century Serbia* (Durham, NC: Duke University Press, 1990), 179, 201–3. On the brief life and later role of Svetozar Marković, see Woodford McClellan, *Svetozar Marković and the Origins of Balkan Socialism* (Princeton: Princeton University Press, 1964); on the influence of French Radicalism and by 1890, British parliamentarism (rule by the majority party), see Milan St. Protić, *Radikali u Srbiji, 1881–1903* (Belgrade: Balkanološki Institut, 1990).

20 Dimitrije Djordjević, "The 1883 Peasant Uprising in Serbia," *Balkan Studies* 20 (1979): 235–55. For further details and references, see Andrija Radenić, *Iz istorije Srbije i Vojvodine, 1838–1914* (Novi Sad: Matica srpska, 1973), 439–556.

21 Stokes, *Politics as Development*, 291–306, provides a concluding summary of the author's argument.

22 Lampe and Jackson, *Balkan Economic History*, 208–12.

23 Ibid., tables 4.2, 6.7–6.8, and 6.13. The strongest evidence of the limitations facing nineteenth-century Serbian agriculture is presented by Michael R. Palairet, "Fiscal Pressure and Peasant Impoverishment in Serbia before World War I," *Journal of Economic History* 39 (September 1979): 331–62.

24 Lampe and Jackson, *Balkan Economic History*, 159–86.

25 Michael R. Palairet, "The Culture of Economic Stagnation in Montenegro," *The Maryland Historian* 17 (1986): 17–42. For further detail, see Žarko Bulajić, *Agrarni odnosi Crne Gore, 1878–1912* (Agrarian relations of Montenegro) (Titograd, 1959).

26 Mirjana Gross, "Croatian National-Integrational Ideologies from the End of Illyrianism to the Creation of Yugoslavia," *Austrian History Yearbook* 15–16 (1979–80): 4–21.

27 Mirjana Gross and Agneza Szabo, *Prema hrvatskome gradjanskom društvu* (Toward Croatian bourgeois society) (Zagreb: Globus, 1992), 266–68. For a summary of recent scholarship on the *Ausgleich*, see Alan Sked, *The Decline and Fall of the Habsburg Empire, 1815–1918* (London: Longman, 1989), 187–97. Hungary had won much broader rights from Vienna the year before under the famous Ausgleich, thereby converting the Habsburg monarchy into the Dual Monarchy of Austria-Hungary.

28 Gross and Szabo, *Prema hrvatskome gradjanskom društvu*, 257–61; MacKenzie, *Ilija Garašanin*, 307–8.

29 The most detailed study of Starčević in English is Mario S. Spalatin, "The Croatian Nationalism of Ante Starčević," *Journal of Croatian Studies* 16 (1975): 19–146. Also see Ivo Banac, *The National Question in Yugoslavia: Origins, History, Politics* (Ithaca, NY: Cornell University Press, 1984), 85–91; on Karadžić and his broader involvement in the Illyrian Movement, culminating in his signature on the 1850 Vienna agreement with Croatian representatives on a common literary language, but for two alphabets and two peoples, see Duncan Wilson, *The Life and Times of Vuk Stefanović Karadžić, 1787–1864* (Oxford: Clarendon Press, 1970), 294–313.

30 Gross and Szabo, *Prema hrvatskom gradjanskom društvu*, 603–7. The only thorough treatment of the Mažuranić era of Croatian liberalism, comparable to the contemporary Serbian era of Vladimir Jovanović, is James Krokar, "Liberal Reform in Croatia, 1872–1875: The Beginnings of Modern Croatia under Ban Ivan Mažuranić" (Ph.D. diss., Indiana University, 1980).

31 Manuela Dobos, "The Nagodba and the Peasantry in Croatia-Slavonia," *The Peasantry of Eastern Europe*, ed. Ivan Volgyes, I (New York: Pergamon Press, 1931), 79–107; and "The Croatian Peasant Uprising of 1883" (Ph.D. diss., Columbia University, 1974).

32 Gunther E. Rothenberg, "The Croatian Military Border and the Rise of Yugoslav Nationalism," *The Slavonic and East European Review* 43–44 (1964): 34–45.

33 See Justin McCarthy, "Ottoman Bosnia, 1800–1878," *The Muslims of Bosnia-Herzegovina*, ed. Mark Pinson (Cambridge, Mass.: Harvard University Press, 1994), 54–83; "The Socialist Republic of Bosnia and Hercegovina," *Enciklopedia Jugoslavije*, 5: 77–90. On early modern Bosnian population, see Traian Stoianovich, *Balkan Worlds*, 146.

34 On the Austrian occupation, see Robert J. Donia, *Islam under the Double Eagle: The Muslims of Bosnia and Hercegovina, 1878–1914* (New York: Columbia University Press, East European Monographs, 1981), 4–29, 41–49, 181–94. On Serbia's role in the Bosnian uprising and subsequent defeat, see David MacKenzie, *The Serbs and Russian Pan-Slavism, 1875–1878* (Ithaca, NY: Cornell University Press, 1967).

35 Peter F. Sugar, *The Industrialization of Bosnia-Hercegovina, 1878–1914* (Seattle, Wash.: University of Washington Press, 1963), 13–45..

36 Robin Okey, "Education and Modernization in a Multi-Ethnic State: Bosnia, 1850–1914," in *Schooling, Educational Policy, and Ethnic Identity*, ed.

Janusz Tomiak (New York: New York University Press, European Science Foundation, 1986), I: 319–41.

37 Ibid., I: 328–39; Mustafa Imamović, "O historiji bošnjačkog pokušaja" (On the history of the Bošniak attempt), in *Muslimani i Bošnjaštvo* (The Muslims in Bosnia), ed. Arif Purivatra (Sarajevo, 1991), 31–70.

38 Mirjana Gross, "The Union of Dalmatia with Northern Croatia," *The National Question in Europe in Historical Context*, ed. Mikulas Teich and Roy Porter (Cambridge: Cambridge University Press, 1993), 270–92.

39 Carole Rogel, *The Slovenes and Yugoslavism, 1890–1914* (Boulder, Colo.: East European Quarterly, 1977), 15–26; Fran Zwitter, "The Slovenes and the Habsburg Monarchy," *Austrian History Yearbook* 3, pt. 2 (1967): 159–88.

3 NEW DIVISIONS, YUGOSLAV TIES, AND BALKAN WARS, 1903–1914

1 John R. Lampe and Marvin R. Jackson, *Balkan Economic History, 1555–1950, From Imperial Borderlands to Developing Nations* (Bloomington, Ind.: Indiana University Press, 1982), 281–97; Jozo Tomasevich, *Peasants, Politics, and Economic Change in Yugoslavia* (Stanford, Calif.: Stanford University Press, 1955), 151–59; and Arnold Suppan, "Die Kroaten," *Die Habsburgermonarchie, 1848–1918*, ed. Adam Wandruszka and Peter Urbanitsh (Vienna: Verlag der ÖAW, 1980), III: 627–33, 694–701.

2 Lampe and Jackson, *Balkan Economic History*, tables 9.1, 9.5.

3 Ibid., tables 6.1–6.5, 9.2, 10.4. The total number of enterprises employing mechanical horsepower and more than twenty workers was roughly one-quarter of that one-half million, divided among 36,000 workers in Slovenia; 24,000 in Croatia-Slavonia; 30,000 in Bosnia-Hercegovina; 16,000 in Serbia; perhaps 10,000 each in Dalmatia and Macedonia; and a negligible number in Montenegro. For a more positive view of economic and industrial growth in the Habsburg borderlands, see David Good, *The Economic Rise of the Habsburg Empire, 1750–1914* (Berkeley, Calif.: University of California Press, 1984).

4 Marina Cattaruzza, "Slovenes, Italians, and Trieste, 1850–1914," *Ethnic Identity in Urban Europe*, ed. Max Engman (New York: European Science Foundation, New York University Press, Dartmouth, 1985), 189–209.

5 This network made a greater contribution to Slovenian than Dalmatian agriculture. Nearly 40 percent of Slovenian agricultural land was in profitable smallholdings of 20 to 40 hectares by 1910, and the debts accumulating for many smaller holdings were sufficiently relieved by the credit unions to prevent foreclosure. The Dalmatian inland peasantry, about four-fifths Croat and one-fifth Serb, continued to confront the sharecropping obligations of the *colonate* system (noted in chapter 2) until the 1930s. Some 86 percent of their own holdings were under 5 hectares, and 59 percent under 2 hectares. The phylloxera epidemic of the 1890s in addition had damaged the vineyards that provided their best cash crop.

Walter Lukan, "The Second Phase of Slovene Cooperation (1894–1918)," *Slovene Studies* 11, 1 (1989): 83–96; Toussaint Hočevar, *The Structure of the Slovenian Economy, 1848–1963* (New York: Studia Slovenica, 1965), 59–73.

6 Carole, Rogel, *The Slovenes and Yugoslavism, 1890–1914* (Boulder, Colo.: East European Quarterly, 1977), 76–87.

7 Bogdan Krizman, "The Croatians in the Habsburg Monarchy in the Nineteenth Century," *Austrian History Yearbook* 3, 2 (1967): 135–40; and Wayne S. Vucinich, "The Serbs in Austria-Hungary," ibid., 23–27.

8 Lampe and Jackson, *Balkan Economic History*, 315–19; Suppan, "Die Kroaten," 679; and Igor Karaman, *Industrializacija gradjanske Hrvatske (1800–1941)* (The industrialization of bourgeois Croatia) (Zagreb: Naprijed, 1991).

9 Lampe and Jackson, *Balkan Economic History*, 287–97; on literacy and schooling in Croatia-Slavonia, see Elinor Murray Despalatović, "The Danish Model and Croatian Peasant Agriculture, 1850–1914," in *Private Agriculture in Eastern Europe*, ed. John R. Lampe (Washington, DC: East European Studies, The Woodrow Wilson International Center for Scholars, 1990), 24–25.

10 Rudolf Signjar, *Statistički atlas Kr. Hrvatske i Slavonije, 1875–1915* (Zagreb: Zemalski statistički ured, 1915), 49.

11 Nicholas Miller, "Two Strategies in Serbian Politics in Croatia and Hungary before the First World War," *Nationalities Papers* 23, 2 (1995): 327–51. Mirjana Gross, *Vladavina Hrvatske-Srpske Koalicije, 1906–1907* (The regime of the Croatian-Serbian coalition) (Belgrade: Jugoslavenski Istorijski Institut, 1960).

12 Elinor Murray Despalatović, "The Peasant Nationalism of Ante Radić," *Canadian Review of Studies in Nationalism* 1 (1978): 86–97; Robert G. Livingston, "Stjepan Radić and the Croatian Peasant Party, 1904–1929" (Ph.D. diss., Harvard University, 1959), 58–63.

13 Peter F. Sugar, *The Industrialization of Bosnia-Hercegovina, 1878–1914* (Seattle, Wash.: University of Washington Press, 1963); Ferdinand Schmid, *Bosnien und die Herzegovenien* (Bosnia and Hercegovina) (Leipzig: [publisher unknown], 1914).

14 For a contrary view that, had war not intervened, the 1908 annexation would have led to the sort of boom in private entrepreneurship after state pump-priming that was under way during the last prewar decade in tsarist Russia, see Michael Palairet, "The Habsburg Industrial Achievement in Bosnis-Hercegovina, 1878–1914: An Economic Spurt That Succeeded?" *Austrian History Yearbook* 24 (1993): 133–52.

15 Schmid, *Bosnien*, 312, 550–52. Also see Tomasevich, *Peasants, Politics*, 107–11.

16 The only clearly successful, official policy, beyond the Brčko promotion of plum cultivation and drying for export in the 1880s, was the spread of poultry raising in the northwestern Bihać triangle after 1900. This precedent, on which Fikret Abdić and his Agrokomerc enterprise would build in the 1970s, emerged from the one pre-1914 case where primarily female labor was employed. Priscilla T. Gonsalves, "Study of the Habsburg Agricultural Programmes in Bosanska Krajina, 1878–1914," *Slavonic and East European Review* 63 (1985): 349–71.

17 Robert J. Donia, *Islam under the Double Eagle: The Muslims of Bosnia and Hercegovina, 1878–1914* (New York: Columbia University Press, East

European Monographs, 1981), 167–94. See also Robin Okey, "Education and Modernization in a Multi-Ethnic Society: Bosnia, 1850–1918," in *Schooling, Educational Policy, and Ethnic Identity*, ed. Janusz Tomiak (New York: European Science Foundation, New York University Press, Dartmouth, 1985), 319–41.

18 On Pašić and Serbia's lively if not ideologically divided political spectrum after 1900, see Wayne S. Vusinich, *Serbia between East and West: The Events of 1903–08* (Stanford, Calif.: Stanford University Press, 1954), 17–21; and Trotsky's neglected but acute observations in *The War Correspondence of Leon Trotsky, The Balkan Years, 1912–13*, ed. George Weisman and Duncan Williams (New York: Monad Press, 1980), 68–111. On Pašić himself, the one detailed study is Vasa Kazimirović, *Nikola Pašić i njegova doba, 1845–1925* (Nikola Pašić and his era), 2 vols. (Belgrade: Nova Evropa, 1990).

19 John R. Lampe, "Austro-Serbian Antagonism and the Economic Background to the Balkan Wars," in *East Central European Society and the Balkan Wars*, ed. Bela Kiraly and Dimitrije Djordjević (New York: Columbia University Press, Social Science Monographs and Atlantic Research and Publications, 1987), 336–45. The definitive study is Dimitrije Djordjević, *Carinski rat Austro-Ugarske i Srbije, 1906–1911* (The tariff war between Austria-Hungary and Serbia) (Belgrade: Istorijski Institut, SANU, 1962). On the role of King Petar, see Dragoljub R. Živojinović, *Kralj Petar I Karadjordjević*, v. II (Belgrade: Beogradski izdavačko-grafički zavod, 1990).

20 This was only the third brief episode of Russian support for Serbia, following the First Uprising in 1806–12 and the Hercegovina revolt of 1876–78. None of the support brought with it the official weight or military force to see Serbia through. There would not be more, unless one counts the equally brief period of Stalin's support for Tito's Communist government in 1944–48, while that government destroyed the last vestiges of the Serbian democratic heritage from its pre-1914 statehood – a multi-party system of parliamentary government under a constitutional monarch. On pre-1914 relations between Serbia and Russia, see Barbara Jelavich, *Russia's Balkan Entanglements, 1804–1914* (Cambridge: Cambridge University Press, 1991), 9–23, 144–77, 235–65.

21 Gale Stokes, "Milan Obrenović and the Serbian Army," *East Central European Society in World War I*, ed. Bela Kiraly and Nandor F. Dreiszinger (New York: Columbia University Press, East European Monographs, 1985), 555–68; David MacKenzie, "Serbian Nationalist and Military Organizations and the Piedmont Idea, 1844–1914," *East European Quarterly* 16, 3 (1982): 333–43.

22 That is the persuasive conclusion to be drawn from the sections on Serbia in Charles Jelavich, *South Slav Nationalisms, Textbooks, and Yugoslav Union before 1914* (Columbus, Ohio: Ohio State University Press, 1990). Serbia's program for primary education, with only 5.8 percent of the total population in school in 1910, lagged behind Bulgaria's 9.3 percent, primarily because of a slow start before 1890. See Holm Sandhaussen, *Historische Statistik Serbiens, 1834–1914* (Munich: R. Oldenbourg Verlag 1989), 551–55.

23 On Skerlić and Belgrade's cultural life, see Jelena Milojković-Djurić, *Tradition and Avant-Garde Literature and Art in Serbian Culture, 1900–1918* (New York: Columbia University Press, East European Monographs, 1981), 129–68; on the "Belgrade style," see Traian Stoianovich, *Balkan Worlds: The First and Last Europe* (Armonk, NY: M. E. Sharpe, 1994), 283–301; and on Belgrade in general, see John R. Lampe, "Modernization and Social Structure: The Case of the Pre-1914 Balkan Capitals," *Southeastern Europe* 5, pt. 2 (1979): 11–32. On Matoš and Zagreb's cultural life, see James Krokar, "National Cultural Centers of the Habsburg Empire before 1914: Zagreb," *Austrian History Yearbook* 19–20 (1983–84): 119–33.

24 Radmila Milentijević, "Serbian Social Democracy Confronts the Nationality Question," *Canadian Review of Studies in Nationalism* 1 (1978): 66–85. A similar split emerged at the Czech-sponsored Neo-Slav meeting of 1909 in St. Petersburg and prevented any Serbs or Croats from Croatia-Slavonia from attending the 1910 meeting in Sofia. Paul Vyšny, *Neo-Slavism and the Czechs* (Cambridge: Cambridge University Press, 1977), 119, 151–52, 191–92.

25 Stephen Raditch, "Autobiography of Stephen Raditch," *Current History* (October, 1928): 5–10. This brief, posthumously translated autobiography, with an introduction by Charles A. Beard, and the above-cited doctoral dissertation of Gerald Livingston provide the only lengthy citations from Radić in English.

26 On the neglected role of Hungarian-Croatian antagonism in the growing South Slav alienation from the Dual Monarchy during the last prewar decade, see Gabor P. Vermes, "South Slav Aspirations and Magyar Nationalism in the Dual Monarchy," in *Nations and Ideology, Essays in Honor of Wayne Vucinich*, ed. Ivo Banac, John G. Ackerman, and Roman Szporluk (New York: Columbia University Press, East European Monographs, 1981), 177–200; and Ivo Banac, "Croat-Magyar Relations, 1904–1914: A New Jelačić or the 'New Course'?" *Slovene Studies* 9, 1–2 (1987): 43–48.

27 Wayne S. Vicinich, "*Mlada Bosna* and the First World War," in *The Habsburg Empire in the First World War*, ed. Robert A. Kann, Bela Kiraly, and Paula S. Fichtner (New York: Columbia University Press, East European Quarterly, 1977), 45–69.

28 Duncan M. Perry, *The Politics of Terror, The Macedonian Revolutionary Movements, 1893–1903* (Durham, NC: Duke University Press, 1988), 196–212. More clearly, the followers of the Internal Macedonian Revolutionary Organization (VMRO) were a peasant minority reacting to exploitation under the persisting *chiftlik* regime of sharecropping in the lowlands and extortion by Albanian and other Muslim warlords in the uplands rather than acting on any sense of Macedonian or Bulgarian national identity. Perry reckons their total number at less than 25,000, or about 1 percent of the three *vilayet*, with supporters adding another 2–4 percent.

29 Steven W. Sowards, *Austria's Policy of Macedonian Reform* (New York: Columbia University Press, East European Monographs, 1989), 25–95.

30 Ernst C. Helmreich, *The Diplomacy of the Balkan Wars, 1912–13* (Cambridge, Mass.: Harvard University Press, 1938). The most recent works are Andrew Rossos, *Russia and the Balkans: Inter-Balkan Rivalries and Russian Foreign*

Policy, 1908–1914 (Toronto: Toronto University Press, 1981); and Samuel R. Williamson, Jr., *Austria-Hungary and the Origins of the First World War* (New York: St. Martin's Press, 1991).

31 Williamson, *Austria-Hungary*, 103–8; Andrej Mitrović, *Srbija u prvom svetskom ratu* (Serbia in the First World War) (Belgrade: Srpska književna zadruga, 1984), 136–37.

32 Miller, "Two Strategies," *Nationalities Papers*, 327–51.

33 Vucinich, "Serbs in Austria-Hungary," 7; Jaroslav Šidak, Mirjana Gross, Igor Karaman, and Dragovan Šepić, *Povijest hrvatskog naroda, 1860–1914* (The history of the Croatian people, 1860–1914) (Zagreb: Školska knjiga, 1968), 284–86.

34 Rogel, *Slovenes and Yugoslavism*, 82–103, 113–16.

35 *The Other Balkan Wars, A 1913 Carnegie Endowment Inquiry in Retrospect* (Washington, DC: Carnegie Endowment Book, 1993), 158–86, 395–97.

36 Danica Milić, "Economic Consequences of the Balkan Wars," *East Central European Society and Balkan Wars*, 386–94; Lampe and Jackson, *Balkan Economic History*, 232–36. For the flurry of German interest in offering some financial support to Serbia in the wake of the Balkan Wars, see Andrej Mitrović, *Prodor na Balkan i Srbija, 1908–1914* (Balkan penetration and Serbia) (Belgrade: Nolit, 1981), 131–76.

37 For a Serbian view, see Alexander Dragnich and Slavko Todorović, *The Saga of Kosovo* (New York: Columbia University Press, East European Monographs, 1984), 95–109.

38 Vucinich, *"Mlada Bosna,"* 59. For a sense of the Montenegrin historical memory of 1876–78, see the novel by Milovan Djilas, *Under the Colors* (New York: Harcourt Brace Jovanovich, 1971).

39 John D. Treadway, *The Falcon and the Eagle: Montenegro and Austria-Hungary, 1908–1914* (West Lafayette, Ind.: Purdue University Press, 1983), 203–12.

40 Milorad Ekmečić, "Impact of the Balkan Wars on Society in Bosnia and Hercegovina," *East Central European Society and the Balkan Wars*, 260–85; *Enciklopedija Jugoslavije: The Socialist Republic of Bosnia and Hercegovina* (Zagreb: Jugoslavenski leksikografski zavod, 1983), 95–97. For details, see Mustafa Imamović, *Pravni položaj i unutrašni politički razvitak Bosne i Hercegovine, 1878–1914* (The legal position and internal political development of Bosnia and Hercegovina) (Sarajevo: Svjetlost, 1976), 236–58.

41 Vucinich, *"Mlada Bosna,"* 56. The most detailed scholarly argument for the independence from Serbian control of Princip and his colleagues is Vladimir Dedijer, *The Road to Sarajevo* (New York: Simon and Schuster, 1966), 175–234. The continuing insistence of Austrian scholarship on Serbian control may be seen in Hellmut Andics, *Der Untergang der Donaumonarchie* (Vienna: Wilhelm Goldmann Verlag, 1981), 86–93

4 THE FIRST WORLD WAR AND THE FIRST YUGOSLAVIA, 1914–1921

1 See the citations in Milorad Ekmečić, "Serbian War Aims," *The Creation of Yugoslavia, 1914–1918*, ed. Dimitrije Djordjević (Santa Barbara, Calif.: ABC

Clio Press, 1980), 25–26; and Bogdan Kirzman, *Hrvatska u prvom svetskom ratu* (Croatia in the First World War) (Zagreb: Globus, 1989), 245–57.

2 Ekmečić, "Serbian War Aims," 19–36. On the Niš Declaration, see Dragoslav Janković, "Niška deklaracija" (The Niš declaration), *Istorija XX veka* 10 (1969): 7–111; on Cvijić and the Serbian scholars, see Ljubinka Trgovčević, *Naučnici Srbije i stvaranje Jugoslovenske države, 1914–1920* (Serbian scholars and the creation of the Yugoslav state) (Belgrade: Narodna knjiga, 1986); and on the 1914 campaigns themselves, Dimitrije Djordjević, "Vojvoda Putnik: The Serbian High Command and Strategy in 1914," in *East Central European Society in World War I*, ed. Bela K. Kiraly and Nandor F. Dreiszinger (New York: Columbia University Press, East European Monographs, 1985), 569–89.

3 Gale Stokes, "The Role of the Yugoslav Committee in the Formation of Yugoslavia," *Creation of Yugoslavia*, 51–72. Also see Ivo Lederer, *Yugoslavia at the Paris Peace Conference* (New Haven, Conn.: Yale University Press, 1963), 3–78; and Dragovan Šepić, *Italija, saveznici i Jugoslovensko pitanje, 1914–18* (Italy, the Allies, and the Yugoslav question) (Zagreb: Školska knjiga, 1970).

4 Andrej Mitrović, *Srbija u prvom svetskom ratu* (Serbia in the First World War) (Belgrade: Srpska književna zadruga, 1984), 312–19. Also see David MacKenzie, *Apis, the Congenital Conspirator: The Life of Colonel Dragutin T. Dimitrijević* (Boulder, Colo.: East European Monographs, 1989).

5 Bogdan Krizman, *Raspad Austro-Ugarske i stvaranje jugoslovenske države* (The fall of Austria-Hungary and the creation of the Yugoslav state) (Zagreb: Školska knjiga, 1977), 262. The most comprehensive work is Dragoslav Janković, *Jugoslovensko pitanje i Krfska deklaracija 1917 g.* (The Yugoslav question and the 1917 Corfu declaration) (Belgrade: Savremena administracija, 1967).

6 Whether any challenge short of massive armed resistance would have been successful is, however, doubtful. On the political-military and socio-economic experience of Bulgaria and its effects in Macedonia for 1915–18, see Richard Crampton, *Bulgaria, 1878–1918* (New York: Columbia University Press, East European Monographs, 1983), 447–510.

7 Richard B. Spence, "The Yugoslav Role in the Austro-Hungarian Army, 1914–18," *East Central European Society*, 354–68.

8 Bogdan Krizman, "The Croatians in the Habsburg Monarchy in the 19th Century," *Austrian History Yearbook* 3, 2 (1967): 146–57; and Krizman, "Plan Stjepana Radića o preuredjenju Habsburške monarhije" (Plan of Stjepan Radić for the transformation of the Habsburg monarchy), *Istorija XX veka* 12 (1972): 31–82.

9 Neda Engelsfeld, *Prvi parliament Kraljevstva Srba, Hrvata i Slovenaca* (First parliament of the Kingdom of Serbs, Croats, and Slovenes) (Zagreb: Globus, 1989), 64–68; Ivo Banac, "Nemiri u severnoj Hrvatskoj u jesen 1918" (Unrest in northern Croatia in the fall of 1918), *Časopis za suvremenu povijest* 24, 3 (1992): 23–43.

10 While no opinion polls are available to support this judgment, contemporary estimates of Austro-Hungarian officials as well as Yugoslav advocates reckon that by the autumn of 1918, popular support for creating such a state had

grown significantly to reach 50 percent in Bosnia-Hercegovina, 60 percent in Croatia-Slavonia, and much higher proportions in Dalmatia and Slovenia. See Ekmečić, "Serbian War Aims," *The Creation of Yugoslavia, 1914–1918*, 25–26.

11 See Richard B. Spence, "General Stephan Freiherr Sarkotić von Lovćen and Croatian Nationalism," *Canadian Review of Studies in Nationalism* 17, 1–2 (1990): 147–55.

12 A comparative accounting of these losses is Jozo Tomasevich, *Peasants, Politics, and Economic Change in Yugoslavia* (Stanford, Calif.: Stanford University Press, 1955), 220–29. For Serbia, see John R. Lampe, "Unifying the Yugoslav Economy, 1918–1921: Misery and Early Misunderstandings," *Creation of Yugoslavia*, 141–42; and Dimitrije Djordjević, "Austro-ugarski okupcioni režim u Srbiji i njegov slom" (Austro-Hungarian occupation regime in Serbia and its fall). *Naučni skup u povodu 50-godišnice raspada Austro-ugarske monarhije* (Scientific gathering on the 50th Anniversary of the fall of Austria-Hungary) (Zagreb: JAZU, 1969), 206–23.

13 Krizman, *Raspad Austro-ugarske*, 270–79; Djordje Stanković, *Nikola Pašić, saveznici i stvaranje Jugoslavije* (Nikola Pašić, the Allies and the creation of Yugoslavia) (Belgrade: Nolit, 1984), 241–50.

14 Krizman, *Raspad Austro-ugarske*, 263–69; Touissant Hočevar, *The Structure of the Slovenian Economy 1848–1963* (NY: Studia Slovenica, 1965), 155–57.

15 Wayne Vucinich, "The Formation of Yugoslavia," *Creation of Yugoslavia*, 183–206; Dragoslav Janković, "Ženevska konferencija 1918 g.," *Istorija XX veka* 5 (1963): 25–62.

16 See Robert Gerald Livingston, "Stjepan Radić and the Croatian Peasant Party, 1904–1929" (Ph.D. diss., Harvard University, 1959), 252; and Jure Krišto, "Katoličko proklanjanje ideologiji jugoslavenstva" (Catholic disposition toward the ideology of Yugoslavism), *Časopis za suvremenu povijest* 24, 2 (1992): 25–45.

17 On the army's growth, initial popularity in restoring order, and subsequent problems with assuming civil functions, see Mile Bjelajac, *Vojska Kraljevine Srba, Hrvata i Slovenaca, 1918–1921* (Army of the Kingdom of Serbs, Croats, and Slovenes) (Belgrade: Narodna knjiga, 1988).

18 Bogdan Krizman, "Medjunarodne priznanje Jugoslavije 1918 g." (International recognition of Yugoslavia, 1918), *Istorija XX veka* 3 (1962): 345–82; Vasa Čubrilović and Andrej Mitrović, eds., *Stvaranje jugoslovenske države 1918* (Belgrade: Naučna knjiga, 1989). For a recent overview of Italian policy as seen by American scholarship and sources, see Arthur Walworth, *Wilson and His Peacemakers, American Diplomacy at the Paris Peace Conference, 1919* (New York: W. W. Norton, 1986), 335–58. A Yugoslav view drawing on all sources is Dragoljub Živojinović, *America, Italy, and the Birth of Yugoslavia, 1917–19* (Boulder, Colo.: East European Monographs, 1972). On the background to Italian claims, see Dennison Rusinow, *Italy's Austrian Heritage, 1919–1946* (London: Oxford University Press, 1969), 15–50.

19 Lederer, *Yugoslavia at the Paris Conference*, 112–14, 138–68, 194, 252, 262–72, 286, 306–8.

20 Rusinow, *Italy's Austrian Heritage*, 119–60; Bogdan C. Novak, *Trieste, 1941–1954* (Chicago, Ill.: University of Chicago Press, 1970), 27–42.

21 Arnold Suppan, "According to the Principle of Reciprocity: The Minorities in Yugoslav–Austrian Relations, 1918–1938," *Ethnic Groups in International Relations*, ed. Paul Smith (New York: European Science Foundation, New York University Press, Dartmouth, 1986), 251–54; Bogdan Krizman, "Jugoslavija i Austrija, 1918–1938," *Časopis za suvremenu povijest* 9 (1977).

22 C. A. Macartney, *Hungary and Her Successors* (London: Oxford University Press, 1937), 390–404; Vuk Vinaver, *Jugoslavija i Madjarska, 1918–1933* (Belgrade: Institut za savremenu istoriju, 1970).

23 The postwar departure of roughly 40,000 Albanians to Turkey or elsewhere trimmed their total in Kosovo to 400,000, but still left them with a two-to-one majority, even after the arrival of some 60,000 Serb colonists during the course of the interwar period. Serbian historians date that Albanian majority only from the period 1878–1912, when roughly 150,000 Serbs were forced out or attracted to Serbia. Alex N. Dragnich and Slavko Todorović, *The Saga of Kosovo* (New York: Columbia University Press, East European Monographs, 1984), 118–21. The Albanian counterclaim is that around 150,000 Kosovar Albanians were forced from the province between 1912 and 1920.

24 Elizabeth Barker, *Macedonia* (1950; reprint, Westwood, Conn.: Greenwood Press, 1980), 23–26.

25 The following section is drawn from Lampe, "Unifying the Yugoslav Economy," 139–56.

26 Ivo Banac, *The National Question in Yugoslavia. Origins, History, Politics* (Ithaca, NY: Cornell University Press, 1983), 248–60; and Banac, "'Emperor Karl has become a Comitadji': The Croatian Disturbances of Autumn 1918," *Slavonic and East European Review* 70, 2 (1992): 284–305.

27 The classic Croatian indictment of the currency conversion is Rudolf Bićanić, *Ekonomska podloga hrvatskog pitanja* (Economic basis of the Croatian question) (Zagreb: Vladko Maček, 1938), 41–46.

28 Engelsfeld, *Prvi parlament*, 263–67.

29 Branislav Gligorijević, *Parlament i političke stranke u Jugoslaviji, 1919–1929* (Parliament and political parties in Yugoslavia) (Belgrade: Institut za savremenu istoriju, 1979), 73–84; and Banac, *National Question in Yugoslavia*, 379–87, offer well-informed but contrasting views of this discrepancy.

30 Ivan Avakumović, *History of the Communist Party of Yugoslavia*, I (Aberdeen: Aberdeen University Press, 1964), 25–59; Ivo Banac, "The Communist Party of Yugoslavia During the Period of Legality, 1919–1921," *The Class War after the Great War: The Rise of Communist Parties in East Central Europe, 1918–1921*, ed. Ivo Banac (Boulder, Colo.: East European Monographs, 1982), 188–230.

31 Charles A. Beard and George Radin, *The Balkan Pivot: Yugoslavia* (New York: Macmillan, 1929), 30–56; Slobodan Jovanović, *Iz istorije i knjižvnosti* (From history and literature) 11, I (Belgrade: BIGZ, 1991), 363–81.

32 Gligorijević, *Parlament i političke stranke*, 94–114; Ferdo Čulinović, *Jugoslavija izmedju dva rata* (Yugoslavia between the two wars) (Zagreb: JAZU, 1961), I: 349–77.

5 PARLIAMENTARY KINGDOM, 1921–1928

1 Charles A. Beard and George Radin, *The Balkan Pivot: Yugoslavia* (New York: Macmillan, 1929), 57–64. In the absence of a scholarly biography needed on Aleksandar, see Stephen Graham, *Alexander of Yugoslavia* (New Haven, Conn.: Yale University Press, 1939), 79–138. A collection of his public statements may be found in Živan Miloradović-Major, *Govori* (Speeches) (Belgrade: Lingua, 1991).

2 The difficulties of the army's transition are detailed in Mile Bjelajac, *Vojska Kraljevine Srba, Hrvata i Slovenaca, 1918–1921* (The army of the Kingdom of Serbs, Croats, and Slovenes) (Belgrade: Narodna knjiga, 1988).

3 Beard and Radin, *Balkan Pivot*, 180–86, 279–99. The annual reports of the British Embassy in Belgrade (Public Record Office, FO 371, London), although sometimes inclined to give the king the benefit of the doubt, provide the most comprehensive and insightful accounts of Yugoslavia available from the diplomatic records of the 1920s.

4 See Djordje Stanković, *Nikola Pašić, saveznicvi i stvaranje Jugoslavije* (Nikola Pašić, the Allies, and the creation of Yugoslavia) (Belgrade: Nolit, 1984); and also his psychological portrait of Pašić in *Iskušenja jugoslovenske istorografije* (Disappointments of Yugoslav historiography) (Belgrade: Rad, 1988), 273–85, for a more critical analysis than the one biography in English, Alex N. Dragnich, *Serbia, Nikola Pašić, and Yugoslavia* (New Brunswick, NJ: Rutgers University Press, 1974).

5 Arif Purivatra, *Jugoslovensksa muslimanska organizacija u političkom životu Kr. SHS* (Yugoslav Muslim Organization in the political life of the Kingdom of Serbs, Croats, and Slovenes) (Sarajevo: Svetlost, 1974), 11–47, 539–47. Also see Ivo Banac, "Bosnian Muslims," in *The Muslims of Bosnia-Herzegovina*, ed. Mark Pinson (Cambridge, Mass.: Harvard University Press, 1994), 129–54.

6 Janko Prunkt, *Slovenski narodni vzpon* (The Slovenian national ascent) (Ljubljana: Državna Založba Slovenije, 1992), 201–55; Momčilo Zečević, *Na istorijskoi prkretnici: Slovenci u politici jugoslvenske države, 1918–1929* (At an historical turning point: Slovenes in the politics of the Yugoslav state, 1918–1929) (Belgrade: Prosveta, 1985), 251–313.

7 Branislav Gligorijević, *Parlament i političke stranke u Jugoslaviji, 1919–1929* (Parliament and political parties in Yugoslavia, 1918–1929) (Belgrade: Narodna knjiga, 1979), 138–49.

8 The Comintern's Marxist insistence on giving industrial workers priority over peasants in the proposed republics was not a prospect Radić could accept, but other attractions had drawn him to Moscow. For Radić, Slavic romanticism about Russia joined with the chance to promote a Balkan federation that would include Bulgaria and to reject the Prague-based Green International that recognized the existing Yugoslav state. Ferdo Čulinović, *Jugoslavija izmedju dva ratu* (Yugoslavia between the two wars) (Zagreb: JAZU, 1961), I: 402–4. This earlier volume from Zagreb along with Gligorijević's view from Belgrade, provides the most detailed political history of the decade available from the former Yugoslavia's Marxist historiography.

9 Robert Gerald Livingston, "Stjepan Radić and the Croatian Peasant Party, 1904–1929" (Ph.D. diss., Harvard University, 1959), 474–82. Perhaps the

best measure of Radić as a political personality, complete with extensive quotation from his political statements, may be found in Josip Horvat's interwar journalist's account, *Politička povijest Hrvatske 1918–1929* (Zagreb: August Cesarac, 1989 edn.).

10　Glivorijević, *Parlament*, 188–95; Čulinović, *Jugoslavija*, I: 446–54.

11　The most detailed and precise account in English of the 1920–27 elections remains Joseph Rothschild's chapter on Yugoslavia in his *East Central Europe between the Two Wars* (Seattle, Wash.: University of Washington Press, 1974), 205–80. Opposition representatives and even voters were kept away from polling places. Some Radical ballots were cast on behalf of Serbia's wartime dead; British Embassy reporting spoke of one Serbian town where Radical officials had laid out tram tracks only to remove them after the election.

12　Lenard J. Cohen, *The Socialist Pyramid, Elites, and Power in Yugoslavia* (Oakville, Ontario: Mosaic Press, 1989), 259–65. Also see Beard and Radin, *Balkan Pivot*, 266–78.

13　Zečević, *Na istorijskoj prekretnici*, 313–45.

14　Branislav Gligorijević, "Politička istorija, 1919–1929," in *Istorija Beograda*, ed. Vasa Čubrilović (Belgrade: Prosveta, 1974), III: 88–99, 144–49.

15　Ivan Avakumović, *History of the Communist Party of Yugoslavia* (Aberdeen: Aberdeen University Press, 1964), I: 60–92. Citation covers the period 1921–28.

16　Stephen Palmer and Robert King, *Yugoslav Communism and the Macedonian Question* (Hamden, Conn.: Archon Books, 1971), 31–46.

17　Branislav Gligorijević, *Kominterna-jugoslovensko i srpsko pitanje* (The Comintern: The Yugoslav and Serbian question) (Belgrade: Institut za savremenu istoriju, 1992), 1–236, provides a scholarly but newly critical Serbian view of the growing Croatian ascendance in the KPJ during the 1920s.

18　Tomislav Bogovac, *Stanovništvo Beograda, 1918–1991* (Population of Belgrade, 1918–1991) (Belgrade: Beogradski izdavački zavod, 1991), 69–81.

19　Ljubomir Durković-Jakšić, *Jugoslovensko knjižarstvo, 1918–1941* (Yugoslav publishing, 1918–1941) (Belgrade: Narodna knjiga, 1979); J. Dubrovac, "Štamparstvo u Beogradu, 1918–1941" (The press in Belgrade, 1918–1941) in *Istorija Beograda*, III: 419–23.

20　Predrag J. Marković, *Beograd i Evropa, 1918–41* (Belgrade: Savremena administracija, 1992), 51–64. On the milieu, see Jelena Milojković-Djurić, *Tradition and Avant-Garde: The Arts in Serbian Culture between the Two World Wars* (New York: Columbia University Press, East European Monographs, 1984), 9–30; and the various short pieces by Krista Djordjević and Guido Tartalija in *Beograd u sećanjima, 1919–1929* (Belgrade in memory, 1919–1929), ed. Pavle Savić, et al. (Belgrade: Srpska književna zadruga, 1980), 57–83.

21　See Miloslav Janićijević, *Stvaralačka inteligencija medjuratne Jugoslavije* (Creative intelligentsia of interwar Yugoslavia) (Belgrade: Institut društvenih nauka, 1984), 120–25, 131–39, 153–57, 169–73.

22　On urban development, see Draga Vuksanić-Anić, "Urbanistički razvitak Beograda u periodu izmedju dva rata" (Urban development of Belgrade in the period between the two wars), *Istorija XX veka* 20 (1968), 468–509. On education, see Charles Jelavich, "Education, Textbooks, and South Slav Nationalisms in the Interwar Era," in *Allgemeinbildung als Modernizierungsfaktor*, ed. Norbert Reiter and Holm Sundhaussen (Berlin and Weisbaden: Harrassowitz Verlag, 1994), 127–42; and Ljubodrag Dimić, "Kulturna politika moderenizacija jugoslovenskog društva," in *Srbija u modernizacijskim procesima XX veka*, ed. Latinka Perović (Belgrade: Institut za noviju istoriju Srbije, 1994), 193–208.

23 The government allocated barely 1 percent of the 373 million gold marks that it had belatedly received from Germany in reparations by 1924 to buy agricultural equipment. Although the sale of equipment delivered as payment in kind boosted the number of iron ploughs close to 15 per 100 peasant households, the agricultural ministry priced harvester and other mechanical equipment too high and most remained unsold. All this, plus new land and crop taxes, helped keep Serbia's cereal yields 16 percent under the country's average for 1921–25. Momčilo Isić, *Seljaštvo u Srbiji, 1918–25* (Peasantry in Serbia) (Belgrade: Institut za noviju istoriju Srbije, 1995), 55–125.

24 Jozo Tomasevich, *Peasants, Politics, and Economic Change in Yugoslavia* (Stanford, Calif.: Stanford University Press, 1955), 353–82.

25 Cohen, *Socialist Pyramid*, 337–41.

26 C. A. Macartney, *Hungary and Her Successors* (London: Oxford University Press, 1937), 400–4.

27 For an appraisal of Yugoslav agricultural performance during the 1920s in Balkan perspective, see John R. Lampe and Marvin R. Jackson, *Balkan Economic History, 1550–1950. From Imperial Borderlands to Developing Nations* (Bloomington, Ind.: Indiana University Press, 1982), 351–75.

28 Mirjana Kolar-Dimitrijević, *Radni slojevi u Zagrebu od 1918 do 1931* (Working strata in Zagreb from 1918 to 1931) (Zagreb: Institut za historije radničkog pokreta Hrvatske, 1973), 27–100.

29 Lampe and Jackson, *Balkan Economic History*, 394–98, especially table 11.6.

30 Ibid., 384–85; L. Pejić, "Ekonomske ideje Dr. Milan Stojadinovića i balkanski privredni problemi" (Economic ideas of Dr. Milan Stojadinović and Balkan economic problems) *Balkanica* 7 (Belgrade, 1976): 240–58.

31 Lampe and Jackson, *Balkan Economic History*, tables 109.6, 10.13, and 10.14.

32 Linda Killen, *Testing the Peripheries: US–Yugoslav Economic Relations in the Interwar Years* (New York: Columbia University Press, East European Monographs, 1994), 45–96.

33 Piotr S. Wandycz, *The Twilight of French Eastern Alliances, 1926–36* (Princeton: Princeton University Press, 1988), 104: Vuk Vinaver, *Jugoslavija i Francuska izmedju dva rata* (Yugoslavia and France between the two wars) (Belgrade: Institut za savremenu istoriju, 1985), 451–54. On the Little Entente, see Magda Adam, *The Little Entente and Europe, 1920–1929* (Budapest: Akademiai Kiadó, 1993), 90–109, 204–17.

34 Some 300,000 Vojvodina Germans had been denied any right to vote in the 1920 elections for the constituent assembly, but were able to participate in the three parliamentary elections of 1923, 1925, and 1927 under less intimidating conditions than those the Hungarians faced. Macartney, *Hungary*, 380–81, 39–99, 408–16. On Carinthia and Slovenia, see Arnold

Suppan, "According to the Principle of Reciprocity: The Minorities in Yugoslav-Austrian Relations, 1918–1938," in *Ethnic Groups in International Relations*, ed. Paul Smith (New York: New York University Press, 1985), 235–73.

35 See R. J. Crampton, *A Short History of Bulgaria* (Cambridge: Cambridge University Press, 1987), 92–93.

36 See C. M. Woodhouse, *Modern Greece: A Short History*, 5th ed. (London: Faber and Faber, 1991), 212–20; and George Mavrocordatos, *Stillborn Republic: Social Conditions and Party Strategies in Greece, 1922–1936* (Berkeley, Calif.: University of California Press, 1983).

37 Ramadan Marmullaku, *Albania and the Albanians* (Hampden, Conn.: Archon Books, 1975), 33–36; Andrej Mitrović, "Yugoslavia, the Albanian Question, and Italy, 1919–1939," in *Serbs and Albanians in the 20th Century*, ed. Andrej Mitrović (Belgrade: Serbian Academy of Arts and Sciences, 1991), 253–73.

38 Dennison Rusinow, *Italy's Austrian Heritage, 1919–1946* (London: Clarendon Press, 1969), 185–210; Christopher Seton-Watson, *Italy from Liberalism to Fascism, 1870–1925* (London: Methuen, 1967), 666–82; Vuk Vinaver, "Velika Britanija i Taliansko 'Okruženje' Jugoslavije, 1926–1928" (Great Britain and Italian "encirclement" of Yugoslavia), *Istorija XX veka* 8 (1966): 73–164.

39 Čulinović, *Istorija Jugoslavije*, I: 524–30. Čulinović quotes instructively from the crescendo of exchanges, starting with "gypsies" and "liars," and offers a vivid description of the killings. See Zvonimir Kolundžić, *Attentat na Stjepana Radića* (Assassination of Stjepan Radić) (Zagreb: Stvarnost, 1967) for a detailed account.

6 AUTHORITARIAN KINGDOM, 1929–1941

1 The interwar struggle between Serbs from Serbia and Croatia over issues of central versus local government was often more important than ethnic or cultural animosity between Serbs and Croats. On the actions of Maček, Trumbić, and Pribićević before and after the king's decree, see Ljubo Boban, *Maček i politika hrvatske seljačke stranke, 1928–1941* (Maček and the politics of the Croatian peasant party) (Zagreb: Liber, 1974), I: 24–50.

2 Joseph Rothschild, *East Central Europe between the Two World Wars* (Seattle, Wash.: University of Washington Press, 1974), 205–80. The best survey of domestic politics and foreign relations during the 1930s is Wayne S. Vucinich, "Interwar Yugoslavia," in *Contemporary Yugoslavia*, ed. Wayne S. Vucinich (Berkeley, Calif.: University of California Press, 1969), 18–58.

3 Svetozar Pribićević's relentless critique of Aleksandar as totalitarian tyrant and proto-fascist was quickly echoed by Croatian and Communist writings. But the reverential approach of Stephen Graham's volume only a few years after the assassination is not much more helpful. Svetozar Pribićević, *Diktatura kralja Aleksandra* (Belgrade: Prosveta, 1952); Stephen Graham, *Alexander of Jugoslavia* (London: Cassel and Co., 1938).

4 Public Record Office, Yugoslavia, Annual Report, 1930, FO 371: 20–24. As for the 1920s, the British diplomatic reports provide the best continuous

source of foreign observation, joined at the start of the 1930s by those from the Embassy of Czechoslovakia and at the end by those from the American Embassy.

5 For an introduction to pre-1914 and interwar Orthodox organization, see Mathew Spinka, "Modern Ecclesiastical Development," in *Yugoslavia*, ed. Robert J. Kerner (Berkeley, Calif.: University of California Press, 1949), 244–60.

6 Arif Purivatra, *Jugoslovenska muslimanska organizacija u političkom životu Kr. Srba, Hrvata i Slovenaca* (The Yugoslav Muslim Organization in the political life of the Kingdom of Serbs, Croats, and Slovenes) (Sarajevo: Prosveta, 1974), 410–20.

7 Janko Prunkt, "Nacionalni program u slovenskoj političkoj misli" (National program in Slovenian political thought), *Časopis za suvremenu povijest* 18, 1 (1986): 2–5; Ljubo Boban, "Zagrebačke punktacije," *Istorija XX veka*, 4 (1962): 309–66.

8 Royal Institute for International Affairs, *The Balkan States*, vol. I, *Economic* (London: Oxford University Press, 1936) provides the best contemporary overview of the Depression's initial impact on Southeastern Europe.

9 Linda Killen, *Testing the Peripheries: US–Yugoslav Economic Relations in the Interwar Years* (New York: Columbia University Press, East European Monographs, 1994), 125–69.

10 This and subsequent data for this section are drawn from John R. Lampe and Marvin R. Jackson, *Balkan Economic History, 1550–1950: From Imperial Borderlands to Developing Nations* (Bloomington, Ind.: Indiana University Press, 1982), 429–72.

11 Branko Petranović and Momčilo Zečević, *Agonije dve Jugoslavije* (The agony of the two Yugoslavias) (Belgrade: Edicija svedočanstva, 1991), 171. Maček characterizes these efforts as "the boom of the party" in his autobiography, *In the Struggle for Freedom* (University Park, Pa.: Pennsylvania State University Press, 1957), 158–73.

12 Mark Wheeler, "Pariahs to Partisans to Power: The Communist Party of Yugoslavia," in *Resistance and Revolution in Mediterranean Europe, 1939–1948*, ed. Tony Judt (New York: Routledge, 1989), 114–16; and for details, Ivan Očak, *Gorkić, život, rad i pogiba* (Gorkić: life, work, and demise) (Zagreb: Globus, 1988).

13 See Richard Crampton, *A Short History of Modern Bulgaria* (Cambridge: Cambridge University Press, 1987), 102–11.

14 The recent temptation to call the Ustaša radical nationalists in reaction to the long-standing Communist condemnation of them as fascists does not explain the movement's internal organization or Pavelić's personal insistence on fascism as the only antidote to Bolshevism. The standard work on the Ustaša based on German and Italian sources remains Ladislav Hory and Martin Borszat, *Der kroatische Ustasha Staat, 1941–1945* (Stuttgart: Deutsche Verlags-Anstalt, 1964), 14–24; and from Croatian sources on the pre-1941 period, see Fikreta Jelić-Butić, *Ustaše i Nezavisna Država Hrvatske, 1941–1945* (Ustaša and the Independent State of Croatia) (Zagreb: Školska knjiga, 1977), 13–56. An informed view of the 1930s from the Croatian emigration is Jere Jareb, *Pola stoljeće hrvatske politike* (Buenos Aires: Knjižica hrvatske revije, 1960).

15 The most detailed study of Prince Paul's role from this time forward remains the sympathetic treatment in J. B. Hoptner, *Yugoslavia in Crisis, 1934–1941* (New York: Columbia University Press, 1962).

16 See the thoroughly researched volume completed by his colleagues after his death, Todor Stojkov, *Vlada Milana Stojadinovića, 1935–1937* (Regime of Milan Stojadinović) (Belgrade: Institut za savremenu istoriju, 1985), 131–50. The general was the last to leave, after trying to prevent the JRZ from organizing locally and then facing suspicion of involvement in an abortive assassination attempt against Stojadinović in the *Skupština* by an abstaining deputy from the Jevtić faction. Prince Paul wanted the general arrested but settled for Stojadinović's suggestion that he not be asked to join the restructured cabinet of March 7.

17 On the various negotiations from all sides with Maček and the Concordat crisis, see the addendum to Stojkov, *Vlada*, 181–222; and on the fall of Stojadinović, see Dušan Biber, "O padu Stojadinovićeva vlade" (On the fall of the Stojadinović regime), *Istorija XX veka* 8 (1966): 5–75.

18 As late as 1932, however, he was advocating an end to the state's tobacco monopoly as a stimulus to production in Macedonia; it had sagged with the monopoly's repeated reductions in the number of authorized growers. L. Pejić, "Ekonomske ideje Dr. Milana Stojadinovića . . . ," *Balkanistika*, 7 (Belgrade, 1976): 259–64.

19 Petranović and Zečević, *Agonije dve Jugoslavije*, 171–74.

20 This foreign total in turn gave the primarily French and British investors a predominant interest in barely 10 percent of Yugoslav joint-stock industrial enterprises possessing one-quarter of their total capital. Only with the fall of France in 1940 did the German share rise to 20 percent. See Lampe and Jackson, *Balkan Economic History*, table 12.23; and Vladimir Rosenberg and Jovan Kostić, *Ko finansira jugoslovensku privredu* (Who finances the Yugoslav economy) (Belgrade, 1940), 94–231.

21 Lampe and Jackson, *Balkan Economic History*, 482–500; and Stefan Kukoleća, *Industrija Jugoslavije, 1918–1939* (Belgrade, 1941). On Stojadinović and the state's growing role, see Smiljana Djurović, *Državna intervencija u industriji Jugoslavije, 1918–41* (State intervention in Yugoslavia's industry) (Belgrade: Institut za savremenu istoriju, 1986), 197–344.

22 A useful appraisal of the secondary sources on this subject is Frank C. Littlefield, *Germany and Yugoslavia, 1933–1941* (New York: Columbia University Press, East European Monographs, 1988), 37–55. Stojadinović's own view is in his *Ni rat ni pakt* (Neither war nor pact) (Rijeka: Otokar Keršovani, 1970). On the extent to which his policies were a reaction against the failures of French financial and commercial policy, see Nicole Jordan, *The Popular Front and Central Europe: The Dilemma of French Impotence, 1918–40* (Cambridge: Cambridge University Press, 1992), 108–24, 233–43.

23 See Gerhard L. Weinberg, "Germany and Munich," in *Reappraising the Munich Pact*, ed. Maya Latynski (Washington, D.C.: Woodrow Wilson Center Press; Baltimore, Md.: Johns Hopkins University Press, 1992), 9–20.

24 Ivo Vinski, "Nacionalni dohodak i fiskni fondovi na području Jugoslavije, 1909–1959" (National income and investment funds on the territory of Yugoslavia), *Ekonomski pregled* (Zagreb, 1959), 11–12, 840–44; and Eric

Lethbridge, "National Income and Product," *The Economic History of Eastern Europe, 1919–1975* (London: Clarendon Press, 1985), I: 532–41, 573–81.

25 Lampe and Jackson, *Balkan Economic History*, 482–90, 500–2.

26 Doreen Warriner, "Urban Thinkers and Peasant Policy in Yugoslavia, 1918–1939," *Slavonic and East European Review* 38 (December 1959): 62–66.

27 A concise survey of interwar education and the political élite is Lenard J. Cohen, *The Socialist Pyramid: Elites and Power in Yugoslavia* (Oakville, Ontario: Mosaic Press, 1989), 106–16. On public employment, see Lampe and Jackson, *Balkan Economic History*, table 12.22; and on the army see Mile Bjelajac, *Vojska Kr. Srba, Hrvata i Slovenaca/Jugoslavije, 1922–1935* (Armed forces of the Kingdom of Serbs, Croats, and Slovenes/Yugoslavia) (Belgrade: INIS, 1994).

28 Miloslav Janićjević, *Stvaralačka inteligencija medjuratne Jugoslavije* (Creative intelligentsia of interwar Yugoslavia) (Belgrade: Institut društvenih nauka, 1984) provides much of the basis for the following subsection. On the role of Krleža in the Communist left of the 1930s, see Ralph Bogert, *The Writer as Naysayer, Miroslav Krleža and the Aesthetic of Interwar Central Europe* (Columbus, Ohio: Slavica Publishers, 1990), 97–133.

29 Ljubo Boban, relying mainly on Ciano's detailed diaries, has argued that Maček wanted first one and then the other. Ljubo Boban, "Oko Mačekovih pregovora s Grofom Čanom" (Concerning Maček's negotiations with Count Ciano), *Istorija XX veka* 6 (Belgrade, 1964): 302–55.

30 Ivo Banac, "Bosnian Muslims: From Religious Community to Socialist Nationhood to Post-Communist Statehood, 1918–1992," in *The Muslims of Bosnia-Herzegovina*, ed. Mark Pinson (Cambridge, Mass.: Harvard University Press, 1994), 140–41. Such an agreement would not be signed until February 1994, under American auspices in the midst of the Bosnian war.

31 On the Yugoslav Communist Party (KPJ), see Wheeler, "From Pariahs to Partisans," 117–23; on the Ustaša see Bogdan Krizman, *Ustaše i Ante Pavelić* (Ustaša and Ante Pavelić) (Zagreb: Globus, 1977), 527–30; and on Serbian politics, see Mira Radojević, "Demokratska stranka o državnom preuredjenju Kr. Jugoslavije, 1935–1941" (Democratic party concerning the state reordering of the Kingdom of Yugoslavia), *Istorija XX veka* 9, 1–2 (Belgrade, 1991): 36–63.

32 Milos Martić, "Dimitrije Lotić and the Yugoslav National Movement Zbor, 1935–1945," *East European Quarterly* 14, 2 (1980): 219–39.

33 Littlefield, *Germany and Yugoslavia*, 62–130; Srdjan Trifković, "Yugoslavia in Crisis: Europe and the Croat Question, 1939–1941," *European History Quarterly* 23, 4 (October 1993): 537–59.

34 Velimir Teržić, *Jugoslavija u Arprilskom ratu 1941* (Yugoslavia in the April war), 2nd ed., 2 vols. (Belgrade: Partizanska knjiga, 1981), whose evidence on German policy and of Croatian complicity therein is not convincing. Martin Van Creveld, *Hitler's Strategy, 1940–41: The Balkan Clue* (Cambridge: Cambridge University Press, 1973), 8–13, makes the most persuasive Western case against the British decision.

35 Hoptner, *Yugoslavia in Crisis*, 236.

7 WORLD WAR AND CIVIL WAR, 1941–1945

1 On the decisive role that the Special Operations Executive sought but failed to play, see David A. T. Stafford, "SOE and British Involvement in the Belgrade Coup d'Etat of March 1941," *Slavic Review* 36, 3 (September 1977): 399–419; and Mark C. Wheeler, *Britain and the War for Yugoslavia, 1940–1943* (New York: Columbia University Press, East European Monographs, 1980), 34–61.

2 The most detailed argument for Hitler's disposition to attack Yugoslavia before the coup of March 27 is Velimir Teržić, *Slom Kraljevine Jugoslavije* (The fall of the Kingdom of Yugoslavia), 2 vols. (Belgrade: Partizanska knjiga, 1981). Norman Rich, *Hitler's War Aims, Ideology, the Nazi State and the Course of Expansion* (New York: W. W. Norton, 1973), 197–203, summarizes a more persuasive case for Hitler's "cautious restraint in dealing with Yugoslavia" up to that date.

3 These minimal losses and later access to Yugoslav transport routes has led Martin Van Creveld to argue that the eleven German divisions scheduled for the Russian campaign were ready for transfer to the Barbarossa command within ten days of the Yugoslav surrender on April 17. Their physical absence could therefore not explain the further six-week delay in launching Barbarossa that has been celebrated in postwar Yugoslavia as dooming the offensive to the fatal Russian winter. But it is still not clear that Hitler and his generals were psychologically ready, their serious equipment shortages aside, to begin their most fateful endeavor so soon after committing large forces to conquering two countries. Jozo Tomasevich cites the minutes of Hitler's meeting with his generals on March 27 as concluding that the Yugoslav campaign required the attack on Russia "to be postponed up to four weeks" from May 12. Martin Van Creveld, *Hitler's Strategy, 1940–1941: The Balkan Clue* (Cambridge University Press, 1973), 139–85; Jozo Tomasevich, *The Chetniks* (Stanford, Calif.: Stanford University Press, 1975), 87.

4 See Vasa Čubrilović, ed. *Istorija Beograda* (Belgrade: Prosveta, 1974), 3: 188–91, 500–6.

5 On the origins of Mihailović and the Chetniks, see Tomasevich, *Chetniks*, 113–31. Joining the Tomasevich book, with its greater reliance on Yugoslav sources, as standard works in English are two volumes that rely more on Italian and German sources, respectively, Matteo J. Milazzo, *The Chetnik Movement and the Yugoslav Resistance* (Baltimore, Md.: Johns Hopkins University Press, 1975); and Walter R. Roberts, *Tito, Mihailović, and the Allies, 1941–1945* (New Brunswick, NJ: Rutgers University Press, 1973; reprint, Durham, NC: Duke University Press, 1987).

6 Stephen Clissold, *Djilas, The Progress of a Revolutionary* (Hounslow: Maurice Temple Smith, Ltd., 1983), 49–53. On the KPJ attitude during 1940–41 toward other ethnic groups on the issue of Yugoslavia, Macedonians in particular, see Paul Shoup, *Communism and the Yugoslav National Question* (New York: Columbia University Press, 1968), 50–59.

7 The most comprehensive study of the Ustaša remains Ladislas Hory and Martin Broszat, *Die kroatische Ustasha Staat, 1945–1945* (The Croatian Ustaša state) (Stuttgart: Deutsche Verlags-Anstalt, 1964). On their

Hungarian and Romanian counterparts, see Nicholas M. Nagy-Talevera, *The Green Shirts and the Others* (Stanford, Calif.: Hoover Institution Press, 1970).

8 Fikreta Jelić-Butić, *Ustaše i Nezavisna Država Hrvatska, 1941–1945* (Ustaša and the Independent State of Croatia) (Zagreb: Školska knjiga, 1977), 158–67. Also see Yeshayahu Jelinek, "Nationalities and Minorities in the Independent State of Croatia," *Nationalities Papers* 8, 2 (1980): 195–210.

9 Stella Alexander, *The Triple Myth: A Life of Archbishop Aloizije Stepinac* (New York: Columbia University Press, East European Monographs, 1987), 57–106, examines the archbishop's writings and actions from early approval to later disenchantment with the Ustaša regime.

10 Jelić-Butić, *Ustaše*, 170–75; and Tomasevich, *Chetniks*, 101–8, review available evidence from the camps themselves. The initial work relying on census data from before and after the war which reduces the long-accepted, official Yugoslav estimate of 1.7 million dead (originally an estimate including children subsequently unborn) to 1 million actual dead came from the *émigré* Serbian scholar, Bogoljub Kočević, *Žrtve drugog svetskog rata u Jugoslaviji* (Victims of the Second World War in Yugoslavia) (London: Veritas, 1985). Subsequent work by Vladimir Žerjavić and other Croatian scholars have largely confirmed his calculations that some 500,000 Serbs, 200,000 Croats, 90,000 Bosnian Muslims, 60,000 Jews, 50,000 Montenegrins, and 30,000 Slovenes died, accounting for nearly 95 percent of the total.

11 On the persecution of Jews and the reaction of Bosnian Muslims, HSS members and others, see Jelić-Butić, *Ustaše*, 178–220.

12 Milazzo, *Chetnik Movement*, 48–80, 96–106. On the undeclared war between Italian and Ustaša units, and the Italian alliance with Chetnik units that followed by 1942, see Jonathan Steinberg, *All or Nothing: The Axis and the Holocaust, 1941–1943* (London: Routledge, 1990), 28–84.

13 Clissold, *Djilas*, 54–63; Milovan Djilas, *Wartime* (New York: Harcourt Brace Jovanovich, 1977), 149.

14 Walter Manoschek, *"Serbien ist Judenfrei," Militärische Besatzungspolitik und Judenvernichtung in Serbien 1941–42* (Munich: R. Oldenbourg Verlag, 1993) emphasizes the role of the Austrian commander Franz Böhme in using the reprisal campaign against the Partisans as an excuse to execute all Jewish internees. On the subordinate Serbian role, see Milos Martić, "Dimitrije Ljotić and the Yugoslav National Movement Zbor, 1935–19," *East European Quarterly* 14, 2 (1980): 219–39. Some of their number were accomplices in the systematic execution of 11,000 of Belgrade's 12,000 Jews and others from the Vojvodina, mainly at the Sajmište camp in Belgrade, during the Fall of 1941. Nedić's State Guards were also used to arrest, confine, or execute a larger number of Serbs over the next two years. On the contrast based on German sources, between direct Nazi controls in Serbia and their indirect role in the NDH, see Norman Rich, *Hitler's War Aims: The Establishment of the New Order* (London: Andre Deutsch, 1974), 273–98.

15 Roberts, *Tito, Mihailović*, 26–80. Also see Tomasevich, *Chetniks*, 282–303.

16 Not until October 1944 did a concrete British plan take shape, a pincer movement on Trieste with its eastern arm starting from Dubrovnik. By that

time, Tito's forces were strong enough to resist the consolidation of the small, lightly armed Floyd Force that arrived in Dubrovnik from Italy in November. The Commonwealth units left in December when the plan, called Operation Gelignite, was abandoned because of the German counterattacks against Allied forces in both Italy and France. Ian S. O. Playfair, et al., *The War in the Mediterranean and the Middle East* VI (London: HMSO, 1955), 1–112. On the overall British strategy of deception concerning any earlier Balkan invasion, see Michael Howard, *The Mediterranean Strategy in the Second World War* (London: Weidenfeld and Nicolson, 1968), 383–90; and *British Policy Toward Wartime Yugoslavia and Greece*, ed. Phylis Auty and Richard Clogg (London: Macmillan, 1975), 102–14.

17 On the decisive role of Ultra, see Ralph Bennett, *Ultra and Mediterranean Strategy, 1941–45* (New York: William Morrow and Co., 1989), 322–53.

18 Stevan K. Pavlowitch, "Out of Context – The Yugoslav Government in London, 1941–1945," *Journal of Contemporary History* 16 (1981): 89–118; also see Wheeler, *War for Yugoslavia*, 121–62.

19 Roberts, *Tito, Mihailović*, 106–12; Djilas, *Wartime*, 229–45.

20 See Franklin Lindsay, *Beacons in the Night: With the OSS and Tito's Partisans in Wartime Yugoslavia* (Stanford, Calif.: Stanford University Press, 1993) for an eyewitness account. On collaboration and resistance in wartime Slovenia, see Helga H. Harriman, *Slovenia under Nazi Occupation, 1941–1945* (New York: Studia Slovenica, 1977); and on Kocbek's role, Stella Alexander, *Church and State in Yugoslavia since 1945* (Cambridge: Cambridge University Press, 1979), 44–48.

21 Holm Sundhaussen, *Wirtschaftsgeschichte Kroatiens im nationalsozialistischen Grossraum, 1941–1945* (Economic history of Croatia in the Nazi empire) (Stuttgart: Deutsche Verlags-Anstalt, 1983).

22 Jill A. Irvine, *The Croat Question: Partisan Politics in the Formation of the Yugoslav Socialist State* (Boulder, Colo.: Westview Press, 1993), 137–99. Hebrang's reemergence and martyrdom after the war (see below) would however make his wartime precedent for Croatian political autonomy perhaps the only point of present-day nationalist pride in Croatia's Communist past. Witness the renaming of a major street in his honor.

23 See note 10 above. On the Second World War in Bosnia-Hercegovina, see Hory and Borszat, *Ustasha Staat*, 148–62; and Noel Malcolm, *Bosnia, A Short History* (New York: New York University Press, 1994), 174–92.

24 Karl Heinz Schlarp, *Wirtschaft und Besatzung in Serbien 1941–1944* (Economy and occupation in Serbia, 1941–44) (Stuttgart: Franz Steiner, 1986), 286, 412–15; E. A. Radice, "Economic Developments in Eastern Europe under German Hegemony," in *Communist Power in Europe, 1944–1949*, ed. Martin McCauley (New York: Barnes and Noble, 1977), 3–21.

25 Roberts, *Tito, Mihailović*, 254–72; Tomasevich, *Chetniks*, 359–421.

26 Union of Journalists' Associations, *The Trial of Dragoljub-Draža Mihailović* (Belgrade, 1946).

27 Branko Petranović, *Srbija u drugom svetskom ratu, 1939–1945* (Serbia in the Second World War) (Belgrade: Vojna štamparija, 1992), 552–61; Shoup, *Yugoslav National Question*, 104–11.

28 Alexander, *Church and State*, 56–81.

29 Vojislav Koštunica and Kosta Čavoški, *Party Pluralism or Monism? Social Movements and the Political System in Yugoslavia, 1944–1949* (New York: Columbia University Press, 1985), 41–131.

30 The most recent Macedonian scholarship emphasizes that for the period 1944–46, Tito and the republic Communist leadership explicitly excluded any claim to Aegean Macedonia. Mihajlo Minoski, "Makedonskoto prashanje vo megjunarodnite odnosi . . . 1943–44" (Macedonian role in international relations), Institut za Nacionalna Istorija, *ASNOM, pedecet godini makedonska držhava, 1944–94* (ASNOM, fifty years of the Macedonian state) (Skopje: Makedonska Akademija na Naukite i Umetnosti, 1995), 235–56. Emphasizing instead the ambiguity of Tito's Greek policy is Angelos Kofos, "The Impact of the Macedonian Question on Civil Conflict in Greece (1943–49)," in his *Nationalism and Communism in Macedonia* (New Rochelle, NY: Aristide D. Caratzas, Publ., 1993), 253–90.

31 Irvine, *Croat Question*, 219–22; Petranović, *Srbija*, 662, 691–99; Shoup, *Yugoslav National Question*, 100–43. For review of post-1945 decisions on internal borders from current Serbian and Croatian perspectives, see respectively, Bogdan Lekić, "Administrativne granice u Jugoslaviji posle drugog svetskog rata" (Administrative borders in Yugoslavia after the Second World War) *Istorija XX veka* 10, 1–2 (1992): 145–62; and Ljubo Boban, *Hrvatske granice, 1918–92* (Croatian borders) (Zagreb: Školska knjiga, 1992), 51–61.

8 FOUNDING THE SECOND YUGOSLAVIA, 1946–1953

1 The 139 articles of the January 1946 constitution are set down in Robert J. Kerner, ed., *Yugoslavia* (Berkeley, Calif.: University of California Press, 1949), 487–512. On the later suppression of the non-Communist partners in the ruling Popular Front, see Vojislav Koštunica and Kosta Čavoški, *Party Pluralism or Monism? Social Movements and the Political System in Yugoslavia, 1944–49* (New York: Columbia University Press, East European Monographs, 1985), 80–97.

2 Aleksa Djilas, *The Contested Country: Yugoslav Unity and Communist Revolution, 1919–53* (Cambridge, Mass.: Harvard University Press, 1991), 150–74. Also see Ivo Banac, *With Stalin against Tito: Cominformist Splits in Yugoslav Communism* (Ithaca, NY: Cornell University Press, 1988), 98–111; Paul Shoup, *Communism and the Yugoslav National Question* (New York: Columbia University Press, 1968), 101–42; Janko Pleterski, *Nacija-Jugoslavija-Revolucija* (Belgrade: IC Komunist, 1985), 477–531.

3 Carol S. Lilly, "Agitprop in Post-war Yugoslavia," *Slavic Review* 53, 2 (1994): 395–413. On religious restriction and the Catholic and Orthodox priests' associations, see Stella Alexander, *Church and State in Yugoslavia since 1945* (Cambridge: Cambridge University Press, 1979), 178–231.

4 Marko Milivojević, "The Role of the Yugoslav Intelligence and Security Committee," in *Yugoslavia in Transition*, ed. John B. Allcock, John J. Horton, and Marko Milovojević (New York: BERG, 1992), 204–7, 234.

5 Koštunica and Čavoški, *Party Pluralism*, 133–46.

6 The one comprehensive account of the *obnova* is Branko Petranović, *Politička i ekonomska osnova narodne vlasti u Yugoslaviji za vreme obnova* (Political and economic basis of people's power in Yugoslavia during the renewal) (Belgrade: Institut za medjunarodni radnički pokret, 1969), 256–349.

7 John R. Lampe, Russell O. Prickett, and Ljubiša Adamović, *Yugoslav-American Economic Relations since World War II* (Durham, NC: Duke University Press, 1990), 21–25.

8 Ibid., 18–21. For the background to these bad relations, see Michael B. Petrovich, "The View from Yugoslavia," in *Witnesses to the Origins of the Cold War*, ed. Thomas T. Hammond (Stanford, Calif.: Stanford University Press, 1982), 35–58. On the Trieste dispute, see Bogdan C. Novak, *Trieste, 1941–54: The Ethnic, Political, and Ideological Struggle* (Chicago, Ill.: University of Chicago Press, 1970), 202–68.

9 Jozo Tomasevich, "Immediate Effects of the Cominform Resolution on the Yugoslav Economy," in *At the Brink of War and Peace: The Tito-Stalin Split in Historical Perspective*, ed. Wayne S. Vucinich (New York: Columbia University Press, East European Monographs, 1982), 89–100. Branko Horvat, *The Yugoslav Economic System* (White Plains, NY: M. E. Sharpe, 1976), 42–44, 88–90, 172–81, 192–94; Jože Prinčić, *Slovenska industrija v jugoslovanskem primežu, 1945–56* (Slovenian industry in the Yugoslav vice) (Nova Mesto: Dolenska založba, 1992).

10 Ranko M. Brashich, *Land Reform and Ownership in Yugoslavia, 1919–53* (New York: Mid-European Studies Center, 1954), 44–71; Melissa Bokovoy, "A Separate Road to Collectivization: The Communist Party of Yugoslavia's Agrarian Policies, 1941–49" (Ph.D. diss., Indiana University, 1991); Nikola Gačesa, *Agrarna reforma i kolonizacija u Jugoslaviji, 1945–48* (Agrarian reform and colonization in Yugoslavia) (Novi Sad: Matica srpska, 1974).

11 Vladimir Dedijer, *The Battle Stalin Lost: Memoirs of Yugoslavia, 1948–53* (New York: Gossett, 1972), 74–96; Edvard Kardelj, *Reminiscences* (London: Blond & Briggs, 1982), 90–114; Milovan Djilas, *Conversations with Stalin* (New York: Harcourt, Brace & Co., 1962).

12 Dedijer, *The Battle Stalin Lost*, 97–132; Stephen Clissold, ed., *Yugoslavia and the Soviet Union, 1939–1973* (London: Institute for the Study of Conflict, 1975), 42–59, 169–214.

13 Elizabeth Barker, *Macedonia* (1950; reprint, Westport, Conn.: Greenwood Press, 1980), 99–107; Branko Petranović, *Balkanska Federacija, 1943–48* (Belgrade: Zaslon, 1991), 118–35, 176–201.

14 Marijan Matička, *Agrarna reforma i kolonizacija u Hrvatskoj, 1945–1948* (Agrarian reform and colonization in Croatia) (Zagreb: Školska knjiga, 1990), 112–45.

15 Brashich, *Land Reform*, 67–73; Jozo Tomasevich, "Collectivization of Agriculture in Yugoslavia," in *Collectivization of Agriculture in Eastern Europe*, ed. Irwin Sanders (Lexington, Ky.: University of Kentucky Press, 1958), 173.

16 Katherine McCarthy, "Agrarian Politics and Peasant Resistance: The Struggle against Collectivization and Otkup in Central Croatia" (Ph.D. diss., University of Pittsburgh, 1995); Vera Kržišnik-Bukić, *Cazinska buna, 1950* (The Cazin revolt) (Sarajevo: Svjetlost, 1991).

17 Izetbegović was sentented to three years in prison in the first trials of 1946. The organization's origins, in the first years of the war, were entirely outside the Partisan struggle, which tarnished it irretrievably for the Communist regime, despite the absence of any ties, beyond a few individuals, to *Ustaša* or German efforts to mobilize the Bosnian Muslims for their own purposes. See chapter 10 for his further activities and 1983 conviction, before he reemerged to become president of an independent Bosnia-Hercegovina in 1992. On the organization's evolution and Izetbegović's role, see Sead Trulj, *Mladi Muslimani* (Young Muslims) (Zagreb: Globus, 1992), 9–36, 57–70.

18 Banac, *With Stalin against Tito*, 117–42, 243–54. Looking beyond total numbers, the large part of Serbs purged came from the Croatian Krajina and Bosnia, thus reducing their disproportionate share in those local party hierarchies.

19 Tomasevich, "Immediate Effects of the Cominform Resolution," 105–13; James Gow, *Legitimacy and the Military: The Yugoslav Crisis* (New York: St. Martin's Press, 1992), 40–44.

20 Stephen Clissold, *Djilas: The Progress of a Revolutionary* (Hounslow: Maurice Temple Smith, 1983), 210–20; A. Ross Johnson, *The Transformation of Communist Ideology: The Yugoslav Case, 1948–53* (Cambridge, Mass.: MIT Press, 1972), 143–220. For a stenographic record, see Branko Petranović, Ranko Končar, and Radovan Radonjić, eds., *Sednice centralnog komiteta KPJ (1948–52)* (Belgrade: Komunist, 1985).

21 From the late 1940s, American Embassy reports became the most detailed and best informed diplomatic source of information on the second Yugoslavia, as were the British Embassy reports for the interwar period. See the volumes on Central and Southeastern Europe in US Department of State, *Foreign Relations of the United States*, 1945–57 (Washington, DC: Government Printing Office, 1947–88) and the declassified holdings of the National Archives of the United States, File H860 in particular, Washington, DC. The best brief account of the political debate over a new direction remains Dennison Rusinow, *The Yugoslav Experiment, 1948–72* (Berkeley, Calif.: University of California Press, 1974), 51–69, now complemented by the economic emphasis from Susan L. Woodward, *Socialist Unemployment: The Political Economy of Yugoslavia, 1945–90* (Princeton: Princeton University Press, 1995), 151–68.

22 Lampe, Prickett, and Adamović, *Yugoslav-American Economic Relations*, 23–46.

23 Only Vladimir Bakarić, the leading Croatian member of the inner circle since Hebrang's exclusion, stood up for large private holdings. No one favored investing more budgetary resources in private agriculture. Tomasevich, "Collectivization of Agriculture in Yugoslavia," 166–92.

24 On the military maneuvers of the Soviet bloc against Yugoslavia, see the various accounts in Vucinich, *At the Brink*.

25 Dijana Pleština, *Regional Development in Communist Yugoslavia* (Boulder, Colo.: Westview Press, 1992), 20–25.

26 Lampe, Prickett, and Adamović, *Yugoslav-American Economic Relations*, 70–76.

27 Johnson, *Transformation of Communist Ideology*, 143–58; Djilas, *Contested Country*, 176–79.

28 Alexander, *Church and State in Yugoslavia since 1945*, 121–36, 178–206.

29 Clissold, *Djilas*, 290; see also his *Yugoslavia and the Soviet Union*, 55–62, 231–47.

9 TITO'S YUGOSLAVIA ASCENDING, 1954–1967

1 Tito agreed to go to Moscow for its negotiation only after Soviet authorities had finally dissolved the Comintern, and with it the main forum for Stalinist Yugoslavs, in April. Also encouraging was Khrushchev's secret speech that had condemned Stalin to the party congress two months before. It included an admission that "we have paid dearly" for Stalin's "artificially" blowing up a conflict with "a state and people who had gone through a severe school of fighting for liberty and independence." Edvard Kardelj, *Reminiscences* (London: Blond and Briggs, 1982), 130–38; Stephen Clissold, ed., *Yugoslavia and the Soviet Union, 1939–1973* (London: Royal Institute of International Affairs, Oxford University Press, 1975), 62–79.

2 Clissold, *Yugoslavia and the Soviet Union*, 62–72; Charles Gati, *Hungary and the Soviet Bloc* (Durham, NC: Duke University Press, 1986), 127–55.

3 James Gow, *Legitimacy and the Military: The Yugoslav Crisis* (New York: St. Martin's Press, 1992), 43–57.

4 See Vaclav Beneš, Robert F. Byrnes and Nicholas Spulber, eds., *The Second Soviet-Yugoslav Dispute* (Bloomington, Ind.: Indiana University Publications, 1959), 27–28; and for a Yugoslav perspective, see Veljko Mićunović, *Moscow Diary* (New York: Doubleday, 1980).

5 Phyllis Auty, "Yugoslavia's International Relations, 1945–1965," *Contemporary Yugoslavia*, ed. Wayne S. Vucinich (Berkeley, Calif.: University of California Press, 1969), 172–95.

6 Vinod Dubey, et al., *Yugoslavia: Development with Decentralization* (Baltimore, Md.: Johns Hopkins University Press for IBRD, 1975), 403–4.

7 Alvin Z. Rubinstein, *Yugoslavia and the Non-Aligned World* (Princeton: Princeton University Press, 1970), 9, 27–34, 52, 81–114; Jadranka Jovanović, *Jugoslavija u Ujedinjenim Nacijama, 1945–1953* (Yugoslavia in the United Nations) (Belgrade: Institut za savremenu istoriju, 1975).

8 Rubinstein, *Yugoslavia*, 155–83, 214.

9 John R. Lampe, Russell O. Prickett, and Ljubiša Adamović, *Yugoslav-American Economic Relations since World War II* (Durham, NC: Duke University Press, 1990), 49–72.

10 Stephen C. Markovich, "American Foreign Aid and Yugoslav International Policies," *East European Quarterly* 9, 2 (1975): 185–93.

11 Roberto G. Rabel, *Between East and West: Trieste, the United States, and the Cold War, 1941–1954* (Durham, NC: Duke University Press, 1988), 131–62.

12 John H. Moore, *Growth with Self-Management: Yugoslav Industrialization, 1952–1975* (Stanford, Calif.: Hoover Institution Press, 1980), 487–97. For another critical overview, see Harold Lydall, *Yugoslav Socialism: Theory and Practice* (Oxford: Clarendon Press, 1984), 73–82.

13 George Macesich, *Yugoslavia: The Theory and Practice of Development Planning* (Charlottesville, Va.: University of Virginia Press, 1964), 123–57.

14 Dennison Rusinow, *The Yugoslav Experiment, 1948–1972* (Berkeley, Calif.: University of California Press for Royal Institute of International Affairs, 1977), 90–115.

15 Macesich, *Yugoslavia*, 167–79; Branko Horvat, *The Yugoslav Economic System* (White Plains, NY: M. E. Sharpe, Inc., 1976), 76–140.

16 Dijana Pleština, *Regional Development in Communist Yugoslavia* (Boulder, Colo.: Westview Press, 1992), 38, 47–53.

17 Dubey, *Yugoslavia*, 119–22; Susan L. Woodward, *Socialist Unemployment: The Political Economy of Yugoslavia, 1945–90* (Princeton: Princeton University Press, 1995), 268–72, 372.

18 Lampe, Prickett and Adamović, *Yugoslav-American Economic Relations*, 64–65.

19 Macesich, *Yugoslavia*, 106–12; Rusinow, *Yugoslav Experiment*, 116–79.

20 Sabrina P. Ramet, *Nationalism and Federalism in Yugoslavia, 1962–1991*, 2nd ed. (Bloomington, Ind.: Indiana University Press, 1992), 50–53.

21 Rusinow, *Yugoslav Experiment*, 120–33. Also see Pleština, *Regional Development*, 62–64; and Deborah Milenkovitch, *Plan and Market in Yugoslav Economic Thought* (New Haven, Conn.: Yale University Press, 1971).

22 Paul Shoup, *Communism and the Yugoslav National Question* (New York: Columbia University Press, 1968), 205–13.

23 Macesich, *Yugoslavia*, 96–102; Lydall, *Yugoslav Socialism*, 63–64, 83.

24 Dubey, *Yugoslavia*, 38–40; Rudolf Bićanić, *Economic Policy in Socialist Yugoslavia* (Cambridge: Cambridge University Press, 1973), 211–38.

25 Ibid., 154–57; Yugoslav FA Committee, eds., *The Development of Socialist Agriculture in Yugoslavia* (Belgrade: Jugoslovenski pregled, 1975), 42–55, 136–41.

26 Lydall, *Yugoslav Socialism*, 82–88.

27 Woodward, *Socialist Unemployment*, 191–221, 273–75, points to wage differentials favoring skilled labor as a further pressure on increasingly profit-seeking, large enterprises to cut loose unskilled labor. Protests from the fiery Svetozar Vukmanović-Tempo resulted only in his dismissal as trade union chief in 1967.

28 This judgment, drawn from the author's observations as an American Embassy officer in Belgrade at the time, runs counter to the otherwise persuasive account in the Ramet reference. Ramet, *Nationalism and Federalism*, 83–94; Rusinow, *Yugoslav Experiment*, 179–91; Slobodan Stanković, "Yugoslavia: Before and after the Purge of Aleksandar Ranković," *Radio Free Europe Research Report*, July 7–8, 1966.

29 Lampe, Prickett and Adamović, *Yugoslav-American Economic Relations*, 84–85; Patrick J. Nichols, "Western Investment in Eastern Europe: The Yugoslav Example," *The Economics of Eastern Europe*, US Congress, Joint Economic Committee (Washington, DC: US Government Printing Office, 1974), 734–35.

30 Pleština, *Regional Development*, 65, 72–83.

31 Barbara Jancar, "The New Feminism in Yugoslavia," in *Yugoslavia in the 1980s*, ed. Pedro Ramet (Boulder, Colo.: Westview Press, 1985), 201–23.

32 Rusinow, *Yugoslav Experiment*, 142–43. Also see Gertrude Joch Robinson, *Tito's Maverick Media* (Urbana, Ill.: University of Illinois Press, 1977).

33 Stella Alexander, *Church and State in Yugoslavia since 1945* (Cambridge: Cambridge University Press, 1979), 226–88.

34 Sabrina P. Ramet, *Balkan Babel: Politics, Culture, and Religion in Yugoslavia* (Boulder, Colo.: Westview Press, 1992), 133–39, 147–57.

35 Steven L. Burg, *Conflict and Cohesion in Socialist Yugoslavia* (Princeton: Princeton University Press, 1983), 36–74.

36 F. E. Ian Hamilton, *Yugoslavia: Patterns of Economic Activity* (New York: Frederick A. Praeger, 1968), 157–254; Pleština, *Regional Development*, 70–71; Dubey, *Yugoslavia*, 248–88, 371, 374–75.

10 TITO'S YUGOSLAVIA DESCENDING, 1968–1988

1 Precise detail and comparably critical analysis of the gathering crisis for 1979–1985 may be found in two surveys with differing ideological dispositions toward workers' self-management, favorable in Bruce McFarlane, *Yugoslavia: Politics, Economics, and Society* (London: Pinter Publishers, 1988); and unfavorable in Harold Lydall, *Yugoslavia in Crisis* (Oxford: Clarendon Press, 1989).

2 April Carter, *Democratic Reform in Yugoslavia: The Changing Role of the Party* (Princeton: Princeton University Press, 1982), 194–98, 207–18, summarizes the role of student dissent and publication. On *Praxis*, see Gerson S. Sher, *Praxis: Marxist Criticism and Dissent in Yugoslavia* (Bloomington, Ind.: Indiana University Press, 1977).

3 Sabrina P. Ramet, *Nationalism and Federalism in Yugoslavia, 1962–1991*, 2nd ed. (Bloomington, Ind.: Indiana University Press, 1992), 188–94.

4 "Cooperation between Tirana University and the New University of Priština," *Radio Free Europe Research Report*, December 3, 1969.

5 Steven Burg, *Conflict and Cohesion in Socialist Yugoslavia* (Princeton: Princeton University Press, 1983), 88–99. Also see Zdenko Antić, "Slovenians Oppose Government in Road-Building Decision," *Radio Free Europe Research Report*, August 1, 1969.

6 Ramet, *Nationalism and Federalism*, 88–135, details the Croatian perspective on those four and a half years.

7 Slobodan Stanković, "Yugoslav Electoral System," *Radio Free Europe Research Report*, pt. 1, April 9, 1969; and pt. 2, April 16, 1969.

8 Dennison Rusinow, *The Yugoslav Experiment, 1948–1974* (Berkeley, Calif.: University of California Press, 1977), 255–68.

9 Along with Ramet cited in note 6, see Burg, *Conflict and Cohesion*, 83–166, for an account of how the Slovenian and Croatian disputes created a "Yugoslav crisis." Carter, *Democratic Reform in Yugoslavia*, 219–24, provides a summary of the Croatian dispute.

10 On the roles of Veselica and Budiša, see Slobodan Stanković, "Problems in Contemporary Yugoslavia," *Radio Free Europe Research Report*, July 15, 1971; and "Yugoslav Students: Their Successes and Failures," *Radio Free Europe Research Report*, December 9, 1971.

11 On the considerable activity of Croatian émigrés somehow linked to the

escaped Ustaša's leadership, see Bogdan Krizman, *Pavelić u bjekstvu* (Pavelić in flight) (Zagreb: Globus, 1986).

12 Nikezić's only published account of his experience is the memoir recorded in Slavoljub Djukić, *Slom srpskih liberala* (Fall of the Serbian liberals) (Belgrade: Filip Višnjić, 1990), especially pp. 88–171.

13 Slobodan Stanković, "Crisis between Hard-Liners and Soft-Liners in the Yugoslav Party," *Radio Free Europe Research Report*, September 28, 1972; and "Nikezić and Friends Expelled from the Party," *Radio Free Europe Research Report*, April 26, 1974.

14 Burg, *Conflict and Cohesion*, 167–87, surveys the spectrum of party purges outside of Croatia.

15 Slobodan Stanković, "Constitutional Changes in Yugoslavia," *Radio Free Europe Research Report*, August 31, 1971.

16 Burg, *Conflict and Cohesion*, 188–241.

17 Laszlo Sekelj, *Yugoslavia: The Process of Disintegration* (New York: Columbia University Press, Atlantic Research and Publications, 1993), 45–51. The fullest account of the 1974 constitutional system is Monika Beckmann-Petey, *Der jugoslawische Föderalismus* (Munich: R. Oldenbourg Verlag, 1990).

18 Lenard J. Cohen, *The Socialist Pyramid: Elites and Power in Yugoslavia* (Oakville, Ont.: Mosaic Press, 1989), 155–69.

19 Harold Lydall, *Yugoslav Socialism: Theory and Practice* (London: Oxford University Press, 1984), 252–66, analyzes the causes of that inflation. On banking and investment, see Vinod Dubey, et al., *Yugoslavia: Development with Decentralization* (Baltimore, Md.: Johns Hopkins University Press, 1975), 216–33.

20 Laura D'Andrea Tyson and Gabriel Eichler, "Continuity and Change in the Yugoslav Economy in the 1970s and 1980s," US Congress, Joint Economic Committee, *East European Economic Assessment*, pt. 1 (Washington, DC: US Government Printing Office, 1980), 156–61.

21 Slobodan Stanković, "Yugoslavia's Law on Associated Labor," *Radio Free Europe Research Report*, January 13, 1977; and Bogomil Bogo Ferfila, *The Economics and Politics of the Socialist Debacle* (Lanham, Md.: University Press of America, 1991), 115–21, summarize the major provisions.

22 Lydall, *Yugoslav Socialism*, 235–51, reviews the Western evidence against the OOURs, while Sekelj, *Yugoslavia*, 46, cites the critical consensus raised against them by Yugoslav sociologists of the 1980s.

23 Tyson and Eichler, *Continuity and Change*, 161–64.

24 Stephen R. Sachs, *Self-Management and Efficiency: Large Corporations in Yugoslavia* (London: George Allen & Unwin, 1983), 31–38; Saul Estrin, *Self-Management: Economic Theory and Yugoslav Practice* (Cambridge: Cambridge University Press, 1983), 81–126.

25 Lydall, *Yugoslav Socialism*, 267–77.

26 McFarlane, *Yugoslavia*, 152–54.

27 John R. Lampe, Russell O. Prickett, and Ljubiša Adamović, *Yugoslav-American Economic Relations since World War II* (Durham, NC: Duke University Press, 1990), 115–40. Also see Patrick F. R. Artisien, *Joint Ventures in Yugoslav Industry* (Aldershot: Gower Publishing Co., Ltd.), 31–40.

28 Michael Palairet, "The Rise and Fall of Yugoslav Socialism: A Case Study of the Yugoslav Automobile Industry," in *Economic Transformations in East and Central Europe*, ed. David Good and Richard Rudolph (London: Routledge, 1994), 54–92.

29 Lydall, *Yugoslavia in Crisis*, 40–71.

30 Slobodan Stanković, "After Brezhnev's Visit to Belgrade," *Radio Free Europe Research Report*, November 19, 1976.

31 Otmar Nikola Haberl, "Yugoslavia and the USSR in the Post-Tito Era," in *Yugoslavia in the 1980s*, ed. Pedro Ramet (Boulder, Colo.: Westview Press, 1985), 276–306. On nonalignment, see Zachary T. Irwin, "Non-Alignment in the 1980s," ibid., 249–75; Slobodan Stanković, "Yugoslavia in 1976," *Radio Free Europe Research Report*, December 28, 1976; and Zdenko Antić, "Non-Alignment: From Belgrade to Havana and After," *Radio Free Europe Research Report*, September 17, 1979.

32 Lampe, Prickett, and Adamović, *Yugoslav-American Economic Relations*, 156–86. For detail on how the debt accumulated, see Mate Babić and Emil Primorac, "Some Causes of the Growth of the External Yugoslav Debt," *Soviet Studies* 38 (January 1986), 69–88; and Momčilo Cemović, *Zašto, kako i koliko smo se zadužili* (Why, how and how much we became indebted) (Belgrade: Institut za unapredjenje robnog prometa, 1985).

33 John P. Burkett, "Stabilization Measures in Yugoslavia: An Assessment of the Proposals of Yugoslavia's Commission for Problems of Economic Stabilisation," *East European Economies: Slow Growth in the 1980s* 3, Joint Economic Committee, US Congress (Washington, DC: US Government Printing Office, 1986), 561–74.

34 For a complete list and brief biographical data on members of Mikulić's Federal Executive Council and the leaders of the 1986 presidency and Federal Assembly, see Bruce McFarlane, *Yugoslavia: Politics, Economics, and Society* (London: Pinter Publishers, 1988), 61–65.

35 Lampe, Prickett, and Adamović, *Yugoslav-American Economic Relations*, 185–89; Susan L. Woodward, *Socialist Unemployment: The Political Economy of Yugoslavia, 1945–90* (Princeton: Princeton University Press, 1995), 253–59.

36 OECD Economic Surveys, *Yugoslavia, 1989–90* (Paris: Organization for Economic Cooperation and Development, 1990), 46–49.

37 For details on Abdić and the Agrokomerc scandal, see "Yugoslavia – Situation Report," *Radio Free Europe Research Report*, September 30, 1987; and ibid., October 22, 1987.

11 ETHNIC POLITICS AND THE END OF YUGOSLAVIA

1 Susan L. Woodward, *Socialist Unemployment: The Political Economy of Yugoslavia, 1945–90* (Princeton: Princeton University Press, 1995), 353.

2 With over one-half million inhabitants each, the two cities had surpassed Ljubljana and were catching up with Zagreb's 800,000. The socio-cultural role of the rural influx is best studied for Belgrade. See Mirjana Prosić-Dvornić, "The Reurbanization of Belgrade after the Second World War," in *Das Volkskultur Südosteuropas in der Moderne*, ed. Klaus Roth (Munich:

Südosteuropa Gesellschaft, 1992), 75–100; and the accompanying bibliography.

3 Aleksa Milojević, "National and Economic Development in Bosnia and Herzegovina," in *Small Nations and Ethnic Minorities in an Emerging Europe*, ed. Silvo Devetak, Sregej Flere, and Gerhard Seewan (Munich: Slavica Verlag Dr. Anton Kovač, 1993), 146–60; "The National Composition of Yugoslavia's Population, 1991," *Yugoslav Survey* 1 (1992), 3–24.

4 For comprehensive detail on migrations across the postwar period, see Ruža Petrović, *Migracije u Jugoslaviji i etnički aspekt* (Migration in Yugoslavia and the ethnic aspect) (Belgrade: Istraživački izdavački centar, 1987); and Silva Meznarić, *Osvajanje prostora – prekrivanje vremena, migracije umjesto razvoja* (Conquering space and obscuring time: Migration in place of development) (Zagreb: Sociološko društvo Hrvatske, 1991).

5 OECD Economic Surveys, *Yugoslavia, 1989–90* (Paris: Organization for Economic Cooperation and Development, 1990), 58.

6 *Jugoslavije 1918–88, statistički godišnjak* (Belgrade: Savezni zavod za statistiku, 1989), 359–66.

7 On the League of Communists' reaction to Laibach in particular, see Gregor Tomc, "The Politics of Punk," *Independent Slovenia: Origins, Movements and Prospects*, ed. Jill Benderley and Evan Kraft (New York: St. Martin's Press, 1994), 113–34.

8 Andrew Horton, "'Only Crooks Can Get Ahead': Post-Yugoslav Cinema/TV/Video in the 1990s," *Beyond Yugoslavia: Politics, Economics, and Culture in a Shattered Community*, ed. Sabrina P. Ramet and Ljubiša Adamović (Boulder, Colo.: Westview Press, 1995), 414–30.

9 Sabrina Petra Ramet, *Balkan Babel: Politics, Culture, and Religion in Yugoslavia* (Boulder, Colo.: Westview Press, 1992), 140–43. Also see pp. 57–174 on the three major religions, the press, rock music, and gender relations.

10 While a detailed account may be found in the documents assembled in Adil Zulfilkarpašić, ed., *Sarajevski proces: sudjenje muslimanskim intelektualcima 1983 g.* (Sarajevo trial: Sentencing of Muslim intellectuals in 1983) (Zurich: Bosanski Institut, 1987), the best collection in English translation appears in the *South Slav Journal*, passim, 1983–86. On the Islamic philosophy of the principals, see Alija Ali Izetbegović, *Islam between East and West* (Indianapolis, Ind.: American Trust Publications, 1989), and on the mixture of Muslim and Christian customs in local practice, Tone Bringa, *Being Muslim in the Bosnian Way, Identity and Community in a Central Bosnian Village* (Princeton: Princeton University Press, 1995), 224–31.

11 Wolfgang Höpken, "Party Monopoly and Political Chance: The League of Communists since Tito's Death," *Yugoslavia in the 1980s*, ed. Pedro Ramet (Boulder, Colo.: Westview Press, 1985), 29–55; Laszlo Sekelj, *Yugoslavia: The Process of Disintegration* (New York: Columbia University Press and Social Science Monographs, 1992), 92–116; and Vladimir Goati, *Politička atanomija jugoslovenskog društva* (Political anatomy of Yugoslav society) (Zagreb: Naprijed, 1989), 91–98.

12 James Gow, *Legitimacy and the Military: The Yugoslav Crisis* (New York: St. Martin's Press, 1992), 95–111; Zdenko Antić, "New Yugoslav Armed

Forces Chief of Staff," *Radio Free Europe Research Report*, August 20, 1979; and Slobodan Stanković, "Yugoslav Army to Hire Professional Soldiers," *Radio Free Europe Research Report*, April 1, 1985.

13 On Milošević's background and rise to power, see Lenard J. Cohen, "Serpent in the Bosom, Slobodan Milošević and Serbian Nationalism," *State-Society Relations in Yugoslavia, 1945–1992*, ed. Jill Irvine, Melissa Bokovoy and Carol Lilly (New York: St. Martin's Press, forthcoming); and Slavoljub Djukić, *Izmedju slave i antateme, Politička biografija Slobodana Miloševića* (Belgrade: Filip Višnjić, 1992).

14 Stevan K. Pavlowitch reviews the Tito biographies in "Dedijer as Historian of the Yugoslav Civil War," *Survey* 28, no. 3 (1984): 95–110. For a critical overview of Serbian scholarship in the 1980s, see Ivo Banac, "Yugoslavia," *American Historical Review* 97, 4 (1992): 1084–104. For another approach, see Aleksandar Pavković, "The Serb National Idea: A Revival, 1986–92," *Slavonic and East European Review* 72, 3 (1994): 449–55. Pavković points out that the most popular novel of the late 1980s, outselling the ethnically detached, contemporary fiction of Mome Kapor as well as works of Drašković and Ćosić, was historical but hardly an endorsement of Great Serbia. In Danko Popović's *Knjiga o Milutinu*, the aged peasant hero reflects bitterly on the Balkan and Yugoslav wars in which he bravely fought for someone else's vision of wider Serb or Yugoslav interests outside of Serbia, all to no real purpose. On the 1986 Memorandum, see the summary of Mihailo Crnobrnja, *The Yugoslav Drama* (London: I. B. Tauris, 1994), 97–100; and the text in *Nacrt memoranduma Srpske Akademije Nauke u Beogradu* (Toronto: Srpske Narodne Odbrane, 1987).

15 Lenard J. Cohen, *Broken Bonds: Yugoslavia's Disintegration and Balkan Politics in Transition*, 2nd ed. (Boulder, Colo.: Westview Press, 1995), 51–55, 74–75, offers the testimony of an otherwise critical Slovenian journalist to the role of Milošević's speaking skill in the success of these mass meetings; on his use of the Kosovo issue, see Sekelj, *Yugoslavija*, 198–205.

16 Mark Thompson, *A Paper House: The Ending of Yugoslavia* (New York: Pantheon Books, 1992), 3–59; "Yugoslavia – Situation Report," *Radio Free Europe Research Report*, January 22, 1987; June 16, 1988; and July 19, 1988.

17 See Branka Magaš, *The Destruction of Yugoslavia* (London: Verso, 1993), 3–76, 179–217.

18 On the demise of the League, see James Seroka, "Variation in the Evolution of the Yugoslav Communist Parties," *The Tragedy of Yugoslavia*, ed. James Seroka and Vukašin Petrović (Armonk, NY: M. E. Sharpe, 1992), 67–88; and Sabrina P. Ramet, *Nationalism and Federalism in Yugoslavia, 1962–1991*, 2nd ed. (Bloomington, Ind.: Indiana University Press, 1992), 238–51.

19 OECD Economic Surveys, *Yugoslavia, 1988–89*, 49–59.

20 David A. Dyker, *Yugoslavia: Socialism, Development, and Debt* (London: Routledge, 1990), 97–102; McFarlane, *Yugoslavia*, table 12.9, 131.

21 Saul Estrin and Lina Takla, "Reform in Yugoslavia: The Retreat from Self-Management," *Industrial Reform in Socialist Countries*, ed. Ian Jeffries (Aldershot: Edward Elgar, 1992), 267–77.

22 Cohen, *Broken Bonds*, table 3.2, 105. See also Susan L. Woodward, *Balkan Tragedy: Chaos and Dissolution after the Cold War* (Washington, DC: Brookings Institution, 1995), 117–45.

23 Dennison Rusinow, "The Avoidable Tragedy," *Beyond Yugoslavia*, 13–38. The most comprehensive overview of the election campaigns and their results remains Cohen, *Broken Bonds*, 88–162. On the crucial Croatian campaign, see Darko Hudelist, *Banket u Hrvatskoj* (Banquet in Croatia) (Zagreb: Dnevnik, 1991). Perhaps the one common feature was a sharp reduction in the number of women elected, most striking in Bosnia-Hercegovina, which dropped from 27 percent in 1986 to 3 percent in 1990.

24 Laura Silber and Allan Little, *The Death of Yugoslavia* (London: Penguin Books, 1995), 87–96.

25 Helsinki Watch, *War Crimes in Bosnia-Hercegovina* (New York: Human Rights Watch, 1992), 62–63.

26 Misha Glenny has for this reason called his chapter on Sarajevo in 1991–92, "The Paradise of the Damned," in his *The Fall of Yugoslavia: The Third Balkan War*, rev. ed. (London: Penguin Books, 1993), 138–80.

27 The most detailed, detached accounts of these controversial negotiations may be found in Paul Shoup, "The Bosnian Crisis in 1992," *Beyond Yugoslavia*, 155–88; and Woodward, *Balkan Tragedy*, 168–94; and Silber and Little, *Death of Yugoslavia*, 226–54.

28 That war's story, costing the lives of more civilians than soldiers and displacing at least 2 million people, takes us beyond the history of Yugoslavia. Among many publications to address the Bosnian war, the closest account to date is Silber and Little, *Death of Yugoslavia*, 255–388.

Selected further reading
(in English and German)

GEOGRAPHY

Carter, Francis W. "Urban Development in the Western Balkans, 1200–1800." In *A Historical Geography of the Balkans*, ed. Francis W. Carter. New York: Academic Press, 1977.

Hamilton, F. E. Ian. *Yugoslavia: Patterns of Economic Activity*. New York: Frederick A. Praeger, 1968.

Hoffman, George. "The Evolution of the Ethnographical Map of Yugoslavia." In *A Historical Geography of the Balkans*, ed. Francis W. Carter. New York: Academic Press, 1977.

Magocsi, Paul Robert. *Historical Atlas of East-Central Europe*. Seattle, Wash.: University of Washington Press, 1993.

PRE-MODERN PERIOD

Adanir, Fikret. "Tradition and Rural Change in Southeastern Europe during Ottoman Rule." In *The Origins of Backwardness in Eastern Europe*, ed. Daniel Chirot. Berkeley, Calif.: University of California Press, 1989.

Bracewell, Catherine Wendy. *The Uskoks of Senj: Piracy, Banditry, and the Holy War in the 16th Century Adriatic*. Ithaca, NY: Cornell University Press, 1992.

Carter, Francis W. *Dubrovnik (Ragusa): A Classic City-State*. London: Seminar Press, 1972.

Džaja, Srećko. *Konfessionalität und Nationalität Bosniens und der Hercegowina: voremanzipatorische Phase, 1463–1804*. Munich: R. Oldenbourg Verlag, 1984.

Fine, John V. A., Jr. *The Bosnian Church: A New Interpretation*. New York: Columbia University Press, 1975.

The Early Medieval Balkans. Ann Arbor, Mich.: University of Michigan Press, 1983.

The Late Medieval Balkans. Ann Arbor, Mich.: University of Michigan Press, 1987.

Guldescu, Stanko. *History of Medieval Croatia*. The Hague: Mouton, 1964.

The Croatian-Slovenian Kingdom, 1526–1792. The Hague: Mouton, 1970.

Malcolm, Noel. *Bosnia: A Short History*. New York: New York University Press, 1994.

Rothenburg, Gunther E. *The Austrian Military Border in Croatia, 1522–1747*. Chicago: University of Chicago Press, 1960.

The Military Border in Croatia, 1740–1881. Chicago: University of Chicago Press, 1966.

Stoianovich, Traian. *Balkan Worlds: The First and Last Europe*. Armonk, NY: M. E. Sharpe, 1994.

Sugar, Peter F. *Southeastern Europe under Ottoman Rule*. Seattle, Wash.: University of Washington Press, 1977.

Vucinich, Wayne S., and Thomas A. Ammert, eds. *Kosovo: Legacy of a Medieval Battle*. Minneapolis, Minn.: Minnesota Mediterranean and East European Monographs, 1991.

Winnifrith, Tom J. *The Vlachs: The History of a Balkan People*. London: Duckworth, 1987.

NINETEENTH AND EARLY TWENTIETH CENTURIES

Adanir, Fikret. *Die Makedonische Frage, Ihre Entstehung und Entwicklung*. Wiesbaden: Franz Steiner Verlag, 1979.

Austrian History Yearbook 3, pt. 2 (1967). Articles by Dimitrije Djordjević, Charles Jelavich, Barbara Jelavich, Bogdan Krizman, Wayne Vucinich, and Fran Zwitter.

Banac, Ivo. *The National Question in Yugoslavia: Origins, History, Politics*. Ithaca, NY: Cornell University Press, 1984.

Behschnitt, Wolf D. *Nationalismus bei Serben und Kroaten, 1830–1914*. Munich: R. Oldenbourg Verlag, 1980.

Carnegie Endowment. *The Other Balkan Wars: A 1913 Carnegie Endowment Inquiry in Retrospect*. Washington, DC: Carnegie Endowment Book, 1993.

Dedijer, Vladimir. *The Road to Sarajevo*. New York: Simon and Schuster, 1966.

Despalatović, Elinor Murray. *Ljudevit Gaj and the Illyrian Movement*. New York: Columbia University Press, East European Quarterly, 1975.

Donia, Robert J. *Islam under the Double Eagle: The Muslims of Bosnia and Hercegovina, 1878–1914*. New York: Columbia University Press, East European Monographs, 1981.

Jelavich, Barbara. *Russia's Balkan Entanglements, 1806–1914*. Cambridge: Cambridge University Press, 1991.

Jelavich, Charles. *South Slav Nationalisms, Textbooks, and Yugoslav Union before 1914*. Columbus, Ohio: Ohio State University Press, 1990.

MacKenzie, David. *Ilija Garašanin, Balkan Bismarck*. New York: Columbia University Press, East European Monographs, 1985.

McClellan, Woodford. *Svetozar Marković and the Origins of Balkan Socialism*. Princeton: Princeton University Press, 1964.

Perry, Duncan M. *The Politics of Terror: The Macedonian Revolutionary Movements, 1893–1903*. Durham, NC: Duke University Press, 1988.

Petrovich, Michael B. *A History of Modern Serbia, 1804–1918*, 2 vols. New York: Harcourt Brace Jovanovich, 1976.

Pinson, Mark, ed. *The Muslims of Bosnia-Herzegovina*. Cambridge, Mass.: Harvard University Press, 1994.

Rogel, Carole. *The Slovenes and Yugoslavism, 1890–1914.* Boulder, Colo.: East European Quarterly, 1977.

Rossos, Andrew. *Russia and the Balkans: Inter-Balkan Rivalries and Russian Foreign Policy, 1908–1914.* Toronto: Toronto University Press, 1981.

Stokes, Gale. *Legitimacy through Liberalism: Vladimir Jovanović and the Transformation of Serbian Politics.* Seattle, Wash.: University of Washington Press, 1975.

Politics as Development: The Emergence of Political Parties in Nineteenth Century Serbia. Durham, NC: Duke University Press, 1990.

Treadway, John D. *The Falcon and the Eagle: Montenegro and Austria-Hungary, 1908–1914.* West Lafayette, Ind.: Purdue University Press, 1983.

Vucinich, Wayne S. *Serbia between East and West: The Events of 1903–08.* Stanford, Calif.: Stanford University Press.

Williamson, Samuel R., Jr. *Austria-Hungary and the Origins of the First World War.* New York: St. Martin's Press, 1991.

THE FIRST YUGOSLAVIA

Avakumović, Ivan. *History of the Communist Party of Yugoslavia.* Vol. 1. Aberdeen: Aberdeen University Press, 1964.

Barker, Elizabeth. *Macedonia.* 1950. Reprint. Westwood, Conn.: Greenwood Press, 1980.

Beard, Charles A., and George Radin. *The Balkan Pivot: Yugoslavia.* New York: Macmillan, 1929.

Djilas, Aleksa. *The Contested Country: Yugoslav Unity and Communist Revolution, 1919–53.* Cambridge, Mass.: Harvard University Press, 1991.

Djordjević, Dimitrije, ed. *The Creation of Yugoslavia, 1914–1918.* Santa Barbara, Calif.: ABC Clio Press, 1980.

Dragnich, Alexander. *The First Yugoslavia: The Search for a Viable Political System.* Stanford, Calif.: Stanford University Press, 1983.

Friedenreich, Harriet Pass. *The Jews of Yugoslavia: A Quest for Community.* Philadelphia, Pa.: Jewish Publication Society of America, 1979.

Hoptner, Jacob B. *Yugoslavia in Crisis, 1934–1941.* New York: Columbia University Press, 1962.

Kerner, Robert J., ed. *Yugoslavia.* Berkeley, Calif.: University of California Press, 1949.

Lederer, Ivo. *Yugoslavia at the Paris Peace Conference.* New Haven, Conn.: Yale University Press, 1963.

Livingston, Robert Gerald. "Stjepan Radić and the Croatian Peasant Party, 1904–1929." Ph.D. diss. 1959. Cambridge, Mass.: Harvard University.

Pavković, Aleksandar. *Slobodan Jovanović, An Unsentimental Approach to Politics.* New York: Columbia University Press, East European Monographs, 1993.

Rothschild, Joseph. *East Central Europe between the Two Wars.* Seattle, Wash.: University of Washington Press, 1974.

Rusinow, Dennison. *Italy's Austrian Heritage, 1919–1946.* Oxford: Clarendon Press, 1969.

Živojinović, Dragoljub. *America, Italy, and the Birth of Yugoslavia, 1917–19.* Boulder, Colo.: East European Monographs, 1972.

ECONOMIC HISTORY (PRE-1945)

Brashich, Ranko M. *Land Reform and Ownership in Yugoslavia, 1919–53*. New York: Mid-European Studies Center, 1954.

Calic, Marie-Janine. *Sozialgeschichte Serbiens 1815–1941*. Munich: R. Oldenberg Verlag, 1994.

Chirot, Daniel, ed. *The Origins of Backwardness in Eastern Europe*. Berkeley, Calif.: University of California Press, 1989.

Hočevar, Toussaint. *The Structure of the Slovenian Economy, 1848–1963*. New York: Studia Slovenica, 1965.

Killen, Linda. *Testing the Peripheries: US-Yugoslav Economic Relations in the Interwar Years*. New York: Columbia University Press, East European Monographs, 1994.

Lampe, John R., and Marvin R. Jackson. *Balkan Economic History, 1555–1950: From Imperial Borderlands to Developing Nations*. Bloomington, Ind.: Indiana University Press, 1982.

McGowan, Bruce. *Economic Life in Ottoman Europe: Taxation, Trade, and the Struggle for Land, 1600–1800*. Cambridge: Cambridge University Press, 1981.

Sugar, Peter F. *The Industrialization of Bosnia-Hercegovina, 1878–1914*. Seattle, Wash.: University of Washington Press, 1963.

Tomasevich, Jozo. *Peasants, Politics, and Economic Change in Yugoslavia*. Stanford, Calif.: Stanford University Press.

SOCIAL HISTORY AND ANTHROPOLOGY

Among the People: Selected Writings of Milenko S. Filipović, ed. E. A. Hammel et al. Ann Arbor, Mich.: Michigan Slavic Publications, 1982.

Bićanić, Rudolph. *How the People Live: Life in the Passive Regions*, trans. and ed. Joel M. Halpern and Elinor Murray Despalatovic. Amherst, Mass.: University of Massachusetts, Department of Anthropology, 1981.

Bringa, Tone. *Being Muslim the Bosnian Way. Identity and Community in a Central Bosnian Village*. Princeton: Princeton University Press, 1995.

Halpern, Joel M., and Barbara Kerewsky Halpern. *A Serbian Village in Historical Perspective*. New York: Holt, Rhinehart & Winston, 1972.

Lockwood, William G. *European Moslems: Economy and Ethnicity in Western Bosnia*. New York: Academic Press, 1975.

Simić, Andrei. *The Peasant Urbanites: A Study of Rural-Urban Mobility in Serbia*. New York: Seminar Press, 1973.

Trouton, Ruth. *Peasant Renaissance in Yugoslavia, 1900–50: A Study of the Development of Yugoslav Peasant Society as Affected by Education*. London: Routledge and Kegan Paul, 1952.

Winner, Irene. *A Slovenian Village: Žerovnica*. Providence, RI: Brown University Press, 1971.

ECONOMIC AND SOCIAL DEVELOPMENT AFTER 1945

Adizes, Ichak. *Industrial Democracy Yugoslav Style: The Effects of Decentralization on Organizational Behavior*. New York: Free Press, 1971.

Bošković, Blagoje, and David Dašić, eds. *Socialist Self-Management in Yugoslavia, 1950–80: Documents*. Belgrade: Socialist Thought and Practice, 1980.

Denitch, Bogdan. *The Legitimation of a Revolution: The Yugoslav Case*. New Haven, Conn.: Yale University Press, 1976.

Dubey, Vinod, et al. *Yugoslavia: Development with Decentralization*. Baltimore, Md.: Johns Hopkins University Press for IBRD, 1975.

Estrin, Saul. *Self-Management: Economic Theory and Yugoslav Practice*. Cambridge: Cambridge University Press, 1983.

Horvat, Branko. *The Yugoslav Economic System*. White Plains, NY: M. E. Sharpe, 1976.

Lampe, John R., Russell O. Prickett, and Ljubiša Adamović. *Yugoslav-American Economic Relations since World War II*. Durham, NC: Duke University Press, 1990.

Lydall, Harold. *Yugoslav Socialism: Theory and Practice*. Oxford: Clarendon Press, 1984.

Macesich, George. *Yugoslavia: The Theory and Practice of Development Planning*. Charlottesville, Va.: University of Virginia Press, 1964.

Milenkovitch, Deborah. *Plan and Market in Yugoslav Economic Thought*. New Haven, Conn.: Yale University Press, 1971.

Moore, John H. *Growth with Self-Management: Yugoslav Industrialization, 1952–1975*. Stanford, Calif.: Hoover Institution Press, 1980.

OECD Economic Surveys. *Yugoslavia, 1962–90*. Paris: Organization for Economic Cooperation and Development, 1963–90.

Pleština, Dijana. *Regional Development in Communist Yugoslavia*. Boulder, Colo.: Westview Press, 1992.

Sachs, Stephen R. *Self-Management and Efficiency: Large Corporations in Yugoslavia*. London: George Allen & Unwin, 1983.

Woodward, Susan L. *Socialist Unemployment: The Political Economy of Yugoslavia, 1945–90*. Princeton: Princeton University Press, 1995.

Yugoslav Survey. Belgrade, 1960–92.

THE SECOND WORLD WAR

Alexander, Stella. *The Triple Myth: A Life of Archbishop Aloizije Stepinac*. New York: Columbia University Press, East European Monographs, 1987.

Auty, Phyllis, and Richard Clogg, eds. *British Policy toward Wartime Yugoslavia and Greece*. London: Macmillan, 1975.

Djilas, Milovan. *Wartime*. New York: Harcourt Brace Jovanovich, 1977.

Hory, Ladislav, and Martin Broszat. *Der Kroatische Ustasha Staat, 1941–45*. Stuttgart: Deutsche Verlags-Anstalt, 1964.

Irvine, Jill. *The Croat Question: Partisan Politics in the Formation of the Yugoslav Socialist State*. Boulder, Colo.: Westview Press, 1993.

Milazzo, Matteo J. *The Chetnik Movement and the Yugoslav Resistance*. Baltimore, Md.: Johns Hopkins University Press, 1975.

Roberts, Walter R. *Tito, Mihailović, and the Allies, 1941–1945*. New Brunswick, NJ: Rutgers University Press, 1973. Reprint. Durham, NC: Duke University Press, 1987.

Steinberg, Jonathan. *All or Nothing: The Axis and the Holocaust, 1941–1943.* London: Routledge, 1990.

Sundhaussen, Holm. *Wirtschaftsgeschichte Kroatiens im nationalsozialistischen Grossraum, 1941–1945.* Stuttgart: Deutsche Verlags-Anstalt, 1983.

Tomasevich, Jozo. *The Chetniks.* Stanford, Calif.: Stanford University Press, 1975.

Trgo, Fabijan. *The National Liberation War and Revolution in Yugoslavia, 1941–45: Selected Documents.* Belgrade: Military History Institute, 1982.

Van Creveld, Martin. *Hitler's Strategy, 1940–41: The Balkan Clue.* Cambridge: Cambridge University Press, 1973.

Wheeler, Mark C. *Britain and the War for Yugoslavia, 1940–43.* New York: Columbia University Press, East European Monographs, 1980.

FOUNDING THE SECOND YUGOSLAVIA

Banac, Ivo. *With Stalin against Tito: Cominformist Splits in Yugoslav Communism.* Ithaca, NY: Cornell University Press, 1988.

Beckmann-Petey, Monika. *Der jugoslawische Föderalismus.* Munich: R. Oldenbourg Verlag, 1990.

Clissold, Stephen. *Djilas, The Progress of a Revolutionary.* Hounslow: Maurice Temple Smith, Ltd., 1983.

Dedijer, Vladimir. *Tito Speaks.* London: Weidenfeld and Nicolson, 1953.

The Battle Stalin Lost: Memoirs of Yugoslavia, 1948–53., New York: Gossett, 1972.

Djilas, Milovan. *Rise and Fall.* New York: Harcourt Brace Jovanovich, 1985.

Johnson, A. Ross. *The Transformation of Communist Ideology: The Yugoslav Case, 1948–53.* Cambridge, Mass.: MIT Press, 1972.

Novak, Bogdan C. *Trieste 1941–54: The Ethnic, Political, and Ideological Struggle.* Chicago: University of Chicago Press, 1970.

Rabel, Roberto G. *Between East and West: Trieste, the United States, and the Cold War, 1941–54.* Durham, NC: Duke University Press, 1988.

Vucinich, Wayne S., ed. *At the Brink of War and Peace: The Tito–Stalin Split in Historical Perspective.* New York: Columbia University Press, East European Monographs, 1982.

TITO'S YUGOSLAVIA

Alexander, Stella. *Church and State in Yugoslavia since 1945.* Cambridge: Cambridge University Press, 1979.

Auty, Phyllis. *Tito: A Biography.* London: Longman, 1970.

Beneš, Vaclav, Robert F. Byrnes, and Nicholas Spulber, eds. *The Second Soviet–Yugoslav Dispute.* Bloomington, Ind.: Indiana University Publications, 1959.

Burg, Steven L. *Conflict and Cohesion in Socialist Yugoslavia.* Princeton: Princeton University Press, 1983.

Carter, April. *Democratic Reform in Yugoslavia: The Changing Role of the Party.* Princeton: Princeton University Press, 1982.

Clissold, Stephen, ed. *Yugoslavia and the Soviet Union, 1939–1973.* London: Institute for the Study of Conflict, 1975.

Cohen, Lenard J. *The Socialist Pyramid: Elites and Power in Yugoslavia.* Oakville, Ont.: Mosaic Press, 1989.

Grothusen, Klaus-Detlev. *Jugoslawien=Yugoslavia.* Göttingen, Germany: Vandenhoech & Ruprecht, 1975.

McFarlane, Bruce. *Yugoslavia: Politics, Economics, and Society.* London: Pinter Publishers, 1988.

Milivojević, Marko, John B. Allcock, and Pierre Maurer, eds. *Yugoslavia's Security Dilemmas: Armed Forces, National Defense, and Foreign Policy.* New York: BERG, 1988.

Pavlowitch, Stevan K. *Yugoslavia: The Improbable Survivor.* Columbus, Ohio: Ohio State University Press, 1988.

Tito, Yugoslavia's Great Dictator: A Reassessment. Columbus, Ohio: Ohio State University Press, 1992.

Ramet, Sabrina Petra. *Nationalism and Federalism in Yugoslavia, 1962–91.* 2nd ed. Bloomington, Ind.: Indiana University Press, 1992.

Rubenstein, Alvin Z. *Yugoslavia and the Non-Aligned World.* Princeton: Princeton University Press, 1970.

Rusinow, Dennison. *The Yugoslav Experiment, 1948–1974.* Berkeley, Calif.: University of California Press, 1977.

Sher, Gerson S. *Praxis: Marxist Criticism and Dissent in Yugoslavia.* Bloomington, Ind.: Indiana University Press, 1977.

Shoup, Paul. *Communism and the Yugoslav National Question.* New York: Columbia University Press, 1968.

Südost Europa. Südost Institut, Munich, 1951– .

Vucinich, Wayne S., ed. *Contemporary Yugoslavia.* Berkeley, Calif.: University of California Press, 1969.

POST-TITO YUGOSLAVIA

Allcock, John B., John J. Horton, and Marko Milivojević, eds. *Yugoslavia in Transition.* New York: BERG, 1992.

Benderly, Jill, and Evan Kraft, eds. *Independent Slovenia: Origins, Movements and Prospects.* New York: St. Martin's Press, 1994.

Cohen, Lenard J. *Broken Bonds: Yugoslavia's Disintegration and Balkan Politics in Transition.* 2nd ed. Boulder, Colo.: Westview, 1995.

Danforth, Loring M. *The Macedonian Conflict, Ethnic Nationalism in a Transnational World,* Princeton, NJ: Princeton University Press, 1995.

Dyker, David A. *Yugoslavia: Socialism, Development, and Debt.* London: Routledge, 1990.

Glenny, Misha. *The Fall of Yugoslavia.* 2nd ed. rev. and enl. New York: Penguin Books, 1993.

Gow, James. *Legitimacy and the Military: The Yugoslav Crisis.* New York: St. Martin's Press, 1992.

Helsinki Watch. *War Crimes in Bosnia-Hercegovina* 1 and 2. New York: Human Rights Watch, 1992, 1993.

Lydall, Harold. *Yugoslavia in Crisis.* Oxford: Clarendon Press, 1989.

Magaš, Branka. *The Destruction of Yugoslavia: Tracking the Break-up, 1980–92.* London: Verso, 1993.

Poulton, Hugh. *Who Are the Macedonians?* Bloomington, Ind.: Indiana University Press, 1995.

Ramet, Pedro, ed. *Yugoslavia in the 1980s.* Boulder, Colo.: Westview, 1985.

Ramet, Sabrina Petra, and Ljubiša Adamović, eds. *Beyond Yugoslavia: Politics, Economic, and Culture in a Shattered Community.* Boulder, Colo.: Westview Press, 1995.

Silber, Laura, and Allan Little. *The Death of Yugoslavia.* London: Penguin Books, 1995.

Udovički, Jasmina and James Ridgeway, eds. *Yugoslavia's Ethnic Nightmare.* New York: Lawrence Hill Books, 1995.

Woodward, Susan L. *Balkan Tragedy: Chaos and Dissolution after the Cold War.* Washington, DC: Brookings Institution, 1995.

CULTURE AND MEDIA

Adamić, Louis. *The Native's Return.* New York: Harper's, 1934.

Andrić, Ivo. *The Bridge on the Drina.* Chicago: University of Chicago Press, 1977.

Barac, Antun. *A History of Yugoslav Literature.* Ann Arbor, Mich.: Michigan Slavic Publications, 1973.

Beker, Miroslav, ed. *Comparative Studies in Croatian Literature.* Zagreb: Liber, 1981.

Bogert, Ralph. *The Writer as Naysayer: Miroslav Krleža and the Aesthetic of Interwar Central Europe.* Columbus, Ohio: Slavica Publishers, 1990.

Cankar, Ivan. *My Life and Other Sketches.* Ed. and comp. Josip Vidmar. Ljubljana: Društvo slovenskih pisateljev, 1988.

Ćosić, Dobrica. *This Land, This Time.* 4 vols. New York: Harcourt Brace Jovanovich, 1983.

Eekman, Thomas. *Thirty Years of Yugoslav Literature, 1945–75.* Ann Arbor, Mich.: Michigan Slavic Press, 1985.

Goulding, Daniel J. *Liberated Cinema: The Yugoslav Experience.* Bloomington, Ind.: Indiana University Press, 1985.

Holne, Milne and Vasa D. Mihailovich, eds. *Serbian Poetry From the Beginning to the Present.* Colombus, Ohio: Slavica Publications for Yale Russian and East European Publications, 1988.

Hawkesworth, Celia. *Ivo Andrić: Bridge between East and West.* London: Athlone, 1984.

Koljević, Svetozar. *Yugoslav Short Stories.* London: Oxford University Press, 1966.

Krleža, Miroslav. *The Return of Philip Latinowicz.* New York: Vanguard, 1959.

Milojković-Djurić, Jelena. *Tradition and Avant-Guard: The Arts in Serbian Culture between the Two World Wars.* New York: Columbia University Press, East European Monographs, 1984.

Ramet, Sabrina P. *Balkan Babel: Politics, Culture, and Religion in Yugoslavia.* Boulder, Colo.: Westview Press, 1992.

Robinson, Gertrude Joch. *Tito's Maverick Media.* Urbana, Ill.: University of Illinois Press, 1994.

Thompson, Mark. *Forging War: The Media in Serbia, Croatia, and Bosnia-Hercegovina*. Avon: The Bath Press, Article 19, 1994.
Wilson, Duncan. *The Life and Times of Vuk Stefanović Karadžić, 1787–1864*. Oxford: Clarendon Press, 1970.

BIBLIOGRAPHIES

Friedman, Francine, ed. *Yugoslavia: A Comprehensive English Language Bibliography*. Wilmington, Del.: Scholarly Resources, Inc., 1993.
Horton, John J., comp. *Yugoslavia: Revised and Expanded Edition*. Santa Barbara, Calif.: ABC Clio Press, 1990.
Janković, Dragoslav. *The Historiography of Yugoslavia, 1965–1975*. Belgrade: Association of Yugoslav Historical Studies, 1975.
Petrovich, Michael B. *Yugoslavia: A Bibliographic Guide*. Washington, DC: Library of Congress, 1974.
Stanković, Dobrila and Zlatan Moltarić. *Svetska bibliografija o krizi u bivšoj Jugoslaviji* (World bibliography on the crisis in the Former Yugoslavia). Belgrade: Službeni glasnik, 1996.

Index

Abdić, Fikret, 324
absenteeism, worker, 311
Adriatic Sea, commercial access to, 29
Afghanistan, Soviet invasion of, 317
Agency for International Development,
    270
Agitprop, 233
Agrarian Council, 239
Agrarian Party, 208, 225
Agrarian Union, 132, 139
agricultural policy, under Five Year Plan,
    239–41
agriculture, 11–12
    in Bosnia-Hercegovina, 79–81
    estate, in Croatia-Slavonia, 77
    in first Yugoslavia, 116–17, 185–86
    foreign aid for, 254
    in Great Depression, 169–70
    land reform and, 146–48
    in nineteenth-century Serbia, 55–56
    in Ottoman Macedonia, 22
    postwar recovery of, 235
    see also collectivization
Agrokomerc scandal of 1987, 324
    air force, Yugoslav, 199
    airlines, 242
Albania
    accusations of revisionism by, 265
    fascist occupation of, 191
    and partition of first Yugoslavia, 199,
        201
    post-First World War territorial claims,
        114–15
    relations with first Yugoslavia, 151,
        153–54
    relations with second Yugoslavia, 265
Albanians, Kosovar, 94–95
    demonstrations of 1968, 296–98
    rebellion against Partisans, 223
    Slovenian support for, 343–44
Aleksandar, King, 125, 128, 156
Alexander, Stella, 205

Allen, George V., 254
Alliance of Reform Forces, 350
alliances
    ethnic, to resist collectivization, 247–48
    against Ottoman Empire, 59
    among political parties in first
        Yugoslavia, 119–20
    Serb-Croat, first attempt at, 46
    Serb-Croat, Serbian terms for, 59
Allies, 213–17
    relations with Communist regime,
        236–37
amputation, of Croatia and Slovenia, 158
Anderson, Benedict, 40, 42
Anderson, David, 320
Andrić, Ivo, 3, 89, 196
annexation, of Bosnia-Hercegovina by
    Austria, 82–85
Anti-Fascist Liberation Movement for
    Yugoslavia (AVNOJ), 217–18
anti-semitism, of Ustaša, 207
army intelligence (KOS), 248, 284, 343
arrests, political, 244, 248–49, 343
Arrow Cross, Hungarian, 204
Artuković, Andrija, 172, 204
assassination, 89, 96, 98, 102, 127, 137,
    139, 152, 158, 302
    of King Aleksandar, 170–73
Assembly of the Socialist Federal Republic
    of Yugoslavia, 307
Austria
    and borders of first Yugoslavia, 112–13
    relations with first Yugoslavia, 151–52
Austria-Hungary
    annexation of Bosnia-Hercegovina,
        82–85
    breakup of, 108
    and Ottoman Macedonia, 90–91
    Serbian economic dependence on, 56
    Serbian tariff war of 1906–11, 83
authoritarianism, of King Aleksandar,
    161–73

authority, dual, under constitution of
    1953, 257
Autonomists, Dalmatian, 68

Bačka, the, 36
Bailey, S. W., 215
Bajt, Aleksandar, 287
Bakarić, Vladimir, 285, 302
Balkan Entente, 182
Balkan federation, proposal for, 243
Balkan Wars of 1912–13, 71
Banac, Ivo, 6, 32, 248
Banat region, 36–37
bank law of 1987, 323
banking
    Balkan wars and, 94
    after economic reform of 1965, 309–10
    and economic reform of 1965, 281–83
    in first Yugoslavia, 148–50
    in Great Depression, 168–70
    and industrial growth, 149
    post-First World War, 118–19
    pre-First World War, 75
    in second Yugoslavia, 278
Barthou, Louis, 173
Basic Organizations of Associated Labor
    (OOUR), 294, 310, 347
Beard, Charles A., 124, 130
Belgrade
    as administrative capital, 39–40
    Allied bombing of, 221
    as capital city, 85–86, 142–46, 164
    as center for KPJ resistance, 203
    as center for unification, 59
    coronation of King Aleksandar in, 125
    in 1830, 50
    during First World War occupation,
        107–8
    intellectuals in, 188–89
    Nazi bombing of, 200
    population in First World War, 107
    problems of 1980s, 338
    rivalry with Zagreb, 118, 144–45
    "rurbanization" of, 329
Belgrade coup, 196, 198
Belgrade Declaration of 1955, 263
Belgrade Eight, 295
Beria, Levrenti, 262
Bernstein, Eduard, 259
Bevan, Aneurin, 258
Bevin, Ernest, 254
Bićanić, Rudolf, Kako živi narod, 186
Bihać, 247
birth rate, 186, 301
Black Hand. See Union or Death

Blair loan, 151
Bled agreement, 243
Bloc of National Agreement, 175–77
Bogomil heresy, 19–20, 23
Böhme, General Franz, 211
Bor copper refinery, as economic success
    story, 313
Borba, 259, 263, 296
border claims
    first Yugoslavia and, 150–55
    historic, 40
    post-First World War, 99, 111–15
borders, internal
    post-Second World War, 226–28
    of second Yugoslavia, 231
Bošković, Rudjer, 36
Bosnia, 3
    independence of, 355
    medieval, 15, 18–20
    transition from Ottoman to Austro-
        Hungarian rule, 64–68
Bosnia-Hercegovina, 3–4, 167
    as Austro-Hungarian province, 79–81
    Balkan wars and, 96–98
    Croat peasants in, 65
    economic growth of, 80
    elections of 1990, 354
    in First World War, 106–7
    under Habsburg rule, 70
    Hungarian occupation of, 62
    Independent State of Croatia and, 204,
        206–9
    industry in, 79–80
    legacy of Second World War, 218–20
    1992 recognition of, 355
    under Ottoman rule, 22–24
    postwar borders of, 226–28
    pre-First World War, 79–81
    revolt of Serb peasants in, 53
    Serb peasants in, 65
Bosnian crisis of 1908, 82–87
boycott of Slovenian consumer goods,
    346
bratstvo i jedinstvo, 232
Braudel, Fernand, 10
Brezhnev, Leonid, 316
Bricklin, Malcolm, 315
Broz, Josip. See Tito, Josip Broz
Brubaker, Rogers, 8
Budak, Mile, 204–5
Bulatović, Momir, 353–54
Bulgaria, 104–5
    and Macedonia, 90–91
    and partition of first Yugoslavia, 199,
        201

Bulgaria (*cont.*)
    post-First World War territorial claims,
        114–15
    and proposed Balkan federation, 243
    relations with first Yugoslavia, 152–53
    relations with second Yugoslavia, 265
    and Serbia, 100
Bulgarian Communist Party (BKP), 243
bureaucracies, regional, under constitution
    of 1946, 230
Burg, Steven, 298, 306
Burian, Istvan, 80
Burma, Yugoslav relations with, 267
Byzantine Empire, and medieval Serbia,
    16–18

cafes, 144
camps, for political prisoners, 249, 258
    see also concentration camps; death
        camps
Cankar, Ivan, 93
Carinthia, and borders of first Yugoslavia,
    112–14
Carniola, 74
Catholic Action, 174
Catholic church, 174, 176
    and Communist consolidation of power,
        224
    and Habsburgs, 27–28
    and intellectuals, 189
    and opposition to first Yugoslavia, 110
    and opposition to Pavelić regime, 207–8
    role in Croatian persecution of Jews and
        Serbs, 205–6
Čavoški, Kosta, 6, 225
censorship, 162, 174
centralism, 49–51, 130, 162
centralization, 41–42, 279–81
Chamber of Nationalities, 280, 299
Chamber of Republics and Autonomous
    Provinces, 306
Chamber of Republics and Provinces,
    300
Chetnik insignia, Serbian nationalists' use
    of, 341
Chetniks, 200–3, 208
    defeat of, 222–23
    executed by Communists, 224
    Montenegrin, 210
    in NDH, 209
    negotiations with Germans, 220–21
    Slovenia and, 217–18
    see also Mihailović, Draža
China, 263, 265
Christian Social Party, 217

Christian-Social Party of Right (Frankist),
    78
Christianity, 11
    see also Bogomil heresy; Catholic
        church; Serbian Orthodox church
Churchill, Winston, quoted, 198, 214
Ciano, Count, 182, 191, 194
Cincar-Marković, Aleksandar, 191
Civil Croatia
    as center of Illyrianism, 43–46
    in early nineteenth century, 41
    under Habsburg rule, 27, 30–32
    national aspirations in, 58–59
    see also Croatia; Croatian Military
        Border; Independent State of Croatia
civil war, 210, 222–24; *see also* wars of
    Yugoslav succession
Čižinski, Josip (Milan Gorkić), 171
Clissold, Stephen, 258
coalition government of 1924, 135
Cohen, Lenard, 308
collaborators, Communist execution of,
    224
collectivization, 246–47, 254
colonization
    in first Yugoslavia, 146–48
    Serb, in Macedonia, 115
Cominform, 241, 243–44, 246
Commission of Administrators, 211
committees, interrepublic, under amended
    1963 constitution, 305–6
Communist Party (ZKS-SPD), 350
Communist Party of Croatia, 192–93
Communist Party of Yugoslavia (KPJ),
    118, 122, 170–71, 189, 192
    and Belgrade coup, 198–99
    and Macedonian question, 139–41
    resistance to Nazi occupation, 202
    response to Tito-Stalin split, 248
    role in constitution of 1953, 258
    Stalin and, 242–43
    Stalinist charges against, 244
    see also League of Communists (SKJ);
        Partisans
Communist Party policy, international
    coordination of, 242–43
Communists
    consolidation of power in 1945, 222–28
    and elections of 1945, 226
    Italian, Slovenes as, 112
companies, foreign, postwar takeover of,
    236–37
concentration camps, 200, 234
Concordat, 174, 176
confederalism, 305–6

Congress of Public Employees, 131
"Congress of Salvation," 346
Conrad, General, quoted, 107
Constantinople, 20
Constituent Assembly of 1945, 222, 229
constitution
    Croatian, 344–45
    Serbian: amendments to, 343–44; of
        1888, 51, 54, 82; of 1869, 51; under
        Miloš, 50; of 1903, 110; revision of,
        338–39, 341
    Slovenian, 345
    first Yugoslavia, 110, 155, 160–61
    of 1953, 229, 251, 256–59
    of 1946, 230–32
    of 1974, 294, 304–8, 322–23
    of 1963, 279–81, 297; amendments to,
        299–302, 304–6
    of 1931, 166
    of 1921, 119–20, 123–25
conversion
    of Bosnian Slavs to Islam, 23–24
    to Catholic church, 49
    of Croats to Catholic church, 14
    forced, 207
    to Orthodox church, 95
    of Orthodox Serbs to Catholic church,
        37
    of slaves to Islam, 23
    of Slovenians to Christianity, 28
    see also Catholic church
cooperative network, 148, 169–70, 219,
    239
Coordinating Committees for Economic
    Relations, 306
Corfu Declaration, 102–4
corruption, 130, 137, 3109–11
Ćosić, Dobrica, 297, 340
Council for Mutual Economic Assistance
    (CMEA), 265
Council of Nationalities, 230, 300
credit unions, 75; see also banking
Croat National Organization, 81
Croatia, 3–4
    and Balkan wars, 92–93
    banking in, 118
    and Bosnia in pre-First World War
        period, 87–89
    and Communist consolidation of power,
        224
    elections of 1990, 352
    in First World War, 105–6
    legacy of Second World War, 218
    in medieval period, 14–16
    Nazi collaborators in, 199

opposition to royal dictatorship, 166
after partition of first Yugoslavia, 203–6
post-First World War problems of,
    116–17
postwar borders of, 226–28
and regional economic imbalance in
    1950s, 276
Serb minority in, 160
and Stojadinović's economic policy, 179
under terms of Sporazum, 191–92
war with Yugoslav National Army, 354
see also Civil Croatia; Croatian Military
    Border; Independent State of Croatia
    (NDH)
Croatian Catholic Association, 97
Croatian crisis of late 1960s, 298–302
Croatian Democratic Alliance (HDZ),
    346, 352
Croatian Home Army (Domobran), 224
Croatian Liberation Council (ZAVNOH),
    219
Croatian Military Border, 29–30, 41,
    58–59, 62–64
Croatian National Community, 97
Croatian National Council, 116
Croatian National Party, 68, 75–76
Croatian National Peasant Party (HPSS),
    78, 93, 109–10, 116, 138, 155
    see also Radić, Stjepan
Croatian Peasant Party (HSS), 156, 158,
    161, 167, 175, 219
    and Communist consolidation of power,
        225
    excluded from list of subversive
        separatists, 170
    opposition to land reform, 186
    and opposition to Pavelić regime, 207–8
    Zagreb support for, 189
    see also Maček, Vladko
Croatian Republican Peasant Party
    (HRSS), 122, 134–37, 225
Croatian-Serbian Coalition, 77–78, 84,
    87–88, 91–92, 105, 109–10, 132
Croatia-Slavonia
    absorption of Military Border into, 62
    economic growth of, 76–77
    under Habsburg rule, 70
    pre-First World War, 76–79
Croato-Serbian Radical Progressive Youth
    Movement, 88
Croats, 1
    Corfu Declaration and, 103–4
    Načertanije and, 52
Crvenkovski, Krste, 285
Čubrilović, Vasa, 188, 239

cultural policy, Communist, 233
currency, 118–19, 150–51, 256, 272, 277, 282, 348
Cuthiliero, Jose, 355
Cvetković, Dragiša, 191
Cvijić, Jovan, 100
Czechoslovakia, 237, 239, 294

Dabčević-Kučar, Savka, 301
Dalmatia, 36, 68
    Balkan wars and, 92–93
    pre-First World War, 74–76
Danica ilirska, 44
d'Annunzio, Gabriele, 112
Danube river, 12
Davidović, Ljuba, 120, 131–32, 135
Deák, Ferenc, 59
Deakin, F. W. (Bill), 216–17
death camps, for Serbs, 207
decentralization, economic, 251–53, 280
Dedijer, Vladimir, 5, 242, 340
de-étatization, 280–81
defection, in First World War, 105
Defenders of the Constitution, 50
defense production, after Tito-Stalin split, 249–50, 252
delegate selection, under 1974 constitution, 307
Democratic Party, 120, 131, 138, 156, 192, 194, 225–26
    see also Davidović, Ljuba
demographic decline, fear of, 301
Demokratija, 226
demonstrations: Kosovar Albanians (1989), 344; Serbs in Vojvodina (1988), 341
deportation, 106–7, 200, 204–5, 217; see also expulsion
Despalatović, Elinor Murray, 44
d'Esperey, General Franchet, 159
dictatorship, royal, of King Aleksandar, 161–73
dictionary, Serbo-Croatian, 299
Dimitrijević, Dragutin (Apis), 84, 102
Dimitrov, Georgi, 243
Dinaric mountains, 10–12
diplomacy, Tito's, 2, 261
discrimination, 185, 248–49, 258
    see also ethnic antagonism
disease, epidemic, 107
division, religious, in medieval Croatia, 15–16
Djilas, Aleksa, 232
Djilas, Milan, 227–28, 230

Djilas, Milovan
    concern for political reform, 258–59
    expulsion from League of Communists, 262
    as head of Agitprop, 233
    as Partisan leader, 203, 210, 216
    and postwar territorial division, 227–28
    reaction to camps for political prisoners, 249
    second thoughts about second Yugoslavia, 230, 251, 257
    Stalin and, 243
    and workers' self-management, 250
Djordjević, Jovan, 305
Djurišić, Pavle, 210
Dobos, Manuela, 63
Dolanc, Stane, 342
domination: Croatian, fears of, 133; Serbian, in first Yugoslavia, 128–30
Domobran, 224
Donià, Robert, 81
Donovan, William, 196
Drašković, Count Janko, 44
Drašković, Milorad, 139–40
Drašković, Vuk, 340
Drnovšek, Janez, 344
Dubrovnik, 10, 33
Dulles, John Foster, 268
Dušan, King, 18
Džemijet Party, 121–22, 136

Eagleburger, Lawrence, 320
economic change, in early twentieth century, 70–73
Economic Council, 239
economic crisis of 1989, 348
economic growth, 273–74, 315
    in first Yugoslavia, 184–85
    post-Second World War, 234–36
    in 1950s, 260, 272–75
    in late 1960s, 295
economic integration, 7, 278, 342
    in first Yugoslavia, 115–19, 141–42
economic policy
    in first Yugoslavia, 148–50
    of Stojadinović, 177–81
economic problems of second Yugoslavia, 293, 326–34
economic reform, 278
    failure of, 321–24
    of 1965, 261, 279–84, 295–96, 299–301
economic rivalry, regional, 285–86
economic setbacks of second Yugoslavia, 238–41

economy
  of NDH, 218–19
  Serbian, of 1880s, 55
  state sector of, 180
education, 144, 145–46, 287, 296, 332–33
  Catholic church and, 224
  under Communist regime, 233
  in Croatian Military Border, 64
  in first Yugoslavia, 133, 136, 162,
    186–88
  higher, 287, 332–33
  in Kosovo after 1968, 297
  in Macedonia, 90
  in 1980s, 327–34
  in nineteenth-century Bosnia, 67
  in nineteenth-century Croatia, 62
  in nineteenth-century Montenegro, 58
  in second Yugoslavia, 252, 261, 333–34
  secular, in Serbia, 85
  see also schools
Egypt, Yugoslav relations with, 267
Ekmečić, Milorad, 5
Ekonomska politika, 309
elections: (1920), 119–23; (1924), 133;
    (1926), 156; (1931), 167; (May
    1935), 174; (Dec. 1938), 176;
    (1945), 225–26; (Apr. 1968), 300
  multi-party, 325, 346
  multiple-candidate, 300
  municipal, in first Yugoslavia, 138–39
  provincial, in first Yugoslavia, 138
  republic, of 1990, 349–50
electoral system, under constitution of
  1974, 306
emigration, 71, 73, 77, 94, 95, 332–33,
    343, 346, 352
employment
  in first Yugoslavia, 185–88
  industrial, in 1964, 290
  in 1980s, 327–34
  in social sector, 272–73, 283
  in state sector, 130, 252
Enlightenment, the, 37–38
enterprise efficiency, 277, 310–12
enterprise managers, 308–9
enterprises, 312, 329, 347
epic poetry, Serbian folk tradition of, 25,
    49
Estrin, Saul, 312
ethnic accommodation, 40
ethnic antagonism, 3–4, 9, 30
  Austro-Serbian, 83
  and liberal alliance, 285–86
  rural, Austro-Hungarian policy and, 80
  in second Yugoslavia, 294

Serb-Croat, 64, 115, 156, 346, 352
Serb-Muslim, 64, 96–97
ethnic anxieties, 301
ethnic assimilation, 85
ethnic balance, key system of, 257–58,
    305–6, 308 337
ethnic cleansing
  in Bosnia-Hercegovina, 107
  of Italians in Croatia, 227
  as practiced by Pavelić regime, 204–6
  in wars of Yugoslav succession, 356
ethnic homelands, claims of, 40
ethnic identity, 25, 74–75, 129, 232
ethnic mixing, 34–38, 261
ethnic self-determination, principle of, 4
ethnic unity, 278
European Community, mediation attempt
  of 1992, 355
exclusivism, ethnic, popular rejection of,
    233–34
exiles see emigration, Yugoslav Committee
expansionism, Italian, 154
expulsion, 206, 248
extremism, 105, 139, (1930s), 170–73,
    248

FADURK see Fund for Accelerated
    Development of Less Developed
    Republics and Kosovo (FADURK)
fascism
  Stojadinović and, 181–82
  Ustaša and, 172
February Patent of 1861, 59
Federal Assembly, under constitution of
  1953, 257–58
Federal Bloc, 134
Federal Chamber, abolition of, 299–300
Federal Council, under constitution of
  1946, 230
Federal Executive Council (SIV), 298, 305
  under constitution of 1953, 257–58
  plan for national referendum in 1990,
    349–50
federal framework, inadequacy of, 326
Federal People's Republic of Yugoslavia
  (SNRJ), 229; see also Yugoslavia,
    second
Federal Planning Commission, 239
Federalists, 141
Ferdinand of Coburg, Tsar of Bulgaria, 91
film industry, 233–34, 335
Fine, John V. A., Jr., 19
First Balkan War of 1912, 89
First Serbian Uprising, 47–49
Fiume (Rijeka), 34

Five Year Plan, 237–41, 274–75, 278
Foča, massacre at, 209
folk culture, as binding element, 78
food shipments, from United States, 254
forced labor, and postwar economic
    recovery, 235
foreign aid, US, 253–56
foreign debt, 151, 168–69, 268–69, 294,
    315, 319–20, 348
foreign intervention, and First Serbian
    Uprising, 49
foreign investment, 180–81, 185, 286,
    313–15, 347, 348
foreign policy, in 1970s and 1980s,
    316–18
"four equalities," 232
fragmentation: imperial, 19; geographic,
    89; political, 40
France
    aid to second Yugoslavia, 269
    First World War and, 108
    and Illyrian provinces, 41–42
    relations with first Yugoslavia, 151
    support for Serbia before First World
        War, 83
    support for Serbia in 1918, 108, 114
    as trade partner, 179
Frank, Josip, 78
Frankist Party see Party of Pure Right
Franz Ferdinand, Archduke, assassination
    of, 98
Friends of Yugoslavia, 315, 319–20, 323
Fronde, Croatian, 32
Fulbright program, 287
Fund for Accelerated Development of
    Less Developed Republics and
    Kosovo (FADURK), 282, 286, 346

Gaj, Ljudevit, 43–46
Garašanin, Ilija, 50–53, 59
General Agreement on Trade and Tariffs
    (GATT), 277–78
General Agricultural Cooperatives, 240,
    246–47
General Investment Fund (GIF), 271,
    274–76, 282
Geneva Agreement, 109
genocide, claims of, in Kosovo, 340
geography, 10–13
Germanization of Slovenes, 217
Germany
    and destruction of first Yugoslavia,
        198–206
    forces, 209, 210–123
    influence, in Slovenia, 28–29

and partition of first Yugoslavia, 199,
    201
relations with first Yugoslavia, 151
Stojadinović and, 181–83
support for Serbia, 83–84
as Yugoslavia's principal trading
    partner, 179–81
Germany, East, 264
Germany, West, 264, 271–72
Gerö, Erno, 263
glagolitic alphabet, 15
Glas koncila, 335
Gligorov, Kiro, 353–54
gold standard, 169
Goli otok, 249, 258
government reform, under King
    Aleksandar, 162
government, representative, 7
    Karadjordje's view of, 48
government-in-exile, royal, 202, 209,
    215
Great Britain
    aid to second Yugoslavia, 269
    and Belgrade coup, 198
    relations with Communist regime,
        236–37
    relations with first Yugoslavia, 151,
        183
    support for Chetniks, 213
    support for Partisans, 213
"Great Croatia," 8, 15, 78
Great Depression, 168–70, 177
"Greater Illyria," 43
Great Migration of 1690, 25–26
"Great Novena – Thirteen Centuries of
    Christianity among the Croats,"
    335–36
"Great Serbia," 8, 16, 52, 84, 89
Greece
    civil war in, 237, 243
    Mussolini's invasion of, 195
    relations with first Yugoslavia, 152–53
Green Cadres, 106, 117, 146
Grenzer, 29–30, 63
Grol, Milan, 145, 194, 226
Gross, Mirjana, 62
Gross Social Product, concept of, 255
guest workers, 283, 289, 301, 329
gypsies, Croatian persecution of, 204–7

Habsburg Empire, 9–10, 27–32
Habsburg monarchy, Croatian and South
    Slav ideas in, 58–64
Handžar Division, war crimes against
    Serbs, 220

harassment: in elections of 1924, 133–34;
of Serbs in Croatia, 105
Hartwig, Nikolai, 84
HDZ see Croatian Democratic Alliance
(HDZ)
Hebrang, Andrija, 219, 238–39, 244
Helsinki Watch, 353
Henderson, Neville, quoted, 160
Hercegovina, 19, 65
see also Bosnia-Hercegovina
Herder, Johann Gottfried, 44
Hitler, Adolf, 182, 195
and destruction of first Yugoslavia,
198–206
Hobsbawm, Eric, 40
Hoffman, George, quoted, 12
HPSS see Croatian National Peasant Party
(HPSS)
HRSS see Croatian Republican Peasant
Party (HRSS)
HSS see Croatian Peasant Party (HSS)
Hudson, Captain William, 211
humanism, Marxist, 295
Hungarian revolt of 1848, 45–46
Hungarian Revolution, 263
Hungary, 44
and administrative integration of
Croatia-Slavonia, 62–64
attitude toward Croatians, 59
and borders of first Yugoslavia, 113–14
and Croatian-Serbian Coalition, 77–78,
88
and medieval Bosnia, 19
in medieval period, 15
and partition of first Yugoslavia, 199,
201
relations with first Yugoslavia, 151–52
role in German invasion, 199
as source of equipment and raw
materials under Five Year Plan, 239
and Ustaša, 172
see also Austria-Hungary
hyperinflation, of 1989, 348

identities, multiple, 294
identity
Bosnian, Kállay's view of, 67
Bulgarian, 104
ethno-religious, under Ottoman rule, 21
religious, 14
Slovene, 28
South Slav, 58
Yugoslav, 294, 356
Illinden Uprising, 70
illiteracy, 75, 77, 187, 292, 333

"Illyria," revival of term, 41
Illyrian Party, 45
Illyrian provinces, creation of, 41–42
Illyrianism, 40, 43–46
income distribution, in 1938 Yugoslavia,
187
Independent Democrats, 158
Independent National Party, 61
Independent Party, 92
Independent Radical Party, 84, 120, 131–32
Independent State of Croatia (NDH),
199, 203–9, 352–53
see also Croatia
Independent Workers' Party of Yugoslavia
(NRPJ), 139–41
India, Yugoslav relations with, 267
industrial development, 274
effect of Soviet siege on, 249
in first Yugoslavia, 117–18, 148–50,
184–85
and Five Year Plan, 238–39
industrial production
in Croatia-Slavonia, 76–77
decline in, 278
growth after 1900, 72
growth in 1950s, 273
in NDH, 219
postwar recovery of, 235
after Tito–Stalin split, 255
Industrijska Komora, 117
inflation, 3, 278, 284; (1964), 281;
(1966), 283; (1965–85), 311;
(1970s), 310; (1980s), 293, 315;
(1990), 348–49; (NDH), 219
Inform Bureauists, 248
Institute for Economic Planning, Zagreb,
280
intellectual freedom, 261
intellectuals
Croatian, 189, 299–302
Slovenian, 189–90
and Yugoslav idea, 188–90
Interim National Parliament (PNP),
110–11, 119–23
interior ministry (MVD), 243
Internal Macedonian Revolutionary
Organization (VMRO), 88, 90,
140–41, 170–71, 353
International Monetary Fund, 255,
322–23, 347
international relations
of first Yugoslavia, 150–55
in 1970s and 1980s, 316–18
of second Yugoslavia, 262–71
Stojadinović and, 181–83

internment, of Serbs in Bosnia-
    Hercegovina, 106–7
invasion: German, 199; Soviet threat of,
    249–50
investment, 281–82
    credits, promised by Stalin, 242, 249
    funds, bargaining for, 252
    policy, of Tito regime, 276
Iron Guard, Romanian, 204
Iskra enterprise for electrical goods, as
    economic success story, 313
Islam see Muslims
isolation, of rural peasantry, 39
Istorija srpskog naroda, 340
Istria, 75; and borders of first Yugoslavia,
    111–12
Italian Communist Party (PCI), 237
Italian influence: (Dalmatia), 36;
    (Slovenia), 28–29; (Split), 41;
    (Zadar), 41
Italians, Croatian, ethnic cleansing of, 227
Italy
    Albania and, 153
    and borders of first Yugoslavia, 111–12
    and Chetniks, 216
    as export market, 150
    forces, 209, 210
    and partition of first Yugoslavia, 199,
        201
    relations with first Yugoslavia, 151, 154
    role in German invasion, 199
    territorial claims of, 104
    as trading partner, 271–72
    and Ustaša, 172
Izetbegović, Alija, 248, 336, 354

Janićijević, Miloslav, 188
Janša, Janez, 343
Jasenovac, 207
Jelačić, Josip, 46
Jevtić, Bogoljub, 174
Jews
    Croatian persecution of, 204–7
    Nazi persecution of, 200
    Sephardic, 24
JMO see Yugoslav Muslim Organization
    (JMO)
JNA see Yugoslav National Army (JNA)
joint ventures, 313–14
    Yugoslav–Soviet, 238–39, 241–42
Jones, E. L., 10
Jovanović, Arso, 210, 248
Jovanović, Dragoljub, 231, 234
Jovanović, Slobodan, 124, 145, 194, 209,
    215, 223

Jovanović, Vladimir, 51
jugoslovenstvo, 86–87, 257, 278, 281
JUSPAD, 242
JUSTA, 242
justice system
    Communist control of, 234
    in first Yugoslavia, 137–39

Kako živi narod (Bićanić), 186
Kállay, Benjámin, 66–67, 79
Karadjordje, 48–49
Karadjordjević, Aleksandar, 50
Karadjordjević, Petar, 83
Karadžić, Radovan, 354–55
Karadžić, Vuk, 44
    "Serbs All and Everywhere," 61
Kardelj, Edvard, 3, 190, 293
    and Belgrade Declaration, 263
    and "empty box" device, 226
    and fall of Ranković, 284–86
    as framer of Yugoslav constitutions,
        230, 256–57, 280, 298, 305
    and second Yugoslav-Soviet split,
        264
    and Tito–Stalin split, 242–44
    and workers' self-management, 250
Kasche, Siegfried, 209
Kavčić, Stane, 342
Khrushchev, Nikita, 262–65
Khuen-Héderváry, Count Károly, 62
Kidrič, Boris, 238–40, 246, 250, 254
Kingdom of Serbs, Croats, and Slovenes,
    103–4, 109–11
    see also Yugoslavia, first
Kingdom of Yugoslavia, 159
    see also Yugoslavia, first
Klagenfurt, 112
Klugman, James, 215
Kluž clothing enterprise, as economic
    success story, 313
knezovi, 48, 50
Knin, 42
Kocbek, Eduard, 218, 342
Kon, Geca, 144
Kopitar, Jernej, 45
Korošec, Monsignor Anton, 3, 168, 173,
    194
    and demise of parliamentary kingdom,
        158
    as leader of Slovenian People's Party,
        109, 133, 152,
    as member of King Aleksandar's
        cabinet, 162
    as member of Stojadinović's cabinet,
        174

Kosovo, 3–4
  Balkan wars and, 93–96
  in 1986, 338
  as part of Serbia, 71
  post-Second World War, 223–24
  quest for republic status, 296–98
  Serb-Albanian relations in, 330–32
  Serbian recapture of, 91
  Serb view of, 26
Kosovo, Battle of, 55, 98
  1989 commemoration of, 345
Koštunica, Vojislav, 6, 225
Kovačić, Viktor, 145
KPJ see Communist Party of Yugoslavia
  (KPJ)
Kragujevac, massacre at, 211
Kraigher, Sergei, 321
Kraljevo, 211
Krek, Janez, 75
Krleža, Miroslav, 3, 144, 189, 258, 299
Kučan, Milan, 325, 338, 342–45,
  350–52
Kulin, Viceroy, 19
Kun, Bela, 113
Kusturica, Emir, "Underground," 1
Kvaternik, Eugen, 60
Kvaternik, Slavko, 172, 203

land distribution, pre-1914, 72
landlords, Muslim, 80, 115, 123, 132–33,
  147
land reform
  in first Yugoslavia, 146–48, 185–86
  in post-First World War Croatia, 116
  in second Yugoslavia, 240
landholding, 20–22, 26, 71–72
languages, 14
  Albanian, 297
  Croatian, 112, 299
  Croato-Serbian, 44
  German, 97
  glagolica, 58
  Hungarian, 78
  Illyrianism and, 44
  literary, 44–45, 86
  Macedonian, 243
  Magyar, 62
  Serbian, 86
  Serbo-Croatian, 24, 42, 44
  Slovenian, 28–29, 75, 112
  South Slav, 28
  štokavian, 61
  štokavski dialect, 42, 44
Law on Associated Labor (1976), 310,
  347

Law on Legal Status of Religious
  Communities (1953), 258
Law on the Management of State
  Economic Associations by Work
  Collectives, 252
Law on Planned Management, 252
League of Communists of Yugoslavia
  (LCY), 281
League of Communists (SKJ), 251, 258,
  260
  Congress of 1990, 346–47
  Croatian, 301, 346
  Eighth Congress, 281
  end of, 344–47
  failure of, 325
  membership of, 259
  in 1980s, 336–38
  Seventh Congress, 264
  Slovenian, 342
  Thirteenth Congress, 321
legislature, of Yugoslav state, 124–25
liberal coalition, 279, 284–86, 295,
  298–304
liberalism, Croatian, 60–62
Liberation Front (OF), 217
Linhart, Tomas, 28
literature, 86, 299
Little Entente, 151
Ljotić, Dimitrije, 193–94, 211
Ljubljana, 138, 144–45
local government
  in first Yugoslavia, 131, 137–39
  and Nazi collaboration, 200
  under Tito regime, 251–53
  Yugoslav state and, 124–25
Lydall, Harold, 283, 316

Macedonia, 4
  and Balkan wars, 93–96
  and borders of first Yugoslavia, 114–15
  Bulgarian claim to, 152
  under Bulgarian control, 203
  elections of 1990, 353–54
  medieval ethnic composition of, 21
  under Ottoman rule, 21–22, 70
  as part of Serbia, 71
  postwar borders of, 226–28
  and Serbia, 90–92
Macedonian question, 139–41; (1947),
  241
Macedonians, 14; as Serbs, 101
Maček, Vladko, 160, 189, 203, 225
  and Belgrade coup, 198
  excluded from list of subversive
  separatists, 170

Maček, Vladko (*cont.*)
  and first Yugoslavia, 191
  opposition to royal dictatorship, 166–68
  refusal to join JRZ, 175
  resistance to Pavelić regime, 208
  and Stojadinović, 176
McFarlane, Bruce, 313
MacKenzie, David, 52
Maclean, Brigadier Fitzroy, 215
Magaš, Branka, 343
Magyarization, in Croatia, 62
Magyarone Party, 45
  see also Unionist Party
Mamula, Admiral Branko, 337–38, 343
Maribor Program, Slovenian, 69
market reform, 279–92, 338–39, 341, 344,
    347–49
markets, Western, 271–78
Marković, Ante, 325, 344, 347, 348, 350
Marković, Mihailo, 295
Marković, Mirjana, 353
Marković, Sima, 139–41
Marković, Svetozar, 54
Marmont, Auguste, 42
Marshall Plan, 254
Masaryk, Tomás, 79
massacre
  at Foča, 209
  by Hercegovinian Serbs, 209
  at Kragujevac, 211
  at Sutjeska, 216
Matica Hrvatska, 299, 301
Matica Srpska, 299
Matoš, Antun Gustav, 86
Mažuranić, Ivan, *Smrt Smail-aga Čengića,*
    61, 64
MBO Party, 354
media, 287, 326, 334–36
  ethnic politics and, 335
  role in dramatizing Croatian crisis,
    302
Medjugorje, 336
meetings of truth, 345
Memorandum of the Serbian Academy of
    Arts and Sciences (1986), 6, 340
Mešić, Stipe, 352
migration
  of Albanians, 24
  of Anatolians, 22
  of Bosnian Muslims to Constantinople,
    65
  to Croatian Military Border, 29
  of Croats, 14
  of Germans, 28, 37
  of Greeks, 34

internal, 301
of janissaries into Serbia, 48
land reform and, 146–48
Montenegro and, 26
of Muslims to Bosnia-Hercegovina, 97
in 1980s, 327–34
of refugees to Bulgaria, 152
rural–urban, 288–89, 329
seasonal, 71
from Serbia, 47
of Serbs, 37, 49, 56, 64
of 1690, 25–26
of South Slavs, 14
of Vlachs, 22
of Vlach Tsintsars, 34
of Yugoslav population to Western
    Europe, 288–89
see also deportation; emigration; guest
    workers
Mihailović, Draža
  as Chetnik leader, 200–3, 210–13
  retreat to Serbia, 216–17
  show trial and execution of, 223, 233
Mijatović, Čedomil, 55
Mikulić, Branko, 320–24, 341
Mikulić government, failure of economic
    reform, 320–24
military, Bosnian, 64–65
military, Serbian, 53–54, 99–100, 102–3,
    116
  Balkan wars and, 91, 94
  in First World War, 107
  and first Yugoslavia, 110, 128–30
military, Yugoslav, and German invasion,
    199
military aid: Soviet, 264; US, 254–55
military officers
  ethnic origin of, 337
  as party members, 337
  Serb, 198–99, 200–203, 325
military spending, in 1984, 337
millet system, 21, 23, 25
Milošević, Slobodan, 3, 325, 345, 350,
    353
  rise of, 338–41
Milošević Commission, 341
Minić, Miloš, 234
minorities
  Croatian, 160
  in first Yugoslavia, 114, 129, 160
  German, 114, 182
  Hungarian, 114, 152, 227
  Kosovar Albanian, 223
  Serb, in Croatia, 160, 192
Mirković, Bora, 198

mobilization, by KPJ under 1946
    constitution, 232–34
modernism, 86
modernization, 39–40, 71
    Croatia and, 61–62
    differential, 86
    in nineteenth-century Bosnia, 66
    in nineteenth-century Serbia, 55
    and Serbianization, 86
    of Serbia under Garašanin, 51
Moljević, Stevan, 202
Molotov, Vyacheslav, 264
monarchy, abolition of, 229
money supply, 348
Montenegro, 4
    Balkan wars and, 93–96
    Chetnik-Partisan relations in, 209–13
    elections of 1990, 353–54
    and first Yugoslavia, 109–10
    independent, 94
    as nineteenth-century mini-state,
        56–58
    under Ottoman rule, 26–27
    postwar borders of, 226–28
Moore, John, 272
Morava river, 13
Moscow Declaration (1956), 263
"Mountain Wreath" (Njegoš), 57
Movement for Yugoslavia (SK), 350
Mürzsteg Agreement, 90
Muslim Party of Democratic Action
    (SDA), 354
Muslims, Bosnian, 67–68, 97
    aid to persecuted Jews, 208
    and Belgrade coup, 198
    as Croats, 193
    in first Yugoslavia, 165
    as landlords, 80, 115, 123, 132–33,
        147
    in 1980s, 329–30, 336
    and opposition to Pavelić regime, 207–8
    persecution by Pavelić regime, 205
    as purest Croats, 205
    relations with Nazis, 219–20
    resistance to collectivization, 247–48
    role in First Serbian Uprising, 48
    and Second Serbian Uprising, 49
    Serb view of, 2
    support for Partisans, 220
    as "Turks," 355
Muslims, Montenegrin, 95
Muslims, Sandžak, 210
Mussolini, Benito, 112, 154, 182, 191,
    194–95
mystics, Muslim, bektashi order, 24

Načertanije, 52
Nagy, Imre, 263
name, for Yugoslav state, 123–24
Narodna Odbrana, 84
Narodna Skupština, 51
Nasser, Gamal Abdel, 267–68
National Assembly, under constitution of
    1946, 230
National Bank of Yugoslavia (NBJ), 278,
    323, 348–49
National Bloc, 135–36
National Committee for the Liberation of
    Yugoslavia, 217
National Council, 109–11
National Front, 225
National Liberation Front, 225
National Party, 45, 59, 61
nationalism, 8
    "bourgeois," and first Yugoslavia, 5
    Christian, 75
    Croatian, 40, 60–62, 140–41, 336
    ethnic, 288
    Italian, pre-First World War, 75
    literary, 86
    Macedonian, 140–41
    romantic, 40, 52
    Serbian, 40, 52–55, 338–41
    see also politics, ethnic
Nationalist Party, 68
NDH see Independent State of Croatia
    (NDH)
Nedić, General Milan, 195–96
Nehru, Jawaharlal, 267
Nemanja, 16
Nettuno Conventions, 154, 156–58
Neubacher, Hermann, 220
Nikezić, Marko, 267, 285, 303–4
Nikola, King, 96
Ninčić, Momčilo, 152, 154
Niš Declaration, 100–101
Njegoš, Petar Petrović, "The Mountain
    Wreath," 57
nobles, Croatian, Illyrianism and, 44–46
Noli, Fan, 154
Non-Aligned Movement, 2, 261, 266–68,
    316–18
normalization, of Soviet-Yugoslav
    relations, 262–66
Nova Evropa, 145
Nova Revija, 342
Nove vreme, 200
Novi Sad, 34, 37
NRPJ see Independent Workers' Party of
    Yugoslavia (NRPJ)
Nušić, Branislav, 144

Obradović, Dositej, 37
Obrenović, Aleksandar, 55
Obrenović, Michael, 51, 53
Obrenović, Milan, 51, 53–55
Obrenović, Miloš, 46, 49–50
Obznana, 123
occupational structure, in first Yugoslavia, 149
oil crisis of 1979, 293
OOUR see Basic Organizations of Associated Labor (OOUR)
Operation Maritsa, 198
Operation Schwartz, 216
Operation Weiss, 215–16
opposition
  in 1945 elections, 226
  to Popular Front, 231
  to Ustaša regime, 207–8, 219
Organization for the Peoples' Defense (OZNa), 223
Orthodox church, 57
Osijek, 76
Ottoman Empire, 9–10, 20–27
  and Macedonia, 70, 90
  and medieval Bosnia, 19
  and medieval Serbia, 18
  and Second Serbian Uprising, 49
overflights, US, postwar dispute over, 236–37

Pacta conventa, 15
Paču, Lazar, 92
Palairet, Michael, 314
Pan-Slavism, 52
Partisans, 209, 214–16
  see also Communists; Djilas, Milovan; Yugoslav National Army (JNA)
partition, of first Yugoslavia, 199–201
party membership: (1960s), 300; (1982), 336–37
Party of Democratic Renewal, 347
Party of Progress, 88
Party of Pure Right, 78, 92, 97, 105, 110, 122
Party of Right, 60–61, 63
party politics, in Habsburg lands, 74–81
Pašić, Nikola
  and Balkan Wars, 91–92
  and Corfu Declaration, 102–4
  and First World War, 102–4
  and formation of first Yugoslavia, 123, 127–28, 130
  and PNP, 119
  as Radical Party leader, 54–55, 82–83

relations with Pribićević, 131–35
relations with Radić, 134–37
Pašić government, 94, 100, 111
patriotism, Yugoslav, as motive for resistance, 203
Patterson, William, 236
Pauker, Ana, 241
Paul, Prince, 174, 176–77, 194–95, 196
Pavelić, Ante, 172–73, 193, 203
Pavlowitch, Stevan, 6, 215
Peasant International Congress (Moscow), 134
peasant revolts, 39
  Croatian, of 1883, 62–64
  in post-First World War Croatia, 116
peasants, 51, 71, 39–40, 146–48, 246–48, 283, 312
  Croat, 71–72, 105
  Croat and Serb, as one people, 42
  and Croatian National Peasant Party, 78–79
  Dalmatian, 75
  in first Yugoslavia, 139
  Illyrianism and, 46
  in nineteenth-century Bosnia-Hercegovina, 65
  in nineteenth-century Croatia, 62
  resistance to Five Year Plan, 239–40
  Serb, 96–97, 169–70
Peasant-Worker Cooperatives (SRZ), 246–47, 254
Pećanac, Kosta, 202, 211
People's Army, 223
People's Councils (NO), 251
Perović, Latinka, 285, 303
persecution, ethnic
  of Serbs, 105–7, 340
  by Ustaša regime, 204–6
Petar II, King, 215, 229
Petranović, Branko, 227
Petrovich, Michael, 36, 48, 50
Pijade, Moša, 217, 244, 256
PL 480 program, 269–70
Planinc, Milka, 319
Plečnik, Jože, 145
PNP see Interim National Parliament (PNP)
political activity ban, in first Yugoslavia, 139
political culture, of first Yugoslavia, 183–84
political factories, 276
political loyalty, and regional economic imbalance, 276–77

political parties
  and Communist consolidation of power,
    225
  and elections of 1920, 120–23
  in first Yugoslavia, 131–37
  new, 70–71, 345–46
  in nineteenth-century Bosnia, 67
  in nineteenth-century Serbia, 53–55
  in pre-First World War Croatia, 77–79
  in Serbia, 84
  see also names of parties
political parties, ethnic, 70, 155, 157,
    161
  in Bosnia-Hercegovina, 354
political party, national, need for, 350
politicians, in first Yugoslavia, 127
politics, ethnic, 325–26
  in Serbia, 338–41
  in Slovenia, 341–44
Politika, 142
popular culture, 326, 334–36
Popular Front, 230–31, 258
population
  of Belgrade in 1920s, 142
  of Belgrade in First World War, 107
  of Bosnia-Hercegovina in 1908, 82
  of Bosnia in 1980s, 329
  of Civil Croatia, 31
  of Croatian Military Border, 30
  of Croatia-Slavonia, in 1880–1910, 71
  of early modern Sarajevo, 34, 36
  in 1800, 10; 1870, 73
  ethnic, in 1961–91, 320
  ethnic, in 1980s, 329–32
  of first Yugoslavia, in 1921, 129
  of Habsburg Slavonia, 31–32
  of interwar Yugoslavia, 185
  in 1910, 72–73
  of nineteenth-century Bosnia-
    Hercegovina, 65
  of nineteenth-century Montenegro, 57
  of nineteenth-century Serbia, 47, 55–56
  of nineteenth-century Zagreb, 61
  of Ottoman Macedonia, 21–22
  of Ottoman Serbia, 24–25
  of republics, in 1953–88, 328
  of sixteenth-century Sarajevo, 24
  of Trieste, in 1910, 74
population growth, 71, 327, 331
populationism, Habsburg, 36–37, 115
power, royal, limits on, 128
power vacuum, post-Tito, 325
Pozderac, Hambdija, 324
P-P regimes, 135
Pravoslavije, 336

Praxis, 295
presidency, collective, 305, 307, 319, 325,
    341, 343–44
press, 335
  Communist monopoly of, 233
  in first Yugoslavia, 142–44
  royal closing of, 162
  in second Yugoslavia, 287
Pribićević, Svetozar
  and formation of first Yugoslavia, 123,
    127, 158
  as leader of Croatian-Serbian Coalition,
    109
  opposition to royal dictatorship, 162,
    166
  relations with Pašić, 131–34
  relations with Radić, 87, 155–56
  and Serbian Independent Party, 77–78,
    120
price controls, lifting of, 347–48
Prickett, Russell, 279, 320, 323
Princip, Gavrilo, 89, 98
Prizad, 169–70
Prodanović, Jaša, 226, 231
professionals, 286, 295, 300
Progressive Party, 54
propaganda, 232, 237, 258
Protestantism, in Slovenia, 28
Protić, Stojan, 109, 124, 134
pseudo-history, 207
publishing houses, in first Yugoslavia,
    142–44
puppet government, in occupied Serbia,
    211
purge, of liberal party leaders by Tito,
    304

Račan, Ivica, 346
Račić, Puniša, 156, 158
racism, 78, 172, 207
Rački, Franjo, 58–59
Radić, Ante, 78–79
Radić, Marija, 225
Radić, Stjepan, 87, 127, 158
  and formation of first Yugoslavia,
    109–10, 122
  as founder of HPSS, 78–79
  as leader of HPSS, 92–93
  and Mussolini, 154
  relations with Pašić, 134–37
  relations with Pribićević, 155–58
Radical Party, 91–92, 119, 131–34, 155
  in Serbia, 54
  see also Pašić, Nikola
Ragusa, 33

railways, 55, 80, 270
    in first Yugoslavia, 115, 117–18, 153
    in 1930s, 179
    in 1920s, 150
    Second World War destruction of, 235
Rákosi, Mátyás, 263
Ramet, Sabrina P., quoted, 299
Ranković, Aleksandar, 234, 244, 246, 249,
    261, 264, 340
    downfall of, 284–86
    as opponent of market reform, 279
Ravna Gora movement. See Chetniks
Ražnjatović, Željko (Arkan), 353
recentralization, Milošević's call for, 341
recognition, international, for first
    Yugoslavia, 111–15
Red Terror, 209
reform, domestic, in Serbia, 54
regional imbalance
    economic, 169, 275–77, 289–92, 296,
    327
    in first Yugoslavia, 184, 186
reintegration, economic, abandonment of,
    349
relief, postwar, 235
religion, in 1980s, 334–36
religious coexistence, in early modern
    Vojvodina, 37
religious freedom
    under constitution of 1946, 230
    in first Yugoslavia, 184
    republic laws on, 1976–78, 335–36
    under Tito regime, 288
    Yugoslav state and, 123–24
religious problems, in first Yugoslavia,
    165–66
Republican Party, 225
republics
    under constitution of 1946, 230
    under constitution of 1953, 257
    regional economic imbalance among,
    276
    right of secession under 1963
    constitution, 281, 297
Republika, 231
resistance
    Communist, 202
    German response to, 211–13
    non-Communist Serbian, 200–203
    of peasants to collectivization, 246–48
revision, 265
Ribičič, Mitija, 298
Rijeka Resolution, 76–77
road-building, dispute over, 298
Roberts, Walter, 216

Romania, 256
Rothschild, Joseph, 162, 183, 191
R-R government, 136
Rubinstein, Alvin, 267
Rusinow, Dennison, 274, 280, 300, 350
Russia
    and first Yugoslavia, 134
    and Ottoman Macedonia, 90–91
    and Serbia, 82–84
    see also Soviet Union
Russian Orthodox church, 26
Russo-Ottoman War, Montenegro and, 57

Sachs, Stephen, 312
Salonika Front, in First World War, 102
Samouprava, 54
Sandžak, 121, 227
Sarajevo, 10, 148
    as administrative capital, 39–40
    ethnic mixing in, 36
    ethnic politics in, 354
    as trade center, 33–34
    as "Yugoslav" city, 330
Sarkotić, Stefan, 106–7
Sava, Saint, 16
Sava river, 13
Schacht, Hjalmar, 179–80
Schmid, Ferdinand, 79
scholarship, Yugoslav, 5–6
schools
    secular, in first Yugoslavia, 133
    Serb, in Croatia, 105
secession, 281, 297, 345
Second Balkan War of 1913, 91
Second Serbian Uprising, 49
Sekelj, Laszlo, quoted, 307
Sekulić, Isadora, 144
self-management, workers, 250–53,
    277–78, 286–87, 303, 310–11, 313
separatism, Croatian, 161–62, 175–76
Serb-Croat agreement of 1939, 190–94
Serbia
    and Austrian annexation of Bosnia,
    82–85
    and Balkan Wars of 1912–13, 71
    centralism in, 49–51
    Chetnik-Partisan relations in, 209–13
    creation of credit in 1965–66, 284
    elections of 1990, 350
    in First World War, 100–4
    First World War occupation of, 107–8
    fourfold division of, 164
    German occupation of, 200
    "homogeneous," 202
    land reform and, 146

legacy of Second World War, 220–22
and Macedonia, 90–92
medieval state of, 16–18
municipal elections in, 138
national aspirations in, 52–55
in 1903, 70
as nineteenth-century nation-state,
46–56
under Ottoman rule, 24–26, 47–50
ouster of liberal leaders in 1972, 303
after partition of first Yugoslavia, 200–3
post-First World War problems of,
117–19
postwar borders of, 226–28
pre-First World War, 81–87
and Yugoslav constitution of 1921, 123
Serbian Cultural Club, 192, 194
Serbian Democratic Party (SDS), 354–55
Serbian Independent Party, 77, 120
Serbian National Organization, 81, 97
Serbian National Party, 68
Serbian Orthodox church, 85, 176
in first Yugoslavia, 124, 165–66
formation of, 16–17
under Habsburg rule, 29, 37
in medieval Montenegro, 26
Miloš and, 50
in 1980s, 336
in nineteenth-century Bosnia, 66–67
under Ottoman rule, 21, 25
under Tito regime, 288
Serbian Voluntary Guards, 353
Serbianization, 86
Serbo-Bulgarian treaty (March 1912), 91
Serbo-Croat Progressive Organization,
88
Serbs
in Bosnia-Hercegovina, 80–81
Bosnian, 32, 330
Corfu Declaration and, 103–4
in Croatian Military Border, 29–30
as Croats, 193
as Croats and Vlachs, 207
forced conversion of, 207
killing of, in NDH, 207
and nineteenth-century nationalism, 1
persecution of, 106–7, 204–6
rural, opposition to Pavelić regime, 208
as Slavs, 79
as South Slavs, 58
state employment and, 188
unification of, 52
"Serbs All and Everywhere" (Karadžić),
61
Seton-Watson, R. W., 108, 112, 134

sharecropping, 42, 80–81, 96–97, 146–47,
186
shipping, 242
Short History of Yugoslavia (Dedijer et al.),
5
siege, Soviet, 244–50, 262–63
Silverman, Lawrence, 317
similarity, socio-economic, of Serbs and
Croats, 40
Simović, General Dušan, 198, 215
Six Day War, 294
Skerlić, Jovan, 86
SKJ see League of Communists (SKJ)
Skopje, 148
Skupština, 159–60, 166
Slavonia, 15, 27, 30–32
"Slavoserb," as pejorative term, 61
Slavs, Macedonian
Serbia's refusal to recognize, 114
as Serbs and Greeks, 90, 92
Slovene People's Party (SLS), 104, 121
Slovenes, 14
Corfu Declaration and, 103–4
as Italian Communists, 112
as "mountain Croats," 61
as South Slavs, 58
state employment and, 188
and Yugoslav Committee, 101
Slovenia, 3
Balkan wars and, 92–93
and Communist consolidation of power,
224
and disintegration of second Yugoslavia,
341–44
elections of 1990, 350
under Habsburg rule, 27–29, 41
independence of, 354
legacy of Second World War, 217–18
in nineteenth century, 69
postwar borders of, 226–28
pre-First World War, 74–76
and regional economic imbalance in
1950s, 276
road-building dispute of 1969, 298
Slovenian Communist Party, 217
Slovenian Democratic Alliance, 345
Slovenian Liberal Party, 133
Slovenian People's Party (SLS), 75, 93,
119, 133, 138, 162, 175, 218
Slovenian Village Guard, 224
Smrt Smail-aga Čengića (Mažuranić), 61,
64
social contributions, 253
Social Democratic Party, 81, 110
Social Plan for 1976–80, 310

social strains, and disintegration of second Yugoslavia, 326–28
socialism, Yugoslav, 229–30, 246, 250–59
Socialist Alliance of Working People (SSRNJ), 258–59, 285, 346
Socialist Party of Serbia (SPS), 349, 353
socioeconomic indicators, 1953 and 1988, 332–33
Socio-Political Chamber, 300
Sokol youth organization, 217
Sokoli, Mehmed, 25
Sonnenfeldt Doctrine, 316
South Slav culture, 126
South Slav solidarity, 85
South Slav state, 100–3
South Slavs, 14
    Bosnians as, 18
    Croations as, 14
    as descendants of ancient Illyrians, 43
    Serbs as, 16
    as single nationality, 41–46
    and unification, 52, 104
Soviet Union
    collapse of, 325
    Nazi invasion of, 202
    nonaggression treaty with Yugoslavia, 199
    normalization of relations with Yugoslavia, 262–66
    possible link to Croatian crisis, 302
    postwar bilateral trade agreements with Yugoslavia, 237
    relations with Yugoslavia, 316–18
    second split with Yugoslavia, 264–65, 267
    as source of equipment and raw materials under Five Year Plan, 239
    Tito's split with, 229, 241–50
Spaho, Mehmed, 133, 174
Special Operations Executive (SOE), 214–15
Split, 41
Sporazum, 160, 190–94, 204
Srem, the, 36
Srpski književni glasnik, 86, 142
Srškić, Milan, quoted, 167
Stadler, Archbishop Josip, 81, 97, 110
Stalin, Joseph
    1947 meeting with Kardelj, 242
    support for Partisans, 221–22
    Tito's split with, 241–50
Stambolić, Ivan, 339–41
Stambolić, Petar, 303

Stamboliiski, Aleksandar, 152
standard of living
    in 1980s, 316
    in 1960s, 260
Stanojević, Aca, 167
Stanovnik, Janez, 343
Stara Gradiška, 207
Starčević, Ante, 60–61
State Agricultural Bank, 169, 179
state building, 6–8
State Security (SDB), 248, 284, 296
State Security Administration (UDBa), 234, 243, 248
state spending, in 1920s, 150
Stepinac, Archbishop Alojzije, 205, 208, 218, 233
Stjepan, King, 16
Stoianovich, Traian, 19
Stojadinović, Milan, 150, 160, 182
    as prime minister, 173–83
Stokes, Gale, 55, 101
strike, student, of 1968, 295–96
strikes, labor, 274, 311, 343–44
    in 1980s, 327
Strossmayer, Josip Juraj, 58–59
students, political involvement of, 88–89, 93, 97–98, 159, 172, 189, 295–96, 342–43
Šubašić, Ivan, 192, 221, 225
succession, after Tito's death, 319
suffrage, 74, 120–21, 144
Sugar, Peter, 79
Sundhaussen, Holm, 219
Supilo, Frano, 76–77, 101–4
Supremists, 90, 141
Sutjeska, massacre at, 216
Šuvar, Stipe, 352

taxation, local, in nineteenth-century Serbia, 48
technocrats, 308–9
territorial division
    in first Yugoslavia, 130, 162–65
    post-Second World War, 226–28
    in second Yugoslavia, 231
    see also partition
terrorism, 139–40
    Croatian émigré, 302
    individual, 88, 98, 172–73
    as tyrannicide, 97
Third World, Yugoslav relations with, 266
Tigers, 353
timar system, 20–22, 26
Timok rebellion of 1883, 54

Tito, Josip Broz, 2, 73, 223, 258
  and Belgrade coup, 199
  and Brezhnev, 316
  death of, 318
  and Five Year Plan, 238
  initial response to split with Soviet
    Union, 246
  KPJ activities, 171
  organization of Partisans, 203
  as Partisan leader, 210
  plans for postwar Yugoslavia, 221–22
  as political personality, 260–61
  as president of presidency, 305
  recruited to KPJ, 122
  removal of liberals, 303–4
  response to Croatian crisis, 298,
    301–2
  response to Hungarian Revolution,
    263–64
  response to 1974 constitution, 308
  response to Soviet invasion of
    Czechoslovakia, 294
  response to student strike of 1968,
    296
  see also Partisans
Tito regime, consolidation of power,
  222–28
Tito–Stalin split of 1948, 229
Todorović, Mijalko, 285
Tomasevich, Jozo, 147
Tomislav, King, 14
tourism, 289, 300–301
trade
  in Croatian Military Border, 30
  among future Yugoslav lands, 77
  under Habsburgs, 29, 34
  in medieval Bosnia, 19
  among Soviet bloc, 265–66
trade, export, 72
  in first Yugoslavia, 116–17, 150
  under Five Year Plan, 239
  Great Depression and, 168–69
  of livestock, 50, 56–57, 77, 115
  and economic reform of 1965, 295
  in 1960s, 265
  1965–85, 319
  in 1930s, 178
  postwar, 251
  and Soviet siege, 249
  Stojadinović and, 179–81
  after Tito–Stalin split, 255
trade, import, 269
  under Five Year Plan, 239–41
  in 1988, 347
  in 1960s, 265

  in 1965–85, 319
  postwar, 251
  from Soviet bloc, 264, 273
  and Soviet siege, 249
  after Tito–Stalin split, 255
trade, regional, in early moden period,
  33–34
trade deficit, 150
trade union network, 139, 141
transfer of power, peaceful, 50
transition, first, 127
Treaty of Berlin, 57, 65
Treaty of Karlovac, 34
Treaty of London, 101
Treaty of Niš, 152
Treaty of Rapallo, 112, 154
Treaty of San Stefano, 57
Treaty of Tirana, 154
Trepča mines, strike at, 343–44
trials, and Communist consolidation of
  power, 224
Trieste
  economic growth and, 74
  postwar dispute over, 236–37, 272
  as trade center, 34
Tripalo, Mika, 301
Tripartite Agreement (1952), 255
Tripartite Pact, 194–96
Triune Kingdom, 32, 44, 68, 76
Trumbić, Ante, 76–77, 101, 103, 109–11,
  123, 161, 168
Tsankov, Aleksandar, 152
Tucker, Robert, 39
Tucović sugar refinery, as economic
  success story, 313
Tudjman, Franjo, 6, 352
Tvrtko, Ban, 19

UDBa see State Security Administration
  (UDBa)
Ujević, Augustin, 144
unanimous agreement, requirement for, in
  1974 constitution, 307
"Underground" (Kusturica), 1
unemployment, 3, 72, 252, 296
  among Kosovar Albanians, 332–34
  in 1980s, 293, 326–27
  in 1970s, 311–12
  in 1960s, 283
  in 1961, 273
  post-First World War, 118
  "socialist," 283–84
unification, first see Yugoslavia, first
Union or Death, 84, 89, 102
Unionist Party, Croatian, 61

United Nations
  Economic and Social Council, 266
  Relief and Rehabilitation Agency
    (UNRRA), 234–36
  Security Council, 266
  Yugoslav role in, 266
United Opposition of Democrats,
    Agrarians, and Republicans, 175,
    226
United States
  provision of aid, 236, 250–51, 253–56,
    268, 277
  relations with Communist regime,
    236–37
  relations with first Yugoslavia, 151
  relations with second Yugoslavia,
    268–71, 316–18
  support for Partisans, 213
  Embassy, 253–54
  Export-Import Bank, 270
  forces, and Chetniks, 221
urban culture, in second Yugoslavia, 261
urban élites, 71, 354
urbanization, 301
Ustaša, 203–9
  and overthrow of Aleksandar's
    Yugoslavia, 170–73
  Sporazum and, 192–93
  see also Pavelić, Ante
Ustaša units, executed by Communists,
    224
Uzunović, Nikola, 137, 155

Vasić, Dragiša, 202
Venetian empire, 15, 33
veto, right of, 305
Vidmar, Josip, 189
Vienna Manifesto (1924), 141
Vinski, Ivo, 287
Vitezović, Pavao Ritter, 32
Vlasto, A. P., 15
VMRO see Internal Macedonian
    Revolutionary Organization (VMRO)
Vojvodina, 4, 10
  and borders of first Yugoslavia, 112–14
  ethnic mixing in, 36–38
  under Habsburg rule, 27
  Serb revolt in, 53
  Serbs of, 46, 48–49
von Aehrenthal, Alois, 82
von Horstenau, General Edmund Glaise,
    209
von Hötzendorf, General Franz Conrad,
    92
von Ribbentrop, Joachim, 196

voting, in elections of 1920, 120–21
Vreme, 142
Vrhovec, Josip, 322
Vucinich, Wayne, 89
Vukmanović-Tempo, Svetozar, 223,
    274

war crimes, 94
  of Croatians, 204–6, 218
  of Germans, in Serbia, 211
  of Handžar Division, 220
  of Tigers in 1992, 353
war reparations, First World War, 117
war shortages, First World War, 105–8,
    116–17
Warriner, Doreen, 186
wars of Yugoslav succession, 354–56
Weber, Eugen, 8, 85
Western Europe, trade with, 271–78
White Book, 280
White Guard, executed by Communists,
    224
White Hand, 102, 129
Wickham Steed, Henry, 108, 112
Wilson, Woodrow, and formation of first
    Yugoslavia, 111–12
Wilson line, the, 112
Winter Olympics (1984), 3, 322, 334
women, 144, 287, 296
Woodward, Susan, 323
work force, ethnic composition of, in
    Bosnia-Hercegovina, 80
workers' councils, 250, 252–53, 294
working class, sovereignty of, 257
World Bank, 255, 270, 298

Yellow Book, 280
Young Bosnia, 88–89, 106
Young Muslims organization, 248
Young Turk Revolution, 90
youth, rural, support for Communist
    regime, 232
youth brigades, and postwar economic
    recovery, 235
youth culture, in 1980s Slovenia, 342–43
Yugo America, Inc., 315
"Yugonostalgia," 334
"Yugoslav," use of term, 68, 70, 189
Yugoslav Academy of Arts and Sciences,
    Zagreb, 58
Yugoslav Army in the Fatherland see
    Chetniks
Yugoslav Association of Economists,
    280
Yugoslav Committee, 101–4, 108–9

Yugoslav idea, 4–7
    among Bosnian Croats, 97
    in Croatia, 58–62
    and Croatian-Serbian Coalition, 78
    Croatian version, 4
    in Croatia-Slavonia, 106
    in Dalmatia, 68
    failure of, 356
    French support for, 108
    Habsburg version, 4
    intellectuals and, 188–90
    as jugoslovenstvo, 257
    King Aleksandar and, 164
    modernization and, 7
    in nineteenth century, 39–40
    pre-First World War, 70–71
    in Serbia, 84
    Serbian version, 4–5
    in Slovenia, 69, 93
    see also Illyrianism
Yugoslav Investment and Foreign Trade
    Banks, 282
Yugoslav Investment Bank, 274
Yugoslavia, first, 108–11
    administrative structure of, 127–41
    balance sheet for, 183–90
    destruction of, 197–206
    economic problems of, 115–19
    efforts to overthrow, 171–73
    international relations of, 150–55
    opposition to, 109–11
    partition of, 199–201
    political culture of, 183–84
Yugoslavia, Second
    disintegration of, 325–26
    formation of, 229–59
Yugoslavism
    in Bosnia-Hercegovina, 88
    Dalmatian, 76
    end of, 279–81
    of King Aleksandar, 164
    of Strossmayer, 69
Yugoslav Muslim Organization (JMO),
    119, 121, 133–34, 138, 167, 190, 192

Yugoslav National Army (JNA), 234, 264,
    325
    Bosnia-Hercegovina and, in 1992, 355
    ethnic composition of, 250
    in 1980s, 336–38, 342–44
    Slovenia and, 342–44
    US aid to, 254
    and wars of Yugoslav succession,
        355–56
Yugoslav Radical Union (JRZ), 175–77
Yugoslav Social Democratic Party, 93
Yugoslav state
    unitary vs. confederal framework for,
        123–25
    use of term, 92
"Yugospeak," 339

Zadar, 41
zadruga system, 29–30
Zagreb
    as administrative center, 39–40, 76–77
    as center of Illyrianism, 43
    cultural life of, 144–45
    as industrial center, 148–49
    intellectuals in, 189
    National Council in, 109–11
    rivalry with Belgrade, 118, 144–45
    as trade center of first Yugoslavia, 117
Zagreb points of 1932, 167–68
Žanko, Miloš, 301
Zastava, Crvena, as case study, 314–15
Zbor Party, 193–94
Zečević, General, 129
Zečević, Momčilo, 5
Zenica iron works, 180
Zhukov, General Georgy, 264
Zimmermann, Warren, 355
Živković, General Petar, 128, 162,
    164–65, 174
Zogu, Ahmed, 154
Žujović, Sreten, 244
Zulfikarpašić, Adil, 354
Zveno, 171